HAMMERS

and *High Heels*

AN ILLUSTRATED GUIDE *to*

DO-IT-YOURSELF HOME PROJECTS

JO BEHARI ALISON WINFIELD-CHISLETT

PLAIN SIGHT PUBLISHING

AN IMPRINT OF CEDAR FORT, INC.

SPRINGVILLE, UTAH

ISBN 13:978-1-4621-1241-8

Library of Congress Cataloging-in-Publication Data

Behari, Jo, author.
Hammers and high heels : an illustrated guide to do-it-yourself
home projects / Jo Behari and Alison Winfield-Chislett.
     pages cm
Originally published as: The girl's guide to DIY. United Kingdom:
New Holland Publishers, 2011.
Includes bibliographical references and index.
ISBN 978-1-4621-1241-8 (alk. paper)
1. Do-it-yourself work–Amateurs' manuals. 2. Women construc-
tion workers. I. Winfield-Chislett, Alison, author. II. Title.

TT149.B45 2013
684'.080082–dc23
Ingram 12/13
21.99   2012050588

Cover design and typesetting by Angela D. Olsen
Cover design © 2013 by Lyle Mortimer
Edited by Whitney A. Lindsley

Printed in China

10 9 8 7 6 5 4 3 2 1

CONTENTS

INTRODUCTION
How to use this book   6

PART 1: BEFORE YOU BEGIN   10
One step at a time   12
A short guide to house construction   18
All tooled up   25
Material girl   34
Basic skills   36

PART 2: PROJECTS   44
Getting it up   46
Getting a handle on home security   50
Snug as a bug—draft-proofing your home   54
Size doesn't matter—small projects to boost confidence   57
Décor decorum—painting and wallpapering projects   62
On the tiles—removing, choosing, and laying tiles   85
Feeling flush—simple plumbing problems solved   91
Floored—what's going on under your feet   99
On the shelf   105
Wonky furniture—repairing those wobbles and creaks   108
Winning the Swedish war   115
Kitchen revamps—new doors, new surfaces   118
The great outdoors   122

GLOSSARY   132
INDEX   142

INTRODUCTION

YOU ARE ENTERING A WORLD of butt joints, stopcocks and rising heads—welcome to *Hammers and High Heels*. If you carry on a little further, you might just pick up a skill or two, although you may already possess transferable skills you can use to transform your home. Like following a recipe to produce a fantastic dish, a successful do-it-yourself project is the result of thoughtful planning, putting together the right ingredients, using a method that works, keeping an eye on the clock, and adding a splash of flair.

Girls allowed

Despite the title, we hope that everyone can take something from these pages. Even if you are a complete novice, we hope you will be emboldened to give it a go. And don't be daunted by the tools. Think of electric drills as eggbeaters on steroids and remember that jigsaws are just sawdust-making cousins of sewing machines. Some beauticians use woodworking files to remove hardened skin from a client's feet during a pedicure! It's the correct tool if it gets the job done.

This book is intended for people with a range of abilities. By learning about tools and how to use them, you can then put these to use with the appropriate materials and techniques that will become skills when practiced over time. Plan starter projects in less-frequently used rooms if possible—practice might not make perfect but it will DO.

Remember this is DIY, not master crafts. You'll never produce a dish from a famous chef to the same standard that he or she will, so don't expect your DIY project to come out like that of a master carpenter. Even if you think you are ham-fisted, can burn hot water, and are a menace around the house, we hope you will gain courage and confidence. For those in possession of basic skills already, there are plenty of projects to increase your know-how and we think that even the hardened DIYer will find some tips to add to their repertoire.

Let's talk symbols

Whatever your ability now, this book provides a starting point. We have laid out the projects a bit like a recipe book and hinted at where the task fits in with abilities. So let's talk symbols—each project has been graded with the level of skill and confidence you will need to tackle it: one hammer—easy-peasy; two hammers—a little skill required; three hammers—makes use of all your talents and skills. You will also see scattered throughout the book a number of TRADE SECRETS and TECHNIQUES boxes (see box below for Symbols explained).

The first part of the book explains the value of good preparation, what to wear, and how to get yourself ready to DIY. It also outlines how your home works and what's going on behind your walls. We give you a guided tour around basic tools and tell you how to use them, and there is a pretty comprehensive discussion about materials—what to buy, what to look for. And we also give you an idea of when NOT to do it yourself; sometimes it's just not worth all the hassle, and it is better to employ a skilled tradesperson who really knows his or her way around

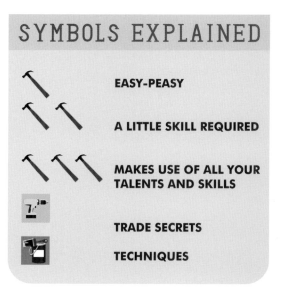

SYMBOLS EXPLAINED

EASY-PEASY

A LITTLE SKILL REQUIRED

MAKES USE OF ALL YOUR TALENTS AND SKILLS

TRADE SECRETS

TECHNIQUES

thorny issues such as plumbing and electricity. The second part of the book—the projects—includes a whole raft of jobs and projects to try, from hanging stuff on walls to decorating and revamping your kitchen cupboards. We have to admit that most of the projects are biased toward us girls. We show storage solutions for housing your shoe collections, how to hang that fab light shade, and how to beautify your home on a budget. To battle against a fear of loud toos, to struggle with new skills, and to suffer the thankless task of clearing up afterwards, the goal has to be worth it. For those with an inclination to climb ladders in the rain to clear out and fix gutters, there are other books with that information.

Eco-friendly too!

Where we can we have suggested materials and methods that are kinder to our planet, and kinder to us too. Because not everything can be recycled with no negative environmental impact yet, we have had to stick with more traditional products in some circumstances. We have encouraged the mantra of "remake, reuse, and recycle." You can feel slightly smug when you breathe new life into an old wardrobe by adding a new shelf, and a tree somewhere will be thanking you for it too!

An argument for brain versus brawn

Not all of us are endowed with big muscles and the stamina of a marathon runner, but being petite isn't a hindrance to successful DIY. There are several ways to compensate for lack of heave-ho.

- Let sharp, good-quality tools do the job. Power tools raised the bar and created a lot of equality as far as strength is concerned.
- Use sharp, good-quality drill bits. Let the drill bits work at their maximum ability.
- Replace blades in the jigsaw and sanding paper as soon as these become dull.
- Grip over-tightened nuts with long-handled pliers and use the extra power of the lever effect to aid you. Mechanics use spanner sets because it's the easiest way to loosen something. So should you.
- Use a cordless screwdriver when possible and a long screwdriver if you are using a manual variety. The extra length increases "torque" and provides more power.
- Loosen screws by spraying WD-40 into the screw. Scratch any hardened paint from the screw slot with a utility knife to maximize the effort.
- When lifting and carrying, carry smaller loads. As long as you get the load moved, it doesn't matter how many trips you make. It's a workout and cheaper than the gym.
- Support heavy stuff by using steps if you have a stepladder or a workbench to hold the other end in place. Use clamps and vices where you can.

TRADE SECRETS

- Screws and nails and drill bits need a place to live. A plastic box with separate compartments works well. Keep the different sizes separated so you don't have to sort through every screw to find what you want.
- Wall plugs and other small bits of stuff can be kept in a box or a bag to start off with (depending on how much you gather).
- Keep old jam jars and jewelry boxes for screws and nails—stick a nail through the top so you know what's in each box before you open it.
- If you invest in a toolbox, make sure it's big and sturdy enough for you. A toolbox isn't just great storage—you can also use it as a mini workbench, and you can stand and sit on it if you don't have anything else around.

Wedging and levers

- You can lift heavy things using a lever made from a garden spade or long length of wood. Use a cold chisel or the claw of a hammer to inch under the heavy item and wedge in a long length of wood. Use the other end of the wood as a lever to lift.
- Take breaks. Don't get discouraged by getting exhausted. A nice sit-down with a cup of coffee and a doughnut provides a short break to raise blood sugar and plan the next stage.
- HALT—Don't do anything when you are Hungry, Angry, Lonely, or Tired. Those strong emotions can help sabotage good work.
- Team up—Two *are* stronger than one. Find a friend who has a project in mind and work together on each other's jobs. Setbacks become challenges that you can talk over and putting heads together can turn up a better creative solution.
- Being smaller means you can fit into tighter corners and being nimble often beats brawn in DIY. Holding tiny panel pins is easier if you have smaller hands.

PART I
BEFORE YOU BEGIN

The door closes. The keys are in your hands. You are finally in your own home. Maybe elation is arising or despair is descending. It can be overwhelming to look at a new home and know where to begin. Perhaps every room needs something changed, but you have to move in regardless. You may hate every color the previous occupant used. If money is tight, there may seem to be no budget to renovate. Whatever the reason, the desire to do everything may clash with a lack of confidence, and the result is that nothing gets done.

Once all your furniture is in place, it can be easy to rationalize that it's too late now, or to allow apathy to gain the upper hand. However, there is always something you can DIY to cheer things up.

ONE STEP AT A TIME

BRACE YOURSELF. YOU *CAN* DO IT. Choose small bits of work. However much that pattern offends, deciding to remove *all* the wallpaper from every room at the same time will invariably leave you exhausted and demotivated. Instead tackle one wall at a time. Set a goal to change one thing about one room every week.

There are several really easy quick fixes that will brighten up your home and help change that depressing space into a happy land. Even if your place is a dingy rental property, changing simple things that can be replaced at the end of the lease will make it seem more like a home. Have a look at the projects section for easy fixes to brighten up your mood and make you feel safe and secure.

GSI (GET SOMEONE IN) VERSUS DIY

Some jobs are simply not suitable for the DIY treatment, either because they are too complex and have safety issues, or because you just don't have time. So if you are going to Get Someone In (GSI as opposed to DIY), here are a few things you need to know before you do.

The best way to get someone who is reliable and trustworthy is to ask people you know for recommendations. Make sure you get a number of estimates. The bigger the job, the more estimates you should get. For something like a bathroom refit, three is a good number, but for something more complex like a loft conversion or extension, then perhaps five.

When a tradesperson visits, he or she should be respectful of your home and listen to what you want. And remember your gut instinct is a powerful tool; if you don't get a good feeling about someone, then don't use that person.

An estimate should come through promptly, showing that the person is serious about the work. It should be detailed and outline all the work that needs doing and include notes that need to be considered when the work is being undertaken, that is, if there might be potential additional work once the job starts.

Getting a quote

People often confuse estimates and quotes. It is a common belief that a quote is a fixed price for the job and an estimate is a rough idea of what it might cost. It is often confusing and it is difficult to separate the two in law, so it is important to clarify with the tradesperson the detail of work they will be doing and, if any additional work is necessary, that you are consulted and the cost agreed upon beforehand.

A good tradesperson will outline each stage of the work and the costs associated. Materials and labor costs should be separated out and if there is likely to be any additional work, a note should be attached to the estimate or quote so you are aware beforehand. This is not always possible because unforeseen problems do arise when work is in progress. If the unforeseen does arise, make sure you see the problems that have occurred and make the effort to see it while the tradesperson is there so he or she can can show you and discuss the solutions.

TRADE SECRET

A good tradesperson will be busy, so if someone says they can start immediately and has no other work lined up, get a reference and check his or her last job.

QUICK TIP

Your cast-offs could be someone else's start-ups. Find out if you have a local online recycling network to pass along anything you will not be using. Charities sometimes take donations, and you will be keeping what you don't want away from landfills.

Don't be afraid to ask questions no matter how dumb they might seem. This is your home, and you have the right to understand the work that is taking place. If you are paying for an estimate, then you should be getting a more consultative approach. It is not uncommon, especially in larger jobs, for tradespeople to provide a less-detailed estimate initially and then, when you have decided to use their services, visit again and spend more time talking through the finer details.

Supporting material

An estimate should be supported by additional materials such as testimonials, copies of insurances, and details of terms and conditions. If they don't provide this kind of information, don't be afraid to ask for it. If you are having a large job done, try to speak to the previous client directly, and if you can, go and see the work yourself. If you build up a friendly relationship with a tradesperson, don't be afraid to ask for advice for projects you want to tackle on your own. Most tradespeople will be flattered enough to share their knowledge.

Even if you feel a job is too advanced to take on, reading this book and learning *how* to do it yourself will make you more comfortable and less intimidated when contracting tradespeople. Next time you hear that infamous sharp intake of breath followed by "That'll cost you!," you'll know if they are talking out of their builder's bum.

Preparation

We are all familiar with cookery programs where the calm chef surrounds him- or herself with a multitude of tiny glass bowls of ingredients in expectation of a smooth performance. You will find that like the TV chef, your project will run much more smoothly if you have taken time to lay out all the tools and materials before starting.

Un-DIYing

Each generation morphs their homes to reflect their individuality and times. In the 1950s when DIY became all the rage, everyone was busy boxing in the banisters

and covering panel doors to simulate "modern" flush doors. Now we are ripping out what went before. More than likely as you become more confident, you will want to take out something old and replace it. Check out the Tool kit section to learn how to hold a cold chisel and claw hammer to remove old work (see page 32).

Scheduling time

Obviously don't plan a project just before a big wedding, going away on vacation, or an important work deadline. Although DIY can become a delightful distraction, it can also drag you down if you are drowning in a project when you should be prioritizing something else. Although toddlers can happily live around bags of dusty plaster, you might find your spirits flagging trying to keep up appearances day in and day out.

Where to work

Consider your work place. You don't need an enormous garage packed with state-of-the-art machinery or even a humble shed at the back of the garden; they are luxuries that aren't required to get a DIY job done well. The most practical area in many homes is the kitchen. It is likely to have a work surface that won't wobble and a floor that is easy to clean. The disadvantage is that mealtimes may interrupt grand preparations. You can use kitchen chairs as a simple trestle for cutting wood. Remember to cover them with a drop cloth. If using the work surface, protect it with newspaper or cardboard. A portable

TRADE SECRET

Put your cell phone in a clear plastic sandwich bag before you begin. This extra piece of preparation will be worthwhile if you receive a phone call while your fingers are covered in wood filler or bath sealant.

bench vice will clamp onto a counter or table—protect these with a fold of cardboard. A hallway can be commandeered for a project and stairs make useful work trestles.

Get started

Early. Leave yourself enough time to hunt out the tools and discover any extra items you will need to buy. This includes an inspection of any half-used filler or sealant that may have hardened over time. There is potential for exasperation if you arrive at the hardware shop after it has closed.

What tools will you need? As in following a recipe, you will need to gather your equipment and tools in the work area. Use a bucket to carry tools and have a small cardboard box (a shoe box is ideal!) in which to place small items; that way they won't get kicked into can't-find-it land.

If the work you are doing is messy, think about dustsheets, spare clothes, and rags to wipe down and clean hands. If you gather these first it will save valuable mopping-up time if something spills.

 TRADE SECRET

Wrap your paint-brushes and rollers in plastic wrap or a plastic bag to stop them drying out overnight. If you rinse them out, they may not be dry enough to use the next day, so this works well.

You can also leave them in the freezer overnight, but remember to keep them away from food.

Cleaning up

As with preparation at the beginning, it's also important to leave plenty of time to clean up. It's really tempting once you've finished a job to want to show off your success to friends, but just remember that leaving time for clear up makes the next job go faster. When you are carrying on a project the following day, make sure you have cleaned any gunk (paint, filler, glue) from your tools and leave them somewhere to dry so that they can be used again quickly.

To **clean brushes** properly, use water and dishwashing liquid for soluble paints and mineral spirits for oil-based paints. Run a filling knife down a roller to get the excess paint off and keep the water running. For oil-based paints, leave brushes to soak in mineral spirits for 30 minutes or so, then run through with warm water and dishwashing liquid to clean thoroughly. Dry bushes flat to stop water running into the handle and loosening the bristle adhesive.

Don't be tempted to leave your brushes standing in paint cleaner for days. The bristles will bend out of shape. If you don't clean your brushes properly, they

will go crusty and won't be very effective when used again, and you'll have to buy new brushes.

Clean your filling knives or spatulas quickly, otherwise filler dries on the blade and the bumps make it impossible to get a smooth flat surface when you come back to use them. It's useful to have a narrow spatula and one with a wider blade, and when you clean them, you can use one knife against the other to scrape off the excess gunk. But be careful because the edges of these knives are very sharp and can cause nasty cuts.

Put all your tools away in the right place. No one likes it when something goes missing. Shake your drop cloths outside and away from the wind, otherwise when you next come to use them, they could be the wrong way up, and you will have the last project's dust and debris all over your floor before you even start.

QUICK TIPS

Don't forget to clean yourself. Clean paint off your skin using olive oil if nothing else works and check all over for stray flecks and splotches. It can be quite embarrassing to go out on a Saturday night and have someone kindly point out that you have a big fleck of paint on your back.

WHAT NOT TO WEAR . . .

Many physical activities require specialist clothing. Although you don't need the latest technological ski jacket *en piste*, most of us would not set off downhill in an evening dress. So it is with DIY. Taking a few moments to make sure you are dressed appropriately will help avoid injury and prevent ruining your favorite pair of jeans. Once dressed for the job, you will feel more confident.

- Remove dangly jewelry and bangles. They can get caught up in tools and drag into paint.
- Tie back your long flowing tresses.
- Choose a work outfit. It might be old jeans and a T-shirt, leggings and a sweatshirt, shorts and a crop top, but whatever the look, let it be something that can stand up to a little paint and a bit of sawdust.

- Loose clothing gets caught, billows onto new paint, and isn't a good thing. Bear in mind that a sweater will hold sawdust much more than a T-shirt.
- Choose flat well-fitting shoes with toes—sneakers are ideal. Tripping isn't funny, and dropping a heavy hammer on your bare toes is really not a good look.

DIY accessories

The classic DIY apron has a bib front and wraps around the side. It ends below your knees and has a generous pocket to hold extra screws and small tools when you are working up a ladder. You can wipe your hands on it and keep the rest of your clothing fairly clean.

Make sure you wear **eye goggles** when drilling or sawing wood.

Hunting for a tiny speck of sawdust in your eye takes a lot of time and is painful. A pair of **gardening gloves** instills confidence when picking up rough timber and handling drill bits and the drill.

The best gloves are made of breathable cloth with latex-dipped fingertips for maximum sensitivity combined with protection. Many people fuss over protecting their hands, but for a lot of jobs, the extra dexterity and agility of bare hands is best. Use a good gardening barrier cream before a job and clean up with baby oil and then gentle soap to prevent chapped hands at the end of the day. Plan your next manicure for after your big project is done.

Buy a set of **dust masks** and wear them when sanding or using a jigsaw. A classic

bandana will protect and hold back your hair for that retro look. It will prevent you getting paint splashes and sawdust in your hair, giving you that "premature hint of gray" look. Consider wearing a shower cap for really dusty work or painting ceilings if no one is around. Not glam but it works!

Invest in some kneepads if you are about to begin any flooring job, laying vinyl tiles, or caulking up drafty holes. Most available pads are large and can chafe, but you can make your own by wrapping thermal socks around your knees. A garden kneeling mat can work just as well, although it's not attached to you, so you'll have to keep moving it along the job as you progress.

A SHORT GUIDE TO HOUSE CONSTRUCTION

WALL CONSTRUCTION

Depending on the type of property you are in, your home is likely to have the following types of interior walls. Most modern buildings and flats will have a majority of plasterboard (stud walls), but older properties will have stronger walls.

The walls between two internal rooms can be either stud walls (see below) or solid walls. Solid walls are usually supporting walls—supporting the weight of the walls above. To remove these walls involves major structural work and it is not a job for a

DIYer; if you want to investigate whether you can do this, you will need to get a builder in and possibly take advice from a surveyor or structural engineer. If your wall is non-supporting, then you can remove this fairly easily (however, bear in mind there will be a lot of finishing to do afterward).

Stud walls or plasterboard walls are a simple timber stud frame construction covered with plasterboard. The plasterboard is then skimmed with a layer of finishing plaster and painted according to your decorative tastes.

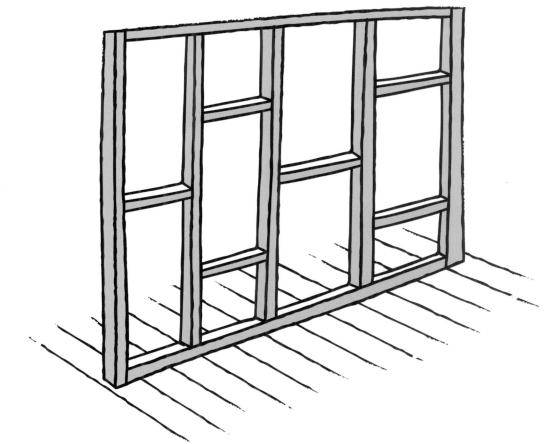

An interior wall is often constructed of timber studs (above) with sheets of plasterboard nailed to it. Whether your wall is framed or solid will affect how you screw things to it.

Solid walls can be made of brickwork and may have a screed (smooth overlay) of concrete. This type of construction can make it difficult to screw into the wall. The load-bearing weight of a solid wall is more than that of a stud wall, so if you have something very heavy to hang then it's worth thinking about putting it on a solid wall.

Also note that above your windows there will be a **"lintel"** (see Glossary page 132) that supports the weight of the wall above the window. These are usually steel or brick and can be difficult to drill in to. To combat this, it is common practice to hang a batten to the wall above the window and fix blinds or curtains to this batten (see 'Fitting a batten,' page 48).

Windows have concrete or metal lintels.

FLOOR COVERINGS

The construction of your floors will depend on the age and style of your property. If you are in an older property, your floors are likely to be wood floorboards on top of a timber frame structure. In newer properties, however, the floors may well be concrete. Whatever your sub-layer, you have many floor covering options available to you. When making a choice about flooring, budget is probably one of the largest considerations; any of these flooring options can range from cheap to very, very expensive.

Carpet is nice and warm underfoot and keeps the heat in, but it can look tired and jaded if not maintained properly. As well as wool and synthetic carpets, there are lovely designs made from grass. Grass grows fast and is happy being harvested.

Sea grass grows in tropical climates on the banks of rivers. The natural fiber is harvested by hand, dried, and hand-spun into cords before being woven into flooring.

Traditional floorboards look beautiful and are nice to restore as an original feature; however they can be drafty in an old house.

available these days. Get a good-quality type—it will last a long time and won't look cheap.

Amtico® is the king of plastic tiles. There is an excellent choice of styles and some are more expensive than wood. Hardwearing and luxurious, Amtico tiles will last for many years.

Marmoleum® is a revival of the old linoleum. Eco-friendly since it is made from resin and linseed oil with jute backing, it is also good for allergy sufferers as it doesn't "off-gas" (give off nasty toxic fumes). Available as tiles and rolls of solid flooring.

Rubber can look a bit industrial, but it comes in some very funky colors and interesting textural designs, and it really suits a small bathroom or kitchen.

WATER, WATER EVERYWHERE

Water coming into a domestic property can be either direct or indirect. To tell which one you have, you will need to look at the type of water system you have. You are likely to have an "indirect" water system if you have a storage water heater or a cold water tank in your attic. The water comes into the property through a mains pipe and gets fed to the storage water heater or cold water storage tank and then is piped to various fixtures (for example, sinks, tubs, showers).

If you have combination boiler (COMBI) system (popular in Europe) or a tankless water heater, then the mains water entry is considered to be "direct." You are able to have hot water instantly and don't need to wait for a tank to fill. This means all the cold taps, showers, kitchen/laundry appliances, toilets, and so are fed water directly from the mains, at mains water pressures.

Many modern properties utilize a "direct" system, which has the advantage of minimizing the amount of plumbing required and means that showers and taps operate at a greater pressure—ideal if you prefer a really powerful shower. The main advantage to an "indirect" system is that you are not without some water supply if there is a temporary mains failure and the water is shut off for a time.

Solid wood floors can be laid over any leveled floor and can really change the look of the room. There are many choices and price ranges too.

Engineered floors involve a surface of real wood veneer being applied to an interior of softwood ply. Bamboo is also available as a composite flooring alternative, a fast-growing resource with a variety of finishes.

Laminate floors have a surface that is a photograph of wood printed on to a thin MDF board. It is easy to damage and impossible to repair. This option is quite cheap, but the style is rather dated now.

Bamboo flooring is one of the hardest natural materials available. Because bamboo is a rapid-growing grass and not a wood, it can be harvested every 3–5 years, unlike 15–25 years for most wood. This makes bamboo a very environmentally friendly product for flooring.

Ceramic tiles are easy to clean but can be cold unless you install underfloor heating; these are best used in wet areas (kitchens, bathrooms, and greenhouses) but can be used anywhere.

Vinyl floors are not as cheap and nasty as you might think; some really funky colors and options are

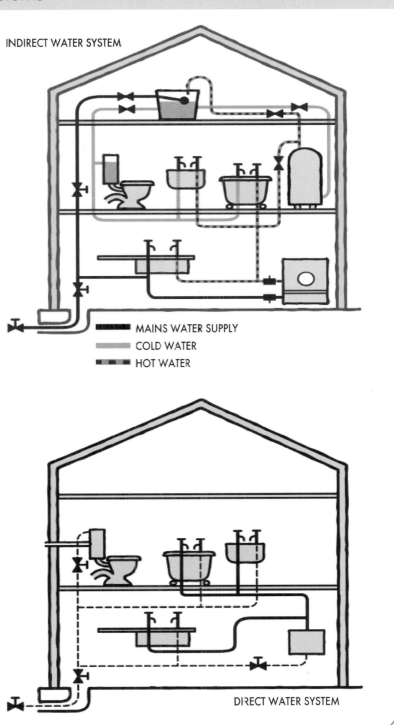

INDIRECT WATER SYSTEM

MAINS WATER SUPPLY
COLD WATER
HOT WATER

DIRECT WATER SYSTEM

If you have a plumbing disaster in your home, the worst thing you can do is panic, and the best thing you can do is be prepared. First of all, you need to know what sort of system you have—indirect or direct. In an indirect cold water system (above right), the water is stored in a tank normally kept in the attic and feeds nearly all the water outlets in the house, whereas in a direct system (below right), all cold water outlets are fed directly from the mains water supply and so have mains pressure.

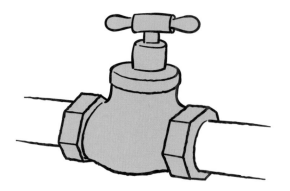

YOUR STOPCOCK WILL LOOK SOMETHING LIKE THIS.

Stopcocks

Before disaster strikes, find out where your stopcock is and if it works. Make sure you know where all your important stopcocks are, because in a plumbing crisis, you will need to stop water coming into your property immediately.

The best way to do this is to turn off your stopcock. The stopcock isolates (shuts off) the mains water supply from the water that runs through your home.

If you are in an apartment, this may be in a communal area such as the hallway, but in most properties it is located near the first source of mains water (usually the kitchen sink taps). It's important to locate and test your stopcock because if you have a leak, you will want to isolate the source of water coming into the property. By turning off the stopcock, you will stop any further water from coming into the property, thereby limiting any further damage from a leak.

Because stopcocks are often left unused for years, they can frequently seize up and are unable to turn, so it's a good idea to find this out before an emergency strikes. This is a lifesaver—and can save you an awful lot of money on an emergency plumber. So put down this book now, yes now, and find your stopcock. Turn it clockwise to turn it off, counterclockwise for on. If a stopcock hasn't been used in a while, it can be really stiff, so spray a bit of lubricating oil in the joints and leave for 10 minutes to let it work its magic. After you have done this, you should be able to turn the valve. If you can't, then you'll need to get the valve replaced. It's best to find out now and get it replaced before you actually need it in an emergency.

Replacing a stopcock is a specialist job for an experienced plumber. It will involve freezing pipework or turning the water off in the street. Outside any property is a mains water stopcock that can be accessed through small panels in the street—you would need a special key to turn this. It's probably something you won't want to tackle yourself, especially if you are in a apartment since you will be turning off the water to the whole building.

Pipework

Inside your property is a series of copper pipes that carries the water around and feeds it to different appliances, such as your shower or toilet. It might be sensible to make sure that each appliance has its own "isolation valve" or mini shutoff valve (it's also known as a service valve).

This will allow the water to any appliance to be isolated and work can take place without having to shut off the mains water. This is handy if you find you have a leaky toilet or shower as you can turn this valve on and off to limit damage and wasted water until the leak is fixed.

The copper pipes running through the house will carry cold water in one set and hot water in another. Cold water will be directed to your hot water system (boiler or tank) and then it will come out into a separate set of pipes that carries hot water around the property.

Waste pipes

Wastewater is carried away from plumbing fixtures through large plastic pipes to the mains drainage system . . . and from there no one needs to know!

ELECTRICAL SYSTEM

Although we take it for granted, electricity is a complex system that needs a level of understanding before we can safely make any electrical changes to our homes. So how does it work?

Electricity is made in a power plant where fossil fuels (such as coal) are used to turn water into steam. This steam powers a turbine that spins a big magnet inside a copper wire. This heat energy is converted to mechanical energy that is then converted to electrical energy—SIMPLE!

From the power plant, the electric current runs through the power lines to a substation, then to an underground transformer or pylon. From here electricity comes into your home through a service box, where your meter is located to measure how much you use. Wires take electricity around your home, powering your lights and all your other electrical appliances. There are multiple power circuits in your home, usually separated into lighting and power. There may also be separate supplies to appliances that require a lot of current.

ELECTRICAL SAFETY ISSUES

Because of the obvious safety issues, there are many electrical tasks you should not do yourself. Remember tampering with electrics can be very dangerous if you don't know what you are doing. The section on projects outlines some safe things you can take on.

There are many restrictions on what electrical work you can do yourself, and there's a good reason for this—poor electrics can and have caused serious fires. This is one area of health and safety that should be taken extremely seriously.

If you are not sure what work you can do yourself, then check with your local building regulations office. When getting someone in to complete certain electrical work for you, that person should provide

you with a certificate at the end of the work detailing what has been completed. This certificate will also be stored with thier professional registration body. If you don't have this certificate then the work is invalid and may even be fitted to illegal standards. This in turn could affect your insurance coverage, so ensure that your contractor provides you with this certificate at the end of the job where appropriate. Don't pay the bill until you've got it. You will especially need this certificate if you decide to rent out your property and also when you are selling your house.

TRADE SECRET

Universal method for tightening and loosening: clockwise to tighten and counterclockwise to loosen. Or remember: "Righty Tighty-Lefty Loosey."

Fuse box

Your fuse box no longer has fuses in it; instead it holds MCBs (Miniature Circuit Breakers) and an RCD (Residual Circuit Breaker), which isolate the source of electricity much like the shutoff valve and service valves in the plumbing system. From here, the wiring is taken to each room of the house and isolated by switches in the walls or on each appliance.

Fuses

Fuses come in a number of varieties, but the ones you will be familiar with are the little glass vials that sit within a plug. A fuse is a metal wire that melts when too much current flows through a circuit—interrupting the circuit to which the item is connected. When a fuse blows, an interruption to the circuit occurs that prevents overheating and fire.

If an appliance doesn't work, it's worth changing the fuse to see if this is the problem. Use a screwdriver to unscrew the two sections of a plug and you will see the fuse sitting neatly in between two clips. Replace this with a new fuse of the same amp (the amp is written on the fuse) and screw the plug back together. Often that will solve the problem.

It's also worth checking what the fuse rating for the appliance is, as the item may be blowing due to having the wrong fuse.

ALL TOOLED UP

BEFORE YOU CAN LAUNCH YOURSELF into your DIY projects, you will need to acquire a basic tool kit and learn a little about the materials you can expect to have to buy and use in the course of doing the projects.

Think of these items as "empower" tools. Dodgy old blunt tools discarded by others will not instill confidence, so take yourself seriously and gather a basic box of tools that you can add to later. Most tools cost less than a bit of makeup and some cost as much as a pair of shoes but could last a lifetime and save a fortune.

Without tools, you will find it difficult to carry out the simplest tasks. If you are camping, you can cook food with a stick and an open fire, but we all know how much easier it is to cook with a range of utensils and it's the same with DIY. If you know what tools you have *and where they are*, you can plan the job and do it whenever you find the time.

When setting up a basic tool kit, buy the best tools you can afford but also acquire the ones you like. More expensive tools tend to perform

CONTAINERS FOR EVERYTHING

Boxes, old cans with lids, plastic containers with lids, and jam jars are just some of the possibilities for storage. You will need containers for:

- Screws, nails, and drill bits. A plastic box with separate compartments works well for these but *sort them*. Keep the different sizes apart so you don't have to sort through every screw to find the size you want.
- Wall plugs. Depending on how many you gather, you can use a box or a bag for these.

- Old jam jars and jewelry boxes for screws and nails. Stick a nail through the top so you know what size is in each jar or box before you open it.

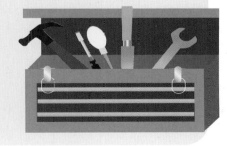

better than cheaper tools and may last longer, but if you only need a tool for one job and you know you won't use it again, then it can't hurt to buy a cheaper version. Learn what each one does by practicing with it before a big project if possible, and by reading its instructions. Trying each tool out and really getting familiar with them will give you more confidence when you use them for real. Every tool is designed to do a specific job, so if you use a tool in the way it was designed, it will make the job run more smoothly. A sure way to damage a tool is to use it for a job it's not designed to do.

Where to buy

Think of choosing tools as you would choose a pot— there's a lot of choice with regard to color, material,

A basic tool kit

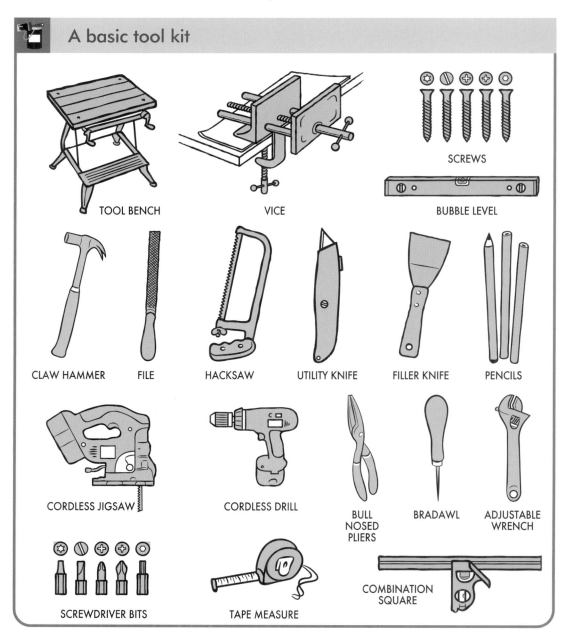

TOOL BENCH

VICE

SCREWS

BUBBLE LEVEL

CLAW HAMMER   FILE   HACKSAW   UTILITY KNIFE   FILLER KNIFE   PENCILS

CORDLESS JIGSAW   CORDLESS DRILL   BULL NOSED PLIERS   BRADAWL   ADJUSTABLE WRENCH

SCREWDRIVER BITS   TAPE MEASURE   COMBINATION SQUARE

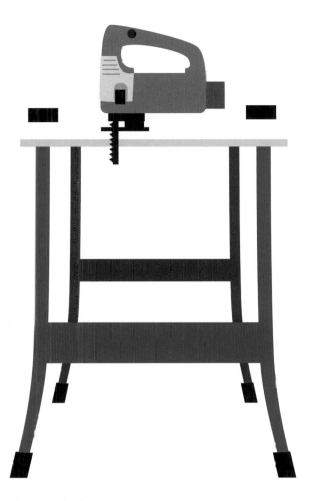

and design, but ultimately it just boils water! Good places to browse are catalogs from online tool supply companies to your local mid-sized hardware store. The advantage of buying from a hardware store or DIY outlet is that you can ask a lot of questions. Ask the assistant to show you how to change a blade on a hacksaw, for instance. Watching someone do it is the best way to learn. Once you know what to look for, you can pick up tools from market stalls and garage sales.

Where to put your tools

A place for everything and everything in its place. You're all set to go, but where is that screwdriver and hammer? Start keeping everything together. Shoeboxes can hold your tools until you expand your collection, and then it can hold all the clips, staples, spare blades, and so on. Good tool storage places include under the stairs, in the bottom of a closet in a special box, or in a trunk doubling as a coffee table. I'm sure that there are any number of places in your home where tools can be stored out of sight. If you invest in a toolbox, make sure it's big enough and sturdy enough for you. A toolbox isn't just great storage, but in a pinch, it can also be used as a mini workbench, and you can stand and sit on it if you don't have a stepladder around.

The workplace

A foldable workbench is the right height for working at, will hold your wood tightly while you work, and is a fabulous friend that will keep your furniture from being ruined. There are several lightweight, adjustable, foldable workbenches on the market that fit into the back of a closet. If you can't find room for a bench, then don't despair; buy a removable table vice and attach it to a worktop or a table when needed. Use a section of cardboard to protect the surface of the table and make it secure with masking tape.

MEASURING AND MARKING TOOLS

"Measure twice, cut once" so the saying goes. I'll add my own tip—measure it again if you have taken

a coffee break before cutting it. Also mark the section to be kept and the section to be discarded so that you will know which is which. But in order to measure you need the right tools:

Sixteen-foot (5 m) retractable tape. Try some out in the shop—unroll it and see how long you can unreel it till it "breaks" (bends). The longer the tape, the better and more handy if you are measuring things by yourself. It should have clear readable numbers that you can understand.

Combination square. This is used for marking right angles, perpendicular marks, and 45-degree angles. Look for clear measurements on the straight part. Most have a small pin that unscrews and can be used for scribing (scratching the line to be marked).

Bubble level. Used for checking and marking horizontal and vertical lines. Look for easy-to-read "bubbles," both horizontal and vertical. Long versions can also be used as a straight edge to cut against. Smaller ones can be used as a plumb line too.

Pencil. *Sharpness* is the key to accuracy. Ask yourself "What side of the pencil line am I cutting against?" Buy two wide, flat carpenter's pencils. They are oval in shape so that when you put them down, they don't roll way. Buy two because a pencil's main aim in life is to hide from you during a project.

Bradawl. Like a very small screwdriver but used for making a very small hole in wood. This is called a "pilot" hole before drilling a bigger hole. It makes the hole more accurate and well worth the extra step. Look for a comfortable handle—some have a flat head, some have a square rod.

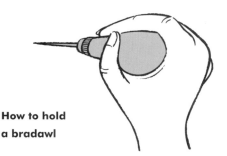

**How to hold
a bradawl**

Miter box. This useful device will help guide you to cut small lengths of wood at angles when finishing a wooden floor.

CUTTING TOOLS

There is an assortment of tools for cutting various materials, so you will need several tools to accomplish the cutting you will do.

Utility knife/all-purpose cutting knife and **a set of spare blades**. This is an invaluable tool for cutting vinyl tiles and carpet and for scoring lines. It is also brilliant for sharpening pencils. Look for a sturdy well-fitting handle; the blade should not rattle when the screw is tightened. Learn how to replace the blade.

Junior hacksaw with a **set of replaceable blades**. A non-powered option for cutting small pieces of wood, especially if you have to hold it near the edge. Also brilliant for cutting curtain track, plastic pipe, dowel, and carpet strip. It won't cut anything larger than the distance between the blade and the back. Look for a fairly comfortable handle. Learn how to change the blade since it becomes blunt eventually, and too much exertion may make the blade snap. It's OK—this is normal. Practice changing the blade when you aren't in a hurry—it's a technique that requires pressure against the saw handle.

Hacksaw and **set of replaceable blades**. Look for a fairly comfortable handle. Hold the saw firmly and level and stand square on to the work you are cutting. It helps to keep the cut vertical. Holding your first finger straight against the saw will help to keep it steady (see below).

Electric powered jigsaw. Look for a bigger motor (18v) since the more it will cut through like butter, the less sweat you will produce. Cordless tools make working up a ladder and in the garden more convenient but are heavier. However, working with these will have a beneficial effect on any bingo wings. The speed needs to be variable so you can cut fast for wood and very slow for metal (it gets hot). The base plate can be adjusted to cut at 45-degree angles so it can cut molding and frames. If it can collect the sawdust then less mess for you to clear up and if it has a laser guide for cutting it's about perfect. Get an assortment of blades—a pack of "rough cut," a pack of "fine cut" and a pack for metal cutting.

A set of pliers. Flat nose, round nose, saw nose will be plenty to start. These are extra hands to help hold and cut wire and cable.

NAILING AND SCREWING IMPLEMENTS

Claw hammer. For nailing and removing nails. Look for a firm head and a very fine V in the claw for removing nails. The flat face should be gently rounded to not dent the surface of the wood when driving nails home. Heavy is good. Remember that the weight of a tool can make up for the lack of muscle strength.

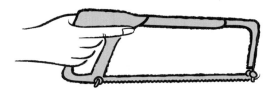

How to hold a hacksaw

How to hold a hammer

effective method of undoing or unscrewing objects—very Edward Scissorhands.

Ratchet screwdriver. Helps keep the screwdriver in the head of the screw, helps to make the turn and doesn't waste muscle power when turning the screwdriver the other way. The ratchet device operates to both screw and unscrew and can be 'locked' to operate as an ordinary screwdriver.

Cordless electric screwdriver. It's a fab toy. Buy a good one with a long battery life—it will save time and muscle and is vital for Flat-pack Queens.

Set of assorted screwdriver bits. A set will have slot heads, cross heads as well as a hex head to assemble flat-pack furniture fast.

DRILLING TOOLS

Cordless drill with a "keyless" chuck. The *best* thing in a girl's tool kit. It is heavier than a drill with a cord, but fabulously freeing when up a ladder or walking across a room—you won't need to use an extension cord. Not only will it drill all the holes you will ever need, you can also use it as a really powerful screwdriver, though I recommend that you have an additional cordless screwdriver (see above) if you are planning a big project so you won't have to change bits from drills to screwdriver heads.

Smaller ball/pein hammer. (pein or peen—it's a metal worker thing . . .). It's used for starting nails and pins on intricate jobs. Look for lighter but still firmly fixed head.

Nail sets. Steel instrument used for hammering in nails below the surface.

Pincers. Used for removing nails. You can use pincers in one hand and pliers in the other for an

Terrified of using a drill?

Are you terrified of hairdryers? Unlikely. Terrified of a food mixer? Even less likely. A drill uses a rotary motor (it makes things go round) and you hold it like a hairdryer. Go to a big hardware store that has plenty of drills on display and pick some up and point them away from you. Go on—it won't hurt anything (they are not charged). How to choose a drill? The same sort of choices as a hairdryer or a sewing machine—how much power you need, how many options you want. Pick an amount you want to spend and buy one you can move all the switches or—remember some will feel stiff because they are designed to avoid getting knocked on or off accidentally. They do tend to be designed for bigger hands, so you may have to reach a bit further but even very dainty paws manage to use drills. The drill bits fit into the drill by gripping into the three jaws that open when the chuck tightens. Learn how to use it. Get it home and charge the battery like a cell phone. You can play with it to learn what it does. Variable speeds mean you can cut metal slowly and ease your way through thick wood. Buy an 18v drill if possible (use the power of the tool to compensate for lack of muscle strength). Buy a "combi" drill. This will have a "hammer action" option and is great for drilling into wall. Get one with two batteries. A battery may run down before a job is finished so it's handy to have a spare on charge.

Set of drill bits. The spiral-bladed things that drill the holes are called bits. You need three sets of bits: one for wood, one for metal, and one for concrete/brick. Buying a complete set of drill bits means you know you have all the sizes you will ever need. The bits will blunt eventually, like pencils, and you can buy replacements individually as you go along. Expensive bits will be worth the money—they are sharper and will last longer. If you don't want screw heads to rest above the surface, then buy a countersink bit to use after drilling the hole.

SMOOTHING AND SHAPING TOOLS

Sanding block. Look for ones made from a wood block with felt on one side and a slit for securing the sandpaper. Others are made of hard rubber or cork. A block will ensure that the surface being sanded has constant pressure and is flat.

Sandpaper. The grittiness is measured by number, so 40 is very coarse and 240 is very fine. Buy an assorted pack and keep all the sheets together with the sanding block in

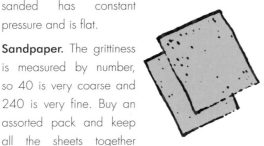

a supermarket bag, then you aren't hunting for the block when you need it. If you are doing a lot of decorating, it's cheaper to buy sandpaper by the yard/meter from a trade store.

Electric sander. Sheet sanders are easy to use—like using an iron from Mad Max. On some machines, the sandpaper even attaches by VELCRO! Beware the orbital sander, as they are more likely to gouge into the wood and leave bad semicircle memories. Small mouse sanders are great for getting into small places and look cute too.

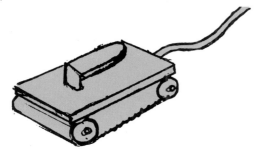

Files. Three assorted hand files with handles to smooth wood and metal. Round, triangular, and flat in shape from rough to fine. The midsize crosscut file

is called a bastard. Keep a straight face when asking for one in a hardware shop. To keep a straight edge when filing, stand behind the work and use long, smooth, even strokes. Files can be used to make fine adjustments to wood, great when you need to shave a thin area off a shelf or can be used to create channels for cables.

Cold chisel. Not expensive but very empowering. You can remove tiles, flooring, skirting boards, stuff that's stuck with a cold chisel and a hammer. Often the first tool on a job.

This list isn't comprehensive, but will enable you to assemble a set of tools to embark on many projects in this book. Beside the tools, there are various must-have items that can be used on almost any project.

How to hold a cold chisel

Screws and nails. Buy assorted packs of screws and nails. These contain a selection of the most popular sizes. Until you begin a job, it's impossible to know what you will need. Crosshead screws are easier to use and require less muscle than traditional slotted head screws. There are lots of brands with "Turbo" and "Max" in the names. These are even easier to drive home (screw into material).

Masking tape. Marvelous for holding down, light clamping, marking out on shiny objects, picking up annoying bits of sawdust off the floor and off of you. Remember to remove it or it will become stickier and turn into MARKING tape.

GLUES AND SOLVENTS

Cartridge gun. Cheaper and much easier to use than little tubes, the cartridge gun will apply sealant, glue and caulk quickly and with style, making you look and feel like a pro.

Woodwork glue. Also called PVA glue (polyvinyl acetate). Wipe off excess quickly; it's harder to remove once it dries. Water solvent, PVA is like school glue, so if you get any on your hands you may delight in peeling it away and reveling in school-day memories.

Other glues. Invest in a pack of two-part epoxy glue, a tube of superglue, and some impact adhesive. As you get in the DIY groove you can decide which is the best glue for a job.

Grab adhesive. When you discover grab adhesive, your confidence level will soar. This brilliant stuff is very viscous and very strong. It sticks everything to everything as well, so be careful when using it because you don't want to stick your clothes to your new shelves.

Can of WD-40. (Water Displacement—40th attempt). The inventor was a persistent guy. This versatile spray repels moisture and loosens things like squeaky doors and helps unstick overtightened joints.

Can of orange-scented goo remover. Great for removing sticky labels and old stickers.

Mineral spirits. For cleaning oil-based paints from brushes and rollers.

Dishwashing liquid. An underrated DIY helper. It acts as a surfactant and dissolves grease on contact. Add a teensy drop to paint where the area is too smooth (glass or shiny metal) to hold.

Baby oil. Great for removing stubborn stains on skin and hard surfaces.

SPECIAL TOOLS FOR SPECIFIC USES

ELECTRICAL PROJECTS

- **Insulated screwdrivers** and **pliers** with a thick rubber handle to limit shocks.
- **Stud/wire detector** to check that you aren't going to drill into cables.
- **Small screwdrivers** for connection boxes.
- **Wire cutters**.
- **Rubber-soled shoes**. You may thank the earth one day . . .

PLUMBING PROJECTS

- **Toilet Auger.** A metal rod with a curly end for unblocking a toilet. It costs a fraction of what an emergency plumber will charge and may save friendships if you share a place with someone who uses a roll of toilet paper every day.
- **PTFE tape**. A special tape that works like a washer when fitting plastic pipes. It's special because it is both slippery and can grip. (Polytetrafluoroethylene, if you are scientifically minded . . .)
- **Adjustable spanners**. Preferably two so you can use them both for grip.
- A **bucket** and **old rags**. No matter how hard you try, there will always be spillage.
- **Pipe cutter.** A whizzy little tool that easily cuts closet rails and metal curtain rods when not being a plumber's mate.
- **Hole saws** for cutting holes for pipework.

TILING PROJECTS

- **Tile spacers.**
- **Trowel** or **spatula** to spread adhesive.
- **Grout float** or **spatula**.
- **Tile cutters.** Either hand-held like big scissors or bigger like a paper cutter.
- **Nibbler.** A type of pincers that will nibble away at a small amount of a tile.

MATERIAL GIRL

SINCE DIY PROJECTS USE A VARIETY of materials, you will need to get to know your way around a building supply store or your local DIY store. And while you are there, you will want to look like you know what you are doing. Wood in all its many forms has different properties and you will need to pick the types to suit your needs. Read on . . .

Solid wood

Solid wood can be bought in various shapes, sizes, and permutations. The upside of using wood is that it looks natural and is easy to join together; screws do not need wall fixings; and DIY stores sell lengths of soft woods in long lengths. The downsides are that wood has knots that are hard to drill and cut and it can continue to move or warp for years. Natural soft wood will need sanding and finishing with stain or paint to make it moisture-proof.

MDF

Medium density fiberboard (MDF) has been around since the 1980s and quite simply, is mashed-up wood fiber held together with resin. Many online companies will cut and deliver shapes for you. The upside of using MDF is that it has no grain; allows for a smooth finish to surfaces; is great for shelves and simple forms that do not have to be attached to each other; special screws will help hold pieces together; and is less expensive than solid wood. MDF has downsides, however. The resins contain urea formaldehyde, which can cause irritation (wear goggles and respiratory mask when cutting and sanding); unless it is a special waterproof variety, MDF will absorb moisture, so it takes longer to paint; it's harder to joint well since fibers are soft and will pull apart; it is heavier than decorative-faced particleboard (see below) because the resin is heavy. Consider this when judging the span of a shelf.

Chipboard

Chipboard has a fairly smooth surface and is made from chips of wood held together with resin. The upside of chipboard is that it is less dense and less expensive than MDF. The downside, however, is that it requires a lot of finishing for a good effect, and it needs knockdown joints to hold it together.

Decorative-faced particleboard

A chipboard with a thin melamine surface, its cut edges can be finished by applying an iron-on edging, purchased separately. The upsides of this board are that it is available in several different wood-effect finishes and white, and the surfaces are water-resistant and can be wiped down. The downside of decorative-faced particleboard, like with MDF, is its weakness if screwed into directly. Use special knockdown fittings to join surfaces or dowel joint it together.

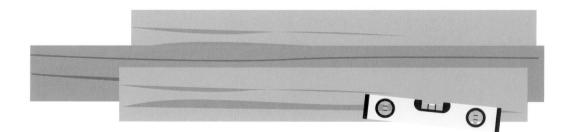

⚙ Buying Wood or How to Swagger in a Lumberyard

Some small local hardware stores carry a stock of precut soft wood, mostly pine. It comes in a large variety of sizes. Browse the selection and make a note of the sizes available. These shops will often have a variety of cornicing or quarter-round beading used for finishing the edges of a floor when laying new flooring if you haven't removed the skirting boards. There is often a range of sizes that can be used as battens. These can also be used for slats for easy-to-make sheves inside cupboards. Round dowels can be used for small rails.

To make sure that the wood you are buying is straight and "true," hold one end of the length and sight your eye down to the other end (see photograph above). Check both width and depth. If it has a bend or curve in it, put it back.

BASIC SKILLS

MASTERING A FEW BASIC SKILLS— measuring and cutting wood, joining two pieces of wood together, and drilling holes in walls—will mean that you can tackle a whole range of projects. But first things first.

Joining Pieces of Wood Together

Once you have mastered the art of joining two pieces of wood/MDF/chipboard together, you can give free rein to your imagination and begin to create your own wonderful item. Use a square to make sure the boards are at right angles to each other. Opposite are three methods of joining two pieces of material together, ranging from the easy to quite demanding.

1° CUTTING WOOD DOWN TO SIZE

First, measure the board with a tape measure and mark a short line with a sharp pencil. Then measure it again, just to make sure. Remember to measure twice, cut once. If the board is wider than the combi square, measure in two places and use a long straight edge to mark the cutting line. If you are using decorative-faced particleboard, use masking tape to cover the area to be cut. This helps keep the melamine surface from chipping. Cut the correct side of the pencil line. The blade of the saw will remove some wood and that needs to be taken into account. Don't be tempted to measure lots of lengths from the same

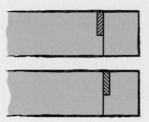

board before cutting. Cut one piece then measure the next one. Avoid using one piece because a template as a form of telephone can ensure that the whole job becomes inaccurate. Use a jigsaw and a straight edge to cut the boards to size. Wait until you have assembled the piece before applying

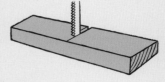

the decorative edges to decorative particleboard in case the length needs adjusting. Point the saw in the direction you want the sawdust to end up. The vent in the saw blows a cascade in front of your work. Wear goggles so you don't waste time getting the flying sawdust out of your eye.

ALL JOINED UP—PUTTING IT TOGETHER

Using rigid joint blocks

You can use **rigid joint blocks** to join two pieces of material together—the easy option. These blocks are often made of plastic and have screw holes on both flat surfaces. Start by making sure that your boards are at right angles to each other. Place the rigid joint block at the inside joint and mark with a pencil where each screw hole needs to go. Start each screw hole with a bradawl and then, using a cordless screwdriver, join the pieces together using the joint block and the screws. Use screws

pieces of wood together. Finish the hole with filler or a purchased plastic cap. (The illustration below left is a butt joint using joint blocks. If you are using the direct drilling method, you would not use blocks but would be making your drill mark on the top board and screwing from the top to join the top horizontal board to the vertical piece of wood.)

Dowel joints

Using **dowel rods** is an age-old and skilled method for joining boards. If you are neat, patient, and accurate, there is something very satisfying about the invisible way that dowels work. The skill is in the marking and drilling. Everything has to be aligned perfectly and at right angles. Use purchased dowels and the same size drill bit. Mark the ends of the board and transfer the marks to the corresponding surface using a combi square and pencil. The dowels are glued for extra security. You will need a sash clamp to hold the pieces together or wedge between furniture to dry. Make sure it is square before the glue dries.

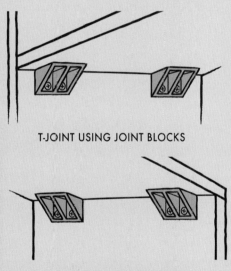

T-JOINT USING JOINT BLOCKS

BUTT JOINT USING JOINT BLOCKS

with threads all the way up to the head and make sure the screws are shorter than the depth of the board. Note that the two illustrations above show a T-joint and a butt joint held together using rigid joint blocks.

Direct drilling joints

This method requires skill. If you don't mind seeing screw head marks on the surface of the board, mark the place where the joint is to be made and mark a center line for the drill hole. Drill a hole through the side with a countersink bit, then hold the joint in place, and screw the two

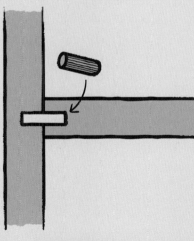

T-JOINT USING DOWEL JOINT

A TURNING POINT IN DIY SKILLS

THIS IS IT. DRILLING! From this single skill mighty projects can grow. At first, a heavy picture can hang on a wall instead of lounging on the floor, and a shelf can hold books at last, but after that? Fixing a batten and then a curtain? A closet? A stud wall? A house extension? OK, let's not run before we can walk.

A supported shelf uses several principles of physics. The shelf is on the outside of the wall while the screw acts as a cantilever inside. Forces are also pushing down on the shelf or bracket and back into the wall. All these factors dictate what will crash down in the middle of the night and what will hold the weight of a ton of books. It is highly recommended that the largest and strongest fixing be used when possible.

Practice **playing with your drill** before starting a project if this is a new skill. Any new tool is like a new phone. Relax and get to know your drill until you can find your way around it with ease. You could even read the manual.

FIXING A SCREW INTO A WALL

DIFFICULTY RATING

TIME FRAME

This will depend on what the screw is designed to hold, but roughly 30 minutes.

YOU WILL NEED

pencil
bradawl
drill
drill bits
plastic wall fixings
hammer
screwdriver
screws
masking tape
paper envelope
bubble level

There are two basic kinds of wall: solid brickwork or concrete blocks with plaster on the surface and hollow timber frame (stud walls) covered by plasterboard or plaster on laths. Knock on a wall with your knuckles. If it hurts, it's probably brick. If it makes a hollow sound, it's probably . . . hollow. Knock along a whole wall and listen carefully for changes in the sound. Studs will run from top to bottom of the wall about 16 inches (40 cm) or 24 inches (60 cm) apart.

Unless the wall is made of wood, a screw placed directly into the wall will have no strength. If the wall is brick, a screw will not secure in the dust and will be easy to pull out. If it is hollow, white plaster dust will give way to air, and anything directly screwed into the wall will loosen. To make a strong hold into the wall, the screw must be screwed into a plastic plug (fixing) that is fitted into a drilled hole.

Drilling the hole

When you have measured or decided where the hole is to be made, use a sharp pencil to mark the spot with an X. It's easier to locate an X on a wall and is more accurate than a round blob of a spot. Yes, I have drilled a hole where a fly had marked the wall instead of my tiny pencil mark. Use a bradawl to make a small hole in the exact center of the X mark. This is a hugely beneficial piece of preparation since it will stop the drill skidding and will make the hole more accurate. If you are drilling into brickwork or concrete, place a length of masking tape over the approximate position and mark on top of that. If that won't stick to the surface, use a chino marker/chalk in a contrasting color. Use masking tape to tape an open envelope under where the hole will be. This will catch all the debris and dust as it falls out of the hole and make clearing up a breeze (see below). When attaching shelves, blinds or rails to the wall, place the item on the

wall where you want it to be fixed and mark the position of the screw holes with a sharp pencil or a bradawl. Make sure it is level by using a bubble level if necessary. Wonky won't do. What size hole? The choice of fixing will dictate the size and depth of the hole. The hole must be deep enough for the fixing to fit flush to the surface.

CARRY THAT LOAD!

The size and type of fixing and the size of screw will depend on the load it will be carrying.

Very light loads	Calendars, key racks, pictures
Light loads	Wardrobe shelves, bathroom fittings, small oil paintings
Medium loads	Shelf for pots and pans, big mirror, small cabinet, hanging basket
Heavy loads	Kitchen worktop, TV, radiator, bike rack

What size hole?

The choice of fixing will dictate the size and depth of the hole. The hole must be deep enough for the fixing to fit "flush" to the surface. The bigger and heavier the thing to be attached, the bigger and deeper the hole. Not sure what you are drilling into? Then start small.

Drilling a pilot hole

Drilling a very small hole (known as a pilot hole) will help ensure accuracy and save time in the long run. Use a small masonry bit and drill a pilot hole. Take the drill and gently place it on the tiny hole made by the bradawl. Turn the drill on—a variable speed drill will get up to speed slowly as you press harder on the trigger. Hold the drill firmly and make sure it is level. This is easier if you are drilling at about eye level or shoulder height. If the drill produces white dust then gives into free space, it's a hollow wall. If the wall resists the drill a little and brick or cement dust emerges, it's solid. By making the small hole first, the hole is drilled as a gradual process and will be a lot more accurate and easier to do. Remember, if you don't have muscles, then rely on the tools. Choose a wall fixing suitable for the wall and load. Read the package for guidance. Drill as deep as the fixing. There is no point in drilling deeper than necessary so wrap

WHAT FIXING AND HOW TO CHOOSE

Some items such as blinds and curtain rails arrive with little packages containing screws and wall fixings. Inspect them closely and regard with great suspicion. Often they are of inferior quality. Hardware stores sell a variety of designs, and manufacturers never stop competing for the Holy Grail of perfect wall fixing. Call me when you find it. Buy a pack of assorted sizes of fixings for hollow and solid walls. When you drill into a wall, you will find out more about the substrate, and you will already have the answer in your toolbox. *Read the pack instructions.*

Packs of fixings clearly state what type of wall they are designed for and all have the correct drill size and range of screw sizes that can be used printed on the packaging. If you are a knitter, you will be familiar with the wraps around the yarn that suggests the needle and tension size. For heavier objects in hollow walls, use a toggle type of fixing with wings or collapsible anchor type. These have an expanding plug that remains in place if the screw is removed. They work by opening as the screw or bolt is tightened.

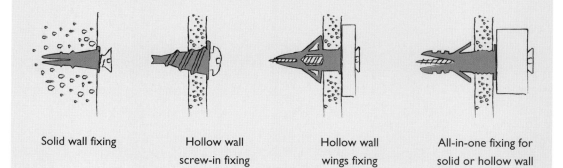

| Solid wall fixing | Hollow wall screw-in fixing | Hollow wall wings fixing | All-in-one fixing for solid or hollow wall |

a small piece of masking tape around the drill bit as a depth gauge. This is also a good idea if you are partly drilling into a piece of wood and don't want to drill right through. Place the fixing against the drill bit and mark the depth of hole required with a small piece of masking tape wrapped around the bit. If you have a combi drill, use the "hammer" action on the drill if drilling into cement or brick. The drill knocks forward and back while it is drilling and makes a satisfying growling noise. This is essential if you are hanging a bracket for a hanging basket or an extendable clothesline on an outside wall. This setting isn't necessary if drilling into wood or plaster. Keep the drill running while slowly removing occasionally while you are drilling. This will pull all the debris out and make sure the drill is clean. Try to keep your hand steady, since too much wobbling will make the hole too big. When the hole is drilled and clear, gently tap the fixing into the wall with a hammer. If the fixing is tight and flush with the wall, your work is done. Use the screw size recommended on the wall fixing package. These usually supply a range of length and thicknesses that can be used. The screw should be as long as possible for greater strength.

Choosing the screw

The choices and properties extolled by screw companies are like the myriad options when choosing a toothbrush or razor. They are available in double thread, turbo max, gold plus tip cutting blah blah, but for the majority of simple tasks, a hardened metal countersunk wood screw will do the job. Some are self-tapping, which means they do not require a pilot hole to be drilled first. The advantage of using designer screws is that they will often bite in easier and require less muscle. Once you have mastered placing a screw into a wall, you have a core skill for tackling many of the projects in this book. Finally, screw the hardware—toilet paper roll holder, key rack, or batten into the wall. Pat yourself on the back.

SCREW SIZES

Screws are measured by gauge (diameter of shank) and length. Popular gauge sizes are: 6 for hinges and catches; 8 for light doors and shelves; 10 for external doors and heavy work. Lengths are measured from end of thread to surface and are available from ¼ inch to 6 inches (6 mm to 150 mm). Use as large a screw as you can for extra strength. Remember that the length of screw will include the measurement of the batten or bracket as well as the depth of plastic fixing.

GLUING STUFF TO THE WALL

There are some absolutely amazing bonding adhesives available and sometimes they can take the place of (or supplement) a nail or screw in a wall. The bond is only as good as the surface it is sticking to, so if you glue something to a flaky wall, the flakes will stick to the glue and will fall off. Paint may separate from plaster, and wallpaper may come loose from the wall, so don't expect to cheat the laws of nature. Make sure that the surfaces are dust-free and dry. Glue will not stick to a greasy surface.

Hot glue

A hot glue gun is a great way to hold small, lightweight items. It is not so good over a large area as the glue quickly cools and loses its stickiness. Work quickly and in small areas at a time. Hot glue will always remain somewhat flexible, so it can't be used to fill holes where a screw is going to be inserted.

Nail-substitute glue

Often these glues come in handy tubes to use with a cartridge gun. Lock and load the tube and cut off the tip. These glues are great for gluing uneven surfaces and will fill fairly big gaps and can hold up skirting boards and cornices. Because they are so viscous and dry quite quickly, the work will not slide while it is wet. *But* tape it or hold it in place if you think it may move. Once it is dry, it is difficult to remove, so take care. It can also be used for additional strength when attaching a batten.

Velcro

Don't dismiss this haberdashery staple. Hook and loop tape is available with a sticky back and can hold items on a wall up to about the weight of an iron. Use larger thicker strips to maximize hold.

Sticky pads

If you use sticky-backed hooks to hold light items such as tea towels, taking a little bit of time will produce a neat result. Use a bubble level if you are aligning more than one hook, and wash and dry the surface first to remove any grease. This is an optimum solution in a rented property since hooks can be removed by gently inserting "goo remover" behind fixing and slowly wiggling it free. Wipe off excess with more goo remover.

 TRADE SECRET

If the hole you have drilled is slightly too big and the fixing isn't tight, push a matchstick or three into the hole to make it slightly smaller and try the fixing again. This isn't a quick-fix solution; it's a trick that many builders use all the time. If you can't make the hole deep enough and you can't try in a different place on the wall, mix a little fast-setting two-part epoxy glue to fill the hole and pack with matchsticks. Then use a shorter, thicker screw. Remember though, that this will not be as strong as a well-fitting hole and wall fixing.

PART II
PROJECTS

Now we can begin to have fun! After an overview of basic tools and skills, we can embark on combining some of those skills to achieve an endless number of personalized DIY solutions. Be guided by our difficulty-rating system, but jump in if you feel more confident. Gather your tools, materials, and courage and get started.

GETTING IT UP

ONE OF THE MOST frustrating aspects of not being able to *do it yourself* is revealed when you go shopping. There to tantalize you is a lovely toilet paper roll holder and matching towel rack—but you don't know how to get those items on to your wall unless some handy person comes by. Instead you buy another freestanding item to add to already-crowded shelves. Shelves? (We will go there later.)

It's all about loading. How heavy is the item you are trying to hang? Let's start with a toilet paper roll holder. As long as you aren't trying to lift yourself up by it, it doesn't need to be hung on the wall by anything more than the wall fixings mentioned in "What fixing and how to choose" (see page 40). The same goes for a coat or towel hook—with two fixings and screws the right length, the weight of what is normally hung there will not pull the hook off the wall.

However, a roller blind or curtains will need some more thought. Not only does the fixing need to support the weight of the blind or curtain and poles, but it will also need to bear the extra stress when the curtains are opened and closed, or when the cat climbs up them. Read on and all will be revealed!

HANGING A BLIND OR CURTAIN

YOU WILL NEED

- stepladder
- drill
- drill bits
- bubble level
- pencil
- screws
- wall fixings
- mastic gun
- nail substitute glue
- batten
- sandpaper
- bradawl
- masking tape

BATTEN ATTACHED ABOVE A WINDOW

Depending on where the blind is to be hung, several screws holding the bracket in place might suffice. If the blind is being secured onto a wooden window frame, then it does not need not be held by wall fixings, but secured directly into the wood.

If the blind is to be recessed into a window alcove, the brackets will be fixed directly into the plaster wall above or on either side of the window. If the blind or pole is to be fixed directly above the window, there may be a metal or cement lintel or beam that provides support across the window. This can be very difficult to drill into, and often a wooden batten fixed onto the wall using screws and nail substitute glue will provide a much stronger solution (see illustration).

Drilling above a window is fraught with surprises, besides the above-mentioned lintel. In older houses, there is a complete void! The drill finds a cavity inside the plaster when trying to make a pilot hole. All these reasons point toward the fitting of a batten (see page 35 about buying wooden battens).

Fitting a batten

Decide where the top of the curtains will be. Measure the length of the blind or pole and add 4 inches (10 cm) so that the brackets won't be attached right at the end of the wood where it may split. Mark the required length on the batten with a square and after measuring *twice*, cut it using a jigsaw or small hacksaw. Finish the wood with fine sandpaper to remove splinted wood at the end.

Use a bubble level to make a fine pencil line along the bottom of where the batten will be fixed. Because it is up high, it's easier to mark the underside rather than the top line. Consider how many screws to fit— as few as possible since we are busy people, but enough to hold the weight.

Drill three or more holes (1 inch/5mm bit) evenly spaced along the batten. These holes will take the screws and are used to mark the position of any drilling into the wall. If you don't drill a hole through the wood, the screw will split it.

Position the batten against the pencil line and mark the center hole through the batten holes. If you have an accomplice, he or she can hold the wood length while you mark all the holes, but since the wood can slip when you are working alone, drill and fix the middle screw first and then mark and drill the rest of the holes once you have one in place to hold itself level.

When the wood has been marked with the center hole, fit an appropriate wall fixing (see "What fixing" on page 40). Then place a screw into the batten and tighten into the wall. Now mark the wall through the rest of the holes using the bradawl with the batten level against the pencil line. Loosen the holding screw so that the batten rotates slightly and reveals the marks. Drill into the marks and fit wall fixings. Rotate the batten back to level and tighten onto the wall with the remaining screws.

If there isn't any chance of being able to screw into a wall or even a part of the depth because there is a restriction and a drill won't fit, a combination of glue and screws can be used.

If using *only* nail substitute glue, bear in mind that it will need to be held in place until the glue sets. If so, predrill small pilot holes in batten and tap a nail through. The batten can be held temporarily by the nails that can just grip the wall surface, even if it's concrete. Use long nails and leave the heads above the wood so that they can be removed easily once the glue has set.

The batten can now be painted the same color as the wall and, once the curtain pole or blind has been fitted, will hardly be visible.

Some blinds and poles are quite heavy, particularly wooden or metal ones, so use the longest screws possible to hold the pole in place. The length will be decided by the maximum depth you can screw into. Decide the size of the wall fixing first.

GETTING A HANDLE ON HOME SECURITY

THERE IS SOMETHING THRILLING about closing the door of your own place, whether it's the door to an apartment, a house, or just a room of your own. But once you're in, how do you make sure that the only people who come in are people you invite? There are several easy ways to beef up your security without resorting to bars on the windows. If the place isn't your own and you would still like more security, ask your landlord for permission to add some safety features. They may even pay for the hardware, as it will remain with the property. If they won't, then consider adding a keyless door lock—the sort used on hostels and hotel rooms; it's removable and does not require elaborate fitting.

LOCKS, BOLTS, AND SPYHOLES

DOORS

The front door into your property will probably be the strongest and the one that needs to be the most secure. If you have a garden or balcony door, make sure these have excellent security as well. Check the existing lock on the door and, if possible, get another set of keys cut to leave with a family member or reliable neighbor. Check that the door has all the screws fitted and that these are fully tightened. Make sure that the latch fits into the doorframe and can't be forced from the outside.

Deadbolt lock

A simple deadbolt can be fitted as an extra safety feature. It will also help to stop the door rattling and scaring the bejeezus out of you at night. Make sure it is fitted as far away from the door glass, if there is any, so that prying hands can't undo it.

Spy hole

A spy hole or door viewer offers a wide field of vision to ensure that you have the best opportunity to identify your visitor before deciding whether to open the door or not. Most spy holes are designed for use in doors up to 2 inches (50 mm) thick and only require drilling a ½ inch (12 mm) hole to install. Center the spy hole by measuring the width of the door and halving it.

Door guard

Bogus solicitors who use distraction burglary techniques don't like door chains or door guards since they offer an opportunity to observe a visitor face-to-face without giving them access to your property. This is a vital deterrent to an intruder. Door guards are a better alternative than a door chain as the solid construction is stronger than a chain and offers less chance of being opened by a smaller hand. Use long steel screws and follow the directions on the fitting.

Safety chain and mirror

Safety chains can be fitted to the inside of the door and do not require specialist equipment. Remember to use the longest screws possible and make sure that the distance between the lock and the fitting place for the chain is as far apart as possible. Door chain mirrors are a really simple addition to your door if visibility is restricted when you use a door chain. A small mirror can be stuck onto the doorframe, making it possible to see the visitor without removing the chain.

WINDOWS

Locks can also be fitted to every type of window for added security.

Sash windows

Locks can be fitted onto the wooden part of sash windows. They work by immobilizing the window into which the lock has been installed—a bolt is screwed to the outer sash that passes over the top of the inner sash so both windows are secure. To let some fresh air in but nothing else, place the bolt about 4 inches (10 cm) lower than the closed level of the window. This way, the window can be opened a little but not enough to allow a person to get in. This also stops small children from falling out. Keep the keys to your window locks out of sight and safe from anyone opening the window without permission.

Casement windows

There are locking devices that work in a similar way to the sash window lock. They work like a door chain, but as there is no loose chain, the window will not be damaged. The product is non-handed and can be used for inward and outward opening windows. There are many different solutions to locking windows. Some are suitable for both wood and UPVC. The most common is a standard window bolt. It is well worth the trouble, time, and small investment to fit window locks.

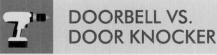

DOORBELL VS. DOOR KNOCKER

Consider both. A door knocker doesn't break down or need batteries, but if you live five stories up, you may not hear it. Door knockers require drilling through the door and fixings tightened from the inside. If the door is hollow, fit an extra large washer to the inside of the door fixing. For some reason, folks love to use the knocker as a pull handle and may end up wrenching it from the door. If there is a doorbell that no longer works, remove it by prying off the cover to reveal one or two screws holding it on. This way, you will not incur the wrath of friends visiting for the first time who have been standing waiting for an answer that will never come. If you have a bell, use your initials rather than your first name to identify the bell as yours. To save time and a lot of unsightly wiring, fit a wireless doorbell, which consists of the bell push and the chimes, and can be fitted anywhere inside your home. Each half can be opened up and fitted using one or two screws. Ding dong!

Letterbox security

Consider fitting a letterbox cover if it is possible to insert a hand through your letterbox from outside or if it's possible to see into your home. A cover will also deter key fishing—using a fishing rod to snag any keys lying around on hallway tables or stands. Attractive brass covers can be fitted to the inside of your door that allow the visor to open about a third of the way, so letters can get in but prying eyes can't. These will also keep out drafts.

SNUG AS A BUG—
DRAFT-PROOFING YOUR HOME

RATTLING SASH WINDOWS and Arctic-style drafts blowing through the gaps sound familiar? One of the simplest ways to ensure your home is environmentally friendly and save yourself huge amounts on heating bills is to make sure your home is draft-proofed. This is especially true if you live in a period property.

Simple techniques can be used to reduce heat loss and your fuel costs. However, damming up all the gaps has its disadvantages too, since a house needs ventilation to get rid of moisture generated by steamy baths, cooking pots, and even us.

If you feel cold air coming in, then warm air is certainly escaping—a simple way to check for drafts is to light a candle and move it around the frames of windows and doors. Where the flame flickers most is where you have a draft. Once you find it, you can then deal with it.

DRAFT-PROOFING DOORS AND WINDOWS

DIFFICULTY RATING

What's a draft and what's ventilation?

Ventilation is good; it keeps the house fresh and healthy. The air inside your home needs to be replaced with air from outside so that it doesn't become stale and damp. Homes need to be fitted with vents in the right spaces—extractor fans above stoves and in bathrooms, as well as wall vents and trickle vents in modern window construction. Drafts, however, are caused by accidental gaps. Some gaps can be filled safely, but care needs to be taken when treating rooms with open fires or open flues as it's important that these have good ventilation. Care is also needed in moisture-producing rooms such as bathrooms, kitchens, and laundry rooms. A build up of condensation causes the dreaded DAMP!

TIME FRAME

An hour or so for each small project

YOU WILL NEED

Foam or rubber strips
Scissors
Damp cloth
Fine sanding paper
Brush strip
Hacksaw
Measuring tape
Pencil
File

There are several methods of draft-proofing doors and windows and one of the easiest methods uses self-adhesive foam strips purchased from most DIY stores. If you are installing these on doors and windows that open regularly, bear in mind the strips can wear quickly. Use self-adhesive rubber strips instead as these are more hardwearing. Make sure that there is

7 Chimneys and fireplaces

If you don't use your fireplace, your chimney may be a big source of unnecessary drafts. You can board up the fireplace with a piece of MDF screwed or glued in place and then painted, or buy a chimney balloon—a sort of inflatable cushion that blocks up the chimney. Quick, easy, and effective!

enough clearance for the draft-proof strip by running a piece of card around the frame (or area that you are fitting the strips). If the card sticks in a certain area then you may not have enough clearance for the draft proofing; it also means that you are less likely to have a draft in this area. Make sure the surface you are sticking the strips to is clean so these adhere properly. Brush strips are another great way to eliminate drafts and are effective in areas that move a lot such as front doors or letterboxes. If you feel cold air around the frames of your doors and windows, the simplest and cheapest solution is to fit lengths of foam strip in the gaps. To reduce the loss of heat from under the door, fit a double-sided draft excluder made from foam,

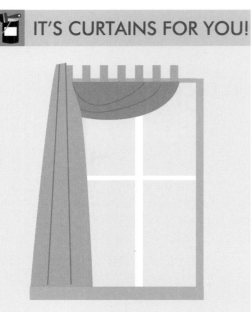

IT'S CURTAINS FOR YOU!

A fun way of keeping the cold out is to put up some nice thick curtains—more exciting than self-adhesive foam strips, and you can change the look of a room with some really interesting fabrics. Think about switching curtains from summer to winter. In the winter you can have nice velvety drapes and switch to softer, flowing fabrics in the summer.

or window frame and sand down any nibs in the paintwork that will prevent the tape from sticking. Use the draft tape to measure lengths as it isn't so important to be very accurate. Remove the glue paper from the tape slowly as you work from top to bottom of the door or window. If using the brush strip method, measure the size of each section to be fitted with a strip. Cut with a hacksaw and file off burrs to make smooth. Doors can be draft-proofed in the same way as windows but don't forget the keyhole and letterbox. You can fit a specially made metal cover to help with drafts. Remember to measure the letterbox before you buy a cover.

OTHER DRAFT-PROOFING POSSIBILITIES

Floorboards and skirtings

Masses of air circulates behind the walls of a house. This is especially true if you happen to live in a period house. You can block cracks in floorbords and skirting boards using flexible filler since these expand and contract with the seasons. Fillers block gaps permanently so be careful when you apply them and wipe off any excess or mess with a damp cloth before it dries. Fillers may break down over time, but can easily be reapplied.

Cellars and lofts

If you are lucky enough to have a cellar or loft, then an easy way to keep the drafts at bay is to board the ceiling of the cellar or the floor of the loft. Applying sheets of plasterboard is relatively easy as you just screw it into the wooden joists. Not only will this make your cellar or loft less drafty but it will make it a nicer environment to spend time in. If you do decide to do this, don't cover any pipework or cables without marking where they are on the plasterboard. This is also a great opportunity to get a proper light fitted, although this is a job for a professional.

which will allow the door to move but stop some of the heat escaping. The simplest just slide under the door, but some need to be screwed onto the wood. You can use short screws for this as it does not require much strength. There are two options if you have casement windows that open—foam/rubber tape or brush strip. Foam tape is an inexpensive solution and can be fitted without tools. Take care to use the correct depth of tape; too small and there will still be a draft but if it's too big the window won't close and could be damaged. The foam strip doesn't last very long and will have to be replaced every few years. If using the tape method, make sure the surfaces are clean and dry. Wipe off any dust around the door

SIZE DOESN'T MATTER – SMALL PROJECTS TO BOOST CONFIDENCE

IT'S UNDERSTANDABLE TO BE DAUNTED by a kitchen refit. but a great way to feel your way into DIY is to tackle projects that con't require drilling deep holes into your walls. Here are a few suggestions to get you thinking. Adapt any idea to suit your own tastes and requirements.

SPACE SAVERS

Additions inside existing storage areas can double the amount of stuff you can stuff into them. It's a great way to gain confidence and you can close the door on any less-than-perfect results!

Shoe organizer and half-shelf

To turn a slim cupboard into a shoe organizer, place the shelves at an angle to hold the shoes in place. You can fit more shoes in this way.

Sometimes, just adding an extra half-shelf in a cupboard will be enough to double your storage. Melamine-coated particle board comes in many depths and is perfect for this add-on extra. Buy extra metal shelf supports and drill into your cabinet walls; insert the shelf supports and your new shelf.

ANTIQUE ANTICS

If you have furniture that has seen better days, there are several quick-fix solutions to bring it back to life. If you know a bit about revamping old furniture you can hunt for bargains in yardsales and thrift stores and transform your home with secondhand wonders. If you have a piece of old furniture that looks a bit shabby and you think it would be better suited to the dump, think again! (Especially in these days of the three Rs—reuse, recycle, revamp.) There are ways you can rescue said item. Anything can be painted, including melamine and laminate veneers (mainly the flat-pack stuff). The key to painting anything is ironically the "key." A key is a finely scratched surface to which paint or varnish will adhere. You need to make sure that you prepare the surface properly and use the correct paints.

Wooden furniture

Let's say you have an old pine chest of drawers. You can revamp the wood by oiling it to give it a more matte and natural finish or paint it a pretty color! To begin, you will need to prepare the surface: make

HALF-SHELF TO MAXIMIZE STORAGE

PULL-OUT STORAGE CADDY

Screw casters on to a board and you have a contraption you can move around. You can use this principle to build a cube or a tower of open shelves to add extra storage inside a closet or make use of space under spare beds by creating custom-made storage boxes

sure the item is clean and dry and if it's been sitting around for a long time, clean it with some sugar soap solution to get rid of general grime and dirt (see "Preparation—Decor Decorum" page 66).

Once it's dry, sand the surface to provide a key for the new finish. Use grade 120 or finer sandpaper and lightly sand all the surfaces in the direction of the grain. If there are any stubborn nicks or cracks, sand these with a finer grade of paper. Clean the surface using a tack cloth to wipe away all the small, barely visible specks of sanding dust. Tack cloths are special cloths you can buy that are slightly waxy and designed to pick up very fine sanding dust. Remove any removable parts and handles, and if there are drawers take these out and work on them separately. If you are finding it difficult to take the handles off, then cover them in masking tape so these don't get painted or varnished. This is also a great opportunity to replace the handles for something more personal—new handles can really jazz up an old item of furniture, so get hunting in thrift stores or online for something that fits the new style. If you find any holes or cracks, now is the time to fill them. If you are keeping the wood a natural color by oiling or varnishing it, then choose a filler that is a similar color to the finish you are aiming for. Colored wood fillers are a bit pricier, but they are well worth the money if you are planning to keep wood natural—white filler would look truly horrible. Once the filler is dry, sand the area so that the filler is flat and seamlessly blends with the piece of furniture.

Oiling wooden furniture

Oiling provides a soft satin sheen to wood that is very durable. This treatment is only suitable for new wood or wood that has been stripped bare or previously oiled. If you have a varnished piece of wood, then all the varnish will need to be removed before you can apply an oil coat. Several types of oil are available. Try boiled linseed oil for a rich deep finish or Danish oil for a lighter effect. Apply oils with a lint-free cloth and add further

layers after coats have dried to achieve your desired finish. This is a satisfying process because you are nurturing the wood and can get fantastic results. This finish is not resistant to water stains so to avoid white glass rings, use coasters or some protective surface on your revamped piece of furniture.

Waxing furniture

Completely different from oils, wax provides a great finish to furniture and is easy to maintain. Waxed surfaces can be marked by heat and water and they can get dirty easily because the wax makes

When using a claw hammer to remove picture hooks and nails, place a bit of cardboard between the wall and the claw of the hammer to prevent scuff marks.

the surface slightly sticky. Therefore, it is best to use waxes on items that are not used every day. Wax can be applied to new or newly stripped wood or to oiled surfaces. The most commonly used wax

finish is beeswax, which varies in color—bleached and white varieties are also available. Carnuba wax is often added to beeswax to reduce its slight tackiness and improve its durability. Paraffin wax is a soft wax, mainly used in less-expensive polishes. This is sometimes added to high-quality wax polishes to make them softer and easier to apply.

Painting furniture

A lick of paint can make a huge difference to a shappy old piece of furniture—to paint wooden furniture follow all the preparation steps above. Once the item is prepared, apply a primer to the wood and then a topcoat. Depending on the color, you might need to apply two coats. If you want to create a distressed look, once the top coat is dry, roughly sand the piece and then apply a lighter color of paint to the item, but water this down so it's a bit thinner and lighter in color. If you want to paint melamine furniture, you will need to sand the item well to create a good key for the paint. Also the piece of furniture will need to be primed properly and you will need a very robust paint such as an epoxy or oil-based paint to cover the surface. You may need to source these from specialist paint stores; ask your local paint store what is best for your particular item. Spray paints can also work well for these types of surfaces.

Furniture reviving polish

Old, dingy, and dusty wooden furniture can be treated with a traditional furniture reviver mix made like a salad dressing in an old bottle. The theory behind the ingredients is that the vinegar cuts through the dirt on the furniture, the turpentine slightly dissolves the old wax polish buildup without stripping and removing the patina of age, and the boiled linseed oil feeds and nourishes the wood. Buy linseed oil and the turpentine from a good hardware store and the vinegar from the supermarket. Use white distilled vinegar rather than the aged balsamic (you aren't making a salad, after all)!

YOU WILL NEED

⅓ part boiled linseed oil
⅓ part turpentine
⅓ part white distilled vinegar
Empty bottle
Old toothbrush
Soft cloths

Shake the mixture in the bottle until it emulsifies, just like making salad dressing. It will smell a bit like an antique shop. Before you launch into reviving your piece of furniture, test the mixture first. Pour a little mixture on a soft cloth and test the result on a hidden area of the furniture. This works well on neglected, thirsty wood, but it can be too harsh for finely finished pieces. Rub the surface in small circles and see if the dirt/old wax comes off on the cloth. Leave the area

to dry for 24 hours and then buff to a shiny finish. (If the surface has gone cloudy or has become sticky, then don't use the mixture on the rest of the piece.) Use an old toothbrush dipped in the mixture to clean fiddly bits of molding that have filled with dust. Protect the surrounding area with dustsheets as the brushing may cause splatters. If the finish on the piece is beyond hope and it isn't *Antiques Roadshow*—worthy, a coat of paint in the same shade as the wall will help it blend into the background while retaining its usefulness.

DECOR DECORUM—PAINTING AND WALLPAPERING PROJECTS

OKAY, NOW THE FUN BEGINS and you can really get to grips with your DIY mania. Changing the decor in a room has to be one of the most satisfying ways to make a real difference to your home. On the following pages, we cover DIY painting and decorating, including how to prepare surfaces, fill cracks and holes, and select paint and paper.

Once you've assembled all your tools, equipment, and materials, you can begin. We have outlined the order of work for painting ceilings, walls, and woodwork, as well as how to tackle that tricky paneled door and sash window. There are also detailed instructions on how to wallpaper—where to begin and how to match tricky patterns.

PAINTING A ROOM

Of all the projects possible, the most gratifying is to decorate a room. Fresh paint and clean walls lift the spirits and welcome friends and family. If you are starting over again, decorating gives you a chance to cover those memories and move on. The energy produced while carrying out the task produces endorphins and lifts depression so happiness isn't *just* in the choice of paint color or wallpaper.

If you are nervous about color, keep to pale ivories and warm shades of cream. White is great if you like an "art gallery" feel but it can seem cold and heartless in a way that warm off-whites don't. You can paint the walls the same color as the woodwork to maximize the illusion of spaciousness. Bold colors used just on woodwork allow you to be brave without going overboard.

If you are feeling more adventurous and know what colors you love, exercise a little restraint and paint bold colors on one wall at a time. They will look lightest and brightest on a wall opposite the window and often one wall is enough. Paint a wall the same color as the sofa for a confident complement.

The time required to complete a painting project is a moveable feast and will depend on the amount of time you spend preparing (sometimes the most time-consuming part). Sanding a skirting board to a mirror finish might not be worth it if it will be hidden by a sofa all its life. However, having to stare at a bump on the wall by the TV every night can be avoided if you spend a little more time sanding before painting.

What color?

Start by looking at paint swatches on a card. Because the perception of color changes depending on the color next to it, take several cards of each color, cut them out and join the swatches to make a bigger swatch. Now move it around the room and see how it looks on all the walls. The color will look different on the wall by the window compared with the wall

TIME FRAME

3–4 days depending on scope of project

YOU WILL NEED

Sandpaper
Sanding block/sander
Drop cloths
Stepladder
2-inch (50 mm) paintbrush
Roller and tray
Radiator roller if you have tight places to paint
Rags to wipe up splashes
Mineral spirits (for cleaning brushes and rollers)

on which the sun shines. If you can, buy a small tester can and apply the paint to the wall. Remember to test it on several walls in the same room and take into account the effect of the color beneath it.

Where to start

Empty the room. If this isn't possible then move out what you can and cover the remaining furniture with plastic dust sheets and newspaper. Move as much stuff into the center of the room so you have easy access to the walls. Use masking tape to protect areas you don't want painted but remember to remove the tape as soon as possible because it gets difficult to remove if left too long.

 FILLING HOLES AND CRACKS

Fill small holes where a wall fixing or picture hook has been removed by pressing filler into the hole with a spatula or filler knife. Wait until it is dry and sand lightly using a sand-paper block to achieve a flat sur-face. Picture hooks can be removed with a claw ham-mer; for stubborn ones, try a tap with a screwdriver in between the wall and the hook for a bit of friendly persuasion. If the wall fixings are in hollow walls, leave them be. You might end up removing more of the wall than you want. Take a hammer and a nail set and gently tap them just below the surface. Now you

can skim them over with wall filler and a filler knife. If the hole is about the size of a fist or a foot, pick away any loose plaster and pour some wood glue on an old newspa-per and scrunch it into the hole. Wait for it to dry and then fill the hole with filler. This way, the filler won't just fall into the cavity. If plaster is ba-sically sound, fill with white powder filler or ready-mixed filler. If plaster is loose and crumbly, you may need to cut out and replaster.

1. After clearing crack of dust and debris, use a scrap of wood to mix filler by adding water.

2. With the loaded fill-er knife, apply the filler across the crack and press in well.

3. Apply filler in the opposite direction and smooth off any excess. Leave to dry.

4. Wipe excess from the filler knife against the board and wash clean before filler sets.

Preparing the surfaces

Wash all the woodwork. Use sugar soap to remove grease and then rinse to remove the sugar soap. Sugar soap is a cleaning material, commonly composed of sodium carbonate, sodium phosphate, and sometimes sodium silicate as an abrasive. Other chemicals might be added to modify the performance or preserve the product. The dry powder looks like table sugar, hence the name. Wear gloves as it is a strong alkaline and will sting.

Lightly sand all woodwork to provide a "key," a finely scratched surface that will hold the paint well. Scars left by removed pictures, scuffs from suitcases and furniture, and accidental damage are hard to live with. Removing the signs of past lives can be cathartic and is easy to do.

Sand woodwork following the grain of the wood to provide a key for fresh paint.

Get rid of old grease stains from blue poster putty by rolling a ball of white bread over the mark. Stubborn stains may need a tiny dab of dry-cleaning fluid. To remove old stickers, use a non-toxic adhesive remover poured on a rag.

Water stains on walls and ceilings from overflowing baths or burst pipes have long memories and if you paint over them with ordinary paint they will reappear again and again. "Die" you say, "die," but they don't. A small can of stain block will go a long way and only needs to be painted over the offending streaks. Wait until it dries and then paint over the water block patch with the desired paint.

MURALS AND STICKERS

A fabulously easy way to make a quirky and individual design statement is to apply ready-made mural stickers to create maximum "wow" factor. If you are feeling adventurous, paint your own mural using sample pots of paint. The sky is the limit.

Old wallpaper

If you are planning to paint over wallpaper ensure that it is securely stuck to the wall, otherwise strip it off. Heavy patterns may show through paint, so try a test patch first. Red ink often comes through a covering layer of paint, but if you paint over the red bits with silver paint (I know it's odd but it acts as a barrier) then the red won't show through.

Porous/flaky surfaces

Clean down and paint porous or flaky surfaces with a sealer or primer paint. PVA glue thinned with water can be used as a sealer coat.

Black mold

Treat this problem with a fungicidal wash and remember to find the cause and cure it (condensation or damp walls) before you paint, otherwise you will simply be postponing the problem and the mold will return. After the wash, use a fungicidal paint.

Fittings

Remove or loosen light fittings and fixtures and protect with masking tape and/or plastic bags. Remember to switch off the electrical source when unscrewing sockets, switch covers, and ceiling roses.

Cover light fixtures with old plastic bags or newspaper to avoid that speckled look!

Paint coverage per quart/liter

Vinyl silk	17–19 sq yards (14–16 meters sq)
Vinyl matt emulsion	16–20 sq yards (13–17 meters sq)
Undercoat	19 sq yards (16 meters sq)
Gloss	20 sq yards (17 meters sq)

This is a rough guide; as mentioned below, read the info supplied on the can.

How much paint?

Measure the area you wish to paint and use the information above and on the paint can to calculate how much paint to buy. Remember to subtract the areas of the doors and windows. When buying paint, read the paint can label. It will tell you how many square yards/meters can be covered. But keep in mind that this can only be a guide as more paint will be required if changing a Goth cave into an angel haven.

Painting tools and equipment

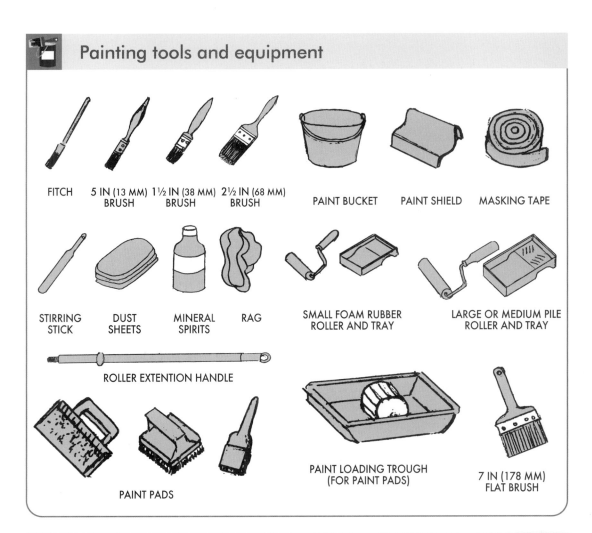

FITCH

5 IN (13 MM) BRUSH

1½ IN (38 MM) BRUSH

2½ IN (68 MM) BRUSH

PAINT BUCKET

PAINT SHIELD

MASKING TAPE

STIRRING STICK

DUST SHEETS

MINERAL SPIRITS

RAG

SMALL FOAM RUBBER ROLLER AND TRAY

LARGE OR MEDIUM PILE ROLLER AND TRAY

ROLLER EXTENTION HANDLE

PAINT PADS

PAINT LOADING TROUGH (FOR PAINT PADS)

7 IN (178 MM) FLAT BRUSH

Order of work

Paint downward. If you are painting the ceiling as well as the walls, start with that. It's also good to know that it's the hardest and most backbreaking task of all. Wipe off any spills or drips on the walls as you go—it's easier to wipe off wet paint than sand off dry paint. Don't be discouraged by the strain; the rest of the room will be plain sailing by comparison.

Matte or silk?

The choice is all yours. Matte paint has no shine and helps hide defects if you have a lumpy uneven wall. Silk/satin has a slight sheen and is great for reflecting a little more light. Gloss is a choice for metal or woodwork—it is really shiny and will need to be applied with care because every sag will show.

Getting started

If the new color is very different from the old one, apply the first coat thinned with water as an undercoat, using about 1 part water to 8 parts paint. Check that the brand of paint *can* be diluted with water. Be careful when using more than one can of specially mixed paint since there can be color differences. To ensure an even color, mix them together in a plastic bucket and stir well before painting.

Painting the ceiling

Flat paint is the traditional choice for ceilings as it hides lumps and bumps, but if you have a good finish on your ceiling, then why not try a sheen? It bounces light off and makes the room brighter. First paint around the edges of the cornices and edge of the ceiling with a well-filled brush that has been gently wiped against the side of the paint can. Feather out paint at the edges. Pour paint from your can into a paint tray to about a third full. Dip in the roller and work paint into the fleece of the roller by rolling against the slope on the tray. This "charges" the roller. Working from a window side of the room, paint the ceiling in a series of crosshatch strokes. Reload the roller as it becomes dry and maintain a single coat as you paint. Finish off each section of paint by lightly rolling over in one direction to even out the paint (this is known as laying off).

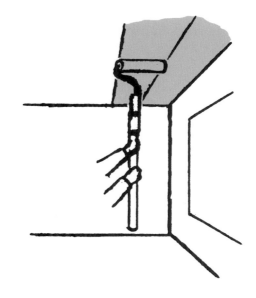

Use an extension pole to roller the ceiling. It's quicker and easier than constantly moving a ladder. Work in manageable strips.

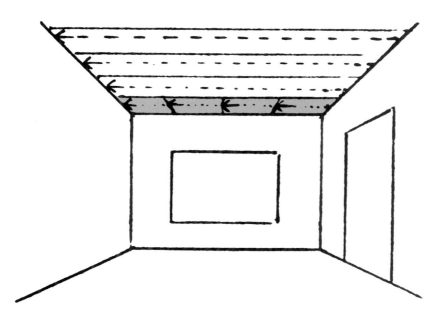

Start painting the ceiling with a roller from the window side of the room and work toward the back of the room. Work in strips and finish one before you move to the next.

Walls

First paint the corners and edges of walls with a smallish brush, feathering out the paint as you go. When using the roller work from the top of a wall to the bottom in bands of crosshatched patches. Allow each coat to dry for 4 hours minimum before applying the next coat.

- WORK ON! Never leave a wall or ceiling half done as you will always notice the join.

- WASH UP. Wash the roller right away with lots of water (if using a water-soluble paint). One method of cleaning the fleece is to use a paint scraper to squeeze all the paint off under running water. If you are taking a short break in between walls, put the roller and tray into a plastic bag and seal it. This way it won't develop a crust. Wipe away any paint drips right away with a damp cloth, so they don't harden.

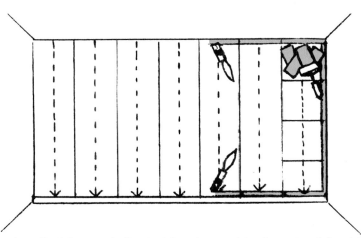

Start to paint the walls of the room by "cutting in"—using a small brush to paint all the tricky edges around the ceilings, skirtings, windows, and door before you start to roll on the paint. When rolling on paint, work in a series of crosshatched patches (see right-hand corner of drawing).

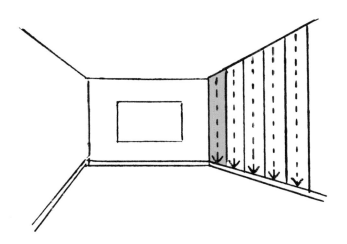

Starting from the window side (the light source) of the room, apply paint with a roller in wide strips using the crosshatching action. Work from the top of the wall to bottom and finish that strip before you start rolling and crosshatching the next one.

PAINTING A ROOM—WOODWORK, WINDOWS, AND DOORS

Gloss and semi-matte are the paints of choice for these surfaces, and like the previous project this one requires similar levels of preparation before you can get started.

YOU WILL NEED

Dust sheets
Set of appropriate brushes
Mineral spirits/brush cleaner
Jam jars for cleaning brushes
Stepladder
Old newspapers and rags for spills
Stir sticks
Screwdriver to remove the paint pot lid
Enough paint for the job

Preparation

If painting new wood, sandpaper it till smooth. Paint knots with a special sealant—if you don't, the resin will continue to seep through the paint leaving ring marks. Apply a primer coat and allow to it dry for at least 12 hours.

If painting over already-painted wood, wash down the surface with sugar soap and water. If the previous paint is oil-based, then sand down lightly with fine sandpaper to remove any paint lumps and bumps and provide a key. Apply wood primer to any bare spots and remove any cracked or peeling areas with a paint scraper and fill with fine filler. Fill cracks

For a good paint finish, only dip your brush into the paint to halfway up the bristles. Gently wipe the brush against the inside lip of the can or paint jar to remove any excess paint. This prevents overloading the brush and avoids runs down half your wall and your arm. Not such a good look!

and small holes with filler. Remove any handles and fittings from doors and windows if possible and apply masking tape over the closing mechanism so that you don't shut yourself in a room without a handle on the door.

Starting to paint

Decant paint into a sturdy pot to avoid carrying a heavy paint can around with you. Wipe the rim of the large paint can and firmly replace the lid to ensure you don't kick it over and say bad words.

Paint your prepared surfaces with undercoat to suit the topcoat. Apply thinly and allow the undercoat to

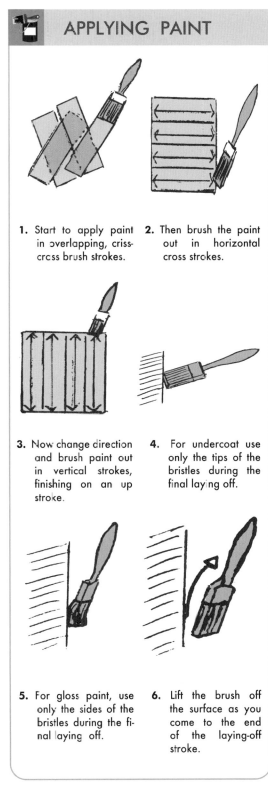

APPLYING PAINT

1. Start to apply paint in overlapping, crisscross brush strokes.

2. Then brush the paint out in horizontal cross strokes.

3. Now change direction and brush paint out in vertical strokes, finishing on an up stroke.

4. For undercoat use only the tips of the bristles during the final laying off.

5. For gloss paint, use only the sides of the bristles during the final laying off.

6. Lift the brush off the surface as you come to the end of the laying-off stroke.

PAINTING A SASH WINDOW

Sash windows are slightly more complicated to paint so plan ahead if you are tackling a sash window. Paint on a fine day in the morning, and if you have to close the windows before the paint is dry, put a matchstick in between the sashes and frame to keep them from drying stuck together. Before starting, make sure the window will still close after an extra layer of paint is applied. Insert a postcard between the window and frame. If you can't do this, then you will have to sand or use a heat gun to remove the extra paint layer. Paint in the order shown in the illustration below. Painting a paneled door requires a similar treatment. This minimizes the look of "joined" paint caused by applying fresh paint next to a drying surface. Paint in the order shown in the illustration opposite.

1. Move lower sash up and top sash down, then paint bottom section of top sash and bottom section of lower sash. Next paint all the exposed runner sides.

2. Now move the top sash toward top, lower sash to bottom. Paint the rest of the top sash and the exposed top runner tracks (see shaded area).

3. Finally, paint the lower sash, including the top edge, as well as the surrounding moldings, the tracks and the window sill. Leave to dry.

dry for 24 hours. Apply the topcoat evenly. Do not overload the brush or the paint will run. It's a good idea to use new brushes for the undercoat; it will help to get rid of any loose bristles. Use a series of cross strokes in flat areas, brushing and smoothing out across the panel. Complete a section at a time or finish the whole area. On panels, work from the edges in toward the middle. Brush over drips or runs as they happen. Do not allow them to harden. If they *do* harden, let them dry, sand down, and repaint the area. For panel doors, decide what color you want to paint the edges—normally it's the same as the inside of the frame. For flush doors, paint the edges first, then paint a series of square areas down the door, painting each square up and down, then sideways. Finish off with light vertical strokes toward the finished area. Work on the next section right away and don't stop. For windows, paint the glazing bars with an angled brush. Paint the edges close to the glass first, then finish off with even strokes across the bar.

PAINTING A PANELED DOOR

 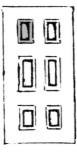

1. Start by wedging the door open, then paint the edge of the door.

2. Next paint the moldings and panel. Continue to paint all the other panels.

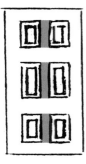 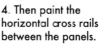

3. Now paint the vertical center rails between the panels.

4. Then paint the horizontal cross rails between the panels.

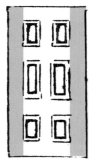 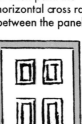

5. Paint the two outer vertical areas (called styles).

6. Finally, paint the surrounding doorframe.

Cleaning and storing brushes

After use, squeeze any remaining paint off the brush against the edge of the paint can, then use an old rag or newspaper to clean any excess paint from the ferrule and handle. Pour 3 in (8 cm) of brush cleaner or mineral spirits into a jar and  mash the brush gently against the bottom of the jar to open the bristles and allow the solvent to work its way into the middle of the brush. Remove as much paint as you can in this way. Now place the brush in an empty sink and pour dishwashing liquid over the bristles. Work the suds into the bristles with your fingers (use rubber gloves). When the mineral spirits and the dishwashing liquid have emulsified, rinse well under warm running water. Don't forget to gently open the middle of the brush and get at the roots. If there is still paint on the brush, pour new mineral spirits into the jar and repeat the process. Leave to dry in the air so the bristles will keep their shape.

TRADE SECRET

If you have to take a short break, cover your paint tray, brush or roller in plastic wrap to prevent it from drying out.

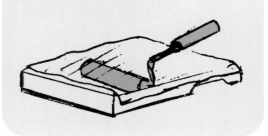

WALLPAPERING A ROOM

DIFFICULTY RATING

YOU WILL NEED

Pasting table
Utility knife and long scissors
Paperhanging brush
Paste
Plastic buckets for paste and water
Stirring sticks
Bubble level
Big sponge (a clean car wash one is fine)
Clean damp cloths for wiping excess paste
Wallpaper
Tape measure or folding rule

Preparation

For all DIY projects, the end results often depend on the amount of effort that goes into preparation before you actually get to the good part—which in this case is papering a room with lovely wallpaper. What preparation you do before wallpapering depends on the surface of your walls.

- **Painted plaster**. Wash down the walls and use a scraper to get rid of any flaky paint. Fill cracks and holes with filler. Seal the surface of the wall

WALLPAPERING TOOLS AND EQUIPMENT

PAPER-HANGING BRUSH

PAPER-HANGING SCISSORS, LONG BLADED

SMALL SHARP SCISSORS

UTILITY KNIFE

SNAP LINE, CHALK, AND DRAWING PINS

PLUMB BOB

PENCILS

WOODEN FOLDING RULE

SEAM ROLLER

SCREWDRIVER

PASTING BRUSH

SPONGE

BUCKET FOR PASTE

BUCKET FOR WATER

STIRRING STICK

with watered-down white glue or wallpaper paste. Apply lining paper first if the wall surface is very uneven.

- **Fresh plaster**. Paint with water-based paint and leave to dry. Allow two weeks for lightweight plaster to dry and up to six weeks for sand and cement to dry before papering.
- **Plasterboard.** If unpainted, paint with a sealer and apply lining paper.
- **Old wallpaper**. It's a really good idea to strip off old wallpaper using a steam stripper (see right), and scraping it off with a stripping knife. Use the steamer in sections of about a meter (a yard) at a time so it doesn't dry out. Score the wallpaper carefully so you don't damage the surface of the plaster underneath. This will help the steam get behind the paper, making it easier to scrape it off. Don't use too much steam or it will seep into the plaster permanently.
- **Skirting boards**. Use decorators' caulk to fill the gaps in between the wall and the skirting boards so that you can achieve a neat finish.

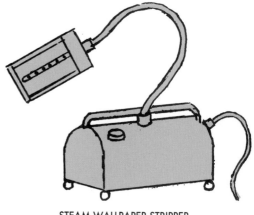

STEAM WALLPAPER STRIPPER

Where to begin

Start from a window. Measure away from the window one roll width less 5 inches (25 mm) and mark a vertical line using a bubble level and a pencil (see the illustration below). Hang the first length with one edge against the vertical line, with the other side trimmed around the window. Work away from the window and around the room, finishing in a corner. Paper the chimney breast and feature walls from the center outward. Measure the center point

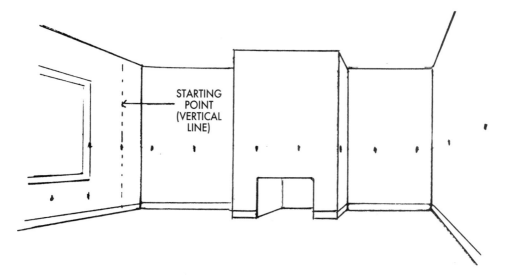

STARTING POINT (VERTICAL LINE)

Use a bubble level and plumb line to create a straight vertical line on your wall. This will be the starting point for your first drop. Then using a roll of wallpaper as a measuring guide, mark the wallpaper widths all around the room in order to see how the joins will work. You don't want to be joining paper on an outside corner, so make adjustments.

HOW MUCH WALLPAPER DO YOU NEED?

Wallpaper comes in rolls of about 33 feet (10 meters) long by 20 in (53 cm) wide. Measure the height of walls (add 6 inches/150 mm for trimming). Measure the total length and subtract areas of window and doors to give the total area of wallpaper required. A standard roll covers about 54 sq ft (5 meters sq), so divide the total wallpaper area by 5 to give you the number of rolls required. For the lovely huge patterns, add 10 percent to the number of rolls to allow for wastage in matching up patterns. You can roughly mark on your walls to help you measure up if need be, using the height of room and width of roll. To calculate for the ceiling, measure the width of room and see how many lengths you can get from the roll at the room width, then mark out how many paper widths you can get into the length of the room.

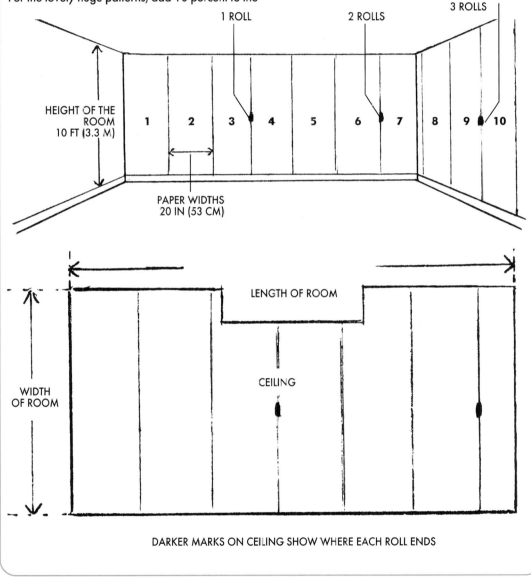

DARKER MARKS ON CEILING SHOW WHERE EACH ROLL ENDS

and then divide the roll width so that there is a drop in the center.

Cutting and pasting

Follow the instructions on the pack and mix up the paste in a bucket. Make sure it's not too sloppy. Cut two lengths to get the hang of it. Add at least 6 inches (150 mm) plus the length of the repeat if your paper has a large pattern (information will be on the roll). Resist the temptation to cut all the lengths until you are confident of your measurements. Once you have pasted a length of paper, or drop (see below), let the paper sit for a few minutes so that it slightly absorbs the paste. This will allow the paper to settle

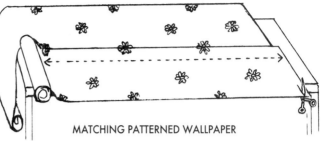

MATCHING PATTERNED WALLPAPER

tightly on the wall as it dries. When you get into your stride, you can paste one drop ahead so there is always a length of paper ready to hang. Place the scissors and a large clean dry brush near your work area—either up the ladder or in your apron pocket.

PASTING AND FOLDING WALLPAPER

Lay the paper on the table with one end at the top and brush the paste from the center outward, and toward the top. Fold over the top so the paste sticks together and move the paper up the table. Paste the other side and fold over that half, then allow the paper to sit.

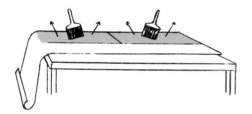

1. With one end of the paper near the end of the table, apply paste by brushing up and outward.

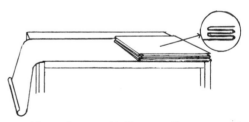

3. Fold over the pasted half onto itself so the pasted surfaces stick together.

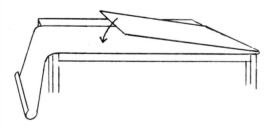

2. If your lengths are very long you may have to concertina-fold the length.

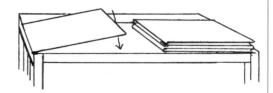

4. Now paste the second half and fold that half over on itself. Allow the length to rest for a few minutes.

- **Drop one.** Hang the pasted wallpaper over your arm and climb the ladder. Unfold one end and place the top against the wall with 3 inches (75 mm) to spare (see box right for step-by-steps). Make sure the edge is against the marked vertical line. If it isn't lined up, gently lift away from the wall and reposition. Gently brush the paper down from the center of the roll, releasing the lower portion when the paper is in position. Brush the paper into the top of the wall, marking a crease gently with the back of the scissors. Do the same with the skirting boards. Lift top and bottom away from wall and cut with scissors and brush back again. Be careful to wipe any excess paste from the ceiling and skirting before it dries.

- **Drop two.** After pasting and resting the next drop, slide the wallpaper into place next to drop one to make a neat butt joint. Wipe the joins gently to remove spare paste. Continue around the room and end at a corner.

HANG UPS

Take the pasted roll to the wall and slide into place. Use a clean brush to push the paper onto the wall; wipe off extra paste that squeezes out the sides.

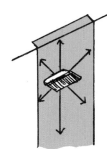

1. Leaving an extra bit at the top, position your first drop, and brush into place.

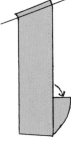

2. Keep the folds together and extend one fold at a time.

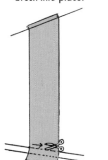

3. With the back of scissors score a line, then lift paper and cut off the excess.

4. Dry-brush paper over the full length and make sure the paper is sitting nicely against the wall.

5. Scribe the top, cutting away surplus paper, then wipe away excess paste on ceiling.

6. Brush the paper into place at the top, brushing from the center of the paper outward.

WALLPAPERING—THE FINER DETAILS

Corners Don't be tempted to take a full roll round the corner; it will crease or create a void. Trim the paper to about 1 inch (25 mm) wide after the corner and overlap with the next sheet. Do this by gently turning the paper around the corners with your fingers, starting from the middle up to the ceiling and then down to the skirting boards.

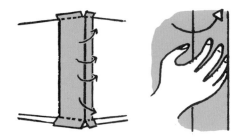

Windows and doors Put the pasted length on the door and brush onto the wall. Feel for the corner of the doorframe and make a diagonal cut. Fold back the two flaps of paper loosely over the frame and gently score the fold line with the back of the scissors. Pull the paper away and cut along the crease.

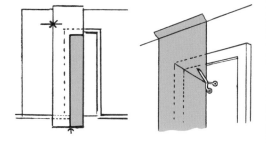

Light switches and fittings. Hang the paper over the switch and make a diagonal cut with a utility knife to the corners of the plate. Fold back, crease around the switch, and cut a little inside the line. If the switch plate has been loosened, use a plastic blade to coax the paper behind the plate. For a pendant light (opposite) brush the paper up to the center of the light. Make a hole in the paper with the point of your scissors, near the center of the fitting, then make three more cuts from the center hole to make a starburst shape. Scribe close to the fitting, continue pasting the length of paper across the ceiling, then go back and cut off the points at the scribed lines; brush snugly against the fitting.

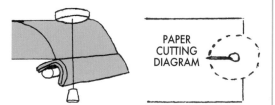

1. Paste paper up to the fixture, make a cut in paper, and proceed to make starburst cuts.

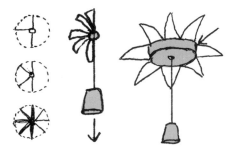

2. Scribe, continue to paper. Trim points snugly against fitting and secure in place.

Air bubbles If you find air bubbles, make a small cut into the wallpaper to release the air, then smooth back with a brush.

LIGHT IT UP

THE LIGHTING IN A ROOM can have a dramatic effect on your mood. A new shade on an old lamp can really lift the decor of a room. Bare lightbulbs from ceiling pendants cast harsh shadows and show up every defect in the room. They also remind you every time you switch on the light that the room is incomplete. Dirty, broken, and uncoordinated shades on ceilings and lamps are very easy to remove and replace.

YOU WILL NEED

Stepladder
New shade
Screwdriver

Choose daytime for this task and always make sure the switch is off. You normally don't need to switch off the power to replace a simple shade. If you are using a stepladder, always make sure it is fully extended and firmly placed on the ground. If you are using a dining chair, test that it is stable by standing on it with shoes off. Place your feet over the legs if possible and don't use a folding chair as any foot movement may knock you off balance. If you feel uneasy about heights, place two chairs together and use a broom as an extra support.

Removing the old lampshade

First remove the lightbulb. Lightbulbs have either screw-in or bayonet connections. If you have never removed a lightbulb before, you can practice on a table lamp before setting off up the ladder. Remember to tackle this when the bulb is cold, otherwise you're in for a nasty burn.

It helps to know how a ceiling light fitting is constructed. If a shade has been on for a long while, the plastic parts may have become brittle and may be difficult to unscrew.

Turn off the power and spray a little WD-40 onto the part of the socket where the old shade is held in place. Wrapping a red rubber band around it helps with friction to remove it.

Paper lampshades

These design classics cost very little, can be bought in a range of shapes and sizes, and are easy to install. Choose a white shade for maximum brightness. They often attach above the light fitting to the wire so don't require any unscrewing. Other fresh and bright lampshades cost very little and are available in many department stores. Remember that big and bold gives the impression of a confident space—smaller lampshades are best for side lights.

ON THE TILES—REMOVING, CHOOSING, AND LAYING TILES

THE BEAUTY OF TILES is that there is a fabulous array of choice. Tiles add color, life, and depth to any surface and if you are looking to revamp a room, tiles are a super option. The knack to tiling well is to choose the appropriate tiles for the job and also to take your time—like all DIY projects, patience and planning are the keys to a good finish. As tiles are waterproof and easy to keep clean, they are great in kitchens and bathrooms. However, a certain amount of maintenance is needed, especially in high water areas—the grout between the tiles can discolor and attract mold. As tiles are rigid objects, consider well before laying them on a springy wooden floor; laying cork tiles or perhaps flexible vinyl tiles might be a better alternative.

TYPES OF TILES

Ceramic tiles are hard-wearing, easier to install and maintain than more complex materials such as glass or natural stone. Ceramic tiles can be glazed or painted so the range is vast. They can be used on floors and walls and are lighter than some natural stone tiles, therefore are great on plasterboard surfaces.

Natural stone tiles are beautiful but are not as uniform as ceramics in color and shade. They take longer to fit than ceramic and some are very hard and difficult to cut. Some stone tiles, especially when polished, can be slippery when wet so be careful if using on floors. Some natural stones absorb anything that is spilled on them so be wary when choosing a stone for the kitchen, for instance. There are special aftercare products that will help to seal out unwanted moisture. This seals the tile and the same process will have to be repeated every year to keep the durability. Limestone, granite, marble, slate, and travertine are all materials used to make tiles, each with their own

TILE FINISHES

Polished	Ground and polished to a sheen or highly reflective (and slippery) surface
Antiqued	Toned down with stains to give that "lived-in" feel
Tumbled	Softened at the edges

plus and minus points.

Glass tiles are really amazing to look at and come in a super range of fun colors. However, they can be extremely difficult to fit as they break into shards when cut. Also they are not recommended for flooring due to their slippery nature.

Mosaic tiles can be made from glass, ceramic, or natural stone. They are laid on a mesh backing, which makes them easier to cut and fit. They are great for borders or to bring in a splash of color if you choose predominantly neutral tiles elsewhere. These can be used on walls, floors, kitchens, bathrooms, and are available in a vast range.

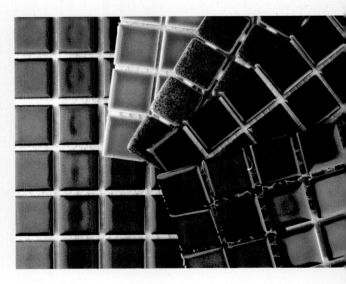

REMOVING OLD TILES

Cold chisel

Hammer

Goggles

Work gloves

Protective drop cloths

Heavyweight garbage bags

This is when you find out just how much adhesive was used to hold your old tiles on the wall. Lay protective drop cloths over the floor and nearby areas, since the edges of tiles could scratch or damage floors and porcelain as they fall. Wear your protective goggles. Starting at an edge or corner, place the cold chisel's tip in between the edge of tile and the wall. Hit the other end with the hammer. Do it cautiously until you get the hang of using the chisel.

As tiles break away, move the chisel toward the next exposed area and work from left to right (if you are right-handed) if possible and from top to bottom. As broken tiles gather, place them in a sturdy rubble bag with strong handles for removal. Continue to use the chisel and hammer to remove excess adhesive still on the wall, taking care not to damage the surface underneath.

TRADE SECRET

Think ahead and place the empty rubble bag close to a point of removal (for example, by the front or back door) and transfer tiles to it. Don't fill it so full that you can't lift it to take it away.

TILING AN AREA

YOU WILL NEED

Tile spacers
Trowel or serrated spatula to spread adhesive
Adhesive
Grout
Grout float or spatula
Tile cutters
Nibblers
Hammer
Bubble level
Screwdriver and screws
Wooden battens
Pencil or china marker
Goggles
Sponge and cloth
Tiles
Barrier cream (this is dry, dusty
work so use this on your hands)

Select a fairly slow-drying **adhesive** if it's the first time you have laid tiles. This will be forgiving if you have to remove a couple to readjust the spacing as you go along. If you buy super-fast-drying adhesive the tiles will be very difficult to remove if you make a mistake.

When choosing **tile spacers**, the size will depend on how thick you want your grout lines. Remember the grout lines need to be in proportion to the size of tile. Don't have large lines on a small tile—it will look odd . . . unless that's your style.

Grout—powdered is better as you can mix up the consistency and amount you require, but ready-mixed is fine for small areas.

Planning ahead—before you even cut a tile!

Remember that you will need to leave the adhesive to dry for 24 hours before grouting and then the grout will need to be left for at least 12 hours before it's dry. So bear this in mind especially when doing a shower or bath area

 HOW MANY TILES?

To calculate how many tiles you need, measure the length of the area by the height if it's a wall or by the width if it's a floor or counter) and multiply the two figures together. This will give you the square area. Always buy 10 percent extra to allow for breakage and wastage of the tiles as you cut. Then measure and calculate again. Remember, measure twice, and you won't be crying that you don't have enough tiles now that the sale is over.

because you won't be able to use the area for two days. The same goes for tiled floors—tile your way out of the room so you don't get stuck in there for 24 hours, and don't walk on the floor until the adhesive is dry!

Think it through

Planning is the most important part of tiling because the first tile laid will determine the end result. If you can, put a plan on paper so that you have laid out each tile before you cut anything or put anything on the wall. The ideal is to have equal-sized tiles at each end of the room (top, bottom, and sides). This will make the tiling look symmetrical. When tiling a bathroom, you need to think about where the fittings (shower, taps, shower screen, etc.) are so that you can factor this into the plan and make sure this works with your tiling arrangement.

Preparing the surface

Once your old tiles are removed you will need to ensure that you have a smooth surface to tile on. This may involve skimming the wall with plaster if the wall is in particularly bad condition or just filling holes where you

YOUR FIRST ROW OF TILES

After you have secured your batten gauge to the wall, use the spreader to spread an even layer of adhesive on to the wall. Once you have covered a reasonable area, use the serrated edge to create horizontal lines in the adhesive.

Lay your first tile against the batten, using your pencil marks as a guide (see "Preparing the surface" above for making and using a batten tile gauge). Press the tile firmly into place, then position the next tile against it using the tile spacers and your gauge as a guide.

Continue until you get to a point when you need to cut tiles. If any adhesive squeezes out onto the tiles, make sure you wipe it off with the damp sponge before it dries. Normally it's best to start at the bottom and work your way along and upward since tiles will sit happily on the lower row. If your design makes this unfeasible, be extra careful to ensure that the tiles are firmly set in place.

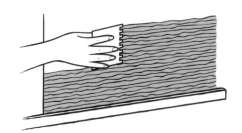

1. Apply adhesive to an area you can tile in about 15 minutes.

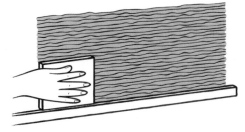

2. Apply tile and add firm pressure to remove air holes.

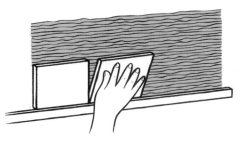

3. Continue to position your tiles along the tile gauge.

can. Skimming is laying a thin coat of plaster on the surface—it's a skill you can acquire with much practice, but it may be more cost effective to get an expert to do this—they can do it quicker and effortlessly. If you need to skim the walls, wait until the plaster is really dry so that no moisture gets trapped behind the tiles risking problems ranging from tiles falling off to mold growth.

You can use adhesive to level a wall to a certain extent, but you don't want to rely solely on this method as little by little, any deviation from a flat surface may increase until you have a hill of tiling.

Before you begin, make a tile gauge by taking one of the battens and laying a row of tiles against it on the floor. Put spacers between the tiles and then use a pencil to mark where the tiles are on the batten gauge stick. Use the gauge stick to help in layout and planning, and marking the wall where the bottom row of tiles will sit. Where possible, make sure this is a full tile and not a cut tile.

Screw the batten gauge stick to the bottom of your horizontal line and use the bubble level to make sure the gauge is level.

Cutting tiles

Your choice of tile will help determine how you cut the tile. You can cut some tiles with a simple glass cutter, though

🔧 TILE-CUTTING TECHNIQUES

There are a number of ways to cut tiles and your choice of tile will help determine which method you use. Nibblers are particularly good for cutting finicky shapes to fit around piping and odd corners.

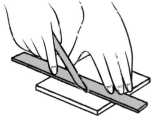

1. Run a tile cutter along a straight edge to score the surface of the tile.

Hold the tile over a small batten and snap along the line.

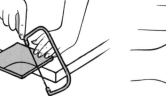

2. For a round cut, score the tile, then use a round-bladed tile cutter

3. Use a nibbler for round and L-shaped cuts.

4. You can get ceramic cutting blades for some jigsaws.

HOW TO MIX GROUT

Place a small amount of powdered grout in a bucket and add water a little at a time, mixing together with a trowel until the grout is the consistency of cake mix. Don't mix too much grout at once otherwise it will set in the bucket, which is not only a waste of grout but also a waste of a good bucket!

this takes practice, so expect to lose a few tiles as you learn. Heavier tiles can be cut on **cutters** that work a bit like paper guillotines (see right). Material such as marble requires a wet cutting machine from a hire shop and is set up where it can make a mess and lots of noise. Don't be afraid of a wet wheel; they are easier to use than you think and make a job run smoothly and more quickly. For some, the grinding of the saw is too dentist-like to make this job a pleasure.

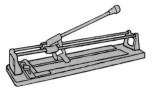

It is especially important to remember "measure twice, cut once" while tiling, since mistakes can be expensive, especially when cutting natural stone. Offer the tile up to the wall and measure the area where the tile needs to fit. You can use a tile gauge if necessary but these are not essential. Mark a line on the tile, showing the area to be cut and then extend the line using a bubble level or long straight edge. Remember to make allowance for grout lines. When you know the area to cut, it's a good idea to hatch lines over the area to be discarded with a pencil so you know which part of the tile is going to be used. This is especially important if you choose to make all your cuts first, then lay them later on.

If you have a very small amount to be removed from a tile, you will need to score a line where the cut is to be made with a glass/tile cutter and use a nibbler to remove the small flakes. Handle the nibbler like nail clipper and remove tiny areas first. Practice on a spare bit of tile before the stress of a real job.

Applying grout

Grout is the fine water-resistant seam between tiles. Once all your tiles have been laid you will need to leave them to dry for 24 hours before applying the grout. The adhesive needs to have air circulated behind it in order to set properly. When it comes to grouting, follow the manufacturers' instructions to mix grout. Apply grout using a grout float or spatula to spread the grout over the lines, pushing it into place to make sure you have a nice full line.

Sometimes, for corners and tight spaces, you may be better off using your fingers to apply the grout like thin face cream—just make sure your fingers are clean. Use a damp sponge to gently clean away any excess

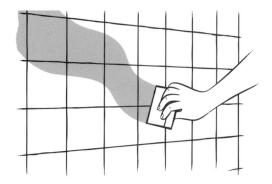

Use the spatula to spread grout between the tiles.

grout, ensuring the grout line is not wiped away. Tidy up grout lines by running down the grout with a thin piece of dowel or round end of a pencil. When you have finished, clean the tiles by wiping with a damp cloth to polish off any grout and adhesive residue.

FEELING FLUSH—SIMPLE PLUMBING PROBLEMS SOLVED

FOR THE MOST PART, PLUMBING is one of those specialist areas where it's sometimes easier to GSI (get someone in). In this case a trained plumber; however, you can do a few things on your own before resorting to the expense of a professional.

UNBLOCKING A U-BEND

Plunger
Vinegar
Baking soda
Bucket
Newspapers
Coat hanger

If you have a clogged sink, you can try to fix it yourself before you call in a plumber. The first thing to try is a plunger on the sink drain—this creates a vacuum effect in the pipes and can shift a blockage in the pipes.

If this doesn't work, you can buy expensive and environmentally harmful products that unclog sinks and drains, but you can make your own just as effectively with some vinegar and baking soda. Pour the bicarbonate of soda down the drain and try and make the drain as dry as possible. Then follow through with vinegar, and when it stops fizzing, flush through with very hot water.

If your sink is still clogged, then you may need to dismantle the U-bend, which isn't as scary as it sounds. The U-bend is the plastic or metal waste pipe under the sink. The nuts on each side of the U-bend should be hand tight, so you shouldn't need tools for this job.

Place a bucket and some newspapers under the U-bend. Then unscrew each side of the U-bend, being careful that the washers inside don't fall out. If you can, keep the U-bend upright and look inside the rims to see where the washers sit. The bucket is there for any residual water to drip into. Remove the washers from the U-bend and place to one side, then tip the U-bend into the bucket to clear the water. If you've managed to lose a piece of jewelry down the drain, now is the time to rescue it!

Then unravel a wire coat hanger (or get some other poking device) and start clearing out the U-bend.

Let's hope your precious ring is safe inside. Once you've cleared the blockage, take the U-bend to another sink to rinse it out. You should also warn anyone else in the property not to use the sink while the U-bend isn't there.

When the U-bend is clean and the blockage has been removed, then reattach, making sure the washers are safely back in place. Screw the nuts so they are hand tight; don't use tools as you can crack the plastic. Run warm water through the sink and check for leaks.

PLUMBING IN WASHING MACHINE/DISHWASHER

DIFFICULTY RATING

YOU WILL NEED

PTFE tape

Most washing machines and dishwashers are a standard size and have flexible hoses that make fitting very easy. Machines are supplied with PVC hoses that have a special valve to link to the water inlet. These valves allow you to turn off the water to the machine and service it or move it to a new place without having to call in a plumber, and without having to affect the water in the rest of the property.

Before you start, read the manufacturer's instructions. A brand-new washing machine will arrive with transit bolts fitted to the back of the machine. These must be removed before installation; otherwise, it won't work properly.

A new machine will come with two inlet hoses, blue for cold and red for hot. These connect to the back of the machine and can be screwed on. The other end connects to the water supply—note that the rubber ends connect to the water pipes and the filter ends connect to the machine. Some machines may only have a cold supply hose as the water is heated in the machine. In this case the fitting is exactly the same—you just need one less hose! Connect the hose/hoses supplied to the back of the machine and the other ends to the coordinating valves of the water supply. These connect by screwing together.

Plug in the machine to the power supply. Turn on the water valves connected to the copper pipes. Check for any drips and leaks. If there are any, turn the valves off and wrap some PTFE tape around the threads and then reconnect the valves. Turn the water on again, check again for drips and leaks.

The waste hose at the back of the machine normally just slots into a standpipe or connects to a waste pipe loosely. Scoot the machine back into place and level the machine by adjusting its feet. Follow the makers' instructions for testing the machine and water pressure, then wash your first load!

FIXING A CLOGGED TOILET

Plunger
Snake (auger)

If you flush the toilet and the water rises to the rim, then you have a blockage in the trap or the drain. Don't panic. You can clear this fairly easily by using a plunger or a snake (also known as an auger).

To use the plunger, fit the rubber end snugly over the toilet waste pipe in the bowl and push up and down swiftly to invert the plunger head. This will cause air to be pushed and pulled in and out of the waste pipe, creating a vacuum that should be enough force to push the blockage through. If this clears and the water starts to drain, flush the toilet a few times to really push the blockage out past the waste pipe.

If this doesn't clear the blockage, then you may need to use a snake that winds down the toilet waste pipe and pushes against the blockage to break it up and move it along.

A long piece of stiff wire such as an old uncurled coat hanger can work if you don't have a plunger or an auger

available—particularly handy if you are staying at someone's house and this happens! Not that I'm suggesting you should go around with a coat hanger in your bag "just in case." However, the best way to solve this problem is through taking preventive measures! Don't put anything down the toilet that you think might be difficult to flush, and then you shouldn't get this nasty problem.

FIXING A WONKY TOILET SEAT

If you have a wonky toilet seat or one whose lid won't stay up, you can try to make simple adjustments before deciding that a new seat is needed. The seat is bolted onto the toilet with a screw and washer. If you place your hand under the toilet at the back of the pan, you should be able to feel these washers.

The screws are usually covered with little plastic covers. Lift these up and tighten or adjust depending on your problem. If this doesn't fix the problem, remove the screws and buy a new seat. They are easy to install especially if you have managed to remove the old one—you'll now know how it works!

RESEALING A BATH

DIFFICULTY RATING

YOU WILL NEED

Utility knife
Pliers
Dishwashing liquid
Mineral spirits
Kitchen towel
Cartridge gun
Silicone sealant
Disposable container
Old toothbrush

If you are starting to get black marks on the silicone sealant around your bath, this is a sign that mold is beginning to grow under it, which means that it is no longer watertight. Your sealant could also start cracking and splitting, which will lead to water seeping in and causing damage to the wall behind the bath. If you leave it too long, the gaps can get wider and water can pool on the floor beneath the bath. At best,

it may cause a bad smell; at worst it will discolor the ceiling below if you have one and add another job to your to-do list. Better to do something about it.

Removing the old silicone

Cut a section of the old sealant with the knife and then use it to pry out a section large enough for you to get a grip on it. Holding on to the length of sealant, pull as much of the silicone out as you can. This can take a bit of effort but it's very satisfying! When a section breaks off, repeat until you have all the silicone out. Any extra bits that cling to the walls can be removed by gently cutting it away with the utility knife. There are silicone remover gadgets on the market that help as well.

Clean the area with mineral spirits to get rid of any residual silicone and any dirt. Pour 2 inches (5 cm) mineral spirits into a paper cup and use an old toothbrush to scrub the area covered by the silicone.

If there is a lot of black mold, then use mold and mildew remover or bleach to kill off the mold and clean it out. If you don't clean it out thoroughly, the mold will just grow back under the silicone. Preparation is all important. Cleaning the surface well will pay off as it will be a longer time until you have to do it again. Once the area is clean and dry, you can apply a new bead of silicone—it's best to buy one that is mold-resistant. Also make sure you buy the right color, it's usually either white or clear, but you can buy lots of different colors.

Using sealant

Cut the nozzle of the sealant tube as per the instructions. Don't cut a large section off because this will make for a large bead of silicone, which will be hard to work with. Fill the bath with water so that the bath is at its heaviest while you apply the silicone. If you don't do this, the next time you have a bath it will move away from the wall and the silicone will move, forcing it to crack and split.

Before you start using the silicone on the bath, practice with a cardboard angle made from a cut-down cereal box so you get used to the force needed on the

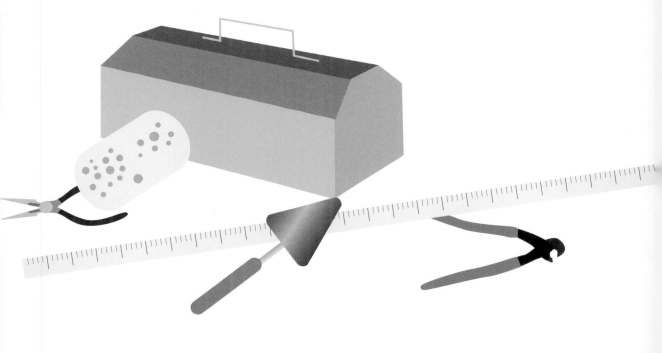

RUNNING A BEAD OF SILICONE AROUND THE BATH

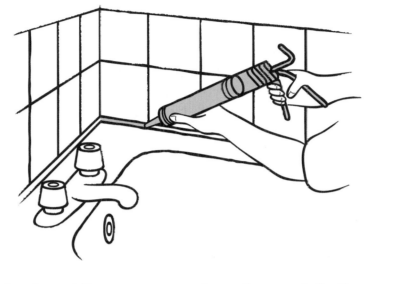

Silicone sealant and a cartridge gun are a menace in the wrong hands. Practice your silicone bead technique on a cardboard box before you allow yourself the pleasure **of resealing your bath. Use even pressure and a steady hand to guarantee an even bead around the rim of the bath, enough to connect tile with bath.**

cartridge gun. Once you are happy with your squirting technique, start running a small bead of silicone around the edge of the bath. When you get to the end of the bath, release the pressure on the gun to stop the silicone flowing out.

Perfecting the finish

It is important to ensure that the sealant is well joined to the wall and the bath. Sealant is extremely sticky and there is a knack to not messing up your beautiful job at this point. Several gadgets on the market can smooth out any bumps you have made while running the sealant around the bath. However, you have a marvelous tool at your fingertips—your fingertip! Cover your

finger with dishwashing liquid and then run it along the middle of the silicone bead you have just created. You need to ensure that the bead spreads enough to join the wall and the side of the bath. When you get a buildup of silicone on your finger, wipe this off with a piece of kitchen towel and then repeat the process until you have created a nice neat seal between the wall and the bath.

Leave the silicone to dry with the water still in the bath for at least 12 hours or longer, depending on the instructions for the product you've purchased. Once dry, clean off the excess dishwashing liquid with warm water—oh, and you can let the water out of the bath now!

FLOORED—WHAT'S GOING ON UNDER YOUR FEET

WHEN YOU ARE REDECORATING, how you treat the floors will have a tremendous impact on any room. You can carpet, paint, or lay laminate flooring, vinyl, or linoleum tiles. Your choice will depend on needs, desires, and good old budget. By reading through how to deal with the different alternatives, you can choose the solutions that are right for you.

If you have already decided that fitted carpet is the way for you, then get some prices for fitting from the store where you buy your carpet. Fitting carpet is a specialized job with some esoteric tools and requires quite a bit of brute force to get the stuff right. The price you pay is probably worth it. A sagging carpet is very annoying.

What flooring

The simplest solution is to **paint** the bare surface. Bare floorboards or concrete flooring can be painted with floor paint, which is more robust than emulsion. There is no going back once it's done, though; you can sand away the paint, but this is a tough job. The next easiest solution is to lay **tiles**; you don't have to move out, and they don't make too much mess. If you do tile, lay the floor in sections and wait until the adhesive is dry before plunking all your furniture back on it.

Linoleum flooring—a little-known fact about lino-leum is that it's an all-natural product, and designs have come on in leaps and bounds since the days that it was fitted in your gran's kitchen. **Marmoleum®** is made from chalk, linseed oil, and natural resins. It's so durable it's probably in your local town hall corridors, but the new colors and ranges are breathtaking in their boldness.

Vinyl tiles are fabulously versa"tile," inexpensive, and really easy to lay. You could choose the classic black-and-white checkerboard pattern for a retro look or use any of the hundreds of designs. The heavier or

🛠 HOW MUCH FLOORING?

To calculate how much flooring you require, measure the length of the room by the width and multiply to get the square yardage/meterage. Always add 10 percent to allow for wastage, cuts, matching patterns, etc. Once you know the area you need to cover, you can get an idea of how much your various options will cost.

more expensive the tile, the less likely it will be to rise because of thinner glue. If you do decide to use an inexpensive option, consider using additional "grab adhesive" to keep it in place, especially if the tile is in the bathroom.

LAYING VINYL TILES

YOU WILL NEED

Tape measure
Utility knife
Kneepads
Vinyl tiles
Adhesive and spreader

All surfaces to be tiled need to be sound, dry, and flat, and when tiling floors, the surface also needs to be level. It's a good idea to draw a scale plan of your floor to work out your pattern (if using one). You then need to find the center of the room, which is where you should start.

Vinyl tiles are easy to cut with a utility knife. Always use a straight edge and a sharp blade when doing this.

Adhesive is applied to the floor using a spreader, and then the tile is laid on top of it. Spread more adhesive and lay the next tile, taking care to butt joint closely to the first tile. Remove any excess adhesive as you go along with a damp cloth (see cutting tiles pages 89–90 for further advice and instructions on cutting, etc.).

Vinyl on a roll is an inexpensive flooring solution as well. However, you will have to remove nearly everything from the room in order to fit it. If you are discarding an old vinyl floor, save the old floor to use as a template. If there are inaccuracies in the old floor, fill in the gaps on the pattern with tape so that the new one fits wonderfully.

SANDING AND VARNISHING WOOD FLOORS

YOU WILL NEED

Sanding machines from a hire shop
Sanding belts
Goggles
Respiratory mask
Nail punch
Hammer
Interior wood varnish
Varnish brush
Kneepads

If you love the wooden floorboards you have found under the carpet, then show them off! However, be aware that this is the Marine Corps end of this DIY book. This is where it gets really quite tough. Sanding your floor can sound like a daunting prospect, but these days many of us have moved away from carpets, and for allergy sufferers a bare floor provides fewer hiding places for the mighty mites.

There's plenty of clip-together wooden flooring available, but if you've got real wooden floorboards, you'd be crazy not to show them off. It's really not that complicated to sand a floor, and it can completely transform a room.

Two things you should know before you decide to embark on sanding your wooden floors. First, this is an incredibly messy job; it's extremely dusty and it's best done when the property is empty. If that's not a possibility, then remove as much furniture as you can to get a clear floor; bear in mind that your walls will get very dusty as well. So if you are thinking of decorating the walls . . . decorate first. It's easier to remove dust from the walls than paint from a finished floor.

Second, if you want to do this work yourself, it can be quite strenuous because of the heavy equipment it requires. Make sure you can control the equipment properly. Go to a rental company and look at the sanding machines. Imagine pushing a really big vacuum cleaner through mud.

If you don't like the sound of either of these elements of the job, then you're better off getting a professional in to complete the work for you. Many companies will do this, but make sure you get some recommendations and view pictures of previous work.

Preparation

To complete the task yourself, you'll need to inspect the condition of the floorboards. If there are any nails sticking up, tap them down with a nail punch and a hammer or remove and replace them; if left exposed, they will rip the sanding belt. Look for patches of tiny holes that could be woodworm. Treat any affected areas with chemicals, and replace any boards that are deeply affected.

You can take replacement boards from other areas of the house or purchase them from a reclaimed timber yard—check the dimensions since there is a variety of standard sizes, depending on the period of the house.

Renting equipment

You will need to rent both a drum flooring sander and an edging sander. Most rental companies will provide a sanding pack with all the equipment you need to complete a standard room, including three grades of sandpaper (coarse, medium, and fine). If your boards are in good condition, medium and fine will do.

Sanding

Block doors to other rooms with a drop cloth and open the windows if possible. Start in the farthest corner of the room with the drum sander and work your way systematically through the room with the medium-grade sanding belt. Then apply the fine grade and work across the room, following the length and grain of the boards.

To finish the areas near the skirting boards and in tight spaces, you will need to use the edging sander. This allows you to get to those areas the drum sander can't reach. Once you have finished the main part of the floor, use the edging sander to blend from the sanded area to the edges. When you are finished sanding, vacuum the floor, then wipe with a damp cloth to remove all the dust.

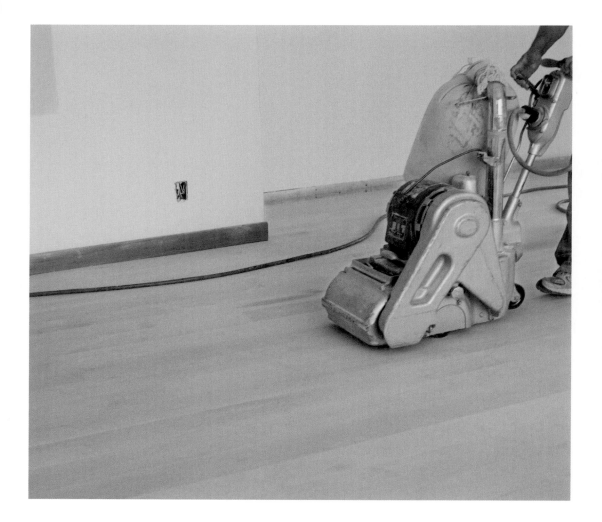

It's a good idea to leave the room for a day before varnishing to allow all the dust in the air to settle. This will reduce the risk of dust settling on the wet varnish. Vacuum the floors again. You'll want to give your walls a good wipe too.

Varnishing

Consider filling the gaps in the floorboards before you begin to varnish (see the section on draft-proofing page 55). Work from the farthest point from the door. Wear kneepads. If you are staining the floor before varnishing, test colors on spare pieces of board similar to the floor itself and wet the sample to show its color after the varnish coat dries. See how the color looks in different parts of the room and at different times of day. What looks striking during the day may look gloomy at night.

There are a number of different varnishes on the market. Many traditional varnishes will have a high odor and need full ventilation, so wear a respiratory mask with replaceable cartridges while using and open all the windows. Think about the other people and pets in the house if you are considering this method.

Modern methods of varnish production have increased the choices of nontoxic and low-odor products that are very durable. If you have small children or fish, these might be preferable. Once you've found one you like, apply with a good brush, following the grain. You will need two coats for depth and durability; allow each coat to dry completely. Make sure you paint your way out of the room and don't walk on the floor with shoes for at least two days! You wouldn't wash your hands after painting your nails, so don't disturb the room until the varnish is completely dry.

FIXING A STICKING DOOR

DIFFICULTY RATING

YOU WILL NEED

Screwdriver
Sandpaper block
Sandpaper
Filler knife
Smoothing plane
Wood file
Stepladder

The problem of sticking doors can easily arise if you have installed a new floor surface and have consequently slightly raised the level of the floor. If you have a door that sticks so it doesn't shut properly, you can fix this fairly easily. If it isn't obvious where the door doesn't fit, be a detective. Take a look at the edge of the door to see if there are any telltale scuff marks to show where the door is rubbing. You can also run a knife blade around the closed door to find the sticking point. The knife will stop at the point where the door sticks. Shut the door as much as you can and with one eye closed, carefully see what areas of the doorframe let light through.

If the door is painted, it may be that there is a buildup of paint causing it to stick. Remove the paint by sanding down the affected area. If this doesn't fix the sticking point, then you will need to use a plane to shave the area. The plane will allow you to remove very thin strips from affected areas. If you don't have a plane, you can use a wood file or a rasp. If the problem is at

Use coarse sandpaper to solve the problem of a sticky door.

the side or the top of the door, then you can usually do this *in situ* by wedging the door open while you work. If the problem is at the bottom of the door, then you will need to remove the door from the frame (making this a slightly more challenging project).

When you remove the door, work the screws off by moving from top hinge to bottom. If you remove one hinge completely before you have even started on the next hinge, it makes the door very difficult to hold in place. Remove the screws from the frame side of the door so that the hinge is left on the door; this makes it much easier to refit once you've completed your task.

Lay the door somewhere flat, preferably on a workbench. A table covered with a drop cloth will also work, but not the floor unless you have a way to raise the part you need to shave off. If the bottom is sticking because you have laid a new floor surface, you may need to trim the door using a jigsaw.

ON THE SHELF

GOT TOO MUCH STORAGE SPACE? Didn't think so. We want it all, but where will we put it? Installing simple shelving need not be a difficult task and adds oodles of satisfaction because all that stuff gets picked up off the floor and placed on the new surface.

The simple truth about floating shelves

Let's face the facts about these. **Floating shelves** may look like the perfect answer since they seem to hang without support and the photo on the pack is of a stylish interior, but take a long look at what is displayed on these shelves. A photo frame. A small vase with a flower. One more feather and the whole thing tumbles to the floor. These shelves are constructed of a hollow box with two holes on one side to fit over a metal frame that

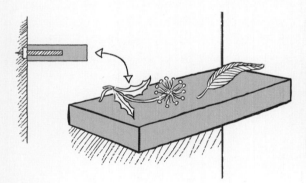

is anchored on the wall. A maximum of six screws hold the metal frame, and so the loadage is going to be proportionate to the length and size of the screws and how securely they are fixed into the wall. The shelves cannot be cut to size; this will weaken the box. Yes, they look great, but if you are looking to load them up with books, think again. Feathers, maybe!

Wired Suspension Shelves

A simple solution is to use a **wired suspension system.** The bracket is the wire that holds the shelf. This requires a wall that can be drilled into, but unlike a floating shelf, the forces that hold the shelf have additional strength because they are directed back into the wall.

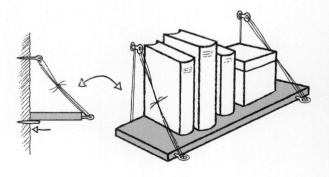

ALCOVE SHELVES

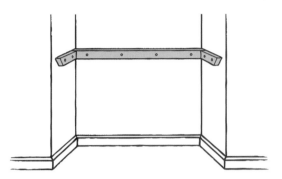

Fit battens to sides and back of alcove to support shelves.

If the shelf required is small and the items are light, a simple solution is to fit battens on the left and right side walls of the alcove to support a free-sitting shelf fitted on top. Cut the battens slightly shorter than the depth of the shelf and maybe cut at an angle to rebate the batten. If the shelf is to carry heavy objects, place a batten on the back wall as well for extra strength (see "Fitting a batten," page 48). The batten *can* be fixed to the front of a shelf instead of, or as well as, a back-wall batten. This look creates a boxy appearance and when it is sanded and painted, lots of novel effects can be achieved.

The simplest shelves to make are those that fit in a recess or inside an existing closet, where the end walls are already in place. The sides of the recess or cupboard provide a surface to attach battens, which in turn support the shelving. Shelves can also be fitted between two cupboards to extend storage.

Attaching a bracket to a wall

If you need to install a shelf where there is no supporting side walls, then plan to use brackets, available from hardware stores or from lots of houseware shops if you are after a decorative look. Consider the length and weight of the shelves and plan to use enough brackets to bear the load and avoid sagging shelves later.

Use a bubble level to draw where the bottom line of the shelf will be. This will mark where the top of the bracket will be. Place brackets slightly in from the end of the shelves and position any additional brackets evenly. Use a bradawl to mark through the holes of the bracket to mark the position of the screws (see "Fixing a screw into a wall," page 38).

YOU WILL NEED

Lengths of batten
Jigsaw
Screws
Drill and bits
Tape measure
Bubble level
Clear varnish or paint
Paintbrush
Wood or melamine board for shelf

WONKY FURNITURE—REPAIRING THOSE WOBBLES AND CREAKS

BEFORE THROWING OUT a less-than-perfect piece of furniture and replacing it with something new and expensive, use it to practice your budding DIY skills and renovate it to its former *(cough)* glory. Even if it's made from chipboard and melamine veneer, restoring it will teach you skills you can use for more challenging projects later. You will also be saving it from a sad and lonely fate in a landfill site. Kind to your wallet and kind to the planet!

HANGING HINGES

DIFFICULTY RATING

Door hinges start to weaken over time, especially if there is a heavy mirror on the door. Take a look at the problem.

YOU WILL NEED

Slot and cross thread screwdrivers
Matchsticks
Glue
Two-part fast-action wood filler

If the doors are held with modern kitchen-style hinges (see opposite) and they are overlapping or one door is higher than the other, then perhaps a simple adjustment with a manual screwdriver is all that is needed. Motor-driven screwdrivers are too enthusiastic and not subtle enough for the fine-tuning within the hinge, so use a manual one. Decide which screws are holding well and which ones aren't working. Remove the door, loosening the screws from the bottom up. Get someone to help you if the door is heavy. If the screws have fallen out of the holes and the holes are now too big to hold them tightly, make the holes smaller by filling with fast-action wood filler or using matchsticks and glue. When the glue or filler has dried, replace the door and use a slightly larger (thicker, not longer) screw if possible, to hold the hinge in place.

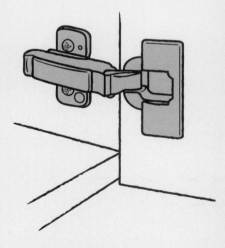

A kitchen-style hinge is easy to adjust

WIBBLY WARDROBE OR BOOKCASE

If you have a leaning tower of wardrobe or bookcase, it is probably because the back has come away from the sides and needs to be repinned.

YOU WILL NEED

Small panel pins
Small hammer
Tape measure
Square
Rubber mallet
Nail set

If it's a big boy, clear a space to lay it down—get a friend to help you place it on its front. If the cabinet has kitchen-style hinges, you can remove them first to make it lighter (see previous page). On many flat-pack pieces of furniture, the back is made from a thin panel of hardboard, and the small nails may have detached over time.

Furniture is strained when it moves, so this often happens after moving it from one place to another. Make sure the frame is square by measuring diagonally from the top left to bottom right, then top right to bottom left, and adjusting the corners with a mallet after working out which way to nudge them with a square. They should all be the same measurement when finished. Sometimes the back panel will help to show which way the frame must be moved to make it square.

Consider using wood glue for extra hold. If you do, run a thin thread of glue in the groove when the frame has been made square. Place the first pin in the middle of one of the sides and the next pin in the middle of the opposite side. Do the same with the top and bottom. Now complete the pinning, with pins placed evenly around the frame. If there *is* a place where a screw could be hidden, then use an extra screw to strengthen the back panel on the main body of the piece.

WOBBLY WOODEN CHAIR AND DROOPY DRAWERS

YOU WILL NEED

Ball of strong yarn/twine
Pencil
Wood glue
Fine sandpaper
Candle

Wobbly Wooden Chair

Didn't your mom tell you not to lean back on chairs? She was right! Over time, the strain of the leaning back on a

chair will weaken the joints where the back leg meets the seat. The back of the chair suffers in the same way. The thorough way of fixing the wobbly legs and back is to sand the glue gently from the joints and reglue the whole thing. But if the legs are too stuck to pull out completely, there are several specialist expanding glues designed to fill the gaps while the joints are still together.

Since clamping such an irregular shape is difficult using G-clamps or one-handed clamps, a way to get everything

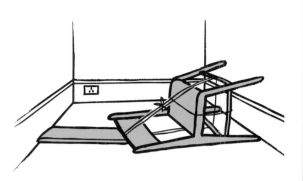

Holding the chair hostage while the glue dries.

to stay together is to use twine wrapped around the chair with a pencil or rod inserted and turned around to form a "tourniquet." Use soft cloths where the twine rubs the chair to avoid scratching the surface. Consider using a heavy object like a sofa to wedge the chair against a wall. Now, how you explain the trussed-up chair to a innocent visitor is entirely up to you.

Droopy drawers

Drawers are constantly under strain to keep our possessions in order, and over time they may become weak and stiff. Fix the drawers one at a time, learning how the work as you go.

Remove the drawer. If it is on runners, there may be a fastening screw close to the front of the drawer, so turn it upside down. Check that all the screws holding the runners, if any, are tight.

Old wooden drawers run on wooden runners that wear and become dry. A traditional method of curing this problem is to take an old candle and rub it on the runners. The base of an old drawer moves, and the base may split.

Once all the drawers have been carefully removed and their positions noted, check that the metal runners (if it has these) still have all their screws in place. If it is a wooden carcass, run the candle on the groove where the drawers run.

This whole operation can be very satisfying and provide a trip down memory lane as you retrieve long-lost socks and old love letters. And maybe, while putting stuff back into the drawer, you can do a bit of a cull and sort out what you really need and recycle the rest.

KNOWING WHEN TO STOP

Flaky veneers and stained wood surfaces may beg for something to be done, but depending on your ability and the value of the object, it may be better to use the skills of a more experienced craftsperson. If you do work on a piece, use white wood glue because it is "reversible," and if more renovation is done at a later date, your work won't have permanently reduced the value. (More on reviving old furniture in "Antique antics," see page 58.)

PIMP MY CLOSET—CUSTOMIZING
AN OLD WARDROBE

Shoes running away from you? Buying things twice because you've forgotten the one lost in the mess? Can't find that belt? You need a closet makeover. Take a day off shopping for new things and spend it sorting out the stuff you've already got. You'll feel like you have a whole new wardrobe because you will have excavated everything you own. Careful thought and a few handy additions to the simplest closet can transform jumbled disorganization into a funky, functional dressing area.

FUN HOUSE VIEW

A word about very cheap mirrors. If the glass is very thin, the image will distort and you will be standing in front of a House of Fun (or Horrors) version of yourself. Place the mirror at an angle on the floor and walk back to take a peek at yourself. Look particularly at anything with a straight edge to make sure the image is true.

YOU WILL NEED

Screwdriver set
Bradawl
Pencil
Level
Jigsaw
Melamine-coated particleboards
Small lengths of batten
Hooks
Mirrors
Mirror fixings/screws

Start with the doors

If you love those changing rooms with mirrors angled in all directions so you can see your gorgeous rear view, perhaps the doors of your closet can be used to re-create the same effect. Sometimes you can hang one mirror on a wall of the room and another on the outside or inside of a wardrobe door so that there is ample posing area in between.

Wall mirrors need special fixings, either corner fittings or special screws with domed screw tops. Since mirrors are heavy, ask a friend to help you when you install it because it's quite a challenge to balance the screw and the mirror at the same time. Not only will breaking a mirror bring seven years' bad luck, it can also result in a lot of clearing up and some very bad language indeed!

Half shelves

Often, there is enough space above a shelf to put in another that is half as deep. This stops too many sweaters having to be piled on top of each other. Using white melamine particleboard instead of wood will ensure that the resin from the wood will not stain clothes that are left on the shelf. This technique of installing an extra half-shelf works in the kitchen too. Use the same techniques for installing shelves to alcoves by inserting batten supports (see "Alcove shelves," page 106, and refer to "Fixing a screw into a wall," page 38–42).

Shoe story

Shoes will be better behaved and come when they are called if kept in a rack. Add a simple shelf to your wardrobe, angled toward the front. Put a small metal rod on the front of the shelf to form a lip that will stop your shoes from sliding down. A length of particleboard held with metal rods can be screwed onto a door or a wall, and shoes can be kept off the floor. Racks can also be made entirely with metal rods.

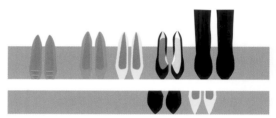

Hooks galore

DIY stores sell a variety of hooks, from simple white clothes hooks to ornate and classic styles. It's up to you if you want to make the inside of your closet razzmatazz or minimalist style. Hang a double hook to hold belts, while plenty of single hooks will hold strappy bags and silky scarves.

CLOTHING ROD

YOU WILL NEED

Chrome rod 1 inch (25 mm) in diameter
End caps for fitting pole to wardrobe walls
Centre rail for extra support
Bradawl
Screwdriver

If you hoard clothes, you may need a heavier clothes rail—an extra-strong rail will hold a lot more. Make sure you leave enough of a gap between the shelf above, if you have one, to lift out a clothes hanger; 3 inches (75 mm) is normally enough. Check the location of the clothes rail by holding a clothes hanger against the wall of the closet. Place the rail so that there is a small clearance between the back of the hanger and the back of the closet.

WINNING THE SWEDISH WAR

IT'S A CLASSIC SCENARIO and the example often given by many people when they define their DIY capabilities: "I can't even build flat-pack furniture." Assembling flat-pack furniture doesn't have to be that painful, and you don't need a design degree to get to grips with putting the bits together.

Do a bit of planning before you go flat-pack shopping at the warehouse or via catalogue. If you are ordering online and the flat-pack is being delivered, think about access to your building.

I recently wandered past a forlorn group in the street consisting of a disappointed woman and two frustrated delivery men trying to persuade a very large sofa into an apartment building.

Measure the doorway and space into which your desired item is going to fit. Don't build the bed in the living room and expect to carry it into the correct room because it might not fit through the door. If you are building tall units that are put together on their backs, make sure you have enough clearance space to stand them up.

... AND BECOMING THE FLAT-PACK QUEEN

DIFFICULTY RATING

YOU WILL NEED
Flat-pack of your choice
Cordless screwdriver and hex bit
Screwdriver bits
Tape measure
Mallet
Hammer
Wood glue
Combi square

Time frame: longer than you might think. Don't berate yourself because it's not done in five minutes. The reason we pay less for receiving furniture in a flat-pack is because we aren't paying for the air inside the item when it's shipped, and the company isn't paying for professionals to assemble it.

If you can, get someone to help you; it will make for a more efficient job since two pairs of hands ease the frustration of trying to hold something up and screw the joint in at the same time. Clear as much space as you can wherever you have decided to build the furniture. Remove anything precious that could be knocked over.

Preparation

Open the box and extract the instructions and diagrams and any clear plastic packs containing teeny tiny bits. Make a soothing non-alcoholic drink, then sit and try to absorb the instructions. The time spent with eyes glazed over incomprehensible words and microscopic diagrams will pay off later. Look out for phrases that begin "DO NOT REMOVE" or "DO NOT GLUE." Seeing, believing, and hoisting these instructions onboard will help make the construction process run much more smoothly and will prevent the onset of a great deal of unladylike language.

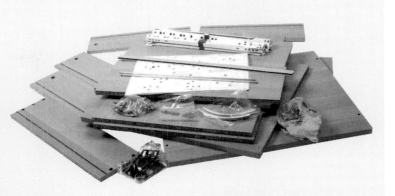

Find an empty egg box or roasting pan and tip the contents of the plastic packs into this container. It will deter the teeny tiny pieces from escaping under the sofa. Sort out all the different pieces, making lines and groups of all the different screws, dowel pegs, bolts, and separate pieces you don't recognize. Hold a roll call. Counting them and matching them up to the picture in the instructions will help you become familiar with them.

The most common problem when building flat-packs is using the wrong screw and running out of the parts you need.

Follow the diagram AND the instructions

A wild and wacky idea, I know, but it really is the key to success when waging the Swedish war. Use the picture as a guide for which way a panel has to go. Look carefully at the layout of the holes, for example, and match up with the real panel. Some diagrams are known as "exploded isometrics." They have illustrated how everything would "un-fit" together. Try the same thing yourself. Lay all the panels where they are in the diagram and work out what screw goes where.

Use a hex bit in a cordless screwdriver instead of the Allen key (the tool that comes with the piece of furniture) if possible. It saves time and doesn't make your hands so sore.

As you build the furniture, don't tighten the screws completely until all the pieces are in place.

Use a combi square to check that everything is at right angles and make the appropriate adjustments.

Once all the parts are together, go round and tighten everything *really tight*. If the furniture fits together with wooden dowels, think about gluing these in place; certainly if you had bought a solid piece of ready-made furniture, it would be glued together. Drawers, in particular, take a lot of strain from the amount of stuff we expect them to hide (see "Droopy drawers" on page 111 to see what happens when we overload these useful storage places).

Maintenance

If you haven't glued the piece of furniture together, it helps make it last longer if you occasionally retighten the screws and bolts.

KITCHEN REVAMPS—
NEW DOORS,
NEW SURFACES

IF YOUR KITCHEN IS LOOKING a bit shabby and worn at the edges, you can give it a whole new look and feel in a few simple steps, assuming you are happy with the layout and that the units are in pretty good shape. Below you will find several suggestions ranging from the very easy to the quite challenging—pick and chose the ones that suit you to give your kitchen a facelift.

KITCHEN COSMETIC
SURGERY

YOU WILL NEED

DIFFICULTY RATING

Drill
Drill bits
Screwdriver and bits
Tape measure
Jigsaw
Bubble level

Change the handles on the units

This one is really easy, and you can make a real impact quickly. Handles can be changed easily, but remember that you will have holes where the current handles are, so make sure your new handles fit these holes. If your old handles are single knobs, you will find a large selection of choices and you have the option of drilling a second hole for a bar-type handle. If your existing handles have two holes, measure the distance from each hole and select from handles that have the same measurements.

Paint the door fronts

This is a slightly longer and more involved process, but painting the doors will make a big difference to your kitchen décor. Clean all the doors lightly with sugar soap to remove all traces of grease and sand to provide a key for the new paint. Use a hard enamel finish for a hardwearing surface. You might find it easier to remove the doors from the units before you begin sanding and painting (see "Hanging hinges," page 108, and refer to preparation sections in "Decor decorum," pages 62–83). This will allow you to move quickly from one door to the next.

Change the doors

If you have a little more money, you might consider replacing the unit doors. There are many online companies selling brand-new doors for kitchen units, and most will show you what measurements you need. Some companies send a person around who will do all the measuring for you,

7 ⚒ SOFT-CLOSING DOORS

The luxury of modern kitchens is symbolized by smug, silent, soft-closing doors. By fitting damper mechanisms to the insides of your kitchen doors, you can enjoy the silence in your own kitchen. You will find packs of these in the kitchen section of large DIY stores—they are easily fitted with screws to the underside of your shelves.

but these tend to be a little more expensive. If you are happy to do it alone, the first thing to do is measure your old doors carefully. If you are lucky and your doors are fairly new but maybe not to your taste, your units will be the same standard size as units sold in large DIY stores.

If your doors don't match any of the standard sizes widely available, try to find a company that will also cut the hinge holes for you. Fitting the new doors will then be a breeze. If you measure the position of the hinge holes on your existing cupboards, the company can drill the holes in the appropriate position in your new doors.

If you change the unit doors, you can either reuse the hinges or buy new adjustable hinges. Don't despair if the door doesn't fit perfectly when you hang it; the hinges will take some adjusting for the door to fit properly. Use a hand screwdriver and slowly turn each adjustable screw of the hinge until the door fits well.

Revamp the backsplash

Retiling the backsplash is a great way to refresh the look of your kitchen, especially if you choose some really funky, bright ceramic or glass tiles. (See "On the tiles," page 85, for more information on tiling.) If you can't face the upheaval of removing the old tiles, then consider painting over the existing tiles in a new zingy color. Make sure the old tiles are completely free of grease by washing with sugar soap and scrubbing them until they are squeaky clean. Thoroughly rinse off the sugar soap. Use gloss paint so that the new surface can be wiped down and cleaned easily.

Another method of revamping the backsplash is to use Amtico® tiles instead of ceramic ones. Like vinyl tiles, they don't have to be grouted and so will have a seamless finish. Ensure that the backsplash area is thoroughly cleaned with sugar soap before you begin and use a high-impact adhesive to hold the tiles. Don't use this method near the cooktop because the tiles may get too warm and melt!

Change the cooktop backsplash

Add a new look by changing the backsplash behind the cooktop. Replace stainless steel by unscrewing the panel and install brightly colored tempered glass. These panels are made in several different sizes and are treated to withstand high temperatures.

THE GREAT OUTDOORS

IF YOU ARE LUCKY ENOUGH to have some outdoor space, then you will want it to be as pretty and practical as possible. That means taking care of outdoor furniture and adding a few DIY embellishments—hanging baskets, solar lights, maybe even an artificial lawn!

HANGING THINGS ON EXTERIOR WALLS

YOU WILL NEED

Drill
Masonry drill bits (or wooden ones, depending on wall)
Bradawl
Chalk/marker pen
Masking tape
Goggles
Wall fitting/screws
Brackets etc
Masonry/wood paint
Brushes

We have talked through the basics of drilling into walls and how to hang things to interior walls (see fixing things to walls, pages 38–41). Well, outside is no different. You will need to use masonry drill bits on masonry walls (brick) and wood bits on wooden areas such as decking and fencing. Simple objects, such as a door number or a "Beware of the Cat" sign, will require only 1 inch (25 mm) or smaller screws. If you *are* putting a number on your house, consider the viewpoint of someone in a car. Bigger numbers or clear markings on a gate will make your delivery person a happy chappy.

If you want to put up something like a hanging basket, you will need to mark the wall where you want the basket to go, bearing in mind that if it's too high you won't be able to water it. Ask someone to hold it in place for you to make sure you like where it is before you start fixing it to the wall. Mark the wall with something visible such as a black marker pen or chalk (pencil really isn't going to show up on brickwork). You can even apply some masking tape to the area and then mark your hole on that.

Use a bradawl to create a tiny hole for the drill bit to grip into, and start making your hole with the appropriate drill bit. If you are struggling to make a hole to start with, then try a smaller pilot hole before going for a bigger drill bit. Drilling into masonry is quite hard work and can take a bit of effort and power, so make sure your drill is in

TRADE SECRET

Use galvanized or coated screws to stop them from rusting. If the screws rust, they become brittle and weak, can break easily, and also look really nasty!

hammer mode if it has that setting. Needless to say, you should be wearing your protective goggles!

Fit the chosen wall fixing into the hole you have made and then screw in the hanging basket bracket. Make sure it is secure because you will be adding weight every time you water the plants.

Use the same method for hanging anything—from an outdoor canopy to external lights. With lighter items, you might just get away with nailing them into place, especially if you are only planning to leave these items outside during the summer months—light fairy lights and lanterns spring to mind.

Lighting

Exterior lighting means that you can use your garden any time of the day or night, weather permitting. For lights that are wired in, you will need to get an electrician to put in the appropriate external wiring, but there is plenty of solar-powered lighting on the market that is easy to fit. Being solar powered means that energy is stored during the day to be used at night; don't worry—it doesn't require brilliant sunshine for it to work.

Most of these lights can be fitted to the wall using the steps outlined above for fixing things to walls. These are great for security, and you can buy ones with sensors that light up if there are intruders in the garden (although they do light up when cats and foxes creep across the grass in the middle of the night too!). Consider it a free floorshow and be glad the lights are working.

Bringing color into the garden

Not everyone has green fingers, but you can bring color into your garden without touching a trowel! Paint for wooden fences now comes in a vast array of shades, which means you can add a splash of color and cover those boring shades of green and brown. Painting a wooden fence doesn't just make it look good, but it protects the wood from weathering, so it's vital to do this every few years.

If you have brick walls in your garden, you can also paint these funky colors—shop online for interesting color masonry paints. You can't use normal emulsion because it won't be sturdy enough to weather the winter. The ranges of masonry paints are still less vibrant than indoor emulsions, but with a bit of imagination and research, you'll be able to find something of interest.

Consider some outdoor artwork; create your own with some help from a spray can (you know you've always wanted to give those graffiti artists a run for their money). You can also put up outdoor mirrors (usually made of robust plastic) to increase the feeling of space. If you choose a glass mirror, make sure you are comfortable with it tarnishing and pitting over time. Secure it safely with "grab it" adhesive or brackets so that your serenity isn't interrupted with a smashing bit of bad luck.

TRADE SECRET

When you paint, be aware of seepage through to the neighbor's fence! There are a number of flashy gizmos on the market that claim you can spray-paint your fence really quickly; however, these can cause a lot of paint to fly through the cracks in your fence into your neighbor's garden. So if you don't want to spray-paint their roses a dark brown, then you are best off sticking with a brush. It's good for the bingo wings (if a little tedious).

FITTING A WATER BUTT

DIFFICULTY RATING

YOU WILL NEED

Masking tape
Hacksaw
Water butt and water butt kit
Diverter (if not included in your kit)
Drill

If you want to make your garden a bit more environmentally friendly, you can do one simple thing: fit a water butt to collect rainwater. It's usually made of soft molded plastic and can be purchased from most decent hardware stores or online retailers. It can be fitted to your drainpipe and collects the rainwater that drains off the roof. You can then use the water to clean your car or water the plants, both saving on water bills and saving the planet.

1. Position butt near pipe, then measure line on pipe level with top of butt. Cut out section where marked.

2. Fit hose-fitting section to the down pipe and seal with PTFE if necessary.

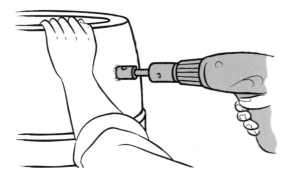

3. Drill hole in butt the same size as the hose connector.

4. Fit flexible hose to connectors.

The second method involves cutting a small hole in the drainpipe and installing a rainwater diverter (see illustrations on page 125). You will need to use a hacksaw or a wallboard saw to cut the hole out of the drainpipe. To make this easier, drill a couple of small holes (being careful not to drill through to the other side of the drain pipe) along the line you need to cut; this acts as a guide and also makes it less tiring on your arm muscles.

Locate a suitable downpipe with plenty of space around it for the water butt. Place the water butt on its stand in front of the downpipe and mark the height on the downpipe. Use a hacksaw to cut the down-pipe about 3 cm (1 inch) below this mark and fit the rainwater diverter here. Attach the rainwater diverter to the water butt with the supplied fittings and ensure the water butt is secure on its stand. If it looks like it may wobble when full, then attach to the wall using a bracket.

Fit the rainwater diverter to the cut-out section of the butt. When the water butt is full, the water will be diverted back to the drainpipe as originally de-signed. Remember when fitting your water butt that the tap should be facing forward and there should be enough room for you to fit a watering can or bucket underneath. If you have a large water butt, you need to make sure it is sitting level on the ground, otherwise it may topple over when full (possibly taking the drain-pipe with it). Sit it on a paving slab, or attach it to the wall with brackets.

Water butts usually stand on the ground, but smaller ones can be fixed to the wall if you are limited on space. If you want to connect a water butt to your down pipes, you will need to ensure that your pipes are plastic and not old-fashioned lead ones, which are much harder to cut into and not recommended at all. Depending on the water butt fitting kit you have bought, your butt should have a rainwater diverter with it. If it doesn't, you can purchase this separately.

Installation

There are two main methods for installing a water butt. The first involves removing the bottom section of the drainpipe and fitting the butt underneath so that the water collects directly into the butt (see photo above for this attachment). Make sure the water butt has an overflow pipe directed into the drain so that when the butt is full, the water can drain away as designed (rather then flooding your garden).

FAKING IT—ARTIFICIAL LAWN

DIFFICULTY RATING

Ahh, the sound of the mower and the smell of newly mowed grass. NOT!

If you live in a basement and your only outside space can't keep ivy alive, consider how sumptuous it would be to walk and laze on a soft grassy surface—enter the world of new types of artificial lawn. Small patches of real lawn can be tough to maintain in a shady and badly drained area; the sad tufts of grass that do make it through the moss, mud, and weeds require cutting and necessitate storing or borrowing a lawn mower. Thousands of gallons of harmful chemicals get poured onto lawns to encourage them to perfection.

You can lay artificial grass on anything: concrete is transformed without having to go through sledgehammer hell. If you are laying it on bare earth, level out the ground with a long piece of plank and a rake. Take your time; it is going to be worth it in the end. Work out how much you need using the same criteria as laying carpet, vinyl tiles or wood flooring (see "Floored" page 99).

Artificial grass has a grain, so if you are patching, be aware that the grass will look different from different angles. You will need an underlay—a weed barrier—and that is easily cut with a sharp utility knife. The artificial grass is joined together with green sealant. After installation, spread fine sand over the grass to fall into the mesh and hold it down.

To maintain artificial grass, you only need to sweep it with a hard broom. Don't get carried away with thinking it's real—stubbing out cigarettes will cause permanent damage—and remember that if you choose to do DIY on your artificial lawn, you need to be careful not to paint it, singe it, or smother it with sawdust because *it won't grow back!*

MAINTAINING OUTSIDE FURNITURE AND WOODWORK

DIFFICULTY RATING

YOU WILL NEED

Preserving oil or varnish
Paint brush or pad
Solvent to clean up
Plastic or latex gloves
Plastic drop cloth
Plastic furniture studs for tables and chairs
Sandpaper

Maintaining outside furniture provides a good workout and is an excellent way to get rid of the winter blahs. Buy wood varnish in advance as the days grow longer and use the first warm morning to blow the cobwebs off your garden furniture and out of your head. Most purchased garden furniture will have been treated with a preserving oil during its manufacture, but to extend its life, you should really apply another coat before you actually put it outside.

Lay down a protective plastic dust sheet so that drips don't mark the ground surface. You can use old newspaper or cardboard, but plastic is less likely to stick to the furniture as it dries. Wear plastic or latex gloves, since you will need to handle the wet furniture as you move it around. Use either a brush or a pad to apply the wood preserver. Needless to say, read and follow the instructions on the can!

Turn the chair, table, or box upside down and paint the ends of the feet. The more preservative you can get into the end grain, the longer it can withstand sitting in the gloomy rain. To provide extra protection, knock in plastic furniture studs to lift the wood away from the wet ground. Treat all the surfaces you can get to while the object is upside down, working in a methodical manner from upturned feet down to the ground—this ensures that falling drips get wiped away.

Turn the object on its side and now work methodically, painting each side, then turn it around. Finally, stand the chair, table or box up and treat the surface areas. Modern preservers are quick-drying and can be sanded in between coats. Once dry, finish table-

tops and arms of chairs by scouring very lightly with steel wool.

If the furniture has to stay outside under snow and months of wetness, not even the most rigorous routine will win the battle of aging. Help it last longer by putting it in the shed or swathing with plastic covers during the winter months.

If you choose not to maintain hardwood, it will develop a cool silver appearance, and the grain will open slightly with the seasons and mellow. Small cracks are normal and won't affect the stability. Unpainted softwood will absorb moisture, rot eventually, and one day may lose you some of your hard-won dignity when a chair breaks beneath you. Don't say you weren't warned!

CAT OR DOG FLAP

If Felix or Fido is testing your patience with attention-grabbing presents in the litter box or performing the world famous "Look at me, I want to be on the other side of the door" routine, then it's time to cut those apron strings and wake up to Independence day.

YOU WILL NEED

Cat or dog flap kit
Tape measure
Marking square
Pencil
Drill and bits
Jigsaw
Screws
Screwdriver
Mastic and gun

You might consider fitting a pet flap and collar combo that allows your Felix or Fido into the house, but keeps out all the other Toms, Dicks, and Harrys. The collar acts as a key!

CHICKEN RUN/GARDEN CLOCHE

A simple wooden framework can be knocked together using basic screwing and joining techniques and adapted to a lot of different uses:

- Covered in chicken wire, it will be a haven for your egg-laying fluffies. Wear gloves to cut the chicken wire because it is a bit aggressive in its springiness. Use a staple gun to hold the wire onto the frame or use staple nails and a hammer.
- To cosset cucumbers, cover the frame in polythene and let the sun shine in. Polythene can be cut with a utility knife. Use galvanized nails with wide heads to hammer and hold onto frame.
- A frame covered in chicken wire can also be a temporary protection system to protect fishponds from unwanted visitors.

Decide where the flap will best suit cat or dog and staff (you)—it might be a panel in a back door. Ensure that the animal in question will be at the correct height to approach it from both sides. You may need to make a step with a couple of bricks outside if the ground is on a different level.

Cat flaps are made for different thicknesses of wood or glass, so make sure you buy one that is suitable for the task. Read the instructions on the back to find out the size of opening you will need to cut. To cut a hole in a wooden panel, measure and mark the rectangle needed, and make a pilot hole with a drill. Increase the size of the hole so that it large enough to use a pad saw or insert the blade of a jigsaw. Screw the flap into the panel and enjoy the unbridled thanks from your cat—or not, as the case may be.

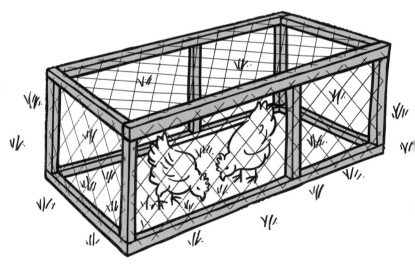

A simple frame can be made into a daytime chicken run or cold frame.

GLOSSARY

ONE OF THE BIGGEST COMPLAINTS directed at tradespeople is their tendency to use overly complex technical language to try to justify the fee for the job they've been asked to do. Most people would prefer straightforward language so they can understand what they are getting and what they are paying for. So jargon busting . . .

Aggregate sand and/or **stone chippings:** added to cement to create concrete. Can also be mixed with paint to create a textured finish.

Air brick: a brick with holes through it that allows air to circulate through a room. It can be installed at the bottom or top of a wall to alleviate condensation.

Airlock: where air has caught in your plumbing pipes; can cause funny noises and inhibit the efficiency of radiators.

Architrave: decorative wooden molding that sits around doors and windows, covering the gaps left between the frame and the wall.

Asbestos: an outdated material used for insulation. Very hazardous to health and must be removed by a specialist. If you suspect you have asbestos don't touch it.

Asphalt: tar-like adhesive usually applied to flat roofs.

Auger: mechanical tool used to bore holes. Drain augers can be used to unblock drains and toilets.

Baluster: chunky post that supports a handrail on a staircase.

Balustrade: safety barrier that runs along staircase or landing.

Banister: handrail that runs up a staircase.

Batten: a piece of wood used to fix things into place.

Beading: small convex wood molding used to cover expansion gaps in floors or as general trim.

Blown plaster: plaster that has become detached from the wall and turned to powder.

Breeze block: various types of building blocks, usually made from cement.

Building regulations: laws that outline what materials, building layouts, and methods can be used in certain building work to ensure durability and safety.

Carpenter: Specialized craftsperson who makes cabinets and furniture.

Cavity wall: continuous gap between inner and outer brickwork. Cavity wall insulation is where this gap is filled with foam or polystyrene beads to increase insulation.

Chase: a channel cut out of masonry or brick to house electrical cable or pipework.

Chipboard: material used for flat-pack furniture or kitchen units. Made of wood chips glued together in sheets and can be covered with melamine.

Circuit: a complete wiring path through which electrical current flows.

Cistern tank for storing water.

Combi: combination gas boiler that heats water instantly so you don't need water tanks and hot water cylinders. Space-saving and energy-efficient, also gives better water pressure than other types of boilers.

Combi drill: a tool that is a combination of drill and hammer drill for harder surfaces.

Condensation: occurs when warm air meets a cold surface, causing water drops on surfaces such as ceilings and windows. When this water forms on absorbent surfaces it can soak in and lead to mold. The solution is improved ventilation.

Consumer Unit: used be to called a fuse board. This box takes the mains electricity into a property and distributes it to various circuits.

Coping/coping stone: a decorative stone or concrete finish that sits on the top of a wall to prevent rainwater from soaking into the wall.

Cornice/coving: decorative molding fitted at the top of a wall where it joins the ceiling.

CORGI: see Gas Safe Register.

Countersink: a hole that allows a bolt or screw to fit flush with the surface.

Dado rail: decorative wooden molding that sits around the lower part of an interior wall.

Damp proof course (DPC): a layer of waterproof material that stops water soaking into the brick of a building from the ground.

Door jamb: vertical pieces of wood on each side of the doorframe.

Dormer window: a window placed in the slope of a roof.

Dry rot: a fungus that attacks wood, causing it to crumble and become structurally unsound. Usually happens in moist environments.

Earth: electrical connection to the ground and to channel a reliable conductive path to the ground.

Eave: overhang of the roof beyond the wall.

Elbow: right-angle joint for pipework and ducting.

Edging strip/bead: molded wood or veneer trim over the edge of furniture to hide the chipboard and provide a tidy finish.

Epoxy: synthetic resin that provides super-strong adhesive—very tough stuff!

Expansion: gap space left when fitting wooden floors to allow for natural expansion and contraction of the wood.

Exterior paint: durable paint with binder and pigments to ensure it can resist the elements.

Fascia: strip of wood that covers the end of the rafters and where guttering is fixed.

Feather: to gently wear away until an edge is covered, can be done with paint, sanding, or delicate woodworking.

Fire door: highly resistant door that often has a self-closing mechanism and provides an additional 30 minutes of protection in the case of a fire. It is a legal requirement to fit these as internal doors in apartments, to minimize the risk of fire spreading.

First fix: when the pipework, electrical cables, and carpentry is done before the plastering.

Flashing: normally made from metal this material sits over roof joints to prevent leaks.

Flat roof: a roof with only a very small gradient for drainage, essentially looks flat.

Flexible hose: a hose made from interlocking metal that can be fitted in tight spaces where hard pipework is not possible. Usually found on taps and under baths.

Floor joist: light beam that supports the floor.

Flue: a duct to allow heat and gas to escape from a boiler or fireplace.

Flush door: flat-faced door.

Formica: high-pressure laminate that can be used for furniture, work surfaces.

French door: exerior double doors, mainly glazed.

Fuse board: see consumer unit.

Fuse spur: a fused power outlet to which an electrical cable is connected directly without the need of a plug.

Gas Safe Register: the official registration body for gas engineers (people that are legally qualified to work on gas plumbing) in the UK. A similar organization in the Unites States is called the American Society of Gas Engineers

Gate valve: a valve that stops the flow of water by an internal gate being lifted or dropped within the valve.

Galvanize: to cover in a protective zinc layer.

Gang: group of sockets (2 gang = double socket).

Grain: the direction of the wood fibers within timbers.

Grout: powder mixed with water to provide the material between tiles.

Guttering: the pipework that filters rainwater from the roof to the drainage system.

Hacksaw: lightweight metal cutting tool.

Hairline cracks: very fine cracks that appear on the surface but do not penetrate.

Half-round: molding used for decorative finishes.

Hammer drill: pneumatically powered mechanism within the drill that allows the drill to penetrate harder surfaces.

Header tank: small tank that feeds water to the central heating system.

Hearth: fire-resistant section on the floor in front of a fireplace.

Hipped roof: a pitched roof where the sides are also sloped.

Hollow wall: continuous gap between the inner and outer brick to allow for air circulation (usually a 2 inch/50 mm gap).

Impermeable: material that does not allow the passage of liquid.

Inspection chamber: a small space covered by a manhole cover to inspect drains and sewer systems.

In situ: to work on something in its place rather than removing it and reinstalling.

Insulation: materials used to cover or protect from heat items, such as electrical wires, and cold water pipes or to reduce the transmission of heat and sound.

Inhibitor: oxidant added to coatings and pipework to stop corrosion and other undesired effects.

Intake valve: pipe or area where gas and water comes into property.

Interior wall: a wall that has no external face.

Isolation valve: small valve on water pipes that allows water to be stopped to that appliance.

Jigsaw: electric saw that allows free and easy cuts.

Joist: timber beam used in ceiling, floor, or roof construction.

Junction box: a small box that allows electric cables to run off in different directions.

Key: a scratch on the surface of paint to provide a rough area for the paint to adhere.

Knot: hard cross-grain section on wood where a branch has met the trunk.

Knotting solution: thin varnish to stabilize the weak point in the wood; this stops the knot from showing through paint work over time and can prevent it from warping the wood.

Lagging: insulation around pipework and tanks to prevent frost.

Laminate: type of wood covered with veneer; can be used for work surfaces or flooring.

Lathe and plaster: an old method of finishing a timber-framed wall or ceiling. Narrow strips of wood (lathes) are nailed to the studs (wall) or joists (ceiling) to provide a supporting framework for plaster.

Lean-to sloping structure that sits against the side of a wall; can be used as a conservatory or utility area.

Lintel: structural wood, steel or brick section above a window that supports the wall above the window opening.

Linoleum: inexpensive floor covering made from cork and linseed oil, very natural and environmentally friendly.

Load-bearing wall: a wall that supports the load from above; if you want to remove one of these you will need to install an RSJ (rolled steel joist) in its place.

Making good: repairing an area of damage and providing the finishing touches.

eco paint

Mantel: shelf or trim above fireplace.

Marine ply: exterior-grade plywood, can get wet.

Mastic: waterproof silicone sealant used to seal joints.

Mark-up: price that is added to materials or work to cover sourcing fees.

Membrane: impervious layer of materials used in roofing, tanking.

Mezzanine: an additional half-floor inserted between floor and ceiling (usually in high buildings).

Mist coat: thin coat of paint used on newly plastered walls to prime the walls for paint (mix 10 percent water into emulsion paint).

Miter: a 45-degree cut or joint in wood.

Mortar: sand and cement mix used in between bricks.

Mortise and tenon: joint in wood that is very strong, the mortise is a hole cut into the wood and the tenon is the piece that goes into the mortise. Can be glued or screwed together.

Nail: pointed metal with a head at the end for joining materials together.

Nail set/nail punch: tapered steel rod that allows nails to be driven under the surface of the material.

Needle-nose pliers: very thin pointed pliers for use in confined spaces.

Newel: large post supporting the staircase handrail at the bottom of the stairs.

Nibblers: tool used to snip small sections of tile away.

P-trap: fitted under sinks and toilets to provide a water seal.

Panel door: a door with panelled patterns in wood.

Panel pin: very small thin nail to attach wood moldings.

Parapet (wall): low wall along the edge of a roof or balcony.

Parting bead: strip of wood that sits between two sash windows.

Parquet: flooring composed of small blocks of wood in geometric patterns.

Party wall: a wall shared between neighboring properties, where both parties have equal rights over the wall.

Pebble dash: exterior render with stones/glass bits embedded in it for decorative effect.

Pendant: central light fitting that drops from ceiling to which a shade can be fitted.

Pilot hole: a small hole drilled before to give a screw guidance.

Pitch: the angle at which a roof slopes.

Plane: a tool used to skim small slivers of wood from a surface to make fine alterations such as when a door is sticking.

Plasterboard: prefabricated boards used for interior wall and ceiling coverings.

Pliers: pincer-like tool.

Plumb line: cord with a weight (plumb bob) on the end to create a straight vertical line.

Pointing: smooth outer edge of the mortar between bricks.

Prime: first coat of paint that protects a surface and stops absorption from other coatings, usually a thinner layer of paint.

Profile: the outline of an object.

PTFE: plumbers' tape of polyurethane that helps seal threaded joints.

Public liability insurance: insurance covering liability of the insured for negligent acts resulting in bodily injury or death, and property damage.

Rafter: a sloping beam forming the structure of the roof.

Ratchet: device that permits movement in one direction only.

Rake out: action to remove debris from crack.

Rawl plug: brand name of wall fixing.

Render: a general wall covering, usually plaster but can be cement, pebble dash, or stucco.

Repointing: needed when mortar between bricks crumbles and needs to be replaced.

Retaining wall: a wall used to support earth or any pressure from the other side.

RCD (Residual Current Device): fuse that monitors the flow of electrical current through the live and neutral wires of a circuit. When an RCD detects an imbalance caused by earth leakage, it cuts off the supply of electricity as a safety measure. Normally fitted to high-current devices such as electric showers and cookers.

Ring: main power circuits for wall sockets.

Rising damp: moisture absorbed from the ground causing damage to brick, wood, plaster, and decoration. Normally a sign of a missing or damaged damp-proof course.

Rock wool: coarse insulating material made from fiberglass.

Rout: to cut a large groove or gap (usually with a router), for decoration or sealants, etc.

RSJ (rolled steel joist): installed to support the load when a load bearing/supporting wall is removed.

Sash window: usually wooden windows that slide parallel to each other.

Screed: layer of fine concrete normally applied to walls for a flat finish.

Second fix: finishing work normally done after the plastering; fitting and connecting sockets and switches, sinks, basins, doors, etc.

Sanding block: small piece of wood wrapped in sandpaper to allow for a better grip and a flatter surface when sanding.

Short circuit: where the current is accidentally rerouted and increases the flow, thereby causing the fuse to blow.

Siphon: mechanism within the toilet.

Skim top: layer of finishing plaster.

Snagging list: once a project has been finished a snagging list notes all the areas where touch ups or further work needs to be done to complete the job.

Soil pipe: vertical pipe that carries sewage directly from the building into the sewer.

Stack: vertical pipes that carry waste from toilets and sinks to the soil pipe.

Staff bead: innermost section of wood that holds a sash window in place.

Stud wall: interior wall (not load-bearing) built from 2 x 4 timber frame and covered with plasterboard to divide two rooms.

Stopcock: isolating tap valve that stops mains water from entering the property.

Subsidence: where the soil has moved beneath or beside a property, causing the property to move. Can be caused by water being taken from the soil by tree roots, or drainage systems flushing away the soil.

Tanking: installing a membrane to ensure an area is waterproofed; for example, behind tiles or in basements.

Trap: waste pipe under a sink that carries away the water.

TRV (thermostatic radiator valve): allows you to adjust the temperature of one radiator.

Undercoat: a layer of paint that provides a good seal for timber and better adhesion for the top coat.

Underlay: soft spongy material used under carpets and flooring to create a flexible surface; can be made from rubber, foam or fiberboard.

Underpinning: normally needed due to subsidence, this method of construction involves providing support beneath a column or a wall, without removing the superstructure, in order to increase the load capacity or improve the original structure of the building.

Veneer: thin decorative laminate covering over chip board.

Washer: flat rubber/metal device used to create a watertight seal in plumbing.

Warp: twist in materials such as wood.

Wet rot: damage and decay of timber as a consequence of water, this is less serious than dry rot but needs to be treated quickly.

Wet trades: refers to plastering and rendering.

Wood filler: specific filler for timber, this paste or liquid dries hard enough to fix things into it.

INDEX

adhesives (glues) 33
  types 43
alcove: shelves for 106
Amtico® 20
apron 17

backsplash: retiling 121
bamboo flooring 10
bath: resealing 95–97
batten: fixing 48–49
black mold 67
blinds: hanging 48–49
bookcases: repairing 110
bradawl 28
brushes:
  cleaning 16, 75
  storing 15, 75
bubble level 28

carpet 19
cartridge gun 33
cat flap 130–31
ceiling: painting 70
cellars: draft-proofing 56
cell phone: protecting 14
ceramic tiles: for floors 20
chairs: wobbly: repairing
  110–11
chicken run 131
chimneys: blocking up 55
chipboard 34
chisels 32
claw hammer 29
clearing up 16
cloche 131
closets 58
cupboards: increasing shelf
  space 58
clothing 17

containers: for storage 8, 25
cooktop: backsplash 121
cracks: in walls: filling 64
curtains 56
  hanging 48–49
cutting: tools for 29

deadbolt lock 51
decorating 62–82
  painting 63–75
  wallpapering 76–82
decorative-faced particleboard
  34, 36
direct drilling joints 37
dishwasher: plumbing in 93
door bells 53
door chain and mirror 51–53
door guard 51
doors:
  draft-proofing 55–56
  panelled: painting 75
  papering round 82
  security 51–53
  sticking: fixing 104
door knockers 53
dowel joints 37
draft-proofing 54–56
drafts: locating 54
drawers: droopy: repairing 111
drilling:
  techniques 38–41
  tools for 30–31
dust masks 17

electrical projects: tools for 33
electrical system 23–24
  fuses 24
  safety 23
estimates 12–13

files 32
fixings: types 40
flaky surfaces: painting 67
flat-packs: assembling 115–17
floor coverings 19–20, 99
  quantities 99
floorboards 19
  draft-proofing 56
floors 99–103
  laying vinyl tiles 100
  painting 99
  wooden: sanding and
    varnishing 101–3
furniture:
  flat-pack 115–17
  oiling 59
  outdoor: maintaining
    128–129
  painting 60–61
  preparing 59
  renovating 58–61
  reviving 61
  waxing 60
  wonky furniture: repairing
    108–14
fuse box 24
fuses 24

garden cloche 131
glues 33
  types 43
goggles 17
grout 87
  applying 90
  mixing 88

hacksaws 29
hammers 29–30
hinges: hanging 108

holes:
  drilling 39
  fixings 40
  pilot 40
  size 40
  too large: correcting 43
home security 50–53

jigsaw 29
joints: types 37

kitchen units:
  doors:
    changing 120–21
    soft-closing 120
  handles: changing 118
  painting 120
kitchens: revamping 118–21
knee pads 17
knives 29
  cleaning 16

laminates, flooring 20
lampshades: replacing 83
lawns, artificial 127
letter boxes: security 53
light fittings:
  painting round 67
  papering round 82
lighting 83
  exterior 124
linoleum flooring 99
lintels 19
locks:
  door 51
  window 53
lofts: draft-proofing 56

marking: tools for 28–29
masking tape 32
masks 17
materials 34–35
MDF 34

measuring 36
  tools for 28–29
mirror: hanging on
  wardrobe 112
miter box 29
mold, black 67
murals 66

nail sets 30
nailing: tools for 29–30
nails 32

paint:
  applying 73
  cleaning 13
  coverage 67
  finishes 67
  quantities 67
  spray: outdoor use 124
painting 63–75
  ceiling 70
  colours 63–64
  equipment 68
  order of work 69–71
  preparations 64–67
  walls 71
  woodwork 72–75
pincers 30
pliers 29
plumbing:
  mains water 20
  pipework 22
  plumbing in machines 93
  projects 91–97
    tools for 33
  stopcocks 22
  systems 20–21
  toilet: unblocking 94
  unblocking U-bend 92
  waste pipes 22
porous surfaces: painting 67
preparation 14–15

recycling 16
red ink: painting over 67
rigid joint blocks 37
rollers: storing overnight 15
rooms:
  painting ceiling and walls
    63–75
  order of work 69–71
  painting woodwork 72–75
  wallpapering 76–82
rubber flooring 20

safety: electrical 23
sanders: electric 32
sanding 102–3
sanding block 32
sandpaper 32
screwdrivers 30
screwing: tools for 29–30
screws 32
  choosing 41–43
  fixing into wall 38–43
  sizes 41
sea grass 19
sealant:
  removing 96
  using 96–97
security: home 50–53
shaping: tools for 32
shelves 105–6
  in alcove 106
  floating 105
  wire suspension 105
shoe racks 114
stopcocks 22
skills 36–43
skirting boards:
  draft-proofing 56
  filling gaps 78
smoothing tools 32
solvents 33
space savers 58
spatulas: cleaning 16

spy hole 51
steam strippers 78
storage:
  containers for 8, 25
  cupboard fittings 58
  places for 27
storage caddy 58
stud walls 18–19
symbols 6

telephone: protecting 14
tile spacers 87
tiles:
  calculating requirements 87
  cutting 89, 90
  finishes 85
  old: removing 86
  types 85
tiling 85–90
  preparing surface 88–89
  splash-back 121
  technique 87–90
  tools for 33
toilet: blocked: fixing 94
toilet seat: wonky: fixing 94
tool box 27
tools 25–33
  basic kit 26
  buying 27
  cleaning 16
  for cutting 29
  for drilling 30–31
  for measuring and marking
    28–29

for nailing and screwing
  29–30
for smoothing and shaping 32
storage places 27
tradespeople:
  advice from 13
  employing 12–14
U-bend: unblocking 92

varnishing 103
vinyl flooring 20
vinyl tiles 99
  laying 100

wallpaper: painting over 67
wallpapering 76–82
  air bubbles 82
  in corners 82
  cutting and pasting 80–81
  hanging paper 81
  light fittings 82
  order of work 78
  preparations 76–78
  quantities 79
  stripping 78
  tools and equipment 76
  windows and doors 82
walls:
  filling holes and cracks 64
  fixing screws into 38–43
  gluing stuff to 43
  hanging things on 19,
    123–124
  painting 71

removing hooks and nails
  from 60
types of construction 18–19
wardrobes:
  adding clothes rail 114
  adding shelves 112–14
  customizing 112–14
  leaning: repairing 110
washing machines:
  plumbing in 93
water butt: installing 125–26
water supply: direct and
  indirect 20–21
windows:
  draft-proofing 55–56
  locks 53
  papering around 82
  sash: painting 74
  security 53
wood:
  buying 35
  cutting to size 36
  floors: sanding and
    varnishing 101–3
  joining pieces 36–37
  measuring 36
  solid 34
woodwork:
  outdoor: maintaining
    128–29
  painting 72–75
    preparations 66, 72–73
work bench 27

PICTURE CREDITS

0 26575 12418 7

Approaching Great Ideas

APPROACHING GREAT IDEAS

CRITICAL READINGS
FOR COLLEGE WRITERS

Lee A. Jacobus
University of Connecticut

bedford
st.martin's
Macmillan Learning
Boston | New York

For Bedford/St. Martin's

Vice President, Editorial, Macmillan Higher Education Humanities: Edwin Hill
Editorial Director, English and Music: Karen S. Henry
Publisher for Composition, Business and Technical Writing, Developmental Writing: Leasa Burton
Executive Editor: John E. Sullivan III
Developmental Editor: Alicia Young
Senior Production Editor: Gregory Erb
Production Supervisor: Robert Cherry
Marketing Manager: Joy Fisher Williams
Copy Editor: Mary Lou Wilshaw-Watts
Photo Researcher: Connie Gardner
Director of Rights and Permissions: Hilary Newman
Senior Art Director: Anna Palchik
Text Design: Laura Shaw Feit
Cover Design: William Boardman
Cover Art: Portman Square, Home House, by Robert Adam (1728–92), Adam, Robert (1728–92)/Courtesy of the Trustees of Sir John Soane's Museum, London/Bridgeman Images; inset photos: (butterfly) Lisa Thornberg/Getty Images; (gold bars) f9photos/Getty Images; (ballot box) Ken Reid/Getty Images; (books) luoman/Getty Images; (justice scales) Comstock/Getty Images
Composition: Jouve
Printing and Binding: RR Donnelley and Sons

Manufactured in the United States of America.

0   9   8   7   6   5
f   e   d   c   b   a

For information, write: Bedford/St. Martin's, 75 Arlington Street, Boston, MA 02116 (617-399-4000)

ISBN 978-1-4576-9994-8 (Student Edition)
ISBN 978-1-319-00823-9 (Instructor's Edition)

Acknowledgments

Text acknowledgments and copyrights appear at the back of the book on pages 455–56, which constitute an extension of the copyright page. Art acknowledgments and copyrights appear on the same page as the art selections they cover. It is a violation of the law to reproduce these selections by any means whatsoever without the written permission of the copyright holder.

Preface for Instructors

⊞

Approaching Great Ideas: Critical Readings for College Writers is a student-centered book introducing some of the best writers examining some of the most important ideas inherent in our culture. The idea for this book grew out of my work on *A World of Ideas: Essential Readings for College Writers*. My aim with that text was to get my first-year composition students writing about important ideas rather than responding to popular writers and journalists centering on personal observations. My students responded positively to reading what they considered to be college-level material written by familiar, famous names such as Plato, Aristotle, Lucretius, James Madison, Andrew Carnegie, Friedrich Nietzsche, Jean-Jacques Rousseau, and Martin Luther King Jr. My purpose was to make the most important ideas of our time available to all my students by providing them with the materials that ultimately permitted them to develop a high-level understanding of how these ideas mattered to the world.

However, in recent years, I have seen an increasing need to show students how ideas from history's greatest thinkers still affect their lives today and to make those ideas as accessible as possible for students whose abilities require additional support. To that end, *Approaching Great Ideas: Critical Readings for College Writers* accounts for the continued examination of great ideas by modern writers such as James Baldwin, John Rawls, Oliver Sacks, Michio Kaku, Jane Jacobs, Thomas Nagel, Peter Singer, Cornel West, bell hooks, Jennifer Ackerman, Kwame Anthony Appiah, and many more. Perspectives from these writers, when presented alongside the foundational work of the classic authors mentioned above, help show students how the ideas in this book continue to be relevant, develop, and flourish in today's world, and carefully structured reading and writing instruction support students' full engagement with the selections.

A FOCUS ON READING

The first part of this book, "Reading and Writing about Great Ideas," provides approaches for critical reading and writing.

Chapter 1, "Examining Ideas," focuses on critical reading. This chapter depends on a modification of the standard reading strategy SQ3R:

Survey, Question, Read, Recite, and Review, as developed in my book *Improving College Reading*, Seventh Edition.

The section "Strategies for Critical Reading about Great Ideas" begins with "Prereading, Titles, and Subheadings." This strategy is a form of surveying the selection before beginning to read it closely. For example, the title of John Dewey's "Education and Morality" introduces two subjects, both of which are related. The section on prereading is followed by "Looking at Opening Paragraphs," which reminds students that reading the opening paragraph of a selection carefully is a strategy that will give them a sense of the overall subject of the essay. The next section, "Annotating" advocates this critical reading strategy because it highlights the notes the student adds to the text, the questions that must be answered, the comments that give the student material for writing, and the important moments in the text.

"Questioning" is a section of utmost importance to students because their critical reading should involve questioning the text rather than merely accepting it passively. Questioning the text can be part of the process of annotation. Such questions will provide subjects for writing brief and longer essays about the ideas of important thinkers. For example, Jane Jacobs's selection, "Stagflation," immediately raises a question: What is stagflation? Beginning with that question initiates the dialogue between the reader and the writer.

"Reviewing" covers a strategy that increases comprehension, especially of complex selections, such as Aristotle's discussion of ethics in "The Aim of Man." Short modern essays may not need much annotation, but longer essays benefit from annotation, analysis, and more time to reflect on their meaning. Reviewing helps the student retain the material and develop ideas for writing.

"Discussing," the last strategy section, deals with a crucial aspect of critical reading. Classroom discussion is a form of recitation that makes a big difference in how one understands the ideas of writers like Aristotle, Robert Dahl, and John Rawls. Being able to talk in a setting that admits of amplification, contradiction, and analysis is a gift. Students benefit from listening to the way others interpret a selection, especially those who call their own ideas into question. Sometimes good class discussion leads to students changing their minds about important issues; this should be seen not as a weakness but rather as a willingness of students to be flexible and allow their ideas to develop and mature.

"Examining Ideas" ends with an excerpt from Alfred North Whitehead's famous essay "Religion and Science." The text provides a space for student annotation, with some sample annotations in the margin. Samples of questions and an analysis of the problems discussed in the text as well as the ways in which the issues apply to modern thought follow the selection. Since this is only an introduction, referring to it again later will be useful when the entire essay appears in "How Science Reads the Book of Nature," where Whitehead is in good company, with Charles Darwin and Steve Jones, who also talk about the issues that sometimes impinge on religious beliefs.

A FOCUS ON WRITING

Approaching Great Ideas is a book for writers. The ideas of authors such as Alfred North Whitehead, Andrew Carnegie, Elizabeth Warren, and Peter Singer invite responses on the part of careful readers. My view is that student writers have much more to say about the kinds of ideas presented here than they might in a book whose ideas are less significant or less well expressed. This material is a stimulus to good thinking and thus to good writing.

As a means of aiding instruction in writing, **Chapter 2, "Writing about Ideas,"** concentrates on some basic rhetorical strategies. We begin with "Generating Topics for Writing," which opens with questions that arise while reading the selection at hand. Some selections will immediately provide subjects for writing because they irritate the reader, instruct the reader, or touch the reader in a personal way. For example, Leslie T. Chang's essay on factory girls in China will likely stimulate any student who has worked in a factory to write about his or her own experience. Elizabeth Warren's essay, "The Vanishing Middle Class," may stimulate a response from any student who is or expects to be part of the middle class. A number of selections are about ideas that have direct pertinence for all of us; as a result, finding a topic for writing will, in such cases, be relatively easy.

Working with some other selections may prove more challenging. In those cases, the questions developed in the act of reading through the piece will be of great use. Moreover, the discussion of a selection in class will generate a great many possible topics for writing an essay that analyzes, challenges, or interprets a range of ideas presented by authors such as Aristotle, Michael Gazzaniga, Adam Smith, Alexis de Tocqueville, and many others. The very fact that many modern writers are still discussing the work of classic writers such as Plato and Rousseau tells us that every age needs to reconsider the basic ideas of freedom, wealth, science, and morality.

Getting student writers involved in the process of contributing to the dialogue is the first step in asking them to write. "Thinking Critically" is a pivotal section that covers the best preparation for developing good ideas for an essay. Each selection has some critical questions that might precipitate an essay, but the best questions come from the writers themselves. A selection like Alfred North Whitehead's raises a specific question: "How can one define terms like Religion and Science?" In the case of Jean-Jacques Rousseau, we would naturally ask, "What is a social contract?"

General questions that apply to virtually every selection are also listed in this section. They are questions such as:

- What is the main point of this selection?
- Is this author presenting an argument or an observation of fact?
- Is the author objective or biased? What might constitute bias in this selection?
- Does the author have adequate evidence to support the claims of the selection?
- How significant is this selection for me personally?

Once an approach to writing has been established, most writers find "Creating a Thesis Statement" to be a real help in crafting their essay. The discussion in that section points out that many professional writers spread a thesis throughout their essay; thus, their essays seem to have no thesis statements. But fashioning a thesis statement is a real advantage in that it provides a focus for writing and a clear direction to guide the whole essay. This discussion provides a number of examples drawn from Alfred North Whitehead's essay. Many kinds of thesis statements will be possible in writing about any of the selections in this book. Three types, among a number discussed, are

- A thesis that states a position: "In any conflict between religion and science, science always wins."
- A thesis that establishes a cause: "Religious belief depends on faith, while scientific belief depends on evidence; therefore, the claims of one should not cause a conflict with the other."
- A thesis that states an opinion: "A religious community should not pass laws that prevent scientific truths from being taught at any level of schooling, whether public or private."

Several more kinds of topic sentences are illustrated in the text, but the important point is that students are given concrete examples that can work for any selection. Further, the emphasis on the topic sentence helps the writer get a good beginning, something that even highly competent writers may have trouble with.

This section ends with two different topic sentences developed into two first paragraphs that each could be developed into full essays. These sample opening paragraphs should lead by example and encourage your students to find their own voices in the ongoing dialogue.

"Supporting Your Thesis" moves on to the question of how the thesis statement can be worked up into a fully developed essay. Many student writers compose paragraphs that sometimes consist of a progression of sentences that could themselves be topic sentences. They make declarations but do not go on to explore the issues. The thesis statement is only the beginning.

Once the student formulates a good thesis, careful development will make the essay both interesting and possibly convincing. This section presents some of the most basic rhetorical methods of development, with examples based on selections from the book. None of these methods is rigid or narrow in scope. They act here as aids, not rules, for development. The examples are presented in such a way as to demonstrate simplicity. They respect the way most of us think about ideas and the way we approach any material we wish to write about. Among them, with paragraphs derived from several essays in the text, are rhetorical methods that show

- Development by definition
- Development by comparison
- Development by example
- Development by analysis of cause and effect

This section is followed by "Establishing Your Argument," which introduces the concept of the essay as a form of argument, a defense of a thesis that tries to establish a position on a serious issue. The point is made that arguments in writing are not contentious, like many arguments between antagonists or even between friends. As a way of illustrating the nature of the argument, I provide some discussion and some examples. Because there is more than one way to argue a case, I also provide instruction in shaping different forms of arguments. The text provides treatment of three basic forms:

- **Classical argument:** An effort to convince readers by the use of facts, evidence, and logical analysis of the important elements of the stated position.
- **Toulmin argument:** An effort to convince readers to take a specific stand on a question of importance. It is distinctive because it relies on shared assumptions that most people take for granted and has three basic parts: a claim, grounds, and a warrant.
- **Rogerian argument:** An argument designed to find common ground on which most readers will agree. The idea behind Rogerian argument is that if a writer recognizes other opinions or arguments about a topic, then the writer creates common ground with as many readers as possible.

Each of these forms of argument appears in selections included in the text. The classical argument is illustrated by Emile Durkheim's "The Intellectual Elite and Democracy," in which he argues that writers and scholars, of which he is one, have an obligation to participate in "public life." This essay offers a good view of how the classical argument can work and, therefore, how it might be used by the student.

The Toulmin argument is exemplified in Cornel West's "The Deep Democratic Tradition in America." West makes his *claim* in his opening paragraph:

"To many, our democratic system seems so broken that they have simply lost faith that their participation could really matter. The politics of self-interest and catering to narrow special interests is so dominant that so many ask themselves, Why vote?" Underlying his essay is the shared assumption that voting is highly desirable, in a sense even a necessity, in a democracy.

Rogerian argument is deftly handled in Alfred North Whitehead's "Religion and Science." Whitehead tries to defuse a potentially explosive situation. His thesis, in his second paragraph, is posed as a possible truth, but one that needs some explanation: "The *conflict* between religion and science is what naturally occurs to our minds when we think of this subject. It seems as though, during the last half-century, the results of science and the beliefs of religion had come into a position of frank disagreement, from which there can be no escape, except by abandoning either the clear teaching of science, or the clear teaching of religion." Obviously, the last sentence seems to present a gulf that could hardly be bridged, even by well-meaning people. But Whitehead's essay, which has never been out of print, uses the best argumentative approach to make the case.

Finally, "Writing about Ideas" ends with a sample student essay that uses Whitehead's "Religion and Science" to generate a useful argument. It is titled "Religion and Science Today," and each paragraph is identified for its method of development. A range of means of development — definition, analysis of circumstances, comparison, example, and cause and effect — demonstrates how the power of common methods of developing paragraphs can achieve a fullness of expression in the essay.

CLASSIC AND CONTEMPORARY PERSPECTIVES ON GREAT IDEAS

Part Two, "The Readings," features selections in five thematic chapters, each of which considers an important area of thought that is detailed and discussed by classic authors to whom most contemporary writers look for basic theory. These authors' selections are then followed by works from contemporary writers exploring the idea from a modern perspective.

Chapter 3, "How Democracy Relates to Human Rights," connects the thinking of the theorists of ancient and modern democracies, such as Plato and James Madison, with the concern for human rights as expressed by the Marquis de Lafayette, Mary Wollstonecraft, and Alexis de Tocqueville. Those issues are developed further by Robert A. Dahl and Fareed Zakaria, who make a case for human rights as essential for a healthy democracy. The argument throughout is that one of government's responsibilities is to preserve and protect human rights, though as Emile Durkheim and Cornel West argue, citizens also have a responsibility to participate in maintaining their democracy. The authors in this section argue that democracies are the most likely, of all forms of government, to promote human rights.

Chapter 4, "How Freedom Depends on Justice," includes Franklin Delano Roosevelt's famous "Four Freedoms" speech to Congress, in which he establishes some of the key liberties that are still withheld from citizens in some parts of the world. Jean-Jacques Rousseau and Lucy A. Delaney delve into matters of slavery, and Martin Luther King Jr. expresses the ideals that propelled the civil rights struggle for justice in the 1960s, which was also when James Baldwin's famous epistle to his nephew remarked harshly on the hundredth anniversary of the Emancipation Proclamation. John Rawls and Amartya Sen clarify some of the modern thinking on how justice should be expressed in a society, and feminist bell hooks joins with Mary Wollstonecraft in discussing women's ongoing quest for justice in a patriarchal society.

The close observation of nature is the focus of Chapter 5, "How Science Reads the Book of Nature," beginning with the Roman poet Lucretius' observations about sleep, which provide a simple introduction to the ways in which we can learn to observe closely. Charles Darwin's discussion of the development of life by a process of evolution — which is still not a universally accepted theory — is followed by Alfred North Whitehead's plea for a resolution of the dispute between science and religion, concerns that continue to resonate. Contemporary writers Oliver Sacks, Michio Kaku, and Jennifer Ackerman discuss matters of perception, artificial intelligence, and genetics, all areas of great importance to the future of humankind and nature. Steve Jones is also concerned about the future of humankind, and he discusses what will happen to the masculine gender now that the idea of the "natural" superiority of males has eroded.

Among many contemporary social issues, few are as widely commented on in the popular press as the inequities of wealth in highly developed nations. Chapter 6, "How Society Regards Wealth and Poverty," begins with Adam Smith, whose focus is on the nature and value of labor during the early years of the Industrial Revolution. Andrew Carnegie, by way of contrast, examines the force of capital and the results of enormous wealth in the hands of a few. He and Smith thought that great wealth in the hands of the few was inevitable and desirable. Charlotte Perkins Gilman acknowledges the value of the domestic arts while championing the idea of more educational and nondomestic opportunities for women, which were radical ideas in her lifetime. John Kenneth Galbraith examines the inequality produced by modern economies, and Elizabeth Warren warns that the middle class — the pride of a rising democracy — is threatened by burgeoning inequities. Jane Jacobs examines the theories of classic economists in order to understand the stagnant economy of her own time. Leslie T. Chang echoes some of Adam Smith's interests in her discussion of factory girls in modern China.

Chapter 7, "How Ethics and Morality Interact," addresses a question that has become increasingly important in an age in which institutional religion plays less of a role in such concerns than it once did. Aristotle, for example, insists that the most important goal for anyone is to achieve happiness and says that in order to achieve long-lasting happiness one must live a life of virtue. Aristotle makes it clear why a life of virtue is rewarding and important, and he does so without reference to any religion or any deity. Friedrich Nietzsche, a philosopher who was born into a family of ministers, argues that building the inner strength of the individual by analyzing the good and the bad values in society is the best way to combat a decline in religious adherence (and potentially, therefore, in morality). John Dewey argues that the individual in a democracy has a moral obligation to seek as much education as possible. Thomas Nagel explores morality to attempt to find a basis for ethical behavior that goes beyond the subjective teachings of religious groups. Ethics involves choices in general social circumstances, and Michael Gazzaniga investigates evolutionary development to see how ethical behavior may be central to the evolution of our species. Peter Singer and Jim Mason accuse humans of "speciesism" in limiting ethical concerns to our own species, and Francis Fukuyama asks us to consider human rights in relation to the rights of animals. Finally, Kwame Anthony Appiah explores the concepts that Aristotle introduces at the beginning of the chapter, arguing that the standards for "good" that people set for themselves nowadays are too low to produce true happiness.

HELPFUL PROMPTS FOR WRITING AND DISCUSSION

At the end of each essay, a number of key questions help develop class discussion of the selection. These questions are designed to begin a critical analysis of the selection as a means of clarifying key ideas and helping increase understanding not only of the main ideas but also of some of the implications of the ideas for the individual student.

Understanding Ideas questions test students' comprehension of the key ideas presented within a reading, and Responding to Ideas questions provide prompts for writing. Each of these writing questions is labeled as a **Definition**, **Comparison**, **Example**, **Cause and Effect**, **Testimony**, **Research**, **Response**, or **Analysis of Circumstances** question. These questions derive from the means of development discussed in Chapter 2, "Writing about Ideas." These are prompts that can direct the entire essay or segments of the essay. In every instance, regardless of the label, the prompts are flexible enough to permit essays to be developed in a variety of ways.

A response prompt asks the student writer to examine the ideas expressed in the selection in relation to the student's own situation. How do these ideas affect the student? What part of the student's life is at stake here? The question usually makes it clear that we are all invested in what the author has said and that it is important for us to understand the author's ideas and to take issue where necessary.

The research prompt will be useful for those courses in which there is an opportunity to use library and online resources to build an essay that goes beyond the limits of the selection alone. In some cases, a bibliographic item or an online source will be suggested as a way to get going. In all cases of the research prompt, I make a point of indicating that relying only on online sources alone is not sufficient in a thoroughly researched essay.

A definition prompt will ask the student to define in writing a key term or key idea. For questions labeled comparison, students will be asked to focus on comparing ideas or positions that are presented within a single reading.

Finally, each reading concludes with a set of Comparing Ideas questions, which involve comparing ideas among two or more authors. For example, the student is prompted to compare Plato's ideas on democracy with the fears expressed by Fareed Zakaria. James Madison's Bill of Rights and Mary Wollstonecraft's "A Vindication of the Rights of Woman" offer an interesting comparison and a good opportunity to write about the role of women in a changing society. Emile Durkheim's essay on the responsibilities of the elite in a democracy provides a good comparison with the ideas of Cornel West, who sees a deep democratic tradition in the United States. Friedrich Nietzsche's concept of morality as a social construct offers a contrast with Michael Gazzaniga's theories implying an evolutionary role in forming moral values. Peter Singer and Jim Mason provide an opportunity to compare their views on the rights of animals and the implications of speciesism with the views of Madison, Lafayette, and Tocqueville.

These questions are designed to widen the range of responses to the ideas in this book, all of which can be seen interacting with many different authors in many different eras.

INSTRUCTOR'S RESOURCE MANUAL

I have prepared a detailed manual, *Resources for Teaching Approaching Great Ideas*, with suggestions for developing a course that makes good use of the material on reading, the material on writing, and the selections and their discussion and usefulness for stimulating good essays on the part of the students. The material I provide for the instructor develops further some of the ideas in the introductions that help set the selections in their time.

I offer some comments on the importance of each selection and provide some material useful in class discussions. Most of the selections in the book are relatively short and can therefore be easily reread. For the few longer essays, I provide a discussion of the key issues so as to help the instructor focus on the important ideas and how they are developed. As much as possible, *Resources for Teaching Approaching Great Ideas* will make the class run smoothly and help students get the most out of the experience of approaching great ideas.

You can download the manual from **macmillanhighered.com /greatideas/catalog**.

ACKNOWLEDGMENTS

I am indebted to a great many creative people at Bedford/St. Martin's, whose support is invaluable. I want particularly to thank Karen Henry, editorial director for English and music; John Sullivan, executive editor for readers; Leasa Burton, publisher for composition, business and technical writing, and developmental writing; and Steve Scipione, senior executive editor, all of whom offered many useful ideas and suggestions, especially in the early stages of development, and kept their sharp eyes on the project throughout. My editor, the extraordinary Alicia Young, has been a steady, guiding hand, discussing material with me and providing help where necessary and when timely. She has been an inspiration in dealing with sometimes intractable problems and responding with encouragement and the kind of help only the best editors can provide. One of the pleasures of working on this and other Bedford books is that my editors have also become my friends.

Assisting her were a number of hardworking individuals, including editorial assistant Jennifer Prince. Gregory Erb, senior production editor, also helped with innumerable important details and suggestions. Mary Lou Wilshaw-Watts, copy editor, improved the prose and watched out for inconsistencies. Thanks also to several staff members and researchers: Jenn Kennett cleared text permissions, Billy Boardman designed the cover, and Connie Gardner secured permission for all the images.

The following professors were generous with criticism, praise, and detailed recommendations for this text: David Elias, Eastern Kentucky University; Christina Lovin, Eastern Kentucky University; Betsy McCormick, Mt. San Antonio College; Janet Mitchell-Wagner, Pasadena City College; Marjory Thrash, Pearl River Community College; Greg Underwood, Pearl River Community College; Justin Williamson, Pearl River Community College; and Susan Wozniak, Westfield State University and Springfield College.

Lee A. Jacobus

GET THE MOST OUT OF YOUR COURSE
WITH *APPROACHING GREAT IDEAS*

Bedford/St. Martin's offers resources and format choices that help you and your students get even more out of your book and course. To learn more about or to order any of the following products, contact your Bedford/St. Martin's sales representative, e-mail sales support (**sales_support@bfwpub.com**), or visit the Web site at **macmillanhighered.com/greatideas/catalog**.

SELECT VALUE PACKAGES

Add value to your text by packaging one of the following resources with *Approaching Great Ideas*. To learn more about package options for any of the following products, contact your Bedford/St. Martin's sales representative or visit **macmillanhighered.com/greatideas/catalog**.

Writer's Help 2.0 is a powerful online writing resource that helps students find answers whether they are searching for writing advice on their own or as part of an assignment.

- **Smart search**

  Built on research with more than 1,600 student writers, the smart search in *Writer's Help* provides reliable results even when students use novice terms, such as *flow* and *unstuck*.

- **Trusted content from our best-selling handbooks**

  Choose *Writer's Help 2.0 for Hacker Handbooks* or *Writer's Help 2.0 for Lunsford Handbooks* and ensure that students have clear advice and examples for all their writing questions.

- **Adaptive exercises that engage students**

  Writer's Help includes LearningCurve, game-like online quizzing that adapts to what students already know and helps them focus on what they need to learn.

Student access is packaged with *Approaching Great Ideas* at a significant discount. Order ISBN 978-1-319-05678-0 for *Writer's Help 2.0 for Hacker Handbooks* or ISBN 978-1-319-05679-7 for *Writer's Help 2.0 for Lunsford Handbooks* to ensure your students have easy access to online writing support. Students who rent a book or buy a used book can purchase access to *Writer's Help 2.0* at **macmillanhighered.com/writershelp2**.

Instructors may request free access by registering as an instructor at **macmillanhighered.com/writershelp2**.

For technical support, visit **macmillanhighered.com/getsupport**.

LaunchPad Solo for Readers and Writers allows students to work on whatever they need help with the most. At home or in class, students learn at their own pace, with instruction tailored to each student's unique needs. *LaunchPad Solo for Readers and Writers* features:

- **Pre-built units that support a learning arc**

  Each easy-to-assign unit is composed of a pretest check, multi-media instruction and assessment, and a posttest that assesses what students have learned about critical reading, the writing process, using sources, grammar, style, mechanics, and English for multilingual writers.

- **A video introduction to many topics**

  Introductions offer an overview of the unit's topic, and many include a brief, accessible video to illustrate the concepts at hand.

- **Adaptive quizzing for targeted learning**

  Most units include LearningCurve, game-like adaptive quizzing that focuses on the areas in which each student needs the most help.

- **The ability to monitor student progress**

  Use our gradebook to see which students are on track and which need additional help with specific topics.

LaunchPad Solo for Readers and Writers can be **packaged at a significant discount**. Order ISBN 978-1-319-06503-4 to ensure your students can take full advantage. Visit **macmillanhighered.com/catalog/readwrite** for more information.

Portfolio Keeping, **3rd Edition, by Nedra Reynolds and Elizabeth Davis**, provides all the information students need to use the portfolio method successfully in a writing course. *Portfolio Teaching*, a companion guide for instructors, provides the practical information instructors and writing program administrators need to use the portfolio method successfully in a writing course. To order *Portfolio Keeping* packaged with this text, contact your sales representative for a package ISBN.

MAKE LEARNING FUN WITH *RE:WRITING 3*

bedfordstmartins.com/rewriting
Bedford's free and open online resource includes videos and interactive elements to engage students in new ways of writing. You'll find tutorials about using common digital writing tools, an interactive peer-review game,

Extreme Paragraph Makeover, and more. Visit **bedfordstmartins.com /rewriting** for more information.

INSTRUCTOR RESOURCES

macmillanhighered.com/greatideas/catalog
You have a lot to do in your course. Bedford/St. Martin's wants to make it easy for you to find the support you need — and to get it quickly.

Resources for Teaching Approaching Great Ideas is available as a PDF that can be downloaded from the Bedford/St. Martin's online catalog at the URL above. In addition to chapter overviews and teaching tips, the instructor's manual includes a sample syllabus, further background on every selection, additional comprehension questions, and suggestions for essays.

Teaching Central offers the entire list of Bedford/St. Martin's print and online professional resources in one place. You'll find landmark reference works, sourcebooks on pedagogical issues, award-winning collections, and practical advice for the classroom — all free for instructors. Visit **macmillanhighered.com/teachingcentral**.

Bedford *Bits* collects creative ideas for teaching a range of composition topics in a frequently updated blog. A community of teachers — leading scholars, authors, and editors such as Andrea Lunsford, Elizabeth Losh, Jack Solomon, and Elizabeth Wardle — discuss assignments, activities, revision, research, grammar and style, multimodal composition, technology, peer review, and much more. Take, use, adapt, and pass the ideas around. Then, come back to the site to comment or share your own suggestions. Visit **bedfordbits.com**.

Contents

PREFACE FOR INSTRUCTORS   *v*

PART ONE

READING AND WRITING ABOUT GREAT IDEAS

1. Examining Ideas   *3*

STRATEGIES FOR CRITICAL READING ABOUT GREAT IDEAS   *4*

    Prereading, Titles, and Subheadings *4*

    Looking at Opening Paragraphs *7*

    Annotating *10*

    Questioning *11*

    Reviewing *12*

    Discussing *12*

        Sample Annotated Passage for Review and Discussion 13

    Forming Your Own Ideas *18*

2. Writing about Ideas   *19*

GENERATING TOPICS FOR WRITING   *20*

    Thinking Critically *20*

CREATING A THESIS STATEMENT   *22*

    Sample Opening Paragraphs *23*

    Supporting Your Thesis *26*

        Development by Definition 27

        Development by Comparison 28

      Development by Example *30*

      Development by Analysis of Cause and Effect *31*

      Development by Analysis of Circumstances *32*

      Development by Testimony *33*

      Development by Rhetorical Question *35*

    Questions for Reading and Writing *36*

ESTABLISHING YOUR ARGUMENT   *37*

    Classical Argument *38*

    Toulmin Argument *39*

    Rogerian Argument *40*

A SAMPLE STUDENT ESSAY   *42*

PART TWO

THE READINGS

3. How Democracy Relates to Human Rights   *49*

INTRODUCTION   *51*

SEEING IDEAS   *54*

PLATO (427–347 B.C.E.)

    Democracy and the Democratic Man   *56*

    We can see at once that a society cannot hold wealth in honor and at the same time establish a proper self-control in its citizens. One or the other must be sacrificed.

JAMES MADISON (1751–1836)

    The Bill of Rights   *65*

    The Convention of a number of the States, having at the time of their adopting the Constitution, expressed a desire, in order to prevent misconstruction or abuse of its powers, that further declaratory and restrictive clauses should be added: And as extending the ground of public confidence in the Government, will best ensure the beneficent ends of its institution.

MARQUIS DE LAFAYETTE (1757–1834) AND THE NATIONAL ASSEMBLY
OF FRANCE (1789)

Declaration of the Rights of Man and Citizen

71

The representatives of the French people, organized in National
Assembly, considering that ignorance, forgetfulness, or contempt of
the rights of man, are the sole causes of the public miseries and of
the corruption of governments, have resolved to set forth in a solemn declaration the natural, inalienable, and sacred rights of man[.]

MARY WOLLSTONECRAFT (1759–1797)

A Vindication of the Rights of Woman

77

[I]f woman be allowed to have an immortal soul, she must have, as
the employment of life, an understanding to improve.

ALEXIS DE TOCQUEVILLE (1805–1859)

The Idea of Rights in the United States

84

Next to the general conception of virtue, I know of none finer than
that of rights, or rather these two ideas are inseparable. The idea of
rights is no more than the concept of virtue applied to the world
of politics.

EMILE DURKHEIM (1858–1917)

The Intellectual Elite and Democracy

90

Writers and scholars are citizens. It is therefore obvious that they
have a strict duty to participate in public life.

ROBERT A. DAHL (1915–2014)

Why Democracy?

96

In the face of so much history, why should we believe that democracy is a better way of governing the state than any nondemocratic
alternative? Let me count the reasons.

CORNEL WEST (b. 1953)

The Deep Democratic Tradition in America

111

The deep democratic tradition did not begin in America and we
have no monopoly on its promise. But it is here where the seeds of
democracy have taken deepest root and sprouted most robustly.

FAREED ZAKARIA (b. 1964)

Illiberal Democracy

120

Russia and China are the two most important countries in the world
that are not liberal democracies. Their search for political and economic systems that work for them is of enormous global significance.

4. How Freedom Depends on Justice   *129*

INTRODUCTION   *131*

SEEING IDEAS   *134*

JEAN-JACQUES ROUSSEAU (1712–1778)

Of Slavery and the Social Pact   *136*

Since no man has natural authority over his fellows, and since Might can produce no Right, the only foundation left for legitimate authority in human societies is Agreement.

LUCY A. DELANEY (c. 1828–1890)

Struggles for Freedom   *146*

How I did hate him! To hear him talk as if I were going to take a pleasure trip, when he knew that if he sold me South, as he intended, I would never see my dear mother again.

FRANKLIN DELANO ROOSEVELT (1882–1945)

The Four Freedoms   *153*

Certainly this is no time for any of us to stop thinking about the social and economic problems which are the root cause of the social revolution which is today a supreme factor in the world. For there is nothing mysterious about the foundations of a healthy and strong democracy.

JOHN RAWLS (1921–2002)

A Theory of Justice   *159*

Just as each person must decide by rational reflection what constitutes his good . . . so a group of persons must decide once and for all what is to count among them as just and unjust.

JAMES BALDWIN (1924–1987)

My Dungeon Shook: Letter to My Nephew on the One Hundredth Anniversary of the Emancipation   *169*

This innocent country set you down in a ghetto in which, in fact, it intended that you should perish. Let me spell out precisely what I mean by that, for the heart of the matter is here, and the root of my dispute with my country.

MARTIN LUTHER KING JR. (1929–1968)

I Have a Dream   *176*

I still have a dream . . . that one day this nation will rise up and live
out the true meaning of its creed — we hold these truths to be self-
evident, that all men are created equa .

AMARTYA SEN (b. 1933)

The Idea of Justice   *183*

When we try to determine how justice can be advanced, there is a
basic need for publc reasoning, involving arguments coming from
different quarters and divergent perspectives.

bell hooks (b. 1952)

Feminist Politics: Where We Stand   *190*

Simply put, feminism is a movement to end sexism, sexist exploitation, and oppression. . . . To understand feminism it implies one has
to necessarily understand sexism.

5. How Science Reads the Book of Nature   *199*

INTRODUCTION   *201*

SEEING IDEAS   *203*

LUCRETIUS (c. 99–c. 55 B.C.E.)

The Nature of Sleep   *206*

And now for *the problem of sleep*: By what contrivance does it flood
our limbs with peace and unravel from our breasts the mind's
disquietude?

CHARLES DARWIN (1809–1882)

Of Sexual Selection and Natural Selection   *212*

This form of selection depends, not on a struggle for existence in
relation to other organic beings or to external conditions, but on a
struggle between the individuals of one sex, generally the males,
for the possession of the other sex.

ALFRED NORTH WHITEHEAD (1861–1947)

Religion and Science   *221*

The difficulty in approaching the question of the relations between
Religion and Science is, that its elucidation requires that we have in

our minds some clear idea of what we mean by either of the terms, "religion" and "science."

OLIVER SACKS (1933–2015)

The Mind's Eye   *236*

Going blind, especially later in life, presents one with a huge, potentially overwhelming challenge: to find a new way of living, of ordering one's world, when the old way has been destroyed.

STEVE JONES (b. 1944)

The Descent of Men   *244*

The final pages of *The Descent of Man*, the model for the present work, contain a lofty account of the natural superiority of men over women[.] . . . In the nineteenth century such ideas seemed self-evident. Now things have changed.

MICHIO KAKU (b. 1947)

Physics of the Impossible   *252*

Critics sometimes point out a pattern, that every thirty years, AI practitioners claim that superintelligent robots are just around the corner. Then, when there is a reality check, a backlash sets in.

JENNIFER ACKERMAN (b. 1959)

Molecules and Genes   *263*

Members of the human family carry traits that have held on down the line not just for generations but for eons, traits that mock all boundaries of time and kind.

6. How Society Regards Wealth and Poverty   *273*

INTRODUCTION   *275*

SEEING IDEAS   *278*

ADAM SMITH (1723–1790)

The Value of Labor   *281*

A man must always live by his work, and his wages must at least be sufficient to maintain him.

ANDREW CARNEGIE (1835–1919)

The Gospel of Wealth　　289

The problem of our age is the proper administration of wealth, so that the ties of brotherhood may still bind together the rich and poor in harmonious relationship. The conditions of human life have not only been changed, but revolutionized, within the past few hundred years.

CHARLOTTE PERKINS GILMAN (1860–1935)

Women and Economics: "Cupid-in-the-Kitchen"　　303

As a natural consequence of our division of labor on sex lines, giving to woman the home and to man the world in which to work, we have come to have a dense prejudice in favor of the essential womanliness of the home duties, as opposed to the essential manliness of every other kind of work.

JOHN KENNETH GALBRAITH (1908–2006)

Inequality　　317

Few things have been more productive of controversy over the ages than the suggestion that the rich should, by one device or another, share their wealth with those who are not.

JANE JACOBS (1916–2006)

Stagflation　　329

Where stagflation has taken hold, remedies have led only to still worse unemployment as a sacrifice to the fight against inflation, or to still worse inflation as a sacrifice to the fight against unemployment.

ELIZABETH WARREN (b. 1949)

The Vanishing Middle Class　　344

The issues of poverty are typically framed around the poor themselves — the causes of their problems and the help they need. But lifting the poor out of poverty means finding a place for them in the middle.

LESLIE T. CHANG (b. 1969)

Factory Girls in Dongguan　　357

Young women from the countryside taught me the city. From them I learned which factories were well run; without ever leaving Dongguan, these workers had figured out the global hierarchy of nations.

7. How Ethics and Morality Interact

7. How Ethics and Morality Interact   *367*

INTRODUCTION   *369*

SEEING IDEAS   *371*

ARISTOTLE (384–322 B.C.E.)
   The Aim of Man   *374*
   Every art and every "scientific investigation," as well as every action
   and "purposive choice," appears to aim at some good; hence the
   good has rightly been declared to be that at which all things aim.

FRIEDRICH NIETZSCHE (1844–1900)
   Good and Bad   *393*
   Quite apart from the fact that this hypothesis about the origin of the
   value judgment *good* is historically untenable, its psychology is
   intrinsically unsound.

JOHN DEWEY (1859–1952)
   Education and Morality   *400*
   The business of childhood is to grow into the independence of
   adulthood by means of the guidance of those who have already
   attained it.

THOMAS NAGEL (b. 1937)
   The Objective Basis of Morality   *406*
   In general, the thought that something is wrong depends on its
   impact not just on the person who does it but on other people. They
   wouldn't like it, and they'd object if they found out.

MICHAEL GAZZANIGA (b. 1939)
   Toward a Universal Ethics   *414*
   Modern knowledge is on a collision course with the ubiquitous personal spiritual belief systems of one kind or another that are held by
   billions of people.

PETER SINGER (b. 1946) AND JIM MASON (b. 1934)
   Ethics and Animals   *430*
   What possible arguments can there be in defense of factory farming?
   We will review some of them and show why they are unconvincing.

FRANCIS FUKUYAMA (b. 1952)

Human Specificity and the Rights of Animals *440*

Much of the work done in animal ethology over the past few generations has tended to erode the bright line that was once held to separate human beings from the rest of the animal world.

KWAME ANTHONY APPIAH (b. 1954)

If You're Happy and You Know It *447*

How many times on TV and in the movies have we heard a parent
tell a child, "I just want you to be happy"? But what does that mean?
Here are a few notions you'll encounter these days.

ACKNOWLEDGMENTS *455*

INDEX *457*

Approaching Great Ideas

Part One

⊞ READING AND WRITING ABOUT GREAT IDEAS

Examining Ideas

⊞

The selections in this book concern themselves with a broad range of great ideas. The development of ideas about democracy and human rights, freedom and justice, science and nature, wealth and poverty, and ethics and morality has occupied our greatest thinkers for centuries. Long before people developed written language to convey their thoughts, these issues had been central to humanity.

Approaching Great Ideas includes readings by some of the world's most celebrated thinkers, such as Plato, Aristotle, Jean-Jacques Rousseau, Mary Wollstonecraft, and Adam Smith, as well as notable contemporary writers who carry on the tradition. Cornel West, Amartya Sen, Jennifer Ackerman, Elizabeth Warren, and Kwame Anthony Appiah continue to write about how we approach great ideas confronting us in our own time. Reading about these complex ideas and seeing how they have developed throughout the ages can help you understand the more challenging parts of these ideas, such as why it is not always easy to see exactly how ethics relates to morality, how justice is sometimes realized or denied, or how wealth and poverty strain the fabric of society.

Because of the significance of the material in this book, and because some of the classical authors wrote in styles unlike they would use were they alive today, it is essential to develop certain reading skills to success-fully engage with the selections. Some of these readings are quite challeng-ing. You may find some of the sentences complex and some of the paragraphs long and difficult. For example, the famous biologist Charles Darwin wrote during the middle of the nineteenth century, when writing commonly included far more words in a sentence than we average today. Additionally, some words that were common to classical writers have fallen out of use over time and may be unfamiliar to you. Because of these factors, when reading authors like Darwin, you have to stop and think, reflect back on what he is saying, and take the time to comprehend his basic points. The contemporary writers in this book assume a general audience and aim at clarity; in previous times, writers assumed a classically educated audience familiar with the Latin roots of English words. As a result, some of these essays may cause you to stop and think. But, then, that really is the point of this book. We all need to stop and think about the great ideas presented here.

To help you get the most out of this book, then, this chapter will introduce you to techniques for critical reading. As the term implies, **critical reading** involves your taking a position on the material you read. In other words, be an **active reader**. Do not let the words slip by without accepting the challenge implied in the writer's argument. Indeed, you should begin by assuming that all the writers in this book are presenting you with arguments. They are trying to convince you and perhaps change your mind about their subject matter. That means you have to decide whether to accept the premises — or assumptions — of the writer's argument or to reject them. And, in turn, that means you need to understand the argument to begin with.

Reading critically, then, means that you need to be on your toes when you read. You should challenge the writer and think about how you might construct an argument of your own that would support a different position. You need not always contradict a writer when you challenge the writer's position; instead, you may want to clarify an important point or develop further an aspect of the argument that you feel is not fully formed or explored.

All of this boils down to you asking questions and taking notes: two important strategies for reading critically.

STRATEGIES FOR CRITICAL READING ABOUT GREAT IDEAS

PREREADING, TITLES, AND SUBHEADINGS

The first, and possibly easiest, critical reading strategy is called **prereading**, or examining the selection for its general subject matter. Usually the title is the best place to begin. "Of Slavery and the Social Pact" (excerpted from his longer work *The Origin of Civil Society*), the title of Jean-Jacques Rousseau's essay in this anthology (p. 136), tells us that he will propose a theory of slavery's position in civilized society. In surveying his selection, you will see that Rousseau includes subheadings in the body of his essay as guideposts for how he develops his thinking. The first section, "Of Slavery," begins with an assertion: "Since no man has natural authority over his fellows, and since Might can produce no Right, the only foundation left for legitimate authority in human societies is Agreement." This is a famous philosophical idea, but it needs to be discussed before a reader can see what Rousseau means by it.

The subheadings in Rousseau's essay are as follows:

Of Slavery

That We Must Always Go Back to an Original Compact

Of the Social Pact

Rousseau devotes only a few pages to each of these major issues. As you review this selection in the act of prereading, you can assume that the material following the first subtitle will talk about the place of slaves in a society and that the material following the second will provide clarification of what Rousseau means by "an original compact." Once you review these clues about the subject matter of the essay, you can begin reading closely, knowing what you are looking for. Prereading provides you with a metaphoric "map" of the selection and helps you find your way through the writer's argument.

This technique of reviewing subheadings is essential for the longer selections in this book, such as Rousseau's "Of Slavery and the Social Pact," which was used as an example in the discussion above; Andrew Carnegie's "The Gospel of Wealth" (p. 289); Charlotte Perkins Gilman's "Women and Economics: 'Cupid-in-the-Kitchen'" (p. 303); and Aristotle's "The Aim of Man" (p. 374).

For shorter essays and those with no subheadings — which include most selections in this book — another prereading strategy that can help you create a "map" of a writer's argument is to search for clues in the opening sentence of each paragraph. Such sentences will not always reveal the major content or even the main idea, but they will give you a feel for the passage and a sense of what concerns the writer. If you make a list of all the opening sentences of the paragraphs from the whole selection, it will often approximate the outline of the passage. (Even if you don't have time to make a list, underlining the opening sentences and reviewing them will accomplish the same objective.)

Here, as an example, is a list of the first sentences from the paragraphs of Leslie T. Chang's "Factory Girls in Dongguan" (p. 357):

I, too, had left home.

Initially, China's appeal for me was pragmatic — in the early 1990s, its booming economy began to attract global attention, and my fluency in Chinese suddenly became an asset.

One of the first things most Chinese Americans do when they go to China is to visit their ancestral hometowns, but for twelve years I lived in Hong Kong, Taiwan, and China without making the journey.

Young women from the countryside taught me the city.

Many things I had read about China's migrants were not true.

I came to like Dongguan, which seemed a perverse expression of China at its most extreme.

Dongguan is invisible to the outside world.

Dongguan was also a city of contradictions, because modern Chinese history had begun here.

But there was another history of this place.

Dongguan was different.

In the early days, there was no train service from Hong Kong.

The local labor supply was soon exhausted and migrants began arriving from neighboring provinces.

In the 1990s, the city's manufacturing shifted to electronics and computer parts.

So Dongguan was a place with conflicting versions of its past — one a high-profile rejection of the foreign presence in China, the other stealthy embrace of it.

I went for months without meeting a native of Dongguan.

Six months after I started coming to Dongguan, I interviewed the deputy mayor.

We already disliked each other.

The interview was useful: Without seeing for myself, I never would have believed how completely the government ignored the migrants.

The deputy mayor then talked of a plan to "lift the quality of the Dongguan people," but the effort excluded those who were not native-born.

This selection continues for another page or so beyond the paragraph beginnings listed above, but just from reading these opening sentences, you already have a sense of Chang's concerns in her essay: Dongguan is a city, unknown to most of the world, but with a history that includes foreign influence. It is so busy that it needs migrants to do most of the work, and the local authority has taken the position that its responsibilities are to the local inhabitants, not to the migrants who have come to labor. Knowing only this much, you will grasp the author's main ideas much sooner than if you were to begin the essay without prereading.

The title of the book from which Chang's essay comes — *Factory Girls: From Village to City in a Changing China* — also alerts you to her concerns. The book is mentioned in her headnote, and the opening sentences listed above further reveal the attention she pays to how the city has evolved since its growth as a manufacturing center in 1990. From these prereading clues, then, you can assume that the effect on the women who do the factory work in Dongguan will be revealed in the selection.

LOOKING AT OPENING PARAGRAPHS

Another strategy for getting a general idea of an author's views is to study the opening paragraph of the entire selection. Generally, the first sentence of the opening paragraph will establish the subject of the passage or make a statement or judgment about it and leave the job of developing that statement or judgment to the following sentences.

Just as the opening sentence is important, the last sentence of the opening paragraph is sometimes even more so because its job is to do one or both of two things: (1) to draw a conclusion from what has been said and/or (2) to make a connection to the next paragraph. The opening paragraphs of the selections in this book will sometimes establish the main idea — or a range of ideas — that will be treated in depth in the rest of the essay.

For example, Andrew Carnegie was an industrialist who led the expansion of the steel industry in America in the late nineteenth and early twentieth centuries, and he was one of the richest men in the world at that time. The opening paragraph of "The Gospel of Wealth" (p. 289) gives you a good idea of what he plans to discuss in his essay:

> The problem of our age is the proper administration of wealth, so that the ties of brotherhood may still bind together the rich and poor in harmonious relationship. The conditions of human life have not only been changed, but revolutionized, within the past few hundred years. In former days there was little difference between the dwelling, dress, food, and environment of the chief and those of his retainers. The Indians are today where civilized man then was. When visiting the Sioux, I was led to the wigwam of the chief. It was just like the others in external appearance, and, even within, the difference was trifling between it and those of the poorest of his braves. The contrast between the palace of the millionaire and the cottage of the laborer with us today measures the change which has come with civilization.

This paragraph is especially wonderful to read because it stimulates so many questions that we would want to have answered in the rest of the essay. For example:

- What are the ties of brotherhood between the rich and the poor?
- Does Carnegie assume there must be a harmonious relationship between rich and poor?
- Why does Carnegie think a chief should live in splendor?
- How is a millionaire like a chief (and who are his retainers)?
- If wealth is a product of civilization, then is poverty also its product?

These important questions are the beginning of critical reading because they imply an examination of the premises of Carnegie's opening paragraph and probably his entire essay. For example, it is obvious that Carnegie is not aiming at getting rid of poverty altogether (a task that would be impossible). Instead, he advocates for a "harmonious relationship" between the poor and the rich. Further, Carnegie seems to be saying that wealth is the product of civilization, and he then says that the Sioux are a primitive people. Obviously, he does not recognize the Sioux as a civilized people, nor does he approve of the way they live — not because they are a people without poverty, but because they are a people without excess disposable wealth.

This opening paragraph is filled with ideas that warrant examination and critical discussion, but the rest of the essay is also packed with ideas that have the support of many people even today. Carnegie was a renowned philanthropist who did a great deal of good with his money and had many interesting ideas about wealth and poverty, some of which may be considered idealistic and some realistic. For example, his idea that it is inevitable that in our society some people will be millionaires — known today as "the 1 percent" — while others will be paupers may seem realistic to certain readers. One of the adventures in reading this famous essay is seeing exactly where Carnegie is going after having begun as he does. What is his argument? Is it reasonable? Do you agree or disagree? Is what he has to say as relevant today as he thought it was in 1889? How would you challenge his views? Given the fear that massive modern wealth may affect our entire society through its influence on political action, we need to pay attention to Carnegie's ideas, if only because so many people still believe in them.

Some opening paragraphs that begin by raising questions will be followed by a paragraph that lays out some of the territory to be covered. Robert A. Dahl's selection (p. 96) begins with an overarching question: "Why Democracy?" He then continues his opening paragraph with more questions:

> Why should we support democracy? More specifically, why should we support democracy in governing the state? The state, remember, is a unique association whose government possesses an extraordinary capacity for obtaining compliance with its rules by (among other means) force, coercion, and violence. Are there no better ways of governing a state? Would a nondemocratic system of government be better?

Note how Dahl probes the subject by posing questions directly to his **audience**. He continues:

Until the twentieth century, most of the world proclaimed the superiority of nondemocratic systems both in theory and in practice. Until very recently, a preponderant majority of human beings — at times, all — have been subject to nondemocratic rulers. And the heads of nondemocratic regimes have usually tried to justify their rule by invoking the ancient and persistent claim that most people are just not competent to participate in governing a state. Most people would be better off, this argument goes, if they would only leave the complicated business of governing to those wiser than they — a minority at most, perhaps only one person. In practice, these rationalizations were never quite enough, so where argument left off coercion took over. Most people never explicitly consented to be ruled by their self-assigned superiors; they were forced to do so. This older view — and practice — is by no means dead even today. In one form or another the contest over government by "the one, the few, or the many" is still with us.

Reflecting on these two paragraphs, we can see that Dahl asks us to look at the long view in which civilization informs us that, for most of history, democratic governments did not exist. Governments were run by "self-assigned superiors" — such as monarchs — who decided what was valuable for the people and what was not. Given the extent of time in which rule was in the hands of just a few members of a society, why do we assume that democracy, in which the power of governance is spread among the many, is in any way more desirable than the historical models of monarchy?

Dahl invites his audience to be critical readers. He asks the questions that you, as a reader, should ask yourself, and you can assume that the rest of his essay will guide you toward some reasonable conclusions. But at the same time, you can see from his opening two paragraphs that he has an argument of his own that he will present. Therefore, as a critical reader, you must develop some of your own questions to evaluate the premises of Dahl's argument. Even if you are willing to accept democracy as a desirable form of government before you read what he has to say, it is imperative that you evaluate his views. If he has good reasons for defending democratic government, then you must understand them or else end up a passive person unable to defend your own views.

Wars have been fought in our time to defend democracy and spread it throughout the world. Yet many nations are absolutely determined to maintain nondemocratic forms of government. Why would this be so? Should democracy be spread even to those nations that do not want it? What moral issues does Dahl raise? Why should we pay attention?

ANNOTATING

Critical reading begins with prereading, which involves surveying the material at hand. You reflect on the selection's title and subtitle; then you review the entire piece to see what its subheadings reveal as a guide to understanding the various ideas it contains. Next, you find the first sentences in the main paragraphs to see where the essay is headed. **Annotating** — taking notes — is the next step.

When you annotate, you should do the following:

- Have a pen or pencil handy when you read.
- Underline sentences you feel are important, such as definitions or declarations.
- Look for key words that are repeated often and underline them.
- Summarize the general content of a paragraph in the margins of the book.
- Jot down any important questions in the margins.
- Note in the margins where there are ideas with which you take issue and that you want to revisit later.
- Note any passages you may wish to quote later.
- Keep track of the author's positions with which you disagree.

Since one of your responsibilities may be to write a response to a selection such as Robert A. Dahl's "Why Democracy?" (p. 96), you will not only need to develop a good understanding of his views but you will also need to keep track of your own ideas as you read.

Annotation has two forms. First, underline or circle the statements in the selection that seem most important to you, such as those that summarize the main ideas or the supporting ideas in the selection. (If you do not wish to underline the statements, then place check marks in the margin or jot down key words or phrases in a notebook.) Try to find the passages in which the author appears to establish an argument designed to convince you of a given position. Those passages should be marked because they provide you with the best opportunity to respond critically. The point is to keep track of what you think is important enough to refer back to later for use in your own writing.

The second form of annotation involves keeping track of your ideas and responses as you read. Find the most interesting ideas the author presents and comment on them in the margin. Or, if you wish to be more extensive, write your response in a notebook, keeping in mind that you may refer back to these comments when you write a formal essay later. As you read carefully and critically, you will generate ideas of your own, and the reality is that there is no better time than when you are reading it to keep track of what you think is important in a selection. Annotation is a form of note taking that most critical readers and writers use as a matter of habit. It is good to develop this habit as early as possible in the act of reading.

QUESTIONING

The key to critical reading throughout the process of annotating and note taking is to generate as many questions as possible. The passive reader will simply absorb some of the ideas the author presents, but the critical reader becomes part of a dialogue with the author. That sometimes involves taking an argumentative position with the author. For example, a critical reader may want to take issue with Andrew Carnegie's apparent view that the Sioux were uniformly poor because they were primitive. Indeed, a critical reader may take issue with the idea that the Sioux were "primitive" in any sense. Likewise, a critical reader may ask why Carnegie disapproves of a people who all live at more or less the same economic level as their chief. All of these thoughts lead to a main question: Why does Carnegie think a society with rich and poor is better than a society without those distinctions? Clearly, this question is still relevant because we live with the consequences of the answer.

Questioning involves evaluating and challenging the author's ideas. For instance, Carnegie may have seen the Sioux's economic system as a form of communism because the Sioux lived in a society that had few economic distinctions. His disapproval may have stemmed from his view that capitalism produced wealth and abundance for many while leaving few in poverty. During the period in which he wrote — the late 1880s — communism was a threat. He lived in a time sometimes described as The Gilded Age, during which huge fortunes were made by many industrialists. A modern critical reader may see Carnegie as a farsighted thinker who anticipated our own age but inquire, Why does Carnegie not ask how to relieve the pains of poverty?

As you read through Carnegie's essay, you will find that he has many ideas that have remained influential. For example, he highly recommends the value of education and suggests that it is desirable to make as much money as possible in the middle years of one's life. Then, he recommends, rich people must give that money away in their later years. This kind of advice may meet with your approval. If so, as you read, your marginal comments and your notes will reveal that you would argue in favor of Carnegie's views. In fact, many people approve of Carnegie's opinions after thinking carefully about the problems that arise from some of his less attractive ideas. The point is that Carnegie's views are profoundly complex when you look at them closely. The critical reader will discover those complexities and be stimulated to respond to them.

REVIEWING

Once you have annotated the text and feel that you have a good grasp of the general ideas being discussed, a careful **review** of your notes, underlinings, and questions will help make everything clear to you. You will get a sense of the author's general argument by looking back on what you noted as you read, the ideas that you took issue with, and the ideas that you felt needed to be reexamined later.

The practice of reviewing is valuable for increasing comprehension, especially of selections that make intense demands on the reader, such as Aristotle's famous discussion of ethics in "The Aim of Man" (p. 374). Whereas short modern essays may not demand quite as much annotation and note taking, longer essays by classical writers will need more annotation and more careful analysis of the text as well as more time to reflect on their meaning. Reviewing the author's work and then gathering your annotations, questions, and marginal responses provide you with material that helps you keep the essay clear in your mind and, at the same time, provide you with material for developing your own ideas.

DISCUSSING

Although it may seem unrelated, **discussion** is a crucial aspect of critical reading. The classroom offers limitless opportunities to try out your ideas in relation to the work of the authors in this book. Talking about these works in a setting that not only encourages but also welcomes contradiction from and analysis with your peers is a gift. Everyone benefits from testing ideas in a forum of people who have read the same material. Your ideas will not seem completely realized to you until you begin to listen to how others have apprehended the same work. One of the most important principles of education is learning enough information to facilitate changing one's mind. If you do not open yourself to the possibility of changing your mind about an idea, you risk not growing into a full understanding of it.

Some suggestions (under the heading "Understanding Ideas") follow the selections as a way to get the discussion under way, but you will probably want to begin any discussion about these selections by trying to establish what you think the main ideas are. In the best case, you may suggest your own views and find that they will be developed by your peers. At the same time, it is beneficial to listen to opposing or different views on what the author seems to be saying and how important or unimportant it may be. Hearing others raise concerns you did not notice is also a gift because it expands your understanding.

Learning how others arrive at their understanding of ideas always helps us find our own way to the discoveries we make. Responding to views completely opposed to or different from our own is important. The process of testing our own ideas is absolutely central to our education. One of the best experiences you can have in a classroom is defending a position that others disagree with. Whether you end up changing your mind or not, the exercise will reveal the limits or the range of your understanding, and that will make a great deal of difference when you come to write about your views. When discussing your ideas, you can test various approaches, learn from your missteps, respond to the criticism of others, and reshape your understanding. When writing, however, you face the prospect of committing yourself to a point of view and a position that, because of discussion and the resultant analysis, you will want to feel is reasonable, sure-footed, and your own.

Sample Annotated Passage for Review and Discussion

Reviewing a selection is much easier when you have underlined and annotated the text. You can look back, refine your observations, and above all, keep track of your thinking as you read. You can also establish what you think are the key ideas in a passage as well as your own reactions to those ideas. If you are planning to write about the passage, then you can begin the process of gathering your thoughts and designing your approach.

What follows is an excerpt from an essay by Alfred North Whitehead on religion and science. This essay first appeared in *The Atlantic* in 1925, though the arguments it makes about the relationship between religion and science are still relevant. Even though these are only the opening pages of a lengthy essay, you can use this excerpt to begin working out your own position on the relationship of religion to science. The annotations throughout this essay show the kinds of questions, ideas, and points for review that might arise as you read.

Alfred North Whitehead

RELIGION AND SCIENCE

The difficulty in approaching the question of the relations between Religion and Science is, that its elucidation requires that we have in our minds some clear idea of what we mean by either of the terms, "religion" and "science." Also I wish to speak in the most general way possible, and to keep in the background any comparison of particular creeds, scientific or religious. We have got to understand the type of connection which exists between the two spheres, and then to draw some definite

Needs definition — what does he mean by each of these terms?

conclusions respecting the existing situation which at present confronts the world.

The *conflict* between religion and science is what naturally occurs to our minds when we think of this subject. It seems as though, during the last half century, the results of science and the beliefs of religion had come into a position of frank disagreement, from which there can be no escape, except by abandoning either the clear teaching of science, or the clear teaching of religion. This conclusion has been urged by controversialists on either side. Not by all controversialists, of course, but by those trenchant intellects which every controversy calls out into the open.

The distress of sensitive minds, and the zeal for truth, and the sense of the importance of the issues, must command our sincerest sympathy. When we consider what religion is for mankind, and what science is, it is no exaggeration to say that the future course of history depends upon the decision of this generation as to the relations between them. We have here the two strongest general forces (apart from the mere impulse of the various senses) which influence men, and they seem to be set one against the other — the force of our religious intuitions, and the force of our impulse to accurate observation and logical deduction.

A great English statesman once advised his countrymen to use large-scale maps, as a preservative against alarms, panics, and general misunderstanding of the true relations between nations. In the same way in dealing with the clash between permanent elements of human nature, it is well to map our history on a large scale, and to disengage ourselves from our immediate absorption in the present conflicts. When we do this, we immediately discover two great facts. In the first place, there has always been a conflict between religion and science; and in the second place, both religion and science have always been in a state of continual development. In the early days of Christianity, there was a general belief among Christians that the world was coming to an end in the lifetime of people then living. We can make only indirect inferences as to how far this belief was authoritatively proclaimed; but it is certain that it was widely held, and that it formed an impressive part of the popular religious doctrine. The belief proved itself to be mistaken, and Christian doctrine adjusted itself to the change. Again in the early Church individual theologians very confidently deduced from the Bible opinions concerning the nature of the physical

What is the conflict?

Whitehead's argument — but does it have to be one or the other?

The future depends on how we resolve the conflict between religion and science.

Are these really the two strongest forces?

Whitehead calls religion and science part of "human nature."

Two great facts: religion and science are always in conflict and always developing.

The end of the world did not come — religion adjusted.

universe. In the year A.D. 535, a monk named Cosmas wrote a book which he entitled, *Christian Topography*. He was a traveled man who had visited India and Ethiopia, and finally he lived in a monastery at Alexandria, which was then a great center of culture. In this book, basing himself upon the direct meaning of biblical texts as construed by him in a literal fashion, he denied the existence of the antipodes, <u>and asserted that the world is a flat parallelogram whose length is double its breadth.</u>

> People thought the world was flat.

In the seventeenth century the doctrine of the motion of the earth was condemned by a Catholic tribunal. A hundred years ago the extension of time demanded by geological science distressed religious people, Protestant and Catholic. <u>And today the doctrine of evolution is an equal stumbling block.</u> These are only a few instances illustrating a general fact. But all our ideas will be in a wrong perspective if we think that this recurring perplexity was confined to contradictions between religion and science, and that in these controversies religion was always wrong, and that science was always right. The true facts of the case are very much more complex, and refuse to be summarized in these simple terms.

> Scientific disagreements persist.

Theology itself exhibits exactly the same character of gradual development, arising from an aspect of conflict between its own proper ideas. This fact is a commonplace to theologians, but is often obscured in the stress of controversy. I do not wish to overstate my case; so I will confine myself to Roman Catholic writers. In the seventeenth century a learned Jesuit, Father Petavius, showed that the theologians of the first three centuries of Christianity made use of phrases and statements which since the fifth century would be condemned as heretical. Also Cardinal Newman devoted a treatise to the discussion of the development of doctrine. He wrote it before he became a great Roman Catholic ecclesiastic; but throughout his life, it was never retracted and continually reissued.

> So science is easier to change than religion.

<u>Science is even more changeable than theology.</u> No man of science could subscribe without qualification to Galileo's beliefs or to Newton's beliefs, or to all his own scientific beliefs of ten years ago.

In both regions of thought, additions, distinctions, and modifications have been introduced. So that now, even when the same assertion is made today as was made a thousand, or fifteen hundred years ago, it is made subject to limitations or expansions of meaning, which were not contemplated at the earlier epoch. We are told by logicians that a proposition must be either

Time may change our opinions/ definitions.

true or false, and that there is no middle term. But in practice, we may know that a proposition expresses an important truth, but that it is subject to limitations and qualifications which at present remain undiscovered. It is a general feature of our knowledge, that we are insistently aware of important truth; and yet that the only formulations of these truths which we are able to make pre-suppose a general standpoint of conceptions which may have to be modified. I will give you two illustrations, both from science: Galileo said that the earth moves and that the sun is fixed; the Inquisition said that the earth is fixed and the sun moves; and Newtonian astronomers, adopting an absolute theory of space, said that both the sun and the earth move. But now we say that any one of these three statements is equally true, provided that you have fixed your sense of "rest" and "motion" in the way required by the statement adopted. At the date of Galileo's controversy with the Inquisition, Galileo's way of stating the facts was, beyond question, the fruitful procedure for the sake of scientific research. But in itself it was not more true than the formulation of the Inquisition. But at that time the modern concepts of relative motion were in nobody's mind; so that the statements were made in ignorance of the qualifications required for their more perfect truth. Yet this question of the motions of the earth and the sun expresses a real fact in the universe; and all sides had got hold of important truths concerning it. But with the knowledge of those times, the truths appeared to be inconsistent.

People did not have all the facts — do we?

Based on the annotations in this essay, here are some of the points that will figure in a response you might give to Whitehead's passage:

- We need concrete definitions for the terms *religion* and *science* even though most people understand what they mean.

- A conflict between religion and science "naturally occurs to our minds."

- Lately the conflict seems to demand that we abandon either science or religion.

- Whitehead feels that the "future course of history" depends on how we resolve the conflict.

- Whitehead calls religion and science the two "strongest general forces" that influence people.

- There are two great facts: (1) religion and science have always been in conflict, and (2) both have been "in a state of continual development."

- Christian doctrine adjusted from predicting the end of the world as well as from the teaching that the world was flat.

- Today the doctrine of evolution is a "stumbling block" to religion.

- Science is more changeable than theology.

- Time can change what we think of as true in both religion and science.

- When Galileo faced the Inquisition, no one as yet had all the facts necessary to decide the truth.

Whitehead wrote this essay some time ago, in 1925, when one of the most important trials of the century was taking place. The Scopes "monkey trial" in Dayton, Tennessee, argued whether or not a science teacher could teach the theory of evolution in public universities and public schools. John Scopes, the teacher, was found guilty of violating a state law that prohibited the teaching of evolution, but the case was eventually dropped. Many people in Tennessee (and elsewhere) insisted that the Bible's teachings took precedence over science. Thus, evolution of humans contradicted the Bible and had to be wrong. Even though the United States Constitution demands separation of church and state and the original Tennessee law was unconstitutional, the Tennessee State Court declared it constitutional. Known as the Butler law, this legislation remained in effect until 1967, when it was challenged again.

Whitehead was aware of the evolution controversy, but his essay is designed to try to find a "big picture" by not focusing on that trial and by pointing instead to the conflict through history. It is possible that he wanted the reader to imagine that in the Scopes trial not all the knowledge was available to make a reasoned judgment. Certainly, it is true that in the last hundred years of scientific research the evidence of evolution has grown exponentially and even many religions accept the science of evolution while preserving their view of how God created mankind.

Nonetheless, the theory of evolution still represents a challenge for religion. Some states, such as Colorado, Missouri, Montana, and Oklahoma, have been considering legislation requiring the biblical version of creation to be taught in public schools. Tennessee and Louisiana have already passed such bills. Textbooks used in those states must include creationist teaching.

Whitehead's position today might stress the possibility that we do not know enough yet to understand fully what the conflict really is. However, Whitehead was himself a major British mathematician and philosopher who ended his career teaching mathematics and physics at Harvard. As a philosopher, he made a number of important contributions to theology and is highly regarded by religious philosophers. As a result, he was in an excellent position to discuss the conflict between science and religion.

When forming your own ideas about Whitehead, you will probably begin with your reactions to some of what he says. You may see, for example, that the theory of evolution is still a problem for some people because of religious issues and religious teaching. You may feel that the conflict is impossible to reconcile because each position presents evidence to support belief. Or you may be a scientist who thinks science has evidence while religion has beliefs. And it is possible that you will or will not accept Whitehead's position that, essentially, the jury is still out on both religion and science. Taking the long, historical view would be reassuring, as Whitehead implies. But taking the short view risks serious conflict.

FORMING YOUR OWN IDEAS

If you were to assign yourself the job of writing in response to Whitehead's opening pages, you might be able to limit yourself to two principal concerns and one ultimate personal statement:

- Your first job may be to provide the definitions of *religion* and *science* that are necessary to a thorough and reasonable discussion of how these strong "general forces" operate in our modern world. Establish their strengths and their characteristics as understood by the general public.

- Second, you must clarify the nature of the conflict that occurs between religion and science. Whitehead talks about the "flat earth" and the theory that the sun moves, but he is really aiming at the contemporary conflict between evolution and biblical truth. Establishing the nature of this conflict will take some doing, including some outside research into contemporary attitudes, especially in schools and churches.

- Finally, your own personal beliefs — belief in science, belief in religion — will take some part in your response to Whitehead. It will be a challenge to be impartial when you examine the evidence of the current conflict between the two. It will be particularly interesting to know how your own thinking will be affected by your research and your thinking on what is clearly still an important issue a hundred years after Whitehead wrote.

CHAPTER TWO

Writing about Ideas

Writing clarifies thinking because it allows you to examine the structure and details of what you develop in the act of writing much more carefully than you can in the act of speaking. For one thing, you have access to a larger body of thought on the page than you can retain from the memory of what you have said. This is true even in the case of discussions that you may have with others.

The written page is a form of commitment. You commit your ideas to the page and thus have the chance to revise, reconsider, and reexamine what you have written. The act of writing and revising naturally sharpens your observations and your argument. You cannot go back and revise what you said yesterday (at least not easily), whereas you can readily revise what you wrote earlier and make it better.

Writing is also a form of self-instruction. You can learn facts from listening to a lecture and learn other points of view from a discussion. However, writing prompts you to learn to think more deeply, more accurately, and with more self-reflection. Writing teaches you more thoroughly than virtually any other process because you learn what it is that you have to do to make your ideas clear and convincing. If the purpose of education is to expand and change your mind, then the process of writing lets you know just how much you have grown and changed because it constantly challenges you to make your ideas clear.

Your audience — your readers — have the chance to examine what you write and to offer suggestions for improvement or challenge you to defend what you may have left vague. All the authors you will read in this book have committed themselves to examining complex ideas and have been subjected to criticism and analysis. For most of these authors, their work was read by friends, teachers, and critics before they published it. As a result, their work has been improved by responding to criticism.

GENERATING TOPICS FOR WRITING

The selections in this book discuss some very important ideas, most of which concern us in our daily life. You will be asked to discuss some of these ideas and to write in response to what the authors have said. Sometimes it will be obvious to you what you should write about, but at other times you may not be sure what to say or how to begin writing, especially if the ideas discussed do not seem relevant to you. Some writers will seem to have said all there is to say on a subject and to have left little room for your ideas. But as you can see from the fact that the topics in this book have been treated by ancient writers and modern writers, there is always room for you to add your own approach. The trick is for you to learn how to develop that approach.

THINKING CRITICALLY

Critical reading pays off when you begin the process of writing. Questioning the text is the best way to begin your analysis of what the author has said and at the same time to begin your own process of developing good topics to write about. Questions need to be answered, so it is important to produce good questions that will provide you with good material to write about. Every selection in this book will generate specific questions, such as Alfred North Whitehead's selection (p. 221), which may prompt you to ask, How can one define terms like *religion* and *science*? In the case of the piece by Jean-Jacques Rousseau (p. 136), you might naturally ask, What is a social contract?

However, there are general questions that can be asked of virtually every selection in this book, and if no specific question comes to mind regarding a selection, you can always rely on general questions such as the following:

- What are the most important ideas presented in this selection?
- Is this author presenting an argument or an observation of fact?
- What is the main point of this selection?
- What seems to be the author's purpose in writing this piece?
- Is the author's purpose explicit? If not, why not?
- What claim or claims does the author make?
- What specifically supports the author's claims?
- Does the author rely on the testimony of other writers?

- Does the author omit information that might contradict the author's claims?

- Is the author objective or biased? What might constitute bias in this selection?

- Does the author have adequate evidence to support the claims of the selection?

- Which elements in the selection are the most convincing?

- How significant is this selection for me personally?

Some of these questions are useful for approaching Whitehead's opening paragraphs. For example, here are some potential responses to the questions above:

- Whitehead's most important ideas concern the ongoing conflict between religion and science and suggest that each side of the conflict has changed its position from time to time.

- Whitehead discusses religion and science because their conflict was relevant when he wrote.

- The main point is that the truth regarding religion and science may not be possible to know because their "truths" change over time.

- Whitehead seems to be hoping to resolve the conflict through reason and by offering a historical perspective.

- Whitehead makes the claim that because both religion and science change over time the truth according to either cannot be taken as absolute.

- Whitehead supports his claims by introducing evidence from history.

- Other authorities, such as Cosmas, a monk, and Cardinal Newman, a Protestant who became a Catholic, and references to Newton and Darwin, both scientists, support his claims.

- The dispute between the church and Galileo is one specific historical instance in which neither religion nor science had all the information necessary to produce "truth."

- Whitehead does not seem specifically biased because he makes an effort to present claims that support both sides of the argument.

- Finally, the significance to each of us will be different depending on our commitments to science and religion.

CREATING A THESIS STATEMENT

A **thesis statement** is a point of view that you can defend; it is the heart of the argument you propose in writing about ideas. While not every writer creates a thesis statement, one of the strategies that will benefit you most when writing about the great ideas in any of the selections in this book is to devise a strong thesis statement.

A thesis statement should come near the beginning of your essay and should be clearly stated. The statement tells your readers what you believe to be true and should be provable in relation to the ideas that you discuss. There can be many different kinds of thesis statements because they can serve different needs. Here are six different thesis statements, all developed from the beginning of Whitehead's essay:

- **A thesis that states a position:** In any conflict between religion and science, science always wins.

- **A thesis that establishes a cause:** Religious belief depends on faith, while scientific belief depends on evidence; therefore, the claims of one should not cause a conflict with the other.

- **A thesis that states an opinion:** A religious community should not pass laws that prevent scientific truths from being taught at any level of schooling, whether public or private.

- **A thesis that analyzes circumstances:** Alfred North Whitehead tries unsuccessfully to resolve the conflict between religion and science by explaining the historical circumstances in which knowledge in both areas was limited and changing.

- **A thesis that defines a condition:** Religion recognizes spiritual truths that depend on the existence of God, while science focuses on knowledge based on mathematical and physical evidence.

- **A thesis that establishes a conclusion:** Throughout history, religious leaders have threatened scientists such as Galileo with torture and imprisonment, while scientists have not threatened to kill religious leaders because of their beliefs.

Some of these statements are better than others, but all of them could sustain careful development into an essay. Like any other statement of purpose, the thesis statement needs support from a variety of sources, both from inside the selection you are writing about and from outside research.

SAMPLE OPENING PARAGRAPHS

Although you have only read the first few pages of Whitehead's selection (p. 13), you could develop a brief essay by using one of the thesis statements listed above. The following is an example of an opening paragraph using one of those statements:

> A religious community should not pass laws that prevent scientific truths from being taught at any level of schooling, whether public or private. In the United States of America, the Constitution says, "Congress shall make no law respecting an establishment of religion, or prohibiting the free exercise thereof." This is the First Amendment and we think of it as guaranteeing the separation of church and state. Today the teaching of biology includes extensive discussion of evolution, much more so than in 1925 because much more is known about genetics and mutations. Viruses like flu mutate every year and new diseases appear as a result of evolutionary mutations. Refusing to teach evolution in schools may have an impact on public health by preventing people from understanding how many diseases behave. Private schools need to find ways to adapt religious teachings to the reality of scientific truths. Alfred North Whitehead implies that it should be possible for religion and science to respect each other's truths.

This opening paragraph begins with an opinion, but it is an opinion that bases itself on the First Amendment to the Constitution and on the fact that biology classes and biology textbooks devote a great deal of attention to evolution because modern science accepts evolution as a reality of nature.

What follows is another beginning for a possible essay on Whitehead's discussion of religion and science. This writer sees an issue that is based not on history but rather on the distinct nature of the kinds of knowledge found in religion and science.

> Religion recognizes spiritual truths that do not depend on physical evidence for proof of the existence of God, while science focuses on knowledge based on mathematical and physical evidence perceptible by people and machines. Faith and belief, both forms of knowledge, are characteristic of religion. Because the Bible says,

"So God created man in his own image" (Gen. 1:27),
religious people believe the Bible is the word of
God and Genesis is the truth. Faith in the Bible
would reject a scientific theory that "man" was
the product of evolution and a descendant of apes.
Science does not operate on faith but requires
evidence backed up by testing and research. Charles
Darwin began testing the theory of evolution by
comparing the development of animals and people
through the geologic record over millions of years.
Today, the discoveries of genetics reinforce the
concept of evolution by showing that humans share
so much of their genetic makeup with other mammals
that testing on mice can result in cures for diseases
in people.

Were either of these first paragraphs to be developed into full essays, brief or long, the thesis statements would need to be supported by a very careful analysis of portions of Whitehead's text as well as by references to outside sources. Outside sources may be drawn from the evidence supplied by other experts in the field or factual research that sheds light on the issues discussed in his essay. Even an opinion piece will not be very convincing if the opinions are not supported by evidence that examines some of the same ideas that Whitehead addresses. If you were to write a detailed essay in response to Whitehead, it would be important to find other writers who address the ideas that Whitehead presents. For example, the Scopes trial of 1925 has been widely written about and your examination of the public responses to that trial may be very important in trying to come to terms with the conflict between religion and science. Online sources will lead you to books that have treated this issue in some detail, such as Adam Shapiro's *Trying Biology: The Scopes Trial, Textbooks, and the Antievolution Movement in American Schools* (2013). There is even a Scopes trial page, with a great deal of historical information and many details from that trial and trials like it, on the University of Missouri–Kansas City Web site.

When writing about a subject as volatile as the conflict between religion and science, it is also valuable to talk with people — whether authorities or not — about their positions. In your own school, you should have access to scientists who will discuss the subject at length. Their viewpoints may very possibly surprise your expectations because many ranking scientists are also very religious.

If your school has a chaplain or ministers in a religious center, be sure to interview them or someone else with a strong opinion on whether there is a conflict between religion and science. Whitehead contends there is a centuries-deep conflict. Because of the Scopes trial in 1925, when he wrote his essay, Whitehead assumes that the conflict has continued. Ask your interviewees whether they think that almost a hundred years later the conflict is ongoing. While you are conducting interviews, be sure to ask your peers. See what their views are and why they think they hold them. All the material you gather will be helpful to your work. Remember, Whitehead himself felt it essential to discuss the writing of experts such as Cosmas, Father Petavius, and Cardinal Newman, all of whom posed some potential challenge to the "truths" of religion.

A good thesis will demand support and analysis. For example, you will need

- evidence that supports the thesis from the author's selection or from outside sources, either factual or drawn from the opinions of experts;

- statements and testimony from authoritative texts that address the thesis concept;

- careful and balanced analysis of the text of the author in question;

- discussion and analysis of counterarguments that might alter the thesis; and

- careful development of the argument or arguments that support the thesis.

One of the most interesting requirements is the consideration of counterarguments, or potential arguments against your position. Any thesis that you choose to develop and defend will be strengthened if you take into consideration the arguments against your position. As a good writer you should be thorough in examining counterarguments, and in the process you might convince yourself that your first position was wrong. If that happens, and sometimes it will, then you must follow the evidence and change your thesis.

Consider this thesis statement:

> Throughout history religious leaders have threatened scientists such as Galileo with torture and imprisonment, while scientists have not threatened to kill religious leaders because of their beliefs.

A possible counterargument is to point out that there are very few scientists on record who have actually been tortured or killed. Even Galileo was given house arrest. Another astronomer, Giordano Bruno (1548–1600), was burned at the stake by the Inquisition, but his heresies were theological as well as scientific. On the other hand, while scientists are not on record as having killed any religious authorities, they can be blamed for threatening religious authority in general by absolutely undermining some religious teaching. For example, the religious teaching that the sun revolved around an unmoving earth was questioned by Nicolaus Copernicus (1473–1543) in a book published in the year of his (natural) death. Copernicus was proved right and the church wrong early in the seventeenth century. That created as much ideological instability as the rejection of the flat-earth theory. Indeed, in the late sixteenth century, Europe suffered a major crisis in the history of thought. Once the absolute certainty of the church's teaching regarding the motion of the planets was proved untenable, people began to question many religious ideas. The Protestant Church broke with the Roman Catholic Church, and many different forms of religious truth proliferated in Europe, causing consternation and wars that lasted for years. Science helped create that instability, which has lasted for centuries.

Critical reading and critical writing both depend on asking serious questions, on not accepting statements at face value without careful investigation. Asking yourself questions about your thinking may also be important. For example, if you were to write about Whitehead's theory of a conflict between religion and science, would you know which side of the conflict you were on before you started to write? Can you detect your own biases? Can you detect the author's biases when you read? Being aware that you come to a piece with many of your own biases will help you read critically, develop a strong thesis, and eventually compose a cogent essay.

SUPPORTING YOUR THESIS

Working up a good thesis statement may be of first importance in writing about the selections in this book, but the thesis statement is only the beginning. When you write, you may find yourself moving on from your thesis with a great many ideas that seem almost to write themselves. But it is more likely that you will have to pause and discover what you must say so that your argument will be clear and full and convincing.

Once you have a good thesis, you will need to develop it carefully so that your overall essay will be both interesting and possibly convincing. Every selection in this book establishes a position and then goes on to use techniques to make that position more understandable and effective. Even if they may not have realized it at the time they wrote, each of the authors has used a variety of rhetorical methods that are fundamental to all writers, regardless of their professional level.

Rhetoric is usually defined as the art of persuasion. It may also be defined as the art of writing, especially prose writing. In the Greek world of Plato and Aristotle, rhetoric was one of the principal arts taught in schools. It was also taught to adults, especially to those in law and in politics. Prized by the ancients, the art of persuasion is just as pertinent in the modern world. I have often told my students that if they do not master the art of rhetoric they run the risk of being mastered by those who have. I think that is generally true, especially today in a world in which digital and other sources of persuasion, especially political and economic, are virtually impossible to avoid.

To develop an argument is to bring to bear a reasonable examination of evidence that eventually points to a truth or to a possible truth about the subject of the argument. The thesis statement establishes what the writer thinks is true, or what might be true, or simply what the writer thinks is most important about the subject. For example, when Plato talks about democracy and oligarchy, he carefully argues by comparing each of these forms of government. Comparison is one of the rhetorical techniques a writer can use. By comparing oligarchy unfavorably with democracy, he attempts to convince the reader to prefer democracy. In our case, we are already predisposed to agree with him, but that would not have been true if we had lived in Germany in 1936, when that nation abandoned democracy for dictatorship.

A writer uses basic rhetorical techniques by devoting a segment — a paragraph or group of paragraphs — of the essay to developing ideas by relying on one or more of the following techniques.

Development by Definition

Development by definition means offering a way of defining the main ideas that you plan to examine so that your reader knows exactly what you are talking about. The first paragraph of Whitehead's essay points to the need for definition, although he puts that off until later in the essay. Today, no writer would use this technique by relying solely on the dictionary to define the term in question. Religion, for example, cannot easily be understood by a dictionary definition because it is a highly complex idea that needs a more thorough analysis. That is one reason Whitehead avoids providing any immediate definitions.

Charlotte Perkins Gilman, in her feminist essay "Women and Economics: 'Cupid-in-the-Kitchen'" (p. 303), undertakes a definition of *cooperation* in part by showing what it is not as much as what it is. The use of definition in developing a good idea is often subtle and much more extensive than simply defining a word or a term. In the paragraphs following, Gilman talks about the nature of the family as well as the responsibilities of women in a family kitchen.

> This does not involve what is known as "cooperation." Cooperation, in the usual sense, is the union of families for the

better performance of their supposed functions. The process fails because the principle is wrong. Cooking and cleaning are not family functions. We do not have a family mouth, a family stomach, a family face to be washed. Individuals require to be fed and cleaned from birth to death, quite irrespective of their family relations. The orphan, the bachelor, the childless widower, have as much need of these nutritive and excretive processes as any patriarchal parent. Eating is an individual function. Cooking is a social function. Neither is in the faintest degree a family function. That we have found it convenient in early stages of civilization to do our cooking at home proves no more than the allied fact that we have also found it convenient in such stages to do our weaving and spinning at home, our soap and candle making, our butchering and pickling, our baking and washing.

As society develops, its functions specialize; and the reason why this great race-function of cooking has been so retarded in its natural growth is that the economic dependence of women has kept them back from their share in human progress. When women stand free as economic agents, they will lift and free their arrested functions, to the much better fulfillment of their duties as wives and mothers and to the vast improvement in health and happiness of the human race.

Cooperation is not what is required for this, but trained professional service and such arrangement of our methods of living as shall allow us to benefit by such service. When numbers of people patronize the same tailor or baker or confectioner, they do not cooperate. Neither would they cooperate in patronizing the same cook. The change must come from the side of the cook, not from the side of the family. It must come through natural functional development in society, and it is so coming. Woman, recognizing that her duty as feeder and cleaner is a social duty, not a sexual one, must face the requirements of the situation, and prepare herself to meet them. A hundred years ago this could not have been done. Now it is being done, because the time is ripe for it. (311–12)

Development by Comparison

Few ways of thinking are more comfortable for us than comparison. It is difficult to mention anything important without thinking of something that compares favorably or unfavorably with it. We use comparison as a means of clarifying the nature of the things or ideas we compare. Often comparing something vague or abstract with something concrete can give us an understanding that we might not otherwise possess. Whitehead spends much of his essay comparing religion and science as a means of helping us understand the nature of each.

In the following sample from "Molecules and Genes" (p. 263), the science writer Jennifer Ackerman compares the genes of microscopic beings, such as algae and yeast, with the genes of human beings. Ackerman expresses surprise that the same, or very similar, genes operate the same way in single-celled plants or small insects as they do in human beings.

> Here is an item from my files. When scientists deciphered the intimate details of mating in yeast, that single-celled fungus that raises our bread and brews our beer, they got a shock. The molecule that draws two yeast cells into sex closely resembles one made by our own brain cells to regulate reproduction.
>
> The likeness seemed a fluke at first. But then other examples popped out of the box: genes that shape the bodies of fruit flies so like our own body-shaping Hox genes[1] that one can put a human Hox gene into a developing fruit fly embryo, and it will carry out the job of the fly's gene without a hitch; genes that shape the marvelous globe of the human eye strangely similar to those that carve the compound eye of a fruit fly; the tiny genetic mechanisms that drive our biological rhythms, keeping us in tune with the big swings of night and day, matching those in algae. So, too, do we share with other organisms the ancient genes that dictate cell death, the phenomenon that underlies metamorphosis, turning tadpoles into frogs and caterpillars into butterflies and also shapes our bodies, whittling away the webbing between fingers before birth, eliminating inappropriate sexual organs. Common to all of us, as well, is a suite of small, sturdy messenger molecules, offering clues to such mysteries as why the cells of the human brain respond to the chemical messages of the poppy plant and to the potent sexual attractants of a Himalayan deer.
>
> What are chemicals found in the human body doing in plants, fungi, bacteria? How can genes that shape a fruit fly be near twins of my own? (265)

---

[1] **Hox genes** Group of genes that plan the structure of the body in the developing embryo.

Development by Example

One of the ways abstract concepts or ideas can be made concrete and under-standable is to provide an example. An example can come from historical instances, from the experience of individuals, from events that are current or ancient, or from personal observation. Every selection in this book offers examples to help us understand the author's argument and convince us of the author's overall thesis. Most of us naturally introduce examples when we discuss any important ideas with each other. Examples are naturally convincing, especially if they are chosen very carefully. Because the burden of proof often rests on example, you need to be sure that the examples you choose are authentic, that they tend to prove your argument, and that they are important rather than trivial. Whitehead offers us Galileo as an example of a scientist who was in conflict with the church. If nothing else, this should convince us that there has been conflict between religion and science in the past.

You will find that many of the writers in this book include examples, and sometimes in great numbers, to demonstrate the virtues of their argu-ments. Robert A. Dahl, in "Why Democracy?" (p. 96), makes a point early in his essay when he says, "Perhaps the most fundamental and persistent prob-lem in politics is to avoid autocratic rule" (para. 6). Essentially, he tells us, even in modern society dictators, or "strong men," are still evident, and he offers some models:

> Consider a few examples from the twentieth century. Under Joseph Stalin's rule in the Soviet Union (1929–1953), many mil-lions of persons were jailed for political reasons, often because of Stalin's paranoid fear of conspiracies against him. An esti-mated twenty million people died in labor camps, were executed for political reasons, or died from the famine (1932–33) that resulted when Stalin compelled peasants to join state-run farms. Though another twenty million victims of Stalin's rule may have managed to survive, they suffered cruelly. Or consider Adolph Hitler, the autocratic ruler of Nazi Germany (1933–1945). Not counting tens of millions of military and civilian casualties resulting from World War II, Hitler was directly responsible for the death of six million Jews in concentration camps as well as innumerable opponents, Poles, gypsies, homosexuals, and mem-bers of other groups he wished to exterminate. Under the des-potic leadership of Pol Pot in Cambodia (1975–1979), the Khmer Rouge killed a quarter of the Cambodian population: an instance, one might say, of self-inflicted genocide. So great was Pol Pot's fear of the educated classes that they were almost exterminated:

wearing spectacles or having uncalloused hands was quite literally a death warrant. (98)

Dahl's examples are drawn from the twentieth century, but anyone writing today could find examples in a number of countries. What his examples point to is that autocratic rule can produce horrors that affect millions of people. They stand as a warning for all of us and offer one answer to the question he uses as the title of his essay.

Development by Analysis of Cause and Effect

One of our natural inclinations is to try to understand what causes something. Once we begin to understand the cause, we naturally want to know its effects. Of course, in the natural order of things we usually see the results first and then try to figure out what has caused them. This means of development is somewhat more subtle than the use of definition, comparison, or example. It requires analysis — a testing of possibilities — as you consider what might have caused something that has already happened or what might happen if a given cause were invoked. Whitehead offers three causes for conflict between science and religion: the church's condemnation of the earth's motion; the extension of geological time (the early church thought the earth was a little more than 4,000 years old); and the doctrine of evolution. He follows with his analysis of the effects of these causes.

Steve Jones, in his "The Descent of Men" (p. 244), talks about a number of issues related to evolution and the behavior of people. One of his important points concerns the question of health, especially among men. He sees some disturbing behavior that causes some very disturbing results. Here is one of his uses of cause and effect as a way of developing his argument:

Each year in the United States, more than twenty million man-years of life are lost to a demise that could, in principle, be avoided. Smoking, fat, and stress all specialize in one segment of society. From gout to hernias (four and nine times more common in males), men suffer while their partners are spared.

Even for men, smoking is now a minority interest, but is far from extinct. Girls have been lured into the habit by tobacco companies (and lung cancer has overtaken breast cancer as their commonest malignancy) but have not yet faced the full consequences. When it comes to alcohol, the difference is starker. Although there are arguments about the safe limit, many recommend a maximum of a quart of beer, or half a bottle of wine, a day. Almost half of young British men drink close to, or above, the limit; and a respectable minority of dangerous drinkers believe that they drink either "a little" or "hardly at all." Those who soak up more than the recommended amount die at twice the rate of those who imbibe very little. A small dose has a minor — and much publicized — beneficial effect, but overall alcohol is a killer. Drink causes cancer of the pancreas and throat and damages the liver, and is associated with the majority of murders and deaths in fires. (248)

This particular passage combines cause and effect with reference to reports of the results of drinking specific quantities of alcohol. But Jones's claim is relatively general, and if one wished to be more convincing it would be good to cite published statistics. On the other hand, Jones knows that one can easily find references to the kind of information he mentions. Nothing he says is out of line with what the reader would expect, but the result of men's dying prematurely because of certain behavior is made much clearer by his use of cause and effect.

Development by Analysis of Circumstances

The circumstances of a given time period, of a given political system, and of a given relationship with family, friends, and contemporaries will all affect our thinking and our understanding. The circumstances of any piece of writing will affect our sense of its importance. This particular means of development depends on two parts: first, the question of what is possible or impossible in the circumstances; and second, what has been done in the past, since if it has been done before, it may be done again. A historical review of any given situation or topic will result in an analysis of circumstances. Normally a writer using this technique will clarify the question of what is possible or impossible, review history to reflect on the present, and offer a view of what seems to be possible today by examining current circumstances. Whitehead uses this method of development for most of the beginning of his essay because he offers primarily a historical review of the past conflict between science and religion. And by mentioning evolution, he points to a current circumstance that fits into the subject of his essay.

Amartya Sen, in his consideration of the idea of justice (p. 183), makes the point that in any society it is imperative that justice appears to be done. That justice is done is simply not enough if people are to take comfort in feeling that justice will serve them. This is not so much a question of historical circumstances as it is of present circumstances, even though Sen illustrates with a historical reference. As you can see from what he says, using circumstance as a means of development requires a broad view, not only of history but also of the question of possibility. In essence, Sen is asking a question: Is it possible for the appearance of justice being done to be as important as the fact that it is done? The way he works out that question in the following two paragraphs from his essay is instructive.

> Consider an often-repeated proposition in a closely related field, the practice of law. It is frequently asserted that justice should not only be done, but also be "seen to be done." Why so? Why should it matter that people actually agree that justice has been done, if it has in fact been done? Why qualify, or constrain, or supplement a strictly juridical requirement (that justice be done) by a populist demand (that people in general can observe that it is being done)? Is there a confusion here between legal correctness and popular endorsement — a confounding of jurisprudence with democracy?
>
> It is not, in fact, hard to guess some of the instrumental reasons for attaching importance to the need for a decision to be *seen to* be just. For one thing, the administration of justice can, in general, be more effective if judges are seen to be doing a good job, rather than botching things up. If a judgment inspires confidence and general endorsement, then very likely it can be more easily implemented. Thus there is not much difficulty in explaining why that phrase about the need for justice to be "seen to be done" received such ringing endorsement and approving reiteration right from the time it was first uttered by Lord Hewart in 1923 (in *Rex* v. *Sussex Justices Ex parte McCarthy* [1923] All ER 233), with his admonishment that justice "should manifestly and undoubtedly be seen to be done." (186–87)

Development by Testimony

In this case, *testimony* means using outside sources to quote or refer to as support for your position. Evidence of fact is one kind of support, just as specific examples that seem to help prove your point are. Testimony is very powerful in its ability to persuade a reader. Quotations from Plato can be very convincing when you argue about political systems, just as carefully chosen quotations from Aristotle can be very important if you are writing an essay about ethical behavior. Outside sources can come from classic authors, modern authors, or important public figures. Scholarly books, popular treatises, magazines, and many varieties of online sources can all provide testimony that will bolster your argument. However, it is also important to realize that when you quote an author it is necessary that you provide analysis of what the author says in order to make it clear why it is important to your argument. In his opening paragraphs about the conflict between religion and science, Whitehead does not quote from authority, but he does refer to the testimony of Cosmas and Petavius. In addition, he paraphrases a major authority when he says, "A great English statesman once advised his countrymen to use large-scale maps, as a preservative against alarms, panics, and general misunderstanding of the true relations between nations" (para. 4). Whitehead relies on comparison, suggesting that his own discussion will be like using a large-scale map because he goes back in history to get the "large view."

Francis Fukuyama, in his essay "Human Specificity and the Rights of Animals" (p. 440), establishes that there are remarkable similarities between human behavior and animal behavior. He cites work done in animal ethology, the study of human behavior and/or the study of animal behavior. The writers whose testimony he cites are Charles Darwin, who saw a link between the animal and human worlds in the nineteenth century, and Frans de Waal, an expert on monkeys and other primates, who himself cites the work of Japanese primatologists in the 1950s. The first sentence of this passage could be taken as a thesis statement for much of his essay.

> Much of the work done in animal ethology over the past few generations has tended to erode the bright line that was once held to separate human beings from the rest of the animal world. Charles Darwin, of course, provided the theoretical underpinning for the notion that man evolved from an ancestral ape, and that all species were undergoing a continuous process of modification. Many of the attributes that were once held to be unique to human beings — including language, culture, reason, consciousness, and the like — are now seen as characteristic of a wide variety of nonhuman animals.
>
> For example, the primatologist Frans de Waal points out that culture — that is, the ability to transmit learned behaviors across generations through nongenetic means — is not an exclusively human achievement. He cites the famous example of the potato-washing macaques that inhabit a small island in Japan. In the 1950s a group of Japanese primatologists observed that one macaque in particular (an Albert Einstein, so to speak, among monkeys) developed a habit of washing potatoes in a local stream. This same individual later discovered that grains of barley could be separated from sand by dropping them in water. Neither was a genetically programmed behavior; neither potatoes nor barley were part of the macaques' traditional diet, and no one had ever before observed these behaviors taking place. Yet both the potato washing and barley separation were

observed among other macaques on the island some years later, well after the original monkey who had discovered these techniques had passed away, indicating that he had taught it to his fellows and they in turn had passed it on to the young. (442)

Development by Rhetorical Question

Although it is common enough in conversation, the rhetorical question is used infrequently by the authors in this book. The rhetorical question is intended to be answered by the person who asks it. Under some conditions, it can be a powerful means of development because it gives you the built-in strategy of aiming at supplying answers. This is especially true if the question or questions have arisen from a critical reading or critical analysis of the subject. For example, the title of Robert A. Dahl's essay "Why Democracy?" (p. 96) is a rhetorical question, and we naturally expect him to provide us with a range of answers. It is a big question and will certainly need the entirety of his essay to reach an answer.

The psychologist Oliver Sacks begins his essay "The Mind's Eye" (p. 236) with more than one rhetorical question and begins his answers with both an example and, eventually, a reference to the testimony of an expert author. The following excerpt from Sacks's piece shows his use of rhetorical questions and example:

> To what extent are we the authors, the creators, of our own experiences? How much are these predetermined by the brains or senses we are born with, and to what extent do we shape our brains through experience? The effects of a profound perceptual deprivation such as blindness may cast an unexpected light on these questions. Going blind, especially later in life, presents one with a huge, potentially overwhelming challenge: to find a new way of living, of ordering one's world, when the old way has been destroyed. (237)

These questions at the beginning of his essay have the advantage of being of general interest to most of us; therefore, we will want to know what kinds of answers Sacks will offer. In essence, he is talking about what makes us the people we know ourselves to be, but even more importantly, he suggests that the forces of genetics may be trumped by external experience. The experience he wishes to consider is blindness.

These samples give you an idea of the range of possibilities in working up the material you intend to include in your own writing. Your response to the selections in this book may take many forms, including the use of the seven means of development discussed in these pages. As you can see from the samples, these means of development may be expressed in a single paragraph or in a range of paragraphs. Indeed, you might be able to use a single means of development for an entire essay. However, it is much more likely that you will use several of these means of development in any group of paragraphs in your essay. The point is to be flexible and to use these techniques as you feel the need. The reality is that most of us use these techniques without a conscious awareness, but by becoming aware of them, you can control your writing process and make them work for you.

QUESTIONS FOR READING AND WRITING

Each selection is followed by three sets of questions: "Understanding Ideas," "Responding to Ideas," and "Comparing Ideas." "Understanding Ideas" questions test your understanding of the key ideas presented within a reading. "Responding to Ideas" questions provide you with prompts for writing. Each of these questions is labeled as a **Definition**, **Comparison**, **Example**, **Cause and Effect**, **Testimony**, **Research**, **Response**, or **Analysis of Circumstances** question. These labels are meant to give you a sense of how to start responding to the readings and developing your own ideas.

For example, when a question is labeled as Definition, it means that your aim in writing will be to define a key term or key idea (though you can always use other methods of development in the body of your essay). When a question is labeled as Research, it means that you will be asked to consult outside sources in your essay. For Response questions, you will be asked to respond to the ideas in the selection with your views, opinions, or personal understanding of the material. Here, you may use any of the methods of development to construct your essay. The work you are asked to do in this kind of question should come from your personal experience and reflect your understanding. For questions labeled as Comparison, you will be asked to focus on comparing ideas or positions that are presented within a single reading.

Each reading also has a third set of questions called "Comparing Ideas," and these questions will ask you to compare the ideas in the selection at hand with another selection or selections from elsewhere in the book. Doing so will help you to see how the ideas from different writers build off of one another, how they overlap, and where they differ.

These questions are all designed to focus your writing and help you begin crafting a response to the readings. However, you are always free to use other methods of development that suit your needs for a given assignment.

As you read the selections in this volume, try to be aware of how the authors develop their ideas and how they pose their arguments.

ESTABLISHING YOUR ARGUMENT

In rhetoric, an argument is not a dispute. You are not expected to antagonize or admonish your reader or to assume that you are countering a position that some readers might have. Instead, an argument, in the sense that we are using the term here, is a reasoned position that is stated clearly and developed fully enough to be convincing. When you publicly discuss politics, music, art, or anything else that requires a judgment of some sort, you will get feedback from whomever you happen to be talking to. That person may not be content with your ideas and may contend with you. When you are writing, there is no one to respond so directly to your views. Therefore, you have no reason to be defensive in what you write. Instead, you need only concentrate on examining the issues that most interest you and then take a stand that seems both reasonable and convincing. Your thesis sentence — or sentences, since some theses will require more than one — will establish what your position is and herald the approach you will take in making it clear and convincing.

Almost all the selections in this book are constructed as arguments with the intention of convincing you, the reader, of their truth. In some cases, the author will assume that the reader is in agreement with him or her. Andrew Carnegie seems to assume that his reader is friendly and likely to agree with his "gospel." James Baldwin seems to assume that his fifteen-year-old nephew will probably not agree with him right away, and Baldwin recognizes that possibility. Since he is writing a letter (eventually published), it may be difficult to know if he regards you, the reader but not the addressee, as friendly or unfriendly. Charles Darwin, like many scientists, constructs an argument based on facts and observations designed to convince you even if you are opposed or indifferent to his point of view.

Elizabeth Warren tries to convince her readers that the middle class is vanishing in the United States. Her audience may already be convinced of her thesis, but even if that were true, it would be important to understand how she can make such a claim in a nation that has always prided itself on having a thriving middle class. Her argument will need to consider the causes and effects of a vanishing middle class. Charlotte Perkins Gilman, Mary Wollstonecraft, and bell hooks argue for greater opportunities for women. These feminist writers are concerned with politics, economics, and opportunity, and they argue using example, analysis of circumstance, cause and effect, and definition. They seem to assume that their audience — or a measure of that audience — will be hostile to their position, so they develop their ideas clearly and effectively.

While your argument can take a number of different apparent forms, the deep structure will probably follow one of three patterns:

- **Classical argument** is a pattern in which you use facts, evidence, and logical analysis to try to convince your readers of the important elements of your position.

- **Toulmin argument**, in which you try to convince your readers to take a specific stand on a question of importance, relies on a basic assumption that most people take for granted.

- **Rogerian argument** requires that you establish as much common ground as possible with your audience so that you have a better chance of persuading them. Because this tactic appears to be nonthreatening, your reader will not be immediately defensive and will therefore be more open to your argument.

These patterns of argument and how they are used by the authors in this volume are discussed in more detail below.

CLASSICAL ARGUMENT

A good example of a **classical argument** is Emile Durkheim's "The Intellectual Elite and Democracy" (p. 90). He argues that writers and scholars, of which he is one, have an obligation to participate in "public life." However, he observes, such people are busy with their own careers, which are unlikely to be political, for instance, as legislators, unless they have abandoned their roles as writers and scholars. More importantly, he argues that the best politicians are men and women of action, not men and women of contemplation.

This is an interesting argument for him to maintain in 1904, when Theodore Roosevelt was president of the United States. Roosevelt famously took action during the Spanish-American War as a soldier, a "Rough Rider," in Cuba in 1898. If any politician was a person of action rather than contemplation, it was Roosevelt. It is unlikely that anyone trained in scholarship would have done anything like what Roosevelt did. Durkheim implies that intellectuals are not suited to be president. Yet he also says that intellectuals need to take part in public life. His solution is that "above all our action must be exerted through books, seminars, and popular education. Above all, we must be *advisers, educators*" (para. 3). He goes on to attempt to convince us by reference to political experiences he has witnessed.

The question is whether or not Durkheim presents an argument that is strong enough to convince you. What is his evidence? What logical analysis has he offered in defense of his views? Does he demonstrate bias or is he quite neutral? If you agree with him that intellectuals should not become political activists, does that imply that we should be content to be governed by nonintellectuals — or perhaps by anti-intellectuals? His argument is brief but complex.

TOULMIN ARGUMENT

The second form of argument, the **Toulmin argument**, was developed by British philosopher, author, and educator Stephen Toulmin. This type of argument has three basic parts: a claim, grounds, and a warrant. The first part, your *claim*, is the position that you need to prove or defend. Your claim is often included as the most important part of a thesis statement. Then, if the argument is to be made good, it needs to be bolstered by *grounds*, or evidence that supports your claim. The third part of the Toulmin argument is the *warrant*, an assumption or a belief that links the claim to the grounds. The existence of warrants helps convince the reader of your argument.

In "The Deep Democratic Tradition in America" (p. 111), Cornel West makes his claim in his opening paragraph: "To many, our democratic system seems so broken that they have simply lost faith that their participation could really matter. The politics of self-interest and catering to narrow special interests is so dominant that so many ask themselves, Why vote?" He then goes on to provide us with a variety of grounds:

- The politics of self-interest discourages voters.
- Political discourse is formulaic and lacks authenticity.
- Both the Republican and Democratic visions are problematic.
- Middle-class Americans are absorbed in personal comfort.
- The black community is divided.
- Some religious movements have become antidemocratic.
- A review of historic idealism in the writing of Emerson, Twain, Tupac Shakur, and so on shows how democracy has long been valued and defended.
- Artists, activists, and intellectuals have championed democracy in America.

His argument is strengthened by his warrants: the assumption that both he and his readers believe that democracy is not only good but that it is also essential. As he says near the end of his essay, "The deep democratic tradition did not begin in America and we have no monopoly on its promise. But it is here where the seeds of democracy have taken deepest root and sprouted most robustly" (para. 11). The advantage of the Toulmin argument for Cornel West is that he knows his audience is deeply concerned with his assumption that democracy is a worthwhile ideal. This makes it easier for him to examine the issues that worry him: the threats to the democratic ideal through divisive politics, the possibility of imperialism, and the feelings of discouragement on the part of some voters. Ultimately, he feels our deep commitment to democracy will eventually "get out the vote."

ROGERIAN ARGUMENT

The third form of argument, the **Rogerian argument**, was developed by Carl R. Rogers, a psychologist. Rogerian argument is distinct in that it aims to find a common ground on which most people can agree. A Rogerian argument begins by stating a claim, but then it acknowledges potential opposition to that claim, which helps avoid a combative stance. The idea behind Rogerian argument is that if a writer recognizes other opinions or arguments about a topic, then the writer creates common ground with as many readers as possible. The Rogerian argument tends to seem more like a discussion than a typical argument, though its ultimate goal is for two sides to come to a mutual agreement, which still involves convincing readers who might initially disagree with the claim. This style of argument is especially useful in treating a subject that invites readers to immediately line up on one or the other side of an issue. The writer of a Rogerian argument is something of a mediator between two positions in conflict.

Alfred North Whitehead's "Religion and Science" (p. 221) is a good example of an essay in which the writer tries to defuse a potentially explosive situation. His thesis, in the second paragraph, is posed as a possible truth but one that needs some explanation: "The *conflict* between religion and science is what naturally occurs to our minds when we think of this subject. It seems as though, during the last half century, the results of science and the beliefs of religion had come into a position of frank disagreement, from which there can be no escape, except by abandoning either the clear teaching of science or the clear teaching of religion."

Whitehead admits that there is a conflict between religion and science, and he gives a number of examples, most of which are common knowledge. He also spends much of his time demonstrating that he knows a great deal about science and just as much about religion. He acknowledges both sides in the debate in part because he is both a scientist and a theologian. His main effort in his essay is to avoid "abandoning" either science or religion. He insists that there are ways of reconciling their differences by examining what they have in common in terms of belief and understanding.

Some of his statements are designed to foster understanding, while his examples show the limitations and characteristics of science and religion:

- Whitehead uses examples from the history of science and the history of religion.
- The conflict "is a slight matter which has been unduly emphasized" (para. 13).
- "A clash of doctrines is not a disaster — it is an opportunity" (para. 16).
- "Religion will not regain its old power until it can face change in the same spirit as does science" (para. 21).

- "So far, my point has been this: that religion is the expression of one type of fundamental experiences of mankind" (para. 25).
- "Religion is the vision of something which stands beyond, behind, and within, the passing flux of things" (para. 27).

Whitehead's Rogerian argument balances his views of religion with his views of science while helping his reader see that there is a long view, a historic view, of the conflict that warns us against being too hasty in our decisions about which side to take.

Despite which method you choose, most written arguments will have a beginning, a middle, and a conclusion. Each part of the argument serves a specific function and is integral to the other parts.

Beginning of an argument

The beginning of an argument is your first opportunity to engage your reader. Besides grabbing the reader's attention and setting the tone, it also

- introduces or identifies the subject of your argument and its importance;
- suggests, or implies, how you plan to argue your case; and
- embeds your thesis statement (or statements) early in your argument.

Middle of an argument

The middle of your argument is where you flex your analytical muscles, the very ones that the beginning and the conclusion of your argument are relying on for support. Therefore, it is imperative that in this section you

- develop the main parts of your argument by marshaling evidence and
- examine the data — all the varieties of evidence you supply — with careful analysis to support your position.

Conclusion of an argument

Although it comes last, the conclusion is essential to the presentation of your argument. It is your final chance to engage your reader's attention, and for that reason you should use it to

- review the claims you make in your thesis that establish your position and
- summarize the main parts of your argument, what they imply, and what you therefore conclude.

A SAMPLE STUDENT ESSAY

The following sample essay is based primarily on the opening pages of Alfred North Whitehead's "Religion and Science," but it also picks up details from the entire essay, which appears on pages 222–33. The annotations on the text appear in the previous chapter of this book, "Examining Ideas," on pages 13–16. Some of them highlight the following ideas:

- We need a definition (of religion and science).
- What is the conflict between religion and science?
- Must we choose between either science or religion?
- The future depends on how we resolve the conflict between religion and science.
- Two great facts: (1) religion and science are always in conflict and (2) always in a state of continual development.
- Science is more changeable than theology.
- Time may change what we think of as true in both religion and science.
- People did not have all the facts when Galileo faced the Inquisition. Do we have all the facts now?

Not all these annotations will yield good points for an argument, but the ones that do will prove to be of great value. Moreover, the best of them will be excellent starting points. In the essay that follows, the methods of development discussed above form the primary techniques and they are labeled in the margin. The development by testimony is handled by using quotations from sources outside of Whitehead's comments. The purpose of the essay is to relate the issues Whitehead saw as being in conflict with some of the resolutions of our own time. In addition, it considers current conflicts that Whitehead would not have foreseen. The writer explores the issues and takes a specific stand at the end of the essay.

RELIGION AND SCIENCE TODAY

Introduction —
author sets up
essay

Alfred North Whitehead's essay "Religion and Science" was written in 1925, at a time when the teaching of evolution was prohibited by law in the public schools of Tennessee. The school authorities had determined that the theory of evolution contradicted the teaching of the Bible, which in Genesis tells that man was created by God in his image. It does not say anything about humans developing from a natural process of evolution from the family of primates. Since 1925, public schools in the United States have taught evolution in biology classes, but some states' departments of education want to include instruction in creationism. This decision has resulted in a new conflict based on old ideas.

Definition —
writer explains
differences in
key ideas

According to Whitehead, religion and science have long been in conflict because they explain the nature of the world in different ways using different methods. One important difference between them is the fact that religion is older than science and was first to explain the world we live in. Science was practiced in ancient times, but it did not become a major force in our culture until the sixteenth and seventeenth centuries, when Galileo and other astronomers contradicted the teachings of the Catholic Church. This is when the scientific method, the examination of physical evidence tested by experience, changed how people thought. Religion before then—and even now—relied on the Bible and the teaching of prophets and the decisions of early religious conferences, such as the legendary Council of Nicea in 325 CE (Whipps), to decide which religious truths should be taught. Unlike science, religion does not depend on physical evidence or experimentation for its teachings. It relies on accepting the teachings of holy writ and the instruction of the elders of the church.

Analysis of cir-
cumstances —
writer
examines how
conditions
affected devel-
opment

In 1925, Tennessee prevented evolution from being taught in public schools, while today the teaching of evolution is taught but not necessarily accepted as fact. In an article for *Slate* in 2014, Chris Kirk noted that "[a] large, publicly funded charter school system in Texas is teaching creationism to its students" ("Map"). He also said that creationism is taught as an alternative to evolution in a great number of schools throughout Tennessee and Louisiana. Most other states do not do this. Creationism is religious teaching based on faith, not based on observation. I thought that the Constitution said that church and state were separate. Teaching creationism in religious schools is one thing, but teaching it in public schools is another. Creationism teaches that the universe and all its beings were created by a specific act of God. It denies that creation was by natural means and therefore says evolution is false.

Comparison — writer compares two ideas

Creationists assume the God of the Bible created everything, while science does not always refer to God. Some scientists, like Alfred North Whitehead, refer to God and do not necessarily see that there is a complete contradiction between believing in God and believing in evolution. However, creationists cannot see any reason to accept evolution. Science has expanded belief in evolution since 1925 by extensive studies of geology, comparative anatomy, and research in genetics and the human genome. For scientists the essential truth of evolution is accepted as a biological reality. Yet many, like Whitehead, also accept the idea of God as creator.

While most creationists defend the idea of "intelligent design" as an absolute conflict with the theory of evolution, not all religious authorities agree. In fact, Pope Francis said only recently that the church accepts even the concept of the big bang as evidence of the way God's mind works (Whitnall). According to the *Independent*, "Speaking at the Pontifical Academy of Sciences, the Pope made comments which experts said put an end to the 'pseudo theories' of creationism and intelligent design that some argue were encouraged by his predecessor,

Example — writer provides examples to support claims

Benedict XVI" (Whitnall). The pope not only accepts the big bang theory and evolution as scientific truth but also says that they each require a God for them to be true. This is a remarkable position for the church and seems to be a result of the mistake the church made in rejecting Galileo and other scientists. Rabbis are not all in agreement, but

Brad Hirschfield, president of the National Jewish Center for Learning and Leadership, has said that "intelligent design attempt[s] to explain the origins of life and to understand how life takes new forms." Still, he insists that Jewish organizations in the United States oppose teaching intelligent design in public schools because doing so would violate the separation of church and state.

Almost a hundred years after the Scopes trial, it seems that the conflict between religion and science in the United States is still operative. Alfred North Whitehead's efforts to see both sides of the conflict may in the long run be helpful today. The fact that both religion and science continue to change has been apparent to us in recent years. When the pope of the largest Christian church can come out and declare his belief in evolution and in the big bang theory just after the previous pope had the opposite view, we can see that there is hope for reconciliation. However, Pope Francis's view may not satisfy creationists because they say evolution is simply wrong. Giving science the victory in the question of evolution is not acceptable to them.

Finally, I do not think that the teaching of creationism as a substitute for evolution makes much sense. It seems to me to be like denying the truth that Galileo discovered. Science proved him right and that the church was wrong. Even Pope Francis sees the truth of evolution and he is a theologian. Creationism emphasizes that God is the creator, and for all religious people this makes sense. It also makes sense for many scientists, who admit that there is a great deal we do not know about the process of creation both in the universe and on our planet. However, the schools should be free to teach the best scientific research possible and not be hampered by having to teach religious theories as if they were science.

Cause and effect — writer identifies action and its consequences

Conclusion — writer restates claim and wraps up essay

WORKS CITED

Hirschfield, Brad. "The Origins of Life: A Jewish Perspective." *National Public Radio*. Natl. Public Radio, 8 Aug. 2005. Web. 21 Jan. 2015.

Kirk, Chris. "Map: Publically Funded Schools That Are Allowed to Teach Creationism." *Slate*. Slate Media Group, 26 Jan. 2014. Web. 19 Feb. 2015.

Whipps, Heather. "How the Council of Nicea Changed the World." *LiveScience*. Purch, 30 Mar. 2008. Web. 28 Feb. 2015.

Whitehead, Alfred North. "Religion and Science." *Approaching Great Ideas: Critical Readings for College Writers*. Ed. Lee A. Jacobus. Boston: Bedford, 2016. 222–33. Print.

Whitnall, Adam. "Pope Francis Declares Evolution and Big Bang Theory Are Real and God Is Not 'A Magician with a Magic Wand.'" *Independent*. Independent, 3 Jan. 2015. Web. 6 Feb. 2015.

The range of this essay is limited to the question of how evolution and creationism, two conflicting theories of our own time, extend the conflict between religion and science that Whitehead described in 1925. It points out that the conflict continues in Tennessee and Louisiana but that it has taken a somewhat different form. Evolution is not prohibited from public schools, but a contrary theory is now introduced as an alternative. The writer seems to be working out the ideas of the essay while considering the issues. The beginning is a simple survey of what seems to be happening in the modern conflict between religion and science, but it soon centers on the way religion — in the form of the Catholic Church — has adapted to scientific realities that were once distasteful. The declaration of the church's acceptance of evolution is a tipping point in the essay and ultimately results in the writer's final decisions on a recommendation regarding teaching creationism in public schools.

The selections that follow in this book are often intense and challenging. They offer some profound ideas, drawn from the ancients as well as from the moderns. Many of the most important ideas of our culture are durable in that they have been considered and argued over for generations. When you read these works, you will begin taking part in the great intellectual debates of our culture. When you respond to these works by writing an essay, your voice will be added to the dialogue.

Part Two

⊞ THE
READINGS

CHAPTER THREE

How Democracy Relates to Human Rights

PLATO   56

JAMES MADISON   65

MARQUIS DE LAFAYETTE AND THE NATIONAL
   ASSEMBLY OF FRANCE   71

MARY WOLLSTONECRAFT   77

ALEXIS DE TOCQUEVILLE   84

EMILE DURKHEIM   90

ROBERT A. DAHL   96

CORNEL WEST   111

FAREED ZAKARIA   120

"If liberty and equality, as is thought by some, are chiefly to be found in democracy, they will be best attained when all persons alike share in government to the utmost."   — Aristotle

---

"In a democracy the poor will have more power than the rich, because there are more of them, and the will of the majority is supreme."   — Aristotle

---

"We are sadly forced to conclude that we live in a world that is functionally godless and that human rights and dignity depend upon the power of one's community to grant or withhold them from its members."   — Richard L. Rubenstein

---

"Democracy is worth dying for, because it's the most deeply honorable form of government ever devised by man."
— Ronald Reagan

"The spirit of democracy is not a mechanical thing to be adjusted by abolition of forms. It requires change of heart."
— Mahatma Gandhi

"I do protect human rights, and I hope I shall always be looked up as a champion of human rights."   — Aung San Suu Kyi

---

"Democracy cannot succeed unless those who express their choice are prepared to choose wisely. The real safeguard of democracy, therefore, is education."
— Franklin Delano Roosevelt

INTRODUCTION

The nature of tyrannies, dictatorships, and oligarchies is to use powers of suppression to deny citizens political and human rights. The nature of democracy is to find ways to guarantee those rights.

In the nine selections in this chapter, you will find views and opinions that go back to Athens, which our culture looks to as the place in Greece where the concept of democracy — often known as "government by the people" — was first put into action. It is also the place in Greece in which democracy's critics functioned. Plato (427–347 B.C.E.), who witnessed democracy and saw it disappear, was in many ways fearful of its nature. He was afraid that democracy meant that the majority would eventually create a tyranny, enacting laws that primarily benefited themselves, and deny the minority their rights. Throughout time, this fear has remained apparent in all nations and communities that have developed democratic governments.

James Madison (1751–1836), who took part in writing the United States Constitution and authored most of the Bill of Rights, was, like Thomas Jefferson and others who favored the American Revolution, also afraid of mob rule. It took a great deal of courage on the part of the founding fathers, many of them wealthy and great property holders, to create a democratic government that gave power to voters who were less educated, less wealthy, and less powerful than they. The concept of equality, which is developed in the Constitution, was an imaginative leap for people who had lived all their lives under the rule of a monarchy, or governance by rulers such as kings and queens. The concept of the king as ruler was fundamental even in the Bible, but it had long been the standard form of government in England and France, from which the United States inherited its ideas about government in the late eighteenth century. Breaking from that mold was not easy, but it was part of the vision of those who founded the United States.

The French Revolution in 1789 enacted a scenario that Plato predicted in his comments on oligarchy and democracy back in ancient Greece. He said that an oligarchy, or a government in which only a small group of people have power, runs the risk of dissipation because the rich would weaken themselves by doing no work, and the poor would eventually see that their own strength would be enough to overthrow the rich. Plato knew that the poor majority could produce a form of democracy that might be bloody at first, and that was what happened in France in the late 1700s. The Marquis de Lafayette (1757–1834), an aristocrat, joined the revolution first in America, when he fought alongside George Washington and befriended Jefferson. When he returned to France, he joined the revolutionary French government and authored, along with a committee, the Declaration of the Rights of Man, guaranteeing the political and human rights that have come to be the basis of democratic government.

Mary Wollstonecraft (1759–1797), while in France during the French Revolution, became famous by writing *A Vindication of the Rights of Men* in 1790. She followed it two years later with *A Vindication of the Rights of Woman*, a book that is among the most famous feminist documents of all time. In the selection that appears in this chapter, she argues for better education for women and an end to the presumption that women's lives be dominated by sensation and emotion rather than by sense and rationality. Her book and her views are still studied with great care, as they have been since the eighteenth century.

Alexis de Tocqueville (1805–1859), author of *Democracy in America* (1835), the most famous book about how democracy worked in the nineteenth century, knew the work of Madison, Lafayette, Wollstonecraft, and other commentators on government and the rights of citizens in a democracy. Tocqueville was a French aristocrat visiting the United States and studying the ways in which the government functioned in the early 1800s. He was astounded at the sense of equality that each citizen he met felt. As an aristocrat, Tocqueville realized that the world was changing and that his social class was essentially doomed. What he witnessed in his visits to various states and his interactions with various kinds of people, including slaves and Native Americans, made him aware of the strengths and weaknesses of the government. His concern centers on the nature of the rights that any citizen of the United States could expect. Democracy made certain guarantees, both in the Constitution and in the facts of life. And while he was aware of its shortcomings, he realized that democracy in America offered a genuinely new beginning.

The great nineteenth-century sociologist Emile Durkheim (1858–1917) wrote extensively on the nature of society. He took a special interest in the ways in which various religions affected the behavior of individuals in society, sometimes to the point of their developing controversial views. For instance, he felt that certain structures of social organizations, such as religions, contributed to suicide. But in the selection in this chapter, he talks about "elite intellectuals" and their responsibilities in a democratic government. He thinks of intellectuals as poorly suited to be governors but well suited to be advisers. His view is that those chosen as representatives of government must be people of action, not people of reflection. The value of much of what he said in 1904 is still appreciated for its relevance more than a century later.

In using the rhetorical question, *Why Democracy?*, Robert A. Dahl (1915–2014) did not expect his reader to provide an answer. Instead, he merely aimed at reminding us that not every nation has chosen a democratic form of government. It may be that he hoped those who live under a government that restricts citizens' right to vote or to hold office might consider an alternative. For one thing, Dahl emphasizes that democracies are not likely to go to war with one another if only because their economic and other interests are usually interrelated in such a way as to make armed conflict impractical. But he also holds that the ideal of democracy is somewhat different from democracy as it exists. His emphasis is on personal participation in the democratic process, and he tells us that the more citizens participate in matters of government, the healthier the democracy will be. The free-market economy, he feels, is essential to a healthy democracy, in part because it represents one of the forms of freedom that are essential to the rights of the individual. In his discussion, he points to a number of recent tyrannical governments and the ways in which they oppressed their own people. True democracies, he reminds us, support freedom; they do not restrict it.

The philosopher Cornel West (b. 1953) sees some of the faults in our modern democracy, especially in what he considers a form of imperialism: the influence of American businesses and American military abroad. As an expert in Middle Eastern languages and culture, West tells us that Islamic fundamentalism is antagonistic toward the United States because of what it considers U.S. economic and military imperialism. While he is deeply concerned about the effect of the political divide in the United States today, he looks to the great writers and poets of America and their deep commitment to the individual's right to personal freedom and judgment. West is critical of social breakdown in the inner city as well as the "misguided righteousness" of extreme religious groups. Ultimately West takes comfort in what he sees as the deep commitment to the principles of democracy as they were conceived in the beginning of the nation and explicated in the writings of America's greatest writers and thinkers. He sees modern artists, such as John Coltrane and Tupac Shakur, as continuing the tradition of clarifying the nature of American democracy.

Freedom of expression is one of the rights that Fareed Zakaria (b. 1964) talks about when he distinguishes between liberal and illiberal democracies. Restrictions on certain rights, such as freedom of speech, are essentially illiberal, no matter what form of government is thought to exist. Zakaria talks about China and Russia, two very important modern nations that may or may not be moving toward establishing liberal democracies. Each of these nations restricts certain forms of expression. China, Zakaria says, is a more restrictive government despite holding elections and having modernized its government in such a way as to produce more prosperity and economic opportunity than in the past. Russia, he feels, is making more progress toward a liberal democracy, but because of the country's historical decision to give vast powers to its president, it may take longer than was hoped. Zakaria's point is that democracies are not all alike.

SEEING IDEAS

The two images that follow help to show how the relationship between democracy and human rights has been acted out in society over time.

The first image, below, is an engraving from 1863 that shows freed former slaves — or freedmen, as they were called — riding in a wagon celebrating their freedom. President Abraham Lincoln had exercised his executive powers to grant freedom to the slaves in his Emancipation Proclamation in January 1863. The posters on the side of the wagon are used as flags to demonstrate the freedmen's guarantee of rights as free citizens in the United States. The Emanicpation Proclamation was an executive decision under the terms of the Constitution that stipulated that the government would "recognize and maintain the freedom" of former slaves. The January Proclamation is prominent on the wagon and on the raised flagpoles in the engraving.

The image on the following page shows protesters on opposite sides of the topic of gay marriage arguing their cases with posters announcing their positions. Same-sex marriage was a point of contention for many people in

Hulton Archive/Getty Images

David Paul Morris/Getty News Images

the early 2000s. In 2008, those who felt that marriage is between a man and a woman won the vote in California when Proposition 8 was passed, which stated that "only marriage between a man and a woman is valid or recognized in California." The proposition was eventually ruled unconstitutional in 2013 on the grounds that it denied the rights of gay and lesbian couples to enjoy the protection of marriage, and same-sex marriages in the state resumed. Despite their differences in views, the protesters in this image express their views in a peaceful manner. Their mode of nonviolent expression is part of their guarantee of human rights under a liberal democracy.

Democracies depend on laws, but as history tells us, some laws infringe on the rights of certain groups in a society. (For example, in 2015, the Supreme Court of the United States ruled that same-sex couples could marry nationwide, which established a new civil right for a group that had not previously had universal protection under the law.) Rule by the majority in government is ideal, but as Plato, James Madison, Alexis de Tocqueville, and others tell us, rule by majority can sometimes damage minority groups. A carefully crafted constitution — and a judiciary that can uphold it — can protect the rights of underrepresented groups in a society.

© Gianni Dagli Orti/Corbis

PLATO

The Greek philosopher **PLATO** (427–347 B.C.E.) was the son of aristocratic parents and given the finest education possible. He lived in very dangerous times, during part of which his city-state, Athens, was defeated by Sparta and ruled by tyrants. Plato intended to take part in politics until 384 B.C.E., when the philosopher Socrates was unjustly charged with corrupting Athenian youth and forced to commit suicide. After that, Plato withdrew from politics and dedicated himself to teaching and studying at the Academy, a philosophical school he established, situated in an olive grove.

His book *The Republic* is his clearest statement of an ideal political society. It is in the form of a dialogue in which Socrates speaks with younger people, such as Glaucon, as in this selection. Plato's dialogue reveals that he is not convinced democracy is the best form of government. In other sections of *The Republic*, he tells us that the best government would be under a philosopher-king, a benevolent monarch who has the best interests of the people at heart and who maintains justice as one of government's highest values.

A few pages before the part of the dialogue reprinted in this chapter begins, Plato reveals the perils of oligarchy, a form of government in which a small number of immensely wealthy people rule, usually for the purpose of making themselves richer. Plato talks about the corrupting power of money being one of the reasons oligarchic government does not succeed. On the other hand, he approves of a form of government called timocracy, in which only owners of property are permitted to vote. That form of democracy was practiced in the United States during the colonial period and in some states even afterward.

As an aristocrat himself, Plato did not have faith in democracy because he saw that people in general gave in to their appetites too easily and had little self-restraint. In this dialogue, Socrates establishes that the oligarchy, devoted to making money and living soft lives, would produce weak heirs who would be overcome by revolution of the poor, whose lives made them tougher. He thought democracy might produce anarchy — a breakdown of government — because ordinary people were not born to lead. Thus, democracy, he feared, might produce tyrants who would wrest power from the people.

Be sure to practice prereading techniques for a careful, annotated reading of Plato's essay. For a review of prereading strategies, see pages 4–9. ⊞

Democracy and the Democratic Man

DEMOCRACY, I suppose, should come next. A study of its rise and character should help us to recognize the democratic type of man and set him beside the others for judgement.

Certainly that course would fit in with our plan.

If the aim of life in an oligarchy is to become as rich as possible, that insatiable craving would bring about the transition to democracy. In this way: since the power of the ruling class is due to its wealth, they will not want to have laws restraining prodigal young men from ruining themselves by extravagance. They will hope to lend these spendthrifts money on their property and buy it up, so as to become richer and more influential than ever. We can see at once that a society cannot hold wealth in honor and at the same time establish a proper self-control in its citizens. One or the other must be sacrificed.

Yes, that is fairly obvious.

In an oligarchy, then, this neglect to curb riotous living sometimes 5 reduces to poverty men of a not ungenerous nature. They settle down in idleness, some of them burdened with debt, some disfranchised, some both at once; and these drones are armed and can sting. Hating the men who have acquired their property and conspiring against them and the rest of society, they long for a revolution. Meanwhile the usurers, intent upon their own business, seem unaware of their existence; they are too busy planting their own stings into any fresh victim who offers them an opening to inject the poison of their money; and while they multiply their capital by usury, they are also multiplying the drones and the paupers. When the danger threatens to break out, they will do nothing to quench the flames, either in the way we mentioned, by forbidding a man to do what he likes with his own, or by the next best remedy, which would be a law enforcing a respect for right conduct. If it were enacted that, in general, voluntary contracts for a loan should be made at the lender's risk, there would be less of this shameless pursuit of wealth and a scantier crop of those evils I have just described.

Quite true.

But, as things are, this is the plight to which the rulers of an oligarchy, for all these reasons, reduce their subjects. As for themselves, luxurious indolence of body and mind makes their young men too lazy and effeminate to resist pleasure or to endure pain; and the fathers, neglecting everything but money, have no higher ideals in life than the poor. Such being the condition of rulers and subjects, what will happen when they are thrown together, perhaps as fellow travelers by sea or land to some festival or on a campaign, and can observe one another's demeanor in a moment of danger? The rich will have no chance to feel superior to the poor. On the contrary, the poor man, lean and sunburnt, may find himself posted in battle beside one who, thanks to his wealth and indoor life, is panting under his burden of fat and showing every mark of distress. "Such men," he will think, "are rich because we are cowards"; and when he and his friends meet in private, the word will go round: "These men are no good: they are at our mercy."

Yes, that is sure to happen.

This state, then, is in the same precarious condition as a person so unhealthy that the least shock from outside will upset the balance or, even without that, internal disorder will break out. It falls sick and is at war with itself on the slightest occasion, as soon as one party or the other calls in allies from a neighboring oligarchy or democracy; and sometimes civil war begins with no help from without.

Quite true.   10

And when the poor win, the result is a democracy. They kill some of the opposite party, banish others, and grant the rest an equal share in civil rights and government, officials being usually appointed by lot.

Yes, that is how a democracy comes to be established, whether by force of arms or because the other party is terrorized into giving way.

Now what is the character of this new regime? Obviously the way they govern themselves will throw light on the democratic type of man.

No doubt.

First of all, they are free. Liberty and free speech are rife everywhere;   15 anyone is allowed to do what he likes.

Yes, so we are told.

That being so, every man will arrange his own manner of life to suit his pleasure. The result will be a greater variety of individuals than under any other constitution. So it may be the finest of all, with its variegated pattern of all sorts of characters. Many people may think it the best, just as women and children might admire a mixture of colors of every shade in the pattern of a dress. At any rate if we are in search of a constitution, here is a good place to look for one. A democracy is so free that it contains a sample of every kind; and perhaps anyone who intends to found a state, as we have been doing, ought first to visit this emporium of constitutions and choose the model he likes best.

He will find plenty to choose from.

Here, too, you are not obliged to be in authority, however competent you may be, or to submit to authority, if you do not like it; you need not fight when your fellow citizens are at war, nor remain at peace when they do, unless you want peace; and though you may have no legal right to hold office or sit on juries, you will do so all the same if the fancy takes you. A wonderfully pleasant life, surely, for the moment.

For the moment, no doubt.   20

There is a charm, too, in the forgiving spirit shown by some who have been sentenced by the courts. In a democracy you must have seen how men condemned to death or exile stay on and go about in public, and no one takes any more notice than he would of a spirit that walked invisible. There is so much tolerance and superiority to petty consider-   *"And when the poor win, the* ations; such a contempt for all those fine   *result is a democracy."* principles we laid down in founding our commonwealth, as when we said that only a very exceptional nature could turn out a good man, if he had not played as a child among things of beauty and given himself only to creditable pursuits. A democracy tramples all such notions under foot; with a magnificent indifference to the sort of life a man has led before he enters politics, it will promote to honor anyone who merely calls himself the people's friend.

Magnificent indeed.

These then, and such as these, are the features of a democracy, an agreeable form of anarchy with plenty of variety and an equality of a peculiar kind for equals and unequals alike.

All that is notoriously true.

Now consider the corresponding individual character. Or shall we take 25
his origin first, as we did in the case of the constitution?

Yes.

I imagine him as the son of our miserly oligarch, brought up under his father's eye and in his father's ways. So he too will enforce a firm control over all such pleasures as lead to expense rather than profit — unnecessary pleasures, as they have been called. But, before going farther, shall we draw the distinction between necessary and unnecessary appetites, so as not to argue in the dark?

Please do so.

There are appetites which cannot be got rid of, and there are all those which it does us good to fulfill. Our nature cannot help seeking to satisfy both these kinds; so they may fairly be described as necessary. On the other hand, "unnecessary" would be the right name for all appetites which can be got rid of by early training and which do us no good and in some cases do harm. Let us take an example of each kind, so as to form a general idea of them. The desire to eat enough plain food — just bread and meat — to keep in health and good condition may be called necessary. In the case of bread the necessity is twofold, since it not only does us good but is indispensable to life; whereas meat is only necessary in so far as it helps to keep us in good condition. Beyond these simple needs the desire for a whole variety of luxuries is unnecessary. Most people can get rid of it by early discipline and education; and it is as prejudicial to intelligence and self-control as it is to bodily health. Further, these unnecessary appetites might be called expensive, whereas the necessary ones are rather profitable, as helping a man to do his work. The same distinctions could be drawn in the case of sexual appetite and all the rest.

Yes.   30

Now, when we were speaking just now of drones, we meant the sort of man who is under the sway of a host of unnecessary pleasures and appetites, in contrast with our miserly oligarch, over whom the necessary desires are in control. Accordingly, we can now go back to describe how the democratic type develops from the oligarchical. I imagine it usually happens in this way. When a young man, bred, as we were saying, in a stingy and uncultivated home, has once tasted the honey of the drones and keeps company with those dangerous and cunning creatures, who know how to purvey pleasures in all their multitudinous variety, then the oligarchical constitution of his soul begins to turn into a democracy. The corresponding revolution was effected in the state by one of the two factions calling in the help of partisans from outside. In the same way one of the conflicting sets of desires in the soul of this youth will be reinforced from without by a group of kindred passions; and if the resistance of the oligarchical faction in him is strengthened by remonstrances and reproaches coming from his father, perhaps, or his friends, the opposing parties will soon be battling within him. In some cases the democratic interest yields to the oligarchical: a sense of shame gains a footing in the young man's soul, and some appetites are crushed, others banished, until order is restored.

Yes, that happens sometimes.

But then again, perhaps, owing to the father's having no idea how to bring up his son, another brood of desires, akin to those which were banished, are secretly nursed up until they become numerous and strong. These draw the young man back into clandestine commerce with his old associates, and between them they breed a whole multitude. In the end, they seize

the citadel of the young man's soul, finding it unguarded by the trusty senti-
nels which keep watch over the minds of men favored by heaven. Knowledge, right principles, true thoughts, are not at their post; and the place lies
open to the assault of false and presumptuous notions. So he turns again to
those lotus-eaters[1] and now throws in his lot with them openly. If his family
send reinforcements to the support of his thrifty instincts, the impostors
who have seized the royal fortress shut the gates upon them, and will not
even come to parley with the fatherly counsels of individual friends. In the
internal conflict they gain the day; modesty and self-control, dishonored and
insulted as the weaknesses of an unmanly fool, are thrust out into exile;
and the whole crew of unprofitable desires take a hand in banishing moderation and frugality, which, as they will have it, are nothing but churlish meanness. So they take possession of the soul which they have swept clean, as
if purified for initiation into higher mysteries; and nothing remains but to
marshal the great procession bringing home Insolence, Anarchy, Waste, and
Impudence, those resplendent divinities crowned with garlands, whose
praises they sing under flattering names: Insolence they call good breeding,
Anarchy freedom, Waste magnificence, and Impudence a manly spirit. Is not
that a fair account of the revolution which gives free rein to unnecessary
and harmful pleasures in a young man brought up in the satisfaction only of
the necessary desires?

Yes, it is a vivid description.

In his life thenceforward he spends as much time and pains and money 35
on his superfluous pleasures as on the necessary ones. If he is lucky enough
not to be carried beyond all bounds, the tumult may begin to subside as he
grows older. Then perhaps he may recall some of the banished virtues and
cease to give himself up entirely to the passions which ousted them; and
now he will set all his pleasures on a footing of equality, denying to none
its equal rights and maintenance, and allowing each in turn, as it presents
itself, to succeed, as if by the chance of the lot, to the government of his soul
until it is satisfied. When he is told that some pleasures should be sought
and valued as arising from desires of a higher order, others chastised and
enslaved because the desires are base, he will shut the gates of the citadel
against the messengers of truth, shaking his head and declaring that one
appetite is as good as another and all must have their equal rights. So he
spends his days indulging the pleasure of the moment, now intoxicated with
wine and music, and then taking to a spare diet and drinking nothing but
water; one day in hard training, the next doing nothing at all, the third apparently immersed in study. Every now and then he takes a part in politics,
leaping to his feet to say or do whatever comes into his head. Or he will set
out to rival someone he admires, a soldier it may be, or, if the fancy takes

---

[1] **lotus-eaters** Those without ambition, or drugged.

him, a man of business. His life is subject to no order or restraint, and he has no wish to change an existence which he calls pleasant, free, and happy.

That well describes the life of one whose motto is liberty and equality.

Yes, and his character contains the same fine variety of pattern that we found in the democratic state; it is as multifarious as that epitome of all types of constitution. Many a man, and many a woman too, will find in it something to envy. So we may see in him the counterpart of democracy, and call him the democratic man.

We may.

Understanding Ideas

1. According to Plato, why does oligarchy produce "young men too lazy and effeminate to resist pleasure or to endure pain" (para. 7)?

2. Why does Plato seem to disapprove of the fact that in a democracy "[l]iberty and free speech are rife everywhere" (para. 15)?

3. Plato appears suspicious of "liberty and equality." Why? Is this a vote against basic human rights?

4. What does Plato's definition of the democratic man say about how freedom to do anything one wants might appeal to base desires? What are base desires?

Responding to Ideas

1. *Analysis of Circumstances* Analyze the circumstances by which, Plato says, an oligarchic government would give way to a democracy. What situations would be necessary in a modern society for a democracy to take the reins of government from the hands of an oligarchy? Money plays a great role in both creating and destroying an oligarchy. Does Plato's description of that process make sense in our world, or is it only limited to ancient Athens?

2. *Definition* How does Plato define a democracy? What does he say about the democratic man that you agree with? What do you disagree with? He places a great deal of emphasis on liberty and equality. To what extent are those qualities essential ingredients of a democratic form of government? Do you find yourself as cautious about the virtues of those qualities as Plato is? Offer your own definition of democratic government, taking into account the concerns of Plato.

3. *Analysis of Circumstances* Near the end of his essay, Plato worries about the possibility that the democratic man will give over to the forces of "Insolence, Anarchy, Waste, and Impudence" (para. 33). He says that in a democracy, "Insolence they call good breeding, Anarchy freedom, Waste magnificence, and Impudence a manly spirit" (para. 33). Given your observations of people in our society today, defend his description as being appropriate in our time. Or, if you disagree, offer an argument that demonstrates that Plato may have been right in his time but not in ours.

4. *Research* An oligarchy is a government run by a relatively small number of people, usually under 1 percent, who are immensely wealthy and govern in such a way as to protect their best interests. Today, some people are fearful that the large inequities in the distribution of wealth are beginning to produce an oligarchy in the United States. If you feel this is true, research the nature of oligarchies and current data about wealth inequity and defend an argument that establishes your position. Do contemporary conditions favor a possible case in which "the democratic interest yields to the oligarchical" (para. 31)?

5. *Example* Some of the complaints Plato makes of the behavior of people rest on his view of the nature of people's souls. He seems to be using the term in a psychological sense, equivalent to what we would think of as character, especially when he says that bad company will "seize the citadel of the young man's soul" (para. 33) and lead him into bad behavior. He contends that this is a result of people having too much freedom: "Liberty and free speech are rife everywhere; anyone is allowed to do what he likes" (para. 15). Because it corrupts people by making them indolent, democracy, Plato fears, will not produce good government. Attack or defend this view, using examples from modern democracies. Does the success of a democracy depend on the character of its citizens or of its governors?

6. *Cause and Effect* Plato's concept of the common people indicates that he is fearful of giving the power of government over to them. Is it reasonable to assume that having the power of government is a basic human right? How do the descriptions of the way in which money corrupts and weakens character affect our conception of what human rights are? Is dissipation of the kind Plato describes a basic human right? Does democracy produce the kind of dissipation he describes?

Comparing Ideas

1. Plato has some misgivings about democracy, and Fareed Zakaria (p. 120) writes about two kinds of democracy. One is a liberal style

of democracy in which freedom of speech is essential to protecting human rights. The other is an illiberal democracy in which the state functions well enough but at the cost of complete freedom of speech and an abridgment of some rights. Write a brief essay in which you compare the kind of democracy Plato describes with either the liberal or illiberal democracy that Zakaria describes.

2. Write a brief essay addressed to Plato. Explain to him why he should not worry about the problems of democracy that he mentions in his essay. Use the points Cornel West (p. 111) uses to explain why America has a deep democratic tradition. How has West responded to some of the same worries that bothered Plato? West talks about the materialism of society and its effect on our democracy, yet he is very optimistic. Do what you can to cheer Plato on to accept the possibility that democracy is a deep tradition and will survive.

JAMES
MADISON

© Corbis

JAMES MADISON (1751–1836) was born in Virginia and educated at Princeton. He became a member of Congress at the time of the ratification of the Constitution in 1788. His concern for the protection of the rights of citizens who had not been accounted for in the original document led him to propose a number of amendments to the Constitution. Eventually, and after considerable debate, he drafted nine of the first ten amendments, which have become known as the Bill of Rights.

Madison drew his inspiration from items included in some of the state constitutions as well as rights granted historically in the English Magna Carta in 1215, which was issued by King John of England and established for the first time the principle that everybody, including the king, was subject to the law. Madison was also inspired by the English Bill of Rights, which was written in 1689 when the last Stuart king was deposed in England and the British Parliament assumed a greater power than it had had originally.

At first, the amendments to the United States Constitution were intended primarily to guarantee rights under the federal government, not necessarily under the individual states' governments. Later, the states accepted the amendments as well. Madison's view was that the original text of the Constitution was not absolutely clear about religious freedom, freedom of speech and of the press, the right to free assembly, the right to bear arms, the guarantee of a speedy public trial, protection against double jeopardy, or protection against unreasonable search and seizure.

Madison, an elegant writer, had a hand in writing the Constitution itself, and he is credited not only with having written most of the Bill of Rights in 1788 but also with having it ratified in December 1791 as the first amendments to the Constitution. Like many other members of Congress, he owned a large number of slaves, but he argued passionately to end the slave traffic and worked with Thomas Jefferson to buy slaves their freedom and return them to Africa. In a letter from 1831, he described slavery as "the dreadful calamity which has so long afflicted our Country."

In 1803, Madison was a principal agent in acquiring the Louisiana Purchase from France, thus more than doubling the size of the nation. He became America's third president (1809–1817) and suffered through the War of 1812, during which he was forced to abandon the White House to the British, who burned it. The difficulties of this war made Madison change his mind and move toward a stronger federal government and the establishment of a national bank.

Be sure to practice prereading techniques for a careful, annotated reading of the Bill of Rights. For a review of prereading strategies, see pages 4–9. ⌗

The Bill of Rights

CONGRESS OF THE UNITED STATES
BEGUN AND HELD AT THE CITY OF NEW YORK, ON
WEDNESDAY THE FOURTH OF MARCH,
ONE THOUSAND SEVEN HUNDRED AND EIGHTY NINE

THE Convention of a number of the States, having at the time of their adopting the Constitution, expressed a desire, in order to prevent misconstruction or abuse of its powers, that further declaratory and restrictive clauses should be added: And as extending the ground of public confidence in the Government, will best ensure the beneficent ends of its institution.

RESOLVED by the Senate and House of Representatives of the United States of America, in Congress assembled, two-thirds of both Houses concurring, that the following Articles be proposed to the Legislatures of the several States, as amendments to the Constitution of the United States, all, or any of which Articles, when ratified by three-fourths of the said Legislatures, to be valid to all intents and purposes, as part of the said Constitution; viz.

ARTICLES in addition to, and Amendment of the Constitution of the United States of America, proposed by Congress, and ratified by the

Legislatures of the several States, pursuant to the fifth Article of the original Constitution.

AMENDMENT I.

Congress shall make no law respecting an establishment of religion, or prohibiting the free exercise thereof; or abridging the freedom of speech, or of the press, or the right of the people peaceably to assemble, and to petition the Government for a redress of grievances.

AMENDMENT II.

A well regulated Militia, being necessary to the security of a free State, the right of the people to keep and bear Arms, shall not be infringed.

AMENDMENT III.

No Soldier shall, in time of peace be quartered in any house, without the consent of the Owner, nor in time of war, but in a manner to be prescribed by law.

AMENDMENT IV.

The right of the people to be secure in their persons, houses, papers, and effects, against unreasonable searches and seizures, shall not be violated, and no Warrants shall issue, but upon probable cause, supported by Oath or affirmation, and particularly describing the place to be searched, and the persons or things to be seized.

AMENDMENT V.

No person shall be held to answer for a capital, or otherwise infamous crime, unless on a presentment or indictment of a Grand Jury, except in cases arising in the land or naval forces, or in the Militia, when in actual service in time of War or public danger; nor shall any person be subject for the same offense to be twice put in jeopardy of life or limb; nor shall be compelled in any criminal case to be a witness against himself, nor be deprived of life, liberty, or property, without due process of law; nor shall private property be taken for public use, without just compensation.

AMENDMENT VI.

In all criminal prosecutions, the accused shall enjoy the right to a speedy and public trial, by an impartial jury of the State and district wherein the crime shall have been committed, which district shall have been previously ascertained by law, and to be informed of the nature and cause of the accusation; to be confronted with the witnesses against him; to have compulsory process for obtaining witnesses in his favor, and to have the Assistance of Counsel for his defense.

AMENDMENT VII.

In suits at common law, where the value in controversy shall exceed twenty dollars, the right of trial by jury shall be preserved, and no fact tried by a jury shall be otherwise re-examined in any Court of the United States, than according to the rules of the common law.

AMENDMENT VIII.

Excessive bail shall not be required, nor excessive fines imposed, nor cruel and unusual punishments inflicted.

AMENDMENT IX.

The enumeration in the Constitution, of certain rights, shall not be construed to deny or disparage others retained by the people.

AMENDMENT X.

The powers not delegated to the United States by the Constitution, nor prohibited by it to the States, are reserved to the States respectively, or to the people.

Understanding Ideas

1. The Bill of Rights indicates that the states wanted "restrictive clauses" added. What do the states imagine is being restricted, and how?

2. In this document, which rights seem to be more important: those that involve freedom of expression or those that involve freedom of behavior?

3. What powers of government are most limited by these amendments?

4. Do these amendments aim to guarantee basic human rights, or are they only aimed at guaranteeing the rights of U.S. citizens? (Keep in mind the limited nature of who was considered a citizen at the time this document was written.)

Responding to Ideas

1. **Testimony** Assume you have the responsibility of clarifying this part of the First Amendment: "Congress shall make no law respecting an establishment of religion, or prohibiting the free exercise thereof." What do you think Madison meant by this statement? Does the statement guarantee a separation of church and state? If so, how? What rights are guaranteed to what people? Are your rights affected by this amendment? Is this a desirable amendment, or would you rewrite it?

2. **Definition** One of the most controversial amendments is the second, which guarantees citizens the right to have their own weapons. This amendment has been interpreted in a variety of ways. Therefore, it is important to define the key terms. What is a "well regulated Militia"? What is a "free State," and what does it mean to "bear Arms"? What constitutes infringement — or encroachment — of the rights of an individual in this amendment? Does a state or local government have any rights under this amendment?

3. **Analysis of Circumstances** These amendments were designed to guarantee the rights of people living in a democracy. However, they were derived from the guarantees offered to people living under the government of monarchs, such as the king of England. Which of these amendments do you feel are most important to our continuing to maintain our democratic way of life? If our democracy were to begin to crumble, which of our rights would be the first to go?

4. **Research** Which of these amendments do you currently hear about most in the news? Search for key terms online, such as *freedom of speech, impartial jury, speedy trial, excessive bail, common law, freedom of the press,* and *right to bear arms.* To what extent are any of these rights threatened? Is there a threat to human rights in this country as a result of current actions by local, state, or federal government?

5. **Analysis of Circumstances** Under what circumstances are the guarantees of rights likely to be most important for you personally? Describe any situations you may have been in when these rights were threatened or, more importantly, defended. When do these rights become personal? What have you done to protect your rights under these

amendments? And what have you done to protect the rights of other people when they may have been threatened? Have you found that institutions such as colleges and universities, as well as corporations or small businesses, have sometimes ignored the guarantees of these amendments? Argue a case in which institutions, or even states, have the right to ignore some of these amendments. Or, argue the opposite.

6. *Response* Amendment IX indicates that the Constitution, including its amendments, specifies certain rights but that there are "others retained by the people." What important rights do people have in a democracy that are not mentioned in the Constitution? Which of the following would you include (or not include) and why: the right to a higher education; the right to a job; the right to a living wage; the right to housing; the right to food; the right to medical care; the right to Internet access; the right to privacy? What other rights might you add?

Comparing Ideas

1. Compare James Madison's Bill of Rights with Mary Wollstonecraft's "A Vindication of the Rights of Woman" (p. 77). Which of Madison's rights seem to be specifically aimed at men? Which are aimed at women? Which rights does Wollstonecraft discuss that are not specifically addressed in Madison's document? What new amendments might Wollstonecraft include? Do either of these champions of human rights consider the right to privacy as essential to a democracy? Which of these writers seems to be more explicitly describing the rights of people living in a democracy?

MARQUIS DE LAFAYETTE AND THE NATIONAL ASSEMBLY OF FRANCE

© Corbis

Marie Joseph Paul Yves Roch Gilbert du Motier, more commonly known as the **MARQUIS DE LAFAYETTE** (1757–1834), fought in the American Revolution and became friends with Thomas Jefferson (1743–1826). In 1789, back in France, Lafayette took a role in the French Revolution and with the help of Jefferson, and with reference to the U.S. Constitution, he helped write the Declaration of the Rights of Man and Citizen. Like America's Constitution, it was the product of a committee — **THE NATIONAL ASSEMBLY OF FRANCE** — but it was influenced by the great changes taking place in the late eighteenth century. One can see the influence, as well, of Jean-Jacques Rousseau (1712–1778), whose *Social Contract* (1762) is excerpted in this book. Rousseau implied that people entered into a contract with society, agreeing to give up some rights while accepting the guarantee of social order.

Lafayette was not only a skilled military man but also a skilled politician. He absorbed the principles of social equality as they were understood by the founders of the United States. When the French Revolution changed the face of Europe, he did what he could to help guarantee some of the rights that the Revolution had won for the common people. The Revolution stripped the aristocrats of their power in much the same way that Plato had suggested poor people would forcefully take power from wealthy oligarchs. Once that was done, the remaining society required those like Lafayette to begin to establish order and outline the rights of people within their new government.

However, it was not an easy path to bring the revolution under control. In 1791 France's violent Jacobin government formed three armies to attack Austria. Lafayette commanded one of them, but when he began to see that the king and queen were likely to be killed, he was conflicted. When he decided to use his army to protect them, the Assembly declared him a traitor and sent him to prison for five years, first in Prussia, then in Austria. Napoleon eventually had him released, but Lafayette resisted taking a strong role in Napoleon's government. Once Napoleon was defeated, Lafayette returned to French politics and visited the United States, where he was feted and honored not only for his service in America but also for his liberal humanism throughout his career.

Be sure to practice prereading techniques for a careful, annotated reading of the Declaration of the Rights of Man and Citizen. For a review of prereading strategies, see pages 4–9. ⊞

Declaration of the Rights of Man and Citizen

THE REPRESENTATIVES of the French people, organized in National Assembly, considering that ignorance, forgetfulness, or contempt of the rights of man, are the sole causes of the public miseries and of the corruption of governments, have resolved to set forth in a solemn declaration the natural, inalienable, and sacred rights of man, in order that this declaration, being ever present to all the members of the social body, may unceasingly remind them of their rights and their duties; in order that the acts of the legislative power and those of the executive power may be each moment compared with the aim of every political institution and thereby may be more respected; and in order that the demands of the citizens, grounded henceforth upon simple and incontestable principles, may always take the direction of maintaining the constitution and the welfare of all.

In consequence, the National Assembly recognizes and declares, in the presence and under the auspices of the Supreme Being, the following rights of man and citizen.

1.   Men are born and remain free and equal in rights. Social distinctions can be based only upon public utility.

2.   The aim of every political association is the preservation of the natural and imprescriptible rights of man. These rights are liberty, property, security, and resistance to oppression.

3. The source of all sovereignty is essentially in the nation; no body, no individual can exercise authority that does not proceed from it in plain terms.

4. Liberty consists in the power to do anything that does not injure others; accordingly, the exercise of the natural rights of each man has no limits except those that secure to the other members of society the enjoyment of these same rights. These limits can be determined only by law.

5. The law has the right to forbid only such actions as are injurious to society. Nothing can be forbidden that is not interdicted by the law, and no one can be constrained to do that which it does not order.

6. Law is the expression of the general will. All citizens have the right to take part personally, or by their representatives, in its formation. It must be the same for all, whether it protects or punishes. All citizens being equal in its eyes, are equally eligible to all public dignities, places, and employments, according to their capacities, and without other distinction than that of their virtues and their talents.

7. No man can be accused, arrested, or detained, except in the cases determined by the law and according to the forms that it has prescribed. Those who procure, expedite, execute, or cause to be executed arbitrary orders ought to be punished: but every citizen summoned or seized in virtue of the law ought to render instant obedience; he makes himself guilty by resistance.

8. The law ought to establish only penalties that are strictly and obviously necessary, and no one can be punished except in virtue of a law established and promulgated prior to the offense and legally applied.

9. Every man being presumed innocent until he has been pronounced guilty, if it is thought indispensable to arrest him, all severity that may not be necessary to secure his person ought to be strictly suppressed by law.

10. No one should be disturbed on account of his opinions, even religious, provided their manifestation does not derange the public order established by law.

11. The free communication of ideas and opinions is one of the most precious of the rights of man; every citizen then can freely speak, write, and print, subject to responsibility for the abuse of this freedom in the cases determined by law.

12. The guarantee of the rights of man and citizen requires a public force; this force then is instituted for the advantage of *all* and not for the personal benefit of those to whom it is entrusted.

13. For the maintenance of the public force and for the expenses of administration a general tax is indispensable; it ought to be equally apportioned among all the citizens according to their means.

14. All the citizens have the right to ascertain, by themselves or by their representatives, the necessity of the public tax, to consent to it freely, to follow the employment of it, and to determine the quota, the assessment, the collection, and the duration of it.

15. Society has the right to call for an account of his administration from every public agent.

16. Any society in which the guarantee of the rights is not secured, or the separation of powers not determined, has no constitution at all.

17. Property being a *sacred* and inviolable right, no one can be deprived of it, unless a legally established public necessity evidently demands it, under the condition of a just and prior indemnity.

Understanding Ideas

1. In what ways does the use of the words "representatives of the French people" imply that France may be instituting democracy?

2. What does the law forbid, and what does it provide the citizen?

3. What does it mean to say that "the guarantee of the rights of man and citizen requires a public force"? What is a public force?

4. What is the French position on the rights to property?

Responding to Ideas

1. *Research* Examine the Declaration of the Rights of Man and Citizen for its treatment of laws. The U.S. Constitution's Bill of Rights talks about law, but Lafayette treats questions of law a bit differently. How does he interpret the role of law in the life of the citizen? How does the law work to limit the citizen's behavior? How does it protect him? And

what does it protect him from? If possible, research the role of the law in France after the Revolution.

2. **Analysis of Circumstances** The last item on the list of the declaration says, "Property being a *sacred* and inviolable right, no one can be deprived of it." The Bill of Rights (p. 65) says one will not be "deprived of life, liberty, or property, without due process of law." What do you make of the emphasis on the right to possess property in either or both of these documents? Is property a sacred or an inviolable right as far as you are concerned? Why would a democratic government make a special mention of the guarantee of property? Under what circumstances must a democratic government take responsibility for preserving your property?

3. **Definition** What is the position of the Declaration of the Rights of Man and Citizen on religion? During the French Revolution, the Catholic Church was persecuted in part because of its wealth and in part because it supported the aristocracy. Are the rights guaranteed by the declaration different from those that a religious authority would guarantee? Is the declaration supported by religious views as much as it is by political views? Does religion have protection in this document?

4. **Response** The second item in the declaration says, "The aim of every political association is the preservation of the natural and imprescriptible rights of man." *Imprescriptible rights* are rights that cannot be taken away because they are guaranteed by law. Research *natural rights* and establish what they are. Then consider which of those rights are guaranteed by the declaration and which are not. What do you feel are the natural rights of "Man and Citizen"? Do you feel that a democracy is more likely to guarantee those rights than would other forms of government? If you do, argue that position.

Comparing Ideas

1. The Declaration of the Rights of Man and Citizen contains seventeen different statements of rights. The Bill of Rights (p. 65) contains only ten. What does Lafayette include that is not in the Bill of Rights? Are his new inclusions very different from the Bill of Rights, or are they expansions or interpretations of Madison's amendments? It is not clear whether Lafayette could have seen Madison's amendments in 1789, although he was familiar with the U.S. Constitution through Jefferson. Compare Lafayette's declaration with the Bill of Rights as a means of

deciding which is more inclusive in covering the most rights for the most citizens.

2. The word *equal* is used in the Declaration of the Rights of Man and Citizen in part because, before the Revolution, the aristocrats and the clergy were in every sense the social superiors of the people, who had few rights by comparison. Examine the declaration for its emphasis on equality. Do the rights guaranteed in this document protect equality? Do they protect equality to the same extent that the Bill of Rights (p. 65) does? Which document is more passionate about equality? Does the fact that slavery was more common in the United States than in France enter into each document's emphasis on equality?

3. In a brief essay, compare the concerns of the Marquis de Lafayette in his discussion of the rights of man with both the Bill of Rights (p. 65) and the ideas expressed in Plato's discussion of democracy (p. 56). What rights are clearly essential for a democracy to function as it should? How do Plato's views fit into the two great declarations of rights? Which of Lafayette's rights would Plato most likely have omitted from his idea of democracy? Where does freedom of speech figure in the work of these three writers?

MARY
WOLLSTONECRAFT

© Corbis

A woman far ahead of her time, **MARY WOLL-STONECRAFT** (1759–1797) became one of the first English feminists. She grew up in difficult circumstances and had to earn her own living at an early age. She became a governess, then a teacher, and finally a writer. She became well known to some of the most important literary and political figures of the age.

The excitement generated first by the American (1776–1783) and then by the French (1789–1799) revolutions caused Wollstonecraft to react against the conservative views of Edmund Burke (1729–1797), an Irish statesman who served in the House of Commons of Great Britain and wrote *Reflections on the Revolution in France* (1790), a defense of constitutional monarchy, aristocracy, and the Church of England. Wollstonecraft responded with a pamphlet, *A Vindication of the Rights of Men* (1790), which attacked the aristocracy. This publication made her instantly famous. But her book *A Vindication of the Rights of Woman* (1792), which expanded on the ideas she had addressed in her pamphlet, added to her fame and is still widely read.

The selection from *A Vindication of the Rights of Woman* included here concerns itself with the conflict of sense and sensibility, as Jane Austen put it. Wollstonecraft accuses society of relegating women as dominated by emotions, or sensibilities, rather than as possessed of rational powers, or sense. During the eighteenth century, a widespread debate warned that sensibility weakened people, and people were encouraged to think rationally. Indeed, the eighteenth century is known as the "age of reason," and Wollstonecraft was enthusiastic in her embrace of rationality. For example, in defiance of convention, she decided to live with an American named Gilbert Imlay in France, despite their not being married. She had a daughter, Fanny, and also proved herself capable of considerable passion.

Returning to London, she met William Godwin, who had read her work and declared that it could make a man fall in love with her. Their eventual marriage was unfortunately brief, and Wollstonecraft died during childbirth. Her second daughter, Mary, grew up to write the novel *Frankenstein*.

In the following selection, Wollstonecraft encourages reason over emotion and demands that women be given an education as fine as that offered to men. Otherwise, she argues, women must "lie down in the dust from whence we were taken, never to rise again" (para. 3). In just a few pages, Wollstonecraft makes a strong argument designed to right a social wrong.

Be sure to practice prereading techniques for a careful, annotated reading of Wollstonecraft's essay. For a review of prereading strategies, see pages 4–9. ⌗

A Vindication of the Rights of Woman

NOVELS, MUSIC, poetry, and gallantry, all tend to make women the creatures of sensation, and their character is thus formed in the mold of folly during the time they are acquiring accomplishments, the only improvement they are excited, by their station in society, to acquire. This overstretched sensibility naturally relaxes the other powers of the mind, and prevents intellect from attaining that sovereignty which it ought to attain to render a rational creature useful to others, and content with its own station; for the exercise of the understanding, as life advances, is the only method pointed out by nature to calm the passions.

Satiety has a very different effect, and I have often been forcibly struck by an emphatical description of damnation; when the spirit is represented as continually hovering with abortive eagerness round the defiled body, unable to enjoy anything without the organs of sense. Yet, to their senses, are women made slaves, because it is by their sensibility that they obtain present power.

And will moralists pretend to assert that this is the condition in which one-half of the human race should be encouraged to remain with listless inactivity and stupid acquiescence? Kind instructors! what were we created for? To remain, it may be said, innocent; they mean in a state of childhood. We might as well never have been born, unless it were necessary that we should be created to enable man to acquire the noble privilege of reason, the power of discerning good from evil, whilst we lie down in the dust from whence we were taken, never to rise again.

It would be an endless task to trace the variety of meannesses, cares, and sorrows, into which women are plunged by the prevailing opinion, that they were created rather to feel than reason, and that all the power they obtain must be obtained by their charms and weakness:

Fine by defect, and amiably weak![1]

And, made by this amiable weakness entirely dependent, excepting what they gain by illicit sway, on man, not only for protection, but advice, is it suprising that, neglecting the duties that reason alone points out, and shrinking from trials calculated to strengthen their minds, they only exert themselves to give their defects a graceful covering, which may serve to heighten their charms in the eye of the voluptuary, though it sink them below the scale of moral excellence.

Fragile in every sense of the word, they are obliged to look up to man 5
for every comfort. In the most trifling danger they cling to their support, with parasitical tenacity, piteously demanding succor; and their *natural* protector extends his arm, or lifts up his voice, to guard the lovely trembler — from what? Perhaps the frown of an old cow, or the jump of a mouse; a rat would be a serious danger. In the name of reason, and even common sense, what can save such beings from contempt; even though they be soft and fair.

These fears, when not affected, may produce some pretty attitudes; but they show a degree of imbecility which degrades a rational creature in a way women are not aware of — for love and esteem are very distinct things.

I am fully persuaded that we should hear of none of these infantine airs, if girls were allowed to take sufficient exercise, and not confined in close rooms till their muscles are relaxed, and their powers of digestion destroyed. To carry the remark still further, if fear in girls, instead of being cherished, perhaps, created, were treated in the same manner as cowardice in boys, we should quickly see women with more dignified aspects. It is true, they could not then with equal propriety be termed the sweet flowers that smile in the walk of man; but they would be more respectable members of society, and discharge the important duties of life by the light of their own reason. "Educate women like men," says Rousseau, "and the more they resemble our sex the less power they will have over us." This is the very point I aim at. I do not wish them to have power over men; but over themselves.

In the same strain have I heard men argue against instructing the poor; for many are the forms that aristocracy assumes. "Teach them to read and write," say they, "and you take them out of the station assigned them by nature." An eloquent Frenchman has answered them, I will borrow his

---

[1] **Fine . . . weak** Alexander Pope, moral essay II, line 44: "Fine by defect, and delicately weak[.]"

sentiments. "But they know not, when they make man a brute, that they may expect every instant to see him transformed into a ferocious beast. Without knowledge there can be no morality."

Ignorance is a frail base for virtue! Yet, that it is the condition for which woman was organized, has been insisted upon by the writers who have most vehemently argued in favor of the superiority of man; a superiority not in degree, but offense; though, to soften the argument, they have labored to prove, with chivalrous generosity, that the sexes ought not to be compared; man was made to reason, woman to feel: and that together, flesh and spirit, they make the most perfect whole, by blending happily reason and sensibility into one character.

"I come round to my old argument: if woman be allowed to have an immortal soul, she must have, as the employment of life, an understanding to improve."

And what is sensibility? "Quickness of 10 sensation, quickness of perception, delicacy." Thus is it defined by Dr. Johnson;[2] and the definition gives me no other idea than of the most exquisitely polished instinct. I discern not a trace of the image of God in either sensation or matter. Refined seventy times seven they are still material; intellect dwells not there; nor will fire ever make lead gold!

I come round to my old argument: if woman be allowed to have an immortal soul, she must have, as the employment of life, an understanding to improve. And when, to render the present state more complete, though everything proves it to be but a fraction of a mighty sum, she is incited by present gratification to forget her grand destination, nature is counteracted, or she was born only to procreate and rot. Or, granting brutes of every description a soul, though not a reasonable one, the exercise of instinct and sensibility may be the step which they are to take, in this life, towards the attainment of reason in the next; so that through all eternity they will lag behind man, who, why we cannot tell, had the power given him of attaining reason in his first mode of existence.

When I treat of the peculiar duties of women, as I should treat of the peculiar duties of a citizen or father, it will be found that I do not mean to insinuate that they should be taken out of their families, speaking of the majority. "He that hath wife and children," says Lord Bacon,[3] "hath given

---

[2] **Dr. Johnson** Samuel Johnson (1709–1784), author of *The Dictionary* and a friend of Mary Wollstonecraft's and her sister Eliza. He was the ranking lexicographer of his age.

[3] **Lord Bacon** Francis Bacon (1561–1626), politician, essayist, scientist, and champion of reason and author of *Novum Organum* (*The New Organon*), a book advocating replacing Aristotelian thought and method with a new approach to logic and rhetoric.

hostages to fortune; for they are impediments to great enterprises, either of virtue or mischief. Certainly the best works, and of greatest merit for the public, have proceeded from the unmarried or childless men." I say the same of women. But the welfare of society is not built on extraordinary exertions; and were it more reasonably organized, there would be still less need of great abilities, or heroic virtues.

In the regulation of a family, in the education of children, understanding, in an unsophisticated sense, is particularly required — strength both of body and mind; yet the men who, by their writings, have most earnestly labored to domesticate women, have endeavored, by arguments dictated by a gross appetite, which satiety had rendered fastidious, to weaken their bodies and cramp their minds.

Understanding Ideas

1. How does an "overstretched sensibility" relax "the other powers of the mind" (para. 1)?

2. Why does Wollstonecraft feel that women are made slaves to their senses?

3. What does Wollstonecraft feel will be the results of educating women in much the same way men are educated?

4. According to Wollstonecraft, what is the proper place for a woman in society?

Responding to Ideas

1. *Definition* Wollstonecraft accuses "[n]ovels, music, poetry, and gallantry" of tending to make "women the creatures of sensation" (para. 1). Establish how these arts could make people "creatures of sensation," and in the process define what a creature of sensation would be. Why does Wollstonecraft protest against these arts? Do you agree that they pertain more to sensation than to reason? Is that a bad thing or a good thing? Why was a life of sensation a problem for women in the eighteenth century?

2. *Research* This passage has several references to the weakness of women. What weaknesses does Wollstonecraft see in women in her time? Do you see the same weaknesses in our time? Is it true that "all the power they obtain must be obtained by their charms

and weakness" (para. 4)? What evidence do you see in the media that would back up your views? What personal experience do you bring to the argument that would help you convince a reader of your views?

3. *Analysis of Circumstances* The argument against "instructing the poor" is said to emanate from the aristocracy because the aristocracy believes education will "take them [the poor] out of the station assigned them by nature" (para. 8). In other words, education will make the lower classes more the equal of the upper classes. How does this argument relate to the education of women? What role did Wollstonecraft's society think was assigned women "by nature"? How does "nature" enter into the argument? How can nature assign women roles that would make them inferior to men? Could such an argument about the inferiority of women be made today on the basis of what women's natural station in life must be?

4. *Example* In what sense is the education of women critical to creating a democratic mode of government? In what sense does the education of women help achieve the democratic ideal of equality? Is Wollstonecraft's argument an example that defends democracy? What examples from your personal experience can you offer to demonstrate how education can make women equal to men? What examples from current events can you offer that show how educating women fosters democracy?

5. *Response* Wollstonecraft refers to women as having "an immortal soul" (para. 11). Some societies have denied that women have souls, but she refers to the Christian beliefs of her readers. Why does she introduce what seems to be a religious issue into her argument? Why would the circumstances of religious belief make her argument stronger? What qualities of "an immortal soul" make the position of women problematic in her world, as Wollstonecraft interprets it? To whom is she addressing this argument? Why would they pay attention to an argument from religion? To what extent do you feel this is an important part of the argument?

Comparing Ideas

1. Mary Wollstonecraft has been said to have had a wide influence on later political writers. She was well known in France, as she was in England and the United States. By comparing their work, construct an argument that defends the idea that Alexis de Tocqueville (p. 84) not only knew Wollstonecraft's work but also defended her view in his

own work. Tocqueville talks about rights in general, but what alerts you that he was thinking of the rights that Wollstonecraft valued as well as those that James Madison (p. 65) and the Marquis de Lafayette (p. 71) valued?

2. The title of Mary Wollstonecraft's book emphasizes the rights of women. What influences seem to come from the Bill of Rights (p. 65) and from the Declaration of the Rights of Man and Citizen (p. 71), both of which were widely discussed in France and England in Wollstonecraft's lifetime? What rights does she add that pertain particularly to women? How might she have written the Declaration of the Rights of Man and Citizen if she had been given the chance?

ALEXIS
DE TOCQUEVILLE

© Adocs photo/Corbis

The French aristocrat **ALEXIS DE TOCQUE-VILLE** (1805–1859) was born to parents who had barely escaped execution during the French Revolution (1789). After an exile in England they returned to France, where they helped Tocqueville begin a career in law that resulted in his appointment to a minor position in Versailles. That position ultimately allowed him to travel to the United States as an inspector of American prisons. His concern for prisons was soon replaced by his fascination with the way democracy worked in all the states he visited.

Because the United States had done away with aristocracy, Tocqueville studied American policies with great personal interest. He was impressed by the sense of equality that almost every American he met enjoyed. His book *Democracy in America* (1835; 1840) remains one of the most important and thorough analyses of the function of democracy as imagined by the founding fathers.

When Tocqueville arrived in America, there were twenty-four states and a population of thirteen million. He regarded the country as still young. Andrew Jackson (1767–1849), the president at the time of Tocqueville's travels, was born in the backwoods of Carolina and was an example of an American's ability to rise in social station. A wartime general, Jackson defeated the British at New Orleans in 1812. He was often coarse and rough, but Tocqueville observed that the people loved him.

Tocqueville also saw that women in the United States shared the sense of equality common to all the men he met. He expected that the nation would eventually grant rights to women equal to those of men. Noting American materialism, in *Democracy in America* in a section discussing honor in the United States, he said, "To clear, cultivate, and transform the realm of this vast uninhabited continent of his, the American must have the daily support of some energetic passion which can only be the love of money. This love of money has, therefore, never been stigmatized in America and, provided that it does not exceed the limits set by the public order, it is held in high esteem." He was also impressed by the apparent absence of the hand of government as well as the freedom the average citizen enjoyed and the essential practicality of the people he met.

Be sure to practice prereading techniques for a careful, annotated reading of Tocqueville's essay. For a review of prereading strategies, see pages 4–9.

The Idea of Rights in the United States

No great nation is without some idea of rights — How such an idea can be imparted to a nation — Respect for rights in the United States — Source of that respect.

NEXT TO the general conception of virtue, I know of none finer than that of rights, or rather these two ideas are inseparable. The idea of rights is no more than the concept of virtue applied to the world of politics.

Men clarified the definition of license and tyranny by means of the idea of rights. By the light of this idea, each man has achieved an independence without arrogance and an obedience which avoids humiliation. The man who submits to violence bends beneath the degradation; but when he obeys the right to give orders which he acknowledges in his fellow man, to some degree he rises above the very person giving him commands. No great man can exist without virtue; no great nation can exist without respect for rights; one might almost say that there is no society without such respect. For what sort of gathering of rational and intelligent beings have you got where force is the sole bond between them?

I am wondering how, in our time, the idea of rights can be taught to men in order to insert it, so to speak, into their sensual experience. I see only one way and that is to give them the peaceful use of certain rights. That indeed happens with children who are men except in strength and experience. When the child begins to move in the world of external objects, instinct leads him to make use of everything which falls into his grasp. He has no idea of other people's property nor of existence itself; but as he grows aware of the value of things and realizes that he too can be deprived of them, he becomes more circumspect and in the end respects in his fellows what he wants them to respect in him.

What a child does with his toys, later a man does with his belongings. Why in America, this land of democracy par excellence, does no one raise that outcry against property in general which often echoes throughout Europe? Do I need to explain? In America, the proletariat does not exist. Since each man has some private possessions to protect, he acknowledges the right, in principle, to own property.

It is the same in the world of politics. In America, the common man has 5 a lofty conception of political rights because he has such rights himself; he does not attack those of others so as to avoid having his own violated. And whereas in Europe this same man would be reluctant to obey even a sovereign authority, the American obeys without a murmur the authority of the lowest magistrate.

This truth is displayed right down to the smallest details of a nation's life. In France, there are few pleasures exclusively reserved for the upper classes of society; the poor man is admitted almost everywhere the rich are; thus he behaves in a seemly way and respects everything which contributes to the enjoyment he is sharing. In England, where the wealthy have the privilege of enjoying themselves as well as the monopoly of power, the complaint is that when the poor man manages to steal furtively into the exclusive haunts of the rich, he likes to cause pointless damage there. Why be surprised at that? Trouble has been taken to see that he has nothing to lose.

Democratic government allows the idea of political rights to filter down to the least of its citizens, just as the division of possessions places the idea of the right to property within the general grasp of all men. That, in my view, is one of its greatest merits.

I am not saying that teaching all men to avail themselves of their political rights is an easy task; I simply say that, when that aim is achieved, the results are great.

And I would add that if ever there was a century when such an undertaking might be attempted, that century is ours.

Do you not see the decline of religions and the disappearance of the 10 divine conception of rights? Do you not realize that morals are changing and with them the moral notion of rights is being removed?

Do you not notice how, on all sides, beliefs are ceding place to rationality and feelings to calculations? If, amid this general upheaval, you fail to link the idea of rights to individual self-interest, which is the only fixed point in the human heart, what else have you got to rule the world except fear?

So, when I am told that laws are weak and the governed are in revolt, that passions are strong, that virtue is powerless and that in this situation one must not even contemplate increasing democratic rights, my reply is that these are the very things one must contemplate. And, in truth, I think that governments have an even greater incentive to do so than society, for governments perish but society cannot die. However, I have no wish to exploit the example of America too far.

In America, the people have been endowed with political rights at a time when it was difficult for them to abuse them because citizens were few and their customs simple. As they have grown, Americans have not really increased democratic powers, merely extended their domain.

There can be no doubt that the moment of granting political rights to a nation hitherto deprived of them is a time of crisis, one that is often necessary but always perilous.

The child kills when unaware of the value of life; he carries off another's 15 property before realizing that his own may be snatched away. The common man, from the moment that he is granted political rights, stands, in relation to those rights, in the same position as a child faced with the whole of nature. It is then that the famous phrase can be applied to him: *Homo puer robustus.*[1]

> *"Democratic government allows the idea of political rights to filter down to the least of its citizens, just as the division of possessions places the idea of the right to property within the general grasp of all men."*

The truth is evident in America itself. Those states where citizens have enjoyed their rights for the longest time are the ones who still know how best to use them.

It cannot be repeated too often: nothing is more fertile in wondrous effects than the art of being free but nothing is harder than freedom's apprenticeship. The same is not true of tyranny, which often advertises itself as the cure of all sufferings, the supporter of just rights, the upholder of the oppressed and the founder of order. Nations are lulled to sleep amid the brief period of prosperity it produces and when they do wake up, wretched they are indeed. On the other hand, freedom is usually born in stormy weather, growing with great difficulty amid civil disturbances. Only when it is already old can one recognize its advantages.

Understanding Ideas

1. What does Tocqueville mean by "[t]he idea of rights is no more than the concept of virtue applied to the world of politics" (para. 1)?

2. How does democracy benefit the rights of "the least of its citizens" (para. 7)?

---

[1] ***Homo puer robustus*** A man is a boy with strength.

3. Why does Tocqueville place a great deal of emphasis on property?

4. Why does Tocqueville use the comparison of a child to a man when talking about political rights?

Responding to Ideas

1. *Comparison* Examine the comparison Tocqueville makes between the behavior of a child and the behavior of a man. Tocqueville says, "What a child does with his toys, later a man does with his belongings" (para. 4). To what extent does this statement help us understand the meaning of rights in any government? Why is it important for us to use this comparison as a means of understanding how the concept of rights begins to inform an individual in society? Is there any other comparison that you can bring to bear on our understanding of the meaning of rights?

2. *Analysis of Circumstances* Tocqueville says, "[W]hen I am told that laws are weak and the governed are in revolt, that passions are strong, that virtue is powerless and that in this situation one must not even contemplate increasing democratic rights, my reply is that these are the very things one must contemplate" (para. 12). To what extent do you agree with Tocqueville? What current circumstances would warrant us to listen to what he says here? How should we behave? How does this statement relate to events in our time?

3. *Example* At one point, Tocqueville says that in France after the Revolution, there are very "few pleasures exclusively reserved for the upper classes of society; the poor man is admitted almost everywhere the rich are" (para. 6). Is this true in the modern democracy in which you live? If possible, give concrete examples of instances in which Tocqueville's observation is true or false in modern society. What do the examples you provide say about rights in contemporary democracies?

4. *Cause and Effect* Tocqueville says that "no great nation can exist without respect for rights; one might almost say that there is no society without such respect. For what sort of gathering of rational and intelligent beings have you got where force is the sole bond between them?" (para. 2). To what extent do you feel Tocqueville is right? Tyranny exists in our modern world. How do nations that restrict the rights of their citizens function? Tocqueville says such nations will not survive. What is your view on the likelihood of their survival?

5. *Comparison* Near the end of this passage, Tocqueville introduces the question of religion, but he tells us that "beliefs are ceding place to rationality" (para. 11). Further, he bases the concept of rights on

self-interest as "the only fixed point in the human heart" (para. 11). Examine, compare, and contrast the concepts based in these sentences (and the paragraph in which they appear). Explain what you think he means; then examine our social order and determine how self-interest helps guarantee our rights in a democracy.

6. *Response* Define the political rights that Tocqueville recommends to a democratic government. He read the Bill of Rights and the Declaration of the Rights of Man and Citizen as well as Thomas Paine's (1737–1809) *The Rights of Man* (1791), which was a best-seller. He connects rights with virtue in his first paragraph: "The idea of rights is no more than the concept of virtue applied to the world of politics." Explain how the rest of the passage defines that statement. How is virtue connected to the concept of political rights?

Comparing Ideas

1. Alexis de Tocqueville places a considerable emphasis on property rights. Property rights are also mentioned in James Madison's Bill of Rights (p. 65) and the Marquis de Lafayette's Declaration of the Rights of Man and Citizen (p. 71). Why is there so much emphasis on property rights in the declaration of revolutionary governments such as the United States and France? Examine the language used in these documents and explain the importance of property rights in good government. Is the concern for property a form of materialism? If so, why do idealists say so much about property rights?

2. In "The Aim of Man" (p. 374), Aristotle talks about the question of virtue and the life of virtue. At the same time, he talks about political ideas being of extremely high value. Alexis de Tocqueville, too, talks about virtue in relation to the idea of people's rights in a democracy. Write a comparative essay that links the rights that Tocqueville considers most important with Aristotle's concept of happiness. Aristotle tells us that happiness is the primary goal of humankind and that a life of virtue is needed to achieve it. How does protecting the rights of people help produce happiness in a democracy?

EMILE DURKHEIM

© Corbis

EMILE DURKHEIM (1858–1917) is known as the father of modern sociology, which was an area of academic study that had not existed before he started his work. Although he was born in eastern France to a family that had traditionally trained its men to be rabbis, he was an agnostic for most of his life. Because he studied at Lycée Louis-le-Grand, the most elite of the secondary schools in Paris, and went on to the École Normale Supérieure, which produced most of France's intellectuals, Durkheim must be considered one of the intellectual elites about whom he writes in the following essay.

The work Durkheim did in sociology emphasizes social structures and the restrictions they place on people. He was particularly interested in religious organizations and saw that, in France, Protestantism was more varied than Catholicism and placed fewer restrictions on its adherents. Protestantism was looser in structure because there were more choices to be made. Catholicism held to a more rigid system of beliefs and aimed at a moral absolutism (i.e., something was either right or wrong, without room for moral ambiguity). Thus, it was less liberal in its practices. Among his many books is *The Elementary Forms of Religious Life* (1912), which outlines some of his important research.

Another of Durkeim's books, *Suicide: A Study in Sociology* (1897), grew out of his research that suggested suicide was not a problem of individuals but a problem of societies. He found that some suicides were the result of the victims having lived in a society without a clear sense of social norms. On the other hand, he also found that, for some individuals, living in highly regulated societies produced *anomie*, a form of restlessness and lack of direction, which sometimes resulted in suicide. His research suggested that Protestants were more likely to commit suicide than Catholics.

Durkheim, a Jew with a German name, was under suspicion during World War I, but he was an ardent supporter of the French cause. His only son, Andre, himself a sociologist, was killed in 1915 in action. Durkheim died soon after, at the age of fifty-nine.

Be sure to practice prereading techniques for a careful, annotated reading of Durkheim's essay. For a review of prereading strategies, see pages 4–9. ⊞

The Intellectual Elite and Democracy

WRITERS AND scholars are citizens. It is therefore obvious that they have a strict duty to participate in public life. It remains to be seen in what form and to what extent.

Men of thought and imagination, they would not seem to be particularly predestined to a properly political career. For that demands, above all, the qualities of a man of action. Even those whose profession is to contemplate societies, even the historian and the sociologist, do not seem to me more fit for these active functions than the man of letters or the naturalist; for it is possible to have a genius for discovering the general laws which explain social facts of the past without necessarily having the practical sense which allows one to divine the course of action which the condition of a given people at a given moment in its history requires. Just as a great physiologist is generally a mediocre clinician, a sociologist has every chance of making a very incomplete statesman. It is no doubt good that intellectuals be represented in deliberative assemblies. Aside from the fact that their culture permits them to bring to deliberations elements of information which are not negligible, they are more qualified than anyone to defend before the public powers the interests of the arts and sciences. But it is not necessary that they be numerous in the parliament in order to perform this task. Moreover, we may wonder whether — except for a few exceptional cases of eminently gifted geniuses — it is possible to become a deputy or senator without ceasing, to the same degree, to be a writer or a scholar, since these two types of functions imply so different an orientation of mind (*esprit*) and will!

What I mean is that above all our action must be exerted through books, seminars, and popular education. Above all, we must be *advisers, educators*. It is our function to help our contemporaries know themselves in their ideas and in their feelings, far more than to govern them. And in the state of mental confusion in which we live, what is a more useful role to play? More-over, we will perform it that much better for having thus limited our ambi-tion. We will gain the confidence of the people all the more easily if we are attributed fewer selfish, hidden motives. The lecturer of today must not be suspected to be the candidate of tomorrow.

It has, however, been said that the mob was not made to understand the intellectuals, and it is democracy and its so-called dull-witted spirit that have been blamed for the sort of political indifference scholars and artists have evinced during the first twenty years of our Third Republic.[1]

"What I mean is that above all our action must be exerted through books, seminars, and popular education. Above all, we must be advisers, educators."

But what shows how groundless this explanation is, is that this indifference was ended as soon as a great moral and social problem was posed before the country. The lengthy abstention which previously existed, therefore, came quite simply from the absence of any question likely to impas-sion. Our political life was languishing mis-erably in questions of personalities. We were divided over who should have the power. But there was no great impersonal cause to which to consecrate ourselves, no lofty goal to which our wills could cling. We therefore fol-lowed, more or less distractedly, the petty incidents of daily politics without experiencing the need to intervene. But as soon as a grave question of prin-ciple was raised, the scholars were seen to leave their laboratories, the learned to leave their libraries to draw nearer the masses, to involve them-selves in life; and the experience has proved that they know how to make themselves heard.

The moral agitation to which these events gave rise has not been extin- 5 guished, and I am among those who think that it must not be extinguished. For it is necessary. It was our former apathy that was abnormal and which constituted a danger. For better or for worse, the critical period begun with the fall of the *ancien régime*[2] has not ended. It is better to recognize it than to abandon ourselves to a deceptive security. Our hour of repose has not struck. There is too much to do for us not to keep our social energies per-petually mobilized. That is why I believe the course of political events in the

[1] **Third Republic** Government of France from 1870 to 1940, which was intended to be transitional but ended up lasting until the occupation by Germany in World War II.

[2] *ancien régime* Literally, the old order. A reference to the traditional monarchy of France, which ended with the beheading of Louis XVI (1793) during the French Revolution.

last four years preferable to those which preceded them. They have succeeded in maintaining a lasting current of collective activity of considerable intensity. To be sure, I am far from thinking that anticlericalism is enough; indeed, I hope to see society soon attach itself to more objective ends. But the essential thing is not to let ourselves fall back into the state of moral stagnation in which we so long tarried.

Understanding Ideas

1. Who, among the population, is considered to be the intellectual elite?
2. According to Emile Durkheim, why are "men of thought and imagination" less suited for political office than "a man of action" (para. 2)?
3. Who is the "mob" (para. 4), and what is its relation to democracy?
4. How must the intellectual elite participate in public life?

Responding to Ideas

1. *Analysis of Circumstances* Durkheim begins by saying, "Writers and scholars are citizens. It is therefore obvious that they have a strict duty to participate in public life" (para. 1). Is it obvious to you that they have a strict duty to take part in the public life of a democracy? Examine the roles that Durkheim suggests they take. Then examine the roles that you see intellectuals taking in your society. Think in terms of popular books, magazine articles, and television interviews and interviewers, as well as political and other bloggers. Are our intellectuals taking an adequate role in public life?

2. *Comparison* Is it possible that there is a contradiction implied by the title of this essay, "The Intellectual Elite and Democracy"? If equality is one of the chief achievements in a democracy, why would we want to pay more attention to a writer or scholar than to a fashion designer or police officer? In a brief essay, defend the view that a democracy will or will not benefit from giving authority to any elite, whether that person is an intellectual, an athlete, or a spiritual adviser. Is the concept of elitism at odds with democracy? Is it in line with guaranteeing the rights of citizens to express themselves?

3. *Research* Throughout this essay, Durkheim seems to be saying that the intellectual elite are unprepared to take a serious leadership role in government. He would not support a major scholar becoming

president, for instance. He would not vote for a sociologist who wanted to be the governor of a state. Do some research into the backgrounds of some of our presidents to see which of them could be considered among the intellectual elite and how well they did in office. You might begin with Thomas Jefferson, William Howard Taft, Herbert Hoover, Woodrow Wilson, Jimmy Carter, Bill Clinton, or Barack Obama.

4. *Research* For the purpose of comparison, examine the achievements of the presidents who have been considered men of action: George Washington, Andrew Jackson, Zachary Taylor, Ulysses S. Grant, Theodore Roosevelt, and Dwight D. Eisenhower. How well did these presidents do in maintaining the health and vigor of American democracy? To what extent did any of them benefit from advice from elite intellectuals?

5. *Response* Durkheim wrote this essay in 1904 when he felt that a general apathy had spread through French society. The term *apathy* is used frequently to describe the social circumstances of our society today. He also describes a "moral agitation" as being present in society. To what extent could you describe your social world as reflecting a general apathy? In what area of your social circumstances do you notice a moral agitation? In what aspect of your experience do you notice the existence of apathy? How is a democracy affected by the apathy of its citizens? What are the symptoms of such apathy? What are the results of such apathy?

6. *Testimony* When he considers what role the intellectual elite should take in public life, Durkheim says, "It is our function to help our contemporaries know themselves in their ideas and in their feelings, far more than to govern them" (para. 3). Defend or attack this view by reference to popular magazines such as *The Atlantic*, *American Scholar*, *The Economist*, *Foreign Affairs*, *Time*, or *World Affairs*. How good a job do intellectuals do in advising those who govern our democracy? What are their chief concerns? To what extent do they expand your understanding and help you know how to act in our society?

Comparing Ideas

1. Plato (p. 56) talks about the risk of democracy possibly encouraging mob rule. Emile Durkheim is concerned with the role of the intellectual elite in a democracy. Compare the views of these writers on the role of the intellectual in society. Plato is uneasy because he feels that the least capable people may rule, but Durkheim's thinking takes him in another direction. Examine their thoughts and attempt to clarify the positions

they seem to have in common as well as the positions they seem to have in disagreement. What is your view on the fears Plato raises?

2. Cornel West (p. 111) has an optimistic view of the way democracy has developed in the United States. Compare his thinking with that of Emile Durkheim. Is Durkheim as optimistic as West? Would West defend the proposition Durkheim offers, which essentially tells us that intellectuals are not suited to govern in a democracy? West is himself a well-known public intellectual who comments widely on important political issues. How much do these two writers agree on important issues? How much do they disagree?

Michael Marsland/Yale University

ROBERT A.
DAHL

ROBERT A. DAHL (1915–2014) was a distinguished professor of political science until his retirement from Yale University. His views on the nature of democracy have been developed in a number of his most important books, such as *A Preface to Democratic Theory* (1956); *Size and Democracy* (1973), coauthored with Edward R. Tufte; *A Preface to Economic Democracy* (1985); *On Democracy* (1998); and *How Democratic Is the American Constitution?* (2001). His views on the Constitution suggest that if the founders of the nation had better understood the nature of the democracy they were creating, they might have made more effort to enfranchise all citizens. In his books, he has recognized a number of the problems that democracies occasionally have, such as the difficulties some minorities have dealing with the sometimes restrictive decisions of majority rule.

Dahl saw that democracy is an ideal and believed that no democracy could be perfect. He felt that there were five important requirements in any thoroughly functional democracy:

1. Real participation in matters of government
2. All votes counting equally
3. A full understanding of the political choices offered
4. Control over what electoral decisions need to be considered
5. All citizens participating equally in government

While Dahl does not regard any democracy as ideal, he does assert that the reasons for preferring a democratic government over any other are absolutely compelling.

Dahl's techniques are typical of a carefully structured argument. He makes a claim — "democracies do not fight wars with one another" (para. 50) — and then he marshals the evidence from contemporary history, concentrating on events in the twentieth century. He admits that the reasons are not fully understood, but he tries to suggest a few possibilities, such as the likelihood that trade relationships are so interwoven among democracies that any war among them would be counterproductive.

When he contends that democracies produce more prosperity than nondemocratic governments, he does not provide a review of history. Instead, his energies go into his review of the reasons that support his claim. Most of these concern praise for the idea of a market economy, which best functions in a free society and produces wealth. Dahl also admits, however, that wealth in a democracy will not be distributed equally. In a democracy, the result of the free-market system is usually that a small number of people will be much wealthier than the average citizen. The dark side of that fact is the lack of "full political equality among the citizens of a democratic country" (para. 61). Nonetheless, a "modern democratic country is likely also to be a rich country" (para. 58), according to Dahl.

Be sure to practice prereading techniques for a careful, annotated reading of Dahl's essay. For a review of prereading strategies, see pages 4–9. ⊞

Why Democracy?

WHY SHOULD we support democracy? More specifically, why should we support democracy in governing the state? The state, remember, is a unique association whose government possesses an extraordinary capacity for obtaining compliance with its rules by (among other means) force, coercion, and violence. Are there no better ways of governing a state? Would a nondemocratic system of government be better?

Until the twentieth century, most of the world proclaimed the superiority of nondemocratic systems both in theory and in practice. Until very recently, a preponderant majority of human beings — at times, all — have been subject to nondemocratic rulers. And the heads of nondemocratic regimes have usually tried to justify their rule by invoking the ancient and persistent claim that most people are just not competent to participate in governing a state. Most people would be better off, this argument goes, if they would only leave the complicated business of governing to those wiser than they — a minority at most, perhaps only one person. In practice, these rationalizations were never quite enough, so where argument left off coercion took over. Most people never explicitly consented to be ruled by their self-assigned superiors; they were forced to do so. This older view — and practice — is by no means dead even today. In one form or another the contest over government by "the one, the few, or the many" is still with us.

In the face of so much history, why should we believe that democracy is a better way of governing the state than any nondemocratic alternative? Let me count the reasons.

In comparison with any feasible alternative to it, democracy has at least ten advantages. . . .

1. *Democracy helps to prevent government by cruel and vicious* 5 *autocrats.*

Perhaps the most fundamental and persistent problem in politics is to avoid autocratic rule. Throughout all recorded history, including our own times, leaders driven by megalomania, paranoia, self-interest, ideology, nationalism, religious belief, convictions of innate superiority, or sheer emotion and impulse have exploited the state's exceptional capacities for coercion and violence to serve their own ends. The human costs of despotic rule rival those of disease, famine, and war.

Consider a few examples from the twentieth century. Under Joseph Stalin's rule in the Soviet Union (1929–1953), many millions of persons were jailed for political reasons, often because of Stalin's paranoid fear of conspiracies against him. An estimated twenty million people died in labor camps, were executed for political reasons, or died from the famine (1932–33) that resulted when Stalin compelled peasants to join state-run farms. Though another twenty million victims of Stalin's rule may have managed to survive, they suffered cruelly. Or consider Adolph Hitler, the autocratic ruler of Nazi Germany (1933–1945). Not counting tens of millions of military and civilian casualties resulting from World War II, Hitler was directly responsible for the death of six million Jews in concentration camps as well as innumerable opponents, Poles, gypsies, homosexuals, and members of other groups he wished to exterminate. Under the despotic leadership of Pol Pot in Cambodia (1975–1979), the Khmer Rouge killed a quarter of the Cambodian population: an instance, one might say, of self-inflicted genocide. So great was Pol Pot's fear of the educated classes that they were almost exterminated: wearing spectacles or having uncalloused hands was quite literally a death warrant.

To be sure, the history of popular rule is not without its own serious blemishes. Like all governments, popular governments have sometimes acted unjustly or cruelly toward people outside their borders, people living in other states — foreigners, colonials, and so on. In this respect popular governments have behaved no worse toward outsiders than nondemocratic governments, and often they have behaved better. In some cases, as in India, the colonial power has contributed inadvertently or intentionally to the creation of democratic beliefs and institutions. Yet we should not condone the injustices often shown by democratic countries toward outsiders, for in so acting they contradict a fundamental moral principle that . . . helps to justify political equality among the citizens of a democracy. The only solution to this contradiction may be a universal code of human rights that is effectively enforced throughout the world. Important as this problem and its solution are, however, they are beyond scope of this small book.

More directly challenging to democratic ideas and practices is the harm inflicted by popular governments on persons who live within their jurisdiction and are compelled to obey its laws but who are deprived of rights to participate in governing. Although these people are governed, they do not govern. Fortunately, the solution to this problem is obvious, if not always easy to carry out: democratic rights should be extended to members of the

> *"The human costs of despotic rule rival those of disease, famine, and war."*

excluded groups. This solution was in fact widely adopted in the nineteenth and early twentieth centuries when previous limits on the suffrage were abolished and universal adult suffrage became a standard aspect of democratic government.

But wait! you might say. Can't democratic governments also inflict harm 10 on a minority of citizens who do possess voting rights but are outvoted by majorities? Isn't this what we mean by "the tyranny of the majority"?

I wish the answer were simple. Alas! It is much more complicated than you might suppose. The complications arise because virtually every law or public policy, whether adopted by a democratic majority, an oligarchic minority, or a benign dictator, is bound to inflict some harm on some persons. Simply put, the issue is not whether a government can design all its laws so that none ever injures the interests of any citizen. No government, not even a democratic government, could uphold such a claim. The issue is whether in the long run a democratic process is likely to do less harm to the fundamental rights and interests of its citizens than any nondemocratic alternative. If only because democratic governments prevent abusive autocracies from ruling, they meet this requirement better than nondemocratic governments.

Yet just because democracies are far less tyrannical than nondemocratic regimes, democratic citizens can hardly afford to be complacent. We cannot reasonably justify the commission of a lesser crime because others commit larger crimes. Even when a democratic country, following democratic procedures, inflicts an injustice the result is still . . . an injustice. Majority might does not make majority right.

However, there are other reasons for believing that democracies are likely to be more just and more respectful of basic human interests than nondemocracies.

   2. *Democracy guarantees its citizens a number of fundamental rights that nondemocratic systems do not, and cannot, grant.*

   Democracy is not only a process of governing. Because rights are nec- 15 essary elements in democratic political institutions, democracy is inherently also a system of rights. Rights are among the essential building blocks of a democratic process of government.

   Consider, for a moment, the democratic standards described in the last chapter. Is it not self-evident that in order to satisfy these standards a political system would necessarily have to insure its citizens certain rights? Take effective participation: to meet that standard, would not its citizens necessarily possess a *right* to participate and a *right* to express their views on political matters, to hear what other citizens have to say, to discuss political matters with other citizens? Or consider what the criterion of voting equality requires: citizens must have a *right* to vote and to have their votes counted fairly. So with the other democratic standards: clearly citizens must have a *right* to investigate alternatives, a *right* to participate in deciding how and what should go on the agenda, and so on.

   By definition, no nondemocratic system allows its citizens (or subjects) this broad array of political rights. If any political system were to do so, it would, by definition, become a democracy!

   Yet the difference is not just a trivial matter of definitions. To satisfy the requirements of democracy, the rights inherent in it must actually be available to citizens. To promise democratic rights in writing, in law, or even in a constitutional document is not enough. The rights must be effectively enforced and effectively available to citizens in practice. If they are not, then to that extent the political system is not democratic, despite what its rulers claim, and the trappings of "democracy" are merely a facade for nondemocratic rule.

   Because of the appeal of democratic ideas, in the twentieth century despotic rulers have often cloaked their rule with a show of "democracy" and "elections." Imagine, however, that in such a country all the rights necessary to democracy somehow become, realistically speaking, available to citizens. Then the country has made a transition to democracy — as happened with great frequency during the last half of the twentieth century.

   At this point you might want to object that freedom of speech, let us say, 20 won't exist just because it is a part of the very definition of democracy. Who cares about definitions? Surely, you will say, the connection must be something more than definitional. And you are, of course, correct. Institutions that provide for and protect basic democratic rights and opportunities are necessary to democracy: not simply as a logically necessary condition but as an empirically necessary condition in order for democracy to exist.

   Even so, you might ask, isn't this just theory, abstractions, the game of theorists, philosophers, and other intellectuals? Surely, you may add, it would be foolish to think that the support of a few philosophers is enough to create and maintain democracy. And you would, of course, be right. [Among] . . . the conditions that increase the chances that democracy will be maintained . . . is the existence of fairly widespread democratic beliefs among citizens and leaders, including beliefs in the rights and opportunities necessary to democracy.

Fortunately, the need for these rights and opportunities is not so obscure that it lies beyond the comprehension of ordinary citizens and their political leaders. To quite ordinary Americans in the late eighteenth century, for example, it was fairly obvious that they could not have a democratic republic without freedom of expression. One of the first actions of Thomas Jefferson[1] after he was elected to the presidency in 1800 was to bring an end to the infamous Alien and Sedition Acts enacted under his predecessor, John Adams,[2] which would have stifled political expression. In doing so Jefferson responded not only to his own convictions but, it appears, to views widely held among ordinary American citizens in his time. If and when many citizens fail to understand that democracy requires certain fundamental rights, or fail to support the political, administrative, and judicial institutions that protect those rights, then their democracy is in danger.

Fortunately, this danger is somewhat reduced by a third benefit of democratic systems.

3. *Democracy insures its citizens a broader range of personal freedom than any feasible alternative to it.*

In addition to all the rights, freedoms, and opportunities that are strictly 25 necessary in order for a government to be democratic, citizens in a democracy are certain to enjoy an even more extensive array of freedoms. A belief in the desirability of democracy does not exist in isolation from other beliefs. For most people it is a part of a cluster of beliefs. Included in this cluster is the belief that freedom of expression, for example, is desirable in itself. In the universe of values or goods, democracy has a crucial place. But it is not the only good. Like the other rights essential to a democratic process, free expression has its own value because it is instrumental to moral autonomy, moral judgment, and a good life.

What is more, democracy could not long exist unless its citizens manage to create and maintain a supportive political culture, indeed a general culture supportive of these ideals and practices. The relation between a democratic system of government and the democratic culture that supports it is complex. . . . Suffice it to say here that a democratic culture is almost certain to emphasize the value of personal freedom and

---

[1] **Thomas Jefferson** (1743–1826) An author of the Constitution and third president of the United States (1801–1809).

[2] **John Adams** (1735–1826) Second president of the United States (1797–1801).

thus to provide support for additional rights and liberties. What the Greek statesman Pericles[3] said of Athenian democracy in 431 B.C.E. applies equally to modern democracy: "The freedom we enjoy in our government extends also to our ordinary life."

To be sure, the assertion that a democratic state provides a broader range of freedom than any feasible alternative would be challenged by one who believed that we would all gain greater freedom if the state were abolished entirely: the audacious claim of anarchists. But if you try to imagine a world with no state at all, where every person respects the fundamental rights of every other and all matters requiring collective decisions are settled peacefully by unanimous agreement, you will surely conclude, as most people do, that it is impossible. Coercion of some persons by other persons, groups, or organizations would be all too likely: for example, by persons, groups, or organizations intending to rob others of the fruits of their labor, to enslave or dominate those weaker than themselves, to impose their own rule on others, or, indeed, to re-create a coercive state in order to secure their own domination. But if the abolition of the state would produce unbearable violence and disorder — "anarchy" in its popular meaning — then a good state would be superior to the bad state that is likely to follow upon the heels of anarchy.

If we reject anarchism and assume the need for a state, then a state with a democratic government will provide a broader range of freedom than any other.

4. *Democracy helps people to protect their own fundamental interests.*

Everyone, or nearly everyone, wants certain things: survival, food, shel- 30 ter, health, love, respect, security, family, friends, satisfying work, leisure, and others. The specific pattern of your wants will probably differ from the specific pattern of another's. Like most people, you will surely want to exercise some control over the factors that determine whether and to what extent you can satisfy your wants — some freedom of choice, an opportunity to shape your life in accordance with your own goals, preferences, tastes, values, commitments, beliefs. Democracy protects this freedom and opportunity better than any alternative political system that has ever been devised. No one has put the argument more forcefully than John Stuart Mill.[4]

A principle "of as universal truth and applicability as any general propositions which can be laid down respecting human affairs," he wrote, " . . . is that the rights and interests of every or any person are secure from being

---

[3] **Pericles** (c. 495–439 B.C.E.) Athens's greatest general and statesman and a champion of democracy.

[4] **John Stuart Mill** (1806–1873) English political philosopher whose *Considerations on Representative Government* (1861) is a major defense of democracy.

disregarded when the person is himself able, and habitually disposed, to stand up for them. . . . Human beings are only secure from evil at the hands of others in proportion as they have the power of being, and are, self-*protecting*." You can protect your rights and interests from abuse by government, and by those who influence or control government, he went on to say, only if you can participate fully in determining the conduct of the government. Therefore, he concluded, "nothing less can be ultimately desirable than the admission of all to a share in the sovereign power of the state," that is, a democratic government.

Mill was surely right. To be sure, even if you are included in the electorate of a democratic state you cannot be certain that all your interests will be adequately protected; but if you are excluded you can be pretty sure that your interests will be seriously injured by neglect or outright damage. Better inclusion than exclusion!

Democracy is uniquely related to freedom in still another way.

5. *Only a democratic government can provide a maximum opportunity for persons to exercise the freedom of self-determination — that is, to live under laws of their own choosing.*

No normal human being can enjoy a satisfactory life except by living in   35 association with other persons. But living in association with others has a price: you cannot always do just what you like. As you left your childhood behind, you learned a basic fact of life: what you would like to do sometimes conflicts with what others would like to do. You have also learned that the group or groups to which you want to belong follow certain rules or practices that as a member you, too, will have to obey. Consequently, if you cannot simply impose your wishes by force, then you must find a way to resolve your differences peacefully, perhaps by agreement.

Thus a question arises that has proved deeply perplexing in both theory and practice. How can you choose the rules that you are obliged by your group to obey? Because of the state's exceptional capacity to enforce its laws by coercion, the question is particularly relevant to your position as a citizen (or subject) of a state. How can you both be free to choose the laws that are to be enforced by the state and yet, having chosen them, not be free to disobey them?

If you and your fellow citizens always agreed, the solution would be easy: you would all simply agree unanimously on the laws. Indeed, in these circumstances you might have no need for laws, except perhaps to serve as a reminder; in obeying the rules you would be obeying yourself. In effect the problem would vanish, and the complete harmony between you and your fellows would make the dream of anarchism come true. Alas! Experience shows that genuine, unforced, lasting unanimity is rare in human affairs; enduring and perfect consensus is an unattainable goal. So our difficult question remains.

If we can't reasonably expect to live in perfect harmony with all our fellow human beings, we might try instead to create a process for arriving at decisions about rules and laws that would satisfy certain reasonable criteria.

- The process would insure that before a law is enacted you and all other citizens will have an opportunity to make your views known.

- You will be guaranteed opportunities for discussion, deliberation, negotiation, and compromise that in the best circumstances might lead to a law that everyone will find satisfactory.

- In the more likely event that unanimity cannot be achieved, the proposed law that has the greatest number of supporters will be enacted.

These criteria, you will notice, are parts of the ideal democratic process. . . . Although that process cannot guarantee that all the members will literally live under laws of their own choosing, it expands self-determination to its maximum feasible limits. Even when you are among the outvoted members whose preferred option is rejected by the majority of your fellow citizens, you may nonetheless decide that the process is fairer than any other that you can reasonably hope to achieve. To that extent you are exercising your freedom of self-determination by freely choosing to live under a democratic constitution rather than a nondemocratic alternative.

6. *Only a democratic government can provide a maximum opportu-* 40
nity for exercising moral responsibility.

What does it mean to say that you exercise moral responsibility? It means, I believe, that you adopt your moral principles and make decisions that depend on these principles only after you have engaged in a thoughtful process of reflection, deliberation, scrutiny, and consideration of the alternatives and their consequences. For you to be morally responsible is for you to be self-governing in the domain of morally relevant choices.

This is more demanding than most of us can hope to meet most of the time. Yet to the extent that your opportunity to live under the laws of your own choosing is limited, the scope for your moral responsibility is also limited. How can you be responsible for decisions that you cannot control? If you cannot influence the conduct of government officials, how can you be responsible for their conduct? If you are subject to collective decisions, as certainly you are, and if the democratic process maximizes your opportunity to live under laws of your own choosing, then — to an extent that no nondemocratic alternative can achieve — it also enables you to act as a morally responsible person.

7. *Democracy fosters human development more fully than any feasible alternative.*

This is a bold claim and considerably more controversial than any of the others. It is, you will notice, an empirical assertion, a claim as to facts. In principle, we should be able to test the claim by devising an appropriate way of measuring "human development" and comparing human development among people who live in democratic and nondemocratic regimes. But the task is of staggering difficulty. As a consequence, though such evidence as exists supports the proposition, we probably should regard it as an assertion that is highly plausible but unproved.

Just about everyone has views about the human qualities they think are 45 desirable or undesirable, qualities that should be developed if they are desirable and deterred if they are undesirable. Among the desirable qualities that most of us would want to foster are honesty, fairness, courage, and love. Many of us also believe that fully developed adult persons should possess the capacity for looking after themselves, for acting to take care of their interests and not simply counting on others to do so. It is desirable, many of us think, that adults should act responsibly, should weigh alternative courses of action as best they can, should consider consequences, and should take into account the rights and obli-gations of others as well as themselves. And they should possess the ability to engage in free and open discussions with others about the problems they face together.

> "How can you be responsible for decisions that you cannot control? If you cannot influence the conduct of government officials, how can you be responsible for their conduct?"

At birth, most human beings possess the potentiality for developing these qualities. Whether and how much they actually develop them depends on many circumstances, among which is the nature of the political system in which a person lives. Only democratic systems provide the conditions under which the qualities I have mentioned are likely to develop fully. All other regimes reduce, often drastically, the scope within which adults can act to protect their own interests, consider the interests of others, take responsi-bility for important decisions, and engage freely with others in a search for the best decision. A democratic government is not enough to insure that people develop these qualities, but it is essential.

8. *Only a democratic government can foster a relatively high degree of political equality.*

One of the most important reasons for preferring a democratic govern-ment is that it can achieve political equality among citizens to a much greater extent than any feasible alternative. But why should we place a value on political equality? . . . [I]t necessarily follows if we accept several reasonable assumptions that probably most of us do believe in. . . .

The advantages of democracy that I have discussed so far would tend to apply to democracies past and present. But . . . some of the political institutions of the democratic systems with which we are familiar today are a product of recent centuries; indeed, one of them, universal adult suffrage, is mainly a product of the twentieth century. These modern representative systems with full adult suffrage appear to have two additional advantages that could not necessarily be claimed for all earlier democracies and republics.

9. *Modern representative democracies do not fight wars with one* 50 *another.*

This extraordinary advantage of democratic governments was largely unpredicted and unexpected. Yet by the last decade of the twentieth century the evidence had become overwhelming. Of thirty-four international wars between 1945 and 1989 none occurred among democratic countries. What is more, "there has been little expectation of or preparation for war among them either." The observation even holds true before 1945. Well back into the nineteenth century, countries with representative governments and other democratic institutions, where a substantial part of the male population was enfranchised, did not fight wars with one another.

Of course modern democratic governments have fought wars with nondemocratic countries, as they did in World Wars I and II. They have also imposed colonial rule by military force on conquered peoples. They have sometimes interfered in the political life of other countries, even weakening or helping in the overthrow of a weak government. Until the 1980s, for example, the United States had an abysmal record of giving support to military dictatorships in Latin America; in 1954 it was instrumental in the military coup that overthrew the newly elected government of Guatemala.

Nonetheless, the remarkable fact is that modern representative democracies do not engage in war with *one another.* The reasons are not entirely clear. Probably the high levels of international trade among modern democracies predisposes them to friendliness rather than war. But it is also true that democratic citizens and leaders learn the arts of compromise. In addition, they are inclined to see people in other democratic countries as less threatening, more like themselves, more trustworthy. Finally, the practice and history of peaceful negotiations, treaties, alliances, and common defense against nondemocratic enemies reinforce the predisposition to seek peace rather than fight wars.

Thus a more democratic world promises also to be a more peaceful world.

10. *Countries with democratic governments tend to be more prosper-* 55 *ous than countries with nondemocratic governments.*

Until about two centuries ago, a common assumption among political philosophers was that democracy was best suited to a frugal people:

affluence, it was thought, was a hallmark of aristocracies, oligarchies, and monarchies, but not democracy. Yet the experience of the nineteenth and twentieth centuries demonstrated precisely the opposite. Democracies were affluent, and by comparison nondemocracies were, on the whole, poor.

The relation between affluence and democracy was particularly striking in the last half of the twentieth century. The explanation is partly to be found in the affinity between representative democracy and a market economy, in which markets are for the most part not highly regulated, workers are free to move from one place or job to another, privately owned firms compete for sales and resources, and consumers can choose among goods and services offered by competing suppliers. By the end of the twentieth century, although not all countries with market economies were democratic, all countries with democratic political systems also had market economies.

In the past two centuries a market economy has generally produced more affluence than any alternative to it. Thus the ancient wisdom has been turned on its head. Because all modern democratic countries have market economies, and a country with a market economy is likely to prosper, a modern democratic country is likely also to be a rich country.

Democracies typically possess other economic advantages over most nondemocratic systems. For one thing, democratic countries foster the education of their people; and an educated workforce is helpful to innovation and economic growth. In addition, the rule of law is usually sustained more strongly in democratic countries; courts are more independent; property rights are more secure; contractual agreements are more effectively enforced; and arbitrary intervention in economic life by government and politicians is less likely. Finally, modern economies depend on communication, and in democratic countries the barriers to communication are much lower. Seeking and exchanging information is easier, and far less dangerous than it is in most nondemocratic regimes.

> "[A] more democratic world promises also to be a more peaceful world."

In sum, despite some notable exceptions on both sides, modern democratic countries have generally tended to provide a more hospitable environment in which to achieve the advantages of market economies and economic growth than have the governments of nondemocratic regimes. 60

Yet if the affiliation between modern democracy and market economies has advantages for both, we cannot overlook an important cost that market economies impose on a democracy. Because a market economy generates economic inequality, it can also diminish the prospects for attaining full political equality among the citizens of a democratic country. . . .

It would be a grievous error to ask too much of any government, including a democratic government. Democracy cannot guarantee that its citizens will be happy, prosperous, healthy, wise, peaceful, or just. To attain these ends is beyond the capacity of any government, including a democratic government. What is more, in practice democracy has always fallen far short of its ideals. Like all previous attempts to achieve a more democratic government, modern democracies also suffer from many defects.

In spite of its flaws, however, we must never lose sight of the benefits that make democracy more desirable than any feasible alternative to it:

1. Democracy helps to prevent government by cruel and vicious autocrats.

2. Democracy guarantees its citizens a number of fundamental rights that nondemocratic systems do not, and cannot, grant.

3. Democracy insures its citizens a broader range of personal freedom than any feasible alternative to it.

4. Democracy helps people to protect their own fundamental interests.

5. Only a democratic government can provide a maximum opportunity for persons to exercise the freedom of self-determination — that is, to live under laws of their own choosing.

6. Only a democratic government can provide a maximum opportunity for exercising moral responsibility.

7. Democracy fosters human development more fully than any feasible alternative.

8. Only a democratic government can foster a relatively high degree of political equality.

9. Modern representative democracies do not fight wars with one another.

10. Countries with democratic governments tend to be more prosperous than countries with nondemocratic governments.

With all these advantages, democracy is, for most of us, a far better gamble than any attainable alternative to it.

Understanding Ideas

1. Why does Robert A. Dahl think democracies will not go to war with each other? If all nations were democratic, would there be no more wars?

2. According to Dahl, what are the economic advantages of democracies over nondemocratic governments?

3. What does Dahl feel are the threats to equality in modern democracies?

4. In Dahl's view, what rights does a democracy guarantee its citizens?

Responding to Ideas

1. ***Research*** Examine Dahl's claim that democracies are prosperous nations while nondemocratic nations are on the whole poor. Use information gathered in your research concerning the gross national product of various kinds of governments. Find out which nations contain the most billionaires and which the most millionaires. Find out which nations are the poorest by searching for the per capita income of citizens of various countries. When you analyze your information, do you find Dahl's claim to be accurate? In your essay, make your own claims and back them up with your research.

2. ***Response*** In Dahl's discussion of democracies, what role does he feel education plays? Although he does not list education as a separate benefit of a democracy, he implies that it is important. To what extent do you feel that equal access to education will increase equality in a democracy? Why would democracies be stronger when their citizens have better educational advantages?

3. ***Definition*** Dahl refers to "full political equality" (para. 63). His hope is for such political equality in a democracy. How would you define "full political equality" in a democracy? How does Dahl seem to define "full political equality"? Is political equality one of the human rights democracy guarantees? To what extent has such equality been achieved in your nation? In your state? In your city? How can a government achieve political equality in modern society?

4. ***Testimony*** In Dahl's final claims of the ten advantages of democracies, he makes absolute statements. Write an essay that takes issue with his claims. How has your experience with democratic government taught you that his claims may be overstatements? Which of them are actually realized in modern society? Which are most questionable? Which are most desirable but least achievable? What ten claims would you make in their place?

5. ***Analysis of Circumstances*** Dahl admits that a free-market democracy results in general prosperity for the nation. But he also admits that the wealth produced by a free-market democracy is not evenly distributed. Some people will be very wealthy and some people will be very poor. Write an essay that demonstrates that a free-market democracy need not have extreme wealth and extreme poverty because it

is a democracy. How can a democratic nation avoid extreme wealth and extreme poverty? Apart from excess wealth, is it possible to avoid extreme poverty in a free-market democracy? Does the inequity in wealth render a democracy undesirable?

6. *Example* Give a careful description of your views on modern democracy as you currently see them displayed by your government. Which of the five requirements for a functional democracy do you see at work? In what ways have you developed a full understanding of the political choices you are offered? How much do people you know understand about their choices? Cite a specific instance in which your choices were either very clear or very unclear to you. What specific examples can you point to that demonstrate how people feel their vote is "counted equally"? To what extent do your friends consider their right to vote a basic human right? Which parts of Dahl's argument struck you as most personally relevant to your views on democracy?

Comparing Ideas

1. Compare Robert A. Dahl's discussion of the rights that democracies guarantee with the rights that James Madison (p. 65) and the Marquis de Lafayette (p. 71) outline in their selections. How does Dahl regard the question of human rights in a democracy? How does he differ from either Madison or Lafayette? To what extent does his discussion take into account the issues of the rights of women as Mary Wollstonecraft (p. 77) outlines them? Which of the three authors — Madison, Lafayette, or Wollstonecraft — has had the most influence on Dahl's thinking about the nature of human rights?

2. In "The Value of Labor" (p. 281), Adam Smith discusses the power of self-interest in producing a prosperous nation. Robert A. Dahl talks also about the self-determination of the individual in a democracy and mentions the role of a democracy in fostering human development and protecting essential personal interests (para. 43). How close are these two writers in their understanding of the force and benefits of promoting self-interest in society?

CORNEL WEST

Everett Collections, Inc./Alamy

CORNEL WEST (b. 1953) is among America's premier African American intellectuals. Primarily a philosopher, he writes on topics from existentialism to Christianity and from politics to race matters. His appearance on talk shows and in the films *The Matrix Reloaded* and *The Matrix Revolutions* led to his commenting on the significance of those works while connecting him to popular culture. West has held professorships at Princeton, Harvard, and the Union Theological Seminary, where he is professor of theology and Christian practice.

Democracy Matters: Winning the Fight against Imperialism (2004), from which the following passage comes, addresses the influence of the United States on world politics, especially in the Middle East. West views our modern version of democracy as far from perfect. Democracy and imperialism are not comfortable with each other as far as West is concerned. The influence of American corporations and problems with corruption hold U.S. democracy back from its full expression and from fully satisfying the needs of its people. West explains that American democracy seems unaware of its hypocrisy in dealing with the Middle East as its economic forces tend toward domination. Islamic fundamentalism is antagonistic toward the United States in part because of what it perceives as both economic and military imperialism.

Ultimately, West feels that there is a historical commitment in the United States to a genuine democracy and that it is expressed most powerfully in the press for civil rights as expressed in the nonviolent principles of Martin Luther King Jr.

West writes simply but thinks deeply. His audience is the concerned citizen of any age. He begins by asking a rhetorical question, "Why vote?" It is a question asked by many young people for the very reason he begins with: the narrow polarization of the nation today has resulted in the feeling that participating in our democracy is futile. But he has profound faith in the deeper strain of American democracy, such as that expressed in the writings of Ralph Waldo Emerson, whose essays encourage the individual to think for himself or herself. Such a practice might make a difference in the logjam of contemporary politics.

He considers the conditions of white and black America and the breakdown of "the civic and social structure in the inner cities" (para. 5), which are problems that face our modern democracy. Then he considers the rise of religiosity in American politics, arriving at the view that the religious right represents a "misguided righteousness" (para. 6). This view, from a theologian, needs to be examined, but it also needs to be respected.

Be sure to practice prereading techniques for a careful, annotated reading of West's essay. For a review of prereading strategies, see pages 4–9. ⌘

The Deep Democratic Tradition in America

TO MANY, our democratic system seems so broken that they have simply lost faith that their participation could really matter. The politics of self-interest and catering to narrow special interests is so dominant that so many ask themselves, Why vote?

This disaffection stems both from the all-too-true reality of the corruptions of our system and from a deeper psychic disillusionment and disappointment. The political discourse is so formulaic, so tailored into poll-driven, focus-group-approved slogans that don't really say anything substantive or strike at the core of our lived experience; the lack of authenticity of discourse — and the underlying lack of gravitas, of penetrating insight and wisdom on the part of politicians — is numbing. But we must keep in mind that the disgust so many feel comes from a deep desire to hear more authentic expressions of insights about our lives and more genuine commitments to improving them. Many of us long for expressions of real concern both about the pain of our individual lives and about the common good — hence the power of Bill Clinton's claim that he felt our pain — as opposed to the blatant catering to base interests and to narrow elite constituencies. We long for a politics that is not about winning a political game but about producing better lives.

The reality of what we get is so far from this that the hope for the kind of authentic voice in our politics that we want to hear has come to seem almost ridiculously naive. And yet, it is the longing for such honest discourse that was surely behind the passion of the early support for Howard Dean.[1] It was no accident that he so energized younger adults in particular — they tend to be less beaten down by the disillusionments of the system. For this reason the angry anti-Bush rhetoric that Dean had to offer was for a while emotionally satisfying, but it was ultimately too limited. It lacked the substance of deeper insights and a positive democratic vision. Both the Republican "vision" and the Democratic "vision" are deeply problematic. Our national focus has become so dominated by narrow us-versus-them discourse that it has all but drowned out authentic debate over issues. Though many voters are mobilized by the increased polarization of our party politics, there is an underlying disgust about the preoccupation of our political leaders with partisan warfare.

The uninspiring nature of our national political culture has only enhanced the seductiveness of the pursuit of pleasure and of diverting entertainments, and too many of us have turned inward to a disconnected, narrowly circumscribed family and social life. White suburbanites and middle-class blacks (and others) are preoccupied with the daily pursuit of the comfort of their material lives. In many cases they literally wall themselves off into comfortable communities, both physical and social, in which they can safely avert their eyes from the ugly realities that afflict so many of our people. Because they are able to buy the cars and take the vacations they want, they are all too willing to either disregard the political and social dysfunctions afflicting the country or accept facile explanations for them.

The black community is increasingly divided, the upper and middle 5 classes as against the feeble institutions of the inner cities. Too much of the black political leadership has become caught up in the mainstream political game and has been turning away from the deep commitment to a more profound advocacy for poor blacks. Meanwhile a generation of blacks who have suffered from the cataclysmic breakdown of the civic and social structure in the inner cities are consigned to lives of extreme alienation and empty pursuit of short-term gratifications.

The emptiness of our political culture has also driven a surge of civically engaged religiosity in the form of the rise of the religious Right, with its misguided righteousness and its narrow, exclusionary, and punitive perspective on the country's social ills. The impulse to join in this massively energized movement may well come from the desire to rise above the

---

[1] **Howard Dean** (b. 1948) Former governor of Vermont and former chairperson of the Democratic Party.

emptiness of what strikes its followers as a depraved culture that has lost its moral rudder, but the movement is violating the very ethics of compassion and ecumenicalism that it professes to live by. So zealous has this movement become that it has turned into a hugely divisive and antidemocratic force in the country.

As we take a hard look at our democracy, therefore, the resurgent imperialism of the Bush[2] administration must not set the limits of our critique; repudiating the Bush administration is not enough. Turning back to multilateralism, and to tax and social policies that no longer grossly favor the already well-off, are essential missions, but we should take this challenging moment as an opportunity for a deeper soul-searching. Our democracy is suffering from more serious psychosocial ills. This is where what I call the deep democratic tradition becomes so vital.

The dissonance of being both a person who ardently believes in democratic ideals — how can we not fall in love with them if and when we are exposed to them? — and a wide-eyed realist about the dispiriting truths of everyday life in America can be alternately enraging, numbing, and crushing. But that dissonance has also provoked our most impassioned and profound indictments of America's democratic failures, from Ralph Waldo Emerson's[3] championing of the necessity of self-cultivation and his praise of John Brown's[4] radical abolitionism, to Herman Melville's[5] darkly tragic portrayal of Ahab's crazed imperialistic nihilism, to Mark Twain's[6] sly indictment of white supremacy, to James Baldwin's[7] and Toni Morrison's[8] profound explorations of the psychic scars of racism, and to Tupac Shakur's[9] eloquent outrage. The violence-obsessed and greed-driven elements of American culture project themselves out to the world so powerfully — and offensively — that the world has developed a problematic love-hate relationship with America, the ugly extremes of which we are now forced to confront. But legions of Americans have been equally affronted by the perversion of our democratic ideals.

---

[2] **Bush** George W. Bush (b. 1946), forty-third president of the United States.

[3] **Ralph Waldo Emerson** (1803–1882) American essayist, poet, and lecturer.

[4] **John Brown** (1800–1859) American abolitionist who led a raid on Harpers Ferry in an attempt to free the slaves.

[5] **Herman Melville** (1819–1891) Author of *Moby-Dick* (1851).

[6] **Mark Twain** (1835–1910) Author of *The Adventures of Huckleberry Finn* (1884).

[7] **James Baldwin** (1924–1987) Poet, playwright, novelist, and essayist, and author of *The Fire Next Time* (1963).

[8] **Toni Morrison** (b. 1931) Nobel Prize–winning American novelist and author of *Beloved* (1987).

[9] **Tupac Shakur** (1971–1996) Hip-hop musician and actor whose work explored themes of racism and the problems of the inner city.

This democratic vigilance has been disproportionately expressed by artists, activists, and intellectuals in American life. They have and can play a unique role in highlighting the possibilities and difficulties of democratic individuality, democratic community, and democratic society in America. They have been the primary agents of our deep democratic tradition. The penetrating visions and inspiring truth telling of Ralph Waldo Emerson, Walt Whitman,[10] Herman Melville, and Eugene O'Neill,[11] of W. E. B. Du Bois,[12] James Baldwin, John Coltrane,[13] Lorraine Hansberry,[14] and Toni Morrison, exemplify the profound potential of democracy in America.

These are the figures whose ferocious moral vision and fervent democratic commitment have held the feet of the plutocratic and imperial elites to the fire and instilled a sense of purpose to democratic activism on the part of citizens from all colors and classes. They have been the life force behind the deeper individual and civic American commitment to democracy.

The deep democratic tradition did not begin in America and we have no monopoly on its promise. But it is here where the seeds of democracy have taken deepest root and sprouted most robustly. The first grand democratic experiment in Athens was driven by a movement of the demos — citizen-peasants — organizing to make the Greek oligarchs who were abusing their power accountable. Democracy is always a movement of an energized public to make elites responsible — it is at its core and most basic foundation the taking back of one's powers in the face of the misuse of elite power. In this sense, democracy is more a verb than a noun — it is more a dynamic striving and collective movement than a static order or stationary status quo. Democracy is not just a system of governance, as we tend to think of it, but a cultural way of being. This is where the voices of our great democratic truth tellers come in.

The two paradigmatic figures of the deep democratic tradition in America are Ralph Waldo Emerson and Herman Melville, two democratically charged giants who set in motion distinctive streams of this tradition. And the most Emersonian of American democratic intellectuals is James Baldwin, while the most Melvillean of our democratic intellectuals is Toni Morrison.

---

[10] **Walt Whitman** (1819–1892) American poet and author of *Leaves of Grass* (1855).

[11] **Eugene O'Neill** (1888–1953) Nobel Prize-winning American playwright and author of *Long Day's Journey into Night* (1941–1957).

[12] **W. E. B. Du Bois** (1868–1963) American educator, historian, and author of *The Souls of Black Folk* (1903).

[13] **John Coltrane** (1926–1967) American jazz saxophone player who influenced modern jazz.

[14] **Lorraine Hansberry** (1930–1965) American playwright and author of *A Raisin in the Sun* (1959).

The indisputable godfather of the deep democratic tradition in America is Emerson, a literary artist of dramatic and visionary eloquence and the first full-blown democratic intellectual in the United States. Emerson was an intellectual who hungered most of all to communicate to broad publics. He reveled in the burning social issues of his day (the annihilation of Native Americans, slavery), highlighting the need for democratic individuals to be nonconformist, courageous, and true to themselves. He believed that within the limited framework of freedom in our lives, individuals can and must create their own democratic individuality. He understood that democracy is not only about the workings of the political system but more profoundly about individuals being empowered and enlightened (and suspicious of authorities) in order to help create and sustain a genuine democratic community, a type of society that was unprecedented in human history. And he knew that mission required questioning prevailing dogmas as well as our own individual beliefs and biases. A democratic public must continuously create new attitudes, new vocabularies, new outlooks, and new visions — all undergirded by individual commitment to scrutiny and volition. He refused to accept the conventional wisdom of leaders and the narrow pronouncements of experts. In his famous essay "Self-Reliance," he writes:

> *"Democracy is not just a system of governance, as we tend to think of it, but a cultural way of being."*

> Whoso would be a man must be a nonconformist. He who would gather immortal palms must not be hindered by the name of goodness, but must explore if it be goodness. Nothing is at last sacred but the integrity of your own mind.

And also:

> There is a time in every man's education when he arrives at the conviction that envy is ignorance; that imitation is suicide; that he must take himself for better for worse as his portion; that though the wide universe is full of good, no kernel of nourishing corn can come to him but through his toil bestowed on that plot of ground which is given to him to till. The power which resides in him is new in nature, and none but he knows what that is which he can do, nor does he know until he has tried.

Emerson offered the empowering insight that to be a democratic individual is to be flexible and fluid, revisionary and reformational in one's dealings with fellow citizens and the world, not adhering to comfortable dogmas or rigid party lines. He posits that the core of being a democrat is to think for one's self, judge for one's self, trust one's self, rely on one's self, and be serene in one's own skin — without being self-indulgent, narcissistic, or self-pitying. This was not a standard beyond the enactment of everyday people, and the concerns of everyday people were the proper focus of democratic inquiry. In "The American Scholar," Emerson declares:

> The literature of the poor, the feelings of the child, the philosophy of the street, the meaning of household life, are the topics of the time. It is a great stride. It is a sign — is it not? of new vigor when the extremities are made active, when currents of warm life run into the hands and the feet. I ask not for the great, the remote, the romantic; what is doing in Italy or Arabia; what is Greek art, or Provencal minstrelsy; I embrace the common, I explore and sit at the feet of the familiar, the low.

Understanding Ideas

1. Cornel West says that our "democratic system seems so broken" (para. 1) that people have asked themselves, "Why vote?" What evidence does he present to back up this view? What evidence do you have?

2. How fair is West's criticism of religion in politics?

3. What does West mean by *imperialism*? How is imperialism expressed?

4. Why does West recommend that democratic individuals be nonconformists?

5. According to West, what are our democracy's problems and how can they be cured?

Responding to Ideas

1. *Definition* West says, "Democracy is not just a system of governance, as we tend to think of it, but a cultural way of being" (para. 11). As a citizen living in a democracy, define what you perceive to be the "cultural way of being" that West describes. How does the democratic system produce a culture of behavior and a cultural attitude distinct enough to set its citizens apart from those who do not enjoy democracy? As a member of a democratic nation, what are your general expectations about governance and about society?

2. ***Response*** West makes a distinct point of telling us that we are currently engaged in "the pursuit of pleasure and of diverting entertainments" (para. 4); therefore, we are disengaged from the political problems that plague our democracy. Offer an analysis of American society as you understand it and qualify his judgments. In what ways does the pursuit of pleasure in our society disengage us from our problems? Is American society as materialistic as West suggests? And if so, how does materialism affect society's attitude toward democracy as it exists in our time? How does the pursuit of pleasure hamper our ability to change our political system to make it more democratic?

3. ***Testimony*** One of West's most important strategies is to refer to major American writers, such as Ralph Waldo Emerson, Herman Melville, Mark Twain, and Toni Morrison, to bolster his critique of current democracy in America. Choose a piece of writing from one of those writers (or another major American writer of your choice) and demonstrate to what extent that work supports West's views. The work of classic American writers will either support West's argument or not. Which is it?

4. ***Example*** One surprising example in West's discussion is his suggestion that the work of John Coltrane and Tupac Shakur, both modern musicians with a wide popular audience, supports his position by their criticism of the culture. If you know the work of Tupac Shakur, examine his music and his lyrics and explain to someone who may not know him how he supports West's view. Why might contemporary politicians feel that it is inappropriate to cite Tupac as a critic of our culture? What other major musical figures are cultural critics? Is their criticism effective? Is it fair?

Comparing Ideas

1. Compare Cornel West's views on individual rights with Alexis de Tocqueville's understanding of how democracy works in America (p. 84). What do these two writers have in common regarding how exercising one's rights will help democracy function? In what ways do they disagree? What might Tocqueville say to West to reassure him that American democracy will cure its ills in the future? In what ways does Tocqueville's understanding of the strengths of American democracy validate West's optimism?

2. Both Plato (p. 56) and Cornel West talk about the "seductiveness of the pursuit of pleasure" and its likely effect on the political health of a democratic nation. What do these two political commentators have

in common concerning the choice between taking a positive political action in society versus just lying back and focusing on personal pleasure? Which of these writers is more fearful of the failure of the individual to take a serious role in society? Which of these writers is more fearful of the possibility of an oligarchy developing from a weakened democracy? Which of these writers is more optimistic about the future of democracy? In an essay, explain how each writer reacts to the idea of imperialism in a democracy.

3. Robert A. Dahl in his essay "Why Democracy?" (p. 96) covers a great many of the issues that worry Cornel West. Dahl gives a list of ten achievements he calls "desirable consequences" produced by democracy. West discusses some of these achievements, but not all. Why does he omit some and admit others? Based on the fact that in their essays West emphasizes imperialism and Dahl omits it almost entirely, how much agreement do you think they would have in discussing this issue?

© Ramin Talaie/Corbis

FAREED ZAKARIA

FAREED ZAKARIA (b. 1964) appears regularly on television news shows discussing important world developments. A Muslim born in Mumbai, India, he is sometimes called upon to comment on Middle Eastern affairs, but his political competence and concerns range far beyond narrow regional interests.

His most important books are *From Wealth to Power: The Unusual Origins of America's World Role* (1998), *The Future of Freedom: Illiberal Democracy at Home and Abroad* (2003), and *The Post-American World* (2008). In that last book, Zakaria examines the question of whether the rise of the Chinese and Indian economies signals the end of America's position as a world power.

In the selection that follows, Zakaria implies a contrast between the liberal democracies of the West, such as in the United States and major European nations, and the illiberal governments of Russia and China. But in treating this subject, he makes explicit comparisons between Russia and China central to his discussion. He begins with a claim: "Russia and China are the two most important countries in the world that are not liberal democracies" (para. 1). Because both of these nations are huge, wealthy, and ambitious, Zakaria assures us that their significance to world peace and world order is enormous. He contrasts Russia and China in terms of their welcoming or not welcoming free elections. He also discusses their efforts at economic reforms. Because this selection comes from his book *The Future of Freedom* (2007), he devotes his second paragraph to the question of which country, Russia or China, is freer. Despite the fact that the Communist Party maintains China as a closed society, it is experiencing some liberalization, although by no means as much as Russia. However, Russia has given too much power to the president, and as a result, Russia's move toward democracy has produced an illiberal version that restricts freedom and human rights.

Zakaria introduces other comparisons. For example, he discusses political developments in India and South Africa, pointing to alternative ways of creating a democratic government. Much of the last pages of his discussion cover the ways Vladimir Putin has used the extended powers of the Russian presidency to limit the powers of his underlings.

Be sure to practice prereading techniques for a careful, annotated reading of Zakaria's essay. For a review of prereading strategies, see pages 4–9. ⌗

Illiberal Democracy

RUSSIA AND China are the two most important countries in the world that are not liberal democracies. Their search for political and economic systems that work for them is of enormous global significance. Were both to become Western-style liberal democracies, all the major powers in the world would be stable regimes governed by popular consent and the rule of law. This would not mean permanent peace, nor would it abolish international rivalries. But it would likely mean a different and probably more benign world. As of now, however, the two countries are on somewhat different paths. China has moved to reform its economy and, very slowly, other aspects of its legal and administrative system, but it has taken few steps to introduce democracy. Russia, by contrast, moved first and most quickly on political reform. Even under Gorbachev,[1] there was more glasnost (political openness) than perestroika (economic restructuring). After communism, Russia moved rapidly to free and fair elections in the hope that they would produce Western-style liberal democracy. It also initiated a burst of economic reforms, in the early 1990s, in the hope that this would produce Western-style capitalism, but most didn't work. To oversimplify, China is reforming its economics before its politics, whereas Russia did the reverse.

Today, Russia is a freer country than China. It has greater respect for individual rights and press freedoms, and even its economy is in theory more open to competition and foreign investment. China remains a closed society run by the Communist Party, but it is being steadily liberalized along several fronts, chiefly economic and legal. Which will ultimately prove to

---

[1] **Gorbachev** Mikhail Gorbachev (b. 1931), the last president of the Union of Soviet Socialist Republics, began the liberalization of Russia.

have taken a more stable route to liberal democracy? If economic development and a middle class are keys to sustaining democracy, China is moving in the right direction. Its economy has grown dramatically over the last twenty-five years. Russia's gross national product, by contrast, has shrunk almost 40 percent since 1991 and has begun to recover only in the last few years, largely because oil prices moved higher. If China continues on its current path and continues to grow, further develops its rule of law, builds a bourgeoisie,[2] and then liberalizes its politics — and these are huge ifs — it will have achieved an extraordinary transformation toward genuine democracy.

If Russia continues down *its* path — and this, too, is a big if — of slipping toward an elected autocracy with more and more of its freedoms secure in theory but violated in practice, with corruption embedded into the very system of politics and economics, it could well remain democratic and illiberal. It might settle into a version of the regimes that dominated Latin America in the 1960s and 1970s: quasi-capitalist, with a permanent governing alliance among the elites. In Latin America this alliance was between big business and the military; in Russia it is between the oligarchs and the former Communist elite. This type of regime appears to have taken hold in much of the former Soviet Union — Central Asia, Belarus, Ukraine — the notable exceptions being the three Baltic states.[3]

The Russian path has, wittingly or not, violated the two key lessons that one can glean from the historical experience of democratization: emphasize genuine economic development and build effective political institutions. Moscow is failing on both counts.

Russia's fundamental problem is not that it is a poor country struggling to modernize, but rather that it is a rich country struggling to modernize. Schoolchildren in the Soviet era were taught that they lived in the richest country in the world. In this case communist propaganda was true. If natural resources were the measure of national wealth, Russia would probably rank on top globally, with its vast endowments of oil, natural gas, diamonds, nickel, and other minerals. These resources probably prolonged the life of Soviet communism for a generation. They also helped produce a dysfunctional state.

In the never-never land of Soviet communism, the state needed no tax revenues, since it owned the entire economy. Much of the manufacturing sector was, by the 1970s, worthless. In fact products were often "value-subtracted," which is to say that the raw materials were more valuable than the finished goods they were turned into. The Soviet state relied almost entirely on revenues from natural resources to fund itself. Thus, unlike

5

---

[2] **bourgeoisie** The middle class.
[3] **Baltic states** Latvia, Estonia, and Lithuania.

dictatorships in South Korea and Taiwan, it never created rules and policies to facilitate economic growth. Rich regimes with faltering legitimacy often bribe their citizens with benefits so that they don't revolt (e.g., Saudi Arabia). The Soviet Union terrorized them instead. Moscow was not inclined to give away resources to its citizens, having much grander purposes for these funds, such as maintaining a huge defense establishment and propping up Third World proxies.[4] When Soviet communism collapsed, Gorbachev's successors inherited a state strong enough to terrorize its people but too weak to administer a modern economy.

Unfortunately Yeltsin[5] added to the problems of Russia's political development. His supporters have justified his autocratic actions by pointing out, correctly, that the president was fighting well-entrenched and nasty anti-democratic forces. But a political founder must follow his acts of destruction with greater acts of construction. Jawaharlal Nehru[6] spent almost thirteen years in jail fighting the British colonial authorities, but as prime minister of independent India he spent many more years preserving British institutions. Nelson Mandela[7] approved of radical and violent resistance to apartheid, but once in power he reached out to South Africa's whites to create a multiracial South Africa.

But unlike Nehru and Mandela, Yeltsin did little to build political institutions in Russia. In fact he actively weakened almost all competing centers of power — the legislature, the courts, regional governors. The 1993 constitution he has bequeathed to Russia is a disaster, creating a weak parliament, a dependent judiciary, and an out-of-control presidency. Perhaps most lamentably, Yeltsin did not found a political party. He could have done so easily, uniting all the reformist elements within Russia. More than any other action this could have ensured that Russian democracy would deepen and become genuine. But he didn't. This may seem like a small point, but parties are the mechanism through which people in modern societies express, reconcile, and institutionalize their moral and political values. The historian of American democracy Clinton Rossiter[8] once wrote, "No America without democracy, no democracy without politics, no politics without parties." His statement is true everywhere. Without parties, politics becomes a game for individuals, interest groups, and strongmen. That is a fair description of Russian democracy today.

---

[4] **Third World proxies** Soviet-influenced nations, such as Poland and Ukraine.

[5] **Yeltsin** Boris Yeltsin (1931–2007) was the first president of the Russian Federation.

[6] **Jawaharlal Nehru** (1889–1964) First prime minister of India after independence and partition in 1947.

[7] **Nelson Mandela** (1918–2013) South Africa's first black president. He dismantled that nation's policy of apartheid, or the segregation of the races.

[8] **Clinton Rossiter** (1917–1970) Professor of political science at Cornell. Among his books is *The American Presidency* (1956).

Putin[9] has strengthened Yeltsin's chief legacy, which is not liberal reform but rather a superpresidency. In his first year in office, Putin shrank the rest of Russia's government. His main targets have been regional governors, whom he effectively disempowered by appointing seven "supergovernors" to oversee the eighty-nine regions and threw the governors out of parliament where they had seats in the upper house. They were replaced by legislators appointed by the Kremlin. Additionally, any governor can now be fired if the president believes that he has broken the law. Putin also persuaded the Duma[10] to enact legislation reducing the tax revenues sent to the provinces. Putin's other targets have been the media and Russia's infamous oligarchs,[11] whom he has threatened with raids, arrests, and imprisonment. As a strategy of intimidation, it has worked. Freedom of the press in Russia barely exists anymore. In April 2000, a Kremlin-allied consortium took over NTV, the country's last independent nation-wide broadcaster, firing most of its senior staff. And when journalists who resigned over the takeover sought refuge at another TV station owned by NTV founder Vladimir Gusinsky,[12] they found their new employer under immediate assault by the tax authorities. The print media is still nominally independent but now toes the government line on all matters.

In doing all this Putin is following the wishes of his electorate. In a 2000   10 poll conducted by the Public Opinion Fund, 57 percent of Russians approved of his censorship of the media. Even more approved of his attacks on the oligarchs, many of whom are questionable figures. Russia's oligarchs acquired their wealth using shady means and maintain it in even more dubious ways. The regional governors are often local bosses with enormous appetites for corruption. But when Putin unleashes the secret police on businessmen or politicians whom he dislikes, he is undermining the rule of law. A minor oligarch (with a fairly clean reputation) once told me in Moscow, "We have all broken some law or other. You cannot do business in Russia without breaking the law. Putin knows that. So to say that he is simply enforcing the law is nonsense. He is selectively using it for political ends." The use of law as a political weapon perverts the idea of equality under law.

More important is the long-term effect of Putin's whittling down of his opponents. Pluralism rests on competing centers of power. Vladimir

---

[9] **Putin** Vladimir Putin (b. 1952), twice-elected president of the Russia Federation (2000–2008; 2012–).

[10] **Duma** Lower house of the Russian Federation.

[11] **oligarchs** Russian oligarchs are those who became rich, often by illegal means, after the collapse of the Soviet Union. They have huge wealth and some influence on the government and are resented by the general population.

[12] **Vladimir Gusinsky** (b. 1951) Russian oligarch and media tycoon whom Putin has wanted prosecuted. Gusinksky fled to Israel to avoid arrest.

Ryzhkov,[13] one of Russia's few liberals in parliament, made an explicit comparison with Europe's past: "The earls and barons who battled royal power were hardly virtuous themselves. But they kept a check on the crown. Our problem in Russia if Putin succeeds is that there will be absolutely no one left to check the Kremlin. We are left trusting once again in a good czar."[14] Putin is a good czar. He wants to build a modern Russia. He believes that Russia needs order and a functioning state in order to liberalize its economy. Perhaps he

> *"The use of law as a political weapon perverts the idea of equality under law."*

even believes that eventually, Russia will be able to democratize its political system. If he succeeds, Putin could help Russia become a normal industrialized country with some of the liberal features that this moniker implies. "The model for Russia in the early 1990s was Poland after communism. Now it's Chile under [Augusto] Pinochet,"[15] says Ryzhkov. The Pinochet model is certainly possible; Pinochet did eventually lead his country to liberal democracy.

But it is an odd argument in favor of Russia's democratic path to say that it has made possible a leader who crushes the opposition, stifles the media, bans political parties, and then liberalizes the economy by fiat, which will eventually bring true democracy. Illiberal democracy is good, in this thesis, because it has — by chance — produced a liberal autocrat who may eventually lead his country to genuine liberal democracy. This is an argument in favor of liberal autocrats, not democracy. There is always the possibility, of course, that Putin, or more likely one of his successors, will turn out to be a bad czar and use his enormous powers for less noble goals. It has happened in the past.

Understanding Ideas

1. Which nation does Fareed Zakaria expect will develop into a Western-style democracy first: Russia or China?

2. According to Zakaria, why are economic development and a middle class essential to a liberal democracy?

---

[13] **Vladimir Ryzhkov** (b. 1966) Russian liberal politician and cochair of the Republican Party of Russia.

[14] **czar** The name of Russia's historical absolute ruler; equivalent to a king.

[15] **Augusto Pinochet** (1915–2006) Dictator of Chile from 1973 to 1990, when he turned the government over to an elected president.

3. Why are Zakaria's judgments of Boris Yeltsin important? According to Zakaria, what should Yeltsin have done differently?

4. Why is a superpresidency a hallmark of an illiberal democracy?

5. What are the chances, according to Zakaria, that Putin will become a "good czar" (para. 11)?

Responding to Ideas

1. *Comparison* Write a brief essay comparing a liberal-style Western democracy with the illiberal-style democracies Fareed Zakaria discusses. What are the chief qualities of a liberal-style Western democracy? What are the chief qualities of an illiberal democracy? Consider freedom of the press, control by wealthy oligarchs, a powerful presidency, and a representative government. Consider, too, the importance of a reliable judiciary. What kinds of power most threaten the rights of people in society?

2. *Analysis of Circumstances* Zakaria says that in a public opinion poll 57 percent of Russians approved of President Putin's censorship of the media. Why is this an important piece of information? If 57 percent of people in a democracy, liberal or illiberal, wish to censor the newspapers and television media, would that make censorship an acceptable thing? Despite popular opinion, why might it be an unacceptable practice in a democracy? Is there any kind of censorship that is appropriate for a thriving democracy?

3. *Response* One complaint Zakaria makes about Boris Yeltsin is that, although he had the power to do so, he did not create a political party in Russia while he liberalized its political structure. Why are political parties essential to a liberal democracy? What are the benefits and what are the drawbacks of political parties in a liberal democracy? Why should a democratic nation have more than one political party for its democracy to be liberal? Should political parties be strong or weak? How many political parties do you think should be functioning in a liberal democracy?

4. *Cause and Effect* The oligarchs that Zakaria refers to in Russia are extremely wealthy businesspeople, almost all men, who wield considerable power because of the assets they control. Putin keeps them in line by threatening them with legal action. One oligarch explains that breaking some law or other is impossible to avoid if one is to do business in Russia. In liberal democracies, extremely wealthy people are the equivalent of Russian oligarchs. In our democracy, do you detect the power of oligarchs trying to influence government policy? Are those influences for the greater good?

5.   ***Research*** Zakaria says much more about Russia than he does about China. Search information about China's political system and determine how much progress it seems to be making toward becoming a more liberal nation. Consider its economic progress and the influence that its economic development has had in the rest of the world. Judging by how much China has changed recently, what are your predictions for how liberal its political system is likely to become?

Comparing Ideas

1.   Robert A. Dahl (p. 96) says that no democratic nations have waged war against one another. Fareed Zakaria opens his piece by saying that if Russia and China became liberal democracies "all the major powers in the world would be stable regimes governed by popular consent and the rule of law" (para. 1). But he also says, "This would not mean permanent peace" (para. 1). Why does Zakaria disagree with Dahl's thinking that democracies will not wage war against each other? Compare Zakaria's and Dahl's views on the possibility of war among democracies. Where do you stand on this issue?

2.   Plato's (p. 56) ideas about democracy may at times be both liberal and illiberal. Write a brief essay that connects Plato's discussion of democracy with Fareed Zakaria's discussion. How much do these writers have in common? Is the concept of oligarchy present in Zakaria's discussion of illiberal democracies? Explain how Zakaria treats the fears Plato has about the possibility of mob rule in a democracy. What chief concerns do they share? What concerns Plato but does not concern Zakaria? What concerns Zakaria but does not concern Plato?

CHAPTER FOUR

How Freedom Depends on Justice

JEAN-JACQUES ROUSSEAU   136

LUCY A. DELANEY   146

FRANKLIN DELANO ROOSEVELT   153

JOHN RAWLS   159

JAMES BALDWIN   169

MARTIN LUTHER KING JR.   176

AMARTYA SEN   183

bell hooks   190

"Freedom is never voluntarily given by the oppressor;
it must be demanded by the oppressed."
— MARTIN LUTHER KING JR.

"Freedom is the right to tell people what they do not
want to hear." — GEORGE ORWELL

"Freedom means you are unobstructed in ruling your
own life as you choose. Anything less is a form of slavery."
— WAYNE DYER

"What is freedom of expression?
Without the freedom to offend, it ceases to exist."
— SALMAN RUSHDIE

"Justice is itself the great standing policy of civil society;
and any eminent departure from it, under any circumstances,
lies under the suspicion of being no policy at all."
— EDMUND BURKE

"Freedom has a thousand charms to show,
That slaves, howe'er contented, never know." — WILLIAM COWPER

"But what is Freedom? Rightly understood,
A universal license to be good." — HARTLEY COLERIDGE

INTRODUCTION

Justice and freedom have always gone together. The freedom of everyone in a modern social order demands laws that guarantee the basic freedoms of the individual to live without encumbrance or oppression.

Jean-Jacques Rousseau (1712–1778), one of the most enduring eighteenth-century philosophers, addresses the issue of slavery and freedom directly in *The Social Contract, or Principles of Political Right* (1762). His concerns about social justice inspired him to analyze the entire concept of how social order is established. Because he was born in a republic rather than under a monarchy, Rousseau saw that the individual was capable of directing his or her own life without having to take on the burden of a king and court that felt they could sequester an individual's freedom without reason. In his book, Rousseau argues against the position of an earlier philosopher, who approved of monarchical government, and contends that, in some remote past, people had gathered together to devise a way of governing themselves. Rousseau calls this an "original compact," or the social contract. Within that contract, Rousseau saw that the people had lost their freedom by giving themselves over to a king and court. As he says in his famous opening statement, "Man was born free, and everywhere he is in chains." Although Rousseau did not live to see the French Revolution, his work became a centerpiece in the philosophy of freedom, equality, and fraternity.

Slavery in the United States was protected by laws aimed at preserving the property of the slave owners. In 1850, during the life of Lucy A. Delaney (c. 1828–1890), who was a slave in St. Louis, the Fugitive Slave Law was enacted, making it a crime for anyone in the United States to protect an escaped slave. The law required citizens to report an escaped slave or face severe penalties. But Delaney, who escaped to freedom, was able to benefit from other laws that resulted from what were known as "freedom suits." Lucy's mother, who had been born free but was kidnapped and sold into slavery, escaped and used the courts to sue for freedom because she had been freeborn. Then she sued for Lucy's freedom because she was the child of a free woman. There were more than three hundred freedom suits in St. Louis in a twenty-year period before the Civil War, and many of them were won. Lucy Delaney's narrative gives us a good view of life as a slave waiting for justice.

In his January 1941 State of the Union speech, President Franklin Delano Roosevelt (1882–1945) spoke to a nation battered by the Great Depression and fearful of an encroaching war in Europe. Due to the invasion of the Nazis, freedom had been denied to most of the democratic nations of Europe. Despite knowing that war was all but inevitable, Roosevelt guaranteed the very freedoms that had disappeared in Germany, France, Belgium, Spain, Italy, Greece, and other European nations. By focusing on freedom of speech, freedom of worship, freedom from want, and freedom from fear, Roosevelt made clear in his address how powerful the threat of Nazi violence was to the entire world — he knew it was only a matter of time before the war reached the United States. On December 7, 1941, Japan attacked Pearl Harbor, and Roosevelt declared war on both Japan and Germany. Ultimately, Roosevelt restored "the four freedoms" to the battered countries of Europe and worked to extend the same kind of justice to Asian nations as well.

The most admired modern philosopher of the theory of justice, John Rawls (1921–2002), takes issue with one of its most durable theories: utilitarianism. Utilitarians defend the view that the function of government is to provide the greatest good to the greatest number of people. Under that system, some people will undoubtedly feel the sting of injustice. But utilitarians argue that as long as most people benefit from a government then that system is working well. But Rawls wants us to look at the question of freedom and justice from another point of view: as benefiting the individual, not just the community. Therefore, he insists, the measure of any legal or government decision is its effect on "the least advantaged" citizen. What Rawls recommends is justice as fairness. An action produces justice when it benefits everyone and is fair to the individual with the fewest advantages granted by the community.

James Baldwin (1924–1987), one of the finest American writers of the second half of the twentieth century, wrote a letter to his fifteen-year-old nephew in 1962 on the eve of the hundred-year anniversary of the Emancipation Proclamation (1863), which freed American slaves in the Confederacy. In his letter, Baldwin warns his nephew not just about the dangers of racism but also about threats to his freedom. Because his nephew James is African American and was born in "the ghetto," Baldwin cautions, society expects him to stay there and not try to improve or change his life. The letter is interesting because it was written during a time of great racial violence in the South, when justice was being denied African Americans like James. But Baldwin does not think James will entirely believe him when he insists that the "system" is designed to keep James in his place. Baldwin accuses his country of crimes against all African Americans and warns James to think for himself.

Martin Luther King Jr.'s (1929–1968) famous speech "I Have a Dream" was delivered at the March on Washington for Jobs and Freedom in August 1963, a year after James Baldwin's letter was written. The background to the speech was the struggle for civil rights. King and his followers came to Washington to get the government to enact legislation that would guarantee justice to people who were being held down in the South and elsewhere. Segregation was still the norm in many parts of the country, and racism was commonplace. While there was a great deal of police violence in many towns in the South, King urged nonviolent action, certain that change would come sooner if peaceful means were used to pressure lawmakers for justice for all. Although King was assassinated five years later, the work he did in the years before and after his speech resulted in many changes in the law.

The distinguished scholar Amartya Sen was born in India in 1933 and lived there during a period of famine brought on by economic problems. Sen grew up to become an expert on economics, eventually winning the Nobel Prize in Economic Sciences in 1998. His work focuses on the social issues involved with economic decisions and circumstances. The question of justice for him is not at all removed from economics. He has written about the effect of development in poor countries and how it results not only in an improved daily life for individuals but also better chances for the system to deliver justice to the people. One of his most interesting ideas is that it is not enough for justice to be done — it also must *appear* that justice has been done. He explains why this requirement is necessary, but it is curious that the appearance of justice is perhaps as important as the justice itself.

Like Amartya Sen, bell hooks (b. 1952) has based some of her work on the writings of Mary Wollstonecraft and credits Wollstonecraft as being an early feminist. Arriving at the question of justice through feminism, hooks examines the ways our culture oppresses women and denies them independence. Part of her essay is a review of the recent years of the feminist movement. She explains that the portrait of feminism as antimale is not a true picture. She also insists that opponents of feminism are not uniformly male: many women can be counted in their ranks. Moreover, hooks says, in a largely Christian culture, religion may support the view that a woman in a domestic situation must be subordinate to a man. Her view of the political realities of our culture leads her to feel that sexism and racism are related and that women have limited access to justice and personal freedom. Her view of the structure of society is unyielding, and she is concerned that the feminist movement may be losing momentum. Convinced that our culture is structured against the rights of women, hooks feels that as such it denies women the justice they deserve.

SEEING IDEAS

The two images that follow help illustrate how people's freedom within a society is dependent on just and fair laws.

This first image, below, is from the late nineteenth century, a time when women were not allowed to vote. As a result, women did not participate in the legislature of the nation, nor were they represented in the judiciary branch of the government. "Justice" was something that was decided for them by men. In both Great Britain and America in the 1870s, many laws were in place denying women justice, including laws that denied widows the right to inherit any property that had been owned by them and their husbands. Protesters for women's rights like Lydia Becker and her supporters (depicted in the image below) often resorted to disruptive measures to have their voices heard.

Underrepresented groups still must fight for justice. Today, more than 150 years after the Emancipation Proclamation, minority groups are demanding justice in an environment in which they feel threatened by the

Hulton Archive/Getty

police. The protesters in the image above knew that the media was covering their demand for justice following the killing of Walter Scott, an unarmed African American man who was shot in the back by a police officer in North Charleston, South Carolina, in April 2015. The homemade signs demonstrate the protesters' seriousness and their deep feelings at a time when several similar fatal incidents had happened (and more followed closely) across the United States, including the killing of Michael Brown in Ferguson, Missouri; Eric Garner in Staten Island, New York; Justus Howell in Chicago, Illinois; Philip White in Vineland, New Jersey; Eric Harris in Tulsa, Oklahoma; and Freddie Gray in Baltimore, Maryland. Following many of these incidents, several nights of riots erupted in demands for justice — for as Martin Luther King Jr. implied in his "I Have a Dream" speech, without justice there can be no freedom.

© Corbis

JEAN-JACQUES
ROUSSEAU

JEAN-JACQUES ROUSSEAU (1712–1778) was one of the most gifted literary men of his time. He wrote a famous novel, *Emile, or On Education* (1762); an opera, *The Village Soothsayer* (1752); an enduring autobiography, *The Confessions* (written in 1770 and published in 1782); and one of the most important political documents of the age, *The Social Contract* (1762). Because he was born in Switzerland in the Republic of Geneva, Rousseau favored a republican form of government that was democratic in principle.

In the selection from *The Social Contract* that follows, Rousseau enters into an imagined argument with Hugo Grotius (1583–1645), author of a famous book on the laws of war. Grotius, unlike Rousseau, accepted the power of the aristocracy and the absolute authority of the sovereign. Rousseau's essentially liberal interpretation of republican government placed him in jeopardy both in his native Geneva, which became governed by a small number of aristocrats, and in France, whose parliament was offended by his novel and rejected him. He spent most of his later life in uncertainty. His reputation was revived shortly after his death when supporters of the French Revolution adopted much of his philosophy.

The Social Contract, Rousseau's most important political work, begins as follows: "Man is born free, and everywhere he is in chains. Many a man believes himself to be the master of others who is, no less than they, a slave. How did this change take place? I do not know. What can make it legitimate? To this question I hope to be able to furnish an answer." In answering such a large question, Rousseau talks about slavery and property, beginning with war and its aftermath. Traditionally, conquering armies made slaves of the losers, but he can see no justification for such behavior. He claims that Grotius denies that political power is ever exercised in the interest of the governed and uses the institution of slavery in support of his view. For this reason, Rousseau examines slavery with great care.

The social pact is a form of contract that people in society make with each other. Rousseau calls this an Agreement. The people agree to socially acceptable behavior as a means of guaranteeing their own freedom and safety. Whereas Grotius and others assume the power is in the hands of the governors, Rousseau argues that it should be in the hands of the governed. One of his positions is that those he argues against insist on treating what is, while he wishes to treat what should be.

In using the metaphor of the social contract, Rousseau establishes that the people have the power to agree to work with each other to provide the benefits of society for themselves. By contrast, subjecting themselves to "the will of a King" implies a form of slavery. Such views were seen as revolutionary in the eighteenth century.

Be sure to practice prereading techniques before a careful, annotated reading of Rousseau's essay. For a review of prereading techniques, see pages 4–9. ⊞

Of Slavery and the Social Pact

OF SLAVERY

SINCE NO man has natural authority over his fellows, and since Might can produce no Right, the only foundation left for legitimate authority in human societies is Agreement.

If a private citizen, says Grotius,[1] can alienate his liberty and make himself another man's slave, why should not a whole people do the same, and subject themselves to the will of a King? The argument contains a number of ambiguous words which stand in need of explanation. But let us confine our attention to one only — *alienate*. To alienate means to give or to sell. Now a man who becomes the slave of another does not give himself. He sells himself in return for bare subsistence, if for nothing more. But why should a whole people sell themselves? So far from furnishing subsistence to his subjects, a King draws his own from them, and from them alone. According to Rabelais,[2] it takes a lot to keep a King. Do we, then, maintain that a subject surrenders his person on condition that his property be taken too? It is difficult to see what he will have left.

---

[1] **Grotius** Hugo Grotius (1583–1645), a Dutch lawyer who spent some time in exile in Paris. His fame as a child prodigy was considerable; his book on the laws of war (*De jure belli ac Pacis*) was widely known in Europe.

[2] **Rabelais** François Rabelais (c. 1494–1553) a French writer, author of *Gargantua* and *Pantagruel*, satires on politics and religion.

It will be said that the despot guarantees civil peace to his subjects. So be it. But how are they the gainers if the wars to which his ambition may expose them, his insatiable greed, and the vexatious demands of his Ministers cause them more loss than would any outbreak of internal dissension? How do they benefit if that very condition of civil peace be one of the causes of their wretchedness? One can live peacefully enough in a dungeon, but such peace will hardly, of itself, ensure one's happiness. The Greeks imprisoned in the cave of Cyclops[3] lived peacefully while awaiting their turn to be devoured.

To say that a man gives himself for nothing is to commit oneself to an absurd and inconceivable statement. Such an act of surrender is illegitimate, null, and void by the mere fact that he who makes it is not in his right mind. To say the same thing of a whole People is tantamount to admitting that the People in question are a nation of imbeciles. Imbecility does not produce Right.

Even if a man can alienate himself, he cannot alienate his children. They 5 are born free, their liberty belongs to them, and no one but themselves has a right to dispose of it. Before they have attained the age of reason their father may make, on their behalf, certain rules with a view to ensuring their preservation and well-being. But any such limitation of their freedom of choice must be regarded as neither irrevocable nor unconditional, for to alienate another's liberty is contrary to the natural order, and is an abuse of the father's rights. It follows that an arbitrary government can be legitimate only on condition that each successive generation of subjects is free either to accept or to reject it, and if this is so, then the government will no longer be arbitrary.

When a man renounces his liberty he renounces his essential manhood, his rights, and even his duty as a human being. There is no compensation possible for such complete renunciation. It is incompatible with man's nature, and to deprive him of his free will is to deprive his actions of all moral sanction. The convention, in short, which sets up on one side an absolute authority, and on the other an obligation to obey without question, is vain and meaningless. Is it not obvious that where we can demand everything we owe nothing? Where there is no mutual obligation, no interchange of duties, it must, surely, be clear that the actions of the commanded cease to have any moral value? For how can it be maintained that my slave has any "right" against me when everything that he has is my property? His right being *my* right, it is absurd to speak of it as ever operating to my disadvantage.

Grotius, and those who think like him, have found in the fact of war another justification for the so-called "right" of slavery. They argue that since the victor has a *right* to kill his defeated enemy, the latter may, if he so

---

[3] **cave of Cyclops** The cyclops is a one-eyed giant cannibal whose cave is the scene of one of Odysseus' triumphs in Homer's *Odyssey* (9).

wish, ransom his life at the expense of his liberty, and that this compact is the more legitimate in that it benefits both parties.

But it is evident that this alleged *right* of a man to kill his enemies is not in any way a derivative of the state of war, if only because men, in their primitive condition of independence, are not bound to one another by any relationship sufficiently stable to produce a state either of war or of peace. They are not *naturally* enemies. It is the link between *things* rather than between *men* that constitutes war, and since a state of war cannot originate in simple personal relations, but only in relations between things, private hostility between man and man cannot obtain either in a state of nature where there is no generally accepted system of private property, or in a state of society where law is the supreme authority.

Single combats, duels, personal encounters are incidents which do not constitute a "state" of anything. As to those private wars which were authorized by the Ordinances of King Louis IX[4] and suspended by the Peace of God, they were merely an abuse of Feudalism — that most absurd of all systems of government, so contrary was it to the principles of Natural Right and of all good polity.

War, therefore, is something that occurs not between man and man, but   10 between States. The individuals who become involved in it are enemies only by accident. They fight not as men or even as citizens, but as soldiers: not as members of this or that national group, but as its defenders. A State can have as its enemies only other States, not men at all, seeing that there can be no true relationship between things of a different nature.

This principle is in harmony with that of all periods, and with the constant practice of every civilized society. A declaration of war is a warning, not so much to Governments as to their subjects. The foreigner — whether king, private person, or nation as a whole — who steals, murders, or holds in durance the subjects of another country without first declaring war on that country's Prince, acts not as an enemy but as a brigand. Even when war has been joined, the just Prince, though he may seize all public property in enemy territory, yet respects the property and possessions of individuals, and, in so doing, shows his concern for those rights on which his own laws are based. The object of war being the destruction of the enemy State, a commander has a perfect right to kill its defenders so long as their arms are in their hands: but once they have laid them down and have submitted, they cease to be enemies, or instruments employed by an enemy, and revert to the condition of men, pure and simple, over whose lives no one can any longer exercise a rightful claim. Sometimes it is possible to destroy a State without killing any of its subjects, and nothing in war can be claimed as a

---

[4] **King Louis IX** (1214–1270) King of France, also called St. Louis. He was considered an ideal monarch.

right save what may be necessary for the accomplishment of the victor's end. These principles are not those of Grotius, nor are they based on the authority of poets, but derive from the Nature of Things, and are founded upon Reason.

The Right of Conquest finds its sole sanction in the Law of the Strongest. If war does not give to the victor the right to massacre his defeated enemies, he cannot base upon a nonexistent right any claim to the further one of enslaving them. We have the right to kill our enemies only when we cannot enslave them. It follows, therefore, that the right to enslave cannot be deduced from the right to kill, and that we are guilty of enforcing an iniquitous exchange if we make a vanquished foeman purchase with his liberty that life over which we have no right. Is it not obvious that once we begin basing the right of life and death on the right to enslave, and the right to enslave on the right of life and death, we are caught in a vicious circle? Even if we assume the existence of this terrible right to kill all and sundry, I still maintain that a man enslaved, or a People conquered, in war is under no obligation to obey beyond the point at which force ceases to be operative. If the victor spares the life of his defeated opponent in return for an equivalent, he cannot be said to have shown him mercy. In either case he destroys him, but in the latter case he derives value from his act, while in the former he gains nothing. His authority, however, rests on no basis but that of force. There is still a state of war between the two men, and it conditions the whole relationship in which they stand to one another. The enjoyment of the Rights of War presupposes that there has been no treaty of Peace. Conqueror and conquered have, to be sure, entered into a compact, but such a compact, far from liquidating the state of war, assumes its continuance.

Thus, in whatever way we look at the matter, the "Right" to enslave has no existence, not only because it is without legal validity, but because the very term is absurd and meaningless. The words *Slavery* and *Right* are contradictory and mutually exclusive. Whether we be considering the relation of one man to another man, or of an individual to a whole People, it is equally idiotic to say — "You and I have made a compact which represents nothing but loss to you and gain to me. I shall observe it so long as it pleases me to do so — and so shall you, until I cease to find it convenient."

THAT WE MUST ALWAYS GO BACK
TO AN ORIGINAL COMPACT

Even were I to grant all that I have so far refuted, the champions of despotism would not be one whit the better off. There will always be a vast difference between subduing a mob and governing a social group. No matter how many isolated individuals may submit to the enforced control of a single conqueror, the resulting relationship will ever be that of Master and Slave, never of People and Ruler. The body of men so controlled may be an agglomeration; it is not an association. It implies neither public welfare nor a body politic. An individual may conquer half the world, but he is still only an individual. His interests, wholly different from those of his subjects, are private to himself. When he dies his empire is left scattered and disintegrated. He is like an oak which crumbles and collapses in ashes so soon as the fire consumes it.

"A People," says Grotius, "may give themselves to a king." His argument   15 implies that the said People were already a People before this act of surrender. The very act of gift was that of a political group and presupposed deliberation. Before, therefore, we consider the act by which a People chooses their king, it were well if we considered the act by which a People is constituted as such. For it necessarily precedes the other, and is the true foundation on which all Societies rest.

"There will always be a vast difference between subduing a mob and governing a social group."

Had there been no original compact, why, unless the choice were unanimous, should the minority ever have agreed to accept the decision of the majority? What right have the hundred who desire a master to vote for the ten who do not? The institution of the franchise is, in itself, a form of compact, and assumes that, at least once in its operation, complete unanimity existed.

OF THE SOCIAL PACT

I assume, for the sake of argument, that a point was reached in the history of mankind when the obstacles to continuing in a state of Nature were stronger than the forces which each individual could employ to the end of continuing in it. The original state of Nature, therefore, could no longer endure, and the human race would have perished had it not changed its manner of existence.

Now, since men can by no means engender new powers, but can only unite and control those of which they are already possessed, there is no way in which they can maintain themselves save by coming together and pooling their strength in a way that will enable them to withstand any resistance exerted upon them from without. They must develop some sort of central direction and learn to act in concert.

Such a concentration of powers can be brought about only as the consequence of an agreement reached between individuals. But the self-preservation of each single man derives primarily from his own strength and from his own freedom. How, then, can he limit these without, at the same time, doing himself an injury and neglecting that care which it is his duty to devote to his own concerns? This difficulty, insofar as it is relevant to my subject, can be expressed as follows:

"Some form of association must be found as a result of which the whole 20 strength of the community will be enlisted for the protection of the person and property of each constituent member, in such a way that each, when united to his fellows, renders obedience to his own will, and remains as free as he was before." That is the basic problem of which the Social Contract provides the solution.

The clauses of this Contract are determined by the Act of Association in such a way that the least modification must render them null and void. Even though they may never have been formally enunciated, they must be everywhere the same, and everywhere tacitly admitted and recognized. So completely must this be the case that, should the social compact be violated, each associated individual would at once resume all the rights which once were his, and regain his natural liberty, by the mere fact of losing the agreed liberty for which he renounced it.

It must be clearly understood that the clauses in question can be reduced, in the last analysis, to one only, to wit, the complete alienation by each associate member to the community of *all his rights*. For, in the first place, since each has made surrender of himself without reservation, the resultant conditions are the same for all: and, because they are the same for all, it is in the interest of none to make them onerous to his fellows.

Furthermore, this alienation having been made unreservedly, the union of individuals is as perfect as it well can be, none of the associated members having any claim against the community. For should there be any rights left to individuals, and no common authority be empowered to pronounce as between them and the public, then each, being in some things his own judge, would soon claim to be so in all. Were that so, a state of Nature would still remain in being, the conditions of association becoming either despotic or ineffective.

In short, whoso gives himself to all gives himself to none. And, since there is no member of the social group over whom we do not acquire precisely the same rights as those over ourselves which we have surrendered to him, it follows that we gain the exact equivalent of what we lose, as well as an added power to conserve what we already have.

If, then, we take from the social pact everything which is not essential 25 to it, we shall find it to be reduced to the following terms: "each of us contributes to the group his person and the powers which he wields as a person under the supreme direction of the general will, and we receive into the body politic each individual as forming an indivisible part of the whole."

As soon as the act of association becomes a reality, it substitutes for the person of each of the contracting parties a moral and collective body made up of as many members as the constituting assembly has votes, which body receives from this very act of constitution its unity, its dispersed *self*, and its will. The public person thus formed by the union of individuals was known in the old days as a *City*, but now as the *Republic* or *Body Politic*. This, when it fulfills a passive role, is known by its members as *The State*, when an active one, as *The Sovereign People*, and, in contrast to other similar bodies, as a *Power*. In respect of the constituent associates, it enjoys the collective name of *The People*, the individuals who compose it being known as *Citizens* insofar as they share in the sovereign authority, as *Subjects* insofar as they owe obedience to the laws of the State. But these different terms frequently overlap, and are used indiscriminately one for the other. It is enough that we should realize the difference between them when they are employed in a precise sense.

Understanding Ideas

1. In a monarchy, how does a person become "the slave of another" (para. 2) as understood by Jean-Jacques Rousseau?

2. According to Rousseau, what are the legitimate "Rights of Conquest" in war (para. 12)?

3. What does the "original compact" imply about the relationship of a people to the king?

4. How does Rousseau interpret the association that results in the social pact?

Responding to Ideas

1. *Definition* Jean-Jacques Rousseau begins by saying, "since Might can produce no Right, the only foundation left for legitimate authority in human societies is Agreement" (para. 1). What does Rousseau mean by the term *agreement*? How does agreement function in a free society? Does such an agreement seem to be working in the society (or societies) in which you live? Why will it produce "Right"? What do you think Rousseau means by the term *right*? Write a brief essay that defines these terms and establishes their significance for our time.

2. **Research** The king in a monarchy derives all his subsistence from "his subjects." The people provide him with his wealth — he does not provide them with their wealth. Rousseau implies that "a man renounces his liberty" (para. 6) when he gives himself over to his king. To what extent is that a fair description of the relationship of a people to a monarch? What does the monarch provide? Why do you think monarchies survived for such a long time? Are they necessarily bad forms of government? If possible, research some of the monarchies that still exist.

3. **Definition** Rousseau argues against Grotius's "Right of Conquest." Grotius says that in war the army has the right to kill its enemies. If so, says Grotius, the army also has the "'right' of slavery" (para. 7) because the victor can ransom the life of the loser "at the expense of his liberty" (para. 7). Analyze the argument as Rousseau summarizes it and decide how sound his position is in relation to Grotius's. Define what is meant by the *Right of Conquest*. Does such a right seem to pertain today? What political organizations are currently practicing such a right?

4. **Analysis of Circumstances** In discussing "an original compact," Rousseau argues that because Grotius tells us that the people had already been a people before they gave "themselves to a king" (para. 15) there had to have been some form of agreement among them. What could that have been? How do you imagine the people were organized (or not organized) before they submitted to a monarch? Is it possible that, as Grotius implies, they submitted themselves willingly? If so, why would they do so? What would they have given up from their original state when they accepted a king? Is it possible that they would have expected the monarch to provide justice to the society?

5. **Response** Using the material in the latter part of Rousseau's selection, explain what the social pact is that he defends. He uses the terms *compact*, *pact*, and *contract*. Are they all the same, or are there subtle differences among those terms? What form of social contract do you think people today have entered into in a democracy? Are you or your friends aware of having an "agreement" that you have entered into in your society? If you do not think of your agreement as a contract, what is a better way to characterize it?

6. **Analysis of Circumstances** How would the social contract Rousseau proposes help guarantee justice in a nation? In an earlier comment, he says that men are "born free" but "everywhere [are] in chains." He implies that the then current form of government by kings essentially makes slaves of its subjects. In the proposal he makes for a social contract, he does not refer to people as subjects but rather as citizens. Given the nature of the agreement he proposes, why would citizens

enjoy more justice than subjects would? Would laws enacted by citizens be more just than laws enacted by a monarchy?

Comparing Ideas

1. Jean-Jacques Rousseau found himself unwelcome in prerevolutionary France, but after 1789 he was considered one of the premier philosophers of the Revolution. His influence was apparent in the works of James Madison (p. 65), the Marquis de Lafayette (p. 71), and Mary Wollstonecraft (p. 77). Compare the selections by those writers with Rousseau's. Which of Rousseau's ideas are most powerfully developed by those writers and are most clearly influenced by his arguments? In what ways did Rousseau make it possible for revolutionary writers to propound the new ideas of liberty and freedom?

2. Compare the ideas that Rousseau discusses about slavery with what Lucy A. Delaney (p. 146) says in her selection "Struggles for Freedom." What kind of social compact seems to have existed in Delaney's society? What would Rousseau have said to Delaney if he had had a chance? What comfort would Delaney have taken from reading Rousseau? Using your imagination and what you know about how Rousseau writes and thinks, craft a detailed letter from him to Delaney.

Missouri History Museum, St. Louis

LUCY A. DELANEY

While there are a number of African American slave narratives that treat the experiences of slaves before the Civil War, **LUCY A. DELANEY**'s (c. 1828–1890) narrative — *From the Darkness Cometh the Light, or Struggles for Freedom* — appeared after emancipation. In it, Delaney examines the everyday conditions of slavery in St. Louis. Her narrative was published after her death in 1891 and was probably written just before or shortly after her emancipation in 1862. Her story also differs from most slave narratives in that it focuses on her mother, Polly, who had been born free, and her struggles to regain her freedom.

Polly Berry (also known as Polly Wash), a freeborn child, was kidnapped by slave catchers in Illinois, a free state that prohibited slavery, and taken to Missouri, where she was sold into slavery. When she was older, Polly married another slave and had two daughters, Nancy and Lucy. Polly's husband was sold after their owner's death and sent downriver to Mississippi. Now owned by Mary Cox, Polly urged her daughter Nancy to escape to Canada, which she eventually did, but Polly and her younger daughter, Lucy, remained slaves. Polly was sold yet again and fearful for Lucy's future. It was then that she began to take legal action.

What makes Polly and Lucy's story most interesting is that Polly insisted on her freedom on the basis of having been born in Illinois a free person. She found Edward Sproat, a lawyer in St. Louis, who helped her file a "freedom suit" in 1839, which was presented in court on her behalf in 1843. Once she had regained her freedom, Polly continued to work on the freedom suit she had entered on behalf of Lucy in 1842. In 1843, Lucy escaped from her owners and then spent some seventeen months in a lockup while her case was being considered.

146

Fortunately, in 1844 the case went in her favor. Polly and Lucy moved to St. Louis, where they worked together to support themselves. In 1845, Lucy married and moved to Quincy, Illinois, where her mother joined the family. Her husband died in a steamship explosion, and in 1849 Lucy married Zachariah Delaney and the family moved back to St. Louis.

Lucy's narrative is interesting for its detail and description of the interaction of slave and slave owner. It focuses on Lucy's interaction with the Cox family after her older sister had run away to Canada while acting as a maid for Mrs. Mitchell, the Coxes' daughter, on her honeymoon at Niagara Falls. Martha Cox was angry because she lost money when Nancy disappeared, and Lucy's story tells us how she acted when Lucy rebelled.

Be sure to practice prereading techniques before a careful, annotated reading of Delaney's passage. For a review of prereading techniques, see pages 4–9. ⊞

Struggles for Freedom

M RS. COX was always very severe and exacting with my mother, and one occasion, when something did not suit her, she turned on mother like a fury, and declared, "I am just tired out with the 'white airs' you put on, and if you don't behave differently, I will make Mr. Cox sell you down the river at once."

Although mother turned grey with fear, she presented a bold front and retorted that "she didn't care, she was tired of that place, and didn't like to live there, nohow." This so infuriated Mr. Cox that he cried, "How dare a negro say what she liked or what she did not like; and he would show her what he should do."

So, on the day following, he took my mother to an auction room on Main Street and sold her to the highest bidder, for five hundred and fifty dollars. Oh! God! the pity of it! "In the home of the brave and the land of the free," in the sight of the stars and stripes — that symbol of freedom — sold away from her child, to satisfy the anger of a peevish mistress!

My mother returned to the house to get her few belongings, and straining me to her breast, begged me to be a good girl, that she was going to run away, and would buy me as soon as she could. With all the inborn faith of a child, I believed it most fondly, and when I heard that she had actually made her escape, three weeks after, my heart gave an exultant throb and cried, "God is good!"

A large reward was offered, the bloodhounds (curse them and curse 5
their masters) were set loose on her trail. In the daytime she hid in caves and
the surrounding woods, and in the nighttime, guided by the wondrous North
Star, that blessed lodestone[1] of a slave people, my mother finally reached
Chicago, where she was arrested by the negro catchers. At this time the Fugitive Slave Law was in full operation, and it was against the law of the whole
country to aid and protect an escaped slave; not even a drink of water, for the
love of the Master, might be given, and those who dared to do it (and there
were many such brave hearts, thank God!) placed their lives in danger.

The presence of bloodhounds and "nigger catchers" in their midst, created great excitement and scandalized the community. Feeling ran high and
hundreds of people gathered together and declared that mother should not
be returned to slavery; but fearing that Mr. Cox would wreak his vengeance
upon me, my mother finally gave herself up to her captors, and returned to
St. Louis. And so the mothers of Israel have been ever slain through their
deepest affections!

After my mother's return, she decided to sue for her freedom, and for
that purpose employed a good lawyer. She had ample testimony to prove
that she was kidnapped, and it was so fully verified that the jury decided that
she was a free woman, and papers were made out accordingly.

In the meanwhile, Miss Martha Berry had married Mr. Mitchell and
taken me to live with her. I had never been taught to work, as playing with
the babies had been my sole occupation; therefore, when Mrs. Mitchell commanded me to do the weekly washing and ironing, I had no more idea how it
was to be done than Mrs. Mitchell herself. But I made the effort to do what
she required, and my failure would have been amusing had it not been so
appalling. In those days filtering was unknown and the many ways of clearing water were to me an unsolved riddle. I never had to do it, so it never
concerned me how the clothes were ever washed clean.

As the Mississippi water was even muddier than now, the results of my
washing can be better imagined than described. After soaking and boiling
the clothes in its earthy depths, for a couple of days, in vain attempt to get
them clean, and rinsing through several waters, I found the clothes were
getting darker and darker, until they nearly approximated my own color. In
my despair, I frantically rushed to my mother and sobbed out my troubles
on her kindly breast. So in the morning, before the white people had arisen,
a friend of my mother came to the house and washed out the clothes. During all this time, Mrs. Mitchell was scolding vigorously, saying over and over
again, "Lucy, you do not want to work, you are a lazy, good-for-nothing nigger!" I was angry at being called a nigger, and replied, "You don't know nothing, yourself, about it, and you expect a poor ignorant girl to know more

---

[1] **lodestone** A magnet.

than you do yourself; if you had any feeling you would get somebody to teach me, and then I'd do well enough."

She then gave me a wrapper to do up, and told me if I ruined that as I 10 did the other clothes, she would whip me severely. I answered, "You have no business to whip me. I don't belong to you."

My mother had so often told me that she was a free woman and that I should not die a slave, I always had a feeling of independence, which would invariably crop out in these encounters with my mistress; and when I thus spoke, saucily, I must confess, she opened her eyes in angry amazement and cried:

"You *do* belong to me, for my papa left you to me in his will, when you were a baby, and you ought to be ashamed of yourself to talk so to one that you have been raised with; now, you take that wrapper, and if you don't do it up properly, I will bring you up with a round turn."

Without further comment, I took the wrapper, which was too handsome to trust to an inexperienced hand, like Mrs. Mitchell very well knew I was, and washed it, with the same direful results as chronicled before. But I could not help it, as heaven is my witness. I was entirely and hopelessly ignorant! But of course my mistress would not believe it, and declared over and over again, that I did it on purpose to provoke her and show my defiance of her wishes. In vain did I disclaim any such intentions. She was bound to carry out her threat of whipping me.

I rebelled against such government, and would not permit her to strike me; she used shovel, tongs, and broomstick in vain, as I disarmed her as fast as she picked up each weapon. Infuriated at her failure, my opposition and determination not to be whipped, Mrs. Mitchell declared she would report me to Mr. Mitchell and have him punish me.

When her husband returned home, she immediately entered a list of 15 complaints against me as long as the moral law, including my failure to wash her clothes properly, and her inability to break my head for it; the last indictment seemed to be the heaviest she could bring against me. I was in the shadow of the doorway as the woman raved, while Mr. Mitchell listened patiently until the end of his wife's grievances reached an appeal to him to whip me with the strength that a man alone could possess.

Then he declared, "Martha, this thing of cutting up and slashing servants is something I know nothing about, and positively will not do. I don't believe in slavery, anyhow; it is a curse on this land, and I wish we were well rid of it."

"Mr. Mitchell, I will not have that saucy baggage around this house, for if she finds you won't whip her, there will be no living with her, so you shall just sell her, and I insist upon it."

"Well, Martha," he answered, "I found the girl with you when we were married, and as you claim her as yours, I shall not interpose any objections to the disposal of what you choose to call your property, in any manner you see fit, and I will make arrangements for selling her at once."

I distinctly overheard all that was said, and was just as determined not to be sold as I was not to be whipped. My mother's lawyer had told her to caution me never to go out of the city, if, at any time, the white people wanted me to go, so I was quite settled as to my course, in case Mr. Mitchell undertook to sell me.

Several days after this conversation took place, Mrs. Mitchell, with 20 her baby and nurse, Lucy Wash, made a visit to her grandmother's, leaving orders that I should be sold before her return; so I was not surprised to be ordered by Mr. Mitchell to pack up my clothes and get ready to go down the river, for I was to be sold that morning, and leave, on the steamboat *Alex. Scott*, at 3 o'clock in the afternoon.

"Can't I go see my mother, first?" I asked.

"No," he replied, not very gently, "there is no time for that, you can see her when you come back. So hurry up and get ready, and let us have no more words about it!"

> *"My mother had so often told me that she was a free woman and that I should not die a slave, I always had a feeling of independence[.]"*

How I did hate him! To hear him talk as if I were going to take a pleasure trip, when he knew that if he sold me South, as he intended, I would never see my dear mother again.

However, I hastily ran upstairs and packed my trunk, but my mother's injunction, "never to go out of the city," was ever present in my mind.

Mr. Mitchell was Superintendent of Indian Affairs, his office being in 25 the dwelling house, and I could hear him giving orders to his clerk, as I ran lightly down the stairs, out of the front door to the street, and with fleet foot, I skimmed the road which led to my mother's door, and, reaching it, stood trembling in every limb with terror and fatigue.

I could not gain admittance, as my mother was away to work and the door was locked. A white woman, living next door, and who was always friendly to mother, told me that she would not return until night. I clasped my hands in despair and cried, "Oh! the white people have sold me, and I had to run away to keep from being sent down the river."

This white lady, whose name I am sorry I cannot remember, sympathized with me, as she knew my mother's story and had written many letters for her, so she offered me the key of her house, which, fortunately, fitted my mother's door, and I was soon inside, cowering with fear in the darkness, magnifying every noise and every passing wind, until my imagination had almost converted the little cottage into a boat, and I was steaming down South, away from my mother, as fast as I could go.

Late at night mother returned, and was told all that had happened, and after getting supper, she took me to a friend's house for concealment, until the next day.

As soon as Mr. Mitchell had discovered my unlooked-for departure, he was furious, for he did not think I had sense enough to run away; he accused the coachman of helping me off, and, despite the poor man's denials, hurried him away to the calaboose[2] and put him under the lash, in order to force a confession. Finding this course unavailing, he offered a reward to the negro catchers, on the same evening, but their efforts were equally fruitless.

Understanding Ideas

1. What most annoys Mrs. Cox about Lucy's mother's behavior?
2. How difficult was it to sell a slave at that time?
3. What was the procedure for capturing escaped slaves?
4. How much "freedom" did slaves like Polly and Lucy seem to have?

Responding to Ideas

1. **Research** Lucy A. Delaney mentions the Fugitive Slave Act as being in "full operation" (para. 5) when she was young. Research the provisions of this law and explain why Delaney calls our attention to it. The law was designed to protect slave owners from losing property — their slaves. Since the Fugitive Slave Act was in fact the "law of the whole country" (para. 5), are we to consider the return of an escaped slave an act of justice? Why or why not? Is not justice the carrying out of the law?

2. **Analysis of Circumstances** Examine this selection for its portrait of the circumstances of domestic slavery. What does Lucy reveal about the conditions under which she and her mother lived? What does she reveal about the general attitude of the white slave owners? Is there anything about the narrative that surprised you and made you revise your view of slavery in the mid-nineteenth century?

3. **Response** Lucy A. Delaney has often been characterized as a deeply spiritual woman. In later life, when she was free, she joined the African Methodist Episcopal Church and many civic organizations. She took leadership positions in the Daughters of Zion and in the African American

---

[2] **calaboose** The local jail.

Female Union. What aspects of Delaney's narrative give you insight into her spiritual and religious beliefs? Were they helpful to her during her struggle? Or was her religion a narcotic that made slavery tolerable?

4. *Research* There were more than three hundred freedom suits presented in St. Louis courts from 1814 to 1860. They were all efforts to secure freedom through the powers of the justice system. Research these suits and decide how effectively they provided justice to slaves of the period. The history of the circuit courts of St. Louis is available at www.stlcourtrecords.wustl.edu/about-freedom-suits-series.php. To what extent did these suits satisfy the need for justice for the slaves who presented them?

5. *Research* Analyze this narrative for what it reveals about the character of Lucy A. Delaney. What do you learn about her life experiences? What do you learn about her emotional nature? What do you learn about her native intelligence? What does she reveal about her ambitions and her talents? If you wish, you can consult the entirety of her book, *From the Darkness Cometh the Light, or Struggles for Freedom*, at Project Gutenberg online.

Comparing Ideas

1. Compare what Jean-Jacques Rousseau says about slavery in "Of Slavery and the Social Pact" (p. 136) with the realities of slavery in Delaney's narrative. How might Delaney have responded to Rousseau's arguments against Hugo Grotius's support of slavery? In what way might Rousseau have come to the aid of Delaney? What kind of social pact seems to have been in existence in 1840s St. Louis that helped shape the form of slavery that Delaney suffered?

2. How does Lucy A. Delaney's quest for freedom demonstrate the truths of the ideas that Cornel West develops in "The Deep Democratic Tradition in America" (p. 111)? How do her ambitions reflect the traditions that West examines? What might West have to say about Delaney's struggles? How do these two writers connect the desire for freedom with the structure of a democracy? In a brief essay, show the interconnected ideas of these two authors.

3. Which of Amartya Sen's arguments in "The Idea of Justice" (p. 183) fits best with Delaney's and her mother's quests for justice? What aspects of Polly's and Delaney's struggles does Sen seem to regard most sympathetically? How much are the ideas in these selections held in common by both writers? Write a brief essay that describes the ways Sen may be said to have learned about justice by reading Delaney's narrative.

FRANKLIN DELANO
ROOSEVELT

© Oscar White/Corbis

FRANKLIN DELANO ROOSEVELT (1882–1945) was president of the United States from 1933 until his death in 1945. When he came into office, the nation and most of Europe and the West were in the middle of the Great Depression, which had begun in 1929 and resulted in the collapse of the banking and financial systems in most of the capitalist world. Roosevelt's programs, such as the Works Progress Administration (WPA), put many people back to work, and his decision to spend more, rather than less, federal money on major federal and local projects was instrumental in bringing a sense of normalcy back to the nation.

Although Roosevelt was himself a member of an influential and wealthy family and a relative of the earlier president Theodore Roosevelt (1858–1919), his appeal to the American public was extraordinarily widespread. His programs to relieve the social problems of the 1930s helped alleviate the pain of the 25 percent of people unemployed when he took office. He began a relief program to aid the homeless and the hungry. Once he had begun to make progress, he instituted Social Security, passed an act ensuring a minimum wage, and introduced legislation to guarantee the security of bank deposits, all of which continue to exist today.

In 1937, in addition to the problems at home with the continuing depression, Roosevelt saw that Japanese invasions in Asia threatened world peace, while the rise of Nazi Germany, which had begun in 1933, was a major issue in Europe. World War II began in 1939 in Europe, with Germany invading Poland. The United States was neutral and determined to stay out of the war, but Roosevelt knew that the Nazi plans were extensive and had to be stopped. He did not have the power to declare war, even when England was the last free European nation fighting against the Nazis. It was not until December 7, 1941, when the Japanese attacked the United States at Pearl Harbor, Hawaii, that Roosevelt was able to declare war on both Japan and Germany.

Roosevelt's "The Four Freedoms" is part of the State of the Union speech he delivered on January 6, 1941, at the beginning of his fourth term and almost a year before the United States went to war. This speech was brought about by the fact that Europe had been at war for sixteen months and almost all the democratic nations of Europe had lost their freedom to the Nazi invaders. The Nazis had already begun widespread roundups of millions of people, whom they eventually gassed, murdered, or forced into slave labor. Roosevelt saw war coming and used his speech to inspire support for aiding the rest of the world and helping guarantee the continued existence of modern democracy.

Be sure to practice prereading techniques before a careful, annotated reading of Roosevelt's speech. For a review of prereading strategies, see pages 4–9. ⌗

The Four Freedoms

THE NATION takes great satisfaction and much strength from the things which have been done to make its people conscious of their individual stake in the preservation of democratic life in America. Those things have toughened the fiber of our people, have renewed their faith and strengthened their devotion to the institutions we make ready to protect.

Certainly this is no time for any of us to stop thinking about the social and economic problems which are the root cause of the social revolution which is today a supreme factor in the world.

For there is nothing mysterious about the foundations of a healthy and strong democracy. The basic things expected by our people of their political and economic systems are simple. They are:

Equality of opportunity for youth and for others.

Jobs for those who can work.

Security for those who need it.

The ending of special privilege for the few.

The preservation of civil liberties for all.

The enjoyment of the fruits of scientific progress in a wider and constantly rising standard of living.

These are the simple, basic things that must never be lost sight of in the turmoil and unbelievable complexity of our modern world. The inner and abiding strength of our economic and political system is dependent upon the degree to which they fulfill these expectations.

Many subjects connected with our social economy call for immediate 5 improvement. As examples:

We should bring more citizens under the coverage of old-age pensions and unemployment insurance.

We should widen the opportunities for adequate medical care.

We should plan a better system by which persons deserving or needing gainful employment may obtain it.

I have called for personal sacrifice. I am assured of the willingness of almost all Americans to respond to that call.

A part of the sacrifice means the payment of more money in taxes. In my Budget Message I shall recommend that a greater portion of this great defense program be paid for from taxation than we are paying today. No person should try, or be allowed, to get rich out of this program; and the principle of tax payments in accordance with ability to pay should be constantly before our eyes to guide our legislation.

If the Congress maintains these principles, the voters, putting patriotism ahead of pocketbooks, will give you their applause.

In the future days, which we seek to make secure, we look forward to a world founded upon four essential human freedoms.

The first is freedom of speech and expression — everywhere in the 10 world.

The second is freedom of every person to worship God in his own way — everywhere in the world.

The third is freedom from want — which, translated into world terms, means economic understandings which will secure to every nation a healthy peacetime life for its inhabitants — everywhere in the world.

The fourth is freedom from fear — which, translated into world terms, means a worldwide reduction of armaments to such a point and in such a thorough fashion that no nation will be in a position to commit an act of physical aggression against any neighbor — anywhere in the world.

That is no vision of a distant millennium. It is a definite basis for a kind of world attainable in our own time and generation. That kind of world is the very antithesis of the so-called new order of tyranny which the dictators seek to create with the crash of a bomb.

To that new order we oppose the greater conception — the moral order. 15 A good society is able to face schemes of world domination and foreign revolutions alike without fear.

Since the beginning of our American history, we have been engaged in change — in a perpetual peaceful revolution — a revolution which goes on steadily, quietly adjusting itself to changing conditions — without the concentration camp or the quicklime in the ditch.[1] The world order which we seek is the cooperation of free countries, working together in a friendly, civilized society.

This nation has placed its destiny in the hands and heads and hearts of its millions of free men and women; and its faith in freedom under the guidance of God. Freedom means the supremacy of human rights everywhere. Our support goes to those who struggle to gain those rights or keep them. Our strength is our unity of purpose.

To that high concept there can be no end save victory.

Understanding Ideas

1. What does Franklin Delano Roosevelt say are the "foundations of a healthy and strong democracy" (para. 3)?

2. What does Roosevelt say about equality in our democracy?

3. What personal sacrifice does Roosevelt ask of the people?

4. What are the four freedoms?

Responding to Ideas

1. *Example* Which of the four freedoms is most under assault in the world today? If we assume that democracy protects these freedoms and guarantees them to its citizens, why is any freedom under assault anywhere? Why is the one freedom you have selected especially threatening to nondemocratic nations? What is particularly problematic about this freedom for a nation? Give some examples of the ways this particular freedom is not tolerated abroad. Is it an act of injustice to deny this or any of the freedoms Roosevelt describes?

2. *Example* Roosevelt proclaims that these freedoms should be guaranteed not just to other democracies but to the people of the United States particularly. Are any of these freedoms under assault in the United States or in the democracy in which you live? If you do not live

---

[1] **quicklime in the ditch** Quicklime was used in mass graves to eat away at the flesh and prevent identification of the dead.

in a democracy, are these freedoms accepted as normal, or are they under threat? Give examples from personal experience or from current news sources, particularly those describing an injustice.

3. **Response** Which of these four freedoms is so essential that without it none of the other freedoms could be guaranteed? Is it freedom of speech, freedom of religion, freedom from want, or freedom from fear? In what ways does the freedom you have chosen as essential help guarantee the other freedoms? What current legal or other controversies have developed concerning the freedom you have chosen? Do you think they are legitimate controversies, or are they politically motivated? How much news coverage has been given to these controversies?

4. **Analysis of Circumstances** Many people say that freedom is good but that it has its limits. What limits should be applied to each of the four freedoms? Why would anyone impose a limit on his or her own freedom? Or are those who suggest limits thinking of restricting others and not themselves? Can you think of any examples that demonstrate the benefits of limiting the rights of people? Essentially, the question is, Does Roosevelt go too far in defining these freedoms? Do his proposals seem more appropriate to 1941 than to the twenty-first century?

5. **Example** Early in this selection, Roosevelt outlines the "basic things expected by our people of their political and economic systems" (para. 3). In most of these categories, the nation in 1941 was not providing them. Is that still true today? Which of the basic things that people should expect is most important? Which is most important to you? Which is most seriously lacking? What is the prognosis for the current political system's ability to provide the basic things people need? Use examples from your own experience as well as examples from current online or published news and magazine articles to support your argument.

6. **Analysis of Circumstances** The last of the basic things people should expect from their government is the "enjoyment of the fruits of scientific progress in a wider and constantly rising standard of living." Is such enjoyment really achievable in our society? Are you and your friends experiencing enjoyment from the fruits of scientific progress? Why is such enjoyment considered a basic right? What particular fruits of scientific progress are available now that were not available (or not widely available) in 1941? How much do you enjoy them? What do you think Roosevelt meant by *enjoyment*?

Comparing Ideas

1. In his essay "Why Democracy?" (p. 96), Robert A. Dahl discusses many of the same issues that concerned Franklin Delano Roosevelt. Dahl knew Roosevelt's speech, which you can read in its entirety online. Compare the way Roosevelt and Dahl develop their ideas. How much does Dahl seem to rely on Roosevelt? How much further does Dahl go in developing the concept of the basic freedoms that must be maintained in a democracy?

2. Compare Roosevelt's speech about the four freedoms with John Rawls's "A Theory of Justice" (p. 159). Write an essay that argues how important the idea of justice is to Roosevelt. Freedom is important in a democracy, and surely the four freedoms Roosevelt describes are aimed at bolstering the strength of American democracy in 1941, when it was under intense threat. But soon after, in 1942, Roosevelt ordered the imprisonment of many Japanese Americans and many Italian Americans. How many of Rawls's ideas seem to be included in the four freedoms speech? How might Roosevelt have reacted to what Rawls feels is essential to the idea of justice?

JOHN
RAWLS

Steve Pyke/Getty Images

Generally considered one of the most important moral philosophers of the second half of the twentieth century, **JOHN RAWLS** (1921–2002) was Conant University Professor at Harvard University. His most important book, *A Theory of Justice* (1971), from which the following selection comes, became a best-seller. Because it is a serious work of philosophy, Rawls was surprised at the book's wide appeal and its influence. Even today, no serious discussion of the philosophical issues involved in examining the theory of justice can begin without reference to his book.

Prior to Rawls's work, most discussions of justice rested on nineteenth-century theories of utilitarianism, a system of justice that benefits the greatest number of people with the greatest good. Utilitarianism has many benefits and is still viewed as a reasonable way of thinking about justice in a complex society. But Rawls considered the problem of justice in a different way. He developed a theory of justice that moved away from the utilitarian concept and toward a system based on fairness.

Rawls argues that justice in any society must take into account the concerns of not only the greater number of people but also the individual. He says that if a social action were to harm an individual then it should be avoided. In a nod to Rousseau, Rawls talks about an original position, which points to the original planners of a society in which "primary goods" — freedom, equality, opportunity, wealth, powers, and income — are thought to be essential. Rawls feels that the planners of society should make their decisions about who receives these primary goods without reference to gender, race, birth, or talent. He talks about a "veil of ignorance," by which he means that the planners of society, when making such decisions, should not base their decisions on their personal circumstances.

Rawls assumes that everyone is directed by self-interest first, so the "veil of ignorance" would not prevent creation of a social structure benefiting only those who were deciding how justice would be allocated. Above all, Rawls believes that justice must be fair and that the rights of the individual should never be sacrificed for the greater good of society. Personal freedom insofar as it did not impinge on the freedom of others was one of his most sacred values. Underlying all these ideas is the insistence that people are equal and should be treated equally.

One of Rawls's most controversial ideas is often referred to as the "difference principle." He felt that any inequality produced by a social structure must be measured by its effect on the least advantaged people in the society. For instance, a tax structure that produced inequality in a society should be measured not by its effect on the wealthy but by its beneficial or harmful effect on the least wealthy.

Be sure to practice prereading techniques before a careful, annotated reading of Rawls's essay. For a review of prereading strategies, see pages 4–9. ⊞

A Theory of Justice

M Y AIM is to present a conception of justice which generalizes and carries to a higher level of abstraction the familiar theory of the social contract as found, say, in Locke, Rousseau, and Kant.[1] In order to do this we are not to think of the original contract as one to enter a particular society or to set up a particular form of government. Rather, the guiding idea is that the principles of justice for the basic structure of society are the object of the original agreement. They are the principles that free and rational persons concerned to further their own interests would accept in an initial position of equality as defining the fundamental terms of their association. These principles are to regulate all further agreements; they specify the kinds of

---

[1] As the text suggests, I shall regard Locke's *Second Treatise of Government*, Rousseau's *The Social Contract*, and Kant's ethical works beginning with *The Foundations of the Metaphysics of Morals* as definitive of the contract tradition. For all of its greatness, Hobbes's *Leviathan* raises special problems. A general historical survey is provided by J. W. Gough, *The Social Contract*, 2nd ed. (Clarendon Press: Oxford, 1957), and Otto Gierke, *Natural Law and the Theory of Society*, trans. with an introduction by Ernest Barker (Cambridge University Press: Cambridge, 1934). A presentation of the contract view as primarily an ethical theory is to be found in G. R. Grice, *The Grounds of Moral Judgment* (Cambridge University Press: Cambridge, 1967). [Rawls's note]

social cooperation that can be entered into and the forms of government that can be established. This way of regarding the principles of justice I shall call justice as fairness.

Thus we are to imagine that those who engage in social cooperation choose together, in one joint act, the principles which are to assign basic rights and duties and to determine the division of social benefits. Men are to decide in advance how they are to regulate their claims against one another and what is to be the foundation charter of their society. Just as each person must decide by rational reflection what constitutes his good, that is, the system of ends which it is rational for him to pursue, so a group of persons must decide once and for all what is to count among them as just and unjust. The choice which rational men would make in this hypothetical situation of equal liberty, assuming for the present that this choice problem has a solution, determines the principles of justice.

In justice as fairness the original position of equality corresponds to the state of nature in the traditional theory of the social contract. This original position is not, of course, thought of as an actual historical state of affairs, much less as a primitive condition of culture. It is understood as a purely hypothetical situation characterized so as to lead to a certain conception of justice.[2] Among the essential features of this situation is that no one knows his place in society, his class position or social status, nor does any one know his fortune in the distribution of natural assets and abilities, his intelligence, strength, and the like. I shall even assume that the parties do not know their conceptions of the good or their special psychological propensities. The principles of justice are chosen behind a veil of ignorance. This ensures that no one is advantaged or disadvantaged in the choice of principles by the outcome of natural chance or the contingency of social circumstances. Since all are similarly situated and no one is able to design principles to favor his particular condition, the principles of justice are the result of a fair agreement or bargain. For given the circumstances of the original position, the symmetry of everyone's relations to each other, this initial situation is fair between individuals as moral persons, that is, as rational beings with their own ends and capable, I shall assume, of a sense of justice. The original position is, one might say, the appropriate initial status quo, and thus the fundamental agreements reached in it are fair. This explains the propriety of

---

[2] Kant is clear that the original agreement is hypothetical. See *The Metaphysics of Morals*, pt. I (*Rechtslehre*), especially §§ 47, 52; and pt. II of the essay "Concerning the Common Saying: This May Be True in Theory but It Does Not Apply in Practice," in *Kant's Political Writings*, ed. Hans Reiss and trans. H. B. Nisbet (Cambridge University Press: Cambridge, 1970), 73–87. See Georges Vlachos, *La Pensée politique de Kant* (Presses Universitaires de France: Paris, 1962), 326–35; and J. G. Murphy, *Kant: The Philosophy of Right* (Macmillan: London, 1970), 109–12, 133–36, for a further discussion. [Rawls's note]

the name "justice as fairness": it conveys the idea that the principles of justice are agreed to in an initial situation that is fair. The name does not mean that the concepts of justice and fairness are the same, any more than the phrase "poetry as metaphor" means that the concepts of poetry and metaphor are the same.

Justice as fairness begins, as I have said, with one of the most general of all choices which persons might make together, namely with the choice of the first principles of a conception of justice which is to regulate all subsequent criticism and reform of institutions. Then, having chosen a conception of justice, we can suppose that they are to choose a constitution and a legislature to enact laws, and so on, all in accordance with the principles of justice initially agreed upon. Our social situation is just if it is such that by this sequence of hypothetical agreements we would have contracted into the general system of rules which defines it. Moreover, assuming that the original position does determine a set of principles (that is, that a particular conception of justice would be chosen), it will then be true that whenever social institutions satisfy these principles those engaged in them can say to one another that they are cooperating on terms to which they would agree if they were free and equal persons whose relations with respect to one another were fair. They could all view their arrangements as meeting the stipulations which they would acknowledge in an initial situation that embodies widely accepted and reasonable constraints on the choice of principles. The general recognition of this fact would provide the basis for a public acceptance of the corresponding principles of justice. No society can, of course, be a scheme of cooperation which men enter voluntarily in a literal sense; each person finds himself placed at birth in some particular position in some particular society, and the nature of this position materially affects his life prospects. Yet a society satisfying the principles of justice as fairness comes as close as a society can to being a voluntary scheme, for it meets the principles which free and equal persons would assent to under circumstances that are fair. In this sense its members are autonomous and the obligations they recognize self-imposed.

One feature of justice as fairness is to think of the parties in the initial 5 situation as rational and mutually disinterested. This does not mean that the parties are egoists, that is, individuals with only certain kinds of interests, say in wealth, prestige, and domination. But they are conceived as not taking an interest in one another's interests. They are to presume that even their spiritual aims may be opposed, in the way that the aims of those of different religions may be opposed. Moreover, the concept of rationality must be interpreted as far as possible in the narrow sense, standard in economic theory, of taking the most effective means to given ends. I shall modify this concept to some extent, but one must try to avoid introducing into it any controversial ethical elements. The initial situation must be characterized by stipulations that are widely accepted.

In working out the conception of justice as fairness one main task clearly is to determine which principles of justice would be chosen in the original position. To do this we must describe this situation in some detail and formulate with care the problem of choice which it presents. . . . It may be observed, however, that once the principles of justice are thought of as arising from an original agreement in a situation of equality, it is an open question whether the principle of utility would be acknowledged. Offhand it hardly seems likely that persons who view themselves as equals, entitled to press their claims upon one another, would agree to a principle which may require lesser life prospects for some simply for the sake of a greater sum of advantages enjoyed by others. Since each desires to protect his interests, his capacity to advance his conception of the good, no one has a reason to acquiesce in an enduring loss for himself in order to bring about a greater net balance of satisfaction. In the absence of strong and lasting benevolent impulses, a rational man would not accept a basic structure merely because it maximized the algebraic sum of advantages irrespective of its permanent effects on his own basic rights and interests. Thus it seems that the principle of utility is incompatible with the conception of social cooperation among equals for mutual advantage. It appears to be inconsistent with the idea of reciprocity implicit in the notion of a well-ordered society. Or, at any rate, so I shall argue.

> "Yet a society satisfying the principles of justice as fairness comes as close as a society can to being a voluntary scheme, for it meets the principles which free and equal persons would assent to under circumstances that are fair."

I shall maintain instead that the persons in the initial situation would choose two rather different principles: the first requires equality in the assignment of basic rights and duties, while the second holds that social and economic inequalities, for example inequalities of wealth and authority, are just only if they result in compensating benefits for everyone, and in particular for the least advantaged members of society. These principles rule out justifying institutions on the grounds that the hardships of some are offset by a greater good in the aggregate. It may be expedient but it is not just that some should have less in order that others may prosper. But there is no injustice in the greater benefits earned by a few provided that the situation of persons not so fortunate is thereby improved. The intuitive idea is that since everyone's well-being depends upon a scheme of cooperation without which no one could have a satisfactory life, the division of advantages should be such as to draw forth the willing cooperation of everyone taking part in it, including those less well situated. Yet this can be expected only if reasonable terms are proposed. The two principles mentioned seem to be a fair agreement on the basis of which those better endowed, or more fortunate in their social position, neither of which we can be said to deserve, could expect the willing cooperation of others when some workable scheme is a necessary condition of the welfare of all.[3] Once we decide to look for a conception of justice that nullifies the accidents of natural endowment and the contingencies of social circumstance as counters in quest for political and economic advantage, we are led to these principles. They express the result of leaving aside those aspects of the social world that seem arbitrary from a moral point of view.

The problem of the choice of principles, however, is extremely difficult. I do not expect the answer I shall suggest to be convincing to everyone. It is, therefore, worth noting from the outset that justice as fairness, like other contract views, consists of two parts: (1) an interpretation of the initial situation and of the problem of choice posed there, and (2) a set of principles which, it is argued, would be agreed to. One may accept the first part of the theory (or some variant thereof), but not the other, and conversely. The concept of the initial contractual situation may seem reasonable although the particular principles proposed are rejected. To be sure, I want to maintain that the most appropriate conception of this situation does lead to principles of justice contrary to utilitarianism and perfectionism, and therefore that the contract doctrine provides an alternative to these views. Still, one may dispute this contention even though one grants that the contractarian method is a useful way of studying ethical theories and of setting forth their underlying assumptions.

Justice as fairness is an example of what I have called a contract theory. Now there may be an objection to the term "contract" and related expressions, but I think it will serve reasonably well. Many words have misleading connotations which at first are likely to confuse. The terms "utility" and "utilitarianism" are surely no exception. They too have unfortunate suggestions which hostile critics have been willing to exploit; yet they are clear enough for those prepared to study utilitarian doctrine. The same should be true of the term "contract" applied to moral theories. As I have mentioned, to understand it one has to keep in mind that it implies a certain level of abstraction. In particular, the content of the relevant agreement is not to enter a given society or to adopt a given form of government, but to accept certain moral principles. Moreover, the undertakings referred to are purely hypothetical: a contract view holds that certain principles would be accepted in a well-defined initial situation.

---

[3] For the formulation of this intuitive idea I am indebted to Allan Gibbard. [Rawls's note]

The merit of the contract terminology is that it conveys the idea that   10
principles of justice may be conceived as principles that would be chosen
by rational persons, and that in this way conceptions of justice may be
explained and justified. The theory of justice is a part, perhaps the most
significant part, of the theory of rational choice. Furthermore, principles
of justice deal with conflicting claims upon the advantages won by social
cooperation; they apply to the relations among several persons or groups.
The word "contract" suggests this plurality as well as the condition that
the appropriate division of advantages must be in accordance with principles acceptable to all parties. The condition of publicity for principles of
justice is also connoted by the contract phraseology. Thus, if these principles are the outcome of an agreement, citizens have a knowledge of the
principles that others follow. It is characteristic of contract theories to
stress the public nature of political principles. Finally there is the long tradition of the contract doctrine. Expressing the tie with this line of thought
helps to define ideas and accords with natural piety. There are then several
advantages in the use of the term "contract." With due precautions taken, it
should not be misleading.

A final remark. Justice as fairness is not a complete contract theory. For
it is clear that the contractarian idea can be extended to the choice of more
or less an entire ethical system, that is, to a system including principles for
all the virtues and not only for justice. Now for the most part I shall consider only principles of justice and others closely related to them; I make
no attempt to discuss the virtues in a systematic way. Obviously if justice as
fairness succeeds reasonably well, a next step would be to study the more
general view suggested by the name "rightness as fairness." But even this
wider theory fails to embrace all moral relationships, since it would seem
to include only our relations with other persons and to leave out of account
how we are to conduct ourselves toward animals and the rest of nature.
I do not contend that the contract notion offers a way to approach these
questions which are certainly of the first importance; and I shall have to
put them aside. We must recognize the limited scope of justice as fairness
and of the general type of view that it exemplifies. How far its conclusions
must be revised once these other matters are understood cannot be decided
in advance.

Understanding Ideas

1. What does John Rawls mean by the "original position of equality"
    (para. 3) in founding a society?

2. Why is the "veil of ignorance" (para. 3) of such importance to the founders of a society?

3. How is justice as fairness a "contract theory" (para. 9), and why is it an incomplete one?

4. How is justice as fairness different from the utilitarian view of the greatest good for the greatest number?

Responding to Ideas

1. **Definition** John Rawls talks about the way founders of society come to understand what they mean by *justice*. What do you think the founders of the United States meant by *justice*? Rawls does not define the term. How would you go about defining it after reading what he says about it? If it is the product of an agreement among people, what are people agreeing to? How do you see the most important qualities of justice as they operate in your environment?

2. **Analysis of Circumstances** Rawls discusses the concept of equality throughout his essay. Writers on democracy also talk about equality with much the same intensity. If democracy depends on justice, and if both depend on equality, how are we to interpret the success or failure of equality in our culture? Rawls discusses "inequalities of wealth and authority" but says that they "are just only if they result in compensating benefits for everyone" (para. 7). In our contemporary culture, there are considerable inequalities in wealth and authority. Construct an argument defending those inequalities as just. Or construct an argument demonstrating that they are unjust.

3. **Research** The concept of utilitarianism is widely accepted today as an appropriate principle for guiding our society. It was first introduced by the British philosophers Jeremy Bentham (1748–1832) and John Stuart Mill (1806–1873), and it is usually described as a social system that guarantees the greatest good for the greatest number. What is your view of the potential for justice in a utilitarian system? Why would Rawls find utilitarianism unacceptable? Which system of justice would you prefer to live in? Which system seems most democratic in its function?

4. **Definition** Rawls uses the word *moral* several times throughout his essay. He appears to feel that he is engaged in a moral argument. *Moral* usually implies a spiritual value and sometimes religious values. Is justice a moral virtue or simply a legal virtue? Is the notion that justice must be measured by its effect on the least advantaged of our citizens a moral argument? If so, why? What makes the concept of justice in

society a moral issue? Do the religions that you know about discuss justice as if it were a moral issue? Do you?

5. ***Analysis of Circumstances*** In his discussion, Rawls reminds us that he refers to a society in which rational people have shaped the social order and made their judgments rationally. He suggests this is a matter of great importance. He also says that the decisions of social founders should be disinterested, by which he means the founders should put their own interests aside and act on behalf of the whole without expecting special privileges. To what extent do you observe that government leaders behave in a disinterested fashion? Why would putting one's own interests first possibly lead to a pattern of injustice?

6. ***Example*** Look for examples in current circumstances in which justice fails to benefit the least advantaged of our society. What examples can you find in which the least advantaged of our society are actually harmed by the unjust behavior of legislation or government action? By way of contrast, what examples can you find online or in news sources in which the least advantaged in society have benefited from acts of justice? Decide in a brief essay whether or not the kind of justice Rawls proposes should be recommended and whether or not it could be successful. Does it seem to be a goal of our democracy?

Comparing Ideas

1. Compare Rawls's conception of a social agreement with Jean-Jacques Rousseau's (p. 136) conception of a social agreement. Both men talk about the social contract and are therefore "contractarian" in their views of society. What does this mean? Are you contractarian? Should we all be contractarian? Rawls not only read Rousseau but also indicates in his footnotes that he was clearly influenced by him. Explain what you see as the fruit of that influence. What have you agreed to in terms of understanding justice as it should function in your society? What do other people seem to have agreed to in order to make society work and justice possible?

2. Compare the views of John Rawls with those of Andrew Carnegie in "The Gospel of Wealth" (p. 289). To what extent does each author agree on the principles of self-interest in society? To what extent does each believe in similar principles of justice? What might have been Rawls's criticisms of Carnegie's view that wealth in the hands of the few benefited society more than if it were in the hands of the many? Using the principles of one of these authors, write a critique of the other's ideas of justice.

3. Amartya Sen wrote "The Idea of Justice" (p. 183) in part to respond to the work of John Rawls, with whom he disagrees on many key points. After reading Sen's selection from that book, write a brief essay that clarifies the points on which he disagrees with Rawls. In the process of writing that essay, explain your position in relation to each writer. Which points, in the work of either author, do you find yourself most at ease with? Which points are least satisfying to you?

JAMES
BALDWIN

One of America's foremost writers, **JAMES BALDWIN** (1924–1987) grew up in a household in Harlem with a preacher father whose hatred of white people distorted his personality. Seeing what damage hatred could do, and with the help of a schoolteacher who became a counselor, James Baldwin said he found it difficult to hate white people or any people.

© Bettmann/Corbis

Much of Baldwin's work in fiction, drama, and essays focuses on the problems of racism and how they harm both individuals and the nation. His career began when he was fourteen, as a preacher in a Pentecostal church, where he served until he was sixteen, after which he turned his back on Christianity. Baldwin has said that his experiences in church represented a major education in language and affected the way he wrote. His autobiographical novel, *Go Tell It on the Mountain* (1953), takes place on one day in a church in Harlem and draws from his youthful experience.

Racism was a fact of life in the 1940s, and in 1948, Baldwin moved to France, where he could avoid some of the racial pressures he had found in New York City. One of his reasons for choosing France was that Richard Wright, one of America's most famous African American novelists, had chosen to live there. Baldwin became Wright's friend in part because of his respect for his writing. By the 1960s, Baldwin had become an international commuter. He lived in St. Paul de Vence and other places in southern France, as well as in New York City and New England. In a sense, he was a "citizen of the world" and was publishing more and more interesting work.

In the years before and after Baldwin wrote "My Dungeon Shock: Letter to My Nephew on the One Hundredth Anniversary of the Emancipation" (1962), America was going through enormous social changes. The civil rights movement to guarantee basic rights for African Americans throughout the nation had only just begun in earnest, and Baldwin was clearly angered by the struggles African Americans were experiencing everywhere. In 1963, a year after his "Letter," Baldwin published one of his most impassioned and alarming works: *The Fire Next Time*. In *The New Yorker* essay version, titled "Down at the Cross," an allusion to extensive suffering, he begins with an exploration of his encounter with Black Muslim separatists, members of a widespread movement that did not attract him because of its potential for violence. Baldwin had become by then a major voice in the civil rights movement, speaking and writing wherever and whenever he could, and was recognized for his efforts with the distinction of being on the cover of *Time* magazine.

Baldwin supported Martin Luther King Jr.'s nonviolent approach to get the government to change laws about segregation. He belonged to the Congress for Racial Equality and lectured on civil rights in several southern states. Unfortunately, because he was homosexual and because black civil rights organizations were hostile to homosexuality at the time, Baldwin was not embraced by Dr. King, and he was not asked to speak at the civil rights march in Washington in 1963.

Be sure to practice prereading techniques before a careful, annotated reading of Baldwin's letter. For a review of prereading strategies, see pages 4–9. ⊞

My Dungeon Shook: Letter to My Nephew on the One Hundredth Anniversary of the Emancipation

DEAR JAMES:

I have begun this letter five times and torn it up five times. I keep seeing your face, which is also the face of your father and my brother. Like him, you are tough, dark, vulnerable, moody — with a very definite tendency to sound truculent because you want no one to think you are soft. You may be like your grandfather in this, I don't know, but certainly both you and your father resemble him very much physically. Well, he is dead, he never saw you, and he had a terrible life; he was defeated long before he died because, at the bottom of his heart, he really believed what white people said about him. This is one of the reasons that he became so holy. I am sure that your father has told you something about all that. Neither you nor your father exhibit any tendency towards holiness: you really *are* of another era, part of what happened when the Negro left the land and came into what the late E. Franklin Frazier[1] called "the cities of destruction." You can only be destroyed by believing that you really are what the white world calls a *nigger*. I tell you this because I love you, and please don't you ever forget it.

I have known both of you all your lives, have carried your Daddy in my arms and on my shoulders, kissed and spanked him and watched him learn to walk. I don't know if you've known anybody from that far back; if you've loved anybody that long, first as an infant, then as a child, then as a man, you gain a strange perspective on time and human pain and effort. Other people cannot see what I see whenever I look into your father's face, for behind your father's face as it is today are all those other faces which were his. Let him laugh and I see a cellar your father does not remember and a house he does not remember and I hear in his present laughter his laughter as a child. Let him curse and I remember him falling down the cellar steps, and howling, and I remember, with pain, his tears, which my hand or your grandmother's so easily wiped away. But no one's hand can wipe away those tears he sheds invisibly today, which one hears in his laughter and in his speech and in his songs. I know what the world has done to my brother and how narrowly he has survived it. And I know, which is much worse, and this is the crime of which I accuse my country and my countrymen, and for which neither I nor time nor history will ever forgive them, that they have destroyed and are destroying hundreds of thousands of lives and do not know it and do not want to know it. One can be, indeed one must strive to become, tough and philosophical concerning destruction and death, for this is what most of mankind has been best at since we have heard of man. (But remember: *most* of mankind is not *all* of mankind.) But it is not permissible that the authors of devastation should also be innocent. It is the innocence which constitutes the crime.

Now, my dear namesake, these innocent and well-meaning people, your countrymen, have caused you to be born under conditions not very far removed from those described for us by Charles Dickens[2] in the London of more than a hundred years ago. (I hear the chorus of the innocents screaming, "No! This is not true! How *bitter* you are!" — but I am writing this letter to *you*, to try to tell you something about how to handle *them*, for most of them do not yet really know that you exist. I *know* the conditions under which you were born, for I was there. Your countrymen were *not* there, and haven't made it yet. Your grandmother was also there, and no one has ever accused her of being bitter. I suggest that the innocents check with her. She

---

[1] **E. Franklin Frazier** (1894–1962) One of the first African American sociologists, head of the Sociology Department at Howard University.

[2] **Charles Dickens** (1812–1870) British author of *Oliver Twist*, a portrait of the impoverished in London.

isn't hard to find. Your countrymen don't know that *she* exists, either, though she has been working for them all their lives.)

Well, you were born, here you came, something like fifteen years ago; and though your father and mother and grandmother, looking about the streets through which they were carrying you, staring at the walls into which they brought you, had every reason to be heavyhearted, yet they were not. For here you were, Big James, named for me — you were a big baby, I was not — here you were: to be loved. To be loved, baby, hard, at once, and forever, to strengthen you against the loveless world. Remember that: I know how black it looks today, for you. It looked bad that day, too, yes, we were trembling. We have not stopped trembling yet, but if we had not loved each other none of us would have survived. And now you must survive because we love you, and for the sake of your children and your children's children.

This innocent country set you down in a ghetto in which, in fact, it 5 intended that you should perish. Let me spell out precisely what I mean by that, for the heart of the matter is here, and the root of my dispute with my country. You were born where you were born and faced the future that you faced because you were black and *for no other reason*. The limits of your ambition were, thus, expected to be set forever. You were born into a society which spelled out with brutal clarity, and in as many ways as possible, that you were a worthless human being. You were not expected to aspire to excellence: you were expected to make peace with mediocrity. Wherever you have turned, James, in your short time on this earth, you have been told where you could go and what you could do (and *how* you could do it) and where you could live and whom you could marry. I know your countrymen do not agree with me about this, and I hear them saying, "You exaggerate." They do not know Harlem, and I do. So do you. Take no one's word for anything, including mine — but trust your experience. Know whence you came. If you know whence you came, there is really no limit to where you can go. The details and symbols of your life have been deliberately constructed to make you believe what white people say about you. Please try to remember that what they believe, as well as what they do and cause you to endure, does not testify to your inferiority but to their inhumanity and fear. Please try to be clear, dear James, through the storm which rages about your youthful head today, about the reality which lies behind the words *acceptance* and *integration*. There is no reason for you to try to become like white people and there is no basis whatever for their impertinent assumption that *they* must accept *you*. The really terrible thing, old buddy, is that *you* must accept *them*. And I mean that very seriously. You must accept them and accept them with love. For these innocent people have no other hope. They are, in effect, still trapped in a history which they do not understand; and until they understand it, they cannot be released from it. They have had to believe for many years, and for innumerable reasons, that black men are inferior to white men. Many of them, indeed, know better, but, as you will discover, people find it very difficult to act on what they know. To act is to be committed, and to be committed is to be in danger. In this case, the danger, in the minds of most white Americans, is the loss of their identity. Try to imagine how you would feel if you woke up one morning to find the sun shining and all the stars aflame. You would be frightened because it is out of the order of nature. Any upheaval in the universe is terrifying because it so profoundly attacks one's sense of one's own reality. Well, the black man has functioned in the white man's world as a fixed star, as an immovable pillar: and as he moves out of his place, heaven and earth are shaken to their foundations. You, don't be afraid. I said that it was intended that you should perish in the ghetto, perish by never being allowed to go behind the white man's definitions, by never being allowed to spell your proper name. You have, and many of us have, defeated this intention; and, by a terrible law, a terrible paradox, those innocents who believed that your imprisonment made them safe are losing their grasp of reality. But these men are your brothers — your lost, younger brothers. And if the word *integration* means anything, this is what it means: that we, with love, shall force our brothers to see themselves as they are, to cease fleeing from reality and begin to change it. For this is your home, my friend, do not be driven from it; great men have done great things here, and will again, and we can make America what America must become. It will be hard, James, but you come from sturdy, peasant stock, men who picked cotton and dammed rivers and built railroads, and, in the teeth of the most terrifying odds, achieved an unassailable and monumental dignity. You come from a long line of great poets, some of the greatest poets since Homer.[3] One of them said, *The very time I thought I was lost, My dungeon shook and my chains fell off.*[4]

> *"This innocent country set you down in a ghetto in which, in fact, it intended that you should perish. Let me spell out precisely what I mean by that, for the heart of the matter is here, and the root of my dispute with my country."*

You know, and I know, that the country is celebrating one hundred years of freedom one hundred years too soon. We cannot be free until they are free. God bless you, James, and Godspeed.

Your uncle,

James

---

[3] **Homer** (c. 8th century B.C.E.) Greek author of *The Iliad* and *The Odyssey*.

[4] **"The very . . . fell off"** Lines from "You Got a Right," a Negro spiritual.

Understanding Ideas

1. What is James Baldwin's greatest fear for his nephew?
2. Why does Baldwin spend so much time talking about family resemblances?
3. Of what crimes does he "accuse" his "country" (para. 2)?
4. What does Baldwin say about acceptance and love?

Responding to Ideas

1. *Analysis of Circumstances* James Baldwin's nephew is fifteen years old. What are the circumstances in which both Baldwin and his nephew James have grown up? What does Baldwin tell us about the ghetto and the attitude of white society toward James and his friends and family? How does James seem to react to his uncle's descriptions? Does Baldwin expect James to think as he does or accept his evaluation of his circumstances?

2. *Definition* Baldwin uses the term *ghetto* in referring to the area in which James and he were born. Research the term *ghetto* and clarify its nature. Are ghettos just neighborhoods, or are they something produced by an organized society? Are they uniformly bad, or are they simply neutral? If possible, describe the nature of the ghetto that Baldwin and his nephew likely lived in. Are such ghettos still in existence, more than fifty years after Baldwin wrote this letter?

3. *Comparison* In talking about the "society which spelled out with brutal clarity, and in as many ways as possible, that you were a worthless human being" (para. 5), Baldwin is aware that James and others will think he is exaggerating. Examine what Baldwin says about what society expected of James and write a brief essay that compares what Baldwin says with what you have observed about the expectations of society for minorities of all kinds. What has changed? What has not? If Baldwin is exaggerating, why does he do so? What kind of justice does he want?

4. *Definition* At one point, Baldwin says, "If you know whence you came, there is really no limit to where you can go" (para. 5). What does Baldwin mean by this statement? What does he tell James about him and his family that would help make this statement true for him? Thinking of yourself, why would your knowledge of where you came from help

you get to where you want to go? Define the phrase *whence you came.* It does not just refer to a neighborhood or a ghetto, although it may include that idea. What else does it include?

5. **Research** Baldwin says that the problem is not that white people must accept James but that James must accept white people: "You must accept them and accept them with love" (para. 5). How do you react to this advice? Is it limited only to people of different races? This was written more than fifty years ago. Have things changed enough socially for this advice to apply to a wide range of people? Is it valid advice, and do you have any examples of situations in which it has proved valid and important? How does this advice relate to Baldwin's earlier comments on his possible bitterness? How does the power of love operate to help change society?

6. **Analysis of Circumstances** Late in his "Letter," Baldwin uses the words *acceptance* and *integration.* Now, more than fifty years after his letter was written, what are the circumstances of African Americans and other minorities in relation to those words? Is there greater acceptance of minorities on the part of the majority and more acceptance of the majority on the part of minorities? Is the society in which you live more integrated than society in Baldwin's time? What kind of progress has the nation seen since the one-hundredth anniversary of emancipation? Is justice closer to being achieved today?

Comparing Ideas

1. Compare the views regarding justice held by James Baldwin in his "Letter to My Nephew" and by Martin Luther King Jr. in "I Have a Dream" (p. 176). Both write a hundred years after the emancipation of American slaves. How do they address the issues of justice and injustice that still affected African Americans? What is their approach to achieving a just society? How do they see the connection between freedom and justice? Baldwin says that "the country is celebrating one hundred years of freedom one hundred years too soon" (para. 6). What does he mean by this, and how much does King seem to agree with him?

2. Baldwin knew the work of Jean-Jacques Rousseau (p. 136). Write a brief essay that traces the influences of Rousseau in Baldwin's letter. Baldwin talks about the issues that immediately affect him and his nephew, but he also sees further into the main issues of justice and freedom that excited Rousseau into writing his *Social Contract.* With knowledge of what Rousseau wrote, explain to a reader who knows neither work just how much Baldwin's selection relies on the social theory of Rousseau.

© Corbis

MARTIN LUTHER
KING JR.

For more than fifteen years, **MARTIN LUTHER KING JR.** (1929–1968) was the most powerful voice in America arguing for the civil rights of African Americans. He was one of the organizers of the March on Washington for Jobs and Freedom on August 28, 1963. The signs for the march proclaimed a need for employment and liberty for African Americans. Jim Crow, or segregationist, laws in the South limited the freedom of African Americans by preventing blacks from staying at the same hotels, eating in the same restaurants, or attending the same schools as whites. Discrimination prevented African Americans from equal opportunity in hiring.

When Dr. King spoke in Washington, the South had already been the focus of a great many nonviolent demonstrations. However, police and protesters had begun to escalate the demonstrations into violent confrontations in many southern states. Scenes of violence were in the news regularly in the year before the march. Throughout this period, King had been threatened frequently. The southern sit-ins and voter registration programs spurred countless bombings, threats, and murders by members of the white community. King's life was at risk, his home bombed, and his followers harassed and beaten. He was assassinated at the Lorraine Motel in Memphis, Tennessee, on April 4, 1968. By then, however, his work had begun a massive change in laws and behaviors that continues even today.

The idea of a march on Washington had been in the minds of African American activists for many years. In 1941, A. Phillips Randolph (1889–1979), a union leader and president of the Brotherhood of Sleeping Car Porters, proposed a march as a means of provoking President Franklin Delano Roosevelt into improving the economic opportunities of African Americans applying for jobs at defense plants, which had largely been restricted to whites. Roosevelt signed an order for a Committee on Fair

Employment Practice, and Randolph called off the march. In May 1957, there was a march on Washington under the banner Prayer Pilgrimage for Freedom. But there was nothing of the size and scope of the long-hoped-for march on Washington until 1963.

Dr. King's speech echoes his experience in church and his education as a theologian. He ends, for example, with the words of a Negro spiritual. His ability to speak and write poetically, relying on metaphor to intensify his message, was a particular gift. Metaphors, such as "lonely island of poverty," "the bank of justice is bankrupt," and "the palace of justice," enrich his vision and color his speech in such a way as to affect the emotions of his audience. He remains the most memorable of all who spoke in those years from Washington and elsewhere on behalf of justice for African Americans.

Be sure to practice prereading techniques before a careful, annotated reading of King's speech. For a review of prereading strategies, see pages 4–9. ⊞

I Have a Dream

FIVE SCORE years ago, a great American, in whose symbolic shadow we stand today, signed the Emancipation Proclamation. This momentous decree came as a great beacon of light of hope to millions of Negro slaves who had been seared in the flames of withering injustice. It came as a joyous daybreak to end the long night of their captivity.

But one hundred years later, the Negro still is not free. One hundred years later, the life of the Negro is still sadly crippled by the manacles of segregation and the chains of discrimination.

One hundred years later, the Negro lives on a lonely island of poverty in the midst of a vast ocean of material prosperity. One hundred years later, the Negro is still languished in the corners of American society and finds himself an exile in his own land. So we have come here today to dramatize a shameful condition.

In a sense we have come to our nation's capital to cash a check. When the architects of our republic wrote the magnificent words of the Constitution and the Declaration of Independence, they were signing a promissory note to which every American was to fall heir. This note was a promise that all men, yes, black men as well as white men, would be granted the unalienable rights of life, liberty, and the pursuit of happiness.

It is obvious today that America has defaulted on this promissory note 5
insofar as her citizens of color are concerned. Instead of honoring this
sacred obligation, America has given the Negro people a bad check, which
has come back marked "insufficient funds."

But we refuse to believe that the bank of justice is bankrupt. We refuse
to believe that there are insufficient funds in the great vaults of opportunity
of this nation. So we have come to cash this check — a check that will give
us upon demand the riches of freedom and the security of justice.

We have also come to this hallowed spot to remind America of the fierce
urgency of now. This is no time to engage in the luxury of cooling off or
to take the tranquilizing drug of gradualism. Now is the time to make real the promises
of democracy. Now is the time to rise from the dark and desolate valley of segregation
to the sunlit path of racial justice. Now is the time to lift our nation from the quick-
sands of racial injustice to the solid rock of brotherhood. Now is the time to make justice
a reality for all of God's children.

> *"No, we are not satisfied, and we will not be satisfied until justice rolls down like waters and righteousness like a mighty stream."*

It would be fatal for the nation to overlook the urgency of the movement and to underestimate the determination of the Negro. This sweltering
summer of the Negro's legitimate discontent will not pass until there is an
invigorating autumn of freedom and equality. 1963 is not an end but a beginning. Those who hope that the Negro needed to blow off steam and will
now be content will have a rude awakening if the nation returns to business
as usual.

There will be neither rest nor tranquility in America until the Negro
is granted his citizenship rights. The whirlwinds of revolt will continue to
shake the foundations of our nation until the bright day of justice emerges.

But there is something that I must say to my people who stand on the 10
warm threshold which leads into the palace of justice. In the process of
gaining our rightful place we must not be guilty of wrongful deeds.

Let us not seek to satisfy our thirst for freedom by drinking from the
cup of bitterness and hatred. We must forever conduct our struggle on the
high plane of dignity and discipline. We must not allow our creative protest
to degenerate into physical violence. Again and again we must rise to the
majestic heights of meeting physical force with soul force.

The marvelous new militancy which has engulfed the Negro community
must not lead us to a distrust of all white people, for many of our white
brothers, as evidenced by their presence here today, have come to realize
that their destiny is tied with our destiny and they have come to realize that
their freedom is inextricably bound to our freedom. This offense we share,

mounted to storm the battlements of injustice, must be carried forth by a biracial army. We cannot walk alone.

And as we walk, we must make the pledge that we shall always march ahead. We cannot turn back. There are those who are asking the devotees of civil rights, "When will you be satisfied?" We can never be satisfied as long as the Negro is the victim of the unspeakable horrors of police brutality.

We can never be satisfied as long as our bodies, heavy with the fatigue of travel, cannot gain lodging in the motels of the highways and the hotels of the cities. We cannot be satisfied as long as the Negro's basic mobility is from a smaller ghetto to a larger one.

We can never be satisfied as long as our children are stripped of their 15 selfhood and robbed of their dignity by signs stating "for whites only." We cannot be satisfied as long as a Negro in Mississippi cannot vote and a Negro in New York believes he has nothing for which to vote. No, we are not satisfied, and we will not be satisfied until justice rolls down like waters and righteousness like a mighty stream.

I am not unmindful that some of you have come here out of excessive trials and tribulation. Some of you have come fresh from narrow jail cells. Some of you have come from areas where your quest for freedom left you battered by the storms of persecution and staggered by the winds of police brutality. You have been the veterans of creative suffering. Continue to work with the faith that unearned suffering is redemptive.

Go back to Mississippi; go back to Alabama; go back to South Carolina; go back to Georgia; go back to Louisiana; go back to the slums and ghettos of the northern cities, knowing that somehow this situation can, and will be changed. Let us not wallow in the valley of despair.

So I say to you, my friends, that even though we must face the difficulties of today and tomorrow, I still have a dream. It is a dream deeply rooted in the American dream that one day this nation will rise up and live out the true meaning of its creed — we hold these truths to be self-evident, that all men are created equal.

I have a dream that one day on the red hills of Georgia, sons of former slaves and sons of former slave owners will be able to sit down together at the table of brotherhood.

I have a dream that one day, even the state of Mississippi, a state swel- 20 tering with the heat of injustice, sweltering with the heat of oppression, will be transformed into an oasis of freedom and justice.

I have a dream that my four little children will one day live in a nation where they will not be judged by the color of their skin but by the content of their character. I have a dream today!

I have a dream that one day, down in Alabama, with its vicious racists, with its governor having his lips dripping with the words of interposition and nullification, that one day, right there in Alabama, little black boys and black girls will be able to join hands with little white boys and white girls as sisters and brothers. I have a dream today!

I have a dream that one day every valley shall be exalted, every hill and mountain shall be made low, the rough places shall be made plain, and the crooked places shall be made straight and the glory of the Lord will be revealed and all flesh shall see it together.

This is our hope. This is the faith that I go back to the South with.

With this faith we will be able to hew out of the mountain of despair a 25 stone of hope. With this faith we will be able to transform the jangling discords of our nation into a beautiful symphony of brotherhood.

With this faith we will be able to work together, to pray together, to struggle together, to go to jail together, to stand up for freedom together, knowing that we will be free one day. This will be the day when all of God's children will be able to sing with new meaning — "my country 'tis of thee; sweet land of liberty; of thee I sing; land where my fathers died, land of the pilgrim's pride; from every mountain side, let freedom ring" — and if America is to be a great nation, this must become true.

So let freedom ring from the prodigious hilltops of New Hampshire.

Let freedom ring from the mighty mountains of New York.

Let freedom ring from the heightening Alleghanies of Pennsylvania.

Let freedom ring from the snow-capped Rockies of Colorado.   30

Let freedom ring from the curvaceous slopes of California.

But not only that.

Let freedom ring from Stone Mountain of Georgia.

Let freedom ring from Lookout Mountain of Tennessee.

Let freedom ring from every hill and molehill of Mississippi, from every 35 mountainside, let freedom ring.

And when we allow freedom to ring, when we let it ring from every village and hamlet, from every state and city, we will be able to speed up that day when all of God's children — black men and white men, Jews and Gentiles, Catholics and Protestants — will be able to join hands and to sing in the words of the old Negro spiritual: "Free at last, free at last; thank God Almighty, we are free at last."

Understanding Ideas

1. How and why does Martin Luther King Jr. remind us that he speaks next to the Lincoln Memorial?

2. What "promissory note" does King feel the United States "has defaulted on" (para. 5)?

3. What does King want to achieve by leading the March on Washington?

4. What is King's dream?

Responding to Ideas

1. *Analysis of Circumstances* Dr. King talks about coming to Washington to cash a check. He feels that the government had long ago made a promise to all people and that now it had to make good on it for African Americans. What is the promise that he talks about, and in what way does he feel the government had written a promissory note to its people? Explain to an audience that may not know about the circumstances of the early 1960s what King expects to achieve. What were his hopes for the outcome of this march?

2. *Example* King says, "Now is the time to make justice a reality for all of God's children" (para. 7). To what extent do you think justice has become a reality today? Find examples that support your position. Rely on the experiences of family, friends, or acquaintances. Also interview people who you feel are more expert than you and ask them whether there is more justice for minorities today than in King's time. Use concrete examples that bolster your view.

3. *Research* When King was writing, the police in the South sometimes used extreme violence against nonviolent protesters, both white and black. In 1965 in Alabama, two years after the march on Washington, marches from Selma to Montgomery, the seat of Alabama's government, resulted in dramatic tear gas attacks and attacks with dogs and police clubs. Research the three Selma marches and explain why there was so much violence and what, ultimately, was achieved by those who marched the fifty-four miles from Selma to Montgomery.

4. *Research* In 1963, Dr. King complained of police brutality toward African Americans. A number of events in recent years have brought police brutality back into the public eye. To what extent is police brutality still an issue? Is it widespread? Is it primarily a matter of concern for the African American community, or is it a general problem? Research current news and online sources and establish the nature of police brutality and the effort to control it today. Be specific in your response and argue your case with details from your research.

5. *Analysis of Circumstances* The social circumstances of African Americans in 1963 — especially in the South — were not good. As Dr. King said, justice was denied to a great many Americans. Now, more than fifty years later, how much of King's dream do you feel has been achieved? Several civil rights acts have been passed into law since

1963. How effective have they been? How have the social circumstances of both whites and blacks been improved over the decades? What particular social circumstances of our time would most please Dr. King? What social circumstances achieved by King's efforts most please you?

Comparing Ideas

1. James Baldwin was part of the March on Washington and was a strong supporter of Dr. King's philosophy of nonviolent action. Baldwin wrote "My Dungeon Shook: Letter to My Nephew on the One Hundredth Anniversary of the Emancipation" (p. 169) a year earlier, in 1962, in an atmosphere of racial tension and escalating hopes for the advancement of civil rights. Compare the position that Baldwin takes with that of King. How many of their concerns are shared? How close are their positions on racial matters? In what ways are they different?

2. Many of the issues that stimulated Martin Luther King Jr.'s speech were also considered by Robert A. Dahl in "Why Democracy?" (p. 96). Dahl wrote thirty-five years after King's speech and had the advantage of knowing King's legacy in the fight for freedom for African Americans. In what ways does Dahl appear to have taken King's concerns into consideration when he reviews the benefits of democracy? To what extent does Dahl seem to be taking into account the struggles of African Americans and other minorities in our democracy? What important points does Dahl make that would have distinctly encouraged Dr. King? In what ways do both men seem to agree about the ability of a democracy to secure freedom and justice for all?

3. Of the two writers who theorize about justice, John Rawls (p. 159) and Amartya Sen (p. 183), whose work do you think Martin Luther King Jr. would have felt more comfortable using as a theoretical base of his own? Comparing him to Rawls and to Sen, use ideas in "I Have a Dream" to compose a brief theory of justice as King might have written it. For King, what is most important to all members of society if they are to receive justice? What kinds of justice are most important to him? How do his values regarding justice agree or disagree with those of Rawls and of Sen?

AMARTYA SEN

© Co in McPherson/Corbis

The wide-ranging scholar **AMARTYA SEN** (b. 1933) was born in India and holds an appointment as professor of economics and philosophy at Harvard University. He has also been a professor of economics at Trinity College, Cambridge; the London School of Economics; the University of Calcutta; and the Delhi School of Economics and was the Drummond Professor of Political Economy at Oxford University. He has won numerous prizes for his work, including the 1998 Nobel Prize in Economic Sciences. His books have been translated into more than thirty languages, and he serves on international committees for economic development.

Sen's interest in philosophy, a subject about which he read deeply after his work in economics, has affected his writing and research. His studies focus on social issues such as the effect of economic conditions in producing famines. In 1943, he witnessed a famine in Bengal, during which as many as three million people died because they could not afford the rising cost of food in wartime. As he has pointed out, most famines result not from a lack of food but rather from an economic system that makes food unaffordable to the rural poor and urban service people. His studies also resulted in his considering gender issues from an economic standpoint. In a 1990 article called "More Than 100 Million Women Are Missing," Sen argues that, especially in Asia, gender inequality adds to the increased mortality of women.

Among Sen's many books are *Collective Choice and Social Welfare* (1970); *Choice, Welfare, and Measurement* (1982); *Development as Freedom* (1999); and *The Idea of Justice* (2009), from which the selection that follows is taken. Sen has been deeply moved by social concerns of many kinds. In the following selection, Sen begins by referring to the work of Mary Wollstonecraft and her appeal to reason in defending the rights of women. He centers his comments on her demand for justice for all women and refers to it as "a reason-based theory of justice."

He begins his own discussion with a question: Why should "a publicly reasoned agreement" be essential to the "soundness of a theory of justice"? He examines some of the historical circumstances of Wollstonecraft's work and then calls attention to the fact that attending to the issues of women's rights naturally brings us to the entire question of social justice. Can there be justice in a community in which half the population is denied many basic rights, such as the right to vote and the right to train for the professions?

From there, Sen moves on to questions of law and the appearance of justice being done, which he sees as linked to Wollstonecraft's work. It is also linked to the ability of a community to discuss justice reasonably rather than through "frustration and ire."

Be sure to practice prereading techniques before a careful, annotated reading of Sen's essay. For a review of prereading strategies, see pages 4–9. ⊞

The Idea of Justice

RESISTANCE TO injustice typically draws on both indignation and argument. Frustration and ire can help to motivate us, and yet ultimately we have to rely, both for assessment and for effectiveness, on reasoned scrutiny to obtain a plausible and sustainable understanding of the basis of those complaints (if any) and what can be done to address the underlying problems.

The dual functions of indignation and reasoning are well illustrated by the attempts of Mary Wollstonecraft, the pioneering feminist thinker, to achieve a "vindication of the rights of woman." There is plentiful expression of anger and exasperation in Wollstonecraft's discussion of the need for a radical rejection of the subjugation of women:

> Let woman share the rights and she will emulate the virtues of man; for she must grow more perfect when emancipated, or justify the authority that chains such a weak being to her duty. — If the latter, it will be expedient to open a fresh trade with Russia for whips; a present which a father should always make to his son-in-law on his wedding day, that a husband may keep his whole family in order by the same means; and without any violation of justice reign, wielding this

scepter, sole master of his house, because he is the only being in it who has reason.

In her two books on rights of men and women, Wollstonecraft's anger is not aimed only at inequities suffered by women; it is directed also at the treatment of other deprived groups of people, for example slaves in the United States and elsewhere. And yet her classic writings are, ultimately, based on a strong appeal to reason. Angry rhetoric is consistently followed by reasoned arguments that Wollstonecraft wants her opponents to consider. In her letter to M. Talleyrand-Périgord,[1] to whom her book, *A Vindication of the Rights of Woman*, is addressed, Wollstonecraft concludes by reaffirming her strong confidence in relying on reason:

> *"Why should it matter that people actually agree that justice has been done, if it has in fact been done?"*

> I wish, Sir, to set some investigations of this kind afloat in France; and should they lead to a confirmation of my principles, when your [French] constitution is revised the Rights of Woman may be respected, if it be fully proved that reason calls for this respect, and loudly demands JUSTICE for one half of the human race.

The role and reach of reason are not undermined by the indignation that leads us to an investigation of the ideas underlying the nature and basis of the persistent inequities which characterized the world in which Wollstonecraft lived in the eighteenth century, as they do also the world in which we live today. While Wollstonecraft is quite remarkable in combining wrath and reasoning in the same work (indeed, alongside each other), even pure expressions of discontent and disappointment can make their own contributions to public reasoning if they are followed by investigation (perhaps undertaken by others) of whatever reasonable basis there might be for the indignation.

The appeal to reason in public, on which Mary Wollstonecraft insists, is 5 an important feature of the approach to justice I have been trying to present in this book. Understanding the demands of justice is not any more of a solitarist exercise than any other discipline of human understanding. When we try to determine how justice can be advanced, there is a basic need for public reasoning, involving arguments coming from different quarters and

---

[1] **M. Talleyrand-Périgord** Charles Maurice de Talleyrand-Périgord (1754–1838), foreign minister for France after the French Revolution known as a cynical politician active in both Napoleon's government and the succeeding Bourbon restoration. He also was on the committee that drafted the Declaration of the Rights of Man and Citizen.

divergent perspectives. An engagement with contrary arguments does not, however, imply that we must expect to be able to settle the conflicting reasons in all cases and arrive at agreed positions on every issue. Complete resolution is neither a requirement of a person's own rationality, nor is it a condition of reasonable social choice, including a reason-based theory of justice.

JUSTICE BEING SEEN TO BE DONE

A preliminary question may be asked: Why should a publicly reasoned agreement be seen as having any particular status in the soundness of a theory of justice? When Mary Wollstonecraft expressed the hope to M. Talleyrand-Périgord that, given due consideration and open public reasoning, there would be a general agreement on the importance of recognizing "the rights of woman," she was treating such a reasoned agreement as a decisive process in determining whether that really would be an enhancement of social justice (and could be seen to be giving legitimate rights to "one half of the human race"). It is, of course, easy enough to understand that an agreement to do something helps the undertaking of that something. That is a recognition of practical relevance, but going beyond instrumental importance, it can be also asked why an agreement or an understanding should have any special status in assessing the viability of a theory of justice.

Consider an often-repeated proposition in a closely related field, the practice of law. It is frequently asserted that justice should not only be done, but also be "seen to be done." Why so? Why should it matter that people actually agree that justice has been done, if it has in fact been done? Why qualify, or constrain, or supplement a strictly juridical requirement (that justice be done) by a populist demand (that people in general can observe that it is being done)? Is there a confusion here between legal correctness and popular endorsement — a confounding of jurisprudence with democracy?

It is not, in fact, hard to guess some of the instrumental reasons for attaching importance to the need for a decision to be *seen* to be just. For one thing, the administration of justice can, in general, be more effective if judges are seen to be doing a good job, rather than botching things up. If a judgement inspires confidence and general endorsement, then very likely it can be more easily implemented. Thus there is not much difficulty in explaining why that phrase about the need for justice to be "seen to be done" received such ringing endorsement and approving reiteration right from the time it was first uttered by Lord Hewart[2] in 1923 (in *Rex* v. *Sussex*

---

[2] **Lord Hewart** Gordon Hewart (1870–1943), a politician and judge in the United Kingdom.

Justices Ex parte McCarthy [1923] All ER 233), with his admonishment that justice "should manifestly and undoubtedly be seen to be done."

And yet it is difficult to be persuaded that it is only this kind of administrative merit that gives the observability of justice such decisive importance. The implementational advantages of getting approval all around are not of course in doubt, but it would be odd to think that Hewart's foundational principle is based on nothing other than convenience and expediency. Going beyond all that, it can plausibly be argued that if others cannot, with the best of efforts, see that a judgement is, in some understandable and reasonable sense, just, then not only is its implementability adversely affected, but even its soundness would be deeply problematic. There is a clear connection between the objectivity of a judgment and its ability to withstand public scrutiny.

Understanding Ideas

1. What does Amartya Sen mean by a "reasoned scrutiny" (para. 1)?
2. What does Sen praise about Mary Wollstonecraft's defense of the rights of men and women?
3. Sen says that Mary Wollstonecraft combines "wrath and reasoning" (para. 4). What does he mean?
4. Why should people agree that justice has been done when it has been done?

Responding to Ideas

1. *Comparison* Amartya Sen calls our attention to the work of Mary Wollstonecraft, particularly *A Vindication of the Rights of Woman*. He believes she is arguing for justice for women. But his main point is that Wollstonecraft is arguing for women's rights in a reasoned manner. Why is this of such importance to him? Why must we argue matters of justice using reason? Examine Wollstonecraft's selection in this book (p. 77) and evaluate it in terms of Sen's view of her. How much do they have in common in their concerns for justice?
2. *Example* In his opening sentences, Sen tells us that "[r]esistance to injustice typically draws on both indignation and argument" (para. 1). Examine a recent instance of resistance to injustice and qualify Sen's statement. What form or forms did the resistance to injustice take?

What were the outcomes of this resistance, and how did they affect people's attitudes toward the question of justice? If you like, you may choose a historical instance of resistance to injustice and examine it in relation to Sen's ideas.

3. *Response* Underneath it all, Sen is telling us that a reasoned approach to dealing with injustice will be much more effective in the long run than a violent reaction involving destruction or even angry argumentation. Is this true in your experience? Consider some of the injustices that have been the subject of the essays in this section of the book. How do they measure up to Sen's suggestions? Remember that Sen, as an Indian, knew the effectiveness of India's nonviolent rejection of British rule in 1947.

4. *Testimony* Sen says, "When we try to determine how justice can be advanced, there is a basic need for public reasoning, involving arguments coming from different quarters and divergent perspectives" (para. 5). Why should there be a need for public reasoning on this issue? How does Sen's argument relate to Jean-Jacques Rousseau's idea of a social contract and an "original compact"? To what extent does Sen's view support our concepts of democracy in the United States?

5. *Analysis of Circumstances* Examine Sen's argument in favor of the need for justice to appear to be done even when it is truly done. Why do we need to reinforce the appearance? How effective is his argument? Would you defend it or argue against it? Or is it, in fact, a nonissue? If possible, refer to an instance of justice that did not appear to have been done. What was the public reaction? By contrast, refer to an instance of justice that appeared to be done and examine the public reaction. What is the relation between the appearance of and the reality of justice being done?

Comparing Ideas

1. Mary Wollstonecraft (p. 77) was seeking to expand the rights of women, and she is considered an early feminist. Do today's feminists go beyond Wollstonecraft in how they seek justice? What injustices do women in our culture face? How are they going about their demands for justice? Are they following Wollstonecraft's method, what Sen refers to as combining "wrath and reasoning"? Do you think Sen supports the methods of modern feminists? What might he advise them to do?

2. Both Amartya Sen and Martin Luther King Jr. discuss freedom and justice, but they put their emphasis more on one than on the other. Examine "I Have a Dream" (p. 176) in the context of what Sen says

about justice. What are the similarities and differences in the things each author says about the ideas they address? What do they seem to be in total agreement on when talking about the same ideas? Which ideas are unique to Sen and which unique to King? How do these two writers reinforce each other's concepts of freedom and justice?

3. Sen wrote the book from which this selection comes partly as a rebuttal to John Rawls (p. 159), with whom he sometimes agrees and sometimes disagrees. Examine both selections carefully and write an essay that attempts to find the problems Sen has with Rawls's ideas. Which of Rawls's ideas does Sen ignore entirely? Which does he seem to take into account? Which of Rawls's ideas does he appear to take issue with and therefore object to? Whose view of justice seems more desirable to you?

John Pinderhughes

bell
hooks

Gloria Jean Watkins writes under the pseud-
onym **bell hooks** (b. 1952), using small letters to
distinguish herself from her much-admired
great-grandmother, who had the same name.
Born and raised in a small town in Kentucky, hooks eventually went to Stanford University for her undergraduate degree in English and to the University of California at Santa Cruz for her doctorate. Over the years, she has
written more than thirty books, such as *Ain't I a Woman? Black Women and
Feminism* (1981), which she began at age nineteen when she was an undergraduate. The title was taken from Sojourner Truth's (1797–1883) "Ain't I a
Woman?" abolitionist speech that she gave in 1851 in Akron, Ohio.

In *Feminist Theory: From Margin to Center* (1984), hooks addresses
some of the problems that the feminist movement in the United States
faced at the beginning, when it seemed that feminists were attacking
all men and focusing on problems of male domination. However, hooks
believes, on the contrary, it is not men themselves who are the problem so
much as the values of the culture that help support the kinds of oppression
feminism tried to attack. Sexism, racism, classism, imperialism, and other
forms of oppression are all connected, she says.

Among hooks's other books are *Teaching to Transgress: Education as
the Practice of Freedom* (1994), which discusses the problems of oppression she sees in many schools, and *Feminism Is for Everybody: Passionate
Politics* (2000), the book from which the following selection is drawn. In
it, she argues that feminism is not just for women, especially not just for
middle-class and successful women. She sees the feminist movement as a
global issue. But she particularly sees it as a political issue.

In "Feminist Politics: Where We Stand," hooks begins with a definition
of feminism that she had used ten years before: "Simply put, feminism is a
movement to end sexism, sexist exploitation, and oppression." She feels
that this definition is powerful because it is inclusive and because it does

not point to men as the enemy. She goes on to talk about the perception of the feminist movement at different times in recent years. She also discusses the role religion plays in the way we think about women and women's rights. She reviews some of the ways feminists pursued their rights and how racial issues affected the movement, especially during the activist period of the civil rights movement. Finally, fearful of a loss of momentum in the feminist movement, she asks for a fresh definition and to "[l]et the movement begin again."

Be sure to practice prereading techniques before a careful, annotated reading of hooks's essay. For a review of prereading strategies, see pages 4–9. ⊞

Feminist Politics: Where We Stand

S IMPLY PUT, feminism is a movement to end sexism, sexist exploitation, and oppression. This was a definition of feminism I offered in *Feminist Theory: From Margin to Center* more than ten years ago. It was my hope at the time that it would become a common definition everyone would use. I liked this definition because it did not imply that men were the enemy. By naming sexism as the problem it went directly to the heart of the matter. Practically, it is a definition which implies that all sexist thinking and action is the problem, whether those who perpetuate it are female or male, child or adult. It is also broad enough to include an understanding of systemic institutionalized sexism. As a definition it is open-ended. To understand feminism it implies one has to necessarily understand sexism.

As all advocates of feminist politics know, most people do not understand sexism, or if they do, they think it is not a problem. Masses of people think that feminism is always and only about women seeking to be equal to men. And a huge majority of these folks think feminism is antimale. Their misunderstanding of feminist politics reflects the reality that most folks learn about feminism from patriarchal mass media. The feminism they hear about the most is portrayed by women who are primarily committed to gender equality — equal pay for equal work, and sometimes women and men sharing household chores and parenting. They see that these women are usually white and materially privileged. They know from mass media that women's liberation focuses on the freedom to have abortions, to be lesbians, to challenge rape and domestic violence. Among these issues masses of people agree with the idea of gender equity in the workplace — equal pay for equal work.

Since our society continues to be primarily a "Christian" culture, masses of people continue to believe that god has ordained that women be subordinate to men in the domestic household. Even though masses of women have entered the workforce, even though many families are headed by women who are the sole breadwinners, the vision of domestic life which continues to dominate the nation's imagination is one in which the logic of male domination is intact, whether men are present in the home or not. The wrongminded notion of feminist movement which implied it was antimale carried with it the wrongminded assumption that all female space would necessarily be an environment where patriarchy and sexist thinking would be absent. Many women, even those involved in feminist politics, chose to believe this as well.

There was indeed a great deal of antimale sentiment among early feminist activists who were responding to male domination with anger. It was that anger at injustice that was the impetus for creating a women's liberation movement. Early on most feminist activists (a majority of whom were white) had their consciousness raised about the nature of male domination when they were working in anticlassist and antiracist settings with men who were telling the world about the importance of freedom while subordinating the women in their ranks. Whether it was white women working on behalf of socialism, black women working on behalf of civil rights and black liberation, or Native American women working for indigenous rights, it was clear that men wanted to lead, and they wanted women to follow. Participating in these radical freedom struggles awakened the spirit of rebellion and resistance in progressive females and led them towards contemporary women's liberation.

As contemporary feminism progressed, as women realized that males were not the only group in our society who supported sexist thinking and behavior — that females could be sexist as well, antimale sentiment no longer shaped the movement's consciousness. The focus shifted to an all-out effort to create gender justice. But women could not band together to further feminism without confronting our sexist thinking. Sisterhood could not be powerful as long as women were competitively at war with one another. Utopian visions of sisterhood based solely on the awareness of the reality that all women were in some way victimized by male domination were disrupted by discussions of class and race. Discussions of class differences occurred early on in contemporary feminism, preceding discussions of race. Diana Press published revolutionary insights about class divisions between women as early as the mid-'70s in their collection of essays *Class and Feminism*. These discussions did not trivialize the feminist insistence that "sisterhood is powerful," they simply emphasized that we could only become sisters in struggle by confronting the ways women — through sex, class, and race — dominated and exploited other women, and created a political platform that would address these differences.

Even though individual black women were active in contemporary feminist movement from its inception, they were not the individuals who became the "stars" of the movement, who attracted the attention of mass media. Often individual black women active in feminist movement were revolutionary feminists (like many white lesbians). They were already at odds with reformist feminists who resolutely wanted to project a vision of the movement as being solely about women gaining equality with men in the existing system. Even before race became a talked about issue in feminist circles it was clear to black women (and to their revolutionary allies in struggle) that they were never going to have equality within the existing white supremacist capitalist patriarchy.

From its earliest inception feminist movement was polarized. Reformist thinkers chose to emphasize gender equality. Revolutionary thinkers did not want simply to alter the existing system so that women would have more rights. We wanted to transform that system, to bring an end to patriarchy and sexism. Since patriarchal mass media was not interested in the more revolutionary vision it never received attention in mainstream press. The vision of "women's liberation" which captured and still holds the public imagination was the one representing women as wanting what men had. And this was the vision that was easier to realize. Changes in our nation's economy, economic depression, the loss of jobs, etc., made the climate ripe for our nation's citizens to accept the notion of gender equality in the workforce.

Given the reality of racism, it made sense that white men were more willing to consider women's rights when the granting of those rights could serve the interests of maintaining white supremacy. We can never forget that white women began to assert their need for freedom after civil rights, just at the point when racial discrimination was ending and black people, especially black males, might have attained equality in the workforce with white men. Reformist feminist thinking focusing primarily on equality with men in the workforce overshadowed the original radical foundations of contemporary feminism which called for reform as well as overall restructuring of society so that our nation would be fundamentally antisexist.

Most women, especially privileged white women, ceased even to consider revolutionary feminist visions, once they began to gain economic

> *"As contemporary feminism progressed, as women realized that males were not the only group in our society who supported sexist thinking and behavior — that females could be sexist as well, antimale sentiment no longer shaped the movement's consciousness. The focus shifted to an all-out effort to create gender justice."*

power within the existing social structure. Ironically, revolutionary feminist thinking was most accepted and embraced in academic circles. In those circles the production of revolutionary feminist theory progressed, but more often than not that theory was not made available to the public. It became and remains a privileged discourse available to those among us who are highly literate, well educated, and usually materially privileged. Works like *Feminist Theory: From Margin to Center* that offer a liberatory vision of feminist transformation never receive mainstream attention. Masses of people have not heard of this book. They have not rejected its message; they do not know what the message is.

While it was in the interest of mainstream white supremacist capitalist 10 patriarchy to suppress visionary feminist thinking which was not antimale or concerned with getting women the right to be like men, reformist feminists were also eager to silence these forces. Reformist feminism became their route to class mobility. They could break free of male domination in the workforce and be more self-determining in their lifestyles. While sexism did not end, they could maximize their freedom within the existing system. And they could count on there being a lower class of exploited subordinated women to do the dirty work they were refusing to do. By accepting and indeed colluding with the subordination of working-class and poor women, they not only ally themselves with the existing patriarchy and its concomitant sexism, they give themselves the right to lead a double life, one where they are the equals of men in the workforce and at home when they want to be. If they chose lesbianism they have the privilege of being equals with men in the workforce while using class power to create domestic lifestyles where they could choose to have little or no contact with men.

Lifestyle feminism ushered in the notion that there could be as many versions of feminism as there were women. Suddenly the politics was slowly removed from feminism. And the assumption prevailed that no matter what a woman's politics, be she conservative or liberal, she too could fit feminism into her existing lifestyle. Obviously this way of thinking has made feminism more acceptable because its underlying assumption is that women can be feminists without fundamentally challenging and changing themselves or the culture. For example, let's take the issue of abortion. If feminism is a movement to end sexist oppression, and depriving females of reproductive rights is a form of sexist oppression, then one cannot be antichoice and be feminist. A woman can insist she would never choose to have an abortion while affirming her support of the right of women to choose and still be an advocate of feminist politics. She cannot be antiabortion and an advocate of feminism. Concurrently there can be no such thing as "power feminism" if the vision of power evoked is power gained through the exploitation and oppression of others.

Feminist politics is losing momentum because feminist movement has lost clear definitions. We have those definitions. Let's reclaim them. Let's share them. Let's start over. Let's have T-shirts and bumper stickers and postcards and hip-hop music, television and radio commercials, ads everywhere and billboards, and all manner of printed material that tells the world about feminism. We can share the simple yet powerful message that feminism is a movement to end sexist oppression. Let's start there. Let the movement begin again.

Understanding Ideas

1. According to bell hooks, why is it important to understand sexism as related to racism and classism?

2. What does hooks purport is the relation of feminism to equality and justice?

3. In hooks's view, what problems were evident in the early women's liberation movement?

4. Why, according to hooks, did black women not become the "stars" of feminist movement?

Responding to Ideas

1. *Definition* In paragraph 5, hooks says that "women realized that males were not the only group in our society who supported sexist thinking and behavior." First, define *sexist thinking* and *sexist behavior.* Is hooks right when she says men are not the only people who support sexist thinking? Who else has supported that kind of thinking? How do they do it? Why do they do it? Who are these people, and how powerful is their point of view? Use examples to strengthen your argument.

2. *Response* Religion is one of the subjects hooks treats. She tells us that because our culture is essentially Christian many people feel that God has "ordained that women be subordinate to men in the domestic household" (para. 3). In your understanding, do most religions in our culture assume that women must be subordinate to men? What evidence do you see that supports such a view? How can a religious person be a feminist? Must religious people be sexist?

3. *Research* In feminist movement, hooks says, black women "were never going to have equality within the existing white supremacist

capitalist patriarchy" (para. 6). Why does she say this? Is she correct? Is there such a thing as a "white supremacist capitalist patriarchy"? If there is, how does it prevent black women from achieving equality? Interview at least three people who you feel may have a strong opinion on this matter and record their views. How happy would hooks be with their responses? How happy are you with their responses?

4. *Response* The question of abortion is quite controversial even today. Yet, hooks says, if feminism is to end sexist oppression, then no feminist can be antichoice. But any feminist woman can herself choose not to have an abortion and still support choice for others. Where do you stand on this issue? Research recent legal disputes regarding abortion rights. Does our culture seem to have a generally accepted position on the question of abortion? Is the question of sexist oppression part of the debate about abortion? Where do other well-known feminists stand on the question of abortion and women's rights?

5. *Definition* Define feminism in terms of how it has affected you and the institutions that you take part in. How active are feminists on your college campus? What are their primary concerns, and how do they articulate their issues? How well respected are feminists in your community? Is feminism stronger in your college than it is in your community? How are you directly affected by feminism?

6. *Definition* Although she mentions the concept of "gender justice" (para. 5), hooks does not explicitly define the term or explain what it might be. How would you define this term, and what ideas in hooks's essay help you explain what it should mean? Today the term *gender* has a meaning much more wide-ranging than when it was used in this essay, so be sure to be as inclusive as you need to in talking about how gender justice relates to feminism, sexism, and/or racism. What new forms of oppression seem to be at work in the modern field of gender justice?

Comparing Ideas

1. Compare the issues that bell hooks addresses in "Feminist Politics: Where We Stand" with those that Mary Wollstonecraft addresses in her "A Vindication of the Rights of Woman" (p. 77). It is clear hooks is approaching the question of feminism from a political position. Is this also true of Wollstonecraft? What does Wollstonecraft seem to see as significant and important that hooks does not take into account? Which of these two pieces do you think is more likely to press the cause

of feminism further? Which piece makes you more likely to become a feminist or stay one?

2. Alexis de Tocqueville in "The Idea of Rights in the United States" (p. 84) takes a stand on women's rights and has read Mary Wollstonecraft (p. 77), with whom he seems to agree. How much agreement is there on the issue of women's rights among these two writers and hooks? How aware is hooks of what Tocqueville and Wollstonecraft say? Are all three of these writers feminists in approximately the same way, or are there distinct differences that set them apart from each other? Explain in a brief essay how they relate to one another on the issues of feminism and justice and feminism and freedom.

CHAPTER FIVE

How Science Reads the Book of Nature

LUCRETIUS 206

CHARLES DARWIN 212

ALFRED NORTH WHITEHEAD 221

OLIVER SACKS 236

STEVE JONES 244

MICHIO KAKU 252

JENNIFER ACKERMAN 263

"The Great tragedy of Science — the slaying of
a beautiful hypothesis by an ugly fact."
— THOMAS HENRY HUXLEY

"The true science and study of man is man."
— PIERRE CHARRON

"Science is organized knowledge."
— IMMANUEL KANT

"Science moves but slowly, slowly,
creeping on from point to point."
— ALFRED, LORD TENNYSON

"That man can interrogate as well as observe
nature was a lesson slowly learned in his evolution."
— SIR WILLIAM OSLER

"Every great advance in science has issued
from a new audacity of imagination."   — JOHN DEWEY

"We live in a society exquisitely dependent on science and
technology, in which hardly anyone knows anything about
science and technology."   — CARL SAGAN

"Science does not know its debt to imagination."
— RALPH WALDO EMERSON

INTRODUCTION

The practice of science is the discovery of the way nature functions. The earliest scientists may have been concerned primarily with the movement of the moon and the stars because the positions of those heavenly bodies helped predict the best times for harvesting and planting. Some of the greatest discoveries of the cosmos were undoubtedly made in prehistory, before written records were kept. In those thousands of years, there must have been many potential Isaac Newtons and Albert Einsteins who understood some of the workings of nature. The earliest historical records imply that some of those unrecorded geniuses may have been religious figures who used religion to encode the rules they discovered.

We have texts from historical times, particularly the records left by the ancient Greeks, that demonstrate a remarkable and widely spread knowledge of mathematics. Two thousand years before the Greeks, the records of the Egyptians reveal an astonishing — and still not entirely understood — capacity to use mathematics for colossal construction and agricultural prediction. The Romans were careful observers of nature and built their scientific practices on the Greek model. One of these methods was to study closely the behavior of the human body and relate its function to the world of nature. Lucretius (c. 99–c. 55 B.C.E.), the Roman poet and scientist, wrote *On the Nature of Things* as a long poem, which was the normal written format of the time. He understood the concept of the atom and rejected superstition as an explanation for the way nature worked. In the selection included in this chapter, Lucretius explores the nature of sleep.

The naturalist and geologist Charles Darwin (1809–1882) began life thinking he might become a doctor, but a series of curious events provided him with the opportunity to take part in a five-year project from 1831 to 1836 on the British exploratory vessel HMS *Beagle*. The boat took him virtually around the world. He was able to study wildlife and plant life in South America and beyond and make careful notes about what he discovered. His book about his adventure made him famous. But he became even more famous worldwide with the 1859 publication of *On the Origin of Species*, in which he presented the evidence that confirmed what many scientists of the time had suspected: that life on Earth developed through the process of evolution. Research in evolution continues today, aided by the discoveries in the human genome project and the ability to identify the information contained in genes of many kinds of living animals and plants.

Alfred North Whitehead (1861–1947) was a major twentieth-century mathematician teaching and writing in both England and the United States. He taught physics at Harvard and in England, but he was also a philosopher with an interest in theology. He reacted in 1925 to a trial in Tennessee — the Scopes "monkey trial" — that was aimed at preventing teachers from teaching evolutionary biology in the public schools. Despite the implication in the Bill of Rights that there is a separation of church and state, Tennessee wanted only the Bible's version of the creation of mankind to be presented in science classes. The trial ended in a deadlock and the case was thrown out, but the issue was not resolved until another legal challenge in 1964. In the selection included here, Whitehead attempts to referee the conflict between science and religion. Some of what he says is echoed by other science writers in this book.

Oliver Sacks (1933–2015) was a neurologist who was interested in the most unusual neurological disorders, many of which he had a chance to study carefully. He became well known for his study of a group of people essentially frozen in place since they had contracted a version of encephalitis — or sleeping sickness — that had been an epidemic from 1915 to 1920. These people could not move themselves and seemed to be in comas. He used an experimental drug, L-dopa, to "wake them up." His book about his experience working with these patients, *Awakenings* (1973), was made into a movie that was nominated for three Academy Awards, including one for best picture. The book also later became the basis of an opera. Interestingly, Sacks himself had been a neurological patient: he had a very strange disorder called *prosopagnosia*, or face blindness. He could not remember people by their faces, and they had to reintroduce themselves only days after first meeting him. This is an uncommon illness, but it was not without precedent. Sacks also had monocular vision, which is one reason he took such an interest in blindness.

Steve Jones (b. 1944) is an evolutionary biologist with a special interest in the complexities of genetics. Because of his respect for the work of Charles Darwin, Jones undertook to rewrite *On the Origin of Species* using Darwin's chapter subjects and covering much the same material at the same length within his book. Jones calls himself Darwin's ghostwriter and intended to write the book the way he thought Darwin would if he were alive today. Jones took a special interest in human evolutionary biology, which Darwin only later wrote about in *The Descent of Man*; in his version, *Descent of Men*, Jones undertakes to revise Darwin's theory, implying that the male of the species is not superior biologically or, today, even socially. He talks about sexual selection, pointing to a development that suggests that men will have less of a role in biological reproduction and that they risk becoming less important to the species.

In what may at first look like an assault on humanity, Michio Kaku (b. 1947), a prominent physicist with a strong interest in the science of the future, talks about artificial intelligence (AI). Today, AI is a very popular subject in colleges as well as in research in many scientific laboratories with commercial prospects. One ambition that has engaged scientists for more than twenty years is the hope of producing a computer that can think and, even more, is capable of giving the impression that it has common sense, a goal that has proved extremely difficult. Robots are a result of experiments in AI. They are already doing a great deal of work in assembly plants, in the military, and in police work. The hopes for robots are very high, and Kaku reviews the progress and looks to the future to see how probable it is that robots will be in our houses performing some of the tasks we have usually done for ourselves.

Genetics is the immediate interest of Jennifer Ackerman (b. 1959), a science writer with a love of nature and the variety of life that she has witnessed while working on her books. She talks about some extraordinary discoveries made in recent years when the microscopic world of single-celled animals and plants became observable and even manipulable. For example, she was amazed to find that the one-celled fungus yeast, which is so basic in nature and important in bread making, has a molecular gene for mating that is like a molecule in the human brain. Further, she discovered that a human gene can be inserted into the embryo of a fruit fly and there will work perfectly to develop that embryo into an adult fruit fly. She tells us that genetic material in some plants is remarkably like the genetic material in humans and other animals. Such discoveries were impossible fifty years ago but are now practicable because of the inroads made studying and decoding the human genome. Now the genomes of other animals and plants can be studied to see how integrated all life is.

SEEING IDEAS

Science begins with questions and progresses with careful observation of nature, which includes plants, animals, human beings, and all the other things that make up our world. Scientists explore mysteries and try to solve them by creating provable theories based on evidence. However, that exploration has been at odds with many religious beliefs throughout history. For example, in Galileo's (1564–1642) time, the Catholic Church believed that Earth was the center of the universe, and it put Galileo on trial for claiming that Earth revolves around the sun. Galileo paid a heavy price for revealing that truth of science, but today we know Earth spins around the sun and not the other way around.

Time Life Picture Collection/Getty Images

Similarly, the evidence that Charles Darwin used to propose his theory of evolution was only the beginning of the scientific examination of evolutionary patterns: Genetic studies, including the decoding of the human genome, point to the conclusion that all living things developed through a slow process of mutation. Yet many religions do not accept evolution as fact and instead believe in creationism, the idea that God created the earth in seven days, as the Bible says. This conflict is illustrated quite vividly in the photo above of science teacher Dr. Maude Stout teaching creationism at Bob Jones University, Greenville, South Carolina, in 1948. Alfred North Whitehead's essay in this chapter addresses the conflict between the teaching of evolution and the creation story of the Bible and tries to offer a solution. Creationism is still being taught today in some biology classes, but as you will see in this chapter, Oliver Sacks, Steve Jones, and others strive to explain the development of humans without reference to that idea.

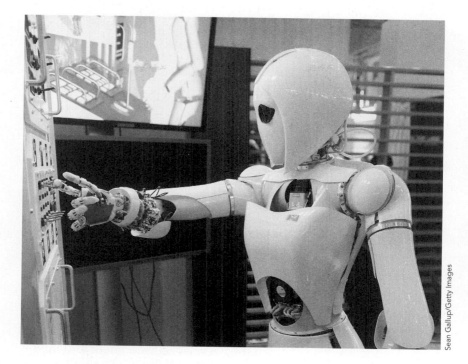

Sean Gallup/Getty Images

The above image shows a different branch of science that causes many people to further examine human nature: artificial intelligence. The study of artificial intelligence is the subject of Michio Kaku's research, which you will read about in this chapter. Since the development of the computer in the twentieth century, the similarity between the way computers work and the way the mind works has alerted scientists to the possibility that a very smart computer might be able to think for itself. After chess-playing machines defeated a world champion people became aware that AI was a possibility. Robots in industry do many jobs better than people and therefore replaced them. Some robotic machines are programmed to learn and make simple adjustments, leading to the development of driverless cars and many other robotic machines that essentially replace human agents. The image above shows an Artificial Intelligence Lightweight Android (AILA) pressing switches on a panel it was able to recognize independently during a demonstration at the German Research Center for Artificial Intelligence in 2013.

Clearly this is an age of discovery of the mysteries of nature. The kind of ambition Galileo had in studying the way Earth circled the sun is at work in scientists today. Inroads in physics, genetics, and artificial intelligence are only the beginning.

Spencer Arnold/Getty Images

LUCRETIUS

TITUS LUCRETIUS CARUS (c. 99–c. 55 B.C.E.) was a Roman poet devoted to the teachings of Epicurus (c. 341–270 B.C.E.), the Greek philosopher who assumed the world was what it seemed, that the senses provided adequate knowledge of the world, and that pleasurable experiences were the best rewards of life. Lucretius addressed his celebrated work, *On the Nature of Things*, to a friend named Memmius and used the poem to explain what he knew about the world.

By following Epicurus, Lucretius developed a scientific theory that is surprising for its resemblance to modern thought. He did not have the benefit of modern technology like the microscope or telescope. He depended on his five senses and his reasoning. He established a principle based on his observations and then demonstrated the likelihood of the truth of this principle by examining the available evidence and drawing the best conclusions possible. The procedure is scientific within its limitations.

The most important point about Lucretius is his curiosity. What interested him was the nature of matter, the nature of space, and the way natural phenomena exist and function. Few in his era were interested in such issues; therefore, his work is especially striking. He believed, for example, in the atomic theory, which he adapted from the work of Democritus (460?–370? B.C.E.). There was no marketplace for scientific ideas in his time, when, as he said, the earth lay "under the dead weight of superstition." Like Epicurus, he was a materialist and did not refer to the Roman deities other than to suggest they may exist but that they took no interest in people. He considered theories of the soul and the afterlife as fictions. However, his views about life were optimistic and encouraging. His emphasis was on the value of life itself and the excitement of the human experience.

In the selection that follows, "The Nature of Sleep," Lucretius demonstrates his method of inquiry in a psychological area that still engages scientific study. We all sleep, and most of us have opinions about the nature of our own experiences as sleepers. Yet little is really known about the phenomenon, especially in animals whose experiences in sleep we can only conjecture. Lucretius brings a nature of inquiry to the subject, explaining to Memmius what he feels to be true about sleep. In the process, he refers to theories of the body that are held today by many healers working in alternative medicine. His language is sometimes metaphoric, as when he describes the sleeping spirit "as smothered fire" that "lurks in a heap of ashes." In his discussion of sleep, he explores an experience that interests and involves all of us.

Be sure to practice prereading techniques before a careful, annotated reading of Lucretius' selection. For a review of prereading strategies, see pages 4–9. ⊞

The Nature of Sleep

A ND NOW for *the problem of sleep*: By what contrivance does it flood our limbs with peace and unravel from our breasts the mind's disquietude? My answer will be persuasive rather than exhaustive: better the fleeting melody of the swan than the long-drawn clangor of cranes high up among the northward-racing clouds. It rests with you to lend an unresisting ear and an inquiring mind. Otherwise you may refuse to accept my explanation as possible and walk away with a mind that flings back the truth, though the blame lies with your own blindness.

In the first place, sleep occurs when the vital spirit throughout the body is discomposed: when part of it has been forced out and lost, part compressed and driven into the inner depths. At such times the limbs are unknit and grow limp. For undoubtedly the sensibility that is in us is caused by the spirit. When sensation is deadened by sleep, we must suppose that this is due to the derangement of the spirit or its expulsion. But it is not all expelled, or else the body would be steeped in the everlasting chill of death. If there were really no lurking particle of spirit left in the limbs, as smothered fire lurks in a heap of ashes, from what source could sentience be suddenly rekindled in the limbs, as flame leaps up from hidden fire? I will explain how this change is brought about and how the spirit can be deranged and the body grow limp. You must see to it that I do not waste my words on the wind.

First, then, a body on its outer surface borders on the gusty air and is touched by it. It must therefore be pelted by it with a continual rain of blows. That is why almost all bodies are covered with hide or shell, rind or bark. In bodies that breathe, the interior also is battered by air as it is inhaled and exhaled. Since our body is thus bombarded outside and in and the blows penetrate through little pores to its primary parts and primal elements, our limbs are subject in a sense to a gradual crumbling. The atoms of body and mind are dislodged from their stations. The result is that part of the spirit is forced out; part becomes tucked away in the interior; part is loosely scattered throughout the limbs, so that it cannot unite or engage in interacting motions, because nature interposes obstacles to combination and movement. This deep-seated change in motion means the withdrawal of sentience. At the same time, since there is some lack of matter to support the frame, the body grows weak; all the limbs slacken; arms and eyelids droop; often, when a man is seeking rest, his knees lose their strength and give way under him.

Food, again, induces sleepiness, because its action, when it is being distributed through all the veins, is the same as that of air. The heaviest kind of sleep is that which ensues on satiety or exhaustion, since it is then that the atoms are thrown into the greatest confusion under stress of their heavy labor. The same cause makes the partial congestion of spirit more deep-seated and the evacuation more extensive, and aggravates the internal separation and dislocation.

Whatever employment has the strongest hold on our interest or has last 5 filled our waking hours, so as to engage the mind's attention, that is what seems most often to keep us occupied in sleep. Lawyers argue cases and frame contracts. Generals lead their troops into action. Sailors continue their pitched battle with the winds. And as for me, I go on with my task, forever exploring the nature of the universe and setting down my discoveries in my native tongue. The same principle generally applies when other crafts and occupations are observed to beguile men's minds in sleep.

Similarly when men have devoted themselves wholeheartedly for days on end to entertainments, we usually find that the objects that have ceased to engage the senses have left wide open channels in the mind for the entry of their own images. So for many days the same sights hover before their eyes: even when awake, they seem to see figures dancing and swaying supple limbs; to fill their ears with the liquid melody and speaking notes of the lyre, and to watch the same crowded theater, its stage ablaze with many-tinted splendor.

Such is the striking effect of interest and pleasure and customary employment, and not on men only but on all animals. You will see mettlesome steeds, when their limbs are at rest, still continuing in sleep to sweat and pant as if straining all their strength to win the palm, or as if the lifted barriers of the starting post had just released them. And the huntsman's hounds, while wrapped in gentle slumber, often toss their legs with a quick jerk and utter sudden whines and draw rapid breaths of air into their nostrils as if they were hot on a newly found scent. Even when awake, they often chase after shadowy images of stags, as though they saw them in full flight, till they shake off the illusion and return to themselves. A litter of good-tempered house-bred puppies are all agog to wriggle their bodies and heave them from the ground, just as if they were seeing the forms and faces of strangers. The fiercer the breed, the more savage must be their behavior in sleep. The various races of birds take to flight and startle the groves of the gods at dead of night with a sudden whir of wings. Doubtless their restful slumber is disturbed by visions of hawks swooping to the fray in fierce pursuit.

Very similar as a rule is the behavior in sleep of human minds, whose massive motions are proportioned to massive effect. Kings take cities by storm, are themselves taken captive, join in battle, and cry aloud as though they felt the assassin's dagger — and all without stirring from the spot. There are many who fight for their lives, giving vent to their agony in groans or filling the night with piercing screams as though they were writhing in the jaws of a panther or a ravening lion. Many talk in their sleep about matters of great moment and have often betrayed their own guilt. Many meet their death. Many, who feel themselves hurled bodily down to earth from towering crags, are startled out of sleep; like men who have lost their wits, they are slow in returning to themselves, so shaken are they by the tumult of their body. The thirsty man finds himself seated beside a river or a delectable spring and is near to gulping down the whole stream. Little boys often fancy when fast asleep that they are standing at a lavatory or a chamber pot and lifting up their clothes. Then they discharge all the filtered fluid of their body, and even the costly splendor of oriental coverlets does not escape a soaking. Those on the verge of manhood, in whose limbs the seed created by maturing age is beginning to gather, are invaded from without by images emanating from various bodies with tidings of an alluring face and a delightful complexion. This stimulates the organs swollen with an accumulation of seed. Often, as though their function were actually fulfilled, they discharge a flood of fluid and drench their covering.

> *"Whatever employment has the strongest hold on our interest or has last filled our waking hours, so as to engage the mind's attention, that is what seems most often to keep us occupied in sleep."*

Understanding Ideas

1. What is the "vital spirit" that Lucretius sees as being "throughout the body" (para. 2)?

2. According to Lucretius, what effect do food and activity have on sleep?

3. What does Lucretius think happens in the sleep of animals?

4. How does Lucretius distinguish the sleep of people from that of animals?

Responding to Ideas

1. *Definition* Lucretius may be a materialist, but he makes a great deal of what he calls spirit and its action throughout the body. In a brief essay, explain what he seems to mean by the term *spirit* and explore the way Lucretius explains its nature. As he uses it, is *spirit* a "spiritual" term, or is it a term for an ordinary quality in the body? In what ways are you aware of possessing a spirit similar to the one that Lucretius assumes is present in you? How does the spirit react to sleep? Are there different stages of activity of the spirit? Does Lucretius provide a scientific examination of the spirit?

2. *Response* Like many of us, Lucretius hypothesizes about what animals are thinking during sleep. He suggests that racehorses move their limbs in such a way as to reveal that they imagine they are just leaving the starting gate. Puppies seem to wriggle in their sleep as if greeting members of their family. More savage breeds of dog seem to have more savage "behavior in sleep" (para. 7). Even birds, he theorizes, sometimes react as if hunted by a hawk. If you have experience with sleeping pets or animals, what is your theory about their dreams? Do you agree with Lucretius? Interview people who raise animals or, if possible, veterinarians to see what they think animals dream about and why. What is the modern reaction to Lucretius' views?

3. *Response* Lucretius considers that people dream in much the way he theorizes that animals dream. But he goes a bit further, suggesting that people sometimes talk in their sleep because of a sense of guilt and thus betray themselves. Kings, he says, "join in battle, and cry aloud" (para. 8), while others groan or scream in their sleep as if they were attacked by a "panther or a ravening lion" (para. 8). If you have had such experiences, describe them and connect them to what Lucretius says. Are his observations about the exclamations of people while asleep confirmed by your experience? What do others say about such events? What kinds of dreams cause you or your acquaintances to shout or scream?

4. *Response* Make your own theory about the nature of sleep by reference to your own experiences. How would you approach the question of sleep scientifically? Lucretius uses several methods: observation,

hypothesizing, and comparison between animals and people. He does not speak of his own experiences in sleep. What are your experiences? Keep a dream journal and decide what your dreams tell you about the purposes of sleep. What do dreams do for you? What kinds of dreams do you most welcome? Do you think dreams tell you something about your personality? Do your dreams have meaning?

5. **Research** Lucretius informs us about the science of sleep two thousand years ago. What are scientists saying about sleep today? Research online and in scientific journals to find out what current sleep specialists say about dreams and sleep. As sources, you might use the Stanford Center for Sleep Sciences and Medicine, the European Sleep Research Society, and the journal *Sleep*. What is being taught in psychology classes about sleep? How much of what is taught today is in agreement with Lucretius' ideas? How much disregards his theorizing?

6. **Research** In discussing dreams, Lucretius focuses on the experiences of men and boys but says nothing about those of women. Do we need a gender-studies version of dream analysis? Collect as much dream content information — especially about recurring dreams — from people who identify themselves as male, female, lesbian, gay, or transgender. Is there a clear difference in their dreams, or is gender irrelevant when it comes to dreaming?

Comparing Ideas

1. Compare the way Lucretius examines the phenomenon of sleep with the way the modern scientist Oliver Sacks (p. 236) discusses the senses. Both writers pay considerable attention to the five senses and treat them with respect because they feel they learn the truth about experience by examining how they function in our lives. What methods of examination and reflection does Sacks use that Lucretius also uses? To what extent do both speculate when they cannot rely on certainty? How does each use his ability to observe experience directly? What seems to be their "scientific method" in reflecting on human psychology? How modern is Sacks compared to Lucretius?

Bob Thomas/Popperphoto/
Getty Images

CHARLES DARWIN

CHARLES DARWIN (1809–1882) was the grandson of one of England's great horticulturists, Erasmus Darwin. He was familiar with the naturalist's process of breeding plants and creating hybrid varieties. In the England of his day, breeding animals, especially livestock and hunting dogs, was a common practice. Portraits of horses in this period attest to the success of breeders in producing strong, fast, and dominant racehorses. Breeders selected animals to mate on the basis of their physical, and sometimes their temperamental, characteristics. This practice of artificial selection had been common since the time of the Egyptians.

Darwin began his studies in medicine at the University of Edinburgh but eventually decided to change direction and train to be a naturalist. The most important event in his young life was his decision to accept an invitation to sail on HMS *Beagle*, a small British warship that had been taken out of military service and refitted for research purposes. Darwin signed on for a five-year voyage (1831–1836) to study and map the coastline of South America and elsewhere for the main purpose of geological studies. Darwin became expert in geology but also collected numerous specimens of plants and animals, as well as many fossils. His subsequent publication *The Voyage of the* Beagle (1839) made him famous and respected as a scientist.

It was during the voyage of the *Beagle* that Darwin began speculating on the varieties of species he observed in many different environments. By 1838, he had begun to formulate his theories about natural selection as the process by which species change and develop. The idea of natural selection had been discussed by a number of other scientists in the early nineteenth century. One of them, Alfred Russel Wallace (1823–1913), sent him a paper he had written on the development of species by natural selection. Wallace had done extensive research in the field, and Darwin recognized their mutual discoveries by publishing a joint paper with Wallace in 1858. Then Darwin moved quickly to publish his own book *On the Origin of Species* in 1859, sending a shock wave into the public imagination that made him the most celebrated scientist in England and possibly the most influential scientist in the world.

Darwin begins the excerpt that follows by commenting on the results of artificial selection of domestic animals that produce hereditary distinctions in either male or female animals. He then reasons that sexual distinctions that appear in domestic breeding can also happen in nature. The distinction between natural selection, or the survival of the fittest, and sexual selection is not the risk of death but rather the risk of not having as many offspring. Darwin considers both forms of selection in this essay.

Be sure to practice prereading techniques before a careful, annotated reading of Darwin's essay. For a review of prereading strategies, see pages 4–9. ⌘

Of Sexual Selection and Natural Selection

SEXUAL SELECTION

I NASMUCH AS peculiarities often appear under domestication in one sex and become hereditarily attached to that sex, so no doubt it will be under nature. Thus it is rendered possible for the two sexes to be modified through natural selection in relation to different habits of life, as is sometimes the case; or for one sex to be modified in relation to the other sex, as commonly occurs. This leads me to say a few words on what I have called sexual selection. This form of selection depends, not on a struggle for existence in relation to other organic beings or to external conditions, but on a struggle between the individuals of one sex, generally the males, for the possession of the other sex. The result is not death to the unsuccessful competitor, but few or no offspring. Sexual selection is, therefore, less rigorous than natural selection. Generally, the most vigorous males, those which are best fitted for their places in nature, will leave most progeny. But in many cases victory depends not so much on general vigor, as on having special weapons, confined to the male sex. A hornless stag or spurless cock would have a poor chance of leaving numerous offspring. Sexual selection, by always allowing the victor to breed, might surely give indomitable courage, length of spur, and strength to the wing to strike in the spurred leg, in nearly the same manner as does the brutal cockfighter by the careful selection of his best cocks. How low in the scale of nature the law of battle descends, I know not; male alligators have been described as fighting, bellowing, and whirling round, like Indians in a war dance, for the possession of the females; male salmons have been observed fighting all day long; male stag beetles sometimes bear wounds from the huge mandibles of other males; the males of certain hymenopterous[1] insects have been frequently seen by that inimitable observer M. Fabre,[2] fighting for a particular female who sits by, an apparently unconcerned beholder of the struggle, and then retires with the conqueror. The war is, perhaps, severest between the males of polygamous animals, and these seem oftenest provided with special weapons. The males of carnivorous animals are already well armed; though to them and to others, special means of defense may be given through means of sexual selection, as the mane of the lion, and the hooked jaw to the male salmon; for the shield may be as important for victory as the sword or spear.

Among birds, the contest is often of a more peaceful character. All those who have attended to the subject, believe that there is the severest rivalry between the males of many species to attract, by singing, the females. The rock thrush of Guiana, birds of paradise, and some others, congregate, and successive males display with the most elaborate care, and show off in the best manner, their gorgeous plumage; they likewise perform strange antics before the females, which, standing by as spectators, at last choose the most attractive partner. Those who have closely attended to birds in confinement well know that they often take individual preferences and dislikes: thus Sir R. Heron[3] has described how a pied peacock was eminently attractive to all his hen birds. I cannot here enter on the necessary details; but if man can in a short time give beauty and an elegant carriage to his bantams, according to his standard of beauty, I can see no good reason to doubt that female birds, by selecting, during thousands of generations, the most melodious or beautiful males, according to their standard of beauty, might produce a marked effect. Some well-known laws, with respect to the plumage of male and female birds, in comparison with the plumage of the young, can partly be explained through the action of sexual selection on variations occurring at different ages, and transmitted to the males alone or to both sexes at corresponding ages; but I have not space here to enter on this subject.

Thus it is, as I believe, that when the males and females of any animal have the same general habits of life, but differ in structure, color, or ornament, such differences have been mainly caused by sexual selection: that is, by individual males having had, in successive generations, some slight

---

[1] **hymenopterous** Relating to insects with two pairs of membranous wings, such as bees and wasps.

[2] **M. Fabre** Jean-Henri Fabre (1823–1915), French scientist who studied insects.

[3] **R. Heron** Sir Robert Heron, 2nd Baronet (1765–1854), maintained a large menagerie on his estate in England.

advantage over other males, in their weapons, means of defense, or charms, which they have transmitted to their male offspring alone. Yet I would not wish to attribute all sexual differences to this agency: for we see in our domestic animals peculiarities arising and becoming attached to the male sex, which apparently have not been augmented through selection by man. The tuft of hair on the breast of the wild turkey-cock cannot be of any use, and it is doubtful whether it can be ornamental in the eyes of the female bird; indeed, had the tuft appeared under domestication it would have been called a monstrosity.

ILLUSTRATIONS OF THE ACTION OF NATURAL SELECTION, OR THE SURVIVAL OF THE FITTEST

In order to make it clear how, as I believe, natural selection acts, I must beg permission to give one or two imaginary illustrations. Let us take the case of a wolf which preys on various animals, securing some by craft, some by strength, and some by fleetness; and let us suppose that the fleetest prey, a deer for instance, had from any change in the country increased in numbers, or that other prey had decreased in numbers, during that season of the year when the wolf was hardest pressed for food. Under such circumstances the swiftest and slimmest wolves have the best chance of surviving, and so being preserved or selected, provided always that they retain strength to master their prey at this or some other period of the year, when they were compelled to prey on other animals. I can see no more reason to doubt that this would be the result, than that man should be able to improve the fleetness of his greyhounds by careful and methodical selection, or by that kind of unconscious selection which follows from each man trying to keep the best dogs without any thought of modifying the breed. I may add that, according to Mr. Pierce,[4] there are two varieties of the wolf inhabiting the Catskill Mountains, in the United States, one with a light greyhound-like form, which pursues deer, and the other more bulky, with shorter legs, which more frequently attacks the shepherd's flocks.

It should be observed that in the above illustration, I speak of the slim- 5 mest individual wolves, and not of any single strongly marked variation having been preserved. In former editions of this work I sometimes spoke as if this latter alternative had frequently occurred. I saw the great importance of individual differences, and this led me fully to discuss the results of unconscious selection by man, which depends on the preservation of all the more or less valuable individuals, and on the destruction of the worst. I saw,

---

[4] **Mr. Pierce** Darwin does not identify him, but it may be a reference to Franklin Pierce (1804–1869).

also, that the preservation in a state of nature of any occasional deviation of structure, such as a monstrosity, would be a rare event; and that, if at first preserved, it would generally be lost by subsequent intercrossing with ordinary individuals. Nevertheless, until reading an able and valuable article in the *North British Review* (1867), I did not appreciate how rarely single variations, whether slight or strongly marked, could be perpetuated. The author takes the case of a pair of animals, producing during their lifetime two hundred offspring, of which, from various causes of destruction, only two on an average survive to procreate their kind. This is rather an extreme estimate for most of the higher animals, but by no means so for many of the lower organisms. He then shows that if a single individual were born, which varied in some manner, giving it twice as good a chance of life as that of the other individuals, yet the chances would be strongly against its

"Thus it is, as I believe, that when the males and females of any animal have the same general habits of life, but differ in structure, color, or ornament, such difference have been mainly caused by sexual selection[.]"

survival. Supposing it to survive and to breed, and that half its young inherited the favorable variation; still, as the reviewer goes on to show, the young would have only a slightly better chance of surviving and breeding; and this chance would go on decreasing in the succeeding generations. The justice of these remarks cannot, I think, be disputed. If, for instance, a bird of some kind could procure its food more easily by having its beak curved, and if one were born with its beak strongly curved, and which consequently flourished, nevertheless there would be a very poor chance of this one individual perpetuating its kind to the exclusion of the common form; but there can hardly be a doubt, judging by what we see taking place under domestication, that this result would follow from the preservation during many generations of a large number of individuals with more or less strongly curved beaks, and from the destruction of a still larger number with the straightest beaks.

It should not, however, be overlooked, that certain rather strongly marked variations, which no one would rank as mere individual differences, frequently recur owing to a similar organization being similarly acted on — of which fact numerous instances could be given with our domestic productions. In such cases, if the varying individual did not actually transmit to its offspring its newly acquired character, it would undoubtedly transmit to them, as long as the existing conditions remained the same, a still stronger tendency to vary in the same manner. There can also be little doubt that the tendency to vary in the same manner has often been so strong that all the individuals of the same species have been similarly modified without the aid of any form of selection. Or only a third, fifth, or tenth part of the individuals may have been thus affected, of which fact several instances could be given. Thus Graba[5] estimates that about one-fifth of the guillemots in the Faroe Islands consist of a variety so well marked, that it was formerly ranked as a distinct species under the name of *Uria lacrymans*. In cases of this kind, if the variation were of a beneficial nature, the original form would soon be supplanted by the modified form, through the survival of the fittest.

To the effects of intercrossing in eliminating variations of all kinds, I shall have to recur: but it may be here remarked that most animals and plants keep to their proper homes, and do not needlessly wander about; we see this even with migratory birds, which almost always return to the same spot. Consequently each newly formed variety would generally be at first local, as seems to be the common rule with varieties in a state of nature; so that similarly modified individuals would soon exist in a small body together, and would often breed together. If the new variety were successful in its battle for life, it would slowly spread from a central district, competing with and conquering the unchanged individuals on the margins of an ever-increasing circle.

It may be worthwhile to give another and more complex illustration of the action of natural selection. Certain plants excrete sweet juice, apparently for the sake of eliminating something injurious from the sap: this is effected, for instance, by glands at the base of the stipules in some Leguminosæ,[6] and at the backs of the leaves of the common laurel. This juice, though small in quantity, is greedily sought by insects; but their visits do not in any way benefit the plant. Now, let us suppose that the juice or nectar was excreted from the inside of the flowers of a certain number of plants of any species. Insects in seeking the nectar would get dusted with pollen, and would often transport it from one flower to another. The flowers of two distinct individuals of the same species would thus get crossed; and the act of crossing, as can be fully proved, gives rise to vigorous seedlings, which consequently would have the best chance of flourishing and surviving. The plants which produced flowers with the largest glands or nectaries, excreting most nectar, would oftenest be visited by insects, and would oftenest be crossed; and so in the long run would gain the upper hand and form a local variety. The flowers also, which had their stamens and pistils placed, in relation to the size and habits of the particular insect which visited them, so as to favor in any degree the transportal of the pollen, would likewise be favored. We might have taken the case of insects visiting flowers for the sake of collecting pollen instead of nectar; and as pollen is formed for the sole purpose of fertilization, its destruction appears to be a simple loss to the plant; yet if

---

[5] **Graba** Carl Julian von Graba (1799–1874), German bird specialist who first studied the Faroe Islands.

[6] **Leguminosæ** Plants within the pea or bean family.

a little pollen were carried, at first occasionally and then habitually, by the pollen-devouring insects from flower to flower, and a cross thus effected, although nine-tenths of the pollen were destroyed it might still be a great gain to the plant to be thus robbed; and the individuals which produced more and more pollen, and had larger anthers, would be selected.

Understanding Ideas

1. According to Charles Darwin, sexual selection among animals usually depends on what weapons?

2. As explained in Darwin's essay, how does sexual selection work in birds?

3. What, according to Darwin, is the likelihood of individual variations in animals being inherited in nature?

4. What does Darwin say about the interdependence of plants and insects?

Responding to Ideas

1. *Research* Charles Darwin discusses sexual selection in both animals and birds. The difference between them is that animals are likely to become violent competing for a mate, while for birds "the contest is often of a more peaceful character" (para. 2). How is the competition for mates carried out by the males and females that you have observed in your social group? Do people in your community differ in their competition for a mate according to gender? Are they closer in behavior to the animals Darwin mentions or to the birds he discusses? Describe carefully how young people in college today practice sexual selection.

2. *Response* Some old movies depict what were then considered typical, sometimes violent, fights between young men, while the woman they compete for stands or sits aside and watches. In those movies, the woman often seems proud to be fought over. If you have witnessed such a scene, how violent was it, and what was the outcome? Does such behavior go on today in your community? How would a young woman today react to such a potentially violent competition?

3. *Research* Assuming that popular culture, such as music, television shows and movies, and dance clubs and bars, aims at somehow aiding sexual selection, how does it do so? Name some of the most important and influential contemporary entertainers who model behavior

that would result in sexual selection. What characteristics of their acts suggest that what they recommend by their behavior will be successful or satisfying? Do these entertainers seem aware of how they influence sexual selection, or does their influence seem mostly unconscious?

4. *Analysis of Circumstances* In discussing natural selection, Darwin talks about slender wolves and heavier wolves. What is the point of his discussion of these wolves? They seem to be particular in that they are not different species but different groups. The slender wolves hunt fleet-footed deer, while the heavier ones usually hunt livestock. Under what conditions is it likely that one group of wolves will survive and breed, while the other will die with few or no offspring? How effective is Darwin's discussion of these wolves? Of what does Darwin convince you?

5. *Response* In discussing "strongly marked variations" (para. 6), Darwin suggests that some variations may be monstrosities and, therefore, would not be transmitted to future generations. But if the variation were "of a beneficial nature" (para. 6), it would be transmitted to future generations, the members of which would supplant the original group. This is a principle of natural selection and is one of Darwin's reasons for arguing natural selection as a basis for evolution. To what extent does this seem reasonable to you? Assuming that evolution is a biological reality, which force — sexual selection or natural selection — do you think is more likely to generate evolutionary change?

6. *Research* In this brief essay, Darwin uses a great many examples to bolster his arguments about sexual selection and natural selection. These arguments support his theory of evolution. Examine the literature of antievolutionists and see how they go about arguing against Darwin. Do they rely as heavily on example for their argument as Darwin does? What is the main argument they have to counter Darwin's views? How effective is their argument? How might Darwin react to their rejection of his position on the results of sexual and natural selection? You might begin with Thomas Fowler, *The Evolution Controversy: A Survey of Competing Theories* (2007).

Comparing Ideas

1. The question of sexual selection is introduced again in Steve Jones's "The Descent of Men" (p. 244). Jones is a committed Darwinist who sees the effects of evolution still at work. Write a brief essay that examines the way Jones studies the present condition of sexual selection and the dangers he sees. How do the theories of Darwin in his "Of

Sexual Selection and Natural Selection" affect Jones's analysis of the current situation in which males are endangered in the modern world? Are both writers sufficiently scientific in their examinations? What is your personal response to what they have to say?

2. Darwin changed a great many people's thinking in the latter half of the nineteenth century. His ideas had interesting influences in the social sciences. For example, in "The Gospel of Wealth" (p. 289), Andrew Carnegie took Darwin very seriously and saw in his work some justification for the enormous inequality of wealth in society. How do the ideas of sexual and natural selection relate to the ideas that Carnegie promoted? Does sexual selection produce the kinds of inequalities in nature that Carnegie saw in economics? How successfully did Carnegie adapt the ideas of Darwin and evolution to his topic?

ALFRED NORTH WHITEHEAD

ALFRED NORTH WHITEHEAD (1861–1947) was educated at Trinity College, Cambridge, and later taught mathematics there. With his student the eminent philosopher Bertrand Russell, Whitehead collaborated on one of the most important modern works on mathematics, the three-volume *Principia Mathematica* (1910–1913). Their project demonstrated the connection between mathematics and formal logic.

After leaving Cambridge, Whitehead taught at Harvard University as a professor of philosophy. He delivered the Lowell Lectures published in 1925 in *Science and the Modern World*, which for some time was an influential best-seller. "Religion and Science" comes from that book. His professional interests and insights successfully encompassed not just science and mathematics but religion and the humanities as well.

"Religion and Science" discusses a controversy over teaching evolutionary biology. The publication of Darwin's *On the Origin of Species* in 1859 had begun a widespread reaction on religious grounds against the idea that people evolved from apes. That issue came to Whitehead's attention because of the celebrated Scopes "monkey trial" in 1925 in Dayton, Tennessee. It was a test of whether or not a science teacher was allowed to teach the theory of evolution in a public school in that state. It was a heightened dramatic event in part because William Jennings Bryan, a brilliant speaker and a three-time presidential candidate, argued for the state. Clarence Darrow, the most respected trial lawyer of the day, acted for the defense. The case was finally thrown out on a technicality, but the issue in Tennessee was not resolved until 1964.

The argument in the case pitched science teachers and the teaching of science against a community that believed evolution was irreligious. The state of Tennessee contended that evolution contradicted the Bible's version of the creation of man. Further, it contended that the Bible was the word of God and, therefore, superseded any and all scientific findings. Today, Tennessee and a few other states do not prevent evolutionary biology from being taught in public schools, but they also teach creationism, which depends on the Bible for its evidence.

In this discussion, Whitehead explains that science and religion have been at odds in Western culture since the late sixteenth century and early seventeenth century, when the astronomer Galileo (1564–1642) first proposed that Earth orbits the sun (instead of the other way around) and the Catholic Church publicly forced him to retract his theory. The church believed that the earth was the center of the universe because the Bible says in several places that the earth is fixed and cannot move. In his essay, Whitehead, who was very knowledgeable in theology, makes an effort to find a way to put the conflict between science and religion into perspective and to soften long-standing disagreements.

Be sure to practice prereading techniques before a careful, annotated reading of Whitehead's essay. For a review of prereading strategies, see pages 4–9. ⊞

Religion and Science

THE DIFFICULTY in approaching the question of the relations between Religion and Science is, that its elucidation requires that we have in our minds some clear idea of what we mean by either of the terms, "religion" and "science." Also I wish to speak in the most general way possible, and to keep in the background any comparison of particular creeds, scientific or religious. We have got to understand the type of connection which exists between the two spheres, and then to draw some definite conclusions respecting the existing situation which at present confronts the world.

The *conflict* between religion and science is what naturally occurs to our minds when we think of this subject. It seems as though, during the last half-century, the results of science and the beliefs of religion had come into a position of frank disagreement, from which there can be no escape, except by abandoning either the clear teaching of science, or the clear teaching of religion. This conclusion has been urged by controversialists on either side. Not by all controversialists, of course, but by those trenchant intellects which every controversy calls out into the open.

The distress of sensitive minds, and the zeal for truth, and the sense of the importance of the issues, must command our sincerest sympathy. When we consider what religion is for mankind, and what science is, it is no exaggeration to say that the future course of history depends upon the decision of this generation as to the relations between them. We have here the two strongest general forces (apart from the mere impulse of the various senses) which influence men, and they seem to be set one against the other — the force of our religious intuitions, and the force of our impulse to accurate observation and logical deduction.

A great English statesman once advised his countrymen to use large-scale maps, as a preservative against alarms, panics, and general misunderstanding of the true relations between nations. In the same way in dealing with the clash between permanent elements of human nature, it is well to map our history on a large scale, and to disengage ourselves from our immediate absorption in the present conflicts. When we do this, we immediately discover two great facts. In the first place, there has always been a conflict between religion and science; and in the second place, both religion and science have always been in a state of continual development. In the early days of Christianity, there was a general belief among Christians that the world was coming to an end in the lifetime of people then living. We can make only indirect inferences as to how far this belief was authoritatively proclaimed; but it is certain that it was widely held, and that it formed an impressive part of the popular religious doctrine. The belief proved itself to be mistaken, and Christian doctrine adjusted itself to the change. Again in the early church individual theologians very confidently deduced from the Bible opinions concerning the nature of the physical universe. In the year A.D. 535, a monk named Cosmas[1] wrote a book which he entitled, *Christian Topography*. He was a traveled man who had visited India and Ethiopia; and finally he lived in a monastery at Alexandria,[2] which was then a great center of culture. In this book, basing himself upon the direct meaning of biblical texts as construed by him in a literal fashion, he denied the existence of the antipodes,[3] and asserted that the world is a flat parallelogram whose length is double its breadth.

In the seventeenth century the doctrine of the motion of the earth[4] 5 was condemned by a Catholic tribunal. A hundred years ago the extension of time[5] demanded by geological science distressed religious people,

---

[1] *Cf.* [William] Lecky's *The Rise and Influence of Rationalism in Europe*, Ch. III. [Whitehead's note]

[2] **Alexandria** City in Egypt; the center of Christianity's Coptic Church.

[3] **antipodes** Whitehead means the North and South Poles; *antipodes* generally means any two places on the earth that are opposite each other.

[4] **motion of the earth** The church taught that the earth was stationary and the sun and moon revolved about it. In 1632, Galileo proved otherwise and was condemned (see note 7).

[5] **extension of time** Calculating from biblical records and genealogies, Archbishop James Usher (1581–1656) established the date of creation as 4004 B.C. Geological science points to a date hundreds of millions of years earlier. Many religions still hold to Usher's dating.

Protestant and Catholic. And today the doctrine of evolution is an equal stumbling block. These are only a few instances illustrating a general fact.

But all our ideas will be in a wrong perspective if we think that this recurring perplexity was confined to contradictions between religion and science; and that in these controversies religion was always wrong, and that science was always right. The true facts of the case are very much more complex, and refuse to be summarized in these simple terms.

Theology itself exhibits exactly the same character of gradual development, arising from an aspect of conflict between its own proper ideas. This fact is a commonplace to theologians, but is often obscured in the stress of controversy. I do not wish to overstate my case; so I will confine myself to Roman Catholic writers. In the seventeenth century a learned Jesuit, Father Petavius, showed that the theologians of the first three centuries of Christianity made use of phrases and statements which since the fifth century would be condemned as heretical. Also Cardinal Newman[6] devoted a treatise to the discussion of the development of doctrine. He wrote it before he became a great Roman Catholic ecclesiastic; but throughout his life, it was never retracted and continually reissued.

Science is even more changeable than theology. No man of science could subscribe without qualification to Galileo's beliefs,[7] or to Newton's beliefs,[8] or to all his own scientific beliefs of ten years ago.

In both regions of thought, additions, distinctions, and modifications have been introduced. So that now, even when the same assertion is made today as was made a thousand, or fifteen hundred years ago, it is made subject to limitations or expansions of meaning, which were not contemplated at the earlier epoch. We are told by logicians that a proposition must be either true or false, and that there is no middle term. But in practice, we may know that a proposition expresses an important truth, but that it is subject to limitations and qualifications which at present remain undiscovered. It is a general feature of our knowledge, that we are insistently aware of important truth; and yet that the only formulations of these truths which we are able to make presuppose a general standpoint of conceptions which may have to be modified. I will give you two illustrations, both from science:

---

[6] **Cardinal Newman** John Henry Newman (1801–1890), an Englishman, published his *Lectures on the Prophetical Office of the Church* (1843) before he converted from Anglicanism to Roman Catholicism (1845). He became a priest and was made a cardinal in 1879. One of his most famous books is *The Idea of a University* (1852).

[7] **Galileo's beliefs** Galileo Galilei (1564–1642), Italian astronomer who proved the Copernican theory that Earth moves around the sun. The Roman Catholic Church, which still officially held otherwise, forced him to recant.

[8] **Newton's beliefs** Isaac Newton (1642–1727), English physicist, discovered the law of gravity and invented calculus. His laws of motion, fluids, and optics are still accurate and applicable in modern physics.

Galileo said that the earth moves and that the sun is fixed; the Inquisition said that the earth is fixed and the sun moves; and Newtonian astronomers, adopting an absolute theory of space, said that both the sun and the earth move. But now we say that any one of these three statements is equally true, provided that you have fixed your sense of "rest" and "motion" in the way required by the statement adopted. At the date of Galileo's controversy with the Inquisition, Galileo's way of stating the facts was, beyond question, the fruitful procedure for the sake of scientific research. But in itself it was not more true than the formulation of the Inquisition. But at that time the modern concepts of relative motion were in nobody's mind; so that the statements were made in ignorance of the qualifications required for their more perfect truth. Yet this question of the motions of the earth and the sun expresses a real fact in the universe; and all sides had got hold of important truths concerning it. But with the knowledge of those times, the truths appeared to be inconsistent.

Again I will give you another example taken from the state of modern   10 physical science. Since the time of Newton and Huyghens[9] in the seventeenth century there have been two theories as to the physical nature of light. Newton's theory was that a beam of light consists of a stream of very minute particles, or corpuscles, and that we have the sensation of light when these corpuscles strike the retinas of our eyes. Huyghens's theory was that light consists of very minute waves of trembling in an all-pervading ether, and that these waves are traveling along a beam of light. The two theories are contradictory. In the eighteenth century Newton's theory was believed, in the nineteenth century Huyghens's theory was believed. Today there is one large group of phenomena which can be explained only on the wave theory, and another large group which can be explained only on the corpuscular theory. Scientists have to leave it at that, and wait for the future, in the hope of attaining some wider vision which reconciles both.

We should apply these same principles to the questions in which there is a variance between science and religion. We would believe nothing in either sphere of thought which does not appear to us to be certified by solid reasons based upon the critical research either of ourselves or of competent authorities. But granting that we have honestly taken this precaution, a clash between the two on points of detail where they overlap should not lead us hastily to abandon doctrines for which we have solid evidence. It may be that we are more interested in one set of doctrines than in the other.

---

[9] **Huyghens** Christian Huyghens (1629–1695), Dutch mathematician and astronomer. He founded the wave theory, discovered the rings of Saturn, invented the pendulum clock, and discovered the laws of centrifugal force. He was an extremely well-known figure.

But, if we have any sense of perspective and of the history of thought, we shall wait and refrain from mutual anathemas.[10]

We should wait: but we should not wait passively, or in despair. The clash is a sign that there are wider truths and finer perspectives within which a reconciliation of a deeper religion and a more subtle science will be found.

In one sense, therefore, the conflict between science and religion is a slight matter which has been unduly emphasized. A mere logical contradiction cannot in itself point to more than the necessity of some readjustments, possibly of a very minor character on both sides. Remember the widely different aspects of events which are dealt with in science and in religion respectively. Science is concerned with the general conditions which are observed to regulate physical phenomena; whereas religion is wholly wrapped up in the contemplation of moral and aesthetic values. On the one side there is the law of gravitation, and on the other the contemplation of the beauty of holiness. What one side sees, the other misses; and vice versa.

"In both regions of thought, additions, distinctions, and modifications have been introduced. So that now, even when the same assertion is made today as was made a thousand or fifteen hundred years ago, it is made subject to limitations or expansions of meaning which were not contemplated at the earlier epoch."

Consider, for example, the lives of John Wesley[11] and of Saint Francis of Assisi.[12] For physical science you have in these lives merely ordinary examples of the operation of the principles of physiological chemistry, and of the dynamics of nervous reactions: for religion you have lives of the most profound significance in the history of the world. Can you be surprised that, in the absence of a perfect and complete phrasing of the principles of science and of the principles of religion which apply to these specific cases, the accounts of these lives from these divergent standpoints should involve discrepancies? It would be a miracle if it were not so.

It would, however, be missing the point to think that we need not trouble ourselves about the conflict between science and religion. In an intellectual age there can be no active interest which puts aside all hope of a vision of the harmony of truth. To acquiesce in discrepancy is destructive of candor, and of moral cleanliness. It belongs to the self-respect of intellect

15

---

[10] **anathemas** Denunciations; in religion, official anathema involved excommunication.

[11] **John Wesley** (1703–1791) English clergyman, founder of the Methodist Church, leader of the religious revival in the eighteenth century.

[12] **Saint Francis of Assisi** (1181–1226) Italian monk, founder of the Franciscan order of monks; like Wesley, he was a powerfully charismatic person who drew many followers. He preached good works, poverty, and charity.

to pursue every tangle of thought to its final unravelment. If you check that impulse, you will get no religion and no science from an awakened thoughtfulness. The important question is, In what spirit are we going to face the issue? There we come to something absolutely vital.

A clash of doctrines is not a disaster — it is an opportunity. I will explain my meaning by some illustrations from science. The weight of an atom of nitrogen was well known. Also it was an established scientific doctrine that the average weight of such atoms in any considerable mass will be always the same. Two experimenters, the late Lord Rayleigh and the late Sir William Ramsay,[13] found that if they obtained nitrogen by two different methods, each equally effective for that purpose, they always observed a persistent slight difference between the average weights of the atoms in the two cases. Now I ask you, would it have been rational of these men to have despaired because of this conflict between chemical theory and scientific observation? Suppose that for some reason the chemical doctrine had been highly prized throughout some district as the foundation of its social order: Would it have been wise, would it have been candid, would it have been moral, to forbid the disclosure of the fact that the experiments produced discordant results? Or, on the other hand, should Sir William Ramsay and Lord Rayleigh have proclaimed that chemical theory was now a detected delusion? We see at once that either of these ways would have been a method of facing the issue in an entirely wrong spirit. What Rayleigh and Ramsay did was this: they at once perceived that they had hit upon a line of investigation which would disclose some subtlety of chemical theory that had hitherto eluded observation. The discrepancy was not a disaster: it was an opportunity to increase the sweep of chemical knowledge. You all know the end of the story: finally argon was discovered, a new chemical element which had lurked undetected, mixed with the nitrogen. But the story has a sequel which forms my second illustration. This discovery drew attention to the importance of observing accurately minute differences in chemical substances as obtained by different methods. Further researches of the most careful accuracy were undertaken. Finally another physicist, F. W. Aston, working in the Cavendish Laboratory at Cambridge in England, discovered that even the same element might assume two or more distinct forms, termed *isotopes*,[14] and that

---

[13] **Rayleigh . . . Ramsay** John William Strutt, Third Baron Rayleigh (1844–1919), and Sir William Ramsay (1852–1916) shared the Nobel Prize for Physics in 1904. Ramsay discovered and worked with inert gases — helium (with Rayleigh); argon (with Morris Travers, another scientist). Together they studied the density of nitrogen produced from air and ammonia, finding the figures persistently different.

[14] *isotopes* Molecules of the same element but having different molecular weights and detectable differences of behavior. Francis William Aston (1877–1945) established the existence of isotopes as a basic phenomenon of nature. The Cavendish Laboratories were founded at Cambridge University by J. C. Maxwell.

the law of the constancy of average atomic weight holds for each of these forms, but as between the different isotopes differs slightly. The research has effected a great stride in the power of chemical theory, far transcending in importance the discovery of argon from which it originated. The moral of these stories lies on the surface, and I will leave to you their application to the case of religion and science.

In formal logic, a contradiction is the signal of a defeat: but in the evolution of real knowledge it marks the first step in progress towards a victory. This is one great reason for the utmost toleration of variety of opinion. Once and forever, this duty of toleration has been summed up in the words, "Let both grow together until the harvest."[15] The failure of Christians to act up to this precept, of the highest authority, is one of the curiosities of religious history. But we have not yet exhausted the discussion of the moral temper required for the pursuit of truth. There are shortcuts leading merely to an illusory success. It is easy enough to find a theory, logically harmonious and with important applications in the region of fact, provided that you are content to disregard half your evidence. Every age produces people with clear logical intellects, and with the most praiseworthy grasp of the importance of some sphere of human experience, who have elaborated, or inherited, a scheme of thought which exactly fits those experiences which claim their interest. Such people are apt resolutely to ignore, or to explain away, all evidence which confuses their scheme with contradictory instances; what they cannot fit in is for them nonsense. An unflinching determination to take the whole evidence into account is the only method of preservation against the fluctuating extremes of fashionable opinion. This advice seems so easy, and is in fact so difficult to follow.

> *"A clash of doctrines is not a disaster — it is an opportunity."*

One reason for this difficulty is that we cannot think first and act afterwards. From the moment of birth we are immersed in action, and can only fitfully guide it by taking thought. We have, therefore, in various spheres of experience to adopt those ideas which seem to work within those spheres. It is absolutely necessary to trust to ideas which are generally adequate, even though we know that there are subtleties and distinctions beyond our ken. Also apart from the necessities of action, we cannot even keep before our minds the whole evidence except under the guise of doctrines which are incompletely harmonized. We cannot think in terms of an indefinite multiplicity of detail; our evidence can acquire its proper importance only if it comes before us marshaled by general ideas. These ideas we inherit — they form the tradition of our civilization. Such traditional ideas

---

[15] The quotation is from Matthew 13:30, an argument against premature "weeding out" of things that might prove useful.

are never static. They are either fading into meaningless formulae, or are gaining power by the new lights thrown by a more delicate apprehension. They are transformed by the urge of critical reason, by the vivid evidence of emotional experience, and by the cold certainties of scientific perception. One fact is certain, you cannot keep them still. No generation can merely reproduce its ancestors. You may preserve the life in a flux of form, or preserve the form amid an ebb of life. But you cannot permanently enclose the same life in the same mold.

The present state of religion among the European races illustrates the statements which I have been making. The phenomena are mixed. There have been reactions and revivals. But on the whole, during many generations, there has been a gradual decay of religious influence in European civilization. Each revival touches a lower peak than its predecessor, and each period of slackness a lower depth. The average curve marks a steady fall in religious tone. In some countries the interest in religion is higher than in others. But in those countries where the interest is relatively high, it still falls as the generations pass. Religion is tending to degenerate into a decent formula wherewith to embellish a comfortable life. A great historical movement on this scale results from the convergence of many causes. I wish to suggest two of them which lie within the scope of this chapter for consideration.

In the first place for over two centuries religion has been on the defen- 20 sive, and on a weak defensive. The period has been one of unprecedented intellectual progress. In this way a series of novel situations have been produced for thought. Each such occasion has found the religious thinkers unprepared. Something, which has been proclaimed to be vital, has finally, after struggle, distress, and anathema, been modified and otherwise interpreted. The next generation of religious apologists then congratulates the religious world on the deeper insight which has been gained. The result of the continued repetition of this undignified retreat, during many generations, has at last almost entirely destroyed the intellectual authority of religious thinkers. Consider this contrast: when Darwin or Einstein proclaim theories which modify our ideas, it is a triumph for science. We do not go about saying that there is another defeat for science, because its old ideas have been abandoned. We know that another step of scientific insight has been gained.

Religion will not regain its old power until it can face change in the same spirit as does science. Its principles may be eternal, but the expression of those principles requires continual development. This evolution of religion is in the main a disengagement of its own proper ideas from the adventitious[16] notions which have crept into it by reason of the expression

---

[16] **adventitious** Borrowed, not original; not essential to something.

of its own ideas in terms of the imaginative picture of the world entertained in previous ages. Such a release of religion from the bonds of imperfect science is all to the good. It stresses its own genuine message. The great point to be kept in mind is that normally an advance in science will show that statements of various religious beliefs require some sort of modification. It may be that they have to be expanded or explained, or indeed entirely restated. If the religion is a sound expression of truth, this modification will only exhibit more adequately the exact point which is of importance. This process is a gain. Insofar, therefore, as any religion has any contact with physical facts, it is to be expected that the point of view of those facts must be continually modified as scientific knowledge advances. In this way, the exact relevance of these facts for religious thought will grow more and more clear. The progress of science must result in the unceasing codification of religious thought, to the great advantage of religion.

The religious controversies of the sixteenth and seventeenth centuries put theologians into a most unfortunate state of mind. They were always attacking and defending. They pictured themselves as the garrison of a fort surrounded by hostile forces. All such pictures express half-truths. That is why they are so popular. But they are dangerous. This particular picture fostered a pugnacious party spirit which really expresses an ultimate lack of faith. They dared not modify, because they shirked the task of disengaging their spiritual message from the associations of a particular imagery.

Let me explain myself by an example. In the early medieval times, Heaven was in the sky, and Hell was underground; volcanoes were the jaws of Hell. I do not assert that these beliefs entered into the official formulations: but they did enter into the popular understanding of the general doctrines of Heaven and Hell. These notions were what everyone thought to be implied by the doctrine of the future state. They entered into the explanations of the influential exponents of Christian belief. For example, they occur in the *Dialogues* of Pope Gregory,[17] the Great, a man whose high official position is surpassed only by the magnitude of his services to humanity. I am not saying what we ought to believe about the future state. But whatever be the right doctrine, in this instance the clash between religion and science, which has relegated the earth to the position of a second-rate planet attached to a second-rate sun, has been greatly to the benefit of the spirituality of religion by dispersing these medieval fancies.

Another way of looking at this question of the evolution of religious thought is to note that any verbal form of statement which has been before

---

[17] *Cf.* Gregorovius's *History of Rome in the Middle Ages*, Book III, Ch. III, Vol. II, English trans. [Whitehead's note] Pope Gregory I (540–604) established the model for the medieval papacy. He used the power of the church to relieve the misery of many people.

the world for some time discloses ambiguities; and that often such ambiguities strike at the very heart of the meaning. The effective sense in which a doctrine has been held in the past cannot be determined by the mere logical analysis of verbal statements, made in ignorance of the logical trap.[18] You have to take into account the whole reaction of human nature to the scheme of thought. This reaction is of a mixed character, including elements of emotion derived from our lower natures. It is here that the impersonal criticism of science and of philosophy comes to the aid of religious evolution. Example after example can be given of this motive force in development. For example, the logical difficulties inherent in the doctrine of the moral cleansing of human nature by the power of religion rent Christianity in the days of Pelagius and Augustine[19] — that is to say, at the beginning of the fifth century. Echoes of that controversy still linger in theology.

So far, my point has been this: that religion is the expression of one type   25 of fundamental experiences of mankind: that religious thought develops into an increasing accuracy of expression, disengaged from adventitious imagery: that the interaction between religion and science is one great factor in promoting this development.

I now come to my second reason for the modern fading of interest in religion. This involves the ultimate question which I stated in my opening sentences. We have to know what we mean by religion. The churches, in their presentation of their answers to this query, have put forward aspects of religion which are expressed in terms either suited to the emotional reactions of bygone times or directed to excite modern emotional interests of nonreligious character. What I mean under the first heading is that religious appeal is directed partly to excite that instinctive fear of the wrath of a tyrant which was inbred in the unhappy populations of the arbitrary empires of the ancient world, and in particular to excite that fear of an all-powerful arbitrary tyrant behind the unknown forces of nature. This appeal to the ready instinct of brute fear is losing its force. It lacks any directness of response, because modern science and modern conditions of life have taught us to meet occasions of apprehension by a critical analysis of their causes and conditions. Religion is the reaction of human nature to its search for God. The presentation of God under the aspect of power awakens every modern instinct of critical reaction. This is fatal; for religion collapses unless its main positions command immediacy of assent. In this respect the

---

[18] **logical trap** A reference to the limits of verbal logic. See Aristotle's cautions in the opening of *The Nichomachean Ethics* on the limits of precision possible in certain inquiries. Matters of faith are not always susceptible to logic.

[19] **Pelagius and Augustine** The argument between Pelagius (360?–?420) and Saint Augustine (354–430) was over the issue of original sin. Pelagius said it was not visited on mankind; Augustine said that it was. The Roman Catholic Church accepts Augustine's view.

old phraseology is at variance with the psychology of modern civilizations. This change in psychology is largely due to science, and is one of the chief ways in which the advance of science has weakened the hold of the old religious forms of expression. The nonreligious motive which has entered into modern religious thought is the desire for a comfortable organization of modern society. Religion has been presented as valuable for the ordering of life. Its claims have been rested upon its function as a sanction to right conduct. Also the purpose of right conduct quickly degenerates into the formation of pleasing social relations. We have here a subtle degradation of religious ideas, following upon their gradual purification under the influence of keener ethical intuitions. Conduct is a by-product of religion — an inevitable by-product, but not the main point. Every great religious teacher has revolted against the presentation of religion as a mere sanction of rules of conduct. Saint Paul[20] denounced the Law, and Puritan divines[21] spoke of the filthy rags of righteousness. The insistence upon rules of conduct marks the ebb of religious fervor. Above and beyond all things, the religious life is not a research after comfort. I must now state, in all diffidence, what I conceive to be the essential character of the religious spirit.

Religion is the vision of something which stands beyond, behind, and within, the passing flux of immediate things; something which is real, and yet waiting to be realized; something which is a remote possibility, and yet the greatest of present facts; something that gives meaning to all that passes, and yet eludes apprehension; something whose possession is the final good, and yet is beyond all reach; something which is the ultimate ideal, and the hopeless quest.

The immediate reaction of human nature to the religious vision is worship. Religion has emerged into human experience mixed with the crudest fancies of barbaric imagination. Gradually, slowly, steadily the vision recurs in history under nobler form and with clearer expression. It is the one element in human experience which persistently shows an upward trend. It fades and then recurs. But when it renews its force, it recurs with an added richness and purity of content. The fact of the religious vision, and its history of persistent expansion, is our one ground for optimism. Apart from it, human life is a flash of occasional enjoyments lighting up a mass of pain and misery, a bagatelle[22] of transient experience.

---

[20] **Saint Paul** The Apostle Paul (d. 64?–?67 A.D.) wrote several letters denouncing morally indefensible Roman laws permitting persecution of Christians. He also repudiated Moses' Law, which he felt was superseded by Christianity.

[21] **Puritan divines** Puritans in England and America in the early seventeenth century insisted that one must follow one's moral conscience even when it directs one to break the law. English Puritans opposed King Charles I (1600–1649) and had him beheaded after they seized power in a bloody civil war.

[22] **bagatelle** Something slight and amusing; a game similar to pool.

The vision claims nothing but worship; and worship is a surrender to the claim for assimilation, urged with the motive force of mutual love. The vision never overrules. It is always there, and it has the power of love presenting the one purpose whose fulfilment is eternal harmony. Such order as we find in nature is never force — it presents itself as the one harmonious adjustment of complex detail. Evil is the brute motive force of fragmentary purpose, disregarding the eternal vision. Evil is overruling, retarding, hurting. The power of God is the worship He inspires. That religion is strong which in its ritual and its modes of thought evokes an apprehension of the commanding vision. The worship of God is not a rule of safety — it is an adventure of the spirit, a flight after the unattainable. The death of religion comes with the repression of the high hope of adventure.

> *"Religion is the vision of something which stands beyond, behind, and within, the passing flux of immediate things[.]"*

Understanding Ideas

1. Why does Alfred North Whitehead consider the conflict between religion and science to be so important?

2. According to Whitehead, which is more changeable, religion or science?

3. Why does Whitehead think religion may be losing its influence?

4. Is Whitehead more worried about religion or science?

Responding to Ideas

1. **Definition** While it is clear that most people think they know what religion is and what science is, the question of clear definitions is still unsettled. Go through Alfred North Whitehead's essay and clarify the various definitions he gives, either specifically or by implication. Explain why you are or are not satisfied with his definitions and offer definitions of your own. Consider the issues of psychology and belief as well as issues of fact.

2. **Testimony** Whitehead says, "A clash of doctrines is not a disaster — it is an opportunity" (para. 16). How does he defend this statement? In what ways is it a key part of his overall argument? Find an example of

a clash of doctrines and show how it has produced opportunities for new development of ideas and achievements. Choose a recent clash between religion and science or find one in which science clashes with popular belief. Global warming is an area in which science today seems to conflict with widely held beliefs. The same may be said for some industrial methods, such as the safety of hydraulic fracturing for gas and oil.

3. **Example** One of Whitehead's chief methods in developing his argument is the use of numerous examples. Analyze his essay for effectiveness of the examples in convincing you of Whitehead's position on matters of religion or of science. Which examples are the most effective, those for religion or those for science? What makes them so effective? What examples might you bring to bear that would make his argument more powerful?

4. **Research** In 1925, the argument between evolution and religion involved the entire population of the United States. Teaching evolution in many states was simply unacceptable. Europe seems to have accepted evolution as a scientific fact without a profound religious conflict. Today Pope Francis has said that the Roman Catholic Church does not have a problem with evolution or even with the big bang theory. What are the circumstances of the clash with evolutionary thought in the nation today? Research online, in the news, and in the library the current thinking on evolutionary doctrine and its effect on religious thought. You might begin with Stephen Jay Gould's *The Structure of Evolutionary Theory* (2002).

5. **Analysis of Circumstances** Is it possible today that either religion or science could actually win as the result of a conflict between them? Which side would you take in the conflict between religion and science and why? If science wins, how does that lessen the impact or importance of religion? If religion wins, how does that diminish the findings of science? What is at stake in a conflict in which religion wins out over science? Are there real possibilities of that happening? What current examples of such conflicts have stimulated attention in recent years?

6. **Response** One way of seeing whether or not there is a current ongoing conflict between religion and science is to conduct a poll. Interview people of different ages and genders and with different backgrounds. Ask them whether they think there is a serious conflict between the way evolution says people developed and the way the Bible says people were created. Press them to take sides on the issue, and see whether or not Whitehead's views about the relation of religion and society still hold. If you have a bias, do your best to present yourself as a neutral interviewer.

Comparing Ideas

1. Alfred North Whitehead presents an argument that balances the interests of religion with the interests of science, using examples that demonstrate the changes in each area of thought and how they relate to each other. One of his concerns is to champion religious values. How is modern religious thought affected by Charles Darwin's ideas in "Of Sexual Selection and Natural Selection" (p. 212)? What religious ideas does Darwin seem to threaten or affect seriously? Why would very religious people argue against the ideas that Darwin presents?

2. In "Good and Bad" (p. 393), Friedrich Nietzsche takes a strong position against religion. He sees the religious teachings on moral behavior as unnatural and destructive. In a sense, Nietzsche behaves as a naturalist in something of the same way Charles Darwin (p. 212) does. How would Whitehead respond to the views that Nietzsche expresses in his essay? How might he have reconciled religion with Nietzsche's examination of moral values?

Bernard Gotfryd/Hulton Archive/
Getty Images

OLIVER
SACKS

OLIVER SACKS (1933–2015) was a professor of neurology at New York University Medical School and a visiting professor at Warwick University and taught for many years at Columbia University. He was a well-known author with many popular and influential books. He was a contributor to *The New Yorker* and *The New York Review of Books*. *The New York Times* referred to him as the "poet laureate of medicine" because of his graceful writing about medical and neurological oddities.

Sacks's books have a wide range. *Awakenings* (1973) was the result of his study of people who were stricken with encephalitis lethargica in the period from 1915 to 1920, when there was an epidemic of that sleeping sickness. The patients he studied were virtually unable to move their bodies for decades. He used a then-experimental drug, L-dopa, to bring them out of their conditions. The playwright Harold Pinter used the book as inspiration for his play *A Kind of Alaska*, while the film *Awakenings* (1990), with Robert De Niro and Robin Williams and which was nominated for three Academy Awards, was also inspired by Sacks's book.

Sacks's *The Man Who Mistook His Wife for a Hat* (1985), a best-seller, discusses a number of neurological disorders, including the inability to recognize people. It was developed into an opera by Christopher Rawlence and Michael Nyman (1986) and inspired a rock band and a number of theatrical productions in Europe and elsewhere. The book is much like Sacks's other studies of neurological oddities: it takes specific examples of disorders and describes them and their treatment with care. Disorders such as Parkinson's disease, schizophrenia, autism, Tourette's syndrome, and Alzheimer's disease also figure in his work.

Sacks's book *A Leg to Stand On* (1984) is a study of one of his own neurological disorders. He had an accident that resulted in his inability to recognize one of his legs as his own, and he recorded his experiences as a patient. He did a good deal of work on visual disorders and their resultant behavior. For instance, he discussed his own disorder: the inability to remember faces, or prosopagnosia, which made it almost impossible for him to recognize people by their faces only a few days or so after having met them.

His later work covered issues associated with color blindness, *The Island of the Colorblind* (1997); deafness, *Seeing Voices: A Journey into the World of the Deaf* (1989); music therapy, *Musicophilia: Tales of Music and the Brain* (2007); and most recently, hallucinations, *Hallucinations* (2012). *The Mind's Eye* (2010), from which the following selection comes, deals with many kinds of visual aberrations, including Sacks's own facial recognition problems and his inability to perceive the world stereoscopically because a tumor in his right eye resulted in its total blindness. Thus, this essay presents his study of a neurological issue very close to his own problems.

Be sure to practice prereading techniques before a careful, annotated reading of Sacks's essay. For a review of prereading strategies, see pages 4–9. ⊞

The Mind's Eye

TO WHAT extent are we the authors, the creators, of our own experiences? How much are these predetermined by the brains or senses we are born with, and to what extent do we shape our brains through experience? The effects of a profound perceptual deprivation such as blindness may cast an unexpected light on these questions. Going blind, especially later in life, presents one with a huge, potentially overwhelming challenge: to find a new way of living, of ordering one's world, when the old way has been destroyed.

In 1990, I was sent an extraordinary book called *Touching the Rock: An Experience of Blindness*, by John Hull, a professor of religious education in England. Hull had grown up partly sighted, developing cataracts at the age of thirteen and becoming completely blind in his left eye four years later. Vision in his right eye remained reasonable until he was thirty-five or so, but there followed a decade of steadily failing vision, so that Hull needed stronger and stronger magnifying glasses and had to write with thicker and thicker pens. In 1983, at the age of forty-eight, he became completely blind.

Touching the Rock is the journal he dictated in the three years that followed. It is full of piercing insights about his transition to life as a blind person, but most striking for me was his description of how, after he became blind, he experienced a gradual attenuation of visual imagery and memory, and finally a virtual extinction of them (except in dreams) — a state that he called "deep blindness."

By this, Hull meant not only a loss of visual images and memories but a loss of the very *idea* of seeing, so that even concepts like "here," "there," and "facing" seemed to lose meaning for him. The sense of objects having appearances, or visible characteristics, vanished. He could no longer imagine how the numeral 3 looked unless he traced it in the air with his finger. He could construct a *motor* image of a 3, but not a visual one.

At first Hull was greatly distressed by this: he could no longer conjure 5 up the faces of his wife or children, or of familiar and loved landscapes and places. But he then came to accept it with remarkable equanimity, regarding it as a natural response to losing his sight. Indeed, he seemed to feel that the loss of visual imagery was a prerequisite for the full development, the heightening, of his other senses.

Two years after becoming completely blind, Hull had apparently become so nonvisual in his imagery and memory as to resemble someone who had been blind from birth. In a profoundly religious way, and in language sometimes reminiscent of that of Saint John of the Cross,[1] Hull entered into the state of deep blindness, surrendered himself, with a sort of acquiescence and joy. He spoke of deep blindness as "an authentic and autonomous world, a place of its own. . . . Being a whole-body seer is to be in one of the concentrated human conditions."

Being a "whole-body seer," for Hull, meant shifting his attention, his center of gravity, to the other senses, and these senses assumed a new richness and power. Thus he wrote of how the sound of rain, never before accorded much attention, could delineate a whole landscape for him, for its sound on the garden path was different from its sound as it drummed on the lawn, or on the bushes in his garden, or on the fence dividing the garden from the road:

> Rain has a way of bringing out the contours of everything; it throws a colored blanket over previously invisible things; instead of an intermittent and thus fragmented world, the steadily falling rain creates continuity of acoustic experience . . . presents the fullness of an entire situation all at once . . . gives a sense of perspective and of the actual relationships of one part of the world to another.

---

[1] **Saint John of the Cross** (1542–1591) Roman Catholic saint who was central to the Counter-Reformation, a period of Catholic revival beginning with the Council of Trent (1545–1563) and continuing to the end of the Thirty Years' War (1648). The Counter-Reformation was a response to the Protestant Reformation.

With his new intensity of auditory experience (or attention), along with the sharpening of his other senses, Hull came to feel a sense of intimacy with nature, an intensity of being-in-the-world, beyond anything he had known when he was sighted. Blindness became for him "a dark, paradoxical gift." This was not just "compensation," he emphasized, but a whole new order, a new mode of human being. With this, he extricated himself from visual nostalgia, from the strain or falsity of trying to pass as "normal," and found a new focus, a new freedom and identity. His teaching at the university expanded, became more fluent; his writing became stronger and deeper; he became intellectually and spiritually bolder, more confident. He felt he was on solid ground at last.[2]

Hull's description seemed to me an astounding example of how an individual deprived of one form of perception could totally reshape himself to a new center, a new perceptual identity. Yet I found it extraordinary that such an annihilation of visual memory as he described could happen to an adult with decades of rich and significant visual experience to call upon. I could not, however, doubt the authenticity of Hull's account, which he related with the most scrupulous care and lucidity.

Cognitive neuroscientists have known for the past few decades that the   10
brain is far less hardwired than was once thought. Helen Neville[3] was one of the pioneers here, showing that in prelingually deaf people (that is, those who had been born deaf or become deaf before the age of two or so) the auditory parts of the brain did not degenerate. They remained active and functional, but with an activity and a function that were new: they were transformed, "reallocated," in Neville's term, for processing visual language. Comparable studies in those born blind, or blinded early, show that some areas of the visual cortex may be reallocated and used to process sound and touch.

---

[2] Despite an initially overwhelming sense of despair on losing their sight, some people, like Hull, have found their full creative strength and identity on the other side of blindness. One thinks especially of John Milton, who started to lose his sight around the age of thirty (probably from glaucoma), but produced his greatest poetry after becoming completely blind a dozen years later. He meditated on blindness, how an inward sight may come in place of outward sight, in *Paradise Lost*, in *Samson Agonistes*, and — most directly — in letters to friends and in a very personal sonnet, "On His Blindness." Jorge Luis Borges, another poet who became blind, wrote about the varied and paradoxical effects of his own blindness; he also wondered how it might have been for Homer, who, Borges imagined, lost the world of sight but gained a much deeper sense of time and, with this, a matchless epic power. (This is beautifully discussed by J. T. Fraser in his 1989 foreword for the Braille edition of *Time, the Familiar Stranger*.) [Sacks's note]

[3] **Helen Neville** Director of the Center for Cognitive Neuroscience at the University of Oregon.

With this reallocation of parts of the visual cortex, hearing, touch, and other senses in the blind can take on a hyperacuity that perhaps no sighted person can imagine. Bernard Morin,[4] the mathematician who showed in the 1960s how a sphere could be turned inside out, became blind at the age of six, from glaucoma. He felt that his mathematical achievement required a special sort of spatial sense — a haptic perception and imagination beyond anything a sighted mathematician was likely to have. And a similar sort of spatial or tactile giftedness has been central to the work of Geerat Vermeij,[5] a conchologist who has delineated many new species of mollusks, based on tiny variations in the shapes and contours of their shells. Vermeij has been blind since the age of three.[6]

"Cognitive neuroscientists have known for the past few decades that the brain is far less hardwired than was once thought."

Faced with such findings and reports, neuroscientists began to concede in the 1970s that there might be a certain flexibility or plasticity in the brain, at least in the first couple of years of life. But when this critical period was over, it was thought, the brain became much less plastic.

Yet the brain remains capable of making radical shifts in response to sensory deprivation. In 2008, Lotfi Merabet, Alvaro Pascual-Leone,[7] and their colleagues showed that, even in sighted adults, as little as five days of being blindfolded produced marked shifts to nonvisual forms of behavior and cognition, and they demonstrated the physiological changes in the brain that went along with this. (They feel it is important to distinguish between such rapid and reversible changes, which seem to make use of preexisting but latent intersensory connections, and the long-lasting changes that occur especially in response to early or congenital blindness, which may entail major reorganizations of cortical circuitry.)

Apparently Hull's visual cortex, even in adulthood, had adapted to a loss of visual input by taking over other sensory functions — hearing, touch,

---

[4] **Bernard Morin** (b. 1931) French mathematician blind since age six.

[5] **Geerat Vermeij** (b. 1946) Professor of geology at the University of California at Davis.

[6] In his book *The Invention of Clouds*, Richard Hamblyn recounts how Luke Howard, the nineteenth-century chemist who first classified clouds, corresponded with many other naturalists of the time, including John Gough, a naturalist blinded by smallpox at the age of two. Gough, Hamblyn writes, "was a noted botanist, having taught himself the entire Linnean system by touch. He was also a master of the fields of mathematics, zoology, and scoteography — the art of writing in the dark." (Hamblyn adds that Gough "might also have become an accomplished musician had his father, a stern Quaker . . . not stopped him playing on the godless violin that an itinerant fiddler had given him.") [Sacks's note]

[7] **Lotfi Merabet, Alvaro Pascual-Leone** Merabet is an optometrist-scientist researching people's adaptations to blindness. Pascual-Leone is a professor of neurology at Harvard Medical School.

smell — while relinquishing the power of visual imagery. I assumed that Hull's experience was typical of acquired blindness, the response, sooner or later, of everyone who loses sight — and a brilliant example of cortical plasticity.

Understanding Ideas

1. According to Oliver Sacks, why is going blind later in life more difficult than early blindness?

2. What were John Hull's experiences with blindness?

3. What does Sacks mean by "cortical plasticity" (para. 14)?

4. Why does Sacks think the brain is "far less hardwired than was once thought" (para. 10)?

Responding to Ideas

1. *Response* Oliver Sacks begins his essay with two rhetorical questions. In a brief essay, answer his question: "To what extent are we the authors, the creators, of our own experiences?" If possible, discuss this question with others in your group to see what kind of responses other people give. If you can conduct an interview about this subject, talk with people of different ages. One area in which people may create experiences is in the memory of long-past events. Examine your own memory and the way it shapes events from long ago. How often does your memory embellish or diminish what really happened?

2. *Response* The way we shape our brains through experience is of interest to people in the arts and the sciences. If you have particular skills in music, you may be aware of the ways you have shaped your brain to respond to sound and to silence. You may also be aware of how your musical skills have affected your motor skills — as, for example, in the coordination needed to play drums or guitar or violin. The skills used in playing piano, including memorization, shape musicians' brains in numerous ways. If you have any such skills, or know someone who does, share your "case history" using as a model Sacks's case history of Hull.

3. *Research* When he refers to St. John of the Cross (1542–1591), Sacks implies that mysticism is neurologically interesting. St. John and St. Teresa (1515–1582), both of Ávila and reformers of the Carmelite Order,

wrote important works with psychological irregularities of the kind Sacks studies. Research either St. John's *The Dark Night of the Soul* or St. Teresa's *The Autobiography of Teresa of Ávila*. Each of these saints had visions that modern neurologists might call hallucinations. Refer to these works, or to the visions of other saints, and decide how the mind creates experiences and how such experiences shape the mind. If possible, compare the descriptions of their visions. Would such visions constitute a medical problem today?

4. *Response* Use yourself as a case study in awareness of sensory experiences. Decide which sense is most dominant in your apprehension of the world. Explain how you rely on that sense for information and how, by habitual selection, you limit the information that sense provides you so that you can function in the world. Then deny yourself the use of that sense long enough for you to begin developing new awarenesses through other senses. What is your experience? Which new sense becomes dominant, and how much of the world does it communicate to you? Under what circumstances is it important that one or another of your senses becomes dominant? Which sense is most reliable for helping you create a world for yourself? What are the effects on you of these experiments?

5. *Response* Write an essay about your five senses. How do they inform you about the world you live in? What are the limitations of each sense, and what are the particular pleasures each sense provides you? Which of your senses is most likely to provide you with information that much later may prove to be misremembered? Some animals may possess more than five senses. If you could invent a new sense, what would it be? What advantages in knowledge would it provide? If you were to rely only on your senses for your experience of the world, how would you be more limited cognitively than you are now?

6. *Definition* Education that emphasizes reasoning and accumulating knowledge does not emphasize the senses, and as a result, it does not do a great deal to educate the senses. Take each of the five senses and explain what someone must do to educate each sense. Be sure to define what you mean by *educate* in your discussion. What does Sacks say that might help you explain what you mean by the education of the senses? What activities help sharpen your visual perception and improve the way your eyes inform you? What activities help educate your sense of touch, your sense of taste, your sense of hearing, and your sense of smell? What commercial activities seem designed to educate your senses? Do you feel your senses are adequately educated, or do you plan to undergo further "education"?

Comparing Ideas

1. Compare Oliver Sacks's observations on the way the senses function under stress with the examples Charles Darwin gives in "Of Sexual Selection and Natural Selection" (p. 212). Darwin connects the selection of mates with the idea of the survival of the fittest. Sacks points out that the brain is "far less hardwired than was once thought" (para. 10). He shows us that there is plasticity in the senses — they respond to trauma by changing. How does his research connect with Darwin's observations of behavior in nature? What issues of evolution and survival are implied by the observations that Sacks makes about the loss of a given sense?

2. In "The Aim of Man" (p. 374), Aristotle talks about the goal of happiness in everyone's life. Aristotle does not talk about individual senses, but he does caution that a life of sensory pleasure does not constitute a life of happiness in his terms. How does Aristotle's theory of how one achieves happiness help us understand the circumstances of the people whom Sacks describes? How does loss of a sense affect the possibility of achieving happiness? To what extent is Sacks concerned about the happiness of the individual?

STEVE
JONES

STEVE JONES (b. 1944), a Welsh biologist who specializes in genetics, has become an expert in evolutionary biology. Although sometimes taunted for his longtime interest in snails and mollusks, he has continued research into their diversity and complexity because he knows that their shells and their fossils hold secrets that pertain to evolution.

Among his many books are several that undertake to review and update Charles Darwin's *On the Origin of Species.* For example, *Almost Like a Whale: The Origin of Species Updated* (1999) was the book, he felt, that Darwin would have written had he lived in the late twentieth century. It went so far as to follow the pattern of Darwin's original book, right down to approximating the length of each chapter in his book with that of Darwin's. In his original edition, Darwin says very little about the evolution of human beings, so Jones includes information that presents the evolutionary evidence for the emergence of the human species from the family tree of primates. In the next year, he updated the book and retitled it *Darwin's Ghost: The Origin of Species Updated*, implying that he was Darwin's ghostwriter.

Jones has become a popular scientific commentator in Great Britain, appearing on television, on the radio, and in newspapers and magazines. His books have been widely published and have stimulated considerable controversy and interest. Plainspoken at times, he has declared that creationism is flatly wrong and that no knowledgeable biologist could believe it. But by the same token, he is absolutely convinced that events can change scientific truths with great suddenness. He holds that science is about disbelief. What we think is true this year may be proved false next year. As an example, he points to 1905, the year Albert Einstein's theories cast a pall on classical physics and opened entirely new ways of reflecting on the nature of things in cosmology and beyond.

Perhaps in a hint at *The Descent of Man, and Selection in Relation to Sex* (1871), Darwin's later book explaining the evolutionary development of humans, Jones published *Y: The Descent of Men* in 2003. The selection that follows comes from this book, whose title honors the Y chromosome, which identifies the male. As Jones points out, all humans begin as female, and the male develops through complex chromosomal and genetic engineering. But the result is that, biologically speaking, men are in many ways inferior to women. For example, men tend to mature later and die younger than women. Jones virtually takes the view that in modern times men are endangered in more ways than we might imagine. The emphasis on sexual selection in Darwin's book is the focus in Jones's work. He sees that today the male may not even play a major part in sexual selection. Jones's views on the future of male humanity are not particularly optimistic.

Be sure to practice prereading techniques before a careful, annotated reading of Jones's essay. For a review of prereading strategies, see pages 4–9. ⊞

The Descent of Men

THE FINAL pages of *The Descent of Man,* the model for the present work, contain a lofty account of the natural superiority of men over women: an ascendancy driven, thought Darwin, by sexual selection. In the nineteenth century such ideas seemed self-evident. Now things have changed.

Males, toward the end of the last millennium, felt a sudden tightening of the bowels with the news that their services had at last been dispensed with. Dolly the sheep — conceived without masculine assistance — had arrived. Her birth reminded half the population of its precarious position. Perhaps, some fear, science will cause nature to return to its original and feminine state and men themselves to fade from view. The Y chromosome, after all, is a mere remnant of a once mighty structure, which might in a few million years disappear. Why should those who bear it feel any more secure?

They have good reason to worry. Even without the help of the cloners, males are wilting away. To be a man has always been a minority interest, but the cruel facts of life and death have made his position even more precarious. From sperm count to social status, and from fertilization to death, as civilization advances those who bear Y chromosomes are in relative decline. Even their place in society — once undisputed — is challenged by the advance of womankind. The flames of Prometheus,[1] the bringer of fire, have been much dimmed since Darwin's day.

At least from the male point of view, not all the news is bad. The world has four hundred billionaires. Nine out of every ten are Prometheans, half of them self-made (and just one of the women, the founder of the Gap fashion chain, earned rather than inherited her money) — but be they plutocrats[2] or paupers, all men pay a high price for their privileges. What once seemed a natural superiority has been lost in the face of a manifold failure to deal with modern times.

Homo sapiens, in the certainty of his dominion, has changed the world. 5 Much is for the better, and both sexes now live longer, healthier, and perhaps happier lives than before. Infant mortality in much of the third world is down to what it was in the West in 1970, and global life expectancy is up by half a decade. For most people, existence is easier than it has ever been, but the minority blessed with a sex-determining gene has not had its fair share. When the going gets tough, the women do better, and when life is good men indulge so much in its vices that they suffer again.

In the nineteenth century, thousands of Mormons traveled west to Salt Lake City. The poorest were forced to push their goods on handcarts, five to a cart. In July 1856 the Willie Party, four hundred strong, set out on the thousand-mile trek across the mountains. With masculine lack of foresight, they started too late, and in the Rockies winter caught up with them. As a survivor wrote, "At first the deaths occurred slowly and irregularly, but in a few days at more frequent intervals, until we soon thought it unusual to leave a camp-ground without burying one or more persons . . . Men who were, so to speak, as strong as lions when we started our journey, and who had been our best supports, were compelled to succumb to the grim monster . . . Many a father pulled his cart, with his little children on it, until the day preceding his death. I have seen some pull their carts in the morning, give out during the day, and die before next morning."

Sixty-eight of the emigrants died. For those over forty, ten times as many men as their partners succumbed, and for the young the rate was twofold. Those with the strength of lions were, when it came to the test, the weaker sex.

For people blessed with a Y, life is hard from the start and gets harder. Fertilization produces a slight excess of male embryos (perhaps because the relevant sperm swim faster), but from then on things go downhill. Even before birth, males cope less well. There are, as a result, more girl twins, as boys do not survive the tough conditions in a shared womb. As the fetus grows, boy babies suffer more brain damage and more birth defects. In

---

[1] **Prometheus** Greek Titan who brought fire to humans.
[2] **plutocrats** Those who depend on wealth for their power.

addition, they experience a whole host of diseases, from color blindness to muscular dystrophy, caused by the damaged genes found on the X which are usually hidden in girls but always exposed in their brothers. At birth they are in a mere 5 percent excess over their sisters, and not for a month does a boy child reach the level of maturity of a newborn girl.

Then the rot sets in. Up to the age of thirty or so, the balance is about even, but at eighty a mere third of the population consists of men, and Queen Elizabeth the Second sends nine times as many congratulatory telegrams to her lady centenarians than to those of the opposite persuasion. From middle age onward it is a woman's world.

Such a large gap between the sexes is new (although Swedish records 10 from the eighteenth century, when life expectancy was half that of today, show that their women already did a little better than the others). A century ago, American husbands and wives died at about the same age. Even at the time of Pearl Harbor, men and women who made it to retirement had just over a decade in which to relax. Now newborn American girls can expect an eight-year advantage. Some of the shift comes from a gain by one group because of healthier childbirth (in the nineteenth century the commonest cause of premature death, but now with a tiny rate of mortality), but more comes from their brothers' inborn frailties and their stubborn refusal to recognize them.

Why do people with the *SRY* gene[3] do so badly? Society plays a part, and stupidity helps, but the testes are much to blame. Some of the harm is direct, for their secretions damage those who bear them. The cells of the immune system die when exposed to testosterone, and the male body, with its vast quantities of the substance, is less able to make antibodies than is its opposite number. As a result men find it more difficult to fight cancer and to resist infection by a variety of diseases, from gonorrhea to rabies. In most animals males die younger than their opposites (by thirty years in sperm whales), as a hint of the importance of chemistry both in its direct effects and as a promoter of rage and lust.

Testosterone is a signpost to several well-trodden paths to oblivion. Suicide is now the main cause of death among young men and is three times more dangerous to sons than to daughters. The incidence among boys has doubled since the 1970s, while in girls the figure has stayed much the same. Other violent deaths, from accident or murder, are on the way down, but — once more — males have been slower to gain and boys still face a doubled risk of accidental death compared to girls. The difference is large even in four-year-olds.

By 2010 a third of all British males will live alone. For bachelors (but not spinsters), mortality is twice that in the population as a whole. Darwin

---

[3] **SRY gene** Gene for maleness on the Y chromosome that determines sex.

248   ⊞   CHAPTER FIVE: HOW SCIENCE READS THE BOOK OF NATURE

noted as much, and *The Descent of Man* gives several paragraphs to the doubled death rate among unmarried, compared to married, Scotsmen of his day (he used the figures to promote the eugenic agenda that the feeblest stay single). Men, it seems, evolved for matrimony, as they gain several more years from the state than do their partners. "Griefe" was entered as a cause of death in the rolls of mortality in the seventeenth century, and widowers still do far worse than widows when forced to deal with their unwelcome situation. Most of them meet their ends from cardiac problems. They die, literally, of a broken heart.

"Up to age thirty or so, the balance is about even, but at eighty a mere third of the population consists of men, and Queen Elizabeth the Second sends nine times as many congratulatory telegrams to her lady centenarians than to those of the opposite persuasion. From middle age onward it's a woman's world."

Misery and violence kill off plenty of males, but neglect destroys far more. Men do not like to bother their doctors, or even themselves. As long ago as 1662, John Gaunt, the founder of demography, noted that physicians had two female patients for each one of the opposite sex. The latter, he thought, died of their vices while women fell victim to the infirmities of their state. He was not far wrong, for females under forty still go to the doctor twice as often as their husbands. Part of the difference comes from the troubles of birth control and pregnancy, but most does not — and that is odd, for males have far worse health.

Each year in the United States, more than twenty million man-years of life are lost to a demise that could, in principle, be avoided. Smoking, fat, and stress all specialize in one segment of society. From gout to hernias (four and nine times more common in males), men suffer while their partners are spared.

Even for men, smoking is now a minority interest, but is far from extinct. Girls have been lured into the habit by tobacco companies (and lung cancer has overtaken breast cancer as their commonest malignancy) but have not yet faced the full consequences. When it comes to alcohol, the difference is starker. Although there are arguments about the safe limit, many recommend a maximum of a quart of beer, or half a bottle of wine, a day. Almost half of young British men drink close to, or above, the limit; and a respectable minority of dangerous drinkers believe that they drink either "a little" or "hardly at all." Those who soak up more than the recommended amount die at twice the rate of those who imbibe very little. A small dose has a minor — and much publicized — beneficial effect, but overall alcohol is a killer. Drink causes cancer of the pancreas and throat and damages the liver, and is associated with the majority of murders and deaths in fires.

The demon in the bottle also acts as chaperone to the biggest assassin of all. Diseases of the heart and circulation account for much of the short-age of men. They cause half of all male deaths before retirement, and the overweight, tobacco-ridden, and stressed inhabitants of any neighborhood bar are in particular danger.

Heart attacks are rather new. From the First World War to the Second, the overall incidence doubled, and from then until 1980, doubled again in men — but dropped among women. Over the past couple of decades, males have done a little better, but less so than their partners, and they now face three times their risk. Young men do even worse, with seven times the rate compared to women of their own age. Estrogen protects the heart, as it increases the release of nitric oxide and relaxes its blood vessels. Those with Y chromosomes lack that shield, and behave in such a way as to dam-age themselves still further. The epidemic of cardiac disease affects a small global minority: men in developed countries. The gender difference is great-est in places with a fatty diet, which allows Scottish males to boast of — among their other undoubted achievements — more heart attacks (and fewer teeth) than anybody else on earth.

Understanding Ideas

1. According to Steve Jones, what was the nineteenth-century position on the superiority of men over women?

2. Why is Dolly the sheep important to Jones's argument?

3. In Jones's view, what evidence suggests that males fare worse biologi-cally than females?

4. Why does Jones believe testosterone is dangerous?

Responding to Ideas

1. **Research** Steve Jones points out that "[m]isery and violence kill off plenty of males, but neglect destroys far more" (para. 14). Women, he says, look after their health much more often than do men. Why do males continue that pattern even today? Research the life expectancy in your country of men and women who are your age and ten, twenty, thirty, and forty years older. When, if ever, does a male's life expectancy come close to that of a female's? What evidence suggests that neglect is a major factor in the "destruction" of men? What examples bear out

Jones's claim? What does the United States Social Security office predict for male and female life expectancy?

2. **Analysis of Circumstances** What has happened to the "natural superiority of men" (para. 1)? Jones is talking about biology on one level, but he also introduces social circumstances that indicate the loss of male superiority. Construct an argument that either defends or attacks his view in terms of the social circumstances of male superiority. Does what Jones says apply to the social circumstances that you are familiar with? Is it possible that he is overstating the case? Or is he understating it? What current developments in our larger culture indicate a lessening of the "superiority" of men?

3. **Response** Assume that you are offering advice to young men in your social environment. Using Jones's statistics and knowledge of biological chemistry, write a brief essay that explains how men could avoid the calamities that Jones feels await them. It may be that some of the calamities are unavoidable, but it is also true that taking action at a young age will improve the chances for increased male survival. Be sure to take into account any counterarguments that will affect your suggestions.

4. **Research** Find out all you can, by researching in your library and online, about the impact alcohol consumption has on men. Either validate or invalidate Jones's argument regarding the effects of drinking on males. Include any observations of drinking behavior that you can bring to bear on the subject. Study societies or religions, such as Mormonism, whose members avoid drinking almost entirely. What is their mortality rate, and how does it compare with Jones's figures? Search for the connection between alcohol consumption and the risk assessment and the coverage offered by insurance companies. What exclusions do insurance companies have in their policies? What legal issues are involved? Write an essay that, like Jones's, informs people of the truth about drinking and its effects on males.

5. **Analysis of Circumstances** Abrahamic religions — religions whose people think Abraham was an important person, such as Judaism, Christianity, and Islam — all adhere to a social policy that credits the superiority of men. How would a member of any of those religions respond to the likelihood that male inferiority will alter profoundly the current relationship between the sexes? As an evolutionary biologist, Jones is talking about a change that seems, at least to him, inevitable no matter how long it will take. How might any of these religions change if men were no longer necessary for procreation? Would such a change mean the end of patriarchy? Would that be a good thing or a bad thing?

6. ***Research*** Prepare a study of population growth or decline among males and females in at least a dozen large nations, such as China, India, Pakistan, the United States, Brazil, Japan, Germany, France, Nigeria, South Africa, Saudi Arabia, Iran, or others of your choice. Considering that some nations still abort female embryos or kill female infants and that the last hundred years have resulted in unknown millions of men dying in continuing warfare, what seems to be the ratio of males to females in those countries? Does your research uncover a historical trend? What does your research demonstrate that will help clarify the views of Jones that suggest the diminishing influence of males in society?

Comparing Ideas

1. With reference to both Charles Darwin's "Of Sexual Selection and Natural Selection" (p. 212) and Jennifer Ackerman's "Molecules and Genes" (p. 263), establish the connection between the comments of Steve Jones on the descent of men and the idea of evolution. Is what Jones describes the result of social changes or evolutionary changes? Is he talking about science or about political science? If Jones is correct about the general inferiority of males in nature, what is the implication about the role evolution favors for females? Why should nature make females superior, and how did it turn out that most human cultures feature males as dominant?

2. Using Charles Darwin's "Of Sexual Selection and Natural Selection" (p. 212), construct an argument that counters Steve Jones's views that human males are naturally inferior to females. Both writers depend on examples to make their arguments, so construct your argument using examples and testimony from other authors where possible. Use personal observations where they will bolster your argument.

MICHIO KAKU

Ted Thai/Getty Images

MICHIO KAKU (b. 1947) has been, since 1973, the Henry Semat Professor of Theoretical Physics at City College of New York. Widely published on superstring theory, supergravity, and string field theory, Kaku has hosted a weekly national radio show on science called *Explorations*, and his science commentaries are carried on more than sixty radio stations. Kaku is a celebrated popularizer of the mysteries of physics and the future prospects of science. He is also concerned about the complications arising from theoretical physics and the dangers of nuclear war. As a result, he has been active in groups that advocate disarmament.

In his book *Physics of the Future: How Science Will Shape Human Destiny and Our Daily Lives by the Year 2100* (2010), Kaku explores the promise of the future of energy, space travel, medicine, nanotechnology, and more. In the selection that follows, Kaku talks about AI, or artificial intelligence, an area of research that has been exciting scientists since the development of the modern computer.

The goal of artificial intelligence has been to construct a machine that can think much as we humans — and many animals — think. The modern evolution of computers began with the primitive machine that Alan Turing (1912–1954), a British mathematician, logician, cryptanalyst, philosopher, and mathematical biologist, developed to break the German code during World War II. After the war, Turing helped develop computers and has been credited with being the "father of AI and computer science." He worked on programming a computer designed to respond to questions in a way that the questioner would not be sure whether the answer was from a machine or a person. Researchers are still working on that project.

Kaku, in the following selection, meditates on the nature of thinking and compares the function of the human brain with the function of the computer. The history of research in AI is marked by unrealistic expectations and failed goals, but that has not stopped the efforts of experimenters. Some of the experimentation has yielded interesting results in the form of robots. Predictions suggest that household robots will be a reality in a few decades. Today robots are conspicuously building automobiles in Detroit and vacuuming floors in many homes. But the question Kaku returns to is not whether robots are effective but whether they can or ever will be able to think. He compares the brain and its operation with the computer and its functions in such a way as to show their differences and how amazing the brain is. In the process, Kaku does not deny that great progress will be made with computers, but he does not hold out hope for a thinking computer in the near future.

Be sure to practice prereading techniques before a careful, annotated reading of Kaku's essay. For a review of prereading strategies, see pages 4–9. ⊞

Physics of the Impossible

HISTORY OF AI

CRITICS SOMETIMES point out a pattern, that every thirty years, AI practitioners claim that superintelligent robots are just around the corner. Then, when there is a reality check, a backlash sets in.

In the 1950s, when electronic computers were first introduced after World War II, scientists dazzled the public with the notion of machines that could perform miraculous feats: picking up blocks, playing checkers, and even solving algebra problems. It seemed as if truly intelligent machines were just around the corner. The public was amazed; and soon there were magazine articles breathlessly predicting the time when a robot would be in everyone's kitchen, cooking dinner, or cleaning the house. In 1965, AI pioneer Herbert Simon[1] declared, "Machines will be capable, within twenty years, of doing any work a man can do." But then the reality set in. Chess-playing machines could not win against a human expert, and could play only chess, nothing more. These early robots were like a one-trick pony, performing just one simple task.

In fact, in the 1950s, real breakthroughs were made in AI, but because the progress was vastly overstated and overhyped, a backlash set in. In 1974,

---

[1] **Herbert Simon** (1916–2001) Nobel Prize–winning political scientist with strong interests in computer science. He was a professor at Carnegie Mellon University.

under a chorus of rising criticism, the U.S. and British governments cut off funding. The first AI winter set in.

Today, AI researcher Paul Abrahams shakes his head when he looks back at those heady times in the 1950s when he was a graduate student at MIT and anything seemed possible. He recalled, "It's as though a group of people had proposed to build a tower to the moon. Each year they point with pride at how much higher the tower is than it was the previous year. The only trouble is that the moon isn't getting much closer."

In the 1980s, enthusiasm for AI peaked once again. This time the Pen- 5 tagon poured millions of dollars into projects like the smart truck, which was supposed to travel behind enemy lines, do reconnaissance, rescue U.S. troops, and return to headquarters, all by itself. The Japanese government even put its full weight behind the ambitious Fifth Generation Computer Systems Project, sponsored by the powerful Japanese Ministry of International Trade and Industry. The Fifth Generation Project's goal was, among others, to have a computer system that could speak conversational language, have full reasoning ability, and even anticipate what we want, all by the 1990s.

Unfortunately, the only thing that the smart truck did was get lost. And the Fifth Generation Project, after much fanfare, was quietly dropped without explanation. Once again, the rhetoric far outpaced the reality. In fact, there were real gains made in AI in the 1980s, but because progress was again overhyped, a second backlash set in, creating the second AI winter, in which funding again dried up and disillusioned people left the field in droves. It became painfully clear that something was missing.

In 1992 AI researchers had mixed feelings holding a special celebration in honor of the movie *2001*, in which a computer called HAL 9000 runs amok and slaughters the crew of a spaceship. The movie, filmed in 1968, predicted that by 1992 there would be robots that could freely converse with any human on almost any topic and also command a spaceship. Unfortunately, it was painfully clear that the most advanced robots had a hard time keeping up with the intelligence of a bug.

In 1997 IBM's Deep Blue accomplished a historic breakthrough by decisively beating the world chess champion Garry Kasparov.[2] Deep Blue was an engineering marvel, computing 11 billion operations per second. However, instead of opening the floodgates of artificial intelligence research and ushering in a new age, it did precisely the opposite. It highlighted only the primitiveness of AI research. Upon reflection, it was obvious to many that Deep Blue could not think. It was superb at chess but would score zero on an IQ exam. After this victory, it was the loser, Kasparov, who did all the talking to

---

[2] **Garry Kasparov** (b. 1963) World chess champion at age twenty-two who retired in order to devote attention to Russian politics.

the press, since Deep Blue could not talk at all. Grudgingly, AI researchers began to appreciate the fact that brute computational power does not equal intelligence. AI researcher Richard Heckler says, "Today, you can buy chess programs for $49 that will beat all but world champions, yet no one thinks they're intelligent."

But with Moore's law[3] spewing out new generations of computers every eighteen months, sooner or later the old pessimism of the past generation will be gradually forgotten and a new generation of bright enthusiasts will take over, creating renewed optimism and energy in the once-dormant field. Thirty years after the last AI winter set in, computers have advanced enough so that the new generation of AI researchers are again making hopeful predictions about the future. The time has finally come for AI, say its supporters. This time, it's for real. The third try is the lucky charm. But if they are right, are humans soon to be obsolete?

IS THE BRAIN A DIGITAL COMPUTER?

One fundamental problem, as mathematicians now realize, is that they made a crucial error fifty years ago in thinking the brain was analogous to a large digital computer. But now it is painfully obvious that it isn't. The brain has no Pentium chip, no Windows operating system, no application software, no CPU, no programming, and no subroutines that typify a modern digital computer. In fact, the architecture of digital computers is quite different from that of the brain, which is a learning machine of some sort, a collection of neurons that constantly rewires itself every time it learns a task. (A PC, however, does not learn at all. Your computer is just as dumb today as it was yesterday.)

So there are at least two approaches to modeling the brain. The first, the traditional top-down approach, is to treat robots like digital computers, and program all the rules of intelligence from the very beginning. A digital computer, in turn, can be broken down into something called a Turing machine, a hypothetical device introduced by the great British mathematician Alan Turing.[4] A Turing machine consists of three basic components: an input, a central processor that digests this data, and an output. All digital computers are based on this simple model. The goal of this approach is to have a

10

---

[3] **Moore's law** Gordon Moore in 1965 predicted a doubling of computer power every two years.

[4] **Alan Turing** (1912–1954) British mathematician, logician, cryptanalyst, philosopher, and mathematical biologist who worked at Bletchley Park in World War II, cracking German codes using a complex computer-like machine. His later research contributed to the development of the programmable computer.

CD-ROM that has all the rules of intelligence codified on it. By inserting this disk, the computer suddenly springs to life and becomes intelligent. So this mythical CD-ROM contains all the software necessary to create intelligent machines.

However, our brain has no programming or software at all. Our brain is more like a "neural network," a complex jumble of neurons that constantly rewires itself.

Neural networks follow Hebb's rule: every time a correct decision is made, those neural pathways are reinforced. It does this by simply changing the strength of certain electrical connections between neurons every time it successfully performs a task. (Hebb's rule can be expressed by the old question: How does a musician get to Carnegie Hall? Answer: practice, practice, practice. For a neural network, practice makes perfect. Hebb's rule also explains why bad habits are so difficult to break, since the neural pathway for a bad habit is so well-worn.)

Neural networks are based on the bottom-up approach. Instead of being spoon-fed all the rules of intelligence, neural networks learn them the way a baby learns, by bumping into things and learning by experience. Instead of being programmed, neural networks learn the old-fashioned way, through the "school of hard knocks."

Neural networks have a completely different architecture from that of digital computers. If you remove a single transistor in the digital computer's central processor, the computer will fail. However, if you remove large chunks of the human brain, it can still function, with other parts taking over for the missing pieces. Also, it is possible to localize precisely where the digital computer "thinks": its central processor. However, scans of the human brain clearly show that thinking is spread out over large parts of the brain. Different sectors light up in precise sequence, as if thoughts were being bounced around like a Ping-Pong ball.

Digital computers can calculate at nearly the speed of light. The human brain, by contrast, is incredibly slow. Nerve impulses travel at an excruciatingly slow pace of about 200 miles per hour. But the brain more than makes up for this because it is massively parallel, that is, it has 100 billion neurons operating at the same time, each one performing a tiny bit of computation, with each neuron connected to 10,000 other neurons. In a race, a superfast single processor is left in the dust by a superslow parallel processor. (This goes back to the old riddle: If one cat can eat one mouse in one minute, how long does it take a million cats to eat a million mice? Answer: one minute.)

In addition, the brain is not digital. Transistors are gates that can either be open or closed, represented by a 1 or 0. Neurons, too, are digital (they can fire or not fire), but they can also be analog, transmitting continuous signals as well as discrete ones.

TWO PROBLEMS WITH ROBOTS

Given the glaring limitations of computers compared to the human brain, one can appreciate why computers have not been able to accomplish two key tasks that humans perform effortlessly: pattern recognition and common sense. These two problems have defied solution for the past half century. This is the main reason why we do not have robot maids, butlers, and secretaries.

The first problem is pattern recognition. Robots can see much better than a human, but they don't understand what they are seeing. When a robot walks into a room, it converts the image into a jumble of dots. By processing these dots, it can recognize a collection of lines, circles, squares, and rectangles. Then a robot tries to match this jumble, one by one, with objects stored in its memory — an extraordinarily tedious task even for a computer. After many hours of calculation, the robot may match these lines with chairs, tables, and people. By contrast, when we walk into a room, within a fraction of a second, we recognize chairs, tables, desks, and people. Indeed, our brains are mainly pattern-recognizing machines.

Second, robots do not have common sense. Although robots can hear 20 much better than a human, they don't understand what they are hearing. For example, consider the following statements:

- children like sweets but not punishment
- strings can pull but not push
- sticks can push but not pull
- animals cannot speak and understand English
- spinning makes people feel dizzy

For us, each of these statements is just common sense. But not to robots. There is no line of logic or programming that proves that strings can pull but not push. We have learned the truth of these "obvious" statements by experience, not because they were programmed into our memories.

The problem with the top-down approach is that there are simply too many lines of code for common sense necessary to mimic human thought. Hundreds of millions of lines of code, for example, are necessary to describe the laws of common sense that a six-year-old child knows. Hans Moravec,[5] former director of the AI laboratory at Carnegie Mellon, laments, "To this day, AI programs exhibit no shred of common sense — a medical diagnosis

---

[5] **Hans Moravec** (b. 1948) Former professor at the Robotics Institute at Carnegie Mellon University who now works for a company designing robots that can negotiate terrain by using video sensors.

program, for instance, may prescribe an antibiotic when presented a broken bicycle because it lacks a model of people, disease, or bicycles."

Some scientists, however, cling to the belief that the only obstacle to mastering common sense is brute force. They feel that a new Manhattan Project, like the program that built the atomic bomb, would surely crack the common-sense problem. The crash program to create this "encyclopedia of thought" is called CYC,[6] started in 1984. It was to be the crowning achievement of AI, the project to encode all the secrets of common sense into a single program. However, after several decades of hard work, the CYC project has failed to live up to its own goals.

> *"Our brain is more like a 'neural network,' a complex jumble of neurons that constantly rewires itself."*

CYC's goal is simple: master "100 million things, about the number a typical person knows about the world, by 2007." That deadline, and many previous ones, has slipped by without success. Each of the milestones laid out by CYC engineers has come and gone without scientists being any closer to mastering the essence of intelligence.

MAN VERSUS MACHINE

I once had a chance to match wits with a robot in a contest with one built by MIT's Tomaso Poggio.[7] Although robots cannot recognize simple patterns as we can, Poggio was able to create a computer program that can calculate every bit as fast as a human in one specific area: "immediate recognition." This is our uncanny ability to instantly recognize an object even before we are aware of it. (Immediate recognition was important for our evolution, since our ancestors had only a split second to determine if a tiger was lurking in the bushes, even before they were fully aware of it.) For the first time, a robot consistently scored higher than a human on a specific vision recognition test.

The contest between me and the machine was simple. First, I sat in a chair and stared at an ordinary computer screen. Then a picture flashed on the screen for a split second, and I was supposed to press one of two keys as fast as I could, if I saw an animal in the picture or not. I had to make a decision as quickly as possible, even before I had a chance to digest the picture. The computer would also make a decision for the same picture.

---

[6] **CYC** Short for *encyclopedia*; name of the project to encode 250,000 commonsense rules and now located at Cycorp in Austin, Texas.

[7] **Tomaso Poggio** (b. 1947) Director of the Center for Biological and Computational Learning at MIT who researches the nature of intelligence in brains and the problem of intelligence in computers.

Embarrassingly enough, after many rapid-fire tests, the machine and I performed about equally. But there were times when the machine scored significantly higher than I did, leaving me in the dust. I was beaten by a machine. (It was one consolation when I was told that the computer gets the right answer 82 percent of the time, but humans score only 80 percent on average.)

The key to Poggio's machine is that it copies lessons from Mother Nature. Many scientists are realizing the truth in the statement, "The wheel has already been invented, so why not copy it?" For example, normally when a robot looks at a picture, it tries to divide it up into a series of lines, circles, squares, and other geometric shapes. But Poggio's program is different.

When we see a picture, we might first see the outlines of various objects, then see various features within each object, then shading within these features, etc. So we split up the image into many layers. As soon as the computer processes one layer of the image, it integrates it with the next layer, and so on. In this way, step by step, layer by layer, it mimics the hierarchical way that our brains process images. (Poggio's program cannot perform all the feats of pattern recognition that we take for granted, such as visualizing objects in 3-D, recognizing thousands of objects from different angles, etc., but it does represent a major milestone in pattern recognition.)

Later, I had an opportunity to see both the top-down and bottom-up 30 approaches in action. I first went to Stanford University's artificial intelligence center, where I met STAIR (Stanford artificial intelligence robot), which uses the top-down approach. STAIR is about 4 feet tall, with a huge mechanical arm that can swivel and grab objects off a table. STAIR is also mobile, so it can wander around an office or home. The robot has a 3-D camera that locks onto an object and feeds the 3-D image into a computer, which then guides the mechanical arm to grab the object. Robots have been grabbing objects like this since the 1960s, and we see them in Detroit auto factories.

But appearances are deceptive. STAIR can do much more. Unlike the robots in Detroit, STAIR is not scripted. It operates by itself. If you ask it to pick up an orange, for example, it can analyze a collection of objects on a table, compare them with the thousands of images already stored in its memory, then identify the orange and pick it up. It can also identify objects more precisely by grabbing them and turning them around.

To test its ability, I scrambled a group of objects on a table, and then watched what happened after I asked for a specific one. I saw that STAIR correctly analyzed the new arrangement and then reached out and grabbed the correct thing. Eventually, the goal is to have STAIR navigate in home and office environments, pick up and interact with various objects and tools, and even converse with people in a simplified language. In this way, it will be able to do anything that a gofer can in an office. STAIR is an example of the top-down approach: everything is programmed into STAIR from the very beginning. (Although STAIR can recognize objects from different angles, it is still limited in the number of objects it can recognize. It would be paralyzed if it had to walk outside and recognize random objects.)

Later, I had a chance to visit New York University, where Yann LeCun[8] is experimenting with an entirely different design, the LAGR (learning applied to ground robots). LAGR is an example of the bottom-up approach: it has to learn everything from scratch, by bumping into things. It is the size of a small golf cart and has two stereo color cameras that scan the landscape, identifying objects in its path. It then moves among these objects, carefully avoiding them, and learns with each pass. It is equipped with GPS and has two infrared sensors that can detect objects in front of it. It contains three high-power Pentium chips and is connected to a gigabit Ethernet network. We went to a nearby park, where the LAGR robot could roam around various obstacles placed in its path. Every time it went over the course, it got better at avoiding the obstacles.

> *"Embarrassingly enough, after many rapid-fire tests, the machine and I performed about equally. But there were times when the machine scored significantly higher than I did, leaving me in the dust. I was beaten by a machine."*

One important difference between LAGR and STAIR is that LAGR is specifically designed to learn. Every time LAGR bumps into something, it moves around the object and learns to avoid that object the next time. While STAIR has thousands of images stored in its memory, LAGR has hardly any images in its memory but instead creates a mental map of all the obstacles it meets, and constantly refines that map with each pass. Unlike the driverless car, which is programmed and follows a route set previously by GPS, LAGR moves all by itself, without any instructions from a human. You tell it where to go, and it takes off. Eventually, robots like these may be found on Mars, the battlefield, and in our homes.

On one hand, I was impressed by the enthusiasm and energy of these researchers. In their hearts, they believe that they are laying the foundation for artificial intelligence, and that their work will one day impact society in ways we can only begin to understand. But from a distance, I could also appreciate how far they have to go. Even cockroaches can identify objects and learn to go around them. We are still at the stage where Mother Nature's lowliest creatures can outsmart our most intelligent robots.

35

---

[8] **Yann LeCun** (b. 1960) Professor of computer science at New York University and head of Facebook's artificial intelligence laboratory in New York City.

Understanding Ideas

1. According to Michio Kaku, what were the early predictions, in the 1950s, of what computers would be able to do?

2. In Kaku's view, what institutions in society were most interested in AI?

3. As explained by Kaku, how does a human brain differ from an advanced computer?

4. In Kaku's estimation, what are the problems with robots?

Responding to Ideas

1. *Definition* In a brief essay, develop a definition for what researchers like Michio Kaku mean by *artificial intelligence*. What does he say about it that helps you define the term? What are some of the achievements in computer science that come closest to producing AI? Is the chess program that regularly beats most human players practicing AI? If it is not an example of AI, what kind of intelligence is the human using while losing to the machine? Write as if you are explaining AI to someone who has never heard of it.

2. *Cause and Effect* Kaku gives two examples of how robots have been developed. In the case of the robots developed at New York University, the question of learning is introduced. The LAGR, or learning applied to ground robots, is not a scripted robot. It has not been told explicitly what to do. Instead it learns by doing. It learns by experience where things are and how to avoid them. But the basic point is that it learns. How do humans learn? Are humans scripted at an early age? Do they learn from experience at an early age? How do humans learn at an advanced age? Write an essay on what you feel causes a human to learn using non–artificial intelligence.

3. *Response* How long will it be before household robots become a reality in advanced societies? What jobs will they do? Who will they replace? If they are a success, how will society adjust to the possibility that certain kinds of work will not be available any longer? Computers have already replaced many people in jobs requiring record keeping. They have replaced many manufacturing jobs in the automotive industry and elsewhere. How has society reacted to losing those jobs?

4. *Response* The concept of common sense is referenced a few times in Kaku's essay. What constitutes common sense, and why is it common? When people talk about the presence or the absence of common

sense, what do they mean? Do you think that a machine could be programmed to have common sense? Why is that such an important quest for those who value computers and prize artificial intelligence? If you were to measure whether or not a machine, either a computer or a robot, had common sense, how would you go about it?

5. *Research* Research artificial intelligence and see how much progress has been made since Kaku wrote his book. In what areas has the most interesting work been done, and what is the prognosis for further development? Under what circumstances does new research seem to produce the best results? What are the greatest hopes for those working in this field today? In what ways does the work being done give you enough confidence to predict positive results? How many decades from now will we see those results?

6. *Analysis of Circumstances* Kaku writes about the excitement and the progress of those who are researching and studying artificial intelligence. He writes about the production of machines that, however rudimentarily, seem to have the promise of thinking. It seems that most people want machines that think. Write an essay in which you argue that thinking machines are not desirable now or in the future. What are the dangers of AI? How are thinking machines a potential threat to human life? How would our culture fare if machines could think much as people think? Would our world be better or worse?

Comparing Ideas

1. Michio Kaku seems somewhat pessimistic about the possibility of creating a thinking robot. However, he is looking only a hundred years ahead. A thousand years from now, such robots may well exist. If they do, how will religions that base their beliefs on our current holy books respond to the robots' existence? Connect the religious perspective of Alfred North Whitehead (p. 221) with the ideas that dominate Kaku's concerns about artificial intelligence. What are the most likely fears that most religions would raise?

2. Thomas Nagel's essay "The Objective Basis of Morality" (p. 406) concerns itself with the ways we conceive of morality and moral behavior. How would he react to the idea of a thinking robot? Compare his essay with Kaku's. Which is more optimistic about the future of such things as artificial intelligence? What, if any, are Kaku's views on the morality of creating a thinking robot? What are your views? Comment on how you think each writer might react to the other's essay. How many of their concerns seem to be shared?

JENNIFER
ACKERMAN

Robert Lewellyn

JENNIFER ACKERMAN (b. 1959) is a science and health writer whose work covers a
range of subjects from genetics to medicine.
She is well known for her 2008 book, *Sex
Sleep Eat Drink Dream,* which was named a
New York Times Editors' Choice. In that book,
Ackerman reveals the way the body's clock regulates itself in an average
day. She begins with the awakening of the senses and ends with drift-
ing into sleep. *Notes from the Shore* (1995) is a record of the activities
of nature in Lewes, Delaware, where Ackerman lived on the edge of the
water and watched a great variety of wildlife. *Chance in the House of Fate:
A Natural History of Heredity* (2001), the book from which the following
selection is taken, addresses the genetic mysteries we all live with: questions of who inherits what traits from which ancestors, and how those traits
are transmitted.

When we think about heredity, we naturally think in terms of our physical makeup: what we inherited from our parents, for example, our father's
eye color, our mother's hair, their physical strength, or their height. Some
of us may look like our mother but not our father or vice versa. Ackerman
addresses these issues, although not directly. She talks about the kinds of
genetically inherited traits that might date back to an enormously remote
time beyond our imaginings. We must carry traits that date to prehistory,
and the mechanism for such transmission is mysterious.

Ackerman marvels at similarities in nature. She talks about the ways
genes that have existed in the same form for millions of years do their work
not only in fruit flies but in people. She remarks on discoveries that show
how one single-celled yeast fungus mates with another by a mechanism
that is replicated in the human brain. The similarities of these functions
have only recently been learned because decoding the human genome
and other genomes has permitted such analysis. Ackerman is eager for us

share her wonder in the ways nature links us all through the microscopic molecular gene and not just through the obvious physical similarities that are apparent in the classroom, in the theater, or at the zoo.

Be sure to practice prereading techniques before a careful, annotated reading of Ackerman's essay. For a review of prereading strategies, see pages 4–9. ⌗

Molecules and Genes

THERE ARE mysteries in all families. Those that arrest me, that set me back on my heels, are the mysteries of heredity — the past whispered in bone and blood; the dozens of ancestors rolled up in one skin, to be read in "curve and voice and eye," as Thomas Hardy[1] wrote, "the seeds of being that heed no call to die" but turn up again and again on the doorstep like a ne'er-do-well uncle. It seems astonishing that a sweep of eleven generations hardly modifies the night blindness of one family or the trembling jaw of another, that fifty or a hundred years may fail to alter a familial pattern of whorled eyebrow or "wolf's" teeth, the musical genius of the Bach family, or the dimpled chin of my husband's tribe.

In the last decade or so, a startling new message has come out about the long hold of heredity. Members of the human family carry traits that have held on down the line not just for generations but for eons, traits that mock all boundaries of time and kind. Scientists probing the deep workings of organisms from yeast to humans have turned up news that despite our outward differences of life and limb, we are run by similar genes and proteins, similar cell parts and mechanisms, which have weathered evolution over ages, passing nearly intact through hundreds of millions of years of rising and falling forms. These shared molecules and routines affect nearly all the turnings of life, from birth and growth to perception and behavior.

This book is a pilgrimage to the heart of heredity. It is a natural history not in the literal sense of a systematic inquiry, but rather in the etymological sense, a telling of stories about life, lineage, chance, and fate; about family, kin, and kind. It explores both the projecting traits of the human family — the one we're born into and the one we create — and also the bigger, deeper inheritance that ties us to the rest of life in profound, even shocking ways.

I like to hang around the doorway of biological surprise. For years I have collected news of curious findings, of young spiders that eat their mothers,

---

[1] **Thomas Hardy** (1840–1928) English novelist and poet.

of a giant fungus infecting miles of Michigan forest spawned by a single spore in the last ice age, of fish with fingers, caterpillars with lungs, genes with secrets. I don't profess to worship everything, but I do harbor strange sympathies fired by such discoveries, a kind of naturalist's faith. This is the news that sweeps me away, the gnomic workings of the living order, nature's inventive jack-in-the-box surprises that shift our view of life like the sudden twist of a kaleidoscope.

Here is an item from my files. When scientists deciphered the intimate 5 details of mating in yeast, that single-celled fungus that raises our bread and brews our beer, they got a shock. The molecule that draws two yeast cells into sex closely resembles one made by our own brain cells to regulate reproduction.

The likeness seemed a fluke at first. But then other examples popped out of the box: genes that shape the bodies of fruit flies so like our own body-shaping Hox genes,[2] that one can put a human Hox gene into a developing fruit fly embryo, and it will carry out the job of the fly's gene without a hitch; genes that shape the marvelous globe of the human eye strangely similar to those that carve the compound eye of a fruit fly; the tiny genetic mechanisms that drive our biological rhythms, keeping us in tune with the big swings of night and day, matching those in algae. So, too, do we share with other organisms the ancient genes that dictate cell death, the phenomenon that underlies metamorphosis, turning tadpoles into frogs and caterpillars into butterflies and also shapes our bodies, whittling away the webbing between fingers before birth, eliminating inappropriate sexual organs. Common to all of us, as well, is a suite of small, sturdy messenger molecules, offering clues to such mysteries as why the cells of the human brain respond to the chemical messages of the poppy plant and to the potent sexual attractants of a Himalayan deer.

What are chemicals found in the human body doing in plants, fungi, bacteria? How can genes that shape a fruit fly be near twins of my own?

Disparate organisms, it seems, are more radically alike than we ever imagined. Our deepest selves — our very cells and molecules — are alive with reminders of old, enduring connections with other creatures, resemblances that run right down to the root of the tree of life. These items of shared inheritance have formed a library of wonders in my mind's eye. That there is a certain sameness among life's various forms follows from the notion that we all arose, ultimately, from a common ancestor. We are shaped by fate, by what came before. But life has chanced to venture in wildly different directions. In learning to suck energy from sunlight and in swallowing shocking amounts of oxygen, in heaving up from the beneficent chemical

---

[2] **Hox genes** Group of genes that plan the structure of the body in the developing embryo.

crucible of the sea and in exploring leafy interiors and desiccated desert, life has split into discrete identities, strewn about fresh designs, unimaginably varied feet, teeth, tongues, antennae, wings, leaves, brains.

In this world of dreamlike change, the lexicon of genes, like human languages, is thought to evolve along unreturning tracks. We know that nature is constantly making random changes in almost all genes, and that two species that diverged from a common ancestor hundreds of millions of years ago are likely to have accumulated a lot of little alterations. As eons pass, so do variants of genes, vanishing on the same wind that took the tyrannosaurs. It seems strange and wonderful that among organisms so spirited with individuality and detail — pepper frog, salp,[3] dragonfish, basset hound — there should be so much solid common ground.

Over the last few years I have wandered the body, looking for these 10 legacies and slim continuances, seeking to ferret them out of their holes and sun them a little, to brush their surface in places, give them a stab or pinch them to the bone if I could. I have a tracked the labyrinthine world of laboratories, too, asking about the molecular bricks that underlie the splendid medley of living forms: What makes them work so beautifully that they have demanded little change in hundreds of millions of years? What happens if they go awry? If organisms of such diverse stripes are made of similar genes, how is newness born in the world?

By exploring this deep-down world, I hope to create new shelves in my mind for the recent profusion of genetic discoveries, the news of the sequencing of genomes from the tubercle bacillus to *Homo sapiens*, the findings of genes linked with cancer, Alzheimer's disease, migraine, and baldness, passed down from father to son, grandmother to granddaughter; genes affecting intelligence, sexual preference, spatial ability, anxiety, sense of well-being — some of them discovered in small, so-called model organisms such as worms, fruit flies, mice.

What is a gene, anyway? Are there genes "for" particular traits? Are the letters DNA and RNA[4] an Open Sesame[5] to all the familial secrets of life? Can we starve all of nature's mysteries into molecular oneness, explain the fruit solely by its root?

And what does one make of the notion that our genes mirror those in yeast? Two decades ago scientists discovered that humans and chimpanzees appear to have in common about 98 percent of their DNA. Chimps are one thing, yeast is quite another. The news that, when it comes to molecules,

---

[3] **salp** A plankton that moves by pumping water through its barrel-shaped body.

[4] **DNA and RNA** Large molecules that transmit genetic information. Deoxyribonucleic acid and ribonucleic acid are strung together in a specific synthesis to store and transmit hereditary characteristics in the gene.

[5] **Open Sesame** Magic words in the Arabic *One Thousand and One Nights* that open a cave filled with treasure.

we are so perilously close to our tailed, finned, and spoorish brethren goes against the stories I grew up on, biblical tales of human supremacy and uniqueness, stories of how I was "fearfully *and* wonderfully made," as it is written in the Psalms, to get up before the sun and buy a river, to buzz above all creatures, "over the fish of the sea, over the fowl of the air, over the cattle, over every creeping thing that creepeth upon the earth."

Fear not therefore: ye are of more value than many sparrows.

(Luke 12:7)

We have for so long picked ourselves out from the horde of other crea-tures, reckoned ourselves the peak and point of nature's whole history. What to do now, with this news of our deep-down similarity, our profound kinship, with "lowly" organisms?

The physicist Michio Kaku once wrote that finding the key to weather 15 and seasons required a leap into another dimension, up into outer space. Understanding humanity's place in the matrix of life requires just such a leap, but downward, into the diminutive world of genes and cells.

Raised as I was on gerbils and birds, on the love of the whole organism, not its microscopic parts, I find it a stretch to descend into the darkness of a molecular world. I know my bats, weasels, and wood frogs far better than I do the crabbed atoms of a hemoglobin molecule. I am far more comfort-able exploring the elements of the violet family than those of the periodic table. The human mind may have mastered the black hole and the quark, but most of us have difficulty grasping the very big and the very small. We tend to think easily only of things on our own scale, midway between the atom and the sun. The first microscopists, confronted with the bizarre creatures swimming beneath their lenses, sought desperately to see bodies like their own, searched for sign of head or tail, denied as long as they could the many orifices and multiple stomachs, the brainless chunks of transparent flesh. So, too, we may seek in vain the familiar in the minute parallel planet of genes and proteins.

To make things worse, the language of this world veers into the cold domain of chemistry, where the common nouns are "nucleic acids" and "amino acids"; the common verbs, "regulate," "synthesize," and "catalyze." One scientist grappling with the absence of a precise definition for the term "gene" offered this to snarl the brain: "It is the nucleotide sequence that stores the information which specifies the order of the monomers in a final functional polypeptide or RNA molecule, or set of closely related isoforms."

But despite the dull terminology used to describe it, the cosmos of molecules and cells has surprising beauties and minute dramas every bit as beguiling as those of a bushmaster or a Bengal tiger. In DNA, proteins, even in the molecules of water encapsulated in our cells, are shapely details, beautiful clues that hold the key to everything from the acuity of the eye to the memory of the immune system. In their daily workings are tales of seduction, compromise, duplicity, deception, stubbornness, art, magic, death.

I first learned of the Hox body-shaping genes when I was a few months pregnant with my second child. The idea that the molecular mechanisms shaping my baby's growth were the same as those fashioning the fruit fly I found oddly comforting. Think of all the bending and breaking in the boughs of life. The notion that species as remotely related as humans and flies are shaped by the same genes — genes that have slipped in and out of the Cambrian, the Devonian, the Permian, the Pleistocene,[6] requiring little revision in all that time — suggests that they must perform their task beautifully and will not easily be wrenched off course.

Fish, fruit flies, wondrous babies: we may be a feast of distinct entities, 20 but we share the odd economies of nature from birth to death. I'm thrilled to find that we're connected with other organisms, not by something as vague or slippery as animal nature, but by a strong ribbon of measurable molecules, molecules so alike that they can be swapped between species separated by half a billion years of evolution.

I think our minds are built for the pleasure of discovering likenesses or links between vastly different things. It is why we delight in learning that the words "fate" and "symphony" share an ancient root meaning "to speak"; that the opening of Beethoven's Fifth neatly repeats the call of the white-breasted wood wren; that pointing a single finger to draw attention to something of interest is bound tightly to the learning of language. (The earlier a baby extends a demonstrative digit, the more words he or she will know by the age of two.) It is why we love syzygies[7] and rhymes and why we are undone by Romeo's words when he finds Juliet in the tomb and thinks her dead: "Death hath suckt the honey of thy breath." It is why we believe Emerson[8] when he tells us that "the world is a Dancer; it is a Rosary; it is a Torrent; it is a Boat; a Mist; a Spider's snare."

The language of science holds a hunch here. Though some scientific terms are Latinate and pompous, or simply weedy (*deoxyribonucleic acid*, for instance, a great millipede of a term that puts the mind off with its literalness), there are other terms — pithy, germinal, long-lived, and prophetic — that link the unlike and suggest the blooming mysteries of both language and

---

[6] **Cambrian . . . Pleistocene** Geological epochs marked by glaciation and other major shifts in the geology of the earth. The Pleistocene period ended 11,000 years ago and began more than 2.5 million years ago.

[7] **syzygies** In poetry, a *syzygy* is the combination of two metrical feet into a single unit, usually achieved by the omission of a sound or syllable (e.g., *e'er*).

[8] **Emerson** Ralph Waldo Emerson (1803–1882), one of the most important poets, essayists, and philosophers of nineteenth-century America.

life. The word "gene" goes back to an Indo-European root word that meant beginning and birth. This gave rise to the Old English *gecynd,* meaning family, kin, or kind. The Greek and Latin variants blossomed into a bunch of *gen* words with a multitude of jobs: genus, genius, gender, gentle, generous, generation, genealogy, genesis. One Latin stem became *gnatus,* unfurling into innate, native, natural.

> "It seems strange and wonderful that among organisms so spirited with individuality and detail — pepper frog, salp, dragonfish, basset hound — there should be so much solid common ground."

That so short and spare a word as "gene" would persist through the revolutions of language and pop up in all these new, masterful forms impresses me. So do these shared ancestral genes, which are something like word roots. Knowing them is a way of prizing what is essential in our common heritage. That we are still abob with these ancient bits of biological wisdom, that they have endured over eons in creatures as genealogically distant as worms and widowed aunts, is to me as much a cause for celebration as a Bach cantata or bird song.

These fragments of shared biology arose by chance and became fate. I have come to think of them as points of entry or small portholes through which to view the natural history of heredity. Or, perhaps, like the scriptural mustard seed cast into the family garden, from which one might draw radii to every corner of nature.

Understanding Ideas

1. How has evolution affected the genes Jennifer Ackerman describes?
2. What surprises Ackerman about the genetic molecule in yeast?
3. In terms of genetics, how does the microscopic world differ from the world we see?
4. How has the word *gene* evolved in modern language?

Responding to Ideas

1. **Research** What does heredity mean to you? Using your family as the source of your research, learn what you can about your ancestral relatives. What qualities or traits did they have that persist in your family today? What traits do older members of your family see in you that you

cannot see in yourself? Some traits will be physical, but others will be temperamental. First, establish the physical traits you share with others in your family. Then describe the behavioral qualities that you possess, for example, intelligence, sense of humor, aggressiveness, ambition, or proneness to anger or calmness. How recognizable are most of the traits and qualities you have inherited? In what way might your genetic inheritance be considered a kind of fate?

2. *Analysis of Circumstances* How disturbing might Ackerman's observations be for someone committed to a religious view of the creation of life? How can a religious person recognize the realities of genetics and still maintain a healthy religious view of the world? Write a brief essay designed to give comfort to anyone who is disturbed by the thought that a human gene can be inserted into a fruit fly's "developing embryo" and produce a perfectly functioning fruit fly.

3. *Research* The question of fate is on Ackerman's mind when she thinks about the many different ways life might have developed, given the flexibility of genes. Do some research online and in your library to find which human diseases seem to be hereditary in some populations. Ackerman mentions cancer, Alzheimer's disease, and migraines, among others. If some diseases are passed on genetically, what does that tell us about the way evolution works? What would be the evolutionary value of passing on disease? Is this what Ackerman means by *fate*?

4. *Definition* The "precise definition for the term 'gene'" (para. 17) Ackerman provides is not intelligible to the nonspecialist biologist. Yet, in order for us to communicate and understand the ideas presented here, we need a reasonable definition for what the gene is, how it exists, where it exists, what it does, and how it does it. Write an essay that provides that definition for an audience with a basic, but not detailed, knowledge of the term *gene*. Use Ackerman's technique and produce a number of examples to help establish your definition. If possible, test your definition on someone before finalizing your essay. How difficult is it to define the term? How important is it to you that you know what a gene is and how it does what it does?

5. *Analysis of Circumstances* What can you do to protect your genetic inheritance? What can you do to be sure that your genes will be healthy and strong when you pass them on to your own progeny? Some behaviors virtually guarantee damage to genes. What are they? How do you go about daily life avoiding the worst of these behaviors that might damage your genetic gifts to your children? To what extent is it important for you to behave in a manner that will protect the health of your genes? What is the most important thing you can do to impart healthy genes to an embryo?

6. ***Research*** This selection was published in 2001 and written at least a year before that. Genetics is a rapidly developing field. A great many new developments have been published regarding the human genome, which has been explored in some detail since 2000. What new developments in the study of the human genome are most interesting to you? Which are most important for society, and which are particularly important for you? What were some of the ethical, legal, and social implications addressed by the human genome project? You might begin your research with Victor K. McElheny, *Drawing the Map of Life: Inside the Human Genome Project* (2010); Francis Collins, *The Language of God: A Scientist Presents Evidence for Belief* (2006); and *Genetics Home Reference* (2013).

Comparing Ideas

1. Compare the ways Jennifer Ackerman and Steve Jones (p. 244) use their information on the effect of genes in humans. Which of them makes the most dramatic claims? Who provides the most remarkable information about how genes function? Both are proponents of evolutionary biology, and both attempt to convince us that evolution is a fact. Analyze the arguments of each writer and decide which is more convincing. Which author's argument is most likely to affect the way you see yourself?

2. Which of the writers in this chapter — Lucretius (p. 206), Charles Darwin (p. 212), Alfred North Whitehead (p. 221), Oliver Sacks (p. 236), Steve Jones (p. 244), Michio Kaku (p. 252), or Ackerman — inspires you most to have a career in science? Whose work most makes you feel that scientific research is important to you? Ackerman is not a professional scientist but rather a journalist interested in science. To what extent does her essay suggest a possible career for you? Why is it important to write about scientific ideas?

CHAPTER SIX

How Society Regards Wealth and Poverty

ADAM SMITH   281

ANDREW CARNEGIE   289

CHARLOTTE PERKINS GILMAN   303

JOHN KENNETH GALBRAITH   317

JANE JACOBS   329

ELIZABETH WARREN   344

LESLIE T. CHANG   357

"In general it may be said that demand is quite as necessary to the increase of capital as the increase of capital is to demand."   — THOMAS MALTHUS

"The farmer and manufacturer can no more live without profit than the laborer without wages."
— DAVID RICARDO

"Labor, therefore, is the real measure of the exchangeable value of all commodities."   — ADAM SMITH

"A society which reverences the attainment of riches as the supreme felicity will naturally be disposed to regard the poor as damned in the next world, if only to justify itself for making their life a hell in this."
— R. H. TAWNEY

"Surplus wealth is a sacred trust which its possessor is bound to administer in his lifetime for the good of the community."   — ANDREW CARNEGIE

"For my part I think that capitalism, wisely managed, can probably be made more efficient for attaining economic ends than any alternative system yet in sight, but that in itself it is in many ways extremely objectionable."
— JOHN MAYNARD KEYNES

INTRODUCTION

As John Kenneth Galbraith tells us, modern society has produced vastly more wealth than was ever imagined in the ancient world. Of course there were immensely wealthy rulers and nobles in ancient times, going all the way back to the ancient Egyptians, whose society began to form around 3150 B.C.E. Even the Bible comments on the rich and poor in statements such as, "Wealth maketh many friends; but the poor is separated from his neighbor" (Prov. 19:4). But until modern times the vast majority of people and nations were very poor.

Today, wealth in developed nations has increased to such an extent that, according to some commentators, it is a problem because it has not contributed to the eradication of poverty. One major problem is the unequal distribution of wealth and what can or should be done about such inequity. Another problem has to do with the relationship of capital to labor and the value of labor in developing nations. The question of whether the wealthy have an obligation to society to use their wealth wisely is always in the background of any discussion of modern economics.

Adam Smith (1723–1790) was a moral philosopher who, in *The Wealth of Nations* (1776), established a baseline for all contemporary discussions of how wealth is amassed and what its effects are on a society. His view was that laborers must be paid wages that allow them to build a reserve, although he knew that in the late eighteenth century many people worked for wages that barely enabled them to survive. Because his focus was on the economics of the city in relation to that of the countryside, he did not make many comments on international trade. However, he did remark on the circumstances of wealth and business in both China and North America, which at that time were important trading sources for Britain. Smith recognized the value of capital for creating and maintaining a healthy economy. At the time he wrote, the Industrial Revolution had taken root in England and was on the verge of revolutionizing not just production but also the lives of all workers and all businesses.

As a child, Andrew Carnegie (1835–1919) came to the United States from Scotland at a time of great innovation in technology. Businesses in oil, railroads, steel, and banking were all expanding at astonishing rates during the latter half of the nineteenth century. As a young boy, Carnegie worked for the telegraph, which was an example of cutting-edge technology during the American Civil War. He eventually found work in the Pennsylvania Railroad and used his earnings to buy into other businesses. By the end of the Civil War, he had immense holdings in steel in Pittsburgh and oil in Pennsylvania. At one time, he was believed to be the wealthiest man in the United States.

Competition was Carnegie's byword. He was taken with Charles Darwin's (p. 212) theory of evolution and influenced by the social Darwinists, who believed in the "survival of the fittest." Carnegie thought that ruthless competition weeded out the weakest men in business and favored the strongest. As the benefactor of competition, he believed that the leaders of industry were the elite in society. However, he also believed that wealth in his hands should be redistributed in ways that benefited society. He founded 2,509 libraries, along with concert halls and a great university, Carnegie Mellon University, which still exists. Carnegie also liberally supported the arts, spending the last part of his life giving his money away. Carnegie felt certain that he was able to put money to better use than those who worked for him could.

Like Mary Wollstonecraft (p. 77), Charlotte Perkins Gilman (1860–1935) focused on the economic conditions of women during her lifetime. Her essay "Women and Economics: 'Cupid-in-the-Kitchen'" describes the circumstances of the housewife whose primary environment is her home and whose job, in great measure, is providing food and sustenance to her family. Gilman describes the situation in some detail, emphasizing, for instance, that housewives are basically amateur cooks and not likely to provide the best nourishment to their husbands and children. What they do is provide what their husbands like to eat rather than what they should eat.

Gilman's solution would be to change the way people live. Instead of having separate homes with kitchens, she proposes a system in which people reside in apartment buildings or communal housing developments that have a separate kitchen run by professional cooks who serve everyone. By this means, women would be free from a great deal of labor and could enrich their lives with more intellectual and artistic pursuits. One of the results of Gilman's work is to call attention to the drabness of the lives of most married women in 1898. She was arguing for change and increased respect and recompense for the work women did in their homes.

During his lifetime, John Kenneth Galbraith (1908–2006) was one of the most well-known economists in the United States. He taught at Harvard University and consulted with numerous American presidents, from Franklin Delano Roosevelt to John F. Kennedy. Galbraith's book *The Affluent Society* (1958) establishes that modern society has grown used to being affluent, but the truth is that such affluence was only a recent phenomenon. He has a great deal to say about the poor and their circumstances. But he also examines the inequality in wealth and the resultant attitudes of people about how to deal with it. One of his points is that although inequality is growing, people, in general, have not taken a strong interest in doing much about it.

One of Galbraith's reasons for thinking so is that in former times men of great wealth were prominent in the minds of the people. The Astors, J. P. Morgan, the Rockefellers, and others were always in the news and in the society pages. They were recognized all the time and lived in huge mansions in neighborhoods reserved for the ultrarich. Today, the lives of the ultrarich are unknown to most people. The great businesses are mostly run by men and women who have none of the charisma of those former industrialists.

Famous for her political activism and her major book on American cities, Jane Jacobs (1916–2006) strove to understand the views of the major historical economists. In the essay in this book, she talks about *stagflation*, a word she made up to describe a stagnant economy characterized by high inflation and high unemployment. None of the economists she consulted explained how stagflation could happen, yet it was common in the 1970s. In the process of talking about the theories of Adam Smith, David Ricardo, John Maynard Keynes, and others, Jacobs describes supply-side economics in which the chief force driving the economy is capital. In that scenario, wealthy people supply the money to build factories and produce the products they think people want. Adam Smith was a supply-side economist. Then there are the demand-side economists, who think the economy is driven by the demand of the people for products they want. She feels Karl Marx, the founder of modern communism, was a demand-side economist. John Maynard Keynes, whose theories helped end the Great Depression, was also a demand-side economist. But none of these economists, she says, developed a theory that works all the time, as promised.

Elizabeth Warren (b. 1949), currently a U.S. senator for Massachusetts, is concerned most with the fate of the middle class. She observes that it is under great stress today and presents us with a number of revealing charts that show the realities of income and increased expenditures for what she identifies as the middle class. Her view is that a strong middle class is important to helping the poor. With a background as a law professor, she has researched the bankruptcy laws and how they have affected the middle class. Statistical evidence shows that the middle class has not spent itself into difficulty by wasting money or being profligate. Evidence suggests that two-earner families are under much more pressure than was true in the 1970s. Warren holds that one of the crushing factors in the shrinking of the middle class is debt, especially credit-card debt and subprime mortgage debt. She provides statistical evidence of the changes in the cost of basic needs, especially housing, over a period of years. She suggests that changes in debt structure may be needed to ensure the survival of a healthy middle class.

Labor is the subject Adam Smith talks about in his essay, and Leslie T. Chang (b. 1969), an American writer who spent many years in China, introduces us to some of the realities of the lives of young women laborers in modern China. She focuses on the city of Dongguan and its outlying areas. The province of Dongguan has a long history of interaction with the West, and today it provides the world with a huge percentage of electronic equipment, such as smart phones and computers. But the backdrop is what interests Chang. She tells us that 150 million people have migrated from the country to the giant factories that drive Chinese industry. This migration, one of the largest in the world's history, has created many problems.

The migrant women who now work in the factories have become sophisticated, yet sometimes they feel lonely and lost in the city. Social interaction between the migrants and Dongguan natives is not altogether good. The migrants think of the native inhabitants as hicks living off the rents they charge the newcomers. The natives think the migrants are hicks. It seems that, even in a nation like China, where enormous changes are wrought by a rapidly developing economy, migrant labor produces suspicion and social problems.

SEEING IDEAS

The gap between the wealthy and the poor has sparked revolutions and riots throughout the world since before recorded history. In highly industrialized modern states, the growth of wealth has become extraordinary. Before the Industrial Revolution in the late eighteenth through the mid-nineteenth centuries, most people were agricultural workers or workers in their own homes. The vast majority of people were what we would call poor; only a small number—aristocrats, churchmen, and landowners—had any considerable wealth. For Adam Smith and Andrew Carnegie, whose work you will read in this chapter, the fact that a few people owned massive wealth was accepted as natural, as the way the world had always worked. After the Great Depression, however, modern industrial societies put social programs in place to try to help the struggling poor.

The photograph on the following page was taken by Margaret Bourke-White after the Great Ohio River Flood of 1937 and shows men and women

in Louisville, Kentucky, lining up for food and supplies at a relief station in front of a billboard boasting America as having the "world's highest standard of living." This photograph has endured as a symbol of the Great Depression of the 1930s because it so vividly shows the contrast of the rich and the poor in America—an imbalance that still exists today.

The question of inequalities between the rich and poor has grown more insistent in the twenty-first century because of the explosion of billionaires whose political power can benefit them at the expense of the average citizen, thus threatening political stability. Billionaires may not be able to outright buy elections, but no one without substantial wealth can run for election at the upper levels of government. Perceived inequalities in wealth often inform elections, such as those in Bath, England (shown in the photo on the following page) in 2015. At the time this photograph was taken, Bath had some of the highest housing prices in the United Kingdom yet some of the lowest annual incomes. On average, one of the houses in this picture would have cost ten times the average person's annual income.

Societies throughout history have generally been tolerant of wealth: early cultures indicate that the wealthy were few in number and limited in power. The difference today is that more than half a nation's wealth is controlled by a very small number of people, and their power is substantial. Elizabeth Warren and John Kenneth Galbraith, as you will read in this chapter, are both deeply concerned about modern inequalities. The middle class,

Matt Cardy/Stringer/Getty Images

once the backbone of the nation, is dwindling not only in Bath, but in the United States. Some see this as a threat to democracy.

The selections in this section cover a wide range of issues relative to the uses of wealth and the facts of poverty. Clearly there are no easy solutions to the financial inequality between the wealthy and the impoverished. Whatever the problems are, they will be with us for a long time.

ADAM
SMITH

© Hulton Deutsch Collect on/Corbis

ADAM SMITH (1723–1790) was born in Scotland and went first to Glasgow University
and then took a degree at Balliol College,
Oxford. He returned home and was made
professor of rhetoric at Glasgow University in
1751. Although he is known today as one of
the founding fathers of modern economics
because of his best-known book, *An Inquiry
into the Nature and Causes of the Wealth of Nations* (1776), he taught
logic and was known in his own time as a philosopher. According to his
students, his primary interests in his lectures were theology, ethics, law,
and economics. Before he published on economics, Smith was well known
for his *Theory of Moral Sentiments* (1759), a study of the ways people form
a sense of morality. Smith thought his reputation would rest on this book,
and he continued to revise it throughout his life.

However, *The Wealth of Nations* continues to be the book everyone
thinks of when Smith's name is mentioned. It was written at a period in England when the Industrial Revolution was just getting under way. Smith was
the champion of most of the economic ideas considered relevant today.
Indeed, his terminology still dominates popular economic discussion.
For instance, he championed competition and free trade, asserting that
they would produce wealth. His message was that the economy worked
because people satisfied their own self-interests in any economic trade.
When people look to their own self-interests, they contribute unintention-
ally, by means of an "invisible hand," to the welfare of society. Smith went
as far as to say that people will do more good if in fact they do not set out
to do so. Self-interest is the key because it produces wealth and the nation
is better when there is more wealth.

On the other hand, Smith also observed that when a political system
is dominated by business interests the needs of the public may be ignored

in the rush to use the political system to make money rather than to better the condition of the public. Despite his emphasis on money, Smith was more concerned with the welfare of the community. While he focused on labor and trade, Smith had very little to say about international business, but he had a great deal to say about trade between the occupants of the countryside and city dwellers within Great Britain. Today, modern economics emphasizes trade between nations, but it still sees the value of self-interest as a driving factor in a healthy economy.

Be sure to practice prereading techniques before a careful, annotated reading of Smith's essay. For a review of prereading strategies, see pages 4–9. ❖

The Value of Labor

BUT THOUGH in disputes with their workmen, masters must generally have the advantage, there is however a certain rate below which it seems impossible to reduce, for any considerable time, the ordinary wages even of the lowest species of labor.

A man must always live by his work, and his wages must at least be sufficient to maintain him. They must even upon most occasions be somewhat more; otherwise it would be impossible for him to bring up a family, and the race of such workmen could not last beyond the first generation. Mr. Cantillon[1] seems, upon this account, to suppose that the lowest species of common laborers must everywhere earn at least double their own maintenance, in order that one with another they may be enabled to bring up two children; the labor of the wife, on account of her necessary attendance on the children, being supposed no more than sufficient to provide for herself. But one-half the children born, it is computed, die before the age of manhood. The poorest laborers, therefore, according to this account, must, one with another, attempt to rear at least four children, in order that two may have an equal chance of living to that age. But the necessary maintenance of four children, it is supposed, may be nearly equal to that of one man. The labor of an able-bodied slave, the same author adds, is computed to be worth double his maintenance; and that of the meanest laborer, he thinks, cannot be worth less than that of an able-bodied slave. Thus far at least

---

[1] **Mr. Cantillon** Richard Cantillon (1680–1734), an Irish-French economist who wrote *Essay on the Nature of Trade in General* in 1730. Written in French, the manuscript was circulated widely but not published until 1755. His book is considered one of the first works on political economy.

seems certain, that, in order to bring up a family, the labor of the husband and wife together must, even in the lowest species of common labor, be able to earn something more than what is precisely necessary for their own maintenance; but in what proportion, whether in that above mentioned, or in any other, I shall not take upon me to determine.

There are certain circumstances, however, which sometimes give the laborers an advantage, and enable them to raise their wages considerably above this rate; evidently the lowest which is consistent with common humanity.

When in any country the demand for those who live by wages; laborers, journeymen, servants of every kind, is continually increasing; when every year furnishes employment for a greater number than had been employed the year before, the workmen have no occasion to combine in order to raise their wages. The scarcity of hands occasions a competition among masters, who bid against one another, in order to get workmen, and thus voluntarily break through the natural combination of masters not to raise wages.

The demand for those who live by wages, it is evident, cannot increase 5 but in proportion to the increase of the funds which are destined for the payment of wages. These funds are of two kinds; first, the revenue which is over and above what is necessary for the maintenance; and, secondly, the stock which is over and above what is necessary for the employment of their masters.

When the landlord, annuitant, or monied man, has a greater revenue than what he judges sufficient to maintain his own family, he employs either the whole or a part of the surplus in maintaining one or more menial servants. Increase this surplus, and he will naturally increase the number of those servants.

When an independent workman, such as a weaver or shoemaker, has got more stock than what is sufficient to purchase the materials of his own work, and to maintain himself till he can dispose of it, he naturally employs one or more journeymen with the surplus, in order to make a profit by their work. Increase this surplus, and he will naturally increase the number of his journeymen.

The demand for those who live by wages, therefore, necessarily increases with the increase of the revenue and stock of every country, and cannot possibly increase without it. The increase of revenue and stock is the increase of national wealth. The demand for those who live by wages, therefore, naturally increases with the increase of national wealth, and cannot possibly increase without it.

It is not the actual greatness of national wealth, but its continual increase, which occasions a rise in the wages of labor. It is not, accordingly, in the richest countries, but in the most thriving, or in those which are growing rich the fastest, that the wages of labor are highest. England is certainly, in the present times, a much richer country than any part of North America. The wages of labor, however, are much higher in North America than in any part of England. In the province of New York, common laborers earn three shillings and sixpence currency, equal to two shillings sterling, a day; ship carpenters, ten shillings and sixpence currency, with a pint of rum worth sixpence sterling, equal in all to six shillings and sixpence sterling; house carpenters and bricklayers, eight shillings currency, equal to four shillings and sixpence sterling; journeymen tailors, five shillings currency, equal to about two shillings and ten pence sterling. These prices are all above the London price; and wages are said to be as high in the other colonies as in New York. The price of provisions is everywhere in North America much lower than in England. A dearth has never been known there. In the worst seasons, they have always had a sufficiency for themselves, though less for exportation. If the money price of labor, therefore, be higher than it is anywhere in the mother country, its real price, the real command of the necessaries and conveniencies of life which it conveys to the laborer, must be higher in a still greater proportion.

But though North America is not yet so rich as England, it is much more   10
thriving, and advancing with much greater rapidity to the further acquisition of riches. The most decisive mark of the prosperity of any country is the increase of the number of its inhabitants. In Great Britain, and most other European countries, they are not supposed to double in less than five hundred years. In the British colonies in North America, it has been found, that they double in twenty or five-and-twenty years. Nor in the present times is this increase principally owing to the continual importation of new inhabitants, but to the great multiplication of the species. Those who live to old age, it is said, frequently see there from fifty to a hundred, and sometimes many more, descendants from their own body. Labor is there so well rewarded that a numerous family of children, instead of being a burthen is a source of opulence and prosperity to the parents. The labor of each child, before it can leave their house, is computed to be worth a hundred pounds clear gain to them. A young widow with four or five young children, who, among the middling or inferior ranks of people in Europe, would have so little chance for a second husband, is there frequently courted as a sort of fortune. The value of children is the greatest of all encouragements to marriage. We cannot, therefore, wonder that the people in North America should generally marry very young. Notwithstanding the great increase occasioned by such early marriages, there is a continual complaint of the scarcity of hands in North America. The demand for laborers, the funds destined for maintaining them, increase, it seems, still faster than they can find laborers to employ.

Though the wealth of a country should be very great, yet if it has been long stationary, we must not expect to find the wages of labor very high in it. The funds destined for the payment of wages, the revenue and stock of its inhabitants, may be of the greatest extent; but if they have continued for several centuries of the same, or very nearly of the same extent, the number of laborers employed every year could easily supply, and even more than supply, the number wanted the following year. There could seldom be any scarcity of hands, nor could the masters be obliged to bid against one another in order to get them. The hands, on the contrary, would, in this case, naturally multiply beyond their employment. There would be a constant scarcity of employment, and the laborers would be obliged to bid against one another in order to get it. If in such a country the wages of labor had ever been more than sufficient to maintain the laborer, and to enable him to bring up a family, the competition of the laborers and the interest of the masters would soon reduce them to this lowest rate which is consistent with common humanity. China has been long one of the richest, that is, one of the most fertile, best cultivated, most industrious, and most populous countries in the world. It seems, however, to have been long stationary. Marco Polo, who visited it more than five hundred years ago, describes its cultivation, industry, and populousness, almost in the same terms in which they are described by travelers in the present times. It had perhaps, even long before his time, acquired that full complement of riches which the nature of its laws and institutions permits it to acquire. The accounts of all travelers, inconsistent in many other respects, agree in the low wages of labor, and in the difficulty which a laborer finds in bringing up a family in China. If by digging the ground a whole day he can get what will purchase a small quantity of rice in the evening, he is contented. The condition of artificers is, if possible, still worse. Instead of waiting indolently in their workhouses, for the calls of their customers, as in Europe, they are continually running about the streets with the tools of their respective trades, offering their service, and as it were begging employment. The poverty of the lower ranks of people in China far surpasses that of the most beggarly nations in Europe. In the neighborhood of Canton many hundred, it is commonly said, many thousand families have no habitation on the land, but live constantly in little fishing boats upon the rivers and canals. The subsistence which they find there is so scanty that they are eager to fish up the nastiest garbage thrown overboard from any European ship. Any carrion, the carcass of a dead dog or cat, for example, though half putrid and stinking, is as welcome to them as the most wholesome food to the people of other countries. Marriage is encouraged in China, not by the profitableness of children, but by the liberty of destroying them. In all great towns several

> *"The demand for those who live by wages, therefore, necessarily increases with the increase of the revenue and stock of every country, and cannot possibly increase without it."*

are every night exposed in the street, or drowned like puppies in the water. The performance of this horrid office is even said to be the avowed business by which some people earn their subsistence.

China, however, though it may perhaps stand still, does not seem to go backwards. Its towns are nowhere deserted by their inhabitants. The lands which had once been cultivated are nowhere neglected. The same or very nearly the same annual labor must therefore continue to be performed, and the funds destined for maintaining it must not, consequently, be sensibly diminished. The lowest class of laborers, therefore, notwithstanding their scanty subsistence, must some way or another make shift to continue their race so far as to keep up their usual numbers.

Understanding Ideas

1. Why, according to Adam Smith, must a laborer earn enough to "maintain him[self]" (para. 2)?

2. What seems to have been the economic value of children in Smith's time? Was this value universal, or did it depend on where the children lived?

3. In Smith's view, how did labor in North America differ from that in Great Britain?

4. According to Smith, when masters get surplus money, what do they usually do?

Responding to Ideas

1. *Research* Adam Smith talks about North America's population growth and the value of children to the economy. Today, the United States has low population growth and relatively few children. What is the average age of an American today? What is the primary source of population growth in the United States? What is the economic value of children today? Write a brief essay that updates Smith's concept of the economic circumstances of the United States.

2. *Analysis of Circumstances* The emphasis on wages in relation to the availability of money leads Smith to say that the minimum needed for a laborer is enough to keep him alive and to ensure that he has children who will replace him when he dies. What are the minimum needs of a laborer in today's economy? What must the laborer's wages pay

for if the laborer is to satisfy the normal daily needs of a modern citizen? Consider what you feel are the needs of a middle-class family with two working parents. Do current wages seem to satisfy the needs of a laborer today?

3. *Response* Smith talks about the minimum needs of labor, but he never mentions the idea of a minimum wage. The first minimum wage law in the United States was enacted in 1933, but in 1935 the Supreme Court ruled it unconstitutional. In 1941, the Supreme Court reviewed the Fair Labor Standards Act and approved the minimum wage. What is your view on the minimum wage today? Is it possible that it is unconstitutional? What effect does a minimum wage have on the overall economy? What has been your experience working for wages? If you are a proponent for the minimum wage, how much do you think it should be? Which laborers should be covered by the minimum wage law?

4. *Analysis of Circumstances* Smith talks about masters and common laborers. Nowadays, we talk in terms of management and labor. The U.S. economy is different today than it was in 1776. How has the relationship between management and labor changed? Who has the upper hand today, management or labor? What affects the relationship of labor to management? For labor to have greater power, what needs to happen in the economy? What can a wage earner (laborer) do today to increase his or her value to management? If you expect to work when you graduate, what must you do to tip the balance of power in your favor?

5. *Analysis of Circumstances* In discussing the burgeoning economy of North America, Smith says, "The value of children is the greatest of all encouragements to marriage" (para. 10). What do you think the value of children is to a family in today's economy? Is Smith's statement still valid? Explain why or why not. Smith considers this value as monetary, mentioning one hundred pounds as the value of a child before he or she is old enough to leave the house. How have things changed? What economic circumstances might be "the greatest of all encouragements to marriage" nowadays? Is it still the "value" of children?

Comparing Ideas

1. Adam Smith says a great deal about self-interest and its value in building wealth in a nation. He seems to give his complete approval for a businessperson to act primarily in self-interest. In "A Theory of Justice" (p. 159), John Rawls talks about self-interest as well, but his views are

somewhat different. Write a brief essay that clarifies the views of both writers and then goes on to explain which writer holds to ideas that are more useful for today's society.

2. Robert A. Dahl's "Why Democracy?" (p. 96) talks about prosperity in democracies. Compare his views with those of Smith, who did not live in — nor could even imagine — a democracy. Smith lived in a monarchy that governed relatively liberally for the age. However, both authors believe that a wealthy nation is a good thing. In a brief essay, clarify the principles that seem to unite the thinking of these two writers. What ideas about economy do they share, and what ideas do they hold to independently?

3. Interestingly, Smith talks about China. Portuguese traders established themselves in China in 1557, and Europe benefited from imports of porcelain, among other Chinese wares. The British began contact with China in 1635, so Smith was familiar with conditions there. Write a brief essay comparing Smith's view of China and Chinese labor in 1776 with Leslie T. Chang's (p. 357) view of factory girls in China today. What has changed? What seems to be the value of labor in modern China? Who has the greater power in China, management or labor?

ANDREW CARNEGIE

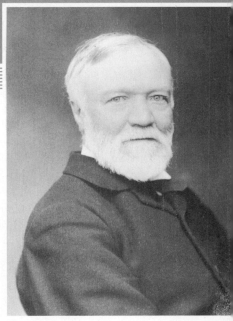

ANDREW CARNEGIE (1835–1919) emigrated with his family from Scotland when he was thirteen. He got a job in a cotton mill in Allegheny, Pennsylvania, working twelve hours a day six days a week for $1.20. He soon became a messenger boy for the telegraph company in Pittsburgh and later took a job with the Pennsylvania Railroad. Both these industries were cutting-edge technologies of the day and offered him opportunities to make money and invest wisely. When the Civil War began in 1861, Carnegie, already wealthy, made more money with investments in oil, steel, armor, and other military materials.

Like Adam Smith (p. 281), Carnegie approved of competition as a lever to produce wealth. He also accepted the inequality that a modern economy produces. Because he was also influenced by Charles Darwin (p. 212), Carnegie agreed with the social Darwinist Herbert Spencer (1820–1903), who coined the phrase "the survival of the fittest." Carnegie believed that competition was a "law" that produced superior people who deserved the greatest benefits of society because their activities resulted in improving civilization.

Carnegie could sometimes be ruthless, cutting the wages of his workers to boost his own wealth because he felt that he would use the money he accumulated in better ways than his workers would. In 1892, his workers went out on strike at Homestead Steel for 143 days. Violence resulted when the Pinkerton guards drove out protesting workers in an assault that left ten men dead. After that, Carnegie's reputation suffered, despite his many philanthropic activities. He sold all his holdings, retired in 1901, and devoted his time to giving his wealth away. Because he loved music, Carnegie endowed Carnegie Hall. Because he loved reading, he built 2,509 libraries throughout the United States and Canada. Because he loved education, he founded Carnegie Mellon University in Pittsburgh. And, although he was not a very religious person, Carnegie paid for the installation of a number of pipe organs in churches because he liked the music they played. All in all, Carnegie used his immense wealth to support the causes he thought were most important. He felt, always, that he knew better than the population at large how to spend money to benefit society.

The following essay was originally published in the *North American Review* in June 1889 with the simple title "Wealth." It was very quickly reprinted and made widely available with its current title, "The Gospel of Wealth." The word *gospel* can refer to a set of principles, beliefs, or truths, but it also invokes the biblical Gospels, which tell the story of Jesus. Thus, even though Carnegie was not a conventionally religious man, his title implies the passionate zealousness verging on religious dogma to be found in his essay on amassing and distributing wealth.

Be sure to practice prereading techniques before a careful, annotated reading of Carnegie's essay. For a review of prereading strategies, see pages 4–9. ⌗

The Gospel of Wealth

THE PROBLEM of our age is the proper administration of wealth, so that the ties of brotherhood may still bind together the rich and poor in harmonious relationship. The conditions of human life have not only been changed, but revolutionized, within the past few hundred years. In former days there was little difference between the dwelling, dress, food, and environment of the chief and those of his retainers. The Indians are today where civilized man then was. When visiting the Sioux, I was led to the wigwam of the chief. It was just like the others in external appearance, and, even within, the difference was trifling between it and those of the poorest of his braves. The contrast between the palace of the millionaire and the cottage of the laborer with us today measures the change which has come with civilization.

This change, however, is not to be deplored, but welcomed as highly beneficial. It is well, nay, essential for the progress of the race, that the houses of some should be homes for all that is highest and best in literature and the arts, and for all the refinements of civilization, rather than that none should be so. Much better this great irregularity than universal squalor.

Without wealth there can be no Maecenas.[1] The "good old times" were not good old times. Neither master nor servant was as well situated then as today. A relapse to old conditions would be disastrous to both — not the least so to him who serves — and would sweep away civilization with it. But whether the change be for good or ill, it is upon us, beyond our power to alter, and therefore to be accepted and made the best of. It is a waste of time to criticize the inevitable.

It is easy to see how the change has come. One illustration will serve for almost every phase of the cause. In the manufacture of products we have the whole story. It applies to all combinations of human industry, as stimulated and enlarged by the inventions of this scientific age. Formerly articles were manufactured at the domestic hearth or in small shops which formed part of the household. The master and his apprentices worked side by side, the latter living with the master, and therefore subject to the same conditions. When these apprentices rose to be masters, there was little or no change in their mode of life, and they, in turn, educated in the same routine succeeding apprentices. There was, substantially, social equality, and even political equality, for those engaged in industrial pursuits had then little or no political voice in the State.

But the inevitable result of such a mode of manufacture was crude articles at high prices. Today the world obtains commodities of excellent quality at prices which even the generation preceding this would have deemed incredible. In the commercial world similar causes have produced similar results, and the race is benefited thereby. The poor enjoy what the rich could not before afford. What were the luxuries have become the necessaries of life. The laborer has now more comforts than the farmer had a few generations ago. The farmer has more luxuries than the landlord had, and is more richly clad and better housed. The landlord has books and pictures rarer, and appointments more artistic, than the King could then obtain.

The price we pay for this salutary change is, no doubt, great. We assemble 5 thousands of operatives in the factory, in the mine, and in the counting-house, of whom the employer can know little or nothing, and to whom the employer is little better than a myth. All intercourse between them is at an end. Rigid Castes are formed, and, as usual, mutual ignorance breeds mutual distrust. Each Caste is without sympathy for the other, and ready to credit anything disparaging in regard to it. Under the law of competition, the employer of thousands is forced into the strictest economies, among which the rates paid to labor figure prominently, and often there is friction between the employer and the employed, between capital and labor, between rich and poor. Human society loses homogeneity.

---

[1] **Maecenas** Gaius Maecenas (c. 74–8 B.C.E.), wealthy patron to great Roman authors.

The price which society pays for the law of competition, like the price it pays for cheap comforts and luxuries, is also great; but the advantages of this law are also greater still, for it is to this law that we owe our wonderful material development, which brings improved conditions in its train. But, whether the law be benign or not, we must say of it, as we say of the change in the conditions of men to which we have referred: it is here; we cannot evade it; no substitutes for it have been found; and while the law may be sometimes hard for the individual, it is best for the race, because it insures the survival of the fittest in every department. We accept and welcome, therefore, as conditions to which we must accommodate ourselves, great inequality of environment, the concentration of business, industrial and commercial, in the hands of a few, and the law of competition between these, as being not only beneficial, but essential for the future progress of the race. Having accepted these, it follows that there must be great scope for the exercise of special ability in the merchant and in the manufacturer who has to conduct affairs upon a great scale. That this talent for organization and management is rare among men is proved by the fact that it invariably secures for its possessor enormous rewards, no matter where or under what laws or conditions. The experienced in affairs always rate the MAN whose services can be obtained as a partner as not only the first consideration, but such as to render the question of his capital scarcely worth considering, for such men soon create capital; while, without the special talent required, capital soon takes wings. Such men become interested in firms or corporations using millions; and estimating only simple interest to be made upon the capital invested, it is inevitable that their income must exceed their expenditures, and that they must accumulate wealth. Nor is there any middle ground which such men can occupy, because the great manufacturing or commercial concern which does not earn at least interest upon its capital soon becomes bankrupt. It must either go forward or fall behind: to stand still is impossible. It is a condition essential for its successful operation that it should be thus far profitable, and even that, in addition to interest on capital, it should make profit. It is a law that men possessed of this peculiar talent for affairs, under the free play of economic forces, must of necessity soon be in receipt of more revenue than can be judiciously expended upon themselves; and this law is as beneficial for the race as the others.

Objections to the foundations upon which society is based are not in order, because the condition of the race is better with these than it has been with any others which have been tried. Of the effect of any new substitutes proposed we cannot be sure. The Socialist or Anarchist who seeks to overturn present conditions is to be regarded as attacking the foundation upon which civilization itself rests, for civilization took its start from the day that the capable, industrious workman said to his incompetent and lazy fellow,

"If thou dost not sow, thou shalt not reap," and thus ended primitive Communism by separating the drones from the bees. One who studies this subject will soon be brought face to face with the conclusion that upon the sacredness of property civilization itself depends — the right of the laborer to his hundred dollars in the savings-bank, and equally the legal right of the millionaire to his millions. To those who propose to substitute Communism for this intense Individualism the answer, therefore, is: the race has tried that. All progress from that barbarous day to the present time has resulted from its displacement. Not evil, but good, has come to the race from the accumulation of wealth by those who have the ability and energy that produce it. But even if we admit for a moment that it might be better for the race to discard its present foundation, Individualism — that it is a nobler ideal that man should labor, not for himself alone, but in and for a brotherhood of his fellows, and share with them all in common, realizing Swedenborg's[2] idea of Heaven, where, as he says, the angels derive their happiness, not from laboring for self, but for each other — even admit all this, and a sufficient answer is, This is not evolution, but revolution. It necessitates the changing of human nature itself — a work of aeons, even if it were good to change it, which we cannot know. It is not practicable in our day or in our age. Even if desirable theoretically, it belongs to another and long-succeeding sociological stratum. Our duty is with what is practicable now; with the next step possible in our day and generation. It is criminal to waste our energies in endeavoring to uproot, when all we can profitably or possibly accomplish is to bend the universal tree of humanity a little in the direction most favorable to the production of good fruit under existing circumstances. We might as well urge the destruction of the highest existing type of man because he failed to reach our ideal as to favor the destruction of Individualism, Private Property, the Law of Accumulation of Wealth, and the Law of Competition; for these are the highest results of human experience, the soil in which society so far has produced the best fruit. Unequally or unjustly, perhaps, as these laws sometimes operate, and imperfect as they appear to the Idealist, they are, nevertheless, like the highest type of man, the best and most valuable of all that humanity has yet accomplished.

We start, then, with a condition of affairs under which the best interests of the race are promoted, but which inevitably gives wealth to the few. Thus far, accepting conditions as they exist, the situation can be surveyed and pronounced good. The question then arises — and, if the foregoing be correct, it is the only question with which we have to deal — What is the proper mode of administering wealth after the laws upon which civilization

---

[2] **Swedenborg's** A spiritual awakening late in life made Emanuel Swedenborg (1688–1771) believe he could speak with angels and visit heaven and hell. His book *Heaven and Hell* (1758) was widely read in the nineteenth century and is still influential.

is founded have thrown it into the hands of the few? And it is of this great question that I believe I offer the true solution. It will be understood that *fortunes* are here spoken of, not moderate sums saved by many years of effort, the returns from which are required for the comfortable maintenance and education of families. This is not *wealth*, but only *competence*, which it should be the aim of all to acquire.

There are but three modes in which surplus wealth can be disposed of. It can be left to the families of the decedents; or it can be bequeathed for public purposes; or, finally, it can be administered during their lives by its possessors. Under the first and second modes most of the wealth of the world that has reached the few has hitherto been applied. Let us in turn consider each of these modes. The first is the most injudicious. In monarchical countries, the estates and the greatest portion of the wealth are left to the first son, that the vanity of the parent may be gratified by the thought that his name and title are to descend to succeeding generations unimpaired. The condition of this class in Europe today teaches the futility of such hopes or ambitions. The successors have become impoverished through their follies or from the fall in the value of land. Even in Great Britain the strict law of entail[3] has been found inadequate to maintain the status of an hereditary class. Its soil is rapidly passing into the hands of the stranger. Under republican institutions the division of property among the children is much fairer, but the question which forces itself upon thoughtful men in all lands is: Why should men leave great fortunes to their children? If this is done from affection, is it not misguided affection? Observation teaches that, generally speaking, it is not well for the children that they should be so burdened. Neither is it well for the state. Beyond providing for the wife and daughters moderate sources of income, and very moderate allowances indeed, if any, for the sons, men may well hesitate, for it is no longer questionable that great sums bequeathed oftener work more for the injury than for the good of the recipients. Wise men will soon conclude that, for the best interests of the members of their families and of the state, such bequests are an improper use of their means.

It is not suggested that men who have failed to educate their sons to   10 earn a livelihood shall cast them adrift in poverty. If any man has seen fit to rear his sons with a view to their living idle lives, or, what is highly commendable, has instilled in them the sentiment that they are in a position to

> "Objections to the foundations upon which society is based are not in order, because the condition of the race is better with these than it has been with any others which have been tried."

---

[3] **law of entail** Law designed to restrict inheritance to only the heirs of the family who owns the property.

labor for public ends without reference to pecuniary considerations, then, of course, the duty of the parent is to see that such are provided for *in moderation*. There are instances of millionaires' sons unspoiled by wealth, who, being rich, still perform great services in the community. Such are the very salt of the earth, as valuable as, unfortunately, they are rare; still it is not the exception, but the rule, that men must regard, and, looking at the usual result of enormous sums conferred upon legatees, the thoughtful man must shortly say, "I would as soon leave to my son a curse as the almighty dollar," and admit to himself that it is not the welfare of the children, but family pride, which inspires these enormous legacies.

As to the second mode, that of leaving wealth at death for public uses, it may be said that this is only a means for the disposal of wealth, provided a man is content to wait until he is dead before it becomes of much good in the world. Knowledge of the results of legacies bequeathed is not calculated to inspire the brightest hopes of much posthumous good being accomplished. The cases are not few in which the real object sought by the testator is not attained, nor are they few in which his real wishes are thwarted. In many cases the bequests are so used as to become only monuments of his folly. It is well to remember that it requires the exercise of not less ability than that which acquired the wealth to use it so as to be really beneficial to the community. Besides this, it may fairly be said that no man is to be extolled for doing what he cannot help doing, nor is he to be thanked by the community to which he only leaves wealth at death. Men who leave vast sums in this way may fairly be thought men who would not have left it at all had they been able to take it with them. The memories of such cannot be held in grateful remembrance, for there is no grace in their gifts. It is not to be wondered at that such bequests seem so generally to lack the blessing.

The growing disposition to tax more and more heavily large estates left at death is a cheering indication of the growth of a salutary change in public opinion. The State of Pennsylvania now takes — subject to some exception — one-tenth of the property left by its citizens. The budget presented in the British Parliament the other day proposes to increase the death-duties; and, most significant of all, the new tax is to be a graduated one. Of all forms of taxation, this seems the wisest. Men who continue hoarding great sums all their lives, the proper use of which for public ends would work good to the community, should be made to feel that the community, in the form of the state, cannot thus be deprived of its proper share. By taxing estates heavily at death the state makes its condemnation of the selfish millionaire's unworthy life.

It is desirable that nations should go much further in this direction. Indeed, it is difficult to set bounds to the share of a rich man's estate which should go at his death to the public through the agency of the state, and by all means such taxes should be graduated, beginning at nothing upon moderate sums to dependents, and increasing rapidly as the amounts swell, until of the millionaire's hoard, as of Shylock's,[4] at least

> — The other half
> Comes to the privy coffer of the state.

This policy would work powerfully to induce the rich man to attend to the administration of wealth during his life, which is the end that society should always have in view, as being that by far most fruitful for the people. Nor need it be feared that this policy would sap the root of enterprise and render men less anxious to accumulate, for to the class whose ambition it is to leave great fortunes and be talked about after their death, it will attract even more attention, and, indeed, be a somewhat nobler ambition to have enormous sums paid over to the state from their fortunes.

There remains, then, only one mode of using great fortunes; but in this we have the true antidote for the temporary unequal distribution of wealth, the reconciliation of the rich and the poor — a reign of harmony — another ideal, differing, indeed, from that of the Communist in requiring only the further evolution of existing conditions, not the total overthrow of our civilization. It is founded upon the present most intense individualism, and the race is prepared to put it in practice by degrees whenever it pleases. Under its sway we shall have an ideal state, in which the surplus wealth of the few will become, in the best sense, the property of the many, because administered for the common good, and this wealth, passing through the hands of the few, can be made a much more potent force for the elevation of our race than if it had been distributed in small sums to the people themselves. Even the poorest can be made to see this, and to agree that great sums gathered by some of their fellow-citizens and spent for public purposes, from which the masses reap the principal benefit, are more valuable to them than if scattered among them through the course of many years in trifling amounts.

If we consider what results flow from the Cooper Institute,[5] for instance, 15
to the best portion of the race in New York not possessed of means, and compare these with those which would have arisen for the good of the masses from an equal sum distributed by Mr. Cooper in his lifetime in the form of wages, which is the highest form of distribution, being for work done and not for charity, we can form some estimate of the possibilities for the improvement of the race which lie embedded in the present law of the accumulation of wealth. Much of this sum, if distributed in small quantities among the people, would have been wasted in the indulgence of appetite,

---

[4] **Shylock** The moneylender in Shakespeare's *The Merchant of Venice.*

[5] **Cooper Institute** Now Cooper Union, founded in 1858 by Peter Cooper as a free school for the sciences and the arts.

some of it in excess, and it may be doubted whether even the part put to the best use, that of adding to the comforts of the home, would have yielded results for the race, as a race, at all comparable to those which are flowing and are to flow from the Cooper Institute from generation to generation. Let the advocate of violent or radical change ponder well this thought.

We might even go so far as to take another instance, that of Mr. Tilden's bequest of five millions of dollars for a free library in the city of New York, but in referring to this one cannot help saying involuntarily, How much better if Mr. Tilden[6] had devoted the last years of his own life to the proper administration of this immense sum; in which case neither legal contest nor any other cause of delay could have interfered with his aims. But let us assume that Mr. Tilden's millions finally become the means of giving to New York a noble public library, where the treasures of the world contained in books will be open to all forever, without money and without price. Considering the good of that part of the race which congregates in and around Manhattan Island, would its permanent benefit have been better promoted had these millions been allowed to circulate in small sums through the hands of the masses? Even the most strenuous advocate of Communism must entertain a doubt upon this subject. Most of those who think will probably entertain no doubt whatever.

Poor and restricted are our opportunities in this life; narrow our horizon; our best work most imperfect; but rich men should be thankful for one inestimable boon. They have it in their power during their lives to busy themselves in organizing benefactions from which the masses of their fellows will derive lasting advantage, and thus dignify their own lives. The highest life is probably to be reached, not by such imitation of the life of Christ as Count Tolstoi[7] gives us, but, while animated by Christ's spirit, by recognizing the changed conditions of this age, and adopting modes of expressing this spirit suitable to the changed conditions under which we live; still laboring for the good of our fellows, which was the essence of his life and teaching, but laboring in a different manner.

This, then, is held to be the duty of the man of Wealth: first, to set an example of modest, unostentatious living, shunning display or extravagance; to provide moderately for the legitimate wants of those dependent upon him; and after doing so to consider all surplus revenues which come to him simply as trust funds, which he is called upon to administer, and strictly bound as a matter of duty to administer in the manner which, in his

---

[6] **Mr. Tilden** Samuel Tilden (1814–1886) bequeathed $4 million to found the New York Public Library after he died. His will was contested and only $3 million was given to found the library.

[7] **Count Tolstoi** Leo Tolstoy (1828–1910), author of *War and Peace* and *Anna Karenina*. Tolstoy lived a spare and simple life in his old age.

judgment, is best calculated to produce the most beneficial results for the community — the man of wealth thus becoming the mere agent and trustee for his poorer brethren, bringing to their service his superior wisdom, experience, and ability to administer, doing for them better than they would or could do for themselves.

We are met here with the difficulty of determining what are moderate sums to leave to members of the family; what is modest, unostentatious living; what is the test of extravagance. There must be different standards for different conditions. The answer is that it is as impossible to name exact amounts or actions as it is to define good manners, good taste, or the rules of propriety; but, nevertheless, these are verities, well known although undefinable. Public sentiment is quick to know and to feel what offends these. So in the case of wealth. The rule in regard to good taste in the dress of men or women applies here. Whatever makes one conspicuous offends the canon. If any family be chiefly known for display, for extravagance in home, table, equipage, for enormous sums ostentatiously spent in any form upon itself — if these be its chief distinctions, we have no difficulty in estimating its nature or culture. So likewise in regard to the use or abuse of its surplus wealth, or to generous, free-handed cooperation in good public uses, or to unabated efforts to accumulate and hoard to the last, whether they administer or bequeath. The verdict rests with the best and most enlightened public sentiment. The community will surely judge, and its judgments will not often be wrong.

The best uses to which surplus wealth can be put have already been   20 indicated. Those who would administer wisely must, indeed, be wise, for one of the serious obstacles to the improvement of our race is indiscriminate charity. It were better for mankind that the millions of the rich were thrown into the sea than so spent as to encourage the slothful, the drunken, the unworthy. Of every thousand dollars spent in so-called charity today, it is probable that $950 is unwisely spent; so spent, indeed, as to produce the very evils which it proposes to mitigate or cure. A well-known writer of philosophic books admitted the other day that he had given a quarter of a dollar to a man who approached him as he was coming to visit the house of his friend. He knew nothing of the habits of this beggar; knew not the use that would be made of this money, although he had every reason to suspect that it would be spent improperly. This man professed to be a disciple of Herbert Spencer;[8] yet the quarter-dollar given that night will probably work more injury than all the money which its thoughtless donor will ever be able to give in true charity will do good. He only gratified his own feelings, saved

---

[8] **Herbert Spencer** (1820–1903) British philosopher who applied Darwinian theories of evolution to the social sciences.

himself from annoyance — and this was probably one of the most selfish and very worst actions of his life, for in all respects he is most worthy.

In bestowing charity, the main consideration should be to help those who will help themselves; to provide part of the means by which those who desire to improve may do so; to give those who desire to rise the aids by which they may rise; to assist, but rarely or never to do all. Neither the individual nor the race is improved by almsgiving. Those worthy of assistance, except in rare cases, seldom require assistance. The really valuable men of the race never do, except in cases of accident or sudden change. Everyone has, of course, cases of individuals brought to his own knowledge where temporary assistance can do genuine good, and these he will not overlook. But the amount which can be wisely given by the individual for individuals is necessarily limited by his lack of knowledge of the circumstances connected with each. He is the only true reformer who is as careful and as anxious not to aid the unworthy as he is to aid the worthy, and, perhaps, even more so, for in almsgiving more injury is probably done by rewarding vice than by relieving virtue.

> "This, then, is held to be the duty of the man of Wealth: . . . becoming the mere agent and trustee for his poorer brethren, bringing to their service his superior wisdom, experience, and ability to administer, doing for them better than they would or could do for themselves."

The rich man is thus almost restricted to following the examples of Peter Cooper, Enoch Pratt of Baltimore, Mr. Pratt of Brooklyn, Senator Stanford,[9] and others, who know that the best means of benefiting the community is to place within its reach the ladders upon which the aspiring can rise — parks, and means of recreation, by which men are helped in body and mind; works of art, certain to give pleasure and improve the public taste; and public institutions of various kinds, which will improve the general condition of the people — in this manner returning their surplus wealth to the mass of their fellows in the forms best calculated to do them lasting good.

Thus is the problem of Rich and Poor to be solved. The laws of accumulation will be left free; the laws of distribution free. Individualism will continue, but the millionaire will be but a trustee for the poor; intrusted for a season with a great part of the increased wealth of the community, but administering it for the community far better than it could or would have done for itself. The best minds will thus have reached a stage in the development of the race in which it is clearly seen that there is no mode of

[9] **Peter Cooper . . . Senator Stanford** Peter Cooper (1791–1883), Enoch Pratt (1808–1896), Charles Pratt (1830–1891), and Leland Stanford (1824–1893) were prominent millionaires and eventual philanthropists, three of whom founded universities.

disposing of surplus wealth creditable to thoughtful and earnest men into whose hands it flows save by using it year by year for the general good. This day already dawns. But a little while, and although, without incurring the pity of their fellows, men may die sharers in great business enterprises from which their capital cannot be or has not been withdrawn, and is left chiefly at death for public uses, yet the man who dies leaving behind him millions of available wealth, which was his to administer during life, will pass away "unwept, unhonored, and unsung," no matter to what uses he leaves the dross which he cannot take with him. Of such as these the public verdict will then be: "The man who dies thus rich dies disgraced."

Such, in my opinion, is the true Gospel concerning Wealth, obedience to which is destined some day to solve the problem of the Rich and the Poor, and to bring "Peace on earth, among men Good-Will."

Understanding Ideas

1. According to Andrew Carnegie, what is the obligation of people with great fortunes?

2. Why, in Carnegie's view, does the law of competition benefit society?

3. Why does Carnegie tolerate financial inequality?

4. What does Carnegie have to say about the "progress of the race" (para. 2)?

Responding to Ideas

1. *Analysis of Circumstances* Andrew Carnegie sometimes cut the wages of his laborers because he felt that he knew how to spend money to benefit the public better than his laborers did. He thought that the average laborer would waste an extra few dollars engaging in undesirable activities, whereas he would use the money for libraries and universities. Analyze his argument. Is it true that a producer of great wealth will use money better than people who work in factories? What benefits would the laborers get for a small wage increase? Why should the laborers be denied the right to spend the money that Carnegie intended to spend on their behalf?

2. *Analysis of Circumstances* Carnegie begins his essay by saying, "The problem of our age is the proper administration of wealth, so that the ties of brotherhood may still bind together the rich and poor in harmonious

relationship." How does this statement relate to the conditions of our own age? Are the rich and poor relating harmoniously? How do we discuss the problem of extreme inequity in our own time? Do people today have a positive view regarding the accumulation of great wealth in the hands of the few? Why should there be a brotherhood binding the rich and the poor? Can it be achieved? What happens if it is not achieved?

3. *Response* Carnegie approves of "the Law of Accumulation of Wealth" and "the Law of Competition" (para. 7). What is your position on these "laws"? In what ways does your community approve of competition? In what circumstances does competition affect you directly? What kinds of competition are socially approved? How have you benefited from competition? Write a brief essay that defines the limits of competition and establishes your position as one who approves or disapproves of competition. Do the same for the concept of the accumulation of wealth. Carnegie says it should be the aim of everyone to accumulate wealth. Where do you stand on that proposition?

4. *Definition* Among his concerns, Carnegie warns of communism and socialism as being destructive of individualism. He also says they are enemies of civilization. Relying on his observations, define what Carnegie means by *civilization*. Explain whether you agree or disagree with his views on civilization. Define what Carnegie means by *communism* and *socialism*. Why does he think that these social institutions, which eliminate competition and inequality, are undesirable? Explain your position on these issues in a brief essay.

5. *Research* Carnegie believes it is the obligation of people who earn a fortune to spend the end of their lives giving their money away to benefit society. However, he believes they might need some prodding by the state's instituting taxes. He says that "most significant of all, the new tax is to be a graduated one. . . . By taxing estates heavily at death the state marks its condemnation of the selfish millionaire's unworthy life" (para. 12). These are strong words. What seems to be the current view on taxing the extremely wealthy? Do some research on the question of taxing the wealthy as it is being debated by politicians today. To what extent are Carnegie's views reflected in the current debate? Where do you stand on the issue of taxing the rich?

Comparing Ideas

1. When Andrew Carnegie wrote "The Gospel of Wealth" in 1889, there was no large middle class as we know it today. In an essay that compares Carnegie's ideas with those of Elizabeth Warren in "The Vanishing

Middle Class" (p. 344), decide how the middle class in the United States may alter Carnegie's most important ideas about wealth and those who possess it. What does Warren believe about the health of the nation and the possession of wealth that would anger or disappoint Carnegie? What would these two writers have to say to one another if they were somehow able to communicate? Would Carnegie have understood Warren's take on the middle class?

2. Neither Carnegie nor Friedrich Nietzsche, in "Good and Bad" (p. 393), reflects very much on the ethical principles of the church. However, Nietzsche claims that the moral teachings that shape the daily lives of most people are handed down by powerful people who desire to control those people with the least power. Compare Nietzsche and Carnegie and explain what Carnegie's ethical principles are and how they are clarified with reference to the concepts of good and bad as outlined by Nietzsche.

3. Both Adam Smith (p. 281) and Carnegie assume that there is a moral value in wealth. How do they treat the question of labor versus the question of accumulated wealth? Write a brief essay that analyzes quotations from both writers and compares their positions. What are the moral concerns of each writer? What are the benefits of wealth to the nation itself, as understood by each writer? What are their positions on the value of labor in society? What are management's moral obligations to labor? How different are Smith and Carnegie? How much do they agree on?

CHARLOTTE
PERKINS GILMAN

CHARLOTTE PERKINS GILMAN (1860–1935) was born in Hartford, Connecticut, into a community of social leaders that included her relative Harriet Beecher Stowe, who wrote *Uncle Tom's Cabin* (1852). Gilman's community actively protested slavery before the Civil War and supported women's rights in the late nineteenth century.

Hulton Archive/Getty Images

Gilman had a difficult upbringing. Her father abandoned his family, and her mother was distant and unsupportive. Gilman attended the Rhode Island School of Design and met and married a Providence artist, Charles Stetson, but the marriage did not last. Gilman had severe postpartum depression after her daughter was born, and she eventually set out on her own. At first she made a living with her art, but she soon turned to writing and lecturing about women's issues.

Gilman published two books of poetry and many short stories. Her collection of stories, *The Yellow Wallpaper* (1892), brought her some lasting recognition. In that collection, she tells stories that explore the stress of married life on women; depression and suicidal thoughts are described in considerable detail in many selections from the collection. Gilman's personal experiences gave dimension to these stories, and in her autobiography, *The Living of Charlotte Perkins Gilman*, published in 1935 after her death, she offers a very intense and detailed story of her emotional development and her personal beliefs.

The selection that follows, "Women and Economics: 'Cupid-in-the-Kitchen,'" was first published in 1898 in the book *Women and Economics: A Study of the Economic Relation between Men and Women as a Factor in Social Evolution*. Gilman was not an economist, but she was a close observer of women's economic issues that professional economists ignored. She said that male economists presumed that women do all the dirty jobs around the house. Women, she said, were essentially unpaid domestic servants in their own houses. Because they depended on the generosity of their husbands, they had to do their best to please them. Among the wealthy, Gilman thought, the situation may have been at its worst: "It is here," she says in an earlier chapter of *Women and Economics*, "that the economic dependence of women is carried to its extreme. The daughters and wives of the rich fail to perform even the domestic service expected of the women of poorer families. They are from birth to death absolutely nonproductive in goods or labor of economic value, and consumers of such goods and labor to an extent limited only by the purchasing power of their male relatives." She was quick to point out that it is not maternity that puts women in this situation but rather the assumption people make about what a woman ought to do with her life.

One of Gilman's most important suggestions is that women should live in houses without kitchens in coed arrangements similar to modern dormitories. This experiment is still forward-looking for some modern colleges and universities.

Be sure to practice prereading techniques before a careful, annotated reading of Gilman's essay. For a review of prereading strategies, see pages 4–9. ⌗

Women and Economics:
"Cupid-in-the-Kitchen"

A S A natural consequence of our division of labor on sex lines, giving to woman the home and to man the world in which to work, we have come to have a dense prejudice in favor of the essential womanliness of the home duties, as opposed to the essential manliness of every other kind of work. We have assumed that the preparation and serving of food and the removal of dirt, the nutritive and excretive processes of the family, are feminine functions; and we have also assumed that these processes must go on in what we call the home, which is the external expression of the family. In the home the human individual is fed, cleaned, warmed, and generally cared for, while not engaged in working in the world.

Human nutrition is a long process. There's many a ship 'twixt the cup and the lip, to paraphrase an old proverb. Food is produced by the human race collectively — not by individuals for their own consumption, but by interrelated groups of individuals, all over the world, for the world's consumption. This collectively produced food circulates over the earth's surface through elaborate processes of transportation, exchange, and preparation, before it reaches the mouths of the consumers; and the final processes of selection and preparation are in the hands of woman. She is the final purchaser: she is the final handler in that process of human nutrition known as cooking, which is a sort of extraorganic digestion proven advantageous to our species. This department of human digestion has become a sex function, supposed to pertain to women by nature.

If it is to the advantage of the human race that its food supply should be thus handled by a special sex, this advantage should be shown in superior health and purity of habit. But no such advantage is visible. In spite of all our power and skill in the production and preparation of food we remain "the sickest beast alive" in the matter of eating. Our impotent outcries against adulteration prove that part of the trouble is in the food products as offered for purchase, the pathetic reiteration of our numerous cookbooks proves that part of the trouble is in the preparation of those products, and the futile exhortations of physicians and mothers prove that part of the trouble is in our morbid tastes and appetites. It would really seem as if the human race after all its long centuries had not learned how to prepare good food, nor how to cook it, nor how to eat it — which is painfully true.

This great function of human nutrition is confounded with the sex relation, and is considered a sex function: it is in the helpless hands of that amiable but abortive agent, the economically dependent woman; and the essential incapacity of such an agent is not hard to show. In her position as private house steward she is the last purchaser of the food of the world, and here we reach the governing factor in our incredible adulteration of food products.

All kinds of deceit and imposition in human service are due to that 5 desire to get without giving, which, as has been shown . . . , is largely due to the training of women as nonproductive consumers. But the particular form of deceit and imposition practiced by a given dealer is governed by the intelligence and power of the buyer. The dilution and adulteration of food products is a particularly easy path to profit, because the ultimate purchaser has almost no power and very little intelligence. The individual housewife must buy at short intervals and in small quantities. This operates to her pecuniary disadvantage, as is well known; but its effect on the quality of her purchases is not so commonly observed. Not unless she becomes the head of a wealthy household, and so purchases in quantity for family, servants, and guests, is her trade of sufficient value to have force in the market. The dealer who sells to a hundred poor women can and does sell a much lower quality of food than he who sells an equal amount to one purchaser. Therefore, the home, as a food agency, holds an essentially and permanently unfavorable position as a purchaser; and it is thereby the principal factor in maintaining the low standard of food products against which we struggle with the cumbrous machinery of legislation.

Most housekeepers will innocently prove their ignorance of these matters by denying that the standard of food products is so low. Let such offended ladies but examine the statutes and ordinances of their own cities — of any civilized city — and see how the bread, the milk, the meat, the fruit, are under a steady legislative inspection which endeavors to protect the ignorance and helplessness of the individual purchaser. If the private housekeeper had the technical intelligence as purchaser which is needed to discriminate in the selection of foods, if she were prepared to test her milk, to detect the foreign substance in her coffee and spices, rightly to estimate the quality of her meat and the age of her fruit and vegetables, she would then be able at least to protest against her supply, and to seek, as far as time, distance, and funds allowed, a better market. This technical intelligence, however, is only to be obtained by special study and experience; and its attainment only involves added misery and difficulty to the private purchaser, unless accompanied by the power to enforce what the intelligence demands.

> *"All kinds of deceit and imposition in human service are due to that desire to get without giving, which . . . is largely due to the training of women as nonproductive consumers."*

As it is, woman brings to her selection from the world's food only the empirical experience gained by practicing upon her helpless family, and this during the very time when her growing children need the wise care which she is only able to give them in later years. This experience, with its pitiful limitation and its practical check by the personal taste and pecuniary standing of the family, is lost where it was found. Each mother slowly acquires some knowledge of her business by practicing it upon the lives and health of her family and by observing its effect on the survivors; and each daughter begins again as ignorant as her mother was before her. This "rule of thumb" is not transmissible. It is not a genuine education such as all important work demands, but a slow animal process of soaking up experience — hopelessly ineffectual in protecting the health of society. As the ultimate selecting agent in feeding humanity, the private housewife fails, and this not by reason of any lack of effort on her part, but by the essential defect of her position as individual purchaser. Only organization can oppose such evils as the wholesale adulteration of food; and woman, the house servant, belongs to the lowest grade of unorganized labor.

Leaving the selection of food, and examining its preparation, one would naturally suppose that the segregation of an entire sex to the fulfillment of this function would insure most remarkable results. It has, but they are not so favorable as might be expected. The art and science of cooking involve a large and thorough knowledge of nutritive value and of the laws of physiology and hygiene. As a science, it verges on preventive medicine. As an art, it is capable of noble expression within its natural bounds. As it stands among us today, it is so far from being a science and akin to preventive medicine, that it is the lowest of amateur handicrafts and a prolific source of disease; and, as an art, it has developed under the peculiar stimulus of its position as a sex function into a voluptuous profusion as false as it is evil. Our innocent proverb, "The way to a man's heart is through his stomach." is a painfully plain comment on the way in which we have come to deprave our bodies and degrade our souls at the table.

On the side of knowledge it is permanently impossible that half the world, acting as amateur cooks for the other half, can attain any high degree of scientific accuracy or technical skill. The development of any human labor requires specialization, and specialization is forbidden to our cook-by-nature system. What progress we have made in the science of cooking has been made through the study and experience of professional men cooks and chemists, not through the Sisyphean[1] labors of our endless generations of isolated women, each beginning again where her mother began before her.

Here, of course, will arise a pained outcry along the "mother's dough- 10 nuts" line. . . . The fact that we like a thing does not prove it to be right. A Missouri child may regard his mother's saleratus[2] biscuit with fond desire, but that does not alter their effect upon his spirits or his complexion. Cooking is a matter of law, not the harmless play of fancy. Architecture might be more sportive and varied if every man built his own house, but it would not be the art and science that we have made it; and, while every woman prepares food for her own family, cooking can never rise beyond the level of the amateur's work.

But, low as is the status of cooking as a science, as an art it is lower. Since the wife-cook's main industry is to please — that being her chief means of getting what she wants or of expressing affection — she early learned to cater to the palate instead of faithfully studying and meeting the needs of the stomach. For uncounted generations the grown man and the growing child have been subject to the constant efforts of her who cooked from affection, not from knowledge — who cooked to please. This is one of the widest pathways of evil that has ever been opened. In every field of life it is an evil to put the incident before the object, the means before the end; and here it has produced that familiar result whereby we live to eat instead of eating to live.

This attitude of the woman has developed the rambling excess called "fancy cookery" — a thing as far removed from true artistic development as

---

[1] **Sisyphean** Arduously repetitious, as in the labors of Sisyphus, a Greek mythical figure who was condemned eternally to roll a great stone to the top of a hill. only to have it roll back down when he neared his goal. See Homer's *Iliad* (Vi.153).

[2] **saleratus** Salt biscuit.

a swinging ice-pitcher from a Greek vase. Through this has come the limitless unhealthy folly of high living, in which human labor and time and skill are wasted in producing what is neither pure food nor pure pleasure, but an artificial performance, to be appreciated only by the virtuoso. Lower living could hardly be imagined than that which results from this unnatural race between artifice and appetite, in which body and soul are both corrupted.

In the man, the subject of all this dining-room devotion, has been developed and maintained that cultivated interest in his personal tastes and their gratification — that demand for things which he likes rather than for things which he knows to be good, wherein lies one of the most dangerous elements in character known to the psychologist. The sequences of this affectionate catering to physical appetites may be traced far afield to its last result in the unchecked indulgence in personal tastes and desires, in drug habits and all intemperance. The temperament which is unable to resist these temptations is constantly being bred at home.

As the concentration of woman's physical energies on the sex functions, enforced by her economic dependence, has tended to produce and maintain man's excess in sex indulgence, to the injury of the race; so the concentration of woman's industrial energies on the close and constant service of personal tastes and appetites has tended to produce and maintain an excess in table indulgence, both in eating and drinking, which is also injurious to the race. It is not here alleged that this is the only cause of our habits of this nature; but it is one of primal importance, and of ceaseless action.

We can perhaps see its working better by a light-minded analogy than 15 by a bold statement. Suppose two large, healthy, nimble apes. Suppose that the male ape did not allow the female ape to skip about and pluck her own cocoanuts [sic], but brought to her what she was to have. Suppose that she was then required to break the shell, pick out the meat, prepare for the male what he wished to consume; and suppose, further, that her share in the dinner, to say nothing of her chance of a little pleasure excursion in the treetops afterward, was dependent on his satisfaction with the food she prepared for him. She, as an ape of intelligence, would seek, by all devices known to her, to add stimulus and variety to the meals she arranged, to select the bits he specially preferred to please his taste and to meet his appetite; and he, developing under this agreeable pressure, would gradually acquire a fine discrimination in foods, and would look forward to his elaborate feasts with increasing complacency. He would have a new force to make him eat — not only his need of food, with its natural and healthy demands, but her need of — everything, acting through his need of food.

This sounds somewhat absurd in a family of apes, but it is precisely what has occurred in the human family. To gratify her husband has been the woman's way of obtaining her own ends, and she has of necessity learned how to do it; and, as she has been in general an uneducated and unskilled worker, she could only seek to please him through what powers she had — mainly those of house service. She has been set to serve two appetites, and to profit accordingly. She has served them well, but the profit to either party is questionable.

On lines of social development we are progressing from the gross gorging of the savage on whatever food he could seize, toward the discriminating selection of proper foods, and an increasing delicacy and accuracy in their use. Against this social tendency runs the crosscurrent of our sexuo-economic relation, making the preparation of food a sex function, and confusing all its processes with the ardor of personal affection and the dragging weight of self-interest. This method is applied, not only to the husband, but, in a certain degree, to the children; for, where maternal love and maternal energy are forced to express themselves mainly in the preparation of food, the desire properly to feed the child becomes confounded with an unwise desire to please, and the mother degrades her high estate by catering steadily to the lower tastes of humanity instead of to the higher.

Our general notion is that we have lifted and ennobled our eating and drinking by combining them with love. On the contrary, we have lowered and degraded our love by combining it with eating and drinking; and, what is more, we have lowered these habits also. Some progress has been made, socially; but this unhappy mingling of sex interest and self-interest with normal appetites, this Cupid-in-the-kitchen arrangement, has gravely impeded that progress. Professional cooking has taught us much. Commerce and manufacture have added to our range of supplies. Science has shown us what we need, and how and when we need it. But the affectionate labor of wife and mother is little touched by these advances. If she goes to the cooking school, it is to learn how to make the rich delicacies that will please rather than to study the nutritive value of food in order to guard the health of the household. From the constantly enlarging stores opened to her through man's activities she chooses widely, to make "a variety" that shall kindle appetite, knowing nothing of the combination best for physical needs. As to science, chemistry, hygiene they are but names to her. "John likes it so." "Willie won't eat it so." "Your father never could bear cabbage." She must consider what he likes, not only because she loves to please him or because she profits by pleasing him, but because he pays for the dinner, and she is a private servant.

Is it not time that the way to a man's heart through his stomach should be relinquished for some higher avenue? The stomach should be left to its natural uses, not made a thoroughfare for stranger passions and purposes; and the heart should be approached through higher channels. We need a new picture of our overworked blind god — fat, greasy, pampered with sweetmeats by the poor worshippers long forced to pay their devotion through such degraded means.

No, the human race is not well nourished by making the process of feed-   20
ing it a sex function. The selection and preparation of food should be in the
hands of trained experts. And woman should stand beside man as the com-
rade of his soul, not the servant of his body.

This will require large changes in our method of living. To feed the
world by expert service, bringing to that great function the skill and experience of the trained specialist, the power of science, and the beauty of art,
is impossible in the sexuo-economic relation. While we treat cooking as a
sex function common to all women and eating as a family function not otherwise rightly accomplished, we can develop no farther. We are spending
much earnest study and hard labor today on the problem of teaching and
training women in the art of cooking, both the wife and the servant; for, with
our usual habit of considering voluntary individual conduct as the cause of
conditions, we seek to modify conditions by changing individual conduct.

What we must recognize is that, while the conditions remain, the conduct cannot be altered. Any trade or profession, the development of which
depended upon the labor of isolated individuals, assisted only by hired servants more ignorant than themselves, would remain at a similarly low level.

So far as health can be promoted by public means, we are steadily
improving by sanitary regulations and medical inspection, by profession-
ally prepared "health foods," and by the
literature of hygiene, by special legislation
as to contagious diseases and dangerous
trades; but the health that lies in the hands
of the housewife is not reached by these
measures. The nine-tenths of our women
who do their own work cannot be turned
into proficient purchasers and cooks any
more than nine-tenths of our men could

"Is it not time that the
way to a man's heart
through his stomach
should be relinquished
for some higher avenue?"

be turned into proficient tailors with no better training or opportunity than
would be furnished by clothing their own families. The alternative remaining to the women who comprise the other tenth is that peculiar survival of
earlier labor methods known as "domestic service."

As a method of feeding humanity, hired domestic service is inferior
even to the service of the wife and mother, and brings to the art of cooking
an even lower degree of training and a narrower experience. The majority of domestic servants are young girls who leave this form of service for
marriage as soon as they are able; and we thus intrust the physical health
of human beings, so far as cooking affects it, to the hands of untrained,
immature women, of the lowest social grade, who are actuated by no higher
impulse than that of pecuniary necessity. The love of the wife and mother
stimulates at least her desire to feed her family well. The servant has no
such motive. The only cases in which domestic cooking reaches anything

like proficiency are those in which the wife and mother is "a natural-born cook," and regales her family with the products of genius, or those in which the households of the rich are able to command the service of professionals.

There was a time when kings and lords retained their private poets to 25 praise and entertain them; but the poet is not truly great until he sings for the world. So the art of cooking can never be lifted to its true place as a human need and a social function by private service. Such an arrangement of our lives and of our houses as will allow cooking to become a profession is the only way in which to free this great art from its present limitations. It should be a reputable, well-paid profession, wherein those women or those men who were adapted to this form of labor could become cooks, as they would become composers or carpenters. Natural distinctions would be developed between the mere craftsman and the artist; and we should have large, new avenues of lucrative and honorable industry, and a new basis for human health and happiness.

This does not involve what is known as "cooperation." Cooperation, in the usual sense, is the union of families for the better performance of their supposed functions. The process fails because the principle is wrong. Cooking and cleaning are not family functions. We do not have a family mouth, a family stomach, a family face to be washed. Individuals require to be fed and cleaned from birth to death, quite irrespective of their family relations. The orphan, the bachelor, the childless widower, have as much need of these nutritive and excretive processes as any patriarchal parent. Eating is an individual function. Cooking is a social function. Neither is in the faintest degree a family function. That we have found it convenient in early stages of civilization to do our cooking at home proves no more than the allied fact that we have also found it convenient in such stages to do our weaving and spinning at home, our soap and candle making, our butchering and pickling, our baking and washing.

As society develops, its functions specialize; and the reason why this great race function of cooking has been so retarded in its natural growth is that the economic dependence of women has kept them back from their share in human progress. When women stand free as economic agents, they will lift and free their arrested functions, to the much better fulfillment of their duties as wives and mothers and to the vast improvement in health and happiness of the human race.

Cooperation is not what is required for this, but trained professional service and such arrangement of our methods of living as shall allow us to benefit by such service. When numbers of people patronize the same tailor or baker or confectioner, they do not cooperate. Neither would they cooperate in patronizing the same cook. The change must come from the side of the cook, not from the side of the family. It must come through natural functional development in society, and it is so coming. Woman, recognizing that her duty as feeder and cleaner is a social duty, not a sexual one, must face the requirements of the situation, and prepare herself to meet them. A hundred years ago this could not have been done. Now it is being done, because the time is ripe for it.

If there should be built and opened in any of our large cities today a commodious and well-served apartment house for professional women with families, it would be filled at once. The apartments would be without kitchens; but there would be a kitchen belonging to the house from which meals could be served to the families in their rooms or in a common dining room, as preferred. It would be a home where the cleaning was done by efficient workers, not hired separately by the families, but engaged by the manager of the establishment; and a roof garden, day nursery, and kindergarten, under well-trained professional nurses and teachers, would insure proper care of the children. The demand for such provision is increasing daily, and must soon be met, not by a boardinghouse or a lodging house, a hotel, a restaurant, or any makeshift patching together of these; but by a permanent provision for the needs of women and children, of family privacy with collective advantage. This must be offered on a business basis to prove a substantial business success; and it will so prove, for it is a growing social need.

There are hundreds of thousands of women in New York City alone who 30 are wage earners, and who also have families; and the number increases. This is true not only among the poor and unskilled, but more and more among businesswomen, professional women, scientific, artistic, literary women. Our schoolteachers, who form a numerous class, are not entirely without relatives. To board does not satisfy the needs of a human soul. These women want homes, but they do not want the clumsy tangle of rudimentary industries that are supposed to accompany the home. The strain under which such women labor is no longer necessary. The privacy of the home could be as well maintained in such a building as described as in any house in a block, any room, flat, or apartment, under present methods. The food would be better, and would cost less; and this would be true of the service and of all common necessities.

In suburban homes this purpose could be accomplished much better by a grouping of adjacent houses, each distinct and having its own yard, but all kitchenless, and connected by covered ways with the eating house. No detailed prophecy can be made of the precise forms which would ultimately prove most useful and pleasant; but the growing social need is for the specializing of the industries practiced in the home and for the proper mechanical provision for them.

The cleaning required in each house would be much reduced by the removal of the two chief elements of household dirt — grease and ashes.

Meals could of course be served in the house as long as desired; but, when people become accustomed to pure, clean homes, where no steaming industry is carried on, they will gradually prefer to go to their food instead of having it brought to them. It is a perfectly natural process, and a healthful one, to go to one's food. And, after all, the changes between living in one room, and so having the cooking most absolutely convenient; going as far as the limits of a large house permit, to one's own dining room; and going a little further to a dining room not in one's own house, but nearby — these differ but in degree. Families could go to eat together, just as they can go to bathe together or to listen to music together; but, if it fell out that different individuals presumed to develop an appetite at different hours, they could meet it without interfering with other people's comfort or sacrificing their own. Any housewife knows the difficulty of always getting a family together at meals. Why try? Then arises sentiment, and asserts that family affection, family unity, the very existence of the family, depend on their being together at meals. A family unity which is only bound together with tablecloth is of questionable value.

There are several professions involved in our clumsy method of housekeeping. A good cook is not necessarily a good manager, nor a good manager an accurate and thorough cleaner, nor a good cleaner a wise purchaser. Under the free development of these branches a woman could choose her position, train for it, and become a most valuable functionary in her special branch, all the while living in her own home; that is, she would live in it as a man lives in his home, spending certain hours of the day at work and others at home.

This division of the labor of housekeeping would require the service of 35 fewer women for fewer hours a day. Where now twenty women in twenty homes work all the time, and insufficiently accomplish their varied duties, the same work in the hands of specialists could be done in less time by fewer people; and the others would be left free to do other work for which they were better fitted, thus increasing the productive power of the world. Attempts at cooperation so far have endeavored to lessen the existing labors of women without recognizing their need for other occupation, and this is one reason for their repeated failure.

It seems almost unnecessary to suggest that women as economic producers will naturally choose those professions which are compatible with motherhood, and there are many professions much more in harmony with that function than the household service. Motherhood is not a remote contingency, but the common duty and the common glory of womanhood. If women did choose professions unsuitable to maternity, Nature would quietly extinguish them by her unvarying process. Those mothers who persisted in being acrobats, horse breakers, or sailors before the mast, would probably not produce vigorous and numerous children. If they did, it would simply prove that such work did not hurt them. There is no fear to be wasted on the danger of women's choosing wrong professions, when they are free to choose. Many women would continue to prefer the very kinds of work which they are doing now, in the new and higher methods of execution. Even cleaning, rightly understood and practiced, is a useful, and therefore honorable, profession. It has been amusing heretofore to see how this least desirable of labors has been so innocently held to be woman's natural duty. It is woman, the dainty, the beautiful, the beloved wife and revered mother, who has by common consent been expected to do the chamber work and scullery work of the world. All that is basest and foulest she in the last instance must handle and remove. Grease, ashes, dust, foul linen, and sooty ironware — among these her days must pass. As we socialize our functions, this passes from her hands into those of man. The city's cleaning is his work. And even in our houses the professional cleaner is more and more frequently a man.

The organization of household industries will simplify and centralize its cleaning processes, allowing of many mechanical conveniences and the application of scientific skill and thoroughness. We shall be cleaner than we ever were before. There will be less work to do, and far better means of doing it. The daily needs of a well-plumbed house could be met easily by each individual in his or her own room or by one who liked to do such work; and the labor less frequently required would be furnished by an expert, who would clean one home after another with the swift skill of training and experience. The home would cease to be to us a workshop or a museum, and would become far more the personal expression of its occupants — the place of peace and rest, of love and privacy — than it can be in its present condition of arrested industrial development. And woman will fill her place in those industries with far better results than are now provided by her ceaseless struggles, her conscientious devotion, her pathetic ignorance and inefficiency.

Understanding Ideas

1. Why does Charlotte Perkins Gilman describe cooking as a "sex function" form of labor?

2. Why should cooking be a professional form of labor, according to Gilman?

3. According to Gilman, why do wives feel they must satisfy the tastes of their husbands?

4. What does Gilman recommend for improving nutrition?

Responding to Ideas

1. **Response** Charlotte Perkins Gilman says that cooking should be a professional activity. Her recommendation is to set up a group of houses that would interconnect with a main kitchen where professional cooks would prepare the meals. If you live, or have lived, in a dormitory, you might be able to argue her case from experience. You may also wish to argue against her case, based on your experience. Write a brief essay in response to Gilman's idea; be sure to ask people about their experiences and include examples that will help your argument.

2. **Research** One of the more controversial points Gilman makes is that the housewife in the home is an amateur cook and is unlikely to be able to get the best food and to prepare it in the best way. Gilman also says that young wives begin their married lives with the same kind of ignorance (and amateurishness) as their mothers. Attack or defend the idea that housewives are amateur cooks. Construct a careful argument that includes evidence from other people's experiences, as well as your own, in defense of your position.

3. **Comparison** Gilman wrote this piece in the late nineteenth century. She focused on cooking and household cleaning because at that time society assigned those roles to women. She also says that "woman, the house servant, belongs to the lowest grade of unorganized labor" (para. 7). Have things changed substantially in the 100-plus years since this essay was published? Explain the differences between a housewife's responsibilities to her family today and those in 1898. How much progress has been made? Why does Gilman call housewives the "lowest grade of unorganized labor"? In what sense do you agree or disagree with that characterization?

4. **Example** Gilman makes the point that cooking is a science with important input from chemistry and nutritional research. She also suggests that it is difficult for a housewife to get the best and most nutritious food where she shops. Further, she claims, because the housewife is dependent on her husband and must please him she caters to his taste and not to his nutritional needs. Is that observation true for families today? What examples can you produce that substantiate or contradict her statements about housewives preparing food that families like rather than what is good for them? What does she mean when she says that "catering to physical appetites" leads to "the unchecked indulgence in personal tastes and desires, in drug habits and all intemperance" (para. 13)?

5. **Analysis of Circumstances** In talking about the value of women's labor, Gilman has chosen to talk almost exclusively about the division of labor

that assigns women to cooking. Gilman stresses the typical wife's lack of training and the problems inherent in pleasing her husband. Gilman's views were very important when she wrote in 1898. But if you were to write a serious essay about the problems inherent in valuing women's labor today, what would you emphasize? What would you point to — and then examine in detail — that would sum up the kinds of issues Gilman addresses? She is concerned with household circumstances, but what circumstances in our time would be more to the point?

Comparing Ideas

1. Charlotte Perkins Gilman talks a great deal about labor and the labor that women do. Indirectly, she is also talking about the role of politics in a woman's life. Both bell hooks in "Feminist Politics: Where We Stand" (p. 190) and Lucy A. Delaney in "Struggles for Freedom" (p. 146) also talk about the work women do and the problems they face in a patriarchal society. Write an essay that helps clarify the nature of women's struggles to achieve freedom and independence over the period of a little more than a hundred years. How deeply committed are these three writers to feminism? Assume you are writing your essay for someone unsympathetic to feminism.

2. Use Adam Smith's concepts in "The Value of Labor" (p. 281) to help convince a reader that Gilman is approaching the value of women's labor from a serious economic position. Be sure to provide a clear definition of each writer's status as an economist. What are the differences in their understandings of labor and its value? How sympathetic would Smith be to Gilman's argument about the value of women's labor in the home? What in his essay implies that he has any concern for the women Gilman discusses?

3. Today, both Mary Wollstonecraft (p. 77) and Gilman are thought of as early feminists. How close is their thinking concerning the value of female labor? What are the primary points of agreement in their main ideas about the social function of women? What points do they perhaps disagree about in terms of women's independence? Describe how each interprets the economic situation of women in their respective eras. Which of their most serious complaints are still valid today?

JOHN KENNETH GALBRAITH

Louis Monier/Getty Images

JOHN KENNETH GALBRAITH (1908–2006) was born in Ontario, Canada, and took his first university degree in agricultural science. He was awarded a scholarship that permitted him to go to the University of California, Berkeley, where he got his Ph.D. in agricultural economics. He taught both at Berkeley and at Princeton University and then moved to Cambridge, where he was professor of economics at Harvard University for many years. He took an interest in politics during the Great Depression and worked in Roosevelt's Office of Price Administration. During the presidential campaigns of Adlai Stevenson in 1952 and 1956, he assisted the Democrats as a speechwriter and economics adviser. He did the same for President John F. Kennedy in 1960. By then he was an American citizen and among the best-known economists in the United States.

As the author of more than fourteen books, Galbraith is best known for *The Affluent Society* (1958; rev. eds. 1969, 1976, 1998), a best-seller that analyzed America's economic ambitions. At that time, the nation's economy was entirely focused on the measurement and growth of the gross national product. Galbraith felt that was a mistake because the emphasis on output would lead to producing things that people did not need and would not benefit from. An economy dependent on creating artificial needs for things that had no ultimate value and had built-in "planned obsolescence" seemed to him wasteful and ultimately destructive.

In "Inequality," drawn from *The Affluent Society*, Galbraith addresses issues that were important in 1958 but that seem even more important today. As each new edition of his book was published, the statistics indicating the respective wealth of the top 10 percent and the bottom 10 percent of Americans have changed, indicating increasing inequality. Galbraith reviews some of the historical attitudes and explanations for such inequality in wealth. Some of his position reflects the ideas of both Adam Smith and Andrew Carnegie. But Galbraith also examines what he sees as the contemporary attitudes of people in general toward the benefits of the rich and the viewpoints of the poor about the rich.

In an earlier part of his book, Galbraith points out that historically almost all countries had been poor through the centuries. In describing ours as an affluent society, he insists that we are only beginning to come to terms with the fact that inequalities of wealth are here and, as Smith would tell us, inevitable. With that idea in the background, Galbraith sets out to examine the nature of inequality and how society deals with it.

Be sure to practice prereading techniques before a careful, annotated reading of Galbraith's essay. For a review of prereading strategies, see pages 4–9. ⊞

Inequality

I

FEW THINGS have been more productive of controversy over the ages than the suggestion that the rich should, by one device or another, share their wealth with those who are not. With comparatively rare and usually eccentric exceptions, the rich have been opposed. The grounds have been many and varied and have been principally noted for the rigorous exclusion of the most important reason, which is simply the unwillingness to give up the enjoyment of what they have. The poor have generally been in favor of greater equality. In the United States this support has been tempered by the tendency of some of the poor to react sympathetically to the cries of pain of the rich over their taxes and of others to the hope that one day soon they might be rich themselves.

. . . [T]he economic and social preoccupation with inequality is deeply grounded. In the competitive society — the society of the central tradition of economics in descent from Ricardo[1] — there was presumed to be a premium on efficiency. The competent entrepreneur and worker were automatically rewarded. The rest, as automatically, were punished for their incompetence or sloth. If labor and capital and land were employed with

---

[1] **Ricardo** David Ricardo (1722–1823), British economist who championed specialization in international trade and admitted some of the kinds of central planning that now figure in international trade agreements among nations.

high efficiency then, *pro tanto*,[2] nothing more, or not much more, could be obtained from the economy in the short run by way of product. And longer-run progress did not necessarily benefit the average man; in the original doctrine, its fruits accrued to others.

So if people were poor, as in fact they were, their only hope lay in a redistribution of income, and especially that which was the product of accu-mulated wealth. Much though Ricardo and his followers might dissent, there were always some — and the number steadily grew — who believed that redistribution might be possible. (Ricardo and those who followed him in the central tradition were never immune from the suspicion that they were pleading a special interest.) All Marxists took the need for a drastic redis-tribution for granted. Consequently, throughout the nineteenth century, the social radical had no choice but to advocate the redistribution of wealth and income by one device or another. If he wanted to change things, this was his only course. To avoid this issue was to avoid all issues.

The conservative defense of inequality has varied. There has always been the underlying contention that, as a matter of natural law and equity, what a man has received save by proven larceny is rightfully his. For Ricardo and his immediate followers, the luxurious income of landlords and of capi-talists was the inevitable arrangement of things. One could tamper with it but only at the eventual price of disrupting the system and making the lot of everyone (including the poor) much worse.

This was essentially the passive defense. With time (and agitation), the 5 case for inequality became a good deal more functional. The undisturbed enjoyment of income was held to be essential as an incentive. The resulting effort and ingenuity would bring greater production and greater resulting rewards for all. In recent times a limit on taxes on earned income has been all but canonized.

Inequality has also come to be regarded as almost equally important for capital formation. Were income widely distributed, it would be spent. But if it flowed in a concentrated stream to the rich, a part would certainly be saved and invested.

There are other arguments. Excessive equality makes for cultural uni-formity and monotony. Rich men are essential if there is to be an adequate subsidy to education and the arts. Equality smacks of communism and hence of atheism and therefore is spiritually suspect.

The cultural misfortunes from excessive equality cannot be pressed too far. As Tawney[3] observed: "Those who dread a dead-level of income

---

[2] ***pro tanto*** So much.

[3] **Tawney** Richard H. Tawney (1880–1962), British economist who fought for social justice for the poor. His most important book is *Religion and the Rise of Capitalism* (1926).

or wealth . . . do not dread, it seems, a dead-level of law and order, and of security of life and property. They do not complain that persons endowed by nature with unusual qualities of strength, audacity, or cunning are prevented from reaping the full fruits of these powers."[4] And in fact, in the conventional wisdom, the defense of inequality does rest primarily on its functional role as an incentive and as a source of capital.

Thus the limited egalitarianism of the present federal income-tax structure has long been held to be seriously dampening to individual effort, initiative, and inspiration or in danger of becoming so. It "destroys ambition, penalizes success, discourages investment to create new jobs, and may well turn a nation of risk-taking entrepreneurs into a nation of softies. . . ."[5] "It destroys the incentive of people to work. . . . It makes it increasingly difficult, if not impossible, for people to save. . . . It has a deadening effect on the spirit of enterprise . . . which has made America."[6]

However, this case is not impeccably consistent. Not many business- 10 men wish to concede that they are putting forth less than their best efforts because of insufficient pecuniary incentive. The typical business executive makes his way to the top by promotion over the heads of his fellows. He would surely endanger his chance for advancement if he were suspected of goldbricking because of his resentment over the inadequacy of his after-tax income. He is expected to give his best to his corporation, and usually he does.

To give individuals large incomes to encourage savings also has elements of illogic. The rich man saves because he is able to satisfy all his wants and then have something over. Such saving, in other words, is the residual after luxurious consumption. This obviously is not an especially efficient way to promote capital formation. Moreover, the empirical evidence on the effect of egalitarianism on capital formation is uncertain. England is often cited as an unfortunate example. But Norway, an even more egalitarian country, had, following World War II, one of the highest rates of capital formation and of economic growth of any country in the non-Communist world.[7] Latin American republics with a highly unequal income distribution have no remarkable record for capital formation.

The *formal* liberal attitude toward inequality has changed little over the years. The liberal has partly accepted the view of the well-to-do that it is

---

[4] R. H. Tawney, *Equality*, 4th ed., rev. (London: Allen & Unwin, 1952), p. 85. [Galbraith's note]

[5] "Taxes and America's Future." Address by Fred Maytag II, before the National Association of Manufacturers, December 1, 1954. [Galbraith's note]

[6] "The Relation of Taxes to Economic Growth." Address by Ernest L. Swigert, before the National Association of Manufacturers, December 6, 1956. [Galbraith's note]

[7] Alice Bourneuf, *Norway: The Planned Revival* (Cambridge, Mass.: Harvard University Press, 1958). [Galbraith's note]

a trifle uncouth to urge a policy of soaking the rich. Yet, on the whole, the rich man remains the natural antagonist of the poor. Economic legislation, above all tax policy, continues to be a contest, however unequal, between the interests of the two. No other question in economic policy is ever so important as the effect of a measure on the distribution of income. The test of the good liberal is still that he is never fooled, that he never yields on issues favoring the wealthy. Other questions occupy his active attention, but this is the constant. Behind him, always challenging him, is the cynical Marxian whisper hinting that whatever he does may not be enough. Despite his efforts, the wealthy become wealthier and more powerful. They lose battles but win wars.

> *"[T]he defense of inequality does rest primarily on its functional role as an incentive and as a source of capital."*

II

However, few things are more evident in modern social history than the decline of interest in inequality as an economic issue. This has been particularly true in the United States. And it would appear, among Western countries, to be the least true of the United Kingdom. While it continues to have a large ritualistic role in the conventional wisdom of conservatives and liberals, inequality has ceased to preoccupy men's minds. And even the conventional wisdom has made some concessions to this new state of affairs.

On the fact itself — that inequality is of declining concern — it is only necessary to observe that for many years no serious effort has been made to alter the present distribution of income.[8] Although in the semantics of American liberalism there is often a tactful silence on the point, since nothing so stirs conservative wrath, the principal public device for redistributing income is the progressive income tax. But the income tax in the years since World War II has greatly regressed as an instrument for income redistribution.

The decline in concern for inequality cannot be explained by the triumph of equality. Although this is regularly suggested in the conventional wisdom of conservatives, and could readily be inferred from the complaints of businessmen, inequality is great and getting greater. In 1970, the one-tenth of families and unattached individuals with the lowest incomes received

15

---

[8] The so-called war on poverty of the Johnson administration was instructive: income redistribution was to be limited to the very poor. The more important improvement in the incomes of the poor was to come from the increased productivity of that group. The ability of all shades of political opinion to endorse aspects of this program suggests the mildness of the effort. [Galbraith's note]

before taxes about 2 percent of the total money income of the country; the tenth with the highest incomes received 27 percent of the total, which is to say their incomes averaged 14 times as much as the lowest tenth. The half of the households with the lowest incomes received, before taxes, only 23 percent of all money income. The half with the highest incomes received 77 percent. In 1972, only about 7 percent of all family units had incomes before taxes of more than $25,000. They received, nonetheless, 21 percent of total income. At the other extreme, 17 percent had before-tax incomes of less than $5,000 and received only 4 percent of the income.[9] In the years since, the share going to the very rich has much increased. Present laws are notably favorable to the person who has wealth as opposed to the individual who is only earning it. With a little ingenuity, the man who is already rich can ordinarily take his income in the form of capital gains and limit somewhat his tax liability. In addition, unlike the man who must earn, he is under no compulsion to acquire a capital stake, either for old age, family, or the mere satisfaction it brings, since he already has one. Accordingly, he need not save. Yet none of these matters nor the numerous more egregious loopholes in the federal income tax arouse the kind of concern which leads on from rhetoric to action.

III

The first reason inequality has faded as an issue is, without much question, that while it has continued and increased, it has not been showing the expected tendency to promote violent reaction. And thus the Marxian prediction, which earlier in this century seemed so amply confirmed by observation, no longer inspires the same depth of fear. In the absence of alarm, inequality is more easily accepted than social reformers in the past have supposed. Emulation or, when this is frustrated, envy has long played a large role in the common view of human motivation. So long as one individual had more than another, the second was presumed to be dissatisfied with his lot. He strove to come abreast of his more favored contemporary; he was deeply discontented if he failed. However, these disenchanting traits are less cosmic than has commonly been supposed. Envy almost certainly operates efficiently only as regards near neighbors. It is not directed toward the distant rich. If the individual's own real income is rising, the fact that unknown New Yorkers, Texans, or West Coast computer entrepreneurs are exceedingly wealthy is not, probably, a matter of prime urgency. It becomes easy, or at least convenient, to accept the case of the conventional wisdom,

---

[9] U.S. Department of Commerce, *Statistical Abstract of the United States.* The 1970 figures are from p. 324 of the 1972 edition; the 1972 figures from p. 382 of the 1974 edition. [Galbraith's note]

which is that the rich in America are both functional and also much persecuted members of the society. And, as noted, to comment on the wealth of
the wealthy, and certainly to propose that it be reduced, has come to be considered bad taste. The individual whose own income is going up has no real
reason to incur the opprobrium of this discussion. Why should he identify
himself, even remotely, with soapbox orators, malcontents, agitators, and
other undesirables?

IV

Another reason for the decline in interest in inequality, almost certainly,
is the drastically altered political and social position of the rich in recent
times. Broadly speaking, there are three basic benefits from wealth. First is
the satisfaction in the power with which it endows the individual. Second
is that in the physical possession of the things
which money can buy. Third is the distinction
or esteem that accrues to the rich man as the
result of his wealth. All of these returns to
wealth have been greatly circumscribed in the
last seventy-five years and in a manner which
also vastly reduces the envy or resentment of
the well-to-do or even the knowledge of their
existence.

> *"The first reason inequality has
> faded as an issue is, without
> much question, that while it has
> continued and increased, it has
> not been showing the expected
> tendency to promote violent
> reaction."*

As recently as the 1920s, the power of the
great business firm was paramount in the
United States and the firm, in turn, was the per-
sonification of the individual who headed it. Men like Morgan, the Rockefeller
executives, Hill, Harriman, and Hearst[10] had great power in the meaningful
sense of the term, which is to say that they were able to direct the actions
and command the obedience of countless other individuals.

In the last seventy-five years, the power and prestige of the United
States government have increased. If only by the process of division, this
diminished the prestige of the power accruing to private wealth. But, in
addition, it also meant some surrender of authority to Washington. Furthermore, trade unions invaded the power of the entrepreneur from another
quarter. But most important, the professional manager or executive took
away from the man of wealth the power that is implicit in running a business. Seventy-five years ago Morgan, Rockefeller, Hill, Harriman, and the
others were the undisputed masters of the business concerns they owned,

---

[10] **Morgan . . . Hearst** J. P. Morgan, John Rockefeller, James J. Hill, Edward Henry
Harriman, and Randolph Hearst were prominent names in banking, oil, the railroads,
and newspapers in the late nineteenth and early twentieth centuries.

or it was indisputably in their power to become so. Their sons and grandsons still have the wealth, but with rare exceptions the power implicit in the running of the firm has passed to professionals.[11]

When the rich were not only rich but had the power that went with active direction of corporate enterprise, it is obvious that wealth had more perquisites than now. For the same reasons, it stirred more antagonism. J. P. Morgan answered not only for his personal wealth but also for the behavior of the United States Steel Corporation which he had put together and which ultimately he controlled. As a man of corporate power, he was also exceedingly visible. Today no sins of similar corporations are visited on their owners, for the latter do not manage the company and almost no one knows who they are. When the power that went with active business direction was lost, so was the hostility.

The power that was once joined with wealth has been impaired in a more intimate way. In 1194, the crusading knight Henry of Champagne[12] paid a visit to the headquarters of the Assassins at the castle at al-Kahf on a rugged peak in the Nosairi Mountains. The Assassins, though a fanatical Moslem sect, had, in general, been on good terms with the Christians, to whom they often rendered, by arrangement, the useful service of resolving disputes by eliminating one of the disputants. Henry was sumptuously received. In one of the more impressive entertainments, a succession of the loyal members of the cult, at a word from the Sheik, expertly immolated themselves. Before, and ever since, the willing obedience of a household coterie has been a source of similar satisfaction to those able to command it. Wealth has been the most prominent device by which it has been obtained. As may indeed have been the case at al-Kahf, it has not always endeared the master to the men who rendered it.

In any case, such service requires a reservoir of adequately obedient or servile individuals. The drying up of this reservoir, no less than the loss of wealth itself, can rob wealth of its prerogatives. The increase in the security and incomes of Americans at the lower income levels has effectively reduced — indeed, for many purposes, eliminated — the servile class. And again the reciprocal is that those who no longer work for the rich (or who have done so or who fear that they might be forced to do so) no longer feel the resentment which such dependence has induced.

---

11 More precisely, to the aggregation of technical and planning talent which I have elsewhere called the technostructure. Cf. *The New Industrial State*, 2nd ed., rev. (Boston: Houghton Mifflin, 1971), Chs. VI, VII and *Economics and the Public Purpose* (Boston: Houghton Mifflin, 1973). [Galbraith's note]

12 **Henry of Champagne** (1166–1197) Eldest son of Count Henry I of Champagne and Marie of France. In 1190, he led the Third Crusade to the Holy Land.

V

The enjoyment of physical possession of things would seem to be one of the prerogatives of wealth which has been little impaired. Presumably nothing has happened to keep the man who can afford them from enjoying his Rembrandts and his home-grown orchids. But enjoyment of things has always been intimately associated with the third prerogative of wealth, which is the distinction that it confers. In a world where nearly everyone was poor, this distinction was very great. It was the natural consequence of rarity. In England, it is widely agreed, the ducal families are not uniformly superior. There is a roughly normal incidence of intelligence and stupidity, good taste and bad, and morality, immorality, homosexuality, and incest. But very few people are dukes or even duchesses, although the latter have become rather more frequent with the modern easing of the divorce laws. As a result, even though they may be intrinsically unexceptional, they are regarded with some residual awe. So it has long been with the rich. Were dukes numerous, their position would deteriorate irretrievably. As the rich have become more numerous, they have inevitably become a debased currency.

Moreover, wealth has never been a sufficient source of honor in itself. It must be advertised, and the normal medium is obtrusively expensive goods. In the latter part of the last century in the United States, this advertisement was conducted with virtuosity. Housing, equipage, female adornment, and recreation were all brought to its service. Expensiveness was keenly emphasized. "We are told now that Mr. Gould's '$500,000 yacht' has entered a certain harbor, or that Mr. Morgan has set off on a journey in his '$100,000 palace car,' or that Mr. Vanderbilt's '$2,000,000 home' is nearing completion, with its '$50,000 paintings' and its '$20,000 bronze doors.'"[13] The great houses, the great yachts, the great balls, the stables, and the expansive jewel-encrusted bosoms were all used to identify the individual as having a claim to the honors of wealth.

Such display is now passé. There was an adventitious contributing 25 cause. The American well-to-do have long been curiously sensitive to fear of expropriation — a fear which may be related to the tendency for even the mildest reformist measures to be viewed, in the conservative conventional wisdom, as the portents of revolution. The depression and especially the New Deal gave the American rich a serious fright. One consequence was to usher in a period of marked discretion in personal expenditure. Purely ostentatious outlays, especially on dwellings, yachts, and associated

---

[13] Matthew Josephson, *The Robber Barons* (New York: Harcourt, Brace, 1934), p. 330. Josephson is paraphrasing W. A. Croffut, Commodore Vanderbilt's biographer, writing in 1885. [Galbraith's note]

females, were believed likely to incite the masses to violence. They were rebuked as unwise and improper by the more discreet. It was much wiser to take on the protective coloration of the useful citizen, the industrial states-man, or even the average guy.

Understanding Ideas

1. What are some arguments for and against income redistribution that John Kenneth Galbraith presents in his essay?

2. According to Galbraith, why is inequality essential to capital formation?

3. Why does Galbraith think that "inequality has faded as an issue" (para. 16)?

4. What, in the view of Galbraith, are the prerogatives of wealth?

Responding to Ideas

1. *Research* John Kenneth Galbraith says that "few things are more evident in modern social history than the decline of interest in inequality as an economic issue" (para. 13). He had said this in an earlier edition of *The Affluent Society* and retained it in 1998. Now, two decades later, is this statement still true? Look at sources in the news and online, as well as in your library, for statements on economic inequality in contemporary society. Write an essay that updates Galbraith's thinking on this issue. If you agree with his view, explain how it can be defended and then defend it.

2. *Research* Galbraith says it is not because there has been more economic equality that economic inequality has not been a major issue in the United States. He presents statistics from 1974 that show the incomes of the highest-earning tenth of the population were fourteen times the incomes of the lowest-earning tenth. In the almost fifty years that have ensued, these numbers have changed. Consult the most recent *Statistical Abstract of the United States* for current numbers. Most recent figures will be available online at the government Web site for the U.S. Census, and comparisons over forty years are available from NPR (try searching for "income inequality"). Once you have the figures and have compared them with those from 1974, what conclusions do you draw?

3. *Analysis of Circumstances* Examine the reasons Galbraith gives for saying that inequality has faded as an issue. How many of them seem

current? He says there is no tendency to violent reaction — such as the revolution expected by the Marxists. Envy, he says, is not a factor. Emulation may be a factor. What do you think the reasons are for the lack of widespread social protest over the extreme inequalities that have recently produced so many billionaires in the United States? As far as you are concerned, is economic inequaity an issue that would stimulate you to social activism?

4. **Response** In talking about the wealth produced by great companies, Galbraith says that none of them are led by prominent men such as J. P. Morgan and John Rockefeller; he says that today we really do not know the names of those who run the companies and possess unusual power. Is that true? Can you name the important wealthy people in the nation who wield unusual power? Is there now a face to go with the wealth, as there was in the late nineteenth and early twentieth centuries? Why would that matter in making economic inequality a prominent issue? f Galbraith is right about us not knowing who runs the great companies, how does this ignorance contribute to the lack of interest in reforming economic inequality?

5. **Response** For those complaints concerning income inequality, there are a number of common reasons that continue to be important. One complaint may be described as a matter of fairness. Is it fair that the richest workers earn one hundred times more than the poorest workers? Another concern is that the wealthiest 1 percent may have more political power and influence over legislators. In that case, economic inequality becomes political inequality. Should the wealthy have more say in the nation's politics than the poor do? What other issues do you see that should worry us about income inequality? Write an essay that either defends today's version of economic inequality or attacks it. Consider the arguments that Adam Smith (p. 281) and Andrew Carnegie (p. 289) make on this subject.

6. **Analysis of Circumstances** Galbraith says that the federal income-tax structure aims at a "limited egalitarianism" (para. 9). This implies that the federal government tries to alleviate inequality. He reviews the complaints about taxation of the wealthy, such as that it destroys the incentive to work and makes it difficult to save. Examine Galbraith's comments on the tax system and the arguments for and against what Andrew Carnegie (p. 289) called a "graduated' tax on the wealthiest. Decide whether you think it is appropriate for the federal government to alleviate income inequality. Is it unconstitutional to tax the rich more than the poor? Would that be unequal treatment under the law? Should local governments levy higher taxes on large homes than they levy on medium-size homes in order to fund education?

Comparing Ideas

1. In "The Vanishing Middle Class" (p. 344), Elizabeth Warren seems to disagree with John Kenneth Galbraith that income inequality has ceased to be an issue of concern in society. What do Galbraith and Warren have in common in terms of their concerns about income inequality and the results of that inequality? In an essay that compares their thinking and their economic concerns, explain how the work of each writer helps us better understand the implications and meaning of inequality in economics today. How has their work affected your own thoughts on income inequality?

2. Both Adam Smith in "The Value of Labor" (p. 281) and Andrew Carnegie in "The Gospel of Wealth" (p. 289) accept income inequality as a matter of fact. Neither complains that a few people have immense wealth and the rest of the people are essentially poor. They even reference the Bible as accepting such distinctions as normal. Compare Galbraith's views on economic well-being with those of Smith and Carnegie. Is Galbraith satisfied with the extreme wealth that Carnegie and other late nineteenth-century industrialists enjoyed? Whose views can you most vigorously defend in your argument?

JANE
JACOBS

JANE JACOBS (1916–2006) was born in Scranton, Pennsylvania, and decided not to go to college right after high school. She was not a good student, although she was constantly reading and was intellectually curious. Instead of continuing in school, she went to New York and lived with her older sister, first in Brooklyn, then in Greenwich Village, which she found more congenial. She worked at several different jobs while writing short pieces that were taken by various publications. For more than ten years, she worked for the magazine *Architectural Digest*, which gave her a chance to write the article on New York City that led eventually to her most famous book, *The Life and Death of Great American Cities* (1961). She attacked the type of city planning that insisted on clearing away neighborhoods and setting high-rise buildings in open spaces. Her preference, largely developed while observing the streets in her Greenwich Village neighborhood, was to crowd people together to get a vibrant community.

Her studies at the Columbia School of General Studies gave her enough of a background in economics that in 1984 she extended her influence with the book *Cities and the Wealth of Nations: Principles of Economic Life*, in a nod to Adam Smith (p. 281). Like Smith, she considers the relationship between residents of the city and the countryside as critical. The city, she says, is the natural economic engine in any country, an idea that counters most economic theory, which she dismisses almost entirely. She is praised not for her knowledge of economics, but for her brilliant intuition.

Stagflation, the subject of the following essay, is defined as a stagnating economy with high inflation and high unemployment. Jacobs begins by referencing Adam Smith but goes on to consider the theories of the eighteenth-century French economist Richard Cantillon, who influenced

329

Smith and many later economists. Her review of the important earlier economic theorists includes John Stuart Mill, the nineteenth-century utilitarian philosopher, and John Maynard Keynes, the twentieth-century economist who was distinguished for helping the United States out of the Great Depression. Jacobs spends a good deal of time considering the supply-side economists, who favor increased capital investment in industry, and the opposing demand-side economists, who, like Keynes, aim at increasing demand for products as a way of stimulating the economy. Jacobs's purpose is to help readers understand why major economic theories have no explanation of stagflation or how it can be avoided.

Be sure to practice prereading techniques before a careful, annotated reading of Jacobs's essay. For a review of prereading strategies, see pages 4–9. ⊞

Stagflation

WHERE STAGFLATION has taken hold, remedies have led only to still worse unemployment as a sacrifice to the fight against inflation, or to still worse inflation as a sacrifice to the fight against unemployment. Behind this terrible dilemma is a terrible theoretical void, for rummage as we may through volumes of economic theory, we will find nothing there that acknowledges the fact of stagflation, much less tells us how to deal with it or what it means.

Cantillon's[1] line of thought was not pursued by Adam Smith,[2] who published forty-five years after Cantillon had proposed his demand-side theory of expansion. Smith was a supply-side economist. That is, he attributed economic expansion to expanding production and trade, with expanding demand as a by-product and consequence. However, unlike later supply-side economists, Smith did not draw a connection between rising prices and falling unemployment or vice versa, nor did he think of money as a factor in depressing or stimulating production.

Smith attributed general price rises solely to rulers' propensities for adulterating coinage with base metal, particularly when they wanted to finance foreign wars; or to sheer increases in the amounts of gold and silver

---

[1] **Cantillon** Richard Cantillon (1680–1734), Irish-French writer whose book *Essay on the Nature of Trade in General* (1730) is said to be one of the first studies of political economy.

[2] **Adam Smith** (1723–1790) Author of *The Wealth of Nations* and one of the founding fathers of modern economics. See page 281.

available for circulation. He thus espoused what we now think of as the government printing-press explanation of inflation. He thought of these "nominal" price changes as being superficial compared with "real" prices of goods and services. True prices, as well as real wealth, he traced to labor. Wealth, considered from every angle and in all its permutations including capital, comes from the toil and trouble, the sheer work that goes into producing it, he said. Thus labor, being the cost of everything, is the real price, "the real measure of the exchangeable value of commodities."

To be sure, said Smith, the money value of labor does fluctuate, depending on the demand for labor by producers and merchants. Where labor is in high demand — unemployment low — wages rise in spite of employers' attempts to combine to keep them down. And conversely, where labor is surplus — unemployment high — wages fall. But Smith was at pains to argue that this does not account for general price rises. He identified those as nationwide, while changes in wage rates are local, he said, owing to their cause. He cited as an example the high wages in England, the low wages in Scotland, although the two places were in the same nation, the United Kingdom, and subject alike to general price rises. In sum, Smith not only offered no explanation for a working connection between general price and unemployment levels, but denied there was a connection.

Nevertheless, one need only discount Smith's insistence that wage rates 5 are local and we have the wage theory of inflation. For if it is true that all costs derive from labor costs, and if it is also true, as it most certainly is, that wages tend to rise when unemployment falls, then the following chain of reasoning seems theoretically plausible: first, a high demand for labor; then wages rise; thus all costs rise; therefore all prices rise. This also seems, at least theoretically, to be a plausible explanation for the countermovements of the seesaw: low demand for labor; wages fall; costs fall; therefore prices fall.

The wage theory has an attractive simplicity and probably for that reason has been perennially popular. But it is too simple. It leaves too much unexplained. Most important, it does not throw any light upon why demand for labor should fluctuate in any case. This is the central problem, which all serious theorists of a price-unemployment relationship, from Cantillon on, have tried to address. The missing piece is crucial. If demand for labor is the force that makes the seesaw move, we are left with a force coming out of nowhere unless the rise and fall of demand for labor can be accounted for, too.

In analogy to the wage theory, or sometimes in association with it, are various other cost-push theories of inflation: costs rise; prices rise; therefore wages must rise; therefore costs rise further; therefore prices rise further; therefore wages rise still further; etc. While this seems plausibly to explain why inflation can spiral, it suffers from the same fatal simplicity as the unadorned wage theory itself.

John Stuart Mill,[3] in 1844, proposed that the crucial force moving the seesaw, including demand for labor, is expansion or contraction of credit advanced by lenders to producers. Mill was a supply-side economist. His ideas about credit complemented the thoughts of David Ricardo[4] in England and Jean Baptiste Say[5] in France, two of the most influential economists of the early nineteenth century. Ricardo and Say argued not only that production takes the lead in economic expansion but also that there is no practical limit to a nation's capacity to use capital productively. Mill propounded the existence of a gratuitous limit. He pointed out that if the working capital available to producers contracts, then production itself must contract, thus reducing demand for labor and, it follows, reducing consumption and demand generally, along with prices. Expansion of credit for producers would have the reverse effects. Mill, like Cantillon and unlike Adam Smith, was stressing a stimulative effect of increased money (in the form of credit), but being a supply-side economist, he reasoned out a path or avenue of stimulation different from Cantillon's.

Karl Marx,[6] whose writings on economics overlapped those of Mill, was infuriated by Ricardo and Say, and by Mill, too, insofar as ideas about credit were concerned. What charlatans! What miserable creatures; what humbug they were spreading! Marx was a demand-side economist. Demand, which he identified as need on the part of a populace, is inherently unlimited, he said, and gratuitous limits on *that* are what limit economic activity. Ricardo and Say had it all backwards with their talk about no inherent limit to uses for capital; Mill, too. It isn't producers who need money to keep economic life expanding, said Marx, but the populace. Lack of money in consumers' and would-be consumers' hands, not in producers' hands, constricts and undermines economic life.

Marx reasoned that since profits come out of the sale price of goods and services, the wage earners who produce the goods and services can't afford, in the aggregate, to buy all they produce. This inexorably leads to overproduction, he said, followed by collapse of both prices and employment. He

10

---

[3] **John Stuart Mill** (1806–1873) British utilitarian philosopher who published widely on the subject of economics. His book *The Principles of Political Economy: With Some of Their Applications to Social Philosophy* (1848) is influential on today's economists.

[4] **David Ricardo** (1722–1823) British economist who championed specialization in international trade. His major book was *On the Principles of Political Economy and Taxation* (1817).

[5] **Jean-Baptiste Say** (1767–1832) French economist, famous for Say's law: Supply creates its own demand.

[6] **Karl Marx** (1818–1883) German philosopher, economist, sociologist, journalist, and revolutionary socialist whose work in economics created the foundation for modern ideas about labor and its relation to capital. His most important work was *The Communist Manifesto* (1848).

thought the built-in discrepancy between wages and prices, by creating a demand gap, led to periodic cyclic crises of unemployment and price collapse, and must also lead before long to a final insurmountable crisis of capitalism, to be followed by socialism, which would eliminate the demand gap by eliminating private profits.

Marx's case was a complicated one to argue because, as he himself well understood, profits do not evaporate out of economic life. In part they are used for buying consumers' goods and services, especially luxuries, he noted. In part they are used for buying capital goods, such as tools, shipping, drained or cleared lands, whatever. These uses of profits all represent demand as surely as the avails of wages do. So how could a fatal demand gap arise?

The trouble, as Marx analyzed it, was largely one of proportion: the proportion of sale prices taken as profits compared to the proportion devoted to wages. He argued that capital inexorably becomes concentrated in fewer hands as time passes, and that monopolization of capital permits capitalists to take ever larger shares of income for themselves, leaving ever smaller shares for wage earners. Capitalist working forces were therefore, he thought, doomed to become increasingly exploited and impoverished. The exorbitant profits would not be used productively, as Ricardo and Say would have one believe; in fact, Marx said, they could not be used productively in view of the impoverishment of customers, the workers.

For many reasons — formation of new enterprises counteracting consolidation of older enterprises, political action, the hard but successful struggles of trade unions, the upward pressures on wages in good times, which Adam Smith had noted — the drama of an increasingly impoverished working force did not unfold in the advanced, capitalist economies of Europe and America as Marx had anticipated. Nevertheless, leaving aside his analysis of how a gap might come about and why, the thought of a gap lends itself to an elegant theoretical explanation for the price-unemployment seesaw.

If it is true that a gap in demand pushes prices down and unemployment up, which is a reasonable-sounding assumption, then the opposite must also be true (as Cantillon had already reasoned). Amplified demand must lower unemployment and push up prices. Furthermore, if unproductively used capital could create a demand gap, the idled funds need not belong to arrant profiteers, as Marx reasoned they must. They could be savings accumulated by workers who weren't being impoverished, or could be savings of both workers and owners.

With these modifications of Marxist thought, we are arriving at the 15 Keynesian theory of the seesaw. John Maynard Keynes,[7] the most influential

---

[7] **John Maynard Keynes** (1883–1946) British economist whose books include *A Treatise on Money* (1930) and *The General Theory of Employment, Interest and Money* (1936).

economist of this century, reasoned that economies undergo periods when investment becomes flaccid, even uneconomic, and yet savings accumulate nevertheless. People defer spending in favor of saving, and the savings don't pull their weight in supporting demand for capital goods or for anything else. The gap in demand leads to falling production of capital equipment, to unemployment, to falling demand for consumers' goods as unemployment increases, and so to further unemployment, to falling prices, to falling and vanishing profits, to bankruptcies, defaults, foreclosures. Savings themselves evaporate in the course of such a debacle and thus the very wherewithal for reversing and retrieving the situation is lost out of the system.

In formulating his theory, Keynes was trying to arrive at an explanation for the Great Depression of the 1930s, with the object of understanding how to combat it and prevent or minimize similar catastrophes in the future. He reasoned that a national government could step into the breach by increasing its own expenditures above and beyond the yield received from taxes. Thus he prescribed deficit financing, not for the purpose of meeting the government's own needs (which would simply have been inflationary according to the Adam Smith or the printing-press theories of inflation), but rather to meet the economy's needs. A government, in short, could deliberately undertake to correct a demand gap incapable of correcting itself. Keynes reasoned that in good times a government could return to balanced budgets. Of course Keynes well understood that more demand requires that more capital be put to work to satisfy growing demand. As a demand-side economist, however, he thought of demand leading the way, with supply following in its wake, which is one reason governments adopting Keynesian deficit financing have tended to favor spending programs and income-transfer schemes that get money into hands of consumers.

Keynes's followers, some of whom in due course became advisers to presidents and prime ministers, and many of whom became government employees throughout the Western world, aimed to use Keynesian fiscal tools responsibly and with precision as far as this could be done within the exigencies of politics. The object was to keep unemployment levels low, yet avoid excess demand — too much money chasing too few goods — which would cause inflationary price rises; the object, in sum, was to keep the seesaw in balance.

The strategy seemed to them so clear, constructive, and correct that Keynesians thought of the problem as being mainly how to refine tactics: tax manipulations, interest-rate manipulations, size and nature of public spending programs, construction of national budgets, choices of how to finance the budgets, and proper timing of whatever interventions were chosen. The Keynesians thus concentrated on creating a science of fiscal intervention — a real science, like chemistry or physics, in which one can count on precise, quantifiable interventions yielding predictable, quantifiable results.

By 1960 it seemed to Keynesians that they had in their hands instruments to serve both as intervention guides and as tables of predictable results. These instruments were known as Phillips curves in recognition of their inventor, the late A. W. H. Phillips,[8] a New Zealand electrical engineer who had become a student, and subsequently a professor, at the London School of Economics.

As an economics student in the years just after World War II, Phillips 20 learned to construct economic models, as all serious economics students did then, and still do. The models are exercises on paper — or nowadays on computer printouts — which purport to demonstrate mathematically how a given economy will behave if various of its factors change, or do not change. Studying Keynes's major work, *The General Theory of Employment, Interest and Money*, Phillips constructed a mathematical model of a Keynesian economy which struck him as looking wonderfully like a description of a hydraulic system. So he proceeded to build a physical model out of pipes, pumps, and valves. Sure enough, when pressure over here was increased, whole successions of valves opened beautifully over there. Phillips's toy enjoyed some success as a teaching device in British, American, and Australian universities (the Ford Motor Co. also acquired it) but Phillips handed the manufacturing over to a British plastics firm and returned to mathematical analyses.

Britain is a splendid mine of data, and among the treasures from the archives which researchers were digging up and putting together in the latter 1940s and 1950s was a table of changes in British price levels for the years 1858–1914, and another of production levels for the same years. Comparing the two in 1954, Phillips found that production had moved upward at times of rising prices and downward at times of falling prices: the familiar seesaw. But Phillips took the relationship a step further. He quantified the seesaw movements by analyzing — in percentages of price rise or fall and production rise or fall — precisely where each end of the seesaw stood each year, and compared the rates of percentage change. He learned that over and over again a given rate of change at one end of the board corresponded to a given rate of change at the other. A few years later he made similar comparisons, this time between unemployment rates in Britain's unionized labor force during the first half of this century, and union wage rates during the same period. In 1958 he distilled his findings into a graph (which actually looked more like a sloping line than a curve). What the graph or curve seemed to show was that any given rate of wage increase was precisely associated with a given rate of unemployment.

---

[8] **A. W. H. Phillips** (1914–1975) Economist who proposed the Phillips curve, a model that established the relationship of inflation to the unemployment rate.

Phillips himself disclaimed that his curve supplied a theory of inflation, and at least at the time he made the curve, he thought of his discovery as merely a refinement of what everybody already knew anyway. But economists trying to make a science out of managing the messy, mysterious, deplorably unpredictable behavior of the real world fell upon the curve with unbounded professional faith and joy. Specific inflation rates corresponded, it seemed, precisely with specific unemployment rates. This could logically be taken to mean that if a government wanted a given change in its national unemployment rate, most likely a reduction, the new rate desired could be gotten by arranging for a predetermined inflation rate, which in turn could be achieved by fiscal intervention; that is, by fiddling with tax and interest rates and spending programs. Conversely, if a government wanted a given inflation rate, most likely a reduction, that too could be achieved by fiscal manipulation, and the cost in jobs would be predictable, therefore could be judged as acceptable or not, and planned for.

> *"The Keynesians thus concentrated on creating a science of fiscal intervention—a real science, like chemistry or physics, in which one can count on precise, quantifiable interventions yielding predictable, quantifiable results."*

In short order, economists far and wide were making and refining their own national Phillips curves, and in schools of economics throughout the Western world, students were being taught how to construct and use them. The first curve based on U.S. data was worked out in 1960, one of its two coauthors being Paul A. Samuelson,[9] the leading American economics textbook author, and subsequently a Nobel laureate in economics. In America an unemployment rate between 3 and 4 percent was deemed to represent full employment on grounds that the slack represents people changing jobs or just entering the labor market for the first time. In Switzerland a rate of 1 percent or less is deemed full employment; differing national mores or expectations of this sort were supposed to be taken into account through the construction of Phillips curves specific to specific countries.

In America the object was to keep the unemployment level at or below a rate of 4 percent. Historically, it seemed that this was associated with an inflation rate of less than 3 percent annually. So that was the balance sought for the seesaw. In 1964, the unemployment rate moved up too high at 5.2 percent. No need to worry; the inflation rate could be taken as being too low, at

---

[9] **Paul A. Samuelson** (1915–2009) Author of one of the most famous economics textbooks of all time, *Economics: An Introductory Analysis*, which was first published in 1948. Samuelson was also the first American to win the Nobel Memorial Prize in Economic Sciences.

1.3 percent. The seesaw need only be brought into better balance through measures that could be counted on to raise the rate of inflation a bit. This was the sort of fine-tuning which had led Presidents Kennedy and Johnson to imagine that the country was entering a new era in which the business cycle was being demystified or at any rate was no longer to be feared.

But by 1967, inflation wasn't quite trading off against sufficient drops in unemployment, and from then on it became increasingly clear that it really wasn't trading off at all. At first the emerging misbehavior of the economy, and of the Phillips curves, was discounted as a temporary aberration, and every few years a new and different circumstantial reason for the misfits was seized upon: insufficient taxation for supporting the Vietnam War and then, later, rising oil prices were favorite explanations. But as early as 1971 a few Keynesians began to suspect that their faith in the curves was misplaced; by 1975, when unemployment in the United States stood at 8.5 percent and the inflation rate at 9.1 percent, most Keynesians, including Samuelson, had to concede the curves were red herrings, though they didn't know why.

Abandoning the curves went hard with Keynesian enonomists because the loss they were suffering was greater than mere loss of faith in a technique or instrument. What was being lost was confidence in Keynesian economics itself. If its prescriptions were not achieving what theory said they should, the theory itself must be suspected of underlying error, or else the economists who had been trying to put it into practice must be suspected of not having understood the theory.

As Keynesianism was succumbing to stagflation, bafflement, and dispute over what Keynes had meant anyhow, monetarists came to the fore. Monetarists are supply-side economists. Their serious theoretical grounding rests largely on the Great Depression theory of the late Irving Fisher,[10] a professor of economics at Yale University, although monetarists became known colloquially as the Chicago School because Fisher's ideas were much refined and further developed at the University of Chicago under the leadership of Milton Friedman,[11] who, like Samuelson, is a Nobel laureate in economics.

Fisher's basic idea was the same as that advanced by John Stuart Mill almost a century earlier, which had subsequently been taken up by American folk and populist economic theorists and by third-party political movements such as the post–Civil War Greenback Labor Party and the Depression-era Social Credit movements. Fisher argued that the cause of the Depression was drastic contraction of credit, owing to panic on the part of bankers who feared — with only too much reason — for the solvency of their banks. He attributed both the fear and its consequences to the fact that banks, quite

---

[10] **Irving Fisher** (1867–1947) Author of *Elementary Principles of Economics* (1913).

[11] **Milton Friedman** (1912–2006) Economist who opposed Keynesian economics. He won the Nobel Prize in Economic Sciences in 1976.

legally, are permitted to lend multiples of their own capital: multiples of the reserves they hold in cash and other assets ultimately backed by government obligations. He reasoned that the way to overcome the Depression was to expand credit to producers, and that the way to prevent similar debacles in future was to stabilize the volume of bank credit, prevent it from fluctuating wildly. To achieve this, he proposed that a government should take full responsibility for issuing all the money its nation's economy requires, instead of relying upon banks to create most of the money by leading beyond their reserves.

Banks, Fisher thought, should be required to hold full reserves against loans, in government-backed obligations. On the one hand, this would make it impossible for bankers to inflate credit above and beyond the government-mandated volume of money; on the other hand, the security conferred upon banks by their 100 percent reserves would make it unnecessary for them to contract credit fearfully, and they would have no reason to do so capriciously because not to lend up to their full reserves would only lose them income. If demand for loans was low, lower interest rates would work as an automatic correction; if high, rising interest rates would be the response. Interest rates, cost of money, would thus fluctuate according to the law of supply and demand, but volume of credit would not.

Fisher proposed further that a government should assume responsi- 30 bility for gradually and steadily increasing the volume of a nation's money at a preordained annual rate calculated to sustain steadily expanding production, but not more, in order to keep prices stable and avoid inflation. Fisher had persuasive statistical data to back up his arguments; in both good times and bad, the gross national product in the United States amounted to about three times the nation's volume of currency plus demand deposits — checking accounts — in banks. Since demand deposits trace back directly and indirectly into bank loans, Fisher said the figures proved that volume of loans determines the volume of economic activity, including rates of employment. Unlike Keynes's prescription, Fisher's were not adopted in America or elsewhere; nevertheless, under Friedman's leadership, monetarism remained alive as an intellectual force.

For many technical reasons it is difficult to define what "money" is, and this has become increasingly a problem since Fisher's time. To modern monetarists, as to Fisher, money means currency and checks actively used in commercial transactions; but statistically separating this M-1, as it is now called, from savings deposits and other forms of money has become an arcane specialty. It is a specialty of greatest importance to monetarists because the core of their theory continues to be the advisability of a steady, gradual national increase in volume of money. "When money and output grow at the same pace, demand and supply remain in balance and prices on average are stable," as one monetarist summed up the belief in 1981.

To monetarists, therefore, sporadic, remedial injections of money into an economy as prescribed by Keynesians are anathema.

After stagflation had discredited Keynesianism, the governments of Britain, the United States, Chile, and a number of other countries turned to the monetarists for counsel. They were prepared. Since stagflation is a two-headed monster, their proposed remedies were two-pronged. To attack inflation, they prescribed tight money — high interest rates — and cuts in government spending, particularly spending to support demand as opposed to spending for support of production. To attack unemployment, which they traced to insufficient investment in production, they advocated reducing tax rates, the purpose being to release funds for private investment and also to increase incentives for investing by lowering the tax bite on its rewards. Since the lower tax rates were supposed to stimulate production and employment, they were supposed to yield more government revenue than higher rates; another curve, the Laffer curve,[12] suggested that this result could be depended on.

Alas. When these prescriptions were tried in practice, the high interest rates made borrowing uneconomic for producers and bankrupted, or helped bankrupt, many. And at a time when production in reality was contracting and unemployment was soaring, lowered tax rates could not produce the desired yields and could serve only to magnify government deficits. In sum, measures contrived to fight inflation were proving ruinous to producers and their workforces, while measures contrived to help producers were enlarging government deficits. In short order, the two-headed monster had undercut the remedies of monetarists as decisively as it undercut the prescriptions of Keynesians.

> "For many technical reasons it is difficult to define what 'money' is, and this has become increasingly a problem since Fisher's time."

One might suppose that at this point the rulers of Marxist economies would have reason to gloat over the failures of capitalist theory. They could ill afford gloating, however. Stagflation was victimizing them, too. It was veiled by policies of overmanning enterprises with workers who were actually surplus, and by price subsidies which periodically had to give under the pressures of inflation. Furthermore, many Marxist economies had become heavily dependent on American, Japanese, and West European sources for capital which they weren't generating themselves and which, as time passed, it was becoming increasingly evident they were in no position to repay.

---

[12] **Laffer curve** Economic model developed by economist Arthur Laffer (b. 1940) that tracks the relationship of rates of taxation to tax revenue. This model was very popular with the Nixon and Ford administrations (1969–1977).

Small wonder the theories I have touched upon have yielded no ger- 35
mane responses to stagflation. Far from explaining what it is or what can
be done about it, from start to finish they have explained, instead, that
stagflation cannot exist! Going all the way back to Cantillon, that has been
the message. The rising prices of which Cantillon spoke were indissolubly
linked with the increased activity (reduced unemployment) of which he
also spoke. Break that link and his entire chain of reasoning disintegrates to
nothing. It is the same with the wage theory; break the link between rising
prices *and* low unemployment rates and nothing is left. So it is with Mill's
ideas on the effects of credit, and with the ideas of the later monetarists,
too; credit to producers, whether expanding or contracting, does not permit
stagflation, because it powers a seesaw. Break the seesaw and nothing is left
of the reasoning. Marx, who supposed he had so little in common with the
supply-side economists of his time, had this in common: his theory outlawed
stagflation too. Overproduction, after all, mandates *both* unemployment and
falling prices, a point Marx himself made over and over and over and over.
Remove the twin consequences of overproduction from Marx's reasoning
and his logic collapses. But leave them in and stagflation cannot be. Nor
does stagflation enter Keynesian analysis; it is impossible, as the Phillips
curves so seductively demonstrated. We comb through economic theory in
vain when we search there for enlightenment on stagflation.

The late Arthur M. Okun, who was an expert on Phillips curves and who
had served as chief economic adviser to President Lyndon Johnson, was one
of the first Keynesians to become suspicious of his science. After stagflation
had emerged he suggested half seriously and half facetiously that unemployment and inflation rates ought to be merged into one single stagflation figure,
"the economic discomfort index." His analogy was to the Weather Bureau's
summertime discomfort index, a figure that merges the humidity rate and
the temperature into one figure to help people understand why they are so
uncomfortable on muggy days. Okun was making two points. Stagflation
is economically uncomfortable, he said, no matter how you slice it analytically. That is, inflation at 10 percent, say, and unemployment at 6 percent are
not really improved by converting them to inflation at 5 percent and unemployment at 11 percent; either way, the merged rates yield an uncomfortable
16. Actually, he thought, the unemployment component contributes more
heavily to the discomfort than the inflation component, but his point was
that an improvement of the one rate at the expense of the other is illusory.
His second point was political. No matter how the economic discomfort
index is sliced analytically, a high stagflation figure plunges a democratic
government into serious trouble with its voters. Economists found Okun's
wry analogy amusing but didn't take his proposed index seriously. Mixing
apples and oranges may serve to make a political point, but keeping them
separate is supposed to be more enlightening for purposes of analysis.

However, suppose we carry Okun's analogy a little further. The reason the Weather Bureau produces a discomfort index, instead of confining itself only to separately reported factors, is that it wants to depict a condition. Just so, we can think of stagflation as a coherent condition in its own right: a condition of high prices and too little work.

Understanding Ideas

1. Why does Jane Jacobs review the theories of early economists?
2. According to Jacobs, what makes stagflation difficult to explain?
3. What seems to be the seesaw effect of wages and labor, as noted by Jacobs?
4. What is the "economic discomfort index"?

Responding to Ideas

1. *Definition* Jane Jacobs describes John Maynard Keynes as a "demand-side" economist like Cantillon. What is *demand-side econ-omy*? How does it work? Is it in favor in government today, or is it out of favor? How does increased savings among people affect demand for products? How does increased demand for products affect the wages of labor? Jacobs describes how Keynesian economic theory works. It contributed to saving the economy in the Great Depression. Would the economy improve if his theories were implemented? Check to see what economists and politicians are saying about the value of Keynes's theories today.

2. *Research* John Stuart Mill and Adam Smith (p. 281) are described as supply-side economists. In modern times, this has occasionally been dubbed "trickle-down economics." The emphasis in this theory is on supplying capital to industry to produce goods and reducing regula-tion and taxes. Explain to an audience that knows little about econom-ics what supply-side economics is and who the primary economists who champion this form of support for the economy are. After you have analyzed the theory and examined its results in practice, decide whether you champion supply-side economics or not.

3. *Analysis of Circumstances* Jacobs speaks in several places about an economic seesaw in which one aspect of the economy, such as wages, goes up when employment goes down. Study this essay carefully to

see what economic events Jacobs thinks are on each end of the see-saw. She talks about wages, unemployment, inflation, interest, and prices. What does she tell us about the interaction of these economic issues? Which elements on the seesaw are most important to you today? Which will be most important in the future? Is there evidence of Jacobs's seesaw in action now? Is current unemployment one impor-tant factor? Is the interest rate a crucial factor? Explain how you evalu-ate the current economic environment.

4. *Research* Jacobs spends a good deal of time discussing the theories of Karl Marx, a demand-side economist. Marx was author of *Das Kapi-tal (Capital)* and influenced by both Adam Smith (p. 281) and David Ricardo. Marx believed that socialism was the solution to the economic problems of any society. What does Jacobs say the problems are with Marx's theories? Be sure to research Marx's economic ideas and see if Jacobs represents them fairly. What are Marx's views on the value of labor in relation to capital? What are his views on the value of profits and the uses of capital? Jacobs calls Marx a demand-side economist, but many others describe him as a supply-side economist. Can you decide which he is?

5. *Definition* Jacobs says, "For many technical reasons it is difficult to define what 'money' is" (para. 30). Write a brief essay in which you define *money*. We use paper notes for money, but other cultures have used cowrie shells, and some American Indians used wampum. If, the-oretically, anything can be used for money, what then is money? Is gold or silver coinage more truly money than paper notes? Why is defining money such a challenging project? Once you have defined money, test yourself by having others read your essay. Did you convince your read-ers to accept your definition of money?

6. *Analysis of Circumstances* Stagflation, a stagnant economy with high unemployment and high inflation, was a description of the global econ-omy in the 1970s. Jacobs talks about it in such detail because she is looking for a theorist who could explain why it happened. Today we have moderately high unemployment and low inflation. Can the overall econ-omy today be described as productive or stagnant? How close to stag-flation is the current economy? Has unemployment depressed wages? Is there any reason to fear that stagflation will be with us again soon?

Comparing Ideas

1. Jane Jacobs offers us a survey of important economists including Adam Smith and several who have followed his ideas. Compare Adam

Smith's "The Value of Labor" (p. 281) with what Jacobs has to say about labor. Where does she differ with Smith, and on what points does she seem to be in agreement with him? What about her theory of labor either develops from what she knew about Smith's views or develops as a critique of his views? In a short essay, compare the techniques Jacobs and Smith use in their writing to explain what they know about labor and economics.

2. Jane Jacobs does not explain her political positions in relation to economics. She critiques virtually all the economists she discusses, and most of them have clear connections with the conservative, liberal, or radical politics of their time. In comparison with the ideologies revealed in the work of Adam Smith (p. 281), John Kenneth Galbraith (p. 317), and Elizabeth Warren (p. 344), where do you think Jacobs positions herself on the political spectrum? Is she conservative, liberal, or radical in her thinking? Which of those camps does she suggest is most attractive?

ELIZABETH
WARREN

ELIZABETH WARREN (b. 1949) is the senior U.S. senator from Massachusetts and a member of the Democratic Party. She was a Republican until 1995 and has voted for both parties because she feels that one should not be dominant. She was born in Oklahoma City, and when she was twelve, her father, a janitor, had a heart attack and could not work. The family was mired in debt and almost lost their house. Her mother found a job and Elizabeth waitressed in a relative's restaurant. What she saw as a child made Warren sensitive to the issues that the poor and almost poor face on a daily basis.

She went to college on a debating scholarship but suspended her studies to marry her childhood sweetheart. Eventually she returned for a degree in speech pathology at the University of Houston and taught for a short time. She spent important years raising two children, and when her husband was transferred to New Jersey she took a law degree from Rutgers University law school. After working in a firm for two years, she began teaching law at Rutgers. She taught at several other law schools, eventually becoming Leo Gottlieb Professor of Law at Harvard Law School.

Her published works range from a widely used legal textbook, *The Law of Debtors and Creditors: Text, Cases, and Problems* (2008, with Jay Westbrook), to an autobiography, *A Fighting Chance* (2014). She and her daughter, Amelia Warren Tyagi, published *The Two-Income Trap: Why Middle-Class Parents Are Going Broke* (2004), which examines some of the issues that continue to concern her as a senator. "The Vanishing Middle Class," which follows, was one of a collection of essays published in *Ending Poverty in America: How to Restore the American Dream* (2007).

One of Warren's chief concerns is the effect of debt on the middle class. Her Harvard legal research focused on bankruptcy and resulted in important studies that blamed easy credit-card debt and subprime mortgages for miring many families in long-term and damaging debt. As a result of her work, the government established the U.S. Consumer Financial Protection Bureau. Warren has also fought for a bill that would allow students to refinance the (often substantial) loans they take out to attend college.

"The Vanishing Middle Class" makes a case for a strong middle class as a healthy factor in a complex economy. Her charts tell the story visually, observing the historical shifts in the income of two-earner families versus one-earner families. She talks about the historical ratios of savings to debt and reviews the kinds of products the contemporary middle class spends its money on. It is clear from what she tells readers that the middle class in the United States is under a great deal of pressure from modern economic forces.

Be sure to practice prereading techniques before a careful, annotated reading of Warren's essay. For a review of prereading strategies, see pages 4–9. ⊞

The Vanishing Middle Class

A STRONG middle class is the best ally of the poor.

The issues of poverty are typically framed around the poor themselves — the causes of their problems and the help they need. But lifting the poor out of poverty means finding a place for them in the middle.

A middle class that is rich with opportunity opens the paths out of poverty. A middle class that is financially strong can support the programs needed to give the poor a helping hand. A middle class that is prosperous provides the model for how education and hard work pay off. And a middle class that is secure provides the kind of political stability that wards off xenophobia[1] and embraces the pluralism that is critical for the economic and social integration of the poor into mainstream America.

The best ally of the poor is a strong middle class, but America's middle class is under attack economically. Multiple forces are pushing those families closer to the financial brink. What is bad for the middle class is ultimately disastrous for the poor.

---

[1] **xenophobia** Dislike and distrust of strangers or foreigners.

MAKING IT TO THE MIDDLE

What is the middle class? Whatever it is, most Americans believe that they   5
are in it. When asked in an open-ended question to identify their class membership, more than 91.6 percent of the adult population of the United States volunteer an identification with "working" or "middle" class. Although there are people who call themselves upper class and others who call themselves lower class, these identifications are numerically somewhat rare.

Although the U.S. government has defined the poverty level, no government agency defines the middle class. One reason is that class status is not a function merely of money or other easily counted characteristics. The running joke of *The Beverly Hillbillies* was that money did not change the social class of the Clampetts. On the other side, people from "good families" who have fallen on hard times might be described as "high class," but their status is not a matter of current income.

Careful studies of the American population show that Americans determine class identification using many variables, including education, occupational status, cultural factors, lifestyle, beliefs and feelings, income, wealth, and more. Political scientists Kenneth Dolbeare and Janette Hubbell[2] assert, "Middle-class values are by definition those of the American mainstream."

This discussion is concentrated on the economic median — the numerical middle — of America. Few families hit the dead center of the economic spectrum, but there is a large group that is roughly in the middle. Even if we cannot tell precisely where the middle shifts over to the lower class or the upper class, knowing what happens to the exact middle explains a lot about what happens to America's middle class.

HIGHER INCOMES, BUT AT A PRICE

Over the past generation new economic forces have reshaped the middle class. The most profound changes have taken place in family income.

As Figure 1 shows, today's median-earning family is making a lot more   10
money than their parents did a generation ago. (Throughout this discussion all dollar figures will be adjusted for the effects of inflation.) Today the two-parent family right in the middle is earning about $66,000.

But notice that there are two lines on Figure 1. The second line shows what has happened to the wages of a fully employed male over the same time period. The answer is that the typical man working full-time, after

---

[2] **Kenneth Dolbeare and Janette Hubbell** Dolbeare (b. 1930) and Hubbell (b. 1948) are coauthors of *USA 2012: After the Middle-Class Revolution* (1995).

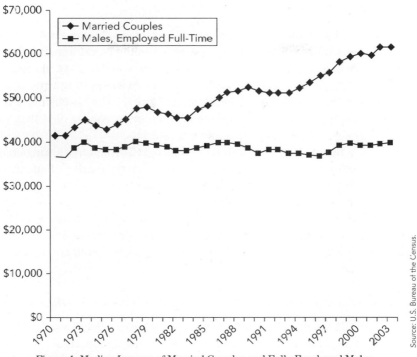

Figure 1. Median Income of Married Couples and Fully Employed Males.
1970–2004

adjusting for inflation, earns about $800 less than his father earned in the early 1970s. After decades of rising incomes earlier in the twentieth century, about thirty years ago wages for middle-class men flatlined.

How did family incomes rise? Mothers of minor children went back to work in record numbers. In the early 1970s the median family lived on one paycheck. Today the family in the middle brings home two paychecks.

The shift from one income to two has had seismic implications for families across America. It means that all the growth in family income came from adding a second earner. Among two-paycheck families median income is now $76,500, but the middle one-paycheck family now earns only $42,300. This means that one-income households — whether they are couples where one works and one stays at home or households with only one parent — have fallen sharply behind. A generation ago a one-earner family was squarely in the middle, but now that average one-earner family has slipped down the economic ladder. Over the past generation critical economic divisions within the middle class have begun to emerge.

SAVINGS AND DEBT

While not every family brought home two paychecks, by the 2000s a substantial majority of families sent both parents into the workforce. For those families, it would seem that the economic picture would be rosy. Not so.

In the early 1970s the typical one-income family was putting away about 11 percent of its take-home pay in savings (Figure 2). That family carried a mortgage, and it also carried credit cards and other revolving debt that, on average, equaled about 1.3 percent of its annual income. 15

By 2004 that picture had shifted dramatically. The national savings rate dropped below zero. Revolving debt — largely credit cards — ballooned, topping 12 percent of the average family's income.

In a single generation the family had picked up a second earner, but it had spent every dollar of that second paycheck. Worse yet, it had also spent the money it once saved, and it had borrowed more besides. By the most obvious financial measures the middle-class American family has sunk financially.

OVERCONSUMPTION — THE STANDARD STORY

There is no shortage of experts who are willing to explain exactly where the money went. The story is all about overconsumption, about families spending their money on things they do not really need. Economist Juliet

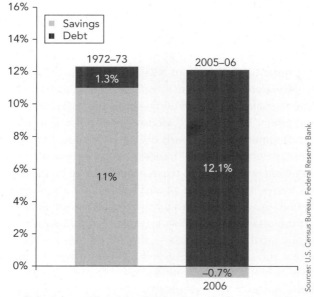

Figure 2. Savings and Revolving Debt as Percentage of Annual Income,
1972–73 to 2005–06

Schor[3] blames "the new consumerism," complete with "designer clothes, a microwave, restaurant meals, home and automobile air conditioning, and, of course, Michael Jordan's ubiquitous athletic shoes, about which children and adults both display near-obsession." Sociologist Robert Frank[4] claims that America's newfound "luxury fever" forces middle-class families "to finance their consumption increases largely by reduced savings and increased debt." John de Graaf[5] and his coauthors claim that "urge to splurge" is an affliction affecting millions of Americans who simply have no willpower. The distinction is critical: overconsumption is not about medical care or basic housing, and it is not about buying a few goodies with extra income. It is about going deep into debt to finance consumer purchases that sensible people could do without.

The beauty of the overconsumption story is that it squares neatly with many of our own intuitions. We see the malls packed with shoppers. We receive catalogs filled with outrageously expensive gadgets. We think of that overpriced summer dress that hangs in the back of the closet or those new soccer shoes gathering dust there. The conclusion seems indisputable: the "urge to splurge" is driving folks to spend, spend, spend like never before. But is it true? Deep in the recesses of federal archives is detailed information on Americans' spending patterns going back for more than a century. It is possible to analyze data about typical families from the early 1970s, carefully sorting spending categories and family size. If today's families really are blowing their paychecks on designer clothes and restaurant meals, then the expenditure data should show that they are spending more on these frivolous items than their parents did a generation earlier. But the numbers point in a very different direction.

> *"The beauty of the overconsumption story is that it squares neatly with many of our own intuitions."*

Start with clothing. Everyone talks about expensive sneakers, designer outfits, and the latest fashions. But how much more is today's typical family of four spending on clothing than the same family spent in the early 1970s? They are spending less, a whopping 32 percent less today than they spent a generation ago. The differences have to do with how people dress (fewer suits and leather shoes, more T-shirts and shorts), where they shop (more discount stores), and where the clothes are manufactured (overseas). 20

---

[3] **Juliet Schor** (b. 1955) A professor of sociology at Boston College who has a background in economics.

[4] **Robert Frank** (b. 1945) Professor of sociology at Cornell University.

[5] **John de Graaf** Executive director of Take Back Your Time, an organization that addresses time, poverty, and overwork in the United States and Canada, and author of *What's the Economy for, Anyway? Why It's Time to Stop Chasing Growth and Start Pursuing Happiness* (2011).

Compared with families a generation ago, today's median earners are down-right thrifty.

How about food? People eat out now more than ever before, and bottled water turns something that was once free into a $2 purchase. So how much more is today's family of four spending on food (including eating out) than the same family in the early 1970s? Once again, they are spending less, about 18 percent less. The reasons are that people eat differently (less meat, more pasta) and shop differently (big discount supercenters instead of corner grocery stores), and agribusiness has improved the efficiency of food production.

What about appliances? Families today have microwave ovens, espresso machines, and fancy washers and dryers. But those appliances are not putting a big dent in their pocketbooks. Today's family spends about 52 percent less each year on appliances than their counterparts of a generation ago. Today's appliances are better made and last longer, and they cost less to buy.

Cars? Surely luxury vehicles are making a difference. Not for the median family. The per car cost of owning a car (purchase, repairs, insurance, gas) was on average about 24 percent lower in 2004 than in the early 1970s.

That is not to say that middle-class families never fritter away any money. A generation ago no one had cable, big-screen televisions were a novelty reserved for the very rich, and DVD and TiVo were meaningless strings of letters. Families are spending about 23 percent more on electronics, an extra $225 annually. Computers add another $300 to the annual family budget. But the extra money spent on cable, electronics, and computers is more than offset by families' savings on major appliances and household furnishings alone.

The same balancing act holds true in other areas. The average family   25
spends more on airline travel than it did a generation ago, but it spends less on dry cleaning; more on telephone services, but less on tobacco; more on pets, but less on carpets. And, when it is all added up, increases in one category are pretty much offset by decreases in another. In other words, there seems to be about as much frivolous spending today as there was a generation ago.

WHERE DID THE MONEY GO?

Consumer expenses are down, but the big fixed expenses are up — way up. Start at home. It is fun to think about McMansions, granite countertops, and media rooms. But today's median family buys a three-bedroom, one-bath home — statistically speaking, about 6.1 rooms altogether. This is a little bigger than the 5.8 rooms the median family lived in during the early 1970s. But the price tag and the resulting mortgage payment are much bigger. In

2004 the median homeowner was forking over a mortgage payment that was 76 percent larger than a generation earlier. The family's single biggest expense — the home mortgage — had ballooned from $485 a month to $854. (Remember that all the numbers have already been adjusted for inflation.)

Increases in the cost of health insurance have also hit families hard. Today's family spends 74 percent more on health insurance than its earlier counterparts — if it is lucky enough to get it at all. Costs are so high that 48 million working-age Americans simply went without coverage in 2005.

The per car cost of transportation is down, but the total number of cars is up. Today's family has two people in the workforce, and that means two cars to get to work. Besides, with more families living in the suburbs, even a one-earner family needs a second car for the stay-at-home parent to get to the grocery store and doctor appointments. Overall transportation costs for the family of four have increased by 52 percent.

Another consequence of sending two people into the workforce is the need for child care. Because the median 1970s family had someone at home full-time, there were no child-care expenses for comparison. But today's family with one preschooler and one child in elementary school lays out an average of $1,048 a month for care for the children.

Taxes also took a bigger bite from the two-income family of 2004. 30 Because their second income is taxed on top of their first income, the average tax rate was 25 percent higher for a two-income family in 2004 than it was for a one-income family in 1972.

The ups and downs in family spending over the past generation are summarized in Figure 3. Notice that the biggest items in the family budget — the mortgage, taxes, health insurance, child care — are on the up side. The down side — food, clothing, and appliances — represents relatively smaller purchases.

Also notice that the items that went down were more flexible, the sorts of things that families could spend a little less on one month and a little more the next. If someone lost a job or if the family got hit with a big medical bill, they might squeeze back on these expenses for a while. But the items that increased were all fixed. It is not possible to sell off a bedroom or skip the health insurance payment for a couple of months. If both parents are looking for work, child-care costs will go on even during a job search.

When it is all added up, the family at the beginning of the twenty-first century has a budget that looks very different from that of its early 1970s counterpart. As Figure 4 shows, there is more income, but the relationship between income and fixed expenses has altered dramatically.

The family of the 1970s had about half its income committed to big fixed expenses. Moreover, it had a stay-at-home parent, someone who could go to work to earn extra income if something went wrong. By contrast, the family of 2004 has already put everyone to work, so there is no extra income to

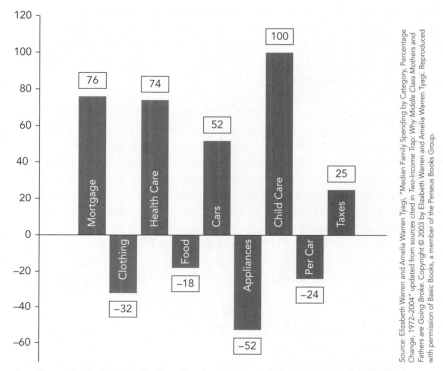

Figure 3. Median Family Spending by Category, Percentage Change, 1972–2004

Source: Elizabeth Warren and Amelia Warren Tyagi, "Median Family Spending by Category, Percentage Change, 1972–2004" updated from sources cited in *Two-Income Trap: Why Middle Class Mothers and Fathers are Going Broke*. Copyright © 2003 by Elizabeth Warren and Amelia Warren Tyagi. Reproduced with permission of Basic Books, a member of the Perseus Books Group.

draw on if trouble hits. Worse yet, even with two people in the workforce, after they pay their basic expenses, today's two-income family has less cash left over than its one-income parents had a generation ago.

NEW RISKS FOR THE MIDDLE CLASS

The numbers make it clear that the cost of being middle class is rising 35 quickly — much more quickly than wages. Many families have tried to cope by sending both parents into the workforce. But that change has helped push up costs, and it has increased the risks these families face. They now have no backup worker. Instead, they now need both parents working full-time just to make the mortgage payment and keep the health insurance. And when they need twice as many paychecks to survive, they face twice the risk that someone will get laid off or become too sick to work — and that the whole house of cards will come tumbling down.

The new two-income family faces other risks as well. In the 1970s, when a child was ill or grandma broke her hip, there was a parent at home

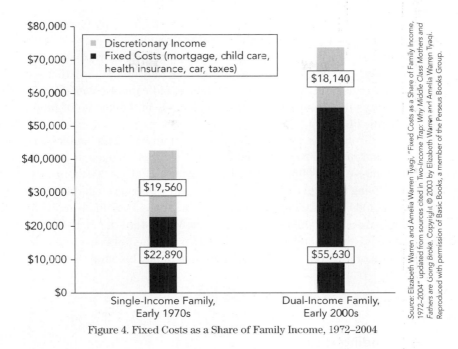

Figure 4. Fixed Costs as a Share of Family Income, 1972–2004

Source: Elizabeth Warren and Amelia Warren Tyagi, "Fixed Costs as a Share of Family Income, 1972–2004" updated from sources cited in Two-Income Trap: Why Middle Class Mothers and Fathers are Going Broke. Copyright © 2003 by Elizabeth Warren and Amelia Warren Tyagi. Reproduced with permission of Basic Books, a member of the Perseus Books Group.

full-time to deal with the needed care, to administer medications, and to drive to doctors' appointments. But someone in the family with no parent at home must take off work whenever anyone else in the family has a serious problem. As a result, problems that were once part of the ordinary bumps of life today have serious income consequences.

New risks keep multiplying. A trip to the emergency room can cost $10,000. The cost of sending a child to college is rising rapidly, while a family's ability to save continues to fall. Retirement presents another risk as generous pensions disappear and even the Social Security backup system looks shaky.

Some will read these data and conclude that one parent should just stay home. Whatever the advantages and disadvantages of that idea from a social perspective, for median earners, it is clearly a losing proposition from an economic perspective. Go back to Figure 1 and look at what a fully employed male can earn (and remember that a fully employed female will earn even less). Then look at the big, fixed expenses. Sure, the family can save on child care, and taxes will be lower, but the house payment and the health insurance stay the same, and car expenses are unlikely to drop much. That leaves the median one-income family with a 71 percent drop in discretionary income compared with a one-income family a generation ago. In other words, the two-income family can barely afford the basics, and the median one-income family is simply out of luck.

What do these data say to one-parent families? These families get the worst of both worlds. They have no partner to provide child care every day and no backup earner when something goes wrong. In those ways they look like the typical two-income family — except that they do not have that second income either. A typical one-parent household cannot cover even the basic expenses that would put that family squarely in the middle of American economic life.

It is no surprise that an increasing number of middle-class families have 40 turned to bankruptcy. From 1980 until federal law was changed in 2005, the number of households filing for bankruptcy quadrupled. By 2004 more children were living through their parents' bankruptcy than through divorce. In fact, households with children were about three times more likely to file for bankruptcy than their childless counterparts. What were the main reasons cited for these bankruptcies? About 90 percent of the families cited some combination of job loss, medical problems, and family breakup.

Understanding Ideas

1. According to Elizabeth Warren, who is in the middle class in the United States?

2. In Warren's view, how important is middle-class overspending today compared with that in 1970?

3. What does Warren say are the most important fixed expenses of people working today?

4. How, according to Warren, does debt affect the circumstances of working couples today?

Responding to Ideas

1. **Definition** Elizabeth Warren explains that there are many definitions for *middle class*. Review what she says, then offer your own definition of the middle class in the United States. Consult published definitions online and elsewhere, analyzing each to confirm its value to your own definition. Think in terms of income, housing, cultural values, moral values, and education. What other yardsticks help clarify your definition? Do you consider yourself part of "mainstream America" and, therefore, middle class? Do your friends consider themselves middle class?

2. **Response** Class is a very touchy topic in the United States. When confronted with demands to tax the rich, some politicians complain that

bending to such demands will invite class warfare. What is the current situation in the United States regarding class stratification? How many social classes do you think are identifiable in today's society? What makes them distinct from one another? In a brief essay, explain to an audience that does not believe there are social classes in our modern culture what it is that distinguishes the various classes that people occupy. Why is the idea of class so repugnant to so many people?

3. **Response** Warren begins her essay by saying, "A strong middle class is the best ally of the poor." Has Warren convinced you that this is true? Why does she think the middle class helps the poor? What is the alternative to having a middle class? Do you think it possible that our middle class will either disappear or become so minimized as to be inconsequential? Today, many politicians and economists say that the middle class is under threat, but why would they worry about that? If there were no middle class, would the nation be worse off? Write a brief essay reflecting on these questions. Or, write a brief essay describing what our society would be like without a middle class.

4. **Analysis of Circumstances** What do you think is the best avenue for a young person today to become part of the middle class? Or, if a young person is already in the middle class, what is the best way for him or her to stay there? Currently, there are widespread complaints that the old American ideal of a future in which children do better than their parents is no longer likely. Judging from your experience, the experiences of people you talk with, and comments in the news and online, how likely is it that most young people will do better financially than their parents? How important is it that young people achieve more than their parents did?

5. **Response** Education is said to be the most important factor in helping a young person achieve a stable financial future. Yet today many college graduates are working at jobs that do not absolutely need a college degree. If that is true, why should people borrow or spend large sums to go to college? What educational choices should people make in college today to help establish themselves in the middle class? How much education should you aim for? What is it about getting a college education, apart from the possibility of making more money, that establishes someone in the middle class? What is the real value of such an education?

6. **Analysis of Circumstances** After reading all the statistics and analyses of the current economic realities affecting the middle class, what is your expectation for its continued survival? Warren implies that those who are now middle class are not overspending, not refusing to work, and not doing anything to make it more difficult for them to be middle

class. If that is true — and be sure to examine that argument and decide if it is — then what can the government do to help the middle class stay strong and healthy in our economy? What should the government not do? How much power do you think the government has to support any social class?

Comparing Ideas

1. How important is the existence of a middle class to a democracy? Compare what Elizabeth Warren has to say about the nature of contemporary economics with what Robert A. Dahl says in "Why Democracy?" (p. 96). Dahl talks about prosperity as one benefit of living in a democracy. Does Warren agree with him? Given what Dahl tells us about democracies, explain why he might be concerned for the continued existence of our democracy if there is no longer a strong middle class in the United States. In your essay, explain where your personal sympathies lie in terms of democracy's link with the middle class. Remember that from the 1700s to the early 1900s American democracy had little or no economic middle class as we know it.

2. In a brief essay, explain why the continued existence of a strong middle class in the United States is a question not just of economics but of justice. Consider Adam Smith's "The Value of Labor" (p. 281) and John Rawls's "A Theory of Justice" (p. 159). Examine Rawls's argument concerning how a just society must work. Rawls discards the utilitarian view that espouses the greatest good for the greatest number — a view that Smith might support. Instead, he focuses on justice for the individual rather than for the social group. How do these writers help Warren's argument for supporting a strong middle class?

LESLIE T. CHANG

Leslie T. Chang

LESLIE T. CHANG (b. 1969) was born near New York City to immigrant parents who insisted on her attending Saturday Chinese school, for which she later became grateful. Raised in an educated family — her father was a physicist specializing in solid-state electronics — she took a degree in American history and literature at Harvard University in 1991. For several years, she lived in China writing for *The Wall Street Journal,* covering how social changes in China affected local and national people and governments. Her articles have appeared in *National Geographic, The New Yorker,* and other magazines. Chang's husband, Peter Hessler, has also written books about China. They live abroad with their twin daughters for Hessler's work, covering the Middle East for *The New Yorker.*

Chang's book *Factory Girls: From Village to City in a Changing China* (2008) won the 2009 PEN USA Literary Award for Research Nonfiction and has been translated into ten languages. When Chang worked in China, her research helped her meet workers and get to know their families and their ambitions. She tells their stories in a way that makes us understand what their experiences have been like. The changes in China since the 1970s have been incredible. Huge factories sprouted up almost overnight, and some are so big they resemble cities. with their own theaters, shopping malls, and even hospitals.

Chinese factory workers often toil for owners in Hong Kong and even for owners in Taiwan, the island nation just off the coast of China. Taiwan is known for computers and other electronics, but it is a nation that has been at war with mainland China since 1949, although there has been no armed conflict in recent years. Hong Kong was a British colony from 1856 to 1997, and as a special economic zone today. it enjoys some independence from Beijing.

The migration of Chinese villagers — mostly young women — has involved almost 150 million people moving from villages, in which their families were often farmers, to cities that are immense by Western standards. Dongguan is a province with a rich history and is now one of the centers in which factories dominate the daily life of every inhabitant. It is in cities such as Dongguan that China manufactures televisions, computers, smart phones, and virtually every product that Westerners buy and at prices much lower than if they were made in the West.

Chang gives readers an inside look at how the young women who work in those factories live. She helps readers understand that while we focus on the ability of China to produce the goods we want at lower prices, there are costs that Chinese individuals must pay for the work that they do.

Be sure to practice prereading techniques before a careful, annotated reading of Chang's essay. For a review of prereading strategies, see pages 4–9. ⊞

Factory Girls in Dongguan

I, TOO, had left home. After graduating from college in America, I moved to Prague, Czechoslovakia. Altogether I lived abroad for fifteen years, going home to see my family once every couple of years, as the migrants did. For a long time I resisted the pull of China. In college, I avoided Chinese American organizations and took only one Chinese-language class; I majored in American history and literature and wrote my undergraduate thesis on Larry McMurtry's novels of the American West. In Prague, I reported on Czech politics and society for an expatriate newspaper. One winter day in 1992, a Chinese couple dragging their suitcases along the slushy sidewalk asked me for directions in Mandarin. I waited a long moment before answering, resentfully, in their language — as if they were forcing me back into a world I had already left behind.

Initially, China's appeal for me was pragmatic — in the early 1990s, its booming economy began to attract global attention, and my fluency in Chinese suddenly became an asset. I went to Hong Kong in 1993 to work as a reporter for the *Wall Street Journal* and began to read books on Chinese history for the first time, eventually to the exclusion of everything else; to me, China has always felt like the test I neglected to study for. When I moved to Taiwan two years later, people there frequently asked me what year I had *chuqu*, gone out, to America — their unspoken assumption that everyone in the world had been born in the Chinese nation. Later after I moved to China,

I often heard the same question. That was one of the ways that Taiwan and China, which until recently had been technically at war, were more alike than they imagined.

One of the first things most Chinese Americans do when they go to China is to visit their ancestral hometowns, but for twelve years I lived in Hong Kong, Taiwan, and China without making the journey. I worried that I wasn't ready to understand what I would find in my family village; secretly, I was afraid it would mean nothing at all. Either way, I understood the factory girls when they spoke of their complicated feelings for home.

Young women from the countryside taught me the city. From them I learned which factories were well run; without ever leaving Dongguan, these workers had figured out the global hierarchy of nations. American and European bosses treated workers best, followed by Japanese, Korean, Hong Kong, and then Taiwanese factory owners. Domestic Chinese factories were the worst, because "they always go bankrupt," one migrant explained to me. They also knew when major policies were about to change — in early 2005, some workers told me that the minimum wage would rise, before it was officially announced.

Many things I had read about China's migrants were not true. They no 5 longer lived in fear of being picked up by the police; instead, the authorities just ignored them. Discrimination from local residents was not really an issue, because migrants almost never encountered locals. And I was surprised to learn that job mobility was high. Almost all the senior people I met in factories had started on the assembly line. The young women I knew did not appear destined to return to the farm because they had never farmed before. They often did not know how much land their family had or when the planting season began. My assumptions had come from studies of Chinese migrant workers done in the mid-1990s: almost a decade later, this world had utterly changed, but things were happening too quickly to be written down.

I came to like Dongguan, which seemed a perverse expression of China at its most extreme. Materialism, environmental ruin, corruption, traffic, pollution, noise, prostitution, bad driving, short-term thinking, stress, striving, and chaos: if you could make it here, you'd make it anywhere. I tried to fit in as much as I could. I ate twenty-five-cent bowls of noodles for lunch and took buses everywhere. I dressed, in jeans and sandals, more plainly than many migrant girls who wore embroidered shirts and high heels when they went out. I was invisible in Dongguan, and I liked that too. In other places in China, a person staring at strangers and writing things in a notebook might attract attention; here, people were too focused on their own affairs to notice me. Only once did someone interfere: I was in the talent market, copying down instructions from a sign on the wall. A guard asked me what I was doing. I told him I was practicing my English, and he left me alone.

Dongguan is invisible to the outside world. Most of my friends in Beijing had passed through the city but all they remembered — with a shudder — were the endless factories and the prostitutes. I had stumbled on this secret world, one that I shared with seven million, or eight million, or maybe ten million other people. Living in Dongguan was like arriving in it for the first time, hurtling down the highway at seventy miles an hour, the scenery changing too fast to keep track of it. Dongguan was a place without memory.

Dongguan was also a city of contradictions, because modern Chinese history had begun here. During the nineteenth century, British smuggling of opium into China devastated the country and drained the treasury. In the summer of 1839, a Qing Dynasty imperial commissioner named Lin Zexu ordered the public incineration of twenty thousand cases of opium in the harbor at Humen, a town in Dongguan. That act set the two nations on course for the First Opium War, which was fought in Guangdong Province and ended quickly when British warships overwhelmed Chinese forces. The Treaty of Nanking ceded Hong Kong to Britain, forced open Chinese ports to international trade, and gave foreign nations unprecedented commercial and legal privileges within China. In the history that is taught in Chinese classrooms, the burning of opium in Humen ignited the modern era: the subjugation to foreign powers, followed by the collapse of the Qing Dynasty, revolution, war, and the Communist victory in 1949.

But there was another history of this place. In the autumn of 1978, the Taiping Handbag Factory of Hong Kong opened the first foreign factory in Dongguan. Income in its first year of operation was one million Hong Kong dollars. The factory processed materials from Hong Kong into finished goods, which were shipped back to Hong Kong to be sold to the world. It established the model for thousands of factories to follow. Over the next two years, China set up four "special economic zones" as testing grounds for free-enterprise practices like foreign investment and tax incentives. The largest zone was Shenzhen, about fifty miles south of Dongguan, which quickly became a symbol of a freewheeling China always open for business. Shenzhen was a planned showcase city, willed into being by leaders in Beijing and supported by government ministries and the companies under them.

Dongguan was different. It rose by no one's decree; it simply grew. 10 While Shenzhen aspired to advanced technology and innovation, Dongguan took what it could get, which meant low-tech factories from Hong Kong and Taiwan that made clothing, toys, and shoes. All they needed was cheap land and labor, as well as local officials who left them alone. What they initially built could not be called modern industry. Many of the early factories were two- or three-story houses where workers sat at desks, fifty to a room, engaged in simple tasks like sewing cloth for a stuffed animal or attaching artificial hair to a doll. Some of the factories were housed in makeshift structures of sheet metal because their owners did not want the expense of real buildings.

In the early days, there was no train service from Hong Kong. Businessmen traveled to the British colony's border with Shenzhen, crossed on foot, and caught a taxi to their Dongguan factory on the other side, passing farms on the way. "There were no roads around here, no cars, no TVs, not even curtains," recalled Allen Lee, a Taiwan shoe industry executive who moved to the city in 1989. "You couldn't buy stuff like that here." In June 1989, he bicycled forty minutes to watch the news on TV about the shooting of protesters around Tiananmen Square.

The local labor supply was soon exhausted and migrants began arriving from neighboring provinces. Lin Xue, the woman I knew who wrote for a migrant magazine, had come to Dongguan from rural Sichuan in 1990. "We came here blind," she told me. "I would go to someone selling tickets and ask, 'Where should I buy a ticket to?' and we would do what they said." Lin Xue got a factory job that paid seventy yuan a month, and her younger sister pressed plywood in a lumber factory.

In the 1990s, the city's manufacturing shifted to electronics and computer parts. Today Dongguan makes 40 percent of the world's magnetic heads used in personal computers and 30 percent of its disk drives. Economic growth over the past two decades has averaged more than 15 percent a year. Some things have not changed. The migrants are still arriving. Labor-intensive factories still dominate, and though their products have gotten more sophisticated, the work itself has not. There are still a great many apartment buildings where workers sit at desks engaged in simple tasks with their hands.

So Dongguan was a place with conflicting versions of its past — one a high-profile rejection of the foreign presence in China, the other stealthy embrace of it. Every Chinese schoolchild learns about the burning of opium. But from the Taiping Handbag Factory, which did not appear in any textbook, I could trace a direct line to everyone I ever met in Dongguan, from the migrants studying Microsoft Word to the self-help gurus to the Mercedes salesman who told me that the priciest S- and E-Class cars sold best in Dongguan because "for a boss to improve his image, this is a good product." For all of them, modern history began with the handbag factory.

I went for months without meeting a native of Dongguan. The world of 15 the factory, from the top managers to the assembly line, was the exclusive domain of migrants, though the top boss was sometimes from Hong Kong or

Taiwan. Local residents spoke the Cantonese dialect, but the factory world functioned in the official dialect of Mandarin, because that was the only way people from different provinces could talk to one another. Migrants held the local residents in low regard: they were uneducated farmers who made a living renting out farmland to factories, and they could not survive a day in the factory's demanding environment. "It's mutual contempt," my friend Lin Xue said, to describe relations between locals and migrants.

"Labor-intensive factories still dominate, and though their products have gotten more sophisticated, the work itself has not."

Six months after I started coming to Dongguan, I interviewed the deputy mayor. His name was Zhang Shunguang and he was a Dongguan native: my first. We sat in a big reception room in a city government building and drank tea out of tiny paper cups. Several of his assistants gathered, speaking to one another in Cantonese. I had never met a Dongguan person and here they all were, inside the government.

"Do you speak Cantonese?" one assistant asked me.

"Sorry, no," I said. No one in the city had ever asked me this question before.

"Is this your first time in Dongguan?"

"No, I've been here many times."

20

"Oh, were they all secret trips?"

"Is it a secret if you don't know about it?"

We already disliked each other. In the middle of the interview, I looked over at the assistant and he stared blankly back at me. The young woman next to him had fallen asleep. The phrase *mutual contempt* popped into my mind.

The interview was useful: without seeing for myself, I never would have believed how completely the government ignored the migrants. The deputy mayor did not have an accurate count of the migrant population — that was up to the national census, not his department. He admitted that the local government lacked the resources to check conditions in the factories. "If I inspected one factory a day," he said, "it would take me fifty years to inspect all the factories. So we must rely on the companies to police themselves."

The deputy mayor then talked of a plan to "lift the quality of the Dong- 25 guan people," but the effort excluded those who were not native born. Like all city people, he had a reflexive contempt for *waidiren*, outsiders, the common term for migrants. "The quality of migrant workers is not high," he said, "but this is the responsibility of the companies. They should be running classes for workers."

I asked the deputy mayor why there were no Dongguan people in the factories, even at the highest levels, and he contradicted what he had just said without missing a beat.

"The people from outside," he said, "have higher quality and lower wages."

After the interview, the deputy mayor shook my hand and praised my knowledge of the city. I didn't tell him my informants were all teenage girls — migrants of low quality and even lower wages.

After a year of visiting the city, I rented a one-bedroom apartment downtown for $160 a month. The high-rise complex was called Dongguan City Holiday, and it targeted single women; hot-pink billboards around town advertised ONE PERSON'S HOUSE, ONE PERSON'S SPLENDOR. I thought I would meet young women and hear their stories, but no one ever said a word to me in the lobbies and elevators, and I never saw a single person in the common room. People were too busy with their own lives to bother with anyone else's. I got most of my news from the bulletin boards in the apartment complex, which portrayed a community of petty crime and round-the-clock construction.

FOR THE PEACE OF RESIDENTS, RENOVATION WILL
STOP ON JANUARY 1. IT WILL RESUME ON JANUARY 2.

WHEN A PERSON KNOCKS ON YOUR DOOR, DO NOT
CASUALLY OPEN IT UNTIL YOU HAVE
CONFIRMED THE PERSON'S IDENTITY.

ANYONE WITH INFORMATION ABOUT THE
THEFT RING IN THE NANCHENG AREA SHOULD CONTACT
THE POLICE.

My landlady had moved to the city years before from rural Guangdong.   30
She often showed up at my apartment in pink pajamas and house slippers to collect the rent, and I once heard her say "Fuck your mother" on the phone to her husband because he had just told her he was returning late from a business trip. She worked the night shift at a hotel, doing sales. I wondered what kind of sales had to be done between midnight and six o'clock in the morning, but I never found the courage to ask. My landlady had a way of deflecting questions.

"How did you have two children?" I asked her once. Most urban families were limited to one.

"How do you think I had two children?" she answered.

The retail environment outside my apartment was in constant flux. On the day I moved in, I was excited to see a BRICK OVEN PIZZA sign beside the entrance to my building, a welcome taste of home. By my next visit, that had morphed into the GREAT AMBITIONS MOBILE PHONE DIGITAL SUPERMARKET. Just what China needed: another store selling mobile phones. Over the following two weeks, the space below my apartment transformed from an empty shell with cables dangling from the ceiling into a full-on mobile-phone store, with robotic salespeople and music blasting from giant speakers into an empty parking lot. On my next stay, marketing had begun, in the form of a young woman who stood at the store entrance and read phone model numbers and prices into a microphone, one after another. Another sign had materialized in front of my building: HAVE KFC AS YOUR NEIGHBOR! EARN 8% ANNUAL INTEREST WITHOUT DOING ANYTHING. I wasn't thrilled to have KFC as my neighbor. The only constant in the neighborhood was the Nescafé plant across the street. On summer days, the smell of coffee enveloped me as soon as I walked outside, a warm bath at once sweet and bitter.

When you lived in Beijing, you were shielded from many things, but in the hinterland cities you could see the strains of China's development up close. Public buses often diverged from their routes to fill up on gas; fuel shortages were common, so an open station was worth a stop even with a load of passengers. Full-day power stoppages were regular events, and factories had to juggle their production schedules because of government rationing. Among the notices on my apartment bulletin board was one that never varied: THE ORIGINAL POWER SUPPLY TRUNK LINE CANNOT KEEP UP WITH THE NEEDS OF DEVELOPMENT AND MUST BE CHANGED.

During the summer of 2005, the power went off for at least one day 35 on each of my trips to Dongguan. With some advance notice I could plan ahead, but sometimes the power went dead without warning, consigning me to a day indoors in ninety-degree heat and as little movement as possible. I would call the building's management office, fuming, but it was not their fault. It was not anyone's fault. China's economy was growing by 10 percent a year, faster in the south, and it was a miracle that things were holding together as well as they were.

Understanding Ideas

1. According to Leslie T. Chang, what kind of job mobility do factory workers have?

2. What are the problems caused by migration into Dongguan that Chang mentions in her essay?

3. What was Chang's early expectation of life in China?

4. Why, according to Chang, is Dongguan a city of contradictions?

Responding to Ideas

1. *Research* The burning of twenty thousand cases of opium in Humen — a town in Dongguan — in 1839 sounds similar to the throwing of cases of tea into Boston Harbor in 1773. A few years after the Boston Tea Party, the British were at war with the American colonies. In China, the British went to war with the Chinese at Dongguan Province — during the infamous Opium Wars. Research each of these events and compare their political motives. Which of these events was more deeply rooted in economic issues? Which has had a more lasting effect?

2. *Analysis of Circumstances* Write a brief essay in which you attempt to establish what the accelerated growth of factories in Dongguan Province has caused in terms of changes in the way of life of the young women who have moved there to work. Compare them, insofar as you can, with the young women who go to work from either high school or college in developed countries in the West. What are the differences in their expectations? What happens to the outlook of workers in the great Chinese factories? What kinds of jobs are available to high school graduates in your town? What differences in economic expectation do you see in residents in Dongguan and residents where you live?

3. *Response* One of the constant complaints made in the United States is that the workers in China have taken jobs away from Americans. Assuming that large factories could be constructed in your town or state and that enough young women could be found to work for low wages in order to keep prices low, would you vote to have such factories built? Write a brief essay in which you take a stand on whether you want to bring back low-wage jobs on a very large scale to the United States or Canada given what Chang has written about the nature of factory work in China. Remember that in order to bring manufacturing back to the United States or Canada we would need to build factories.

4. *Response* If you ever worked in a factory — or if you can interview people who work or have worked in factories — describe the nature of the work and the spirit of the workers. What kinds of factories exist in your immediate neighborhood? What factories are operating in your state or major city? Do they bear any resemblance to the factories that Chang describes? Do you or your classmates want to work in factories either here or abroad? Why? How has Chang affected your attitude about factory work and factory workers?

5. *Analysis of Circumstances* Chang tells us that the local inhabitants of Dongguan considered the migrants "hicks" from the country. They thought them unintelligent and uneducated. The deputy mayor and the local government officials had conflicting attitudes, but they were

generally contemptuous of migrants who came from the country. On the other hand, the migrants were contemptuous of the locals who often lived off the workers' rent money and "could not survive a day in the factory's demanding environment" (para. 15). How close are these attitudes to those in the West with regard to immigrants who take low-level jobs? In what ways does Chang's essay act to sensitize Westerners to problems in their own countries? How has your view of immigration been changed by Chang's essay?

6. **Analysis of Circumstances** Examine Chang's observations of factory life in China in terms of class and class structure. Is there a middle class in Dongguan? Who belongs to it in her essay? Does there seem to be an awareness of class differences? If there is, how is it expressed? What is implied by the fact that Chang hardly worries about the existence or lack of existence of a middle class? How would a middle class make life better for the average factory worker? In view of what Chang has told us, do you think that Dongguan would be happier with a middle class, or would there be dissension in the society?

Comparing Ideas

1. Compare the conditions of the factory girls in Dongguan with the conditions of the women Charlotte Perkins Gilman describes in "Women and Economics: 'Cupid-in-the-Kitchen'" (p. 303). What issues are raised by Gilman that are also discussed or implied in Leslie T. Chang's discussion of the life of factory girls in China? Are the circumstances of factory girls in China a distinct improvement over the conditions and circumstances of women in Gilman's New England?

2. Adam Smith understands the value of labor in his essay (p. 281). How might he have used the information that Chang provides in her discussion to interpret the value factory girls bring to Dongguan? Would he feel that the girls were being valued in the community as they should be? How would he have interpreted the relationship between management and labor in Dongguan? How valuable are Smith's ideas about labor to your understanding of the circumstances of the factory girls Chang describes?

CHAPTER SEVEN

How Ethics and Morality Interact

ARISTOTLE 374

FRIEDRICH NIETZSCHE 393

JOHN DEWEY 400

THOMAS NAGEL 406

MICHAEL GAZZANIGA 414

PETER SINGER AND JIM MASON 430

FRANCIS FUKUYAMA 440

KWAME ANTHONY APPIAH 447

"Happiness is a certain activity of the soul in accordance with perfect virtue."   — ARISTOTLE

"Morality is a subject that interests us above all others: we fancy the peace of society to be at stake in every decision concerning it."   — DAVID HUME

"Democracy and the one, ultimate, ethical ideal of humanity are to my mind synonymous."
— JOHN DEWEY

"You will never be happy if you continue to search for what happiness consists of. You will never live if you are looking for the meaning of life."   — ALBERT CAMUS

"The ethical decision is always the fearsome decision. When something matters enough that we are afraid of the consequences — afraid that even the honorable choice could result in harm or loss or sorrow — that's when ethics are involved."   — HENRY W. BLOCH

"So far, about morals, I know only that what is moral is what you feel good after and what is immoral is what you feel bad after."
— ERNEST HEMINGWAY

"All I'm trying to say is, our world hinges on moral foundations."
— MARTIN LUTHER KING JR.

INTRODUCTION

Philosophy and religion have focused on moral and ethical behavior in part because society cannot function without a sense of morality and people cannot interact peacefully and prosperously without a clear view of ethics.

Religions have set standards in a very general sense, as in the Ten Commandments of the Old Testament. In ancient Greece, philosophy saw the need for a virtuous life to promote what Aristotle called happiness. For Aristotle, ethical and moral behavior — the virtuous life — produced happiness because a vicious life produced only a dispirited and painful life.

While modern industrial societies have explored the issues of ethics and morality in ways that clarify the complexities of behavior that may or may not be moral or ethical, most thinkers look first to Aristotle's (384–322 B.C.E.) *Nichomachean Ethics*, the book he wrote for his son, Nichomachus. In "The Aim of Man," Aristotle considers what must be thought of as the highest good that anyone can aspire to. After some reflection and consideration, he tells us that the highest good for humankind is happiness. He does not mean a temporary state of mind but rather a lasting sense that informs a lifetime. To achieve that state, he urges people to live a life of virtue in which good behavior dominates and one's moral position is firm. Good behavior is needed to achieve the highest good.

Friedrich Nietzsche (1844–1900), a nineteenth-century philosopher and child of a family of ministers, attempts to detach morality from religion. When Aristotle discusses virtue, he does not refer to any divinity, and Nietzsche, the philosopher who said "God is dead," is also talking about ethics and morality with no reference to a divinity. For Nietzsche, the work of modern people was the fashioning of a system of morality that was independent of religion. The concept of *good* and *bad*, he wrote, may be nothing more than a system of belief imposed on the lower classes by the ruling elite of past centuries. What Nietzsche feared was that modern people would fall into despair without religion (which he felt was disappearing in society) to guide them. They would need great strength, he felt, to create a moral system that could guide them.

One of America's most influential philosophers of education, John Dewey (1859–1952) connected the education of the individual with the health of a democracy. As a pragmatist — that is, one who looks closely at the practical side of all actions and the usefulness of the results of those actions — he saw that the individual in a democracy has a moral obligation to seek as much education as possible. Society, he says, is benefited in many ways by education, for "[t]he heart of the sociality of man is in education" (para. 3). What he means by that statement is that education is what supports the conversation of people in every social situation and, the better the education, the fuller the understanding of the people, one to another. Dewey is one of the few philosophers who addresses a specific activity of society and explores its moral implications.

Thomas Nagel (b. 1937) has much to say about the possibility that evolution is not dominated by chance and accident but is, by design, destined to produce consciousness in animals and in ourselves. Our consciousness formulates moral rules, many of which Nagel says are questionable. In looking for an objective basis for morality — the absolutes that we base our moral views on — Nagel questions the kinds of behavior that society rules as wrong. What makes them wrong besides our decision to deem them wrong? This seems to be a fairly basic concept, but Nagel shows us the underlying complexity that most of us never think about. He explores the concept of fairness and unfairness as a basis for morality, just as he explores religious teachings about morality and sees them as inconclusive. By considering ethics as an objective, rather than as a personal and subjective, concept, Nagel forces us to examine our own understanding of right and wrong.

Because he is a scientist of brain activity, Michael Gazzaniga (b. 1939) asks a difficult question: Is the brain hardwired for moral behavior? One of the reasons he can ask this question is that he has observed mental activity in brain scans and has seen that portions of the brain involved in similar thinking light up very much the same way in many different people. There is then a possibility that evolution built in certain tendencies toward altruistic behavior as a means of helping our species survive by aiding social cooperation. This in turn implies the need for ethical behavior to make society function healthily. But it is also likely that our tendency to violence is a product of evolution. Therefore, our way of dealing with our impulse for violent behavior is through self-control. As Gazzaniga tells us, ethical behavior begins with self-control.

Peter Singer (b. 1946) argues that we are largely guilty of *speciesism*, an attitude toward all other species that resembles racism, sexism, or ageism. Singer, along with his coauthor Jim Mason (b. 1934), does not contend that other animals have rights in the sense that humans do but insists that animals should never be treated cruelly. Singer is a widely published ethicist whose positions on highly controversial issues, such as abortion, have drawn fire from churches and other institutions. His views are informed by the utilitarian idea that we must do all we can to produce happiness and avoid pain. Together, Singer and Mason argue strongly against factory farming because it treats animals inhumanely by restricting their living space and limiting their movement. They try to convince readers that humans must treat other animals in an ethical fashion, just as we treat ourselves.

Although he is primarily a political scientist, Francis Fukuyama (b. 1952) has a wide-ranging interest in biotechnology, which he feels is currently a threat to humanity. He begins the essay from which the excerpt in this chapter comes with a discussion of geneticists who promise designer babies, which Fukuyama fears will add to the world's inequality. Moreover, he fears that we will be producing monsters rather than human people. In the discussion included in this chapter, he talks about the qualities of animals and what rights, if any, they have. In response to Peter Singer's charge of *species-ism*, or the idea that humans deserve greater moral rights than nonhumans, Fukuyama describes what he calls species-specific behavior and tells us why it is important to respect behavior that is natural to other species. By doing so, he assures us that we will be better able to behave ethically toward other animals.

Kwame Anthony Appiah (b. 1954), in "If You're Happy and You Know It," talks about the subjective conception of happiness and wonders whether it is a feeling or something else. He begins by taking issue with Aristotle's word *eudaimonia*, which is ordinarily translated as *happiness*. Appiah is not sure this is the best translation because he feels Aristotle means something beyond just feeling happy. He goes on to talk about the standards that people might set themselves to aim for happiness. Appiah says that when these standards are very low they cannot be well regarded as producing happiness. Aristotle's concept of virtue, central to his ideas about happiness, is also of considerable importance to Appiah, who says that those who get pleasure from giving others pain cannot be said to be happy. If the greatest good is not what we aim for or what we feel we have achieved for ourselves, then we cannot expect to be happy.

SEEING IDEAS

Generally, we think of ethics as the rules of behavior that guide us in social interaction, as in developing an ethical position in business or determining an ethical approach in medicine. Ethics consist of decisions that benefit society and fit our place in society. Morals often cross over into ethics and

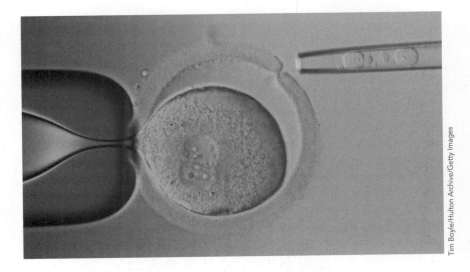

Tim Boyle/Hulton Archive/Getty Images

are sometimes indistinguishable. However, we usually think of morals more as guiding our own personal choices. Morals arise from beliefs and are sometimes (but not always) associated with religious beliefs. For example, a belief in the value of life or proper sexual behavior will usually be thought of as stemming from morals rather than ethics.

The photograph above shows a close-up microscopic image of an embryo being altered at the Reproductive Genetics Institute's Chicago laboratory. Cell manipulation and transplantation procedures such as this one raise both ethical and moral concerns. Ethically, such procedures make us wonder how such a procedure satisfies modern medical ethics and how such procedures may affect our society long-term. Further, the morality of the issue calls into question what we believe about the nature of life itself. Is it moral to alter life by such unnatural means? This procedure to alter an embryo has become more commonplace since this photo was taken in 2000 and will continue to be performed, but who is to decide the ethical or moral limits of this kind of work?

Our ethical responsibility to animals is also of great concern to people all over the world. The photograph on the following page is from a 2012 protest in India against the eating of animals and is hard to forget because the life-size plate does not have a piece of chicken or a steak on it, but a human being. The woman on the plate implies a moral question: How much do we value life? We value human life from a moral point of view. Why not, then, value all animal life from a moral position? Those who do often follow a vegan diet. But are those who eat meat behaving immorally? Peter Singer and Jim Mason, as you will read in this chapter, accuse such people of

"speciesism," and Francis Fukuyama talks about our ethical responsibility to animals, including those we intend to eat.

All the thinkers in this chapter are ultimately addressing the question of what kind of behavior produces satisfaction with life and can be described as happiness. The connection between happiness and moral behavior and ethical standards is a concept that may have begun with Aristotle, but it lives on today in our own experiences and quests for fulfillment.

ARISTOTLE

Dea Picture Library/De Agostini/Getty

ARISTOTLE (384–322 B.C.E.) was the philosopher Plato's most brilliant student. He left Plato's Academy in Athens after Plato's death in 347 B.C.E. and accepted the offer of Philip of Macedon to teach at the royal academy in Macedon. Among Aristotle's students was Alexander the Great. Alexander conquered the known world and spread Greek values everywhere he went. Consequently, it is valuable to know that Aristotle encouraged Alexander to conquer the Persians and to treat them harshly. Alexander would not have read "The Aim of Man" — the essay that follows — because Aristotle wrote it for his own son, Nichomachus, who was born after Aristotle had returned to Athens to teach at his Lyceum. But with Aristotle's emphasis in "The Aim of Man" on statecraft as the highest study a man could pursue, we suspect that much of what Alexander knew about politics he learned from Aristotle.

After Plato died, Aristotle began to reveal the ways he disagreed with Plato. For example, Plato thought the highest good existed only in an ideal realm. In contrast, Aristotle concentrated his attention not on the ideal heavenly world but on the world of the five senses. This shift of attention had great significance for science because Aristotle's methods of relying on sensory observation, recorded in his books on geology, physics, biology, psychology, and more, have led later commentators to describe him as the world's first true scientist.

Aristotle's effort to understand happiness focuses on what we can do in this world to achieve some complete understanding of the good. He makes a distinction between the good as it applies to an individual and the good as it applies to the state as a whole. Ultimately, he feels that the highest good that people can attain is happiness — not the kind that exists only for a few moments but the kind that stays with one for life. Some of his comments are abstract because the Greeks valued abstract reasoning in discussing matters of philosophy. However, some of his analogies help root his ideas in the world of experience.

Rational behavior is essential, Aristotle feels, to achieving happiness. Reason is our guide, he tells us, but he also knows that people often behave irrationally, putting passion ahead of careful thought. If he is truly addressing his son, he is telling him to aim for the kind of happiness that will serve him through life, which means acting thoughtfully and avoiding behavior that harms others. Aristotle's final view is that living a life of virtue will produce the reward of peace and long-lasting happiness. Unlike many later commentators on ethics, Aristotle does not mention the gods or any divinity when giving guidance to his son. He is very realistic and practical and does not point to happiness in heaven as a reward for virtue on earth.

Be sure to practice prereading techniques before a careful, annotated reading of Aristotle's essay. For a review of prereading strategies, see pages 4–9. ⊞

The Aim of Man

DEFINITION OF THE GOOD

EVERY ART and every "scientific investigation," as well as every action and "purposive choice," appears to aim at some good; hence the good has rightly been declared to be that at which all things aim. A difference is observable, to be sure, among the several ends: some of them are activities, while others are products over and above the activities that produce them. Wherever there are certain ends over and above the actions themselves, it is the nature of such products to be better than the activities.

As actions and arts and sciences are of many kinds, there must be a corresponding diversity of ends: health, for example, is the aim of medicine, ships of shipbuilding, victory of military strategy, and wealth of domestic economics. Where several such arts fall under some one faculty — as bridle-making and the other arts concerned with horses' equipment fall under horsemanship, while this in turn along with all other military matters falls under the head of strategy, and similarly in the case of other arts — the aim of the master art is always more choiceworthy than the aims of its subordinate arts, inasmuch as these are pursued for its sake. And this holds equally good whether the end in view is just the activity itself or something distinct from the activity, as in the case of the sciences above mentioned.

PRIMACY OF STATECRAFT

If in all our conduct, then, there is some end that we wish on its own account, choosing everything else as a means to it; if, that is to say, we do not choose everything as a means to something else (for at that rate we should go on *ad infinitum*[1] and our desire would be left empty and vain); then clearly this one end must be the good — even, indeed, the highest good. Will not a knowledge of it, then, have an important influence on our lives? Will it not better enable us to hit the right mark, like archers who have a definite target to aim at? If so, we must try to comprehend, in outline at least, what that highest end is, and to which of the sciences or arts it belongs.

Evidently the art or science in question must be the most absolute and most authoritative of all. Statecraft answers best to this description; for it prescribes which of the sciences are to have a place in the state, and which of them are to be studied by the different classes of citizens, and up to what point; and we find that even the most highly esteemed of the arts are subordinated to it, e.g., military strategy, domestic economics, and oratory. So then, since statecraft employs all the other sciences, prescribing also what the citizens are to do and what they are to refrain from doing, its aim must embrace the aims of all the others; whence it follows that the aim of statecraft is man's proper good. Even supposing the chief good to be eventually the same for the individual as for the state, that of the state is evidently of greater and more fundamental importance both to attain and to preserve. The securing of even one individual's good is cause for rejoicing, but to secure the good of a nation or of a city-state[2] is nobler and more divine. This, then, is the aim of our present inquiry, which is in a sense the study of statecraft.

TWO OBSERVATIONS ON THE STUDY OF ETHICS

Our discussion will be adequate if we are content with as much precision   5
as is appropriate to the subject matter; for the same degree of exactitude ought no more to be expected in all kinds of reasoning than in all kinds of handicraft. Excellence and justice, the things with which statecraft deals, involve so much disagreement and uncertainty that they come to be looked on as mere conventions, having no natural foundation. The good involves a similar uncertainty, inasmuch as good things often prove detrimental: there are examples of people destroyed by wealth, of others destroyed by courage. In such matters, then, and starting from such premises as we do, we

---

[1] *ad infinitum* Endlessly; to infinity.

[2] **city-state** Athens was an independent nation, a city-state (*polis*). Greece consisted of a great many independent states, which often leagued together in confederations.

must be content with a rough approximation to the truth; for when we are dealing with and starting out from what holds good only "as a general rule," the conclusions that we reach will have the same character. Let each of the views put forward be accepted in this spirit, for it is the mark of an educated mind to seek only so much exactness in each type of inquiry as may be allowed by the nature of the subject matter. It is equally wrong to accept probable reasoning from a mathematician and to demand strict demonstrations from an orator.

A man judges well and is called a good judge of the things about which he knows. If he has been educated in a particular subject he is a good judge of that subject; if his education has been well-rounded he is a good judge in general. Hence no very young man is qualified to attend lectures on statecraft; for he is inexperienced in the affairs of life, and these form the date and subject matter of statecraft. Moreover, so long as he tends to be swayed by his feelings he will listen vainly and without profit, for the purport of these [lectures] is not purely theoretical but practical. Nor does it make any difference whether his immaturity is a matter of years or of character: the defect is not a matter of time, but consists in the fact that his life and all his pursuits are under the control of his passions. Men of this sort, as is evident from the case of those we call incontinent,[3] do not turn their knowledge to any account in practice; but those whose desires and actions are controlled by reason will derive much profit from a knowledge of these matters.

So much, then, for our prefatory remarks about the student, the manner of inquiry, and the aim.

THE GOOD AS HAPPINESS

To resume, then: since all knowledge and all purpose aims at some good, what is it that we declare to be the aim of statecraft; or, in other words, what is the highest of all realizable goods? As to its name there is pretty general agreement: the majority of men, as well as the cultured few, speak of it as happiness; and they would maintain that to live well and to do well are the same thing as to be happy. They differ, however, as to what happiness is, and the mass of mankind give a different account of it from philosophers. The former take it to be something palpable and obvious, like pleasure or wealth or fame: they differ, too, among themselves, nor is the same man always of one mind about it: when ill he identifies it with health, when poor with wealth; then growing aware of his ignorance about the whole matter he feels admiration for anyone who proclaims some grand ideal above his comprehension. And to add to the confusion, there have been some philosophers

---

[3] **incontinent** Uncontrolled, in this case by reason.

who held that besides the various particular good things there is an absolute good which is the cause of all particular goods. As it would hardly be worthwhile to examine all the opinions that have been entertained, we shall confine our attention to those that are most popular or that appear to have some rational foundation.

One point not to be overlooked is the difference between arguments that start from first principles[4] and arguments that lead up to first principles. Plato very wisely used to raise this question, and to ask whether the right way is from or toward first principles — as in the racecourse there is a difference between running from the judges to the boundary line and running back again. Granted that we must start with what is known, this may be interpreted in a double sense: as what is familiar to us or as what is intelligible in itself. Our own method, at any rate, must be to start with what is familiar to us. That is why a sound moral training is required before a man can listen intelligently to discussions about excellence and justice, and generally speaking, about statecraft. For in this field we must take as our "first principles" plain facts; if these are sufficiently evident we shall not insist upon the whys and wherefores. Such principles are in the possession of, or at any rate readily accessible to, the man with a sound moral training. As for the man who neither possesses nor can acquire them, let him hear the words of Hesiod:[5]

> Best is he who makes his own discoveries;
> Good is he who listens to the wise;
> But he who, knowing not, rejects another's wisdom
>   Is a plain fool.

CONFLICTING VIEWS OF HAPPINESS

Let us now resume our discussion from the point at which we digressed. 10 What is happiness, or the chief good? If it is permissible to judge from men's actual lives, we may say that the mass of them, being vulgarians, identify it with pleasure, which is the reason why they aim at nothing higher than a life of enjoyment. For there are three outstanding types of life: the one just mentioned, the political, and, thirdly, the contemplative. "The mass of men" reveal their utter slavishness by preferring a life fit only for cattle; yet their

---

[4] **first principles** Concepts such as goodness, truth, and justice. Arguments that lead to first principles usually begin with familiar, less abstract evidence.

[5] *Works and Days*, II. 293–297. [Translator's note] **Hesiod** (eighth century B.C.E.) Well-known Greek author. His *Works and Days* is notable for its portraits of everyday shepherd life and for its moralizing fables. His *Theogony* is a description of the creation, widely taken as accurate in his day.

views have a certain plausibility from the fact that many of those in high places share the tastes of Sardanapalus.[6] Men of superior refinement and active disposition, on the other hand, identify happiness with honor, this being more or less the aim of a statesman's life. It is evidently too superficial, however, to be the good that we are seeking; for it appears to depend rather on him who bestows than on him who receives it, while we may suspect the chief good to be something peculiarly a man's own, which he is not easily deprived of. Besides, men seem to pursue honor primarily in order to assure themselves of their own merit; at any rate, apart from personal acquaintances, it is by those of sound judgment that they seek to be appreciated, and on the score of virtue. Clearly, then, they imply that virtue is superior to honor: and so, perhaps, we should regard this rather than honor as the end and aim of the statesman's life. Yet even about virtue there is a certain incompleteness; for it is supposed that a man may possess it while asleep or during lifelong inactivity, or even while suffering the greatest disasters and misfortunes; and surely no one would call such a man happy, unless for the sake of a paradox. But we need not further pursue this subject, which has been sufficiently treated of in current discussions. Thirdly, there is the contemplative life, which we shall examine at a later point.

As for the life of moneymaking, it is something unnatural. Wealth is clearly not the good that we are seeking, for it is merely useful as a means to something else. Even the objects above mentioned come closer to possessing intrinsic goodness than wealth does, for they at least are cherished on their own account. But not even they, it seems, can be the chief good, although much labor has been lost in attempting to prove them so. With this observation we may close the present subject.

FUNCTIONAL DEFINITION OF MAN'S HIGHEST GOOD

Returning now to the good that we are seeking, let us inquire into its nature. Evidently it is different in different actions and arts: it is not the same thing in medicine as in strategy, and so on. What definition of good will apply to all the arts? Let us say it is that for the sake of which all else is done. In medicine this is health, in the art of war victory, in building it is a house, and in each of the arts something different, although in every case, wherever there is action and choice involved, it is a certain end; because it is always for the sake of a certain end that all else is done. If, then, there is one end and aim

---

[6] An ancient Assyrian king to whom is attributed the saying, "Eat, drink, and be merry: nothing else is worth a snap of the fingers." [Translator's note] **Sardanapalus** (d. 880 B.C.E.) Noted for his slothful and decadent life. When it was certain that he was to die — the walls of his city had been breached by an opposing army — he had his wives, animals, and possessions burned with him in his palace.

of all our actions, this will be the realizable good; if there are several such ends, these jointly will be our realizable goods. Thus in a roundabout way the discussion has been brought back to the same point as before; which we must now try to explain more clearly.

As there is evidently a plurality of ends, and as some of these are chosen only as means to ulterior ends (e.g., wealth, flutes, and instruments in general), it is clear that not all ends are final.[7] But the supreme good must of course be something final. Accordingly, if there is only one final end, this will be the good that we are seeking; and if there is more than one such end, the most complete and final of them will be this good. Now we call what is pursued as an end in itself more final than what is pursued as a means to something else; and what is never chosen as a means we call more final than what is chosen both as an end in itself and as a means; in fact, when a thing is chosen always as an end in itself and never as a means we call it absolutely final. Happiness seems, more than anything else, to answer to this description: for it is something we choose always for its own sake and never for the sake of something else; while honor, pleasure, reason, and all the virtues, though chosen partly for themselves (for we might choose any one of them without heeding the result), are chosen also for the sake of the happiness which we suppose they will bring us. Happiness, on the other hand, is never chosen for the sake of any of these, nor indeed as a means to anything else at all.

We seem to arrive at the same conclusion if we start from the notion of self-sufficiency; for the final good is admittedly self-sufficient. To be self-sufficient we do not mean that an individual must live in isolation. Parents, children, wife, as well as friends and fellow citizens generally, are all permissible; for man is by nature political. To be sure, some limit has to be set to such relationships, for if they are extended to embrace ancestors, descendants, and friends of friends, we should go on *ad infinitum*. But this point will be considered later on; provisionally we may attribute self-sufficiency to that which taken by itself makes life choiceworthy and lacking in nothing. Such a thing we conceive happiness to be. Moreover, we regard happiness as the most choiceworthy of all things; nor does this mean that it is merely one good thing among others, for if that were the case it is plain that the addition of even the least of those other goods would increase its desirability; since the addition would create a larger amount of good, and of two goods the greater is always to be preferred. Evidently, then, happiness is something final and self-sufficient, and is the end and aim of all that we do.

---

[7] **not all ends are final** By *ends* Aristotle means purposes. Some purposes are final — the most important; some are immediate — the less important. When a corporation contributes funds to the Public Broadcasting Service (PBS), for example, its immediate purpose may be to fund a worthwhile program. Its final purpose may be to benefit from the publicity gained from underwriting a PBS program.

But perhaps it will be objected that to call happiness the supreme good 15
is a mere truism, and that a clearer account of it is still needed. We can give
this best, probably, if we ascertain the proper function of man. Just as the
excellence and good performance of a flute player, a sculptor, or any kind of
artist, and generally speaking of anyone who has a function or business to
perform, lies always in that function, so man's good would seem to lie in the
function of man, if he has one. But can we suppose that while a carpenter
and a cobbler each has a function and mode of activity of his own, man qua
man[8] has none, but has been left by nature functionless? Surely it is more
likely that as his several members, eye and hand and foot, can be shown to
have each its own function, so man too must have a function over and above
the special functions of his various members. What will such a function be?
Not merely to live, of course: he shares that even with plants, whereas we
are seeking something peculiar to himself. We must exclude, therefore, the
life of nutrition and growth. Next comes sentient[9] life, but this again is had
in common with the horse, the ox, and in fact all animals whatever. There
remains only the "practical"[10] life of his rational nature; and this has two
aspects, one of which is rational in the sense that it obeys a "rational principle," the other in the sense that it possesses and exercises reason. To avoid
ambiguity let us specify that by "rational" we mean the "exercise or activity," not the mere possession, of reason; for it is the former that would seem
more properly entitled to the name. Thus we conclude that man's function
is an activity of the soul in conformity with, or at any rate involving the use
of, "rational principle."

An individual and a superior individual who belong to the same class
we regard as sharing the same function: a harpist and a good harpist, for
instance, are essentially the same. This holds true of any class of individuals
whatever; for superior excellence with respect to a function is nothing but
an amplification of that selfsame function: e.g., the function of a harpist is to
play the harp, while that of a good harpist is to play it well. This being so, if
we take man's proper function to be a certain kind of life, viz. an activity and
conduct of the soul that involves reason, and if it is the part of a good man
to perform such activities well and nobly, and if a function is well performed
when it is performed in accordance with its own proper excellence; we may
conclude that the good of man is an activity of the soul in accordance with
virtue, or, if there be more than one virtue, in accordance with the best and
most perfect of them. And we must add, in a complete life. For one swallow

---

[8] **man qua man** Man as such, without reference to what he may be or do.

[9] **sentient** Knowing, aware, conscious.

[10] **"practical"** Aristotle refers to the actual practices that will define the ethical nature of
the individual.

does not make a spring, nor does one fine day; and similarly one day or brief period of happiness does not make a man happy and blessed.

So much, then, for a rough outline of the good: the proper procedure being, we may suppose, to sketch an outline first and afterwards to fill in the details. When a good outline has been made, almost anyone presumably can expand it and fill it out; and time is a good inventor and collaborator in this work. It is in just such a way that progress has been made in the various "human techniques,"[11] for filling in the gaps is something anybody can do.

But in all this we must bear constantly in mind our previous warning: not to expect the same degree of precision in all fields, but only so much as belongs to a given subject matter and is appropriate to a particular "type of inquiry." Both the carpenter and the geometer investigate the right angle, but in different ways: the one wants only such an approximation to it as will serve his work; the other, being concerned with truth, seeks to determine its essence or essential attributes. And so in other subjects we must follow a like procedure, lest we be so much taken up with side issues that we pass over the matter in hand. Similarly we ought not in all cases to demand the "reason why"; sometimes it is enough to point out the bare fact. This is true, for instance, in the case of "first principles"; for a bare fact must always be the ultimate starting point of any inquiry. First principles may be arrived at in a variety of ways: some by induction,[12] some by direct perception, some by a kind of habituation, and others in other ways. In each case we should try to apprehend them in whatever way is proper to them, and we should take care to define them clearly, because they will have a considerable influence upon the subsequent course of our inquiry. A good beginning is more than half of the whole inquiry, and once established clears up many of its difficulties.

CONFIRMATION BY POPULAR BELIEFS

It is important to consider our ethical "first principle" not merely as a conclusion drawn from certain premises, but also in its relation to popular opinion; for all data harmonize with a true principle, but with a false one they are soon found to be discordant. Now it has been customary to divide good things into three classes: external goods on the one hand, and on the other goods of the soul and goods of the body; and those of the soul we call good in the highest sense, and in the fullest degree. "Conscious actions," i.e., "active expressions of our nature," we take, of course, as belonging to

---

[11] **"human techniques"** Arts or skills; in a sense, technology.

[12] **induction** A process of reasoning based on careful observation and collection of details upon which theories are based. "A kind of habituation" may refer to a combination of intellectual approaches characteristic of an individual.

the soul; and thus our account is confirmed by the doctrine referred to, which is of long standing and has been generally accepted by students of philosophy. . . .

We are in agreement also with those who identify happiness with vir- 20 tue or with some particular virtue; for our phrase "activity in accordance with virtue" is the same as what they call virtue. It makes quite a difference, however, whether we conceive the supreme good as the mere possession of virtue or as its employment — i.e., as a state of character or as its active expression in conduct. For a state of character may be present without yielding any good result, as in a man who is asleep or in some other way inactive; but this is not true of its active expression, which must show itself in action, indeed in good action. As at the Olympic games it is not merely the fairest and strongest that receive the victory wreath, but those who compete (since the victors will of course be found among the competitors), so in life too those who carry off the finest prizes are those who manifest their excellence in their deeds.

Moreover, the life of those active in virtue is intrinsically pleasant. For besides the fact that pleasure is something belonging to the soul, each man takes pleasure in what he is said to love — the horse lover in horses, the lover of sights in public spectacles, and similarly the lover of justice in just acts, and more generally, the lover of virtue in virtuous acts. And while most men take pleasure in things which, as they are not truly pleasant by nature, create warring factions in the soul, the lovers of what is noble take pleasure in things that are truly pleasant in themselves. Virtuous actions are things of this kind; hence they are pleasant for such men, as well as pleasant intrinsically. The life of such men, therefore, requires no adventitious[13] pleasures, but finds its own pleasure within itself. This is further shown by the fact that a man who does not enjoy doing noble actions is not a good man at all: surely no one would call a man just who did not enjoy performing just actions, nor generous who did not enjoy performing generous actions, and so on. On this ground too, then, actions in conformity with virtue must be intrinsically pleasant. And certainly they are good as well as noble, and both in the highest degree, if the judgment of the good man is any criterion; for he will judge them as we have said. It follows, therefore, that happiness is at once the best and noblest and pleasantest of things, and that these attributes are not separable as the inscription at Delos[14] pretends:

> Perfect justice is noblest, health is best,
> But to gain one's heart's desire is pleasantest.

---

[13] **adventitious** Unnecessary; superfluous.

[14] **inscription at Delos** Delos is the island that once held the Athenian treasury. It was the birthplace of Apollo, with whom the inscription would be associated.

For our best activities possess all of these attributes; and it is in our best activities, or in the best one of them, that we say happiness consists.

Nevertheless, happiness plainly requires external goods as well; for it is impossible, or at least not easy, to act nobly without the proper equipment. There are many actions that can only be performed through such instruments as friends, wealth, or political influence; and there are some things, again, the lack of which must mar felicity, such as good birth, fine children, and personal comeliness: for the man who is repulsive in appearance, or ill-born, or solitary and childless does not meet the requirements of a happy man, and still less does one who has worthless children and friends, or who has lost good ones by death. As we have said, then, happiness seems to require the addition of external prosperity, and this has led some to identify it with "good fortune," just as others have made the opposite mistake of identifying it with virtue.

SOURCES OF HAPPINESS

For the same reason there are many who wonder whether happiness is attained by learning, or by habituation or some other kind of training, or whether it comes by some divine dispensation,[15] or even by chance. Well, certainly if the gods do give any gifts to men we may reasonably suppose that happiness is god given; indeed, of all human blessings it is the most likely to be so, inasmuch as it is the best of them all. While this question no doubt belongs more properly to another branch of inquiry, we remark here that even if happiness is not god sent but comes as a result of virtue or some kind of learning or training, still it is evidently one of the most divine things in the world, because that which is the reward as well as the end and aim of virtuous conduct must evidently be of supreme excellence, something divine and most blessed. If this is the case, happiness must further be something that can be generally shared; for with the exception of those whose capacity for virtue has been stunted or maimed, everyone will have the ability, by study and diligence, to acquire it. And if it is better that happiness should be acquired in this way than by chance, we may reasonably suppose that it happens so; because everything in nature is arranged in the best way possible — just as in the case of man-made products, and of every kind of causation, especially the highest. It would be altogether wrong that what is greatest and noblest in the world should be left to the dispensation of chance.

Our present difficulty is cleared up by our previous definition of happiness, as a certain activity of the soul in accordance with virtue; whereas

---

[15] **divine dispensation** A gift of the gods.

all other sorts of good are either necessary conditions of, or cooperative with and naturally useful instruments of this. Such a conclusion, moreover, agrees with the proposition we laid down at the outset: that the end of state-craft is the best of all ends, and that the principal concern of statecraft is to make the citizens of a certain character — namely, good and disposed to perform noble actions.

Naturally, therefore, we do not call an ox or a horse or any other brute 25 happy, since none of them is able to participate in conduct of this kind. For the same reason a child is not happy, since at his age he too is incapable of such conduct. Or if we do call a child happy, it is in the sense of predict-ing for him a happy future. Happiness, as we have said, involves not only a completeness of virtue but also a complete lifetime for its fulfillment. Life brings many vicissitudes and chance happenings, and it may be that one who is now prosperous will suffer great misfortunes in his old age, as is told of Priam[16] in the Trojan legends; and a man who is thus buffeted by fortune and comes to a miserable end can scarcely be called happy.

HAPPINESS AND THE VICISSITUDES OF FORTUNE

Are we, then, to call no one happy while he lives? Must we, as Solon[17] advises, wait to see his end? And if we accept this verdict, are we to interpret it as meaning that a man actually becomes happy only after he is dead? Would not this be downright absurd, especially for us who define happiness as a kind of vital activity? Or if we reject this interpretation, and suppose Solon to mean rather that it is only after death, when beyond the reach of further evil and calamity that a man can safely be said to have been happy during his life, there is still a possible objection that may be offered. For many hold that both good and evil may in a certain sense befall a dead man (just as they may befall a living man even when he is unconscious of them) — e.g., honors and disgraces, and the prosperity or misfortune of his children and the rest of his descendants. And this presents a further problem: suppose a man to have lived to a happy old age, and to have ended as he lived, there are still plenty of reverses that may befall his descendants — some of them will perhaps lead a good life and be dealt with by fortune as they deserve, others not. (It is clear, too, that a man's relationship to his descendants admits of various degrees.) It would be odd, then, if the dead man were to change along with the fortunes of his descendants, becoming happy and miserable

---

[16] **Priam** King of Troy in Homer's *Iliad*. He suffered a terrible reversal of fortune when Troy was defeated by the Greeks.

[17] **Solon** (638–558 B.C.E.) Greek lawgiver and one of Greece's earliest poets. He was one of the Seven Sages of Athens.

by turns; although, to be sure, it would be equally odd if the fortunes of his descendants did not affect him at all, even for a brief time.

But let us go back to our earlier question,[18] which may perhaps clear up the one we are raising at present. Suppose we agree that we must look to the end of a man's life, and only then call him happy, not because he then *is* happy but because we can only then know him to have been so: Is it not paradoxical to have refused to call him happy during just the period when happiness was present to him? On the other hand, we are naturally loath to apply the term to living men, considering the vicissitudes to which they are liable. Happiness, we argue, must be something that endures without any essential change, whereas a living individual may experience many turns of fortune's wheel. Obviously if we judge by his changing fortunes we shall have to call the same man now happy now wretched, thereby regarding the happy man as a kind of chameleon and his happiness as built on no secure foundation; yet it surely cannot be right to regard a man's happiness as wholly dependent on his fortunes. True good and evil are not of this character; rather, as we have said, although good fortune is a necessary adjunct to a complete human life, it is virtuous activities that constitute happiness, and the opposite sort of activities that constitute its opposite.

The foregoing difficulty [that happiness can be judged of only in retrospect] confirms, as a matter of fact, our theory. For none of man's functions is so permanent as his virtuous activities — indeed, many believe them to be more abiding even than a knowledge of the sciences; and of his virtuous activities those are the most abiding which are of highest worth, for it is with them that anyone blessed with supreme happiness is most fully and most continuously occupied, and hence never oblivious of. The happy man, then, will possess this attribute of permanence or stability about which we have been inquiring, and will keep it all his life; because at all times and in preference to everything else he will be engaged in virtuous action and contemplation, and he will bear the changes of fortune as nobly and in every respect as decorously as possible, inasmuch as he is truly good and "four-square beyond reproach."[19]

But the dispensations of fortune are many, some great, others small. Small ones do not appreciably turn the scales of life, but a multitude of great ones, if they are of the nature of blessings, will make life happier; for they add to life a grace of their own, provided that a man makes noble and good use of them. If, however, they are of an evil kind, they will crush and maim happiness, in that they bring pain and thereby hinder many of our natural

---

[18] I.e., whether we are to call no one happy while he still lives. [Translator's note]

[19] A quotation from Simonides. [Translator's note] **Simonides** (556?–469 B.C.E.) Greek lyric poet who lived and wrote for a while in Athens. His works survive in a handful of fragments; this quotation is from fragment 5.

activities. Yet true nobility shines out even here, if a multitude of great misfortunes be borne with calmness — not, to be sure, with the calmness of
insensibility, but of nobility and greatness of soul.

If, as we have declared, it is our activities that give life its character, 30
then no happy man can become miserable, inasmuch as he will never do
what is hateful or base. For we hold that the truly good and wise man will
bear with dignity whatever fortune sends, and will always make the best
of his circumstances, as a good general makes the most effective use of the
forces at his command, and a good shoemaker makes the best shoes out of
the leather that is available, and so in the case of the other crafts. On this
interpretation, the happy man can never become miserable — although of
course he will not be blessed with happiness in the full sense of the word
if he meets with such a fate as Priam's. At all events, he is not variable and
always changing; for no ordinary misfortunes but only a multitude of great
ones will dislodge him from his happy state, and should this occur he will
not readily recover his happiness in a short time, but only, if at all, after a
long period has run its course, during which he has achieved distinctions of
a high order.

Is there any objection, then, to our defining a happy man as one whose
activities are an expression of complete virtue, and who at the same time
enjoys a sufficiency of worldly goods, not just for some limited period, but
for his entire lifetime? Or perhaps we had better add the proviso that he
shall be destined to go on living in this manner, and die as he has lived; for,
whereas the future is obscure to us, we conceive happiness to be an end,
something altogether and in every respect final and complete. Granting all
this, we may declare those living men to be "blessed with supreme happiness" in whom these conditions have been and are continuing to be fulfilled.
Their blessedness, however, is of human order.

So much for our discussion of this question.

DERIVATION OF THE TWO KINDS OF HUMAN EXCELLENCE

Since happiness is a certain activity of the soul in accordance with perfect
virtue, we must next examine the nature of virtue. Not only will such an
inquiry perhaps clarify the problem of happiness; it will also be of vital concern to the true student of statecraft, whose aim is to make his fellow citizens good and law-abiding. The Cretan and Spartan lawgivers,[20] as well as
such others as may have resembled them, exemplify this aim. And clearly,

---

[20] **Cretan and Spartan lawgivers** Both Crete and Sparta were noted for their constitutions, based on the laws of Gortyn in Crete. These laws were aristocratic, not
democratic as in Athens; they promoted a class system and a rigid code of personal
behavior.

if such an inquiry has to do with statecraft, it will be in keeping with our original purpose to pursue it.

It goes without saying that the virtue we are to study is human virtue, just as the good that we have been inquiring about is a human good, and the happiness a human happiness. By human virtue we mean virtue not of the body but of the soul, and by happiness too we mean an activity of the soul. This being the case, it is no less evident that the student of statecraft must have some knowledge of the soul, than that a physician who is to heal the eye or the whole body must have some knowledge of these organs; more so, indeed, in proportion as statecraft is superior to and more honorable than medicine. Now all physicians who are educated take much pains to know about the body. Hence as students of statecraft, too, we must inquire into the nature of the soul; but we must do so with reference to our own distinctive aim and only to the extent that it requires, for to go into minuter detail would be more laborious than is warranted by our subject matter.

"For none of man's functions is so permanent as his virtuous activities . . . and of his virtuous activities those are the most abiding which are of highest worth, for it is with them that anyone blessed with supreme happiness is most fully and most continuously occupied, and hence never oblivious of."

We may adopt here certain doctrines 35 about the soul that have been adequately stated in our public discourses:[21] as that the soul may be distinguished into two parts, one of which is irrational while the other possesses reason. Whether these two parts are actually distinct like the parts of the body or any other divisible thing, or are distinct only in a logical sense, like convex and concave in the circumference of a circle, is immaterial to our present inquiry.

Of the irrational part, again, one division is apparently of a vegetative nature and common to all living things: I mean that which is the cause of nutrition and growth. It is more reasonable to postulate a vital faculty of this sort, present in all things that take nourishment, even when in an embryo stage, and retained by the full-grown organism, than to assume a special nutritive faculty in the latter. Hence we may say that the excellence belonging to this part of the soul is common to all species, and not specifically human: a point that is further confirmed by the popular view that this part of the soul is most active during sleep. For it is during sleep that the distinction between good men and bad is least apparent; whence the saying that for

---

[21] **our public discourses** Aristotle may be referring to speeches at which the public is welcome, as opposed to his lectures to students.

half their lives the happy are no better off than the wretched. This, indeed, is natural enough, for sleep is an inactivity of the soul in those respects in which the soul is called good or bad. (It is true, however, that to a slight degree certain bodily movements penetrate to the soul; which is the reason why good men's dreams are superior to those of the average person.) But enough of this subject: let us dismiss the nutritive principle, since it has by nature no share in human excellence.

There seems to be a second part of the soul, which though irrational yet in some way partakes of reason. For while we praise the rational principle and the part of the soul that manifests it in the case of the continent and incontinent man alike, on the ground that it exhorts them rightly and urges them to do what is best; yet we find within these men another element different in nature from the rational element, and struggling against and resisting it. Just as ataxic limbs,[22] when we choose to move them to the right, turn on the contrary to the left, so it is with the soul: the impulses of the incontinent man run counter to his ruling part. The only difference is that in the case of the body we see what it is that goes astray, while in the soul we do not. Nevertheless the comparison will doubtless suffice to show that there is in the soul something besides the rational element, opposing and running counter to it. (In what sense the two elements are distinct is immaterial.) But this other element, as we have said, seems also to have some share in a rational principle: at any rate, in the continent man it submits to reason, while in the man who is at once temperate and courageous it is presumably all the more obedient; for in him it speaks on all matters harmoniously with the voice of reason.

Evidently, then, the irrational part of the soul is twofold. There is the vegetative element, which has no share in reason, and there is the concupiscent,[23] or rather the appetitive element, which does in a sense partake of reason, in that it is amenable and obedient to it: i.e., it is rational in the sense that we speak of "having *logos* of" [paying heed to] father and friends, not in the sense of "having *logos* of" [having a rational understanding of] mathematical truths. That this irrational element is in some way amenable to reason is shown by our practice of giving admonishment, and by rebuke and exhortation generally. If on this account it is deemed more correct to regard this element as also possessing reason, then the rational part of the soul, in turn, will have two subdivisions: the one being rational in the strict sense as actually possessing reason, the other merely in the sense that a child obeys its father.

----

[22] **ataxic limbs** Aristotle refers to a nervous disorder of the limbs.

[23] **concupiscent** Sexual; Aristotle corrects himself to refer to the general nature of desire.

Virtue, too, is differentiated in accordance with this division of the soul: for we call some of the virtues intellectual and others moral: wisdom, understanding, and sagacity being among the former, liberality and temperance among the latter. In speaking of a man's character we do not say that he is wise or intelligent, but that he is gentle or temperate; yet we praise the wise man too for the disposition he has developed within himself, and praiseworthy dispositions we call virtues.

Understanding Ideas

1. According to Aristotle, why is statecraft the "the most absolute and most authoritative of all" (para. 4) the arts?

2. How does Aristotle describe "good"?

3. In what ways do people define "happiness, or the chief good" (para. 10), according to Aristotle?

4. Why does Aristotle think of happiness as an end in itself, not as a means to something else?

Responding to Ideas

1. *Response* Aristotle talks about happiness as the greatest good. Achieving it involves living a life of reason. However, he also talks about other kinds of good. For instance, he begins by saying that "every action and 'purposive choice,' appears to aim at some good" (para. 1). Review what Aristotle says here and then write a brief essay that establishes what you feel are the lesser "goods" that you aim at on a regular basis. He talks about various ends that are desirable, such as health, victory, and wealth. What are the kinds of good that you aim for that will help you achieve happiness? To what extent will they help you achieve the virtuous life that will eventually be necessary to achieve happiness?

2. *Analysis of Circumstances* Consider the question of ends and means. Happiness is the highest good because it represents a final end; in other words, happiness does not lead to something higher or better. Given that this is true, what other ends must be achieved in order to establish a life of happiness? How must you evaluate the means that will lead to the ends you desire? How does the idea of virtue dictate the kinds of means that can be used to achieve the ends necessary

to achieve happiness? Will any means justify the ends if the ends are good?

3. **Response** Aristotle says that money and moneymaking are unnatural. Yet he also says that the erd of domestic labor is wealth. Why is this not a contradiction? Aristotle says that wealth is a means to some other end. Money is not the good itself, only a "means to something else" (para. 11). Given that so many people make it their life's purpose to amass wealth, why does Aristotle rot credit wealth with being an important means to the end of happiness? Where do you stand on this issue? Is wealth essential to happiness? Write an essay that examines the modern desire for wealth and why it may be one of those "goods" that can prove detrimental.

4. **Response** Aristotle considers a life "that possesses and exercises reason" (para. 15) as essential to achieving happiness. What does he mean by this? What are the alternatives to possessing and exercising reason? What could make it difficult or impossible for a person to live a life of reason? What kinds of irrationalities affect ordinary people and make it difficult or impossible for them to live the reasonable life Aristotle approves of? What in your own experience has hindered you from living a life of reason? In what ways might it be possible for you to live a happy life and avoid living a life of reason? Describe how you would live a life of reason.

5. **Definition** Aristotle admits that happiness will not be the same for everyone. After considering his discussion, offer as careful a definition of *happiness* as you can. Think of it as a definition for yourself rather than a prescription for others. Or, if you prefer, imagine that like Aristotle you are giving advice to your child (imaginary or real). What are the ways you or your "child" can achieve happiness in the world in which we live? Consider that your recommendations are not for a period but rather for a lifetime of happiness.

6. **Response** Aristotle describes three kinds of life. The first is the life of the vulgar, which is to say the crdinary people. They pursue pleasure as a means to happiness. The second is the life of virtue, which he questions because virtue cannot protect the virtuous from suffering "great misfortunes" (para. 25), and they cannot be considered happy. The third life is the contemplative life, which he says he will describe at a later time (and not in this essay). Aristotle is himself an example of someone who lived a contemplative life. Write an essay that describes each of these kinds of life and which you would prefer to live. Which do you feel is likely to produce happiness?

Comparing Ideas

1. Aristotle has had an influence on most Western writers on politics and ethics. Search through Robert A. Dahl's "Why Democracy?" (p. 96) for evidence of Aristotle's influence. Aristotle talks about "[e]xcellence and justice, the things with which statecraft deals" (para. 5). Compare Dahl's position on nobility and justice in a democracy with Aristotle's views on statecraft. What attention does Dahl pay to theories of ethical behavior? Is the democratic ideal of the pursuit of happiness rooted in Aristotle's ideas about how we achieve happiness in life? Explore these ideas in an essay that argues the influence Aristotle had on Dahl's examination of democracy.

2. In "The Gospel of Wealth" (p. 289), Andrew Carnegie defends his position as a man who has achieved happiness through immense wealth but, possibly, at the expense of a multitude of underpaid laborers. In a brief essay, review the principles of Aristotle in his discussion of happiness and qualify the ethical views that Carnegie either states explicitly or merely implies. Would his justification — that his employees would waste the "extra" wages he might pay them — be ethically acceptable to Aristotle? Explain how Carnegie's views do or do not accommodate Aristotle's prescription for achieving happiness.

FRIEDRICH NIETZSCHE

© Corbis

FRIEDRICH NIETZSCHE (1844–1900) was the German philosopher who declared that "God is dead" (*The Gay Science*, 1882). He said this because he saw that science had altered the balance between humans and nature, that psychology had begun to explain the unconscious mind, and that the commitment to the religious belief of earlier times was giving way. Losing the structure of religion, he thought, would leave people without a sense of hope or purpose unless they could create it for themselves. He feared that only very strong and spiritually resourceful people would be able to face life without despair. To an extent, he was sure that the changes science and psychology had wrought threatened the nature of civilization.

Nietzsche's own life was sometimes difficult. Both his grandfathers were Lutheran ministers. His father was also a Lutheran minister but died of an unspecified brain ailment when Nietzsche was four years old. When Nietzsche finished his studies in theology and philology — the study of the interpretation of primarily biblical and classical texts — he joined the army. A bad accident on a horse left him injured. In the Franco-Prussian War (1870–1871) Nietzsche served in a hospital unit and saw the massive injuries incurred through modern warfare. Having contracted syphilis during this time, he began to show signs of mental illness in 1889. He went to a sanatorium where his mother and sister took care of him for the rest of his life.

Before the war, at age twenty-four, Nietzsche was appointed professor of classical philology at the University of Basel in Switzerland. He published one of his most important books, *The Birth of Tragedy from the Spirit of Music*, in 1872. In that book, he explores two aspects of cultural psychology: Apollonian intellectuality and Dionysian passion. In 1882, after he had been forced to leave the university, he published *The Gay Science*, in which he proposes an alternative to the idea of a life after death. His view of an "eternal recurrence" suggests that we are destined to live this life again, down to every detail. The purpose of his proposing such a possibility was to help us focus on the value of this life and make us determined to live it well.

The Genealogy of Morals (1887), from which the following selection is taken, criticizes contemporary religion, especially Christianity. Nietzsche rejects religion on the basis of its being an attack on our natural human feelings. Good and evil, he argues, are loaded terms that do not exist in nature and are, therefore, suspect. Nietzsche examines the etymology of good and bad to establish their linguistic genealogy. As a professor of philology, the study of words, he was especially qualified to do so.

Be sure to practice prereading techniques before a careful, annotated reading of Nietzsche's essay. For a review of prereading strategies, see pages 4–9. ⊞

Good and Bad

I

THE ENGLISH psychologists to whom we owe the only attempts that have thus far been made to write a genealogy of morals are no mean posers of riddles, but the riddles they pose are themselves, and being incarnate have one advantage over their books — they are interesting. What are these English psychologists really after? One finds them always, whether intentionally or not, engaged in the same task of pushing into the foreground the nasty part of the psyche, looking for the effective motive forces of human development in the very last place we would wish to have them found, e.g., in the inertia of habit, in forgetfulness, in the blind and fortuitous association of ideas: always in something that is purely passive, automatic, reflexive, molecular, and, moreover, profoundly stupid. What drives these psychologists forever in the same direction? A secret, malicious desire to belittle humanity, which they do not acknowledge even to themselves? A pessimistic distrust, the suspiciousness of the soured idealist? Some petty resentment of Christianity (and Plato) which does not rise above the threshold of consciousness? Or could it be a prurient taste for whatever is embarrassing, painfully paradoxical, dubious, and absurd in existence? Or is it, perhaps, a kind of stew — a little meanness, a little bitterness, a bit of anti-Christianity, a touch of prurience, and desire for condiments? . . . But, again, people tell me that these men are simply dull old frogs who hop and creep in and around man as in their own element — as though man were a bog. However, I am reluctant to listen to this, in fact I refuse to believe it; and if I may express a wish where I cannot express a conviction, I do wish whole-heartedly that things may be otherwise with these men — that these micro-scopic examiners of the soul may be really courageous, magnanimous, and proud animals, who know how to contain their emotions and have trained themselves to subordinate all wishful thinking to the truth — any truth, even a homespun, severe, ugly, obnoxious, un-Christian, unmoral truth. For such truths do exist.

II

All honor to the beneficent spirits that may motivate these historians of ethics! One thing is certain, however, they have been quite deserted by the true spirit of history. They all, to a man, think unhistorically, as is the age-old custom among philosophers. The amateurishness of their procedure is made plain from the very beginning, when it is a question of explaining the provenance of the concept and judgment *good*. "Originally," they decree, "altruistic actions were praised and approved by their recipients, that is, by those to whom they were useful. Later on, the origin of that praise having been forgotten, such actions were felt to be good simply because it was the habit to commend them." We notice at once that this first derivation has all the earmarks of the English psychologists' work. Here are the key ideas of utility, forgetfulness, habit, and, finally, error, seen as lying at the root of that value system which civilized man had hitherto regarded with pride as the prerogative of all men. This pride must now be humbled, these values devalued. Have the de-bunkers succeeded?

Now it is obvious to me, first of all, that their theory looks for the gen-esis of the concept *good* in the wrong place: the judgment *good* does not originate with those to whom the good has been done. Rather it was the "good" themselves, that is to say the noble, mighty, highly placed, and high-minded who decreed themselves and their actions to be good, i.e., belonging to the highest rank, in contradistinction to all that was base, low-minded, and plebeian. It was only this *pathos of distance* that authorized them to create values and name them — what was utility to them? The notion of utility seems singularly inept to account for such a quick jetting forth of supreme value judgments. Here we come face to face with the exact oppo-site of that lukewarmness which every scheming prudence, every utilitarian calculus presupposes — and not for a time only, for the rare, exceptional hour, but permanently. The origin of the opposites *good* and *bad* is to be found in the pathos of nobility and distance, representing the dominant temper of a higher, ruling class in relation to a lower, dependent one. (The lordly right of bestowing names is such that one would almost be justified in seeing the origin of language itself as an expression of the rulers' power. They say, "This *is* that or that"; they seal off each thing and action with a sound and thereby take symbolic possession of it.) Such an origin would suggest that there is no a priori necessity for associating the word *good* with altruistic deeds, as those moral psychologists are fond of claiming. In fact, it is only after aristocratic values have begun to decline that the egotism-altruism dichotomy takes possession of the human conscience; to use my own terms, it is the herd instinct that now asserts itself. Yet it takes quite a while for this instinct to assume such sway that it can reduce all moral valuations to that dichotomy — as is currently happening throughout Europe, where the prejudice equating the terms *moral, altruistic,* and *disinterested* has assumed the obsessive force of an idée fixe.

III

Quite apart from the fact that this hypothesis about the origin of the value judgment *good* is historically untenable, its psychology is intrinsically unsound. Altruistic deeds were originally commended for their usefulness, but this original reason has now been forgotten — so the claim goes. How is such a forgetting conceivable? Has there ever been a point in history at which such deeds lost their usefulness? Quite the contrary, this usefulness has been apparent to every age, a thing that has been emphasized over and over again. Therefore, instead of being forgotten, it must have impressed itself on the consciousness with ever increasing clearness. The opposite theory is far more sensible, though this does not necessarily make it any the truer — the theory held by Herbert Spencer,[1] for example, who considers the concept *good* qualitatively the same as the concepts *useful* or *practical*; so that in the judgments *good* and *bad*, humanity is said to have summed up and sanctioned precisely its unforgotten and unforgettable experiences of the *useful practical* and the *harmful impractical*. According to this theory, the *good* is that which all along has proved itself useful and which therefore may lay the highest claim to be considered valuable. As

"The origin of the opposites good *and* bad *is to be found in the pathos of nobility and distance, representing the dominant temper of a higher, ruling class in relation to a lower, dependent one."*

---

[1] **Herbert Spencer** (1820–1903) British philosopher who believed societies evolved just as Darwin said living species evolved.

I have said, the derivation of this theory is suspect, but at least the explanation is self-consistent and psychologically tenable within its limits.

Understanding Ideas

1. Why does Friedrich Nietzsche criticize English psychologists?
2. Why does Nietzsche reject the utilitarian analysis of the word *good*?
3. According to Nietzsche, what is the relation of "good" to altruistic deeds?
4. What does Nietzsche mean by condemning the idea that good is defined by people to whom the good has been done?

Responding to Ideas

1. *Analysis of Circumstances* The British philosopher Herbert Spencer said that the good is what is useful and practical. It would follow then that behavior that is useful is good; behavior that is impractical is bad. In a society in which good deeds are altruistic actions that benefit people, why should we not link the concept of the good with what is useful in social intercourse? In a brief essay, examine the idea that good in society is primarily what is most useful to humans in a social order. Connect the idea of the good to what is practical and can be accomplished in society. Find examples that make your point conclusive and convincing.

2. *Response* When Aristotle talked about the good, he was talking about the value that was most precious to mankind. He did not talk about religion, morality, or belief in a divinity. By contrast, when Nietzsche talks about the good, he is talking about a moral issue. For him, the good is synonymous with a moral life and good morals. Write a brief essay that examines the question of how a philosopher who has declared that God is dead and that religion is not the answer can propose the idea of good morals. Explain how a nonreligious concept of morality can function in society. Why do people think morality depends on religious belief?

3. *Analysis of Circumstances* Nietzsche does not define *good* in the moral sense. Search the word online and in religious encyclopedias, as well as in your college library. Be sure to consult a concordance to the Bible for the word *good*. Write an essay in which you provide a careful definition of the word with reference to quotations from the

authorities you have found. What problems does Nietzsche have with conventional definitions of the word?

4. *Response* The English psychologists that Nietzsche refers to are the utilitarian philosophers Jeremy Bentham, John Stuart Mill, and Herbert Spencer. Utilitarian philosophy insists that society must function in a manner that provides the greatest good to the greatest number. Some people interpret this to mean providing good benefits, good services, and good opportunities. But Nietzsche means good morals. He is angry at the linking of good morals with altruism. Explain in a careful argument why Nietzsche is justified in his feelings.

5. *Analysis of Circumstances* Nietzsche says, "The origin of the opposites *good* and *bad* is to be found in the pathos of nobility and distance, representing the dominant temper of a higher, ruling class in relation to a lower, dependent one" (para. 3). Explain what you think Nietzsche means by this statement. How could you defend his view that the concepts of good and bad moral behavior are the result of a ruling class's definitions designed to regulate not themselves but the lower class, which in Nietzsche's lifetime meant the rest of society? How would you characterize the moral behavior of our "ruling class"?

6. *Example* Find at least three examples of behavior reported on widely in the news or in recent publications that you can defend as good moral behavior. On what basis do you defend them as moral and good? Do the same for behavior that you can defend as immoral and bad. Are your definitions dependent on religious teaching? Are your definitions the same as those of most people? What is the basis of your moral evaluations of these behaviors? Would the utilitarians defend your decisions on the basis of their expectations of usefulness or practicality? How does your approach to this problem differ from Nietzsche's?

Comparing Ideas

1. Friedrich Nietzsche talks about the English psychologists who promote the utilitarian view that society must produce the greatest good for the greatest number. John Rawls in "A Theory of Justice" (p. 159) also critiques the utilitarian view. Write an essay that compares the views of Nietzsche and Rawls, looking for those things on which they disagree and on which they agree most heartily. Rawls read Nietzsche and, like him, does not invoke any religious ideas in constructing his ethical views on justice. How similar are their ethical ideas? Is justice an ethical issue or just a political one? How would these writers answer that question?

2. The Aristotelian ideal of a life in pursuit of happiness was well known to Nietzsche. Examine Aristotle's "The Aim of Man" (p. 374) in an effort to compare his ethical views with those of Nietzsche. Does Aristotle seem to understand the concept of good and bad in the same way Nietzsche does, or are his ideas about virtue different? Aristotle and Nietzsche seem to share the view that ethics is not dependent on belief in a divinity. How do they then distinguish between a life of virtue and a life of vice? What does Nietzsche borrow from Aristotle in order to clarify his views on ethics?

© Corbis

JOHN
DEWEY

JOHN DEWEY (1859–1952) graduated from the University of Vermont at age nineteen. He then became a teacher before moving on to Johns Hopkins University, where he studied the works of the idealist German philosophers Immanuel Kant (1724–1804) and Georg Wilhelm Friedrich Hegel (1770–1831), who both felt that true freedom was connected with reason. Later, Dewey taught at the University of Michigan for ten years and became a professor at the University of Chicago when the school was only four years old. The new department Dewey joined combined studies of psychology, philosophy, and pedagogy. Soon the pedagogy contingent broke off, and Dewey helped turn it into one of the first schools of education.

In 1904, Dewey moved to Columbia University in New York, where he had appointments in the department of philosophy and at Teachers College. His ideas underwent considerable change in his years at Columbia. He joined with the modern pragmatist philosophers William James (1841–1910) and Charles Sanders Peirce (1839–1914). American pragmatism evaluated ideas in terms of their practicality and usefulness. Dewey was a social experimentalist, studying how ideas affected and changed people in the world of action. Unlike the more theoretical idealists, he placed a high value on experience as a way of knowing.

Among Dewey's most influential books is *Democracy and Education* (1916). He also wrote *Human Nature and Conduct* (1922), *Experience and Nature* (1925), *Philosophy and Civilization* (1931), and *Freedom and Culture* (1939). All of these books reveal the practical nature that marked his philosophy. *Reconstruction in Philosophy* (1919), in which the following passage appears, is rooted in his developing commitment to pragmatism.

Dewey's intellectual interests ranged from psychology, the subject of his first book, to politics, in which he studied of the idea of democracy and how it works in the world of politics and the world of education. He saw education as a force for producing responsible businesspeople, responsible professional people, and responsible citizens living in a democracy that values all equally. The moral dimension of education is not usually discussed by people interested in why children must go to school or why high school graduates should go to college. Yet he saw that the moral issues involved in education were always evident in the experience of those who had achieved an education.

Be sure to practice prereading techniques before a careful, annotated reading of Dewey's essay. For a review of prereading strategies, see pages 4–9. ⊞

Education and Morality

I F A few words are added upon the topic of education, it is only for the sake of suggesting that the educative process is all one with the moral process, since the latter is a continuous passage of experience from worse to better. Education has been traditionally thought of as preparation: as learning, acquiring certain things because they will later be useful. The end is remote, and education is getting ready, is a preliminary to something more important to happen later on. Childhood is only a preparation for adult life, and adult life for another life. Always the future, not the present, has been the significant thing in education: acquisition of knowledge and skill for future use and enjoyment; formation of habits required later in life in business, good citizenship, and pursuit of science. Education is thought of also as something needed by some human beings merely because of their dependence upon others. We are born ignorant, unversed, unskilled, immature, and consequently in a state of social dependence. Instruction, training, moral discipline are processes by which the mature, the adult, gradually raise the helpless to the point where they can look out for themselves. The business of childhood is to grow into the independence of adulthood by means of the guidance of those who have already attained it. Thus the process of education as the main business of life ends when the young have arrived at emancipation from social dependence.

These two ideas, generally assumed but rarely explicitly reasoned out, contravene the conception that growing, or the continuous reconstruction of experience, is the only end. If at whatever period we choose to take a person, he is still in process of growth, then education is not, save as a byproduct, a preparation for something coming later. Getting from the present the degree and kind of growth there is in it is education. This is a constant function, independent of age. The best thing that can be said about any special process of education, like that of the formal school period, is that it renders its subject capable of further education: more sensitive to conditions of growth and more able to take advantage of them. Acquisition of skill, possession of knowledge, attainment of culture are not ends: they are marks of growth and means to its continuing.

The contrast usually assumed between the period of education as one of social dependence and of maturity as one of social independence does harm. We repeat over and over that man is a social animal, and then confine the significance of this statement to the sphere in which sociality usually seems least evident, politics. The heart of the sociality of man is in education. The idea of education as preparation and of adulthood as a fixed limit of growth are two sides of the same obnoxious untruth. If the moral business of the adult as well as the young is a growing and developing experience, then the instruction that comes from social dependencies and interdependencies is as important for the adult as for the child. Moral independence for the adult means arrest of growth, isolation means induration. We exaggerate the intellectual dependence of childhood so that children are too much kept in leading strings, and then we exaggerate the independence of adult life from intimacy of contacts and communication with others. When the identity of the moral process with the processes of specific growth is realized, the more conscious and formal education of childhood will be seen to be the most economical and efficient means of social advance and reorganization, and it will also be evident that the test of all the institutions of adult life is their effect in furthering continued education. Government, business, art, religion, all social institutions have a meaning, a purpose. That purpose is to set free and to develop the capacities of human individuals without respect to race, sex, class, or economic status. And this is all one with saying that the test of their value is the extent to which they educate every individual into the full stature of his possibility. Democracy has many meanings, but if it has a moral meaning, it is found in resolving that the supreme test of all political institutions and industrial arrangements shall be the contribution they make to the all-around growth of every member of society.

Understanding Ideas

1. According to John Dewey, why has education been thought of as preparation for something else?

2. Why, in Dewey's opinion, is education needed?

3. What, in Dewey's view, is the business of childhood?

4. In Dewey's philosophy, what is the moral business of the adult?

Responding to Ideas

1. *Analysis of Circumstances* John Dewey talks about education as being perceived as preparation for something else. In fact, he talks about many things in our lives that are preparation for something else. However, Dewey decries this view and insists that education is an experience in itself, not just preparation. Write an essay that explores the idea of education not as preparation for a job or a future career but as something in itself, an experience that unfolds while you are taking part in it. How does such a view meld with the usual thinking that you observed in others throughout your own education?

2. *Analysis of Circumstances* One of Dewey's most interesting statements is, "The heart of the sociality of man is in education" (para. 3). Unlike Aristotle, Dewey feels politics is "the sphere in which sociality usually seems least evident" (para. 3). Why would Dewey think that education, rather than politics, is a primary area for social engagement among people? What does education achieve that helps increase social interaction in modern society? What are the ethical and moral implications of an education that prepares you for taking part in society? How has your education contributed to your social relationships?

3. *Response* The moral dimension of education is constantly on Dewey's mind as he explores the issue. What do you see as the moral dimension of education? Write an essay that explains why, in a democratic society, it may be a moral obligation for each of us to get an education. The founding fathers anticipated a free education through grade school. Why should we fund the education of citizens beyond grade school? How much education should be provided free for modern citizens in this country? How much education is necessary for people to be able to "look out for themselves" (para. 1)?

4. *Response* When Aristotle talks about various arts and their aims, naming in some cases the good that each aspired to, he does not mention education directly. Instead, he refers to the contemplative life. Using your education as an example, describe what "good" it aims at. Or do you think of your education as an end in itself, rather than as a means to an end? What is the most ethical purpose to which you can apply your education? Do you have a moral obligation to the society that provided your education to get as much of an education

as possible? Is there an ethical issue involved in dropping out of high school?

5. *Response* Today's emphasis in education is on attaining skills that will permit people to get specific jobs and increase the nation's ability to compete in a global marketplace. What are the moral implications involved in this kind of emphasis? To what extent should education focus on attaining skills and competing in any marketplace? Is education only training? What does the word *learning* imply beyond training? Consider Aristotle's concept of happiness (p. 374). What kind of education is likely to contribute to your lifelong happiness?

6. *Analysis of Circumstances* What is the moral issue involved in a higher education system that emphasizes training for jobs in computer, electronics, and other technological fields that are in rapid flux? The risk of emphasizing procedures that will be obsolete in ten to twenty years, leaving the trained employee redundant, is very great. People who graduate from college today may experience profound market transformations that lead to job changes three to four times in their lifetimes, perhaps involving employment in yet unknown industries. The computer industry as such did not exist thirty-five years ago. A generation of workers has been replaced by computers and without retraining is unable to be part of the new economy. What kind of education will prevent you from falling victim to such redundancy? What kind of education will render you "capable of further education: more sensitive to conditions of growth and more able to take advantage of them" (para. 2)? What are the ethical implications of a "good education"?

Comparing Ideas

1. John Dewey says, "Democracy has many meanings, but if it has a moral meaning, it is found in resolving that the supreme test of all political institutions and industrial arrangements shall be the contribution they make to the all-around growth of every member of society" (para. 3). Compare what Dewey has to say about a moral meaning in democracy with what Robert A. Dahl says in "Why Democracy?" (p. 96). How far does Dahl go in answering whether democracy has a moral meaning? Construct an argument that explains why these writers see a moral meaning in the idea of democracy.

2. Dewey advocates education in our democracy. Review the essays on human rights written by James Madison (p. 65), the Marquis de Lafayette (p. 71), and Mary Wollstonecraft (p. 77). Using those docu-

ments and John Dewey's defense of education, write an argument that defends the right of every citizen (and noncitizen resident) to a free education. Why should education be considered a human right? How much education should a democracy provide to ensure the "all-around growth of every member of society" (para. 3)? What are the ethical issues involved in providing — or withholding — an education from members of society?

© Dario Pignatelli/Reuters/Corbis

THOMAS NAGEL

THOMAS NAGEL (b. 1937) was born in Belgrade, Serbia. He was educated at Cornell, Oxford, and Harvard universities. He is currently a professor of philosophy at New York University. His influential article "What Is It Like to Be a Bat?" was first published in the *Philosophical Review* in October 1974 and made him a well-known philosopher early in his career. In that article, he reveals how difficult it is to think in terms other than one's own subjective consciousness. He argues that states of consciousness cannot be explained by modern physics and that consciousness is for that reason metaphysical. In his most recent book, *Mind and Cosmos: Why the Materialist Neo-Darwinian Conception of Nature Is Almost Certainly False* (2012), Nagel argues that modern Darwinian biologists are incorrect when they emphasize the evolution of life by chance and accident. Instead, he argues, consciousness is the end to the development of life. In other words, evolution is designed to produce consciousness.

Not every philosopher agrees with Nagel, and many have taken issue with him. The defenders of creationism have praised him and see him as a champion of their position that the universe is designed by a God who has a divine plan that is being played out. However, many philosophers and ethicists have attacked Nagel's proposal that the universe is teleological, or designed. Nagel, who is an atheist and whose ethical views do not depend on a religious basis or on the existence of a divine being, does not agree that his philosophy supports creationism.

Among Nagel's important works are *The Possibility of Altruism* (1970), in which he begins some of his thinking on ethical issues, and *Mortal Questions* (1991), a collection of earlier published essays with titles such as "Moral Luck," "Ruthlessness in Public Life," and "Ethics without Biology." One of Nagel's claims is that the study of ethics is still young and that there is much that he does not know about how ethics works in our or in any culture. He insists that more must be done to investigate "the history and psychology of morals," which he says are "important but undeveloped subjects much neglected by philosophers since Nietzsche."

Be sure to practice prereading techniques before a careful, annotated reading of Nagel's essay. For a review of prereading strategies, see pages 4–9. ⊞

The Objective Basis of Morality

S UPPOSE YOU work in a library, checking people's books as they leave, and a friend asks you to let him smuggle out a hard-to-find reference work that he wants to own.

You might hesitate to agree for various reasons. You might be afraid that he'll be caught, and that both you and he will then get into trouble. You might want the book to stay in the library so that you can consult it yourself.

But you may also think that what he proposes is wrong — that he shouldn't do it and you shouldn't help him. If you think that, what does it mean, and what, if anything, makes it true?

To say it's wrong is not just to say it's against the rules. There can be bad rules which prohibit what isn't wrong — like a law against criticizing the government. A rule can also be bad because it requires something that *is* wrong — like a law that requires racial segregation in hotels and restaurants. The ideas of wrong and right are different from the ideas of what is and is not against the rules. Otherwise they couldn't be used in the evaluation of rules as well as of actions.

If you think it would be wrong to help your friend steal the book, then   5 you will feel uncomfortable about doing it: in some way you won't want to do it, even if you are also reluctant to refuse help to a friend. Where does the desire not to do it come from; what is its motive, the reason behind it?

There are various ways in which something can be wrong, but in this case, if you had to explain it, you'd probably say that it would be unfair to other users of the library who may be just as interested in the book as your friend is, but who consult it in the reference room, where anyone who needs it can find it. You may also feel that to let him take it would betray your employers, who are paying you precisely to keep this sort of thing from happening.

These thoughts have to do with effects on others — not necessarily effects on their feelings, since they may never find out about it, but some kind of damage nevertheless. In general, the thought that something is wrong depends on its impact not just on the person who does it but on other people. They wouldn't like it, and they'd object if they found out.

But suppose you try to explain all this to your friend, and he says, "I know the head librarian wouldn't like it if he found out, and probably some of the other users of the library would be unhappy to find the book gone, but who cares? I want the book; why should I care about them?"

The argument that it would be wrong is supposed to give him a reason not to do it. But if someone just doesn't care about other people, what reason does he have to refrain from doing any of the things usually thought to be wrong, if he can get away with it: What reason does he have not to kill, steal, lie, or hurt others? If he can get what he wants by doing such things, why shouldn't he? And if there's no reason why he shouldn't, in what sense is it wrong?

Of course most people do care about others to some extent. But if 10 someone doesn't care, most of us wouldn't conclude that he's exempt from morality. A person who kills someone just to steal his wallet, without caring about the victim, is not automatically excused. The fact that he doesn't care doesn't make it all right: he *should* care. But *why* should he care?

There have been many attempts to answer this question. One type of answer tries to identify something else that the person already cares about, and then connect morality to it.

For example, some people believe that even if you can get away with awful crimes on this earth, and are not punished by the law or your fellow men, such acts are forbidden by God, who will punish you after death (and reward you if you didn't do wrong when you were tempted to). So even when it seems to be in your interest to do such a thing, it really isn't. Some people have even believed that if there is no God to back up moral requirements with the threat of punishment and the promise of reward, morality is an illusion: "If God does not exist, everything is permitted."

This is a rather crude version of the religious foundation for morality. A more appealing version might be that the motive for obeying God's commands is not fear but love. He loves you, and you should love Him, and should wish to obey His commands in order not to offend Him.

But however we interpret the religious motivation, there are three objections to this type of answer. First, plenty of people who don't believe in God still make judgments of right and wrong, and think no one should kill another for his wallet even if he can be sure to get away with it. Second, if God exists, and forbids what's wrong, that still isn't what *makes* it wrong. Murder is wrong in itself, and that's *why* God forbids it (if He does). God couldn't make just any old thing wrong — like putting on your left sock before your right — simply by prohibiting it. If God would punish you for doing that it would be inadvisable to do it, but it wouldn't be wrong. Third, fear of punishment and hope of reward, and even love of God, seem not to be the right motives for morality. If you think it's wrong to kill, cheat, or steal, you should want to avoid doing such things because they are bad things to do to the victims, not just because you fear the consequences for yourself, or because you don't want to offend your Creator.

This third objection also applies to other explanations of the force of 15 morality which appeal to the interests of the person who must act. For example, it may be said that you should treat others with consideration so that they'll do the same for you. This may be sound advice, but it is valid only so far as you think what you do will affect how others treat you. It's not a reason for doing the right thing if others won't find out about it, or against doing the wrong thing if you can get away with it (like being a hit-and-run driver).

There is no substitute for a direct concern for other people as the basis of morality. But morality is supposed to apply to everyone: And can we assume that everyone has such a concern for others? Obviously not: some people are very selfish, and even those who are not selfish may care only about the people they know, and not about everyone. So where will we find a reason that everyone has not to hurt other people, even those they don't know?

Well, there's one general argument against hurting other people which can be given to anybody who understands English (or any other language), and which seems to show that he has *some* reason to care about others, even if in the end his selfish motives are so strong that he persists in treating other people badly anyway. It's an argument that I'm sure you've heard, and it goes like this: "How would you like it if someone did that to you?"

It's not easy to explain how this argument is supposed to work. Suppose you're about to steal someone else's umbrella as you leave a restaurant in a rainstorm, and a bystander says, "How would you like it if someone did that to you?" Why is it supposed to make you hesitate, or feel guilty?

Obviously the direct answer to the question is supposed to be, "I wouldn't like it at all!" But what's the next step? Suppose you were to say, "I wouldn't like it if someone did that to me. But luckily no one *is* doing it to me. I'm doing it to someone else, and I don't mind that at all!"

This answer misses the point of the question. When you are asked how 20 you would like it if someone did that to you, you are supposed to think about all the feelings you would have if someone stole your umbrella. And that includes more than just "not liking it" — as you wouldn't "like it" if you stubbed your toe on a rock. If someone stole your umbrella you'd *resent* it. You'd have feelings about the umbrella thief, not just about the loss of the umbrella. You'd think, "Where does he get off, taking my umbrella that I bought with my hard-earned money and that I had the foresight to bring after reading the weather report? Why didn't he bring his own umbrella?" and so forth.

When our own interests are threatened by the inconsiderate behavior of others, most of us find it easy to appreciate that those others have a reason to be more considerate. When you are hurt, you probably feel that other people should care about it: you don't think it's no concern of theirs, and that they have no reason to avoid hurting you. That is the feeling that the "How would you like it?" argument is supposed to arouse.

Because if you admit that you would *resent* it if someone else did to you what you are now doing to him, you are admitting that you think he would have a reason not to do it to you. And if you admit that, you have to consider what that reason is. It couldn't be just that it's *you* that he's hurting, of all the people in the world. There's no special reason for him not to steal *your* umbrella, as opposed to anyone else's. There's nothing so special about you. Whatever the reason is, it's a reason he would have against hurting anyone else in the same way. And it's a reason anyone else would have too, in a similar situation, against hurting you or anyone else.

> *"There is no substitute for a direct concern for other people as the basis of morality."*

But if it's a reason anyone would have not to hurt anyone else in this way, then it's a reason *you* have not to hurt someone else in this way (since *anyone* means *everyone*). Therefore it's a reason not to steal the other person's umbrella now.

This is a matter of simple consistency. Once you admit that another person would have a reason not to harm you in similar circumstances, and once you admit that the reason he would have is very general and doesn't apply only to you, or to him, then to be consistent you have to admit that the same reason applies to you now. You shouldn't steal the umbrella, and you ought to feel guilty if you do.

Someone could escape from this argument if, when he was asked, "How would you like it if someone did that to you?" he answered, "I wouldn't resent it at all. I wouldn't *like* it if someone stole my umbrella in a rainstorm, but I wouldn't think there was any reason for him to consider my feelings about it." But how many people could honestly give that answer? I think most people, unless they're crazy, would think that their own interests and harms matter, not only to themselves, but in a way that gives other people a reason to care about them too. We all think that when we suffer it is not just bad *for us*, but *bad, period*.

The basis of morality is a belief that good and harm to particular people (or animals) is good or bad not just from their point of view, but from a more general point of view, which every thinking person can understand. That means that each person has a reason to consider not only his own interests but the interests of others in deciding what to do. And it isn't enough if he is considerate only of some others — his family and friends, those he specially cares about. Of course he will care more about certain people, and also about himself. But he has some reason to consider the effect of what he does on the good or harm of everyone. If he's like most of us, that is what he thinks others should do with regard to him, even if they aren't friends of his.

Understanding Ideas

1. According to Thomas Nagel, why don't rules against behavior make that behavior wrong?

2. In Nagel's view, in what ways does unfairness constitute a wrong?

3. What does Nagel believe is the religious motivation for good behavior?

4. How does the Golden Rule, "Do unto others as you would have them do to you," help establish wrong behavior?

Responding to Ideas

1. **Analysis of Circumstances** Thomas Nagel says, "There is no substitute for a direct concern for other people as the basis of morality" (para. 16). Explain what you think he means by this statement. Why should your good behavior and your avoidance of doing what is wrong be conditioned by your concern for other people? Should you be concerned for other people even when you know they are not concerned for you? Are those who are unconcerned immoral people? Are people who are generally indifferent living immoral lives? Explain in a brief essay why lack of concern for other people does or does not constitute a question of morality.

2. **Response** Imagine a world in which, for a time, you are alone and not in a social situation in which anything you might do could harm or help anyone else. You would not need to concern yourself about other people at all. What then would constitute moral behavior on your part? Is there any ethical or moral behavior that you would maintain in order not to do anything wrong? What ethical or moral value would the words *good* and *bad* have in a circumstance in which you are totally alone? What is your moral obligation to yourself, and how would you fulfill it? If you could do anything — something good or something bad — what would it be?

3. *Analysis of Circumstances* Why is stealing a moral issue? There are many cases in literature and life in which a starving man or woman stole food for his or her family, thus preventing the family from starving to death. Should such thieves be punished for immoral behavior? What are the moral complications implied in any action that prevents the death of people who, by stealing, could save themselves or their families? If you feel that such people are justified in their actions, then what does that tell you about the elasticity of moral values? If such starving people stole food from other starving people, would that change the moral equation in any significant way? Write an essay that tackles this issue. You may want to consult the idea of the sanctity of property rights in the Bill of Rights (p. 65) or the Declaration of the Rights of Man and Citizen (p. 71) as you prepare your essay.

4. *Analysis of Circumstances* Nagel discusses the question of belief in God not just as a way of establishing moral behavior but as a way of qualifying all behavior in terms of morality. Religions provide moral instruction. What moral instruction do religions provide beyond the Ten Commandments set forth in the Bible (Exod. 20:1–17)? Three of the commandments concern respect for God, one tells us to honor our parents, and the rest direct our behavior toward others: do not murder; do not commit adultery; do not steal; do not bear false witness; do not covet other people's property, wives, or servants. Are these the limits of moral behavior? Do religions add other "commandments" that become moral requirements, and, if so, are they fully moral in your judgment? In an essay, consider the power of religion to establish morality in society.

5. *Definition* Thomas Nagel says, "Murder is wrong in itself" (para. 14). In other words, it is wrong without reference to any other value. What does it mean for an action to be "wrong in itself"? How does that then create a moral valuation of murder? What other actions are wrong in themselves? How can a terrorist commit murder and consider it a moral action? By what moral standards can we establish any actions as wrong without reference to religious or political values?

6. *Response* What is the moral status of rape? Philosophers have pointed out that rape may be an evolutionary strategy for increasing the progeny of the strong rather than the weak. In nature some animals, including and especially primates, gather a bevy of females that they guard by force and impregnate. Some religions have maintained polygamy, and often by force. If rape could in some sense be considered a natural behavior, on what objective basis must we condemn it as immoral?

Comparing Ideas

1. Lucy A. Delaney in "Struggles for Freedom" (p. 146) makes reference to the Fugitive Slave Act of 1850, which made harboring escaped slaves a crime. The fines were very high and the possibility of jail almost certain. This was a federal law in a democratic nation. Why did so many people — and even states — feel it was morally correct to ignore the law and protect escaped slaves? Since slaves in 1850 were considered property, why were those who helped them reach freedom not con-sidered thieves? Why is a perceived disjunction between such a law and what people feel is moral behavior a problem? Those who owned slaves felt they were behaving morally and used the Bible to back their views. So on what grounds can we declare that their behavior was immoral? Did those who defied the Fugitive Slave Act invent their own system of morality to justify breaking the law? In a brief essay, answer the following question: When is it ethical to break the law, and who decides?

2. Friedrich Nietzsche (p. 393) suggests that the decision about what is moral and ethical has been made by an elite class of rulers in order to keep everyone else in line. Popular literature suggests that moral behavior varies among social classes and that the most powerful class of people have a moral code that sometimes admits sexual infidelity and various deceptions, financial and otherwise, that shock the middle and working classes. Celebrities in the entertainment and sports worlds often flout ethical values that others live by. Find at least one example of a powerful person or group that you feel often behaves immorally. Write an essay that explains what makes the behavior immoral. What makes it unethical? Does society resent the behavior or condone it? Does the behavior act as a model for people who are not as powerful or who are not celebrities?

MICHAEL GAZZANIGA

MICHAEL GAZZANIGA (b. 1939), a professor of psychology at the University of California, Santa Barbara, is head of the SAGE Center for the Study of the Mind. His primary research has been studying the relationship of the mind to the brain. He was among the first scientists to examine the two hemispheres of the brain as they acted independently once surgery had separated them. (This surgery was performed on people with severe epilepsy, who reported themselves freed of attacks when their hemispheres were separated.) Each hemisphere was seen to specialize in certain functions. For example, the left hemisphere is specialized to handle language, reading, writing, and math skills. The right hemisphere handles music, visual relations, spatial relations, and artistic skills. One of Gazzaniga's early books, *The Bisected Brain* (1970), describes the research that examines the implications of these discoveries.

The selection that follows is from *The Ethical Brain* (2005). In it, Gazzaniga asks a serious question: Is ethical behavior hardwired in the brain through eons of evolution? He begins to answer this question by considering the moral questions raised and answered over the centuries by philosophers and religious thinkers who created what he calls "stories" about the way we should behave. These thinkers worked "in the dark" because they knew nothing about the science of brain development and brain systems. Gazzaniga reminds us that the functions of the brain can be revealed on medical scans with some clarity. The seat of personality and the physical areas involved in moral choice are in the frontal lobe, which does not fully mature until a person is in his or her early twenties.

Gazzaniga's early discussion of evolution and the development of the brain reminds us that we have inherited the genes of the earliest people, from the time when there may have only been ten thousand or so people on Earth. That raises the question of how much of our natural behavior is meant to guarantee survival. The fact that some people are prone to violence may be a holdover from our distant ancestors having lived in the wild. Gazzaniga admits as much, but he also explains that we have been living in social groups for thousands of years and part of the reason for our survival as a group is that we have learned to use self-control. Ethical behavior begins with self-control.

In the long run, Gazzaniga points out, our capacity for empathy, our willingness to come to the aid of others, and our self-control are essential to the survival of the species. His examination of ethics raises issues about the ways the human brain has evolved.

Be sure to practice prereading techniques before a careful, annotated reading of Gazzaniga's essay. For a review of prereading strategies, see pages 4–9. ⊞

Toward a Universal Ethics

EVER-ADVANCING HUMAN knowledge seeps into the assumptions of everyone on earth whether they like it or not. From Harvard Square to a remote village in Sri Lanka, people have concepts of a gene, a brain, the Internet, the good life. Affluent cultures and democracies gain from all this knowledge, even though the lessons of modern knowledge about the nature of the world may produce conflicts with some traditional beliefs. That is what is happening on the surface. Underneath these material gains is another, psychological reality. Modern knowledge is on a collision course with the ubiquitous personal spiritual belief systems of one kind or another that are held by billions of people. Putting it in secular terms, no one has told the kids yet there is no Santa Claus.

We are big animals, and only five thousand generations ago there were just ten thousand of us roaming the world. Our genes stem from those ten thousand people and are 99.9 percent the same. Ever since that time, we have been busy cooking up cultures and stumbling forward. Anyone who does not appreciate this fundamental fact of modern life is either clinging to heartfelt beliefs about the nature of life and the history of the world, or is quite simply out of the loop. This is the single most disturbing reality of modern-day citizenship and our notion of shared values.

Received wisdom — the thoughts of the giants of human history — is stunning, captivating, and intelligent. But for the most part it is based on first guesses, as we know from current scientific and historical information. Aristotle, Socrates, Hume, Locke, Descartes, Aquinas, Darwin,

Hobbes[1] — all put forward explanations of human nature that still reso-nate today. Their thinking about approaches to life are brilliant schemas for how the world must be, based on the information made available to them at the time, and are the products of clear-thinking people. Religious movements throughout human history produced moral codes and interpretations and stories about what it means to be human — indeed, what it means to exist at all. All are part of our rich past. The harsh, cold fact, however, is that these rich, metaphoric, engaging ideas — whether philosophical or religious — are stories, although some are based on more evidence than others. Even if you do not believe or accept this as a given, you should be aware that this is what every modern-day secular university is teaching, either implicitly or explicitly.

What is more fascinating to me is that even though new data provide scientific and historical bases for new views about nature and our past, people can still disagree about whether there even *is* a human nature. As Steven Pinker[2] recently remarked before the President's Council on Bioeth-ics, "In much of the 20th Century, there was a widespread denial of the exis-tence of human nature in Western intellectual life, and I will just present three representative quotations. 'Man has no nature,' from the philosopher José Ortega y Gasset. 'Man has no instincts,' from the anthropologist and public intellectual Ashley Montagu. 'The human brain is capable of a full range of behaviors and predisposed to none,' from the evolutionary biolo-gist Stephen Jay Gould."[3]

Yet we know there *is* something we call human nature, with fixed quali- 5 ties and inevitable expression in any number of situations. We know that some fixed properties of mind come with us from the baby factory, that all humans possess certain skills and abilities other animals don't have, and that all of this makes up the human condition. And we now know that we are the products of an evolutionary process that has shaped our species, for better or for worse. We are big animals. The rest of our stories about our origins are just that, stories that comfort, cajole, and even motivate — but stories nonetheless.

---

[1] **Aristotle . . . Hobbes** Philosophers ranging from early Greeks to nineteenth-century thinkers who posited theories of human behavior and also expressed or implied moral theories.

[2] **Steven Pinker** (b. 1954) Professor of psychology at Harvard University and a student of the evolutionary nature of the language instinct.

[3] **Ortega y Gasset . . . Gould** José Ortega y Gasset (1883–1955) was one of Spain's greatest modern philosophers; Ashley Montagu (1905–1999) was a prominent anthropologist; Stephen Jay Gould (1941–2002) was professor of zoology at Harvard University and author of books studying evidence relating to Darwin's evolutionary theories.

This leaves us in a quandary and with a task. The quandary is daunting: to understand that most of our current beliefs and moral systems derive from theories, perhaps based on the logic of what our species' best minds through the ages, reacting to life's events, could posit about the nature of reality. For those who realize and believe this, the task and the challenge of modern humans is to try to discern whether our highly evolved human nature and culture benefit from an underlying universal ethics, a moral response to life's challenges that has been a feature of our species from the beginning. The question is, Do we have an innate moral sense as a species, and if so, can we recognize and accept it on its own terms? It is not a good idea to kill because it is not a good idea to kill, not because God or Allah or Buddha said it was not a good idea to kill.

GUESSING ABOUT OUR MORAL SENSE

Until recently, the possibility that our species has a built-in moral sense, a basic human capacity to make judgments about right and wrong, has been argued more by assertion and analysis of human behavior than by demonstrated biological fact. Especially rare, if not missing entirely from the argument, has been the fact that we could not draw upon how the brain works in morally challenging situations. Modern social scientists can get only so far in their efforts to understand human behavior. James Q. Wilson[4] used analysis of social science research in his classic 1993 book, *The Moral Sense*, but admitted, "The truth, if it exists, is in the details. . . . I am not trying to discover 'facts' that will prove 'values'; I am endeavoring to uncover the evolutionary, developmental, and cultural origins of our moral habits and our moral sense. But in discovering these origins, I suspect that we will encounter uniformities; and by revealing uniformities, I think that we can better appreciate what is general, nonarbitrary, and emotionally compelling about human nature."[5] Wilson, the distinguished political scientist from Harvard and now UCLA, suggested, "However much the scientific method is thought to be the enemy of morality, scientific findings provide substantial support for its existence and power."[6] Wilson cast an astonishingly wide net to make his case for an innate human moral sense. He reviewed not only the history of philosophy but also evolutionary theory, anthropology, criminology, psychology, and sociology. He concluded that no matter what intellectuals argue, there are certain universal, guiding moral instincts. In fact, they are

---

[4] **James Q. Wilson** (1931–2012) Political scientist and professor of government at Harvard, UCLA , and Pepperdine.

[5] Wilson, J. Q. (1993). *The Moral Sense* (New York: Free Press), p. 26. [Gazzaniga's note]

[6] Ibid., p. xii. [Gazzaniga's note]

so instinctual that they often get overlooked: "Much of the dispute over the existence of human universals has taken the form of a search for laws and stated practices. But what is most likely to be universal are those impulses that, because they are so common, scarcely need to be stated in the form of a rule. . . ."[7] Highest among these are that all societies believe that murder and incest are wrong, that children are to be cared for and not abandoned, that we should not tell lies or break promises, and that we should be loyal to family.

Wilson rejected the idea that morality is purely a social construct — that we are constrained by the need to behave a certain way because of external factors: "For there to be a contract, whether to create a state or manage and exchange, there must first be a willingness to obey contracts; there must be in Durkheim's[8] phrase, some noncontractual elements of contract."

Wilson may have been prescient. A series of studies suggesting that there *is* a brain-based account of moral reasoning have burst onto the scientific scene. It has been found that regions of the brain normally active in emotional processing are activated with one kind of moral judgment but not another. Arguments that have raged for centuries about the nature of moral decisions and their sameness or difference are now quickly and distinctly resolved with modern brain imaging. The short form of the new results suggests that when someone is willing to *act* on a moral belief, it is because the emotional part of his or her brain has become active when considering the moral question at hand. Similarly, when a morally equivalent problem is presented that he or she decides not to act on, it is because the emotional part of the brain does not become active. This is a stunning development in human knowledge because it points the way toward figuring out how the brain's automatic response may predict our moral response.

SCANNING FOR MORAL REASONING

First, to be able to assess moral reasoning, scientists have analyzed the   10
psychology of different moral theories. In other words, they have asked what kinds of decisions or judgments a person needs to make in order to decide what actions to take. This careful assessment of moral reasoning is obviously tricky, and in a laboratory setting, ascertaining what kinds of decisions trigger what kinds of brain reactions is even trickier; but some clever researchers are doing just that.

Evolutionary psychology points out that moral reasoning is good for human survival — the ability to recognize a certain norm for behaving in society and to apply it to others and oneself helps one to survive and thrive.

---

[7] Ibid., p. 18. [Gazzaniga's note]

[8] **Durkheim** Emile Durkheim (1858–1917), considered the father of modern sociology.

As William D. Casebeer,[9] a young philosopher at the Air Force Academy, has written, "We are social creatures, and if we are to flourish in our social environments, we must learn how to reason well about what we should do."[10] The question, then, is whether this skill might be built in to the brain, hard-wired by evolution.

To me, these kinds of issues may be where the true secrets about the uniqueness of the human brain, the human condition, lie. Research long ago recognized that the essential function of the human brain is to make decisions; it is a decision-making device. On no dimension of human consciousness are more decisions made than on social issues, the second-by-second, minute-by-minute judgments we make all day long about our standing and situation in a social group. The enormous cerebral cortex — the huge expansion of capacity in the human brain — may be there for social processes such as our relentless need for social comparison. Could it be that these decisions are influenced by some kind of universal moral compass we all possess? This issue, along with others, is why the new field of social neuroscience is so exciting and potentially enlightening.

When a scientist wants to design experiments to see what brain centers become active during moral reasoning, he or she needs to examine moral reasoning itself. This is difficult, given how many different moral philosophies exist. Nonetheless, a good place to begin is with the three main Western philosophies: utilitarianism, deontology, and virtue theory — represented by the philosophers John Stuart Mill, Immanuel Kant, and Aristotle, respectively. Utilitarians believe in actions that produce the most happiness for the most people; in other words, they look to the bottom line. Deontologists don't worry about the outcome of an action but focus on the intention that produced it — it's more important not to violate another person's rights than to have an ideal outcome. Virtue theorists look to cultivate virtue and avoid vices.[11]

Casebeer reviewed this trio of philosophies and concluded, "Jokingly, then, it could be said that these approaches emphasize different brain regions: frontal (Kant); prefrontal, limbic, and sensory (Mill); the properly coordinated action of all (Aristotle)."[12] That goes to the heart of the question:

---

[9] **William D. Casebeer** Former professor of philosophy at the Air Force Academy and current intelligence officer for the U.S. Air Force. His book is *Natural Ethical Facts: Evolution, Connectionism, and Moral Cognition* (2003).

[10] Casebeer, W. D. (2003). "Moral Cognition and Its Neural Constituents," *Nature Reviews Neuroscience* 4: 840–847. [Gazzaniga's note]

[11] Ibid. [Gazzaniga's note]

[12] **frontal . . . all** The frontal lobe of the brain is the large portion of both hemispheres located behind the forehead; the prefrontal cortex is beneath the forehead and responsible for actions involving moral decisions; the limbic system is responsible for emotional behavior; the sensory is a group of lobes that parse sight, sound, and so on. Casebeer connects each to the philosopher whose "stories" most clearly relate to those portions of the brain.

Are there moral reasoning centers in the brain? It's surely not as simple as that, but it may well be that intricate and distributed neural networks are active when a person is making certain moral decisions. Can they be captured with modern brain-imaging technologies?

Research on moral cognition studies three main topics: moral emotions, theory of mind, and abstract moral reasoning. Moral emotions — those that motivate behavior — are driven mostly by the brain stem and limbic axis, which regulate basic drives such as sex, food, thirst, and so on. *Theory of mind* is the term for our ability to judge what others are thinking so that we can behave appropriately in response to them — an essential in moral reasoning because it guides our social behavior. The "mirror neurons" I discussed [earlier], the orbital frontal cortex, the medial structures of the amygdala, and the superior temporal sulcus are believed to be responsible for theory-of-mind processes. Finally, abstract moral reasoning, brain imaging is showing us, uses many brain systems.

"When a scientist wants to design experiments to see what brain centers become active during moral reasoning, he or she needs to examine moral reasoning itself."

The dilemma in abstract moral reasoning studies most often presented by researchers to volunteers is the trolley problem, one version of which I described [earlier]. In this version, a trolley is hurtling down a track, headed straight for five people. You have to decide whether to let it hit the five people or, up close and personal, throw a person standing next to you onto the tracks to stop the trolley from hitting the other five.

Most people claim they won't throw the nearby person in front of the trolley. At the same time, they will pull a switch and divert the train to another track, which will spare the five people even though the switched train will run into and kill a single person. So the question is, Where do these gut reactions come from? Is there a neural basis for these two prevalent responses? Have they been honed through evolution?

Joshua Greene,[13] a neurophilosopher from Princeton, raises two additional commonly used examples. Say you are driving along in your new car and you see a man on the side of the road. He has been in an accident and is bloody. You could take him to the hospital and save his life; however, you would get blood all over your new car. Is it morally okay to leave him there? Or take another scenario. You receive a request in the mail saying that if you send in $100, you will save the lives of ten starving children. Is it okay to not send in the money?

[13] **Joshua Greene** Professor of psychology at Harvard University and author of *The Moral Brain and How to Use It* (2012).

In analyzing these kinds of dilemmas, Greene and his colleagues found that while the choices are the same on the surface — do nothing and preserve your self-interest, or save lives at little cost to yourself — the difference is that the first scenario is personal whereas the second is impersonal. As already mentioned, Greene's studies found that judgments of personal dilemmas such as those seen in the trolley problem involve more brain activity in areas associated with emotion and moral cognition. Why is this? From an evolutionary perspective the theory is that the neural structures that tie altruistic instincts to emotion may have been selected for over time because helping people immediately is beneficial. Gut instinct, or morality, is a result of processes selected for over the evolutionary process. We have cognitive processes that allow us to make quick moral decisions that will increase our likelihood of survival. If we are wired to save a guy right in front of us, we all survive better. In the case of the money contribution, long-distance altruism just isn't as necessary; out of sight, out of mind. There is no dire need.

This brings us back to the central issue of whether moral truths are 20 really universal truths, or whether they are merely opinions, individual gut instincts. When making moral judgments, are we perceiving external truths or expressing internal attitudes? The new brain imaging results are highly suggestive that our brains are responding to the great underlying moral dilemmas. It is as if all the social data of the moment, the personal survival interests we each possess, the cultural experience we have undergone, and the basic temperament of our species all feed into the subconscious mechanisms we all possess and out comes a response, an urging for either action or inaction. This is the moral spark Wilson was talking about. This is the glue that keeps our species, over the long haul, from destroying itself.

Marc Hauser[14] has addressed this issue, as we saw [earlier]. He reasoned that if moral judgments were derived from rational processes, one would predict that people from different cultures, of different ages and sexes, would respond differently to a common challenge. He also reasoned that they would have readily available and articulate justifications for their decisions. Hauser showed that irrespective of sex, age, and culture, most subjects responded in a similar fashion, making similar moral choices. Further, and most important, none could articulate or justify their responses. In short, there seem to be common subconscious mechanisms that are activated in all members of our species in response to moral challenges. When the participants in Hauser's research were challenged to explain their decision, none of them were particularly rational or logical. Their explanations seemed to be the product of personal interpreters spinning out some theory or other that seemed right to them on the spot.

---

[14] **Marc Hauser** (b. 1959) Professor of psychology at Harvard University until 2011, where he focused on evolutionary biology and cognitive neuroscience.

Most moral judgments are intuitive, as I've noted throughout this book. We have a reaction to a situation, or an opinion, and we form a theory as to why we feel the way we do. In short, we have an automatic reaction to a situation — a brain-derived response. Upon feeling that response, we come to believe we are reacting to absolute truths. What I am suggesting is that these moral ideas are generated by our interpreter, by our brains, yet we form a theory about their absolute "rightness." Characterizing the formation of a moral code in this way puts the challenge directly on us. As Greene points out, "It is one thing to care about the plight of the poor, and another to think that one's caring is objectively correct."[15] It looks like it may be correct after all.

Somehow our brains are cued to be alert to the mental states of others as we struggle to play a productive role in developing a moral code in a social group. Somehow it would seem the universally recognized mechanisms of self-survival have been co-opted and are used to work in more social settings. Evolution is saving the group, not just the person, because it would seem that saving the group saves the person. To do this, we have somehow become mind readers, reflexively.

HOW WE READ MINDS

There are two major theories about how we "read minds" — that is, how we attribute certain mental or emotional states to others in order to explain or predict their behavior. The first is simulation theory (ST), whereby, very simply, we put ourselves in another person's shoes and figure out what we'd do in his or her situation. This requires us to use our imaginations to feed in "fake" data and to be able to hold the fake data separate from real life so that we don't act on it but only imagine what we would do, given the circumstances.[16]

Rivaling ST is the redundant-sounding theory-theory, or TT. "TT maintains that the mental terms and concepts used in understanding human behavior get their predictive and explanatory credentials by being embedded in a folk theory of mind."[17] This folk psychology, the theory goes, is a set of rules that we use to judge and gauge others' behavior. We need not be conscious of this set of rules, or even of using them; they are just there. But where does

25

---

[15] Greene, Joshua (2003). "From Neural 'Is' to Moral 'Ought': What Are the Moral Implications of Neuroscientific Moral Psychology?," *Nature Reviews Neuroscience* 4: 847–850. [Gazzaniga's note]

[16] Gallese, V., and A. Goldman (1998). "Mirror Neurons and the Simulation Theory of Mind-Reading," *Trends in Cognitive Sciences* 2: 493–501; Goldman, A. (1989). "Interpretation Psychologized," *Mind and Language* 4: 104–119. [Gazzaniga's note]

[17] Ibid. [Gazzaniga's note]

the theory come from? Here is where TT comes up against the same problem that Greene raises about where moral truths come from, the nature-nurture dilemma. Are we born with the knowledge, or do the rules exist in the ether, available for us to learn? TT adherents differ on whether the theory is innate or learned, as well as on whether we use a distinct "theory of mind" module in the brain or some more continuous system of representations that produce the same effect. What theory-theorists agree on is that we are in fact using knowledge that is encoded in a theory to judge behavior.

ST, on the other hand, denies that we are using a theory or body of knowledge or rules to judge behavior; "rather our own mental processes are treated as a manipulable model of other minds." Even though we may make generalizations that, say, people tend to do X in circumstances like Y, simulation theorists believe this approach is process driven rather than being based strictly on preexisting knowledge. "The basic idea is that if the resources our own brain uses to guide our own behavior can be put to work as a model of other people, then we have no need to store general information about what makes people tick: We just do the ticking for them."[18]

A long and rich history of psychological research has outlined what is called the empathy altruism hypothesis, which seeks to explain the prosocial behavior we engage in when we watch another human being in distress. We automatically and unconsciously simulate this distress in our minds, which in turn makes us feel bad — not in an abstract way, but literally bad. We become infected by the other person's negative feelings, and in order to alleviate this state in ourselves, we are motivated to action. A number of studies support this idea — that manipulating feelings toward an individual increases helping behavior. Looking at expressions of distress, for example, enhances helping behavior.[19]

Indeed, Adam Smith[20] was onto aspects of this thinking about social contagion. In 1759 he wrote, "When we see a stroke aimed and just ready to fall upon the leg or arm of another person, we naturally shrink and draw back our leg or our own arm; and when it does fall, we feel it in some measure, and are hurt by it as well as the sufferer . . . Persons of delicate

---

[18] Gordon, R. See www.umsl.edu/~philo/Mind_Seminar/New%20Pages/subject.html. [Gazzaniga's note]

[19] Batson, C. D., and J. S. Coke (1981). "Empathy: A Source of Altruistic Motivation for Helping," in *Altruism and Helping Behavior: Social Personality and Developmental Perspectives*, J. P. Rushton and R. M. Sorrentino, eds (Hillsdale, N.J.: Erlbaum), pp. 167–211. Also, Cialdini, R. B., S. L. Brown, B. P. Lewis, C. Luce, and S. L. Neuberg (1997). "Reinterpreting the Empathy-Altruism Relationship: When One into One Equals Oneness," *Journal of Personality and Social Psychology* 73: 481–494; and Hoffman, M. L. (2000). *Empathy and Moral Development: Implications for Caring and Justice* (New York: Cambridge University Press). [Gazzaniga's note]

[20] **Adam Smith** (1723–1790) Professor of moral philosophy at Glasgow University and author of *The Wealth of Nations* (1776).

fibres and weak constitution of body complain, that in looking at the sores and ulcers which are exposed by beggars on the streets, they are apt to feel an itching or uneasy sensation in the correspondent part of their own bodies."[21]

Countless experiments have been carried out to support this general idea. My former colleague at Dartmouth, John Lanzetta,[22] and his colleagues demonstrated repeatedly that people tend to respond to the sense of touch, taste, pain, fear, joy, and excitement of others with analogous physiological activation patterns of their own. They literally feel the emotional states of others as their own.[23] This tendency to react to the distress of others appears to be innate: it has been demonstrated in newborn infants, who cry in response to the distress of other infants within the first days of life.[24]

In considering all these arguments, I believe the STs have it right. From a neuroscience perspective, the mirror neuron could support the ST view of how this works. Mirror neurons are believed to be responsible for "action understanding" — that is, understanding the actions of others. While we can't ethically do single-cell recording of mirror neurons in humans, some neurophysiological and brain imaging experiments suggest that mirror neurons do exist in humans and that they function to help with action understanding as well as action imitation.[25]

The neurophysiology of what might be called social process started in 1954, when Henri Gastaut[26] and his colleagues in Marseille noted in EEG studies that human subjects have a brain wave response not only when performing actions themselves but when watching others perform actions. Gastaut's research has since been confirmed by many studies using both additional brain measurement techniques, such as the more advanced magnetoencephalographic technique, and stimulation techniques, such as transcranial magnetic stimulation (TMS), a noninvasive technique for electrical stimulation of the nervous system. Another important finding of the more recent studies has been that the spinal cord inhibits the execution of the observed action, "leaving the cortical motor system free to 'react' to that

30

---

[21] Hatfield, E., J. T. Cacioppo, and R. L. Rapson (1994). *Emotional Contagion* (New York: Cambridge University Press), p. 17. [Gazzaniga's note]

[22] **John Lanzetta** (1926–1989) Former professor of psychology at Dartmouth College.

[23] Lanzetta, J. T., and B. G. Englis (1989). "Expectations of Cooperation and Competition and Their Effects on Observers' Vicarious Emotional Responses," *Journal of Personality and Social Psychology* 56: 543–554. [Gazzaniga's note]

[24] Simner, M. L. (1971). "Newborn's Response to the Cry of Another Infant," *Developmental Psychology* 5: 136–150. [Gazzaniga's note]

[25] Rizzolatti, G., and L. Craighero (2004). "The Mirror Neuron System," *Annual Reviews in Neuroscience* 27: 169–192. [Gazzaniga's note]

[26] **Henri Gastaut** (1915–1995) French neurologist and specialist in epilepsy.

action without the risk of every movement generation."[27] Rizzolatti[28] and his colleagues point out that, in total, the TMS studies indicate that the human mirror system not only exists, but differs from the monkey system in a key way: it seems to recognize meaningless movements, such as vague gestures, as well as goal-directed movements.

Why is that important? Because these are the skills needed to imitate movements. This could suggest that the human mirror neuronal system is the basis for learning by imitation.

Human imaging studies are seeking to identify the complex network that is activated by the human mirror system. This is important to the search for the biology of moral reasoning. If we know what part of the brain is activated when observing an action, we can start to understand what mechanisms the brain uses to understand the world. For instance, if observing a barking dog activates my motor and visual areas, but seeing a picture of a barking dog activates only my visual area, this suggests not only that we process the information from these two situations differently, but that this different processing may evoke a different psychological experience of the observation. Observing a dog barking activates my motor system and therefore creates a deeper resonance with the observed action; seeing a picture of a barking dog just doesn't get "in my bones" in the same way.

Rizzolatti suggests that when we learn new motor patterns, it is possible we break them down into basic movements, via the mirror mechanism, and that once the mirror system activates these basic motor representations, they are recombined into the action. He goes on to argue, as did Robin Allott[29] before him, that the mirror system, with its role in imitation and action understanding, may be the evolutionary precursor to language.[30] In other words, we went from understanding others' gestures, to understanding abstract representations of meaning — speech. This idea is supported by research suggesting hand and mouth gestures are linked in humans.

V. S. Ramachandran's[31] work on anosognosia patients — the stroke   35 patients who deny their paralysis — indicates another crucial role mirror

---

[27] Rizzolatti and Craighero. "Mirror Neuron System," citing Baldissera, F., P. Cavallari, L. Craighero, and L. Fadiga (2001). "Modulation of Spinal Excitability During Observation of Hand Actions in Humans," *European Journal of Neuroscience* 13: 190–194. [Gazzaniga's note]

[28] **Rizzolatti** Giacomo Rizzolatti (b. 1937) Italian neurophysiologist at the University of Parma.

[29] **Robin Allott** Author of *Motor Theory of Language* (1987) who describes himself as a "higher education professional."

[30] Allott, R. (1991). "The Motor Theory of Language," in *Studies in Language Origins*, vol. 2, W. von Raffler-Enel, J. Wind, and A. Jonker, eds. (Amsterdam: John Benjamins), pp. 123–157. [Gazzaniga's note]

[31] **V. S. Ramachandran** (b. 1951) Professor of psychology at the University of California at San Diego. Among his books is *The Emerging Mind* (2003).

neurons may play in humans. Ramachandran found that some patients deny not only their own paralysis but the obvious paralysis of others — something he suggests may be due to damage to mirror neurons. "It's as if anytime you want to make a judgment about someone else's movements, you have to run a VR [virtual reality] simulation of the corresponding movements in your own brain, and without mirror neurons you cannot do this."[32] If this is so, it would seem that mirror neurons support the simulation theorists' view that the brain is built to feel not only our own experiences but those of others.

The tension between ST and TT gets us back to the universal ethics dilemma. Are the moral truths we seem to live by a set of rules that exist independently of us, rules that we learn and live by? Or are these rules the result of our brains using built-in systems to empathize and thereby predict behavior and act accordingly? Whatever the answer, one thing is clear: the rules exist.

I believe, therefore, that we should look not for a universal ethics comprising hard-and-fast truths, but for the universal ethics that arises from being human, which is clearly contextual, emotion-influenced, and designed to increase our survival. This is why it is hard to arrive at absolute rules to live by that we can all agree on. But knowing that morals are contextual and social, and based on neural mechanisms, can help us determine certain ways to deal with ethical issues. This is the mandate for neuroethics: to use our understanding that the brain reacts to things on the basis of its hardwiring to contextualize and debate the gut instincts that serve the greatest good — or the most logical solutions — given specific contexts.

I am convinced that we must commit ourselves to the view that a universal ethics is possible, and that we ought to seek to understand it and define it. It is a staggering idea, and one that on casual thought seems preposterous. Yet there is no way out. We now understand how tendentious our beliefs about the world and the nature of human experience truly are, and how dependent we have become on tales from the past. At some level we all know this. At the same time, our species wants to believe in something, some natural order, and it is the job of modern science to help figure out how that order should be characterized.

Understanding Ideas

1. According to Michael Gazzaniga, why is it important to understand whether or not the brain is hardwired to make us care for others?

---

[32] Ramachandran, V. S. "Mirror Neurons and Imitation Learning as the Driving Force Behind 'the Great Leap Forward' in Human Evolution," *Third Edge*. See www.edge .org/3rd_culture/ramachandran/ramachandran_p1.html. [Gazzaniga's note]

2. Why, in Gazzaniga's view, must we become mind readers?

3. As Gazzaniga explains it, how do mirror neurons help us understand others?

4. Why does Gazzaniga believe we should be concerned with the search for universal ethics?

Responding to Ideas

1. **Response** When someone is willing to act on a moral belief it is because "the emotional part of his or her brain has become active when considering the moral question at hand" (para. 9). Considering the classic command warning us to be rational rather than emotional in our behavior, what does this brain research tell you about how we process moral concepts? The last time you acted to help someone, what went through your mind? Gazzaniga tells us that most of us act intuitively in offering to help someone. Poll a group of people and gather various stories from them about what happened when they acted to help a person or an animal in distress. Use those stories to develop an essay about a theory of moral behavior.

2. **Definition** "Evolutionary psychology points out that moral reasoning is good for human survival" (para. 11), says Gazzaniga. What is the difference between *moral reasoning* and *moral emotion*? How does moral reasoning work? Are you aware of possessing moral reasoning yourself? What examples of your own behavior have involved moral reasoning? Get examples from your peers about how they have experienced an instance of moral reasoning. What were the outcomes of these examples? How have they contributed, even if only slightly, to the idea that moral reasoning is good for human survival? Write an essay that defines moral reasoning as you understand it and defends it as essential to the human race.

3. **Response** Gazzaniga tells us that we must be mind readers. By this he is saying that we must make an effort to find out what people we interact with are thinking about themselves and about us. Recent cognitive research tells us that one of the most important stages of development in babies is their learning to read and interpret what people around them are thinking. It is a very high level of cognitive function. Write a brief essay describing a situation in which it was necessary for you to "read the mind" of an associate or acquaintance. What was the purpose or need for you to understand what the other person was thinking? Have there been situations in which what the person said was not what you thought he or she was thinking? If you have a pet,

such as a dog, do you have any evidence that it can figure out what you are thinking? If humans have mirror neurons that help us in "reading minds," how likely is it that dogs or cats also possess such neurons?

4. **Research** After reading this selection, consider the question that Gazzaniga poses: "Are there moral reasoning centers in the brain?" (para. 14). Write a brief essay in which you examine evidence in favor of reasoning centers in the brain. At the same time, consider the evidence against there being such centers in the brain. Research moral reasoning online, but be sure to look for articles and books in your library to develop resources to help bolster your argument or to provide counterarguments that you can address. If there are moral-reasoning centers in the brain, why do so many people behave immorally? Could there be immoral-reasoning centers in the brain as well? Or are there simply omissions of moral-reasoning centers in some people?

5. **Research** Much research has been done on people from different cultures with different languages on how they would handle the "trolley problem," a classic thought experiment in ethics. The problem is this: There is a runaway trolley barreling down the railway tracks, straight to where five people are tied up. You are standing next to a lever that can divert the train away from the five people, but if you pull this lever, the trolley will switch to a different set of tracks, where there is one person on the track who will be killed. Either you can do nothing and let the trolley kill five people on the main track or you can pull the lever and kill one person on the side track. In a brief essay, describe which choice you would make and why. Try to analyze your moral reasoning in enough detail that others will understand. Can you imagine what your emotional moral reaction would be? Search online for the "trolley problem" and see how your decision compares with that of others. How different is your solution to the problem?

6. **Research** Gazzaniga claims, "Looking at expressions of distress, for example, enhances helping behavior" (para. 27). Decide whether and to what extent this statement is true. If it is true, would it not also be true that seeing films of people in distress would be extremely helpful in engaging our moral reasoning? Does cinematic art help us become more ethical by stimulating our moral emotions? *Lassie Come Home* and other such films engage our moral responses to seeing the distress of animals and people. If that is true, then is it not also true that literature acts as a means of stimulating our moral emotions by activating the neurons in our brain that affect such emotions? Write an essay in which you examine an important film or piece of fiction that you feel is likely to cause most people to empathize with someone in distress. One example might be *To Kill a Mockingbird* by Harper Lee. Is it possible that film and literature educate our moral sense?

Comparing Ideas

1. Michael Gazzaniga is a scientist talking about ethical issues that may be connected with evolution. Michio Kaku's essay (p. 252) is written from the point of view of a scientist, too. In a brief essay, explain to a reader who knows little about the subject of these essays what ethical issues are in conflict in the creation of artificial intelligence (AI). How is AI different from the possible hardwired behaviors that may be in the human brain? Which author is more concerned about the ethical issues of his scientific research?

2. Friedrich Nietzsche, in "Good and Bad" (p. 393), seems to suggest that moral behavior is entirely a social construct but that beneath that is nature's morality. Evolution may have hardwired some behavior in our brains, as Michael Gazzaniga implies, but social behavior overrides evolution. In an essay that examines the ideas in both Nietzsche's and Gazzaniga's essays, decide how much they agree on the role of nature in establishing moral behavior. Which of these writers is more interested in the moral behaviors that we may have inherited through evolution?

Steve Pyke/Getty Images (top);
Harriet Buchholz (bottom)

PETER **SINGER**
AND JIM **MASON**

PETER SINGER (b. 1946) was born in Melbourne, Australia, to parents who had fled there in 1938 after the Nazi takeover of Austria. Singer was educated at the University of Melbourne and at Oxford University, taking degrees in philosophy. In 1999, he assumed a professorship at Princeton University, where he has served as the Ira W. DeCamp Professor of Bioethics in the University Center for Human Values. It was in Oxford in 1971 that he first met people who were vegetarian, and after reflecting on his own habit of eating meat, he too became a vegetarian — a choice that has informed much of his worldview and his writing.

Singer's ethical positions have drawn some criticism, but he generally agrees with the utilitarian philosophers, whose views support the idea of providing the greatest number of people with the greatest good and avoiding causing pain to others. His position on euthanasia has been clearly on the side of permitting a sick or dying patient the right to end his or her life. Singer is a consequentialist in that he measures ethical values in terms of the consequences of one's actions. For instance, he agrees that abortion is morally reasonable in circumstances in which the consequences of carrying the embryo to term were seriously bad for either the mother or the fetus. Moreover, he also has said that he supports the view that badly disabled babies should be permitted to die rather than to spend a lifetime in agony. Such views have been attacked by churches and even other philosophers. But Singer feels they are consistent with the utilitarian view to elevate happiness and reduce pain.

JIM MASON (b. 1934) is an attorney who is also a journalist, an author, a lecturer, and an editor. His concerns align with those of Singer, as both authors focus on animal rights. Mason grew up on a farm in Missouri and established an early understanding of animals and their behavior.

Singer and Mason focus on the suffering animals endure being made ready for market as food. Raising animals with little or no regard for the consequences of their treatment is, both writers say, a form of *speciesism*. Both writers contend that speciesism is as disgusting and as undesirable as racism or sexism. They do not contend that animals have rights in the same sense that people do, but they argue that animals do not deserve to be treated cruelly. Singer and Mason published *Animal Factories* (1980) as a way of calling attention to the ways animals suffer on a regular basis to provide us with food. What they tell readers in the following selection is an expansion on their philosophical position regarding the relationship of people to animals and our responsibility to them.

Be sure to practice prereading techniques before a careful, annotated reading of Singer and Mason's essay. For a review of prereading strategies, see pages 4–9. ⊞

Ethics and Animals

I N AMERICA, those opposed to factory farming include Matthew Scully, a former speech writer in George W. Bush's White House and the author of *Dominion: The Power of Man, the Suffering of Animals, and the Call to Mercy*. Although "animal rights" tend to be associated with those on the left, Scully makes a case for many of the same goals using arguments congenial to the Christian right. In Scully's view, even though God has given us "dominion" over the animals, we should exercise that dominion with mercy — and factory farming fails to do so. Scully's writings have found support from other conservatives, like Pat Buchanan, editor of the *American Conservative*, which gave cover-story prominence to Scully's essay "Fear Factories: The Case for Compassionate Conservatism — for Animals," and George F. Will, who used his *Newsweek* column to recommend Scully's book.

No less a religious authority than Pope Benedict XVI[1] has stated that human "dominion" over animals does not justify factory farming. When

---

[1] **Pope Benedict XVI** (b. 1927) Pope of the Roman Catholic Church from 2005 until he resigned in 2013.

head of the Roman Catholic Church's Sacred Congregation for the Doctrine of the Faith, the future pope condemned the "industrial use of creatures, so that geese are fed in such a way as to produce as large a liver as possible, or hens live so packed together that they become just caricatures of birds." This "degrading of living creatures to a commodity" seemed to him "to contradict the relationship of mutuality that comes across in the Bible."

On this issue we agree with Scully, Buchanan, Will, Pollan, Fearnley-Whittingstall, Scruton, and Pope Benedict XVI:[2] no one should be supporting the vast system of animal abuse that today produces most animal products in developed nations.

UNSOUND DEFENSES OF FACTORY FARMING

What possible arguments can there be in defense of factory farming? We will review some of them and show why they are unconvincing. First, it is sometimes said that we have no duties to animals, because they are incapable of having duties toward us. This has been argued by those who believe that the basis of ethics is some kind of contract, such as "I'll refrain from harming you, if you refrain from harming me." Animals cannot agree to a contract and thus fall outside the sphere of morality. But so, on this view, do babies and those with permanent, severe intellectual disabilities. Do we really have no duties to them either? An even bigger problem for the contract view of ethics is that it cannot ground duties to future generations. We could save ourselves a lot of money and effort by storing radioactive waste from nuclear-power plants in containers designed to last no more than, say, 150 years. If we only have duties to those who have duties towards us, why would that be wrong? There is an old joke that goes, "Why should I do anything for posterity? What did posterity ever do for me?" The problem with contract theorists is that they don't get the joke.

Second, when ethical issues are raised about eating meat, many people 5 use what might be called "the Benjamin Franklin defense." Franklin was for many years a vegetarian, until one day, while watching his friends fishing, he noticed that some of the fish they caught had eaten other fish. He then said to himself: "If you eat one another, I don't see why we may not eat you." The thought here may be that if a being treats others in a particular way, then humans are entitled to treat that being in an equivalent way. However, this does not follow as a matter of logic or ethics. Quite rightly, we do not normally take the behavior of animals as a model for how we may treat

---

[2] **Scully . . . Pope Benedict XVI** Michael Pollan (b. 1955) writes about food production and nutrition; Hugh Fearnley-Whittingstall (b. 1965) is a celebrity chef who appears on British TV; Roger Scruton (b. 1944) is a conservative British philosopher who hunts and raises meat for his own table.

them. We would not, for example, justify tearing a cat to pieces because we had observed the cat tearing a mouse to pieces. Carnivorous fish don't have a choice about whether to kill other fish or not. They kill as a matter of instinct. Meanwhile, humans can choose to abstain from killing or eating fish and other animals.

Alternatively, the argument could be made that it is part of the natural order that there are predators and prey, and so it cannot be wrong for us to play our part in this order. But this "argument from nature" can justify all kinds of inequities, including the rule of men over women and leaving the weak and the sick to fall by the wayside. Even if the argument were sound, however, it would work only for those of us still living in a hunter-gatherer society, for there is nothing at all "natural" about our current ways of raising animals. As for Franklin's argument about the fish who had eaten other fish, this is a selective use of an argument we would reject in other contexts. Franklin was a sufficiently acute observer of his own nature to recognize how selective he was being, because he admits that he hit upon his justification for eating the fish only after they were in the frying pan and had begun to smell "admirably well."

Third, we have said that the suffering inflicted on animals by factory farming, transportation, and slaughter is unnecessary because — as . . . vegan families demonstrate — there are alternatives to meat and other animal products that allow people to be healthy and well nourished. It might be argued that food from animals is a central part of the standard Western diet and important, if not always central, to what people eat in many other cultures as well. Because animal products are so significant to us, and because we could not buy them as cheaply as we can now without factory farming, factory farming is justifiable despite the suffering it inflicts on animals. But when cultural practices are harmful, they should not be allowed to go unchallenged. Slavery was once part of the culture of the American South. Biases against women and against people of other races have been, and in some places still are, culturally significant. If a widespread cultural practice is wrong, we should try to change it.

It's true that the alternatives to factory farming . . . , whether Cyd Szymanski's eggs or Niman Ranch pork,[3] are more expensive. Let's grant, too, that switching to a totally vegan diet is something that many people would find difficult, at least at first. But these assumptions are still insufficient to justify factory farming. The choice is not between business as usual and a vegan world. Without factory farming, families with limited means would be able to afford fewer animal products, but they would not have to stop buying them entirely. Nutritionists agree that most people in developed

---

[3] **Cyd Szymanski . . . Niman Ranch pork** Cyd Szymanski (b. 1957) created the Happy Egg Company, and William Niman raised beef and pork in a humane fashion.

countries eat far more animal products than they need, and more than is good for their health. Spending the same amount of money and buying fewer animal products would therefore be a good thing, especially if those animal products came from animals free to walk around outside, which would make the meat less fatty, and if the reduced consumption in animal products were offset by increased consumption of fruit and vegetables. That is the recommendation of Hugh Fearnley-Whittingstall, and few people are more devoted to food than he is.

For perhaps a billion of the world's poorest people, hunger and malnutrition are still a problem. But factory farming isn't going to solve that problem, for in developing countries the industry caters to the growing urban middle class, not the poor, who cannot afford to buy its products. In developing countries, factory-farming products are chosen for their taste and status, not for the consumer's good health. The world's largest and most comprehensive study of diet and disease has shown that in rural China, good health and normal growth are achieved on a diet that includes only one-tenth as much animal-based food as Americans eat. Increases in the consumption of animal products above that very low base are correlated with an increase in the "diseases of affluence": heart disease, obesity, diabetes, and cancer.

"But when cultural practices are harmful, they should not be allowed to go unchallenged."

The great suffering inflicted on animals by factory farming is not outweighed by a possible loss in gastronomic satisfaction caused by the elimination of meat from animals raised on factory farms from the diet. The harder question is whether we should be vegan or at least vegetarian? To answer that question, we need to go beyond the rejection of unjustified suffering and ask whether it is wrong to kill animals — without suffering — for our food. We need to ask what moral status animals have, and what ethical standards should govern our treatment of them.

ETHICS AND ANIMALS

The prevailing Western ethic assumes that human interests must always prevail over the comparable interests of members of other species. Since the rise of the modern animal movement in the 1970s, however, this ethic has been on the defensive. The argument is that, despite obvious differences between human and nonhuman animals, we share a capacity to suffer, and this means that they, like us, have interests. If we ignore or discount their interests simply on the grounds that they are not members of our species, the logic of our position is similar to that of the most blatant racists or sexists — those who think that to be white, or male, is to be inherently superior in moral status, irrespective of other characteristics or qualities.

The usual reply to this parallel between speciesism and racism or sexism is to acknowledge that it is a mistake to think that whites are superior to other races, or that males are superior to women, but then to argue that humans really are superior to nonhuman animals in their capacity to reason and the extent of their self-awareness, while claiming that these are morally relevant characteristics. However, some humans — infants, and those with severe intellectual disabilities — have less ability to reason and less self-awareness than some nonhuman animals. So we cannot justifiably use these criteria to draw a distinction between all humans on the one hand and all nonhuman animals on the other.

In the eighteenth century, Jonathan Swift,[4] the author of *Gulliver's Travels*, made a "modest proposal" to deal with the "surplus" of the children of impoverished women in Ireland. "I have been assured," he wrote, "that a young healthy child well nursed is at a year old, a most delicious, nourishing, and wholesome food, whether stewed, roasted, baked, or boiled." The proposal was, of course, a satire on British policy towards the Irish. But if we find this proposal shocking, our reaction shows that we do not really believe that the absence of an advanced ability to reason is sufficient to justify turning a sentient being into a piece of meat. Nor is it the potential of infants to develop these abilities that marks the crucial moral distinction, because we would be equally shocked by anyone who proposed the same treatment for humans born with serious and irreversible intellectual disabilities. But if, within our own species, we don't regard differences in intelligence, reasoning ability, or self-awareness as grounds for permitting us to exploit the being with lower capacities for our own ends, how can we point to the same characteristics to justify exploiting members of other species? Our willingness to exploit nonhuman animals is not something that is based on sound moral distinctions. It is a sign of "speciesism," a prejudice that survives because it is convenient for the dominant group, in this case not whites or males, but humans.

If we wish to maintain the view that no conscious human beings, including those with profound, permanent intellectual disabilities, can be used in ways harmful to them solely as a means to another's end, then we are going to have to extend the boundaries of this principle beyond our own species to other animals who are conscious and able to be harmed. Otherwise we are drawing a moral circle around our own species, even when the members

---

[4] **Jonathan Swift** (1667–1745) Irish satirist, churchman, and author of *Gulliver's Travels*.

of our own species protected by that moral boundary are not superior in any morally relevant characteristics to many nonhuman animals who fall outside the moral circle. If we fail to expand this circle, we will be unable to defend ourselves against racists and sexists who want to draw the boundaries more closely around themselves.

EQUAL CONSIDERATION FOR ANIMALS?

Those who defend our present treatment of animals often say that the animal-rights movement would have us give animals the same rights as humans. This is obviously absurd — animals can't have equal rights to an education, to vote, or to exercise free speech. The kind of parity that most animal advocates want to extend to animals is not equal rights, but equal consideration of comparable interests. If an animal feels pain, the pain matters as much as it does when a human feels pain. Granted, the mental capacities of different beings will affect how they experience pain, how they remember it, and whether they anticipate further pain — and these differences can be important. But the pain felt by a baby is a bad thing, even if the baby is no more self-aware than, say, a pig, and has no greater capacities for memory or anticipation. Pain can be a useful warning of danger, so it is sometimes valuable, all things considered. But taken in themselves, unless there is some compensating benefit, we should consider similar experiences of pain to be equally undesirable, whatever the species of the being who feels the pain. 15

We have now progressed in our argument beyond the avoidance of "unnecessary" suffering to the principle of equal consideration of interests, which tells us to give the same weight to the interests of nonhuman animals as we give to the similar interests of human beings. Let's see whether this principle can help us to decide whether eating meat is unethical.

Understanding Ideas

1. What is *speciesism*?
2. Why do Peter Singer and Jim Mason condemn factory farming?
3. According to Singer and Mason, what is the economic advantage of factory farming?
4. What do Singer and Mason say are the ethical problems with eating meat?

Responding to Ideas

1. *Definition* Peter Singer and Jim Mason mention the term *speciesism*
    several times, with only partial information that would lead to a defini-
    tion of the word. Write a brief essay that explores and defines the idea
    of speciesism in terms of people's general interaction with animals.
    Use your own experience with animals, but also include the experi-
    ences of people you have queried on the subject. Literature is filled
    with examples of interactions with animals, such as Herman Melville's
    Moby-Dick, Jack London's *The Call of the Wild*, and Anna Sewell's
    Black Beauty. Decide in your writing whether speciesism exists or if it
    is just a contrivance of Singer and Mason's arguments against factory
    farming.

2. *Definition* In the Bible, in Genesis 1:26, it says, "And God said, Let us
    make man in our image, after our likeness: and let them have domin-
    ion over the fish of the sea, and over the fowl of the air, and over the
    cattle, and over all the earth, and over every creeping thing that creep-
    eth upon the earth." This text has been used to justify shooting foxes,
    wolves, and other animals that threaten livestock. In a brief essay,
    explain what the word *dominion* means in this passage and what it
    means to us today in our interactions with animals. Is the use of pesti-
    cides to eradicate "every creeping thing" an example of our right to
    dominion over insects? What are our moral obligations to destructive
    insects and predatory animals like wolves?

3. *Research* Utilitarian philosophy predicates actions on the principle
    of increasing the happiness and the welfare of all while doing harm
    to the fewest possible. It is a philosophy addressed to people, not
    to the entire living world that includes plants and animals. Since fac-
    tory farming produces the most meat and the most fish at the lowest
    possible cost, it makes good food available at ower cost to millions
    more people than would be possible under another system. With-
    out factory farming, the poor would be harmed more than the rich.
    If you enjoy eating meat and fish, and if you have been doing it most
    of your life, you are in a position to defend factory farming. Con-
    sider some of Singer and Mason's arguments and defend the use of
    factory farming as a way of satisfying the utilitarian ideal. If possible,
    research current methods of factory farming to help you with your
    argument.

4. *Response* One of the major questions Singer and Mason raise is
    "whether we should be vegan or at least vegetarian" (para. 10). Could
    becoming vegetarian be an ethical requirement? Discuss this ques-
    tion with as many people as possible. Take notes on what vegans

and vegetarians tell you about their experience and their reasons for adopting their eating style. What do you feel are the chief arguments in favor of a vegan or vegetarian diet? What are the chief counterarguments? What are the health issues involved in adopting either of these styles of eating? If you have tried one or the other, draw on your own experiences. If possible, consult a medical professional for a judgment on the nutritional implications of these diets.

5. *Analysis of Circumstances* Evolutionary biology suggests that predatory behavior is not only natural but also essential to maintain the balance of predator to prey. Predators help prevent overpopulation. Predators are distinguished by having their eyes in the front of their head, while prey animals have them on the sides of their head. Humans are anatomically predators. Like other predatory animals with instincts, people also have a natural tendency to hunt and eat their kill. Many people think that repressing our natural instincts will harm us psychologically. Construct an argument in favor of eating meat based on what you learn about the nature of predators and the literature on psychological repression of natural behavior. Is it possible that repressing natural behavior will have a harmful effect on people? To what extent is repressing instincts an ethical issue?

6. *Research* Few crimes arouse the moral anger of people more than the mistreating, harming, torturing, or killing of household pets such as dogs, cats, and songbirds. Find recent news stories about mistreatment of pets and examine them in detail for evidence of concern for the animals that have been harmed. Why is there so much more concern for these animals than for chickens raised for food that have been given only a few square inches of living space? Why is there so much more sympathy for pets than for calves penned in for life so that their meat can be sold as veal? What does your research about cruelty to pets tell you about speciesism? Do people react more as a matter of morality or as a matter of sympathy?

Comparing Ideas

1. At one point, Singer and Mason suggest that it is not their position to establish animal rights. But many people do assume that animals have rights — or should have them. In an essay that references the work of James Madison (p. 65), Alexis de Tocqueville (p. 84), and the Marquis de Lafayette (p. 71), write an argument in favor of establishing the rights of animals. Explain why each of the rights you demand for animals must be accorded to them.

2. In an essay that relies on Michael Gazzaniga's "Toward a Universal Eth-
    ics" (p. 414) and Thomas Nagel's "The Objective Basis of Morality"
    (p. 406), construct an argument that says it is immoral to eat animals.
    Explain why, even though we are predators, we should respect the
    moral obligation not to eat beings that are animals like us. Explain why
    it is moral for us to eat vegetables. If you feel that insects are not ani-
    mals, explain why it is moral for us to eat them. Why is there any moral
    issue involved in eating anything?

Werner Baum/picture-alliance/dpa/
AP Photo

FRANCIS
FUKUYAMA

FRANCIS FUKUYAMA (b. 1952) was born in Hyde Park, near Chicago. A political scientist and economist, he has taught at George Mason University and Johns Hopkins University, and he is now a fellow at the Freeman Spogli Institute for International Studies at Stanford University. The institute is an interdisciplinary center for studies in democracy, international problems, and important issues.

Fukuyama was educated at Cornell University, where he earned a degree in classics, and Harvard University, where he received a doctorate in political science. He was an adviser to President Ronald Reagan and is a prominent conservative thinker. He was involved in political discussions with high-level politicians during the presidency of Bill Clinton and through the George W. Bush years, when he supported the president's program in the Middle East. More recently, he reports having voted for Barack Obama in 2008.

He became well known outside of academia with his publication of *The End of History and the Last Man* (1992), which suggests that with the survival and flourishing of democracies after the defeat of fascism and communism there would be no stable forms of government left to threaten liberal democracy. In other words, the history of political science was at an end. While he had many critics of the views he presented in that book, and he himself published a later work that softened his stance, his position influenced many political scientists, and he was recognized as an important theorist.

Among his later books are *America at the Crossroads: Democracy, Power, and the Neoconservative Legacy* (2006), *The Origins of Political Order* (2011), and *Political Order and Political Decay: From the Industrial Revolution to the Globalization of Democracy* (2014). The selection that follows is from *Our Posthuman Future* (2004), a discussion of the ways bio-technology may permit us to design our children and create more inequality in the world. He feels this is a threat to humanity and an attack on human nature. Genetic advances such as those that allow for the human genetic code to be put on a DVD and for the production of drugs that enhance, perhaps delimit, life spans make Fukuyama fearful of our new ability to produce monsters.

In this se ection, Fukuyama encourages us to consider the nature of humanity and human rights in relation to the rights of animals. What is specific to animals is important when considering the question of animal ethics.

Be sure to practice prereading techniques before a careful, annotated reading of Fukuyama's essay. For a review of prereading strategies, see pages 4–9. ⊞

Human Specificity and the Rights of Animals

THE CONNECTION between rights and species-typical behavior becomes obvious when we consider the issue of animal rights. There is today around the world a very powerful animal rights movement, which seeks to improve the lot of the monkeys, chickens, minks, pigs, cows, and other animals that we butcher, experiment on, eat, wear, turn into upholstery, and otherwise treat as means rather than ends in themselves. The radical fringe of this movement has on occasion turned violent, bombing medical research labs and chicken processing plants. The bioethicist Peter Singer has built his career around the promotion of animal rights and a critique of what he calls the speciesism of human beings — the unjust favoring of our species over others. All of this leads us to raise the question posed by James Watson . . . : What gives a salamander a right?

The simplest and most straightforward answer to this question, which applies perhaps not to salamanders but certainly to creatures with more highly developed nervous systems, is that they can feel pain and suffer. This is an ethical truth to which any pet owner can testify, and much of the moral impulse behind the animal rights movement is understandably driven by the desire to reduce the suffering of animals. Our greater sensitivity to this issue stems in part from the general spread of the principle of equality in the world, but also from an accumulation of greater empirical knowledge about animals.

Much of the work done in animal ethology[1] over the past few generations has tended to erode the bright line that was once held to separate human beings from the rest of the animal world. Charles Darwin, of course, provided the theoretical underpinning for the notion that man evolved from an ancestral ape, and that all species were undergoing a continuous process of modification. Many of the attributes that were once held to be unique to human beings — including language, culture, reason, consciousness, and the like — are now seen as characteristic of a wide variety of nonhuman animals.

For example, the primatologist Frans de Waal[2] points out that culture — that is, the ability to transmit learned behaviors across generations through nongenetic means — is not an exclusively human achievement. He cites the famous example of the potato-washing macaques that inhabit a small island in Japan. In the 1950s a group of Japanese primatologists observed that one macaque in particular (an Albert Einstein, so to speak, among monkeys) developed a habit of washing potatoes in a local stream. This same individual later discovered that grains of barley could be separated from sand by dropping them in water. Neither was a genetically programmed behavior; neither potatoes nor barley were part of the macaques' traditional diet, and no one had ever before observed these behaviors taking place. Yet both the potato washing and barley separation were observed among other macaques on the island some years later, well after the original monkey who had discovered these techniques had passed away, indicating that he had taught it to his fellows and they in turn had passed it on to the young.

Chimpanzees are more humanlike than macaques. They have a language 5 of grunts and hoots and have been trained in captivity to understand and express themselves in a limited range of human words. In his book *Chimpanzee Politics*, de Waal describes the machinations of a group of chimps trying to achieve alpha male status in a captive colony in the Netherlands. They enter into alliances, betray one another, plead, beg, and cajole in ways that would be very familiar to Machiavelli. Chimpanzees also appear to have a sense of humor, as de Waal explains in *The Ape and the Sushi Master*:

> When guests arrive at the Field Station of the Yerkes Primate Center, near Atlanta, where I work, they usually pay a visit to my chimpanzees. Often our favorite troublemaker, a female named Georgia, hurries to the spigot to collect a mouthful of water before they arrive . . . If necessary, Georgia will wait minutes with closed lips until the visi-

---

[1] **ethology** The science and study of animal behavior.
[2] **Frans de Waal** (b. 1948) Dutch ethologist and professor of primate studies at Emory University.

tors come near. Then there will be shrieks, laughs, jumps, and sometimes falls when she suddenly sprays them.

. . . I once found myself in a similar situation with Georgia. She had
taken a drink from the spigot and was sneaking up to me. I looked
straight into her eyes and pointed my finger at her, warning, in Dutch,
"I have seen you!" She immediately stepped back, let some of the water
fall from her mouth, and swallowed the rest. I certainly do not claim
that she understands Dutch, but she must have sensed that I knew
what she was up to, and that I was not going to be an easy target.

Georgia could apparently not just play jokes, but could feel embarrassment
at being caught as well.

Examples like these are frequently cited not only to support the idea
of animal rights but to denigrate human claims of uniqueness and special
status. Some scientists revel in debunking traditional claims about human
dignity, particularly if they are based in religion. . . . There is still a great deal
to the idea of human dignity, but the point remains that a wide variety of
animals share a number of important characteristics with humans. Human
beings are always making sentimental reference to their "shared humanity,"
but in many cases what they are referring to is their shared animality. Elephant parents, for example, appear to mourn the loss of their offspring, and
become highly agitated when they discover the remains of a dead elephant.
It is not too much of a stretch to imagine that a human being grieving for a
lost relative or feeling dread at the sight of a corpse has something very dis-
tantly in common with the elephant (which is perhaps why we paradoxically
call animal protection societies "humane" societies).

But if animals have a "right" not to suffer unduly, the nature and limits of that right depend entirely on empirical observation of what is typical
for their species — that is, on a substantive judgment about their natures.
To my knowledge, not even the most radical animal rights activist has ever
made a case for the rights of AIDS viruses or *E. coli* bacteria, which human
beings seek to destroy by the billions every day. We don't think to accord
these living creatures rights because, not having nervous systems, they
apparently can't suffer or be aware of their situation. We tend to accord
conscious creatures greater rights in this regard because, like humans, they
can anticipate suffering and have fears and hopes. A distinction of this sort
might serve to distinguish the rights of a salamander from those of, say, your
dog Rover — to the relief of the Watsons of the world.

But even if we accept the fact that animals have a right not to suffer
unduly, there is a whole range of rights that they cannot be granted because
they are not human. We would not even consider granting the right to vote,
for example, to creatures that, as a group, were incapable of learning human

language. Chimps can communicate in a language typical of their species, and they can master a very limited number of human words if extensively trained, but they cannot master human language and do not possess human cognition more generally. That some human beings can't master human language either actually confirms its importance to political rights: children are excluded from the right to vote because they do not as a group have the cognitive abilities of a typical adult. In all of these cases, the species-specific differences between nonhuman animals on the one hand and human beings on the other make a tremendous amount of difference to our understanding of their moral status.

"But even if we accept the fact that animals have a right not to suffer unduly, there is a whole range of rights that they cannot be granted because they are not human."

Blacks and women were at one time excluded from the vote in the United States on the grounds that they did not have the cognitive abilities necessary to exercise this right properly. Blacks and women can vote today, while chimps and children cannot, because of what we know empirically about the cognitive and linguistic abilities of each of these groups. Membership in one of these groups does not guarantee that one's individual characteristics will be close to the median for that group (I know a lot of individual children who would vote more wisely than their parents), but it is a good enough indicator of ability for practical purposes.

What an animal rights proponent like Peter Singer calls speciesism is 10 thus not necessarily an ignorant and self-serving prejudice on the part of human beings, but a belief about human dignity that can be defended on the basis of an empirically grounded view of human specificity. We have broached this subject with the discussion of human cognition. But if we are to find a source of that superior human moral status that raises us all above the rest of animal creation and yet makes us equals of one another qua human beings, we need to know more about that subset of characteristics of human nature that are not just typical of our species but unique to human beings. Only then will we know what needs the greatest safeguarding against future developments in biotechnology.

Understanding Ideas

1. According to Francis Fukuyama, what gives a salamander a right?
2. How absolute is the line between human beings and animals in Fukuyama's estimation?

3. Why does Fukuyama say that it is important that a chimpanzee has a sense of humor?

4. Do animals have rights?

Responding to Ideas

1. **Comparison** One of the persistent questions regarding humane societies is whether or not animals have rights. Consider the statements in the Bill of Rights (p. 65) and in the Declaration of the Rights of Man and Citizen (p. 71), and draft a Declaration of the Rights of Animals. What does it mean for an animal to have rights? Rights to what? Rights to do what? Is freedom one of the rights that must be accorded animals, as it is accorded to humans? If animals have rights, is it then criminal to put them in cages? Is it criminal to put them on a leash? How can you help guarantee the rights of animals? How are those rights different than those of humans?

2. **Response** Francis Fukuyama points to the chimpanzees that can be taught a modicum of human language as examples of animals with attributes once considered uniquely human. How does the ability of an animal to communicate its desires and needs change the ethical position of people in regard to that animal? What are the ethical demands that such animals have, and what ethical consideration should other silent animals expect from people? Would people regard animals that could talk or reveal a capacity to think of their own needs and the needs of another animal differently than they would regard silent animals? Why is the possession of language such a powerful stimulus for improving human ethical behavior?

3. **Definition** The question of human nature is important to Fukuyama. He says that "we need to know more about that subset of characteristics of human nature that are not just typical of our species but unique to human beings" (para. 10). In a brief essay, define *human nature* by clarifying the characteristics of human nature that are typical. What is typically human behavior? Explain how you know it is typical. Then describe those characteristics of human nature that you think are unique to humans and not characteristic of other species of animals. We are always impressed by the characteristic behaviors we share with animals, but what behaviors do we have that are not shared?

4. **Research** Fukuyama begins this selection with mention of species-typical behavior. Do some research into what species-typical behavior is. Chose two or three different kinds of animals and write an essay that explains what the species-typical behavior of each animal is. Most

people already think they know what the typical behavior of dogs is and how it differs from the typical behavior of cats. In the course of your writing, try to establish how different the typical behavior is of different species you have studied or observed. Among people you have discussed this idea with, how much agreement is there about the typical behavior of animals?

5. *Research* When considering the nature of animals, Fukuyama says that humans share much more with animals than was once thought. He mentions "language, culture, reason, consciousness, and the like" (para. 3). Examine his statement by referring to findings by animal ethologists to see how they agree or disagree with him. Search *ethology* as well as *animal ethology*. What do you see as the most important similarities in the behaviors we share with animals? Since these behaviors would not be species specific, how are we to regard them? Which are the most surprising to you? Which are most likely to demand an ethical position that includes animals as well as fellow human beings?

6. *Response* What ethical position should people adopt toward animals? Should that position be granted to all animals or just some? Are some species naturally omitted from our ethical concerns? Would poisonous snakes, spiders, or scorpions be omitted? Do we need to have an ethical position regarding "varmints" who plunder livestock such as sheep? How are we to regard the ethical rights of birds, fish, octopi, eels, or jellyfish? Is there any species-specific behavior that releases us from ethical consideration of an animal? What does it ultimately mean for people to have an ethical consideration for animals, especially for dangerous species?

Comparing Ideas

1. Francis Fukuyama speaks about the species-specific behavior of animals. Owners of dogs know a great deal about the species-specific behavior of their pets. Some dogs, such as young beagles, will create havoc in a household. Most dog owners try some kind of training to curtail bad behavior in their pets. John Dewey, in "Education and Morality" (p. 400), recommends educating one's pet. Referencing both Dewey and Fukuyama, construct an argument that explains why it is a moral act to educate one's pet. Explain, too, what it means to educate a dog and what effect that education may have on its species-specific behavior. Use examples where possible, such as the training rescue dogs and other service animals receive, to support your argument.

KWAME ANTHONY APPIAH

Greg Martin

KWAME ANTHONY APPIAH was born in London in 1954 and raised in Kumasi, Ghana. His father, Joe Emmanuel Appiah, was a lawyer and politician in Ghana. His mother, Enid Margaret Appiah, is the daughter of Sir Stafford Cripps, one of England's most notable statesmen. His family tree traces back to the Winthrops in prerevolutionary America and to precolonial Ghanaian rulers. His education was at Clare College, Cambridge, where he took his Ph.D. Formerly a professor of philosophy at Princeton University, Appiah is currently a professor of philosophy at New York University and holds a professorship in NYU's school of law.

Appiah is both a scholar and a novelist. He has written books on a wide range of subjects. Some of the books concern racial issues, such as *In My Father's House: Africa in the Philosophy of Culture* (1992), which explores the question of African identity. In *Color Conscious: The Political Morality of Race* (1998), he examines the entire question of race: what it is, how it is expressed, and how it affects different cultures. In *The Ethics of Identity* (2007), he considers the constraints people put on themselves by joining specific organizations and institutions.

In *Experiments in Ethics* (2008), from which the following selection is taken, Appiah aims to bring philosophy and the social sciences together in a tradition he traces back to Aristotle. He begins his essay with a consideration of Aristotle's word *eudaimonia*, which is ordinarily translated as happiness. He reviews what Aristotle said about happiness being the ultimate good, but in the process he raises questions that need answers that Aristotle did not provide. He talks about virtue and worthwhile aims that qualify the entire idea of happiness in ways that he feels make it difficult to translate *eudaimonia* in any simple way. Appiah goes further and asks us to understand what it means when parents tell a child that all they want is

447

for the child to be happy. We have all heard that expression and seem to understand it, even though upon closer examination neither the parents nor the child likely knows what is fully meant by the statement.

Appiah asks whether we are happy if we think we are. For some people this may be all it takes, but Appiah is looking at the entire circumstance of our awareness of happiness. Is it a feeling? Is it an experience? Is it enough for us to think that we are happy, or is there more involved?

Be sure to practice prereading techniques before a careful, annotated reading of Appiah's essay. For a review of prereading strategies, see pages 4–9. ⌗

If You're Happy and You Know It

ETHICS IS, in that formulation of Aristotle's, about the ultimate aim or end of human life, the end he called *eudaimonia*. Of course, philosophical ethics has not always shared that vision; nor should philosophers be confident that history has given them a special lien upon the subject of human flourishing. There's a sense . . . that the members of my profession became philosophers in the way that the Vlach,[1] after the union of Wallachia and Moldavia in the mid-nineteenth century, became "Romanians," claiming a glorious ancient pedigree through a nomenclatural coup. The slippery movements of group designations are familiar to all historians, not to mention any sports fan who has watched the Jets, who used to be the Titans, play the Titans, who used to be the Oilers.

Still, our names can express our aspirations. In the pages that follow, then, I want to sidle up to that great end of ethics, see how we might best make sense of it, and offer a final accounting of what "naturalism" means within the realm of human values — and within the project of *eudaimonia*.

So what is that devoutly-to-be-hoped-for thing, anyway? If you think of *eudaimonia* as happiness, and believe, as many modern people claim to do, that happiness is just a matter of satisfying your felt desires, you will think that evaluations are just desires gussied up with fancy talk. The antiquity of this temptation is shown by the antiquity of the rebuttals: through more than two millennia, thinkers have vigorously demonstrated that mere subjective contentment isn't a worthwhile aim. One way to deepen our grasp

---

[1] **Vlach** Ancient people from eastern Europe who spoke Latin. Their name means "stranger" and is associated with the Wallachia, an ethnic group living primarily in Romania.

of *eudaimonia* is to understand why "happiness" is, at least for us today, a terribly misleading translation of that Greek word.

How many times on TV and in the movies have we heard a parent tell a child, "I just want you to be happy"? But what does that mean? Here are a few notions you'll encounter these days. First, happiness is a feeling; you are happy if and only if you think you are happy. For a feeling just is a state of mind, like a pain, that you can't have without being aware that you have it. A more sophisticated thought often follows: whether you are happy or not is to be decided by standards set by you. Together, these claims amount to construing happiness as something deeply subjective: it's a feeling; we all know whether we have it, and each of us sets the standards for our own happiness. Call this the *subjective conception of happiness.*

As philosophers have never tired of pointing out, this isn't really a con- 5 ception that withstands scrutiny. No loving and thoughtful parents could mean that they just wanted a child to be subjectively happy. Consider the happiness that comes from a successful relationship. If all that matters is how you feel, then if you *feel* it's going well, it *is* going well, and it's of no consequence if your partner is merely feigning affection, so long as the illusion is maintained. But, of course, what matters in relationships requires that our feelings be apt; it requires the truth of at least some of the beliefs that partially constitute those feelings. When Dad tells his daughter he wants her to be happy, he doesn't mean it's fine if her boyfriend goes on *pretending* to love her. It's not just that a boyfriend who doesn't love you is, no doubt, less reliable than one who does. Daddy, especially a soap-opera daddy, could be rich enough to make it worth the boyfriend's while to keep up the act, and his daughter would still be in trouble. People who don't grasp this — who care only whether their beloveds *appear* to love them — are simply not capable of love.

The philosopher Robert Nozick[2] proposed a famous thought experiment along these lines in *Anarchy, State, and Utopia.* Imagine there was an "experience machine" that would provide any experience you wanted. "Superduper neuropsychologists could stimulate your brain so that you would think and feel you were writing a great novel, or making a friend, or reading an interesting book," he wrote, even though you'd just be floating in a tank with electrodes plugged into your brain. Would you plug in? Films like the Wachowski brothers' *The Matrix* or Cameron Crowe's *Vanilla Sky* — or Alejandro Amenábar's marvelous *Abre los Ojos* (Open Your Eyes), on which it was based — exploit the possibility of something like an experience machine to raise exactly the question Nozick asks. And his answer — that what matters is not only how our life feels, but also whether our

---

[2] **Robert Nozick** (1938–2002) Professor of philosophy at Harvard University and author of *Anarchy, State, and Utopia* (1974).

experiences and achievements are real — is not only right but right in a way that Aristotle would surely have thought obvious. Whatever Aristotle meant by *eudaimonia*, he didn't mean subjective happiness.

To say that feelings aren't the only things that matter is not to go to the other extreme and say that they don't matter at all. No doubt some of the experiences I have in my relationships are part of what is good about them, part of what makes the relationships contribute to my flourishing, to what is good in my life. Loving couples know the feeling of walking hand in hand under the stars, confident in each other's love; lying together at night, conscious of each other's breathing, feeling the warmth of each other's bodies. These experiences are valuable parts of a life in love. Again, though, the experiences must be in some sense apt. The shared life is a good life because two people are really making a life together: if your partner is not a real person but an automaton or an electronic phantasm, you're living in what we appropriately call a fool's paradise. You may think your life is going well, but you're wrong.

What about that thesis that each person sets the standards for his or her own happiness? People find it plausible, I think, because they follow a train of thought that goes like this: "What matters in your life matters because it matters *to you*; because it is one of your aims. Succeeding in what matters to you is what's important — important in the sense that getting it contributes to your happiness, your *eudaimonia*. Anything you care about matters to you. Ergo, getting what you care about contributes to your happiness." Here is one of the many places where morality matters for ethics, and one of the many ways in which *eudaimonia* is shown to be indissolubly social, because the question of what we owe to others — in the classical formulation, *suum cuique tribuens* ("giving to each his due") — is inherently interpersonal. Suppose, like a character in the fantasies of the Marquis de Sade,[3] I take pleasure in humiliating other people. That I care to humiliate people doesn't mean that if I succeed in doing so my life is going well. You can't set success at sadism as one of the aims of your life and thereby make a life of cruelty a good life. So one reason that you can't set your own standards for happiness is that some standards are morally wrong.

This helps explain why so many thinkers, from Socrates on, have connected happiness with virtue. However many things you have achieved, however much pleasure you have experienced, however many friends you have, however wonderful your relationship with your spouse, and however successful your children, if you have achieved all this at the expense

---

[3] **Marquis de Sade** (1740–1814) French nobleman and writer. The words *sadism* and *sadist* derive from him and his erotic writings, most of which involve violence and pain. He spent more than thirty years in prison or in an insane asylum. During the French Revolution, he was freed and elected as a delegate to the National Assembly.

of neglecting your moral obligations, your existence is less successful than it would have been had you paid proper attention to what morality demands. . . . [T]his connection between morality and ethics is internal: doing what is morally right is one of the constituents of human flourishing. So we don't need to believe in a providential invisible hand, assigning happiness to the saints, to insist on the connection between virtue and happiness, properly understood. A sinner may think he's happy. But insofar as he's a sinner, his life is thereby made less successful, whether he knows it or not. Whatever it is that he wants, the rest of us should want him, truly, to be better than he is.

It's also true that some aims, however genuinely desired, are not signifi- 10
cant enough to add to the value of a life. You cannot give a saucer of mud significance in your life simply by announcing you want it; and, indeed, if you find you do want it for no purpose, this is not a reason to go looking for a saucer of mud, but rather a reason to seek clinical help. If the standards were whatever you decided they were, you could make your life a smashing success simply by setting the standards absurdly low.

> "So one reason that you can't set your own standards for happiness is that some standards are morally wrong."

Someone could set as his aim that he should do whatever job came along moderately well and make enough money to have fun from time to time. "I am satisfied," he might say, looking back on his life at the end. "I had fun occasionally, I was a work-to-rule bureaucrat; I avoided the entanglements of love and friendship, which would only have risked my wanting things — like loyalty and reciprocation — that you can't guarantee." And we would say, rightly, that if that is all there was to it, this person, far from having lived well, had wasted his life.

In short, you aren't flourishing just because you're getting what you want. We can grasp the alternative vision, shared by the soulless libertine or lifer — we can imagine a moment when, in Philip Larkin's[4] mordant words, "every life became / a brilliant breaking of the bank, / A quite unlosable game" — but we cannot enter it. What we want has to be *worth* wanting: it has to be consistent with human decency and connected with humanly intelligible values. Aristotle's view was, indeed, that life was a challenge to be faced; that to live well was an achievement.

---

[4] **Philip Larkin** (1922–1985) British poet. The lines Appiah includes in this essay are from Larkin's poem "Annus Mirabilis," from his collection *High Windows* (1974).

Understanding Ideas

1. What is the subjective conception of happiness according to Kwame Anthony Appiah?

2. In Appiah's estimation, to what extent do people set the standard for their own happiness?

3. Why does Appiah say that the illusion of happiness is not enough?

4. According to Appiah, why is doing what is morally right essential to happiness?

Responding to Ideas

1. *Response* Explain why the subjective conception of happiness is not enough. Kwame Anthony Appiah gives a number of possible subjective moments that might spell happiness to some people. But he does not believe it is enough to simply think we are happy just because we feel happy. What must be included in our experience to make happiness more than just a personal feeling? Of course, you may disagree with Appiah on this point, and if you do, explain yourself with the same rigor that Appiah uses in his analysis of subjective happiness, or happiness as a feeling. Analyze his argument and address it yourself in a careful essay.

2. *Response* Amartya Sen, in his selection from *The Idea of Justice* (p. 183), tells us that it is important that when justice is done that it appears to be done. He means that people must think justice is done — its actually having been done is not quite enough. Does this apply to happiness as well? Is it imperative that you think you are happy for you to be truly happy? Is an appearance/reality disjunction possible in the realm of happiness? Some people have said that it is enough to think you are happy for you to experience happiness. How true (or how false) is this in your experience? Explore these questions in a careful essay.

3. *Response* Appiah refers to the philosopher Robert Nozick and his theoretical "experience machine" that could cause someone to feel happiness by electrical stimulation. Why does Appiah feel this kind of machine may seem to produce happiness but that it is not real happiness? Why is real happiness better than artificial happiness if happiness is a feeling? Drugs may be able to produce the euphoria associated with happiness, but Appiah would say it is not real happiness. Why would Appiah argue against a drug-induced state as being happiness? How might Aristotle have responded to the idea of artificial stimulation producing a feeling of happiness? How do you respond to that idea?

4. ***Analysis of Circumstances*** What is the problem with the idea of people setting the standard for their own happiness? Are there experiences or circumstances that regularly give you happiness that would not be "enough" for other people? What is the problem with setting the standard too low? What is the problem with setting it too high? What kinds of standards do you see people around you setting in terms of reaching happiness? What standards do you set for yourself? How do people set such standards? Are they aware of doing so? Does it work? Why is there a problem with setting low standards as long as they produce some form of happiness for the individual? Is Appiah wrong? What ethical issues does Appiah raise when he implies that the standards for happiness may possibly not be set by you?

5. ***Analysis of Circumstances*** The German word *schadenfreude* describes the feeling of pleasure one gets when one sees someone else fail. "It is not enough that one succeed; others must fail" is an expression that describes a similar sentiment regarding people whose happiness derives from others' pain. What ethical issues are at work in either of these descriptions of pleasure? If people do nothing to harm someone else, why would it be unethical for them to take pleasure from other people's failure? Is there a moral issue here? Why would Appiah say that this is not really happiness? What more than taking pleasure in an experience or in a string of experiences is necessary for one to be truly happy? If people are happy watching someone else fail, how can we say that they are not really in possession of happiness, or what Aristotle called the greatest good?

Comparing Ideas

1. Both Aristotle (p. 374) and Kwame Anthony Appiah, with reference to Socrates, tell us that happiness depends on virtue. Leading a virtuous life, they imply, may be essential to achieving happiness. In a brief essay, explain why these philosophers may think virtue is the "soul" of happiness. Are you aware of the effects of virtue — or the lack of it — in producing a sense of happiness in people that you know or know about? What is a life of virtue? How difficult is it to design and live a life of virtue in the environment in which you live? Is it more difficult to live a virtuous life today than it was in the past? What feelings does living a life without virtue produce? Can it produce unhappiness? What insight into the virtuous life does Appiah give us? To what extent do you agree or disagree with him?

2. Kwame Anthony Appiah talks about virtue and happiness. Friedrich Nietzsche in "Good and Bad" (p. 393) talks about virtue indirectly, but he does not talk about happiness. Yet Nietzsche knew the work of Aristotle as well as Appiah does and, therefore, understands that virtue leads to happiness in the Aristotelian sense. Examine Nietzsche's views on what is and is not moral, and explain how his views shed light on Appiah's concepts of happiness. How might Nietzsche define happiness? How much does Nietzsche have in common with Appiah? Appiah knew Nietzsche's work in detail. What influence of Nietzsche is apparent in Appiah's work?

3. In a brief essay, explain how the work of Michael Gazzaniga in "Toward a Universal Ethics" (p. 414) helps clarify Appiah's ideas about happiness. What does Gazzaniga say that Appiah would agree with? How comfortable would Appiah be in reacting to the scientific approach that Gazzaniga uses? Write a brief essay contrasting the methods each writer uses to discuss the moral and ethical issues important to him.

Acknowledgments

Jennifer Ackerman, "Molecules and Genes" from *Change in the House of Fate*. Copyright © 2001 by Jennifer Ackerman. Reproduced with permission of Houghton Mifflin Harcourt Publishing Company. All rights reserved.

Kwame Anthony Appiah, "If You're Happy and You Know It" from *Experiments in Ethics*. Copyright © 2008 by the President and Fellows of Harvard College. Reproduced with permission of Harvard University Press, Cambridge, MA. All rights reserved.

Aristotle, "The Aim of Man" from *Nicomachean Ethics* by Aristotle. Originally published by Pearson. Translation copyright © 1982 by Martin Ostwald. Reproduced with permission of David Ostwald.

James Baldwin, "My Dungeon Shook: Letter to My Nephew on the One Hundredth Anniversary of the Emancipation" originally published in *The Progressive*. Copyright © 1962 by James Baldwin. Collected in *The Fire Next Time*, published by Vintage Books. Copyright renewed. Reproduced in arrangement with the James Baldwin Estate.

Leslie T. Chang, excerpts from *Factory Girls: From Village to City in a Changing China*. Copyright © 2008 by Leslie T. Chang. Reproduced with permission of Spiegel & Grau, an imprint of Random House, a division of Penguin Random House, LLC. All rights reserved.

Robert A. Dahl, "Why Democracy?" from *On Democracy*. Copyright © 1999 by Robert A. Dahl. Reproduced with permission by Yale University Press.

Lucy Delaney, "From Darkness Cometh Light, or Struggles for Freedom" published by J. T. Smith in 1891. Courtesy of the Western Reserve Historical Society.

John Dewey, "Education and Morality" from *Reconstruction in Philosophy*. Copyright © 1971 by John Dewey. Reproduced with permission of Beacon Press in the format "republish in a book" via Copyright Clearance Center.

Francis Fukuyama, "Human Specificity and the Rights of Animals" from "Human Nature" from *Our Posthuman Future: Consequences of the Biotechnology Revolution*. Copyright © 2002 by Francis Fukuyama. Reproduced with permission of Farrar, Straus and Giroux, LLC.

John Kenneth Galbraith, "Inequality" from *The Affluent Society*, Fourth Edition. Copyright © 1958, 1969, 1976, 1984 by John Kenneth Galbraith. Reproduced with permission of Houghton Mifflin Harcourt Publishing Company. All rights reserved.

Michael S. Gazzaniga, "Toward a Universal Ethics" from *The Ethical Brain*. Copyright © 2005 by Michael S. Gazzaniga. Published and reproduced with permission of Dana Press, New York.

bell hooks, "Feminist Politics: Where We Stand" from *Feminism is for Everybody: Passionate Politics*. Copyright © 2000 by bell hooks. Reproduced with permission of Taylor and Francis in the format "republish in a book" via Copyright Clearance Center.

Jane Jacobs, "Stagflation" from *Cities and the Wealth of Nations*. Copyright © 1984 by Jane Jacobs. Reproduced with permission of Random House, an imprint of and division of Penguin Random House, LLC. All rights reserved.

Steve Jones, "The Descent of Men" from *Y: The Descent of Men*. Copyright © 2003 by Steve Jones. Reproduced with permission of Houghton Mifflin Harcourt Publishing Company. All rights reserved.

Michio Kaku, "Physics of the Impossible" from *Physics of the Impossible: A Scientific Exploration into the World of Phasers, Force Fields, Teleportation, and Time Travel*. Copyright © 2008 by Michio Kaku. Reproduced with permission of Doubleday, an imprint of the Knopf Doubleday Publishing Group, a division of Penguin Random House, LLC. All rights reserved.

Index

Ackerman, Jennifer, "Molecules and Genes," 263
active readers, 4
"Aim of Man, The" (Aristotle), 374
analysis, 12, 13, 19, 20, 24, 25, 27, 35, 41, 131
    of cause and effect, 31–32
    of circumstances, 32–33
annotating, 10–11, 16–17
Appiah, Kwame Anthony, "If You're Happy and You Know It," 447
argument, 4, 5, 8, 9, 10, 13, 19, 20, 21, 22, 25, 26, 27, 30, 31, 33–34, 36, 37–41, 42, 131
    classical, 38
    establishing, 37–41
    Rogerian, 38, 40–41
    Toulmin, 38, 39
Aristotle, "The Aim of Man," 374
asking questions, 4, 7–9, 10, 11, 12, 20–21, 26, 370. See also rhetorical questions
audience, 4, 8, 9, 19, 37, 38, 39

Baldwin, James, "My Dungeon Shook: Letter to My Nephew on the One Hundredth Anniversary of the Emancipation," 169
"Bill of Rights, The" (Madison), 65

Carnegie, Andrew, "The Gospel of Wealth," 289
cause and effect, 31–32
Chang, Leslie T., "Factory Girls in Dongguan," 357
circumstances, 32–33
claims, 39

classical arguments, 38
comparisons, 28–29, 34, 36
conclusions, drawing, 7
conflict, 40, 204
critical reading, 4, 9, 20, 26
critical thinking, 20–21

Dahl, Robert A., "Why Democracy?," 96
Darwin, Charles, "Of Sexual Selection and Natural Selection," 212
"Declaration of the Rights of Man and Citizen" (Lafayette and The National Assembly of France), 71
"Deep Democratic Tradition in America, The" (West), 111
definitions, 27–28, 36
Delaney, Lucy A., "Struggles for Freedom," 146
"Democracy and the Democratic Man" (Plato), 56
"Descent of Men, The" (Jones), 244
Dewey, John, "Education and Morality," 400
discussing, 12–13
Durkheim, Emile, "The Intellectual Elite and Democracy," 90

"Education and Morality" (Dewey), 400
"Ethics and Animals" (Singer and Mason), 430
evidence, 39, 204, 277–278
examples, 30–31, 40–41

"Factory Girls in Dongguan" (Chang), 357
"Feminist Politics: Where We Stand" (hooks), 190

"Four Freedoms, The" (Roosevelt), 153

Fukuyama, Francis, "Human Specificity and the Rights of Animals," 440

Galbraith, John Kenneth, "Inequality," 317

Gazzaniga, Michael, "Toward a Universal Ethics," 414

Gilman, Charlotte Perkins, "Women and Economics: 'Cupid-in-the-Kitchen,'" 303

"Good and Bad" (Nietzsche), 393

"Gospel of Wealth, The" (Carnegie), 289

grounds, 39

hooks, bell, "Feminist Politics: Where We Stand," 190

"Human Specificity and the Rights of Animals" (Fukuyama), 440

"Idea of Justice, The" (Sen), 183

"Idea of Rights in the United States, The" (Tocqueville), 84

"If You're Happy and You Know It" (Appiah), 447

"I Have a Dream" (King), 176

"Illiberal Democracy" (Zakaria), 120

"Inequality" (Galbraith), 317

"Intellectual Elite and Democracy, The" (Durkheim), 90

Jacobs, Jane, "Stagflation," 329

Jones, Steve, "The Descent of Men," 244

Kaku, Michio, "Physics of the Impossible," 252

King, Martin Luther, Jr., "I Have a Dream," 176

Lafayette, Marquis de (and The National Assembly of France), "Declaration of the Rights of Man and Citizen," 71

listing, 5–6

Lucretius, "The Nature of Sleep," 206

Madison, James, "The Bill of Rights," 65

Mason, Jim (and Peter Singer), "Ethics and Animals," 430

"Mind's Eye, The" (Sacks), 236

"Molecules and Genes" (Ackerman), 263

"My Dungeon Shook: Letter to My Nephew on the One Hundredth Anniversary of the Emancipation" (Baldwin), 169

Nagel, Thomas, "The Objective Basis of Morality," 406

National Assembly of France, The (and Marquis de Lafayette), "Declaration of the Rights of Man and Citizen," 71

"Nature of Sleep, The" (Lucretius), 206

Nietzsche, Friedrich, "Good and Bad," 393

note taking. See annotating

"Objective Basis of Morality, The" (Nagel), 406

"Of Sexual Selection and Natural Selection" (Darwin), 212

"Of Slavery and the Social Pact" (Rousseau), 136

opening paragraphs, 7–9, 23–26, 34

"Physics of the Impossible" (Kaku), 252

Plato, "Democracy and the Democratic Man," 56

prereading, 4–5, 6, 10

questioning, 4, 7–9, 10, 11, 12, 20–21, 26, 370, 372, 373

quotations, 33

Rawls, John, "A Theory of Justice," 159
reading, critical, 4, 9, 20, 26
"Religion and Science" (Whitehead),
    221
reviewing, 12
rhetoric, 26, 37
rhetorical questions, 35–36
Rogerian arguments, 38, 40–41
Roosevelt, Franklin Delano, "The Four
    Freedoms," 153
Rousseau, Jean-Jacques, "Of Slavery
    and the Social Pact," 136

Sacks, Oliver, "The Mind's Eye," 236
Sen, Amartya, "The Idea of Justice,"
    183
Singer, Peter (and Jim Mason), "Ethics
    and Animals," 430
Smith, Adam, "The Value of Labor," 281
"Stagflation" (Jacobs), 329
statistics, 32, 277–278
"Struggles for Freedom" (Delaney), 146
subheadings, 4–5
subtitles, 6

testimony, 33–35
"Theory of Justice, A" (Rawls), 159
thesis, supporting your, 26–36
thesis statements, creating, 22–36
thinking, critical, 20–21

titles, 4
Tocqueville, Alexis de, "The Idea of
    Rights in the United States," 84
topics, generating, for writing, 20–21
Toulmin arguments, 38, 39
"Toward a Universal Ethics"
    (Gazzaniga), 414

"Value of Labor, The" (Smith), 281
"Vanishing Middle Class, The"
    (Warren), 344
"Vindication of the Rights of Woman,
    A" (Wollstonecraft), 77

warrants, 39
Warren, Elizabeth, "The Vanishing
    Middle Class," 344
West, Cornel, "The Deep Democratic
    Tradition in America," 111
Whitehead, Alfred North, "Religion and
    Science," 221
"Why Democracy?" (Dahl), 96
Wollstonecraft, Mary, "A Vindication of
    the Rights of Woman," 77
"Women and Economics: 'Cupid-in-the-
    Kitchen'" (Gilman), 303
writing, generating topics for, 20–21

Zakaria, Fareed, "Illiberal Democracy,"
    120

RESOURCES FOR TEACHING

Approaching Great Ideas

CRITICAL READINGS FOR COLLEGE WRITERS

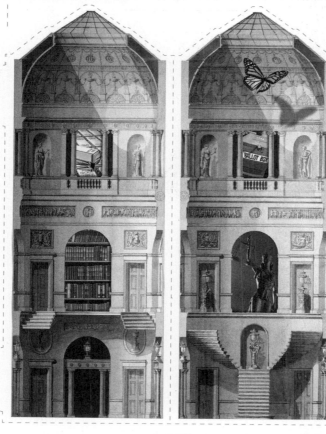

LEE A. JACOBUS

RESOURCES FOR TEACHING

Approaching Great Ideas

RESOURCES FOR TEACHING

APPROACHING GREAT IDEAS

 CRITICAL READINGS
FOR COLLEGE WRITERS

Lee A. Jacobus
University of Connecticut

 bedford
st.martin's
Macmillan Learning
Boston | New York

For information, write: Bedford/St. Martin's, 75 Arlington Street, Boston, MA 02116
    (617-399-4000)

Cover Art: Portman Square, Home House, by Robert Adam (1728–92), Adam, Robert (1728–92)/Courtesy of the Trustees of Sir John Soane's Museum, London/Bridgeman Images; inset photos: (butterfly) Lisa Thornberg/Getty Images; (gold bars) f9photos/Getty Images; (ballot box) Ken Reid/Getty Images; (books) luoman/Getty Images; (justice scales) Comstock/Getty Images

ISBN 978-1-319-03610-2

PREFACE

⊞

Approaching Great Ideas: Critical Readings for College Writers is designed for first-year college English instruction in composition, the level at which I used these essays for my own students. I am aware of the problems involved in trying to teach students to read more carefully and respond to significant authors by writing their own essays. We usually ask our students to read professional essays while they are learning to write them, and I have found that using essays by significant writers is one of the best ways to help students write and keep writing. The material in *Approaching Great Ideas* is important enough to generate good class discussion as well as good essays.

These *Resources*, like the text, are divided into two parts. "Part One: Reading and Writing about Great Ideas" deals with basic issues in teaching reading skills. Using the material in that section of the text should help students learn quickly how to focus their attention and get the most out of the essays in the book. I recommend reading aloud in class, both on the part of the student and on your part as instructor. Students need to hear how some of this material sounds. It helps them ground themselves, and it helps them understand what is most important in the essays they read. I found it exhilarating to discuss Plato, Rousseau, Wollstonecraft, and Darwin with first-year college students. They understand these are writers they ought to know. And because they feel that way, I find it easier to hold their attention and show them how to learn about writing — while learning about other things — from a discussion of the prose before them.

"Part Two: The Readings" in this manual includes discussions of all thirty-nine readings in *Approaching Great Ideas* and provides additional suggestions to supplement those in the book. First, I provide a brief comment on the passage. Then, I provide "Questions for Comprehension" that you can use to check on how well your students have read the passage. Following that, I provide "Suggestions for Essays" that supplement the assignments within the book. You can modify these as you choose.

Resources for Teaching is designed to not get in your way as a teacher. I can't pretend to explain these essays the way you will explain them to your class. Students are all so different that no two discussions of, say, Darwin are ever the same. Even principal areas of focus change from discussion to discussion. Therefore, you probably will not want to use all of the materials — discussion topics, writing assignments, and bibliographies — for each essay that you teach. But you may appreciate knowing that all these options are available, particularly if some of the essays turn out to be more challenging than you thought.

I have had extensive experience in remedial English and understand some of the reading problems that even an average class contains. Yet I have been warmed by the enthusiasm my students showed over the years for the approach I recommend here. Using this book with first-year students implies that we respect their native intelligence, especially if we feel their preparation for college has not been as good as we would wish. The Brunerian hypothesis — that students who are treated as if they were geniuses will perform as such — may not withstand the proof of experience, but I have found that even the most difficult students in an average class can derive benefit from assignments on this kind of material. Granted, one must work hard to help them understand the ideas and grasp the basic rhetorical principles that they must apply. But I find the work is well rewarded.

One genuine reward is the quality of class discussions. I was pleased with the ways my students pursued lines of argument or implications of a thought and then tried to make sense of the essays they read. It is always interesting to discuss Aristotle's concept of happiness, for example — an idea that is important to young people, idealists or otherwise.

Another reward of this approach is the belief that we are contributing to the education of beginning students. Because most composition classes demand that some reading material be used for discussion and models of good writing, I consider it important to provide the best there is. In this case, the best thinkers talking about some of the most vital ideas of all time represent the best stimuli and models for writing. It is surprising to see how each of these authors provides a useful model. Whether the essay presents a specific form of argument, employs images or metaphors, or examines a single idea from many points of view, it remains a model with teaching potential for beginning students.

Contemporary journalistic essays of the sort that appear in most anthologies available today are easy and fun reading for students. But in many cases they are also insubstantial and often do not really offer the kind of model for writing that is truly useful. Most of the essays in this category — by Joan Didion, Tom Wolfe, E. B. White, and other fine writers — fascinate the reader because of the author's style. It is not the invention or the organization that stands out — it is the style. And style is the one element that first-year students cannot learn from such models.

First-year students can learn in their writing course how to use methods of development to help invention. They can also learn about argumentation, narrative, and other organizational principles. But they cannot hope to imitate or learn directly from a mature, polished style. That comes only with time. Meanwhile, the kinds of essays included here have a great deal to offer beginning students of writing. I have tried to make the going as simple as I can to maintain morale and give students the chance to make the most of this valuable opportunity.

The contents of this manual may also be downloaded from **macmillanhighered.com/greatideas/catalog**.

Contents

PREFACE   *vii*

PART ONE
READING AND WRITING ABOUT GREAT IDEAS

1. Examining Ideas   *2*

2. Writing about Ideas   *5*

GENERATING TOPICS FOR WRITING   *6*

THINKING CRITICALLY: ASKING QUESTIONS   *10*

DEVELOPING IDEAS IN WRITING   *12*

SAMPLE ESSAY   *13*

SAMPLE SYLLABUS   *14*

SUGGESTED PAIRINGS OF ESSAYS   *17*

PART TWO
THE READINGS

3. How Democracy Relates to Human Rights   *20*

PLATO
Democracy and the Democratic Man   *21*

JAMES MADISON
The Bill of Rights   *22*

                                                                              xi

MARQUIS DE LAFAYETTE AND THE NATIONAL ASSEMBLY OF FRANCE
Declaration of the Rights of Man and Citizen 23

MARY WOLLSTONECRAFT
A Vindication of the Rights of Woman 25

ALEXIS DE TOCQUEVILLE
The Idea of Rights in the United States 26

EMILE DURKHEIM
The Intellectual Elite and Democracy 29

ROBERT A. DAHL
Why Democracy? 30

CORNEL WEST
The Deep Democratic Tradition in America 32

FAREED ZAKARIA
Illiberal Democracy 33

4. How Freedom Depends on Justice 35

JEAN–JACQUES ROUSSEAU
Of Slavery and the Social Pact 36

LUCY A. DELANEY
Struggles for Freedom 38

FRANKLIN DELANO ROOSEVELT
The Four Freedoms 39

JOHN RAWLS
A Theory of Justice 41

JAMES BALDWIN
**My Dungeon Shook: Letter to My Nephew on the
One Hundredth Anniversary of the Emancipation** 43

MARTIN LUTHER KING JR.
I Have a Dream 44

AMARTYA SEN
The Idea of Justice 46

bell hooks
Feminist Politics: Where We Stand 47

5. How Science Reads the Book of Nature 49

LUCRETIUS
    The Nature of Sleep   50

CHARLES DARWIN
    Of Sexual Selection and Natural Selection   51

ALFRED NORTH WHITEHEAD
    Religion and Science   53

OLIVER SACKS
    The Mind's Eye   55

STEVE JONES
    The Descent of Men   56

MICHIO KAKU
    Physics of the Impossible   58

JENNIFER ACKERMAN
    Molecules and Genes   60

6. How Society Regards Wealth and Poverty 62

ADAM SMITH
    The Value of Labor   64

ANDREW CARNEGIE
    The Gospel of Wealth   66

CHARLOTTE PERKINS GILMAN
    Women and Economics: "Cupid-in-the-Kitchen"   68

JOHN KENNETH GALBRAITH
    Inequality   70

JANE JACOBS
    Stagflation   72

ELIZABETH WARREN
    The Vanishing Middle Class   74

LESLIE T. CHANG
    Factory Girls in Dongguan   75

7. How Ethics and Morality Interact 78

ARISTOTLE
The Aim of Man 79

FRIEDRICH NIETZSCHE
Good and Bad 81

JOHN DEWEY
Education and Morality 82

THOMAS NAGEL
The Objective Basis of Morality 84

MICHAEL GAZZANIGA
Toward a Universal Ethics 86

PETER SINGER AND JIM MASON
Ethics and Animals 88

FRANCIS FUKUYAMA
Human Specificity snd the Rights of Animals 90

KWAME ANTHONY APPIAH
If You're Happy and You Know It 91

⊞ READING AND WRITING ABOUT GREAT IDEAS

CHAPTER ONE

Examining Ideas

⊞

The first step in approaching the material in the text is developing good reading habits. While the material is sometimes challenging, I have chosen it carefully to make it appropriate for students in a standard composition class. The individual pieces are sometimes as short as three or four pages, while only a few are more than ten pages in length. The length of each essay is short because it permits the willing student to review the reading more than once. It also offers you a chance to cover the material in great detail. Critical reading involves paying attention to the large questions and noting the details as carefully as possible. It also involves developing good questions and observations that can later help provide material for the student to discuss with others and, in some cases, to provide stimulus for writing.

The first chapter of *Approaching Great Ideas* uses a modified version of the classic reading strategy called SQ3R: Survey, Question, Read, Recite, Review. It was originally developed by Francis Pleasant Robinson in his 1946 book *Effective Study* and was intended primarily to boost study skills. Today, it is widely employed in reading courses, and I have modified it slightly to reflect its usefulness first in reading the essays in the book and second in helping students contribute to class discussion.

Surveying begins with **Prereading, Titles, and Subheadings**, an overview and anticipation of key ideas in the selection. To an extent, this will also give the student a chance to bring to bear some prior knowledge of the selection's subject matter. The title of the essay is the first place to start because it often gives the basic approach of the author and provides the subject of the essay. Then, noting the subheadings and where they appear will give the reader a reasonable guide to the contents of the essay. **Looking at Opening Paragraphs** also instructs students to survey the selection for key ideas. It is a good place to begin.

I include another aspect of prereading: **Annotating** and note taking are detailed versions of surveying. Annotation helps the reader keep track of what seems important or useful in the first and possibly the next reading of the piece. I suggest using underlining and making notes in the margins of the pages. I know that most students will not mark up their books because they expect to re-sell them later, so I also suggest keeping a separate notebook. I can hardly read anything without annotating the text, but I also know that many students have been prohibited from writing in their books since grade school. It's hard to break old habits. (Maybe if we could convince students that annotation is a form of subversion, they might get the idea.)

The skills of **Questioning**, with numerous examples at different stages of working with selections, help sharpen the student's understanding of the selection's main ideas. Questioning is also the best strategy to prevent the student from being a passive reader. Eventually, questioning will lead students to challenge some of the author's ideas, sharpening their ability to identify and evaluate those ideas. I always asked my students to write their questions in the margins as they read, but most did not. As a result, I always had some questions to use in class discussion to get things underway. Those students who developed their own questions stimulated even more discussion in class.

Reviewing the selection together with notes and underlining helps students focus their attention and increases understanding and comprehension of what they have been reading. This involves examining underlining in the text, prereading questions and answers, and the note taking students did as they read.

The concept of recitation, in Robinson's book, appears here as **Discussing.** This is a most important form of recitation, shaping the students' response to the selection's ideas by offering their own thoughts to the examination of others. Ultimately, class discussion helps build reading skills by sharpening the students' understanding of the text at hand. Other students will interpret the text in slightly different ways, see implications that might have been missed. Class discussion helps students reconsider their understanding in an open forum, improving both understanding and comprehension in a community setting. As an example for instruction, a selection by Alfred North Whitehead is offered for analysis and demonstration of critical reading skills.

These simple steps are easy to talk about and easy to recommend, but we all know that most students will think they can do without them. One way to reach them is to have them read a paragraph or two in class and then discuss what they have been reading. This method may help them see the virtue of being better prepared to talk about this material. In my own classes, I always spent time reading aloud passages of importance from the texts. I suggest you do that as well. When you do, explain that you are pointing out some of the most important moments in the text and that they should underline or annotate those passages for later reference. This procedure gives them a model for effective annotation and effective reading.

The suggestions for reading in the text stem from my commitment to making students in my classes develop important ideas of their own. My hope is to expand their understanding of very important concepts, and in addition, I hope to change some minds. Frankly, changing minds is a key part of education. The students who come to a beginning composition class are possibly the most responsive of all students in the college, and it is always exciting to see how they reconsider "received" ideas as they go through the course.

I know from the experience of students throughout the country that some of them will come to the class after reading some of the essays and express anger because they will disagree strongly with part — or all — of what they read. This is the ideal, of course, because they produce the energy that makes class discussion exciting. Above all, it is essential to give students a chance to develop their own thoughts and challenge the ideas in this text. I want students to be on a quest for truth and deep understanding. The point of *Approaching Great Ideas* is to encourage students to think on an intellectual level that is worthy of them. For some of your students, the material in the book will be their primary exposure to an education in the liberal arts. I hope they will find it challenging and exciting.

CHAPTER TWO

WRITING ABOUT IDEAS

⊞

You know best what kinds of essays or responses you want from your students after they have read the assigned material. I found that I could direct my students toward personal and revealing writing or toward more formal and objective writing. Some suggestions for writing invite a personal response, and for certain students, this is the best kind of response. But for other students, a more reasoned and detached response might be desirable. What kind of response to aim toward lies with you, and *Approaching Great Ideas* is flexible enough to allow you to decide.

I suggest that you hold some discussions with your students about your expectations and discuss openly with them what their expectations in the course are and what kind of writing they feel they need to do. I feel that self-expressive writing is appropriate for some students, but I also feel that most students at the first-year level should attempt less self-expressive writing and should instead practice writing that asks them to reason well, to think clearly, and to work with mature and demanding ideas. For that reason, you will find that most of the assignments direct students toward a kind of writing that is similar to the material they are reading: discursive, demanding, thoughtful, and rooted in universal human experience.

SUGGESTIONS FOR DISCUSSION

1. Hold an open discussion with your students on why they ought to write about these essays instead of just talk about them. Ask them what they think the difference is, for example, between writing an

essay and taking an examination on Plato's selection. I think you will uncover some interesting attitudes and be able to help your students understand the differences between these two processes.

2. In the course of discussing an essay — Andrew Carnegie's "The Gospel of Wealth" should do nicely — you might ask your students to make some observations about the author's tone or attitude toward the audience. These are important issues, and discussing them at an early stage can help you clarify some points. You can also explore with your students the kinds of choices they can make to control tone and use it to their best advantage.

3. It may be dangerously subjective — but also exceptionally human — to ask your students to comment on what they think about the author they are working with. How much of James Baldwin comes through in his "Letter to My Nephew," and in which passages? Or you may prefer to ask your students to decide on the attitude the authors assume. For example, is Nietzsche cynical? Is Tocqueville idealistic? What about Madison or Jacobs? Or Smith, King, or Whitehead?

4. Spend some time in your class discussions on the question of what students might write about. Suggest topics as they occur to you, and ask students to recommend and refine topics for essays. The virtue of this approach is that it encourages students to start thinking about writing topics early on, which in turn motivates them as they read.

GENERATING TOPICS FOR WRITING

You may regard the suggestions for writing at the end of the selections as a last resort for your students, but teachers tell me that the suggestions work. In fact, when I asked one reviewer of the book what I could do to improve it, she recommended only that I include more suggestions for writing, which I have done.

Most students come up with ideas as they discuss the essays, but many also rely on the suggestions for writing and the questions intended to stimulate class discussion. Most students appreciate these suggestions, and students produce surprisingly varied papers based on what they choose.

USING WRITING PROMPTS

All the questions for writing in the text offer a variety of writing prompts, each a method of development identified before the questions for writing. I have included them as a way of helping students connect what is detailed in the text, including the examples I supply of worked-up paragraphs, with their own practice. Naturally, if you find such writing prompts ineffective, simply instruct your students to ignore them. However, some students may find them very valuable, and I recommend your being flexible on this rhetorical issue.

I include a variety of prompts before questions for writing, such as:

- Definition Prompt
- Comparison Prompt
- Analysis of Circumstances Prompt
- Cause and Effect Prompt
- Response Prompt
- Example Prompt
- Research Prompt
- Testimony Prompt (or Analysis of Quotations)

Writing prompts are designed with the student in mind and follow some of the patterns for development already discussed in the text. The prompts follow every selection and provide avenues for investigation of the selection that stimulate a response and help develop a thesis for writing an essay. Some prompts are useful for one- or two-page essays, while some are useful for longer essays. You may wish to use the samples here to illustrate the effectiveness of writing prompts:

- **Definition** In the last paragraph of Alexis de Tocqueville's essay, he says, "nothing is more fertile in wondrous effects than the art of being free but nothing is harder than freedom's apprenticeship." In a brief essay, define the expression "the art of being free" and the expression "freedom's apprenticeship." Are you engaged currently in freedom's apprenticeship? Have you practiced the art of being free? What do these expressions mean?

- **Comparison** Cornel West says that deep in the American culture there is a profound desire for democracy. What would West most approve of in his reading of the Bill of Rights? How thoroughly would West feel Madison considers the questions of human rights in the new nation? What would Cornel West and James Madison be most likely to agree upon in considering how a government should function to best serve its people? What does West take into consideration that Madison does not?

- **Analysis of Circumstances** Like most Virginia gentlemen of the period, James Madison owned slaves. He also approved a plan for gradual emancipation of the slaves, but it was never presented to Congress because the plan would never be passed. Along with Benjamin Franklin and Thomas Jefferson, he approved a scheme to buy slaves and send them back to Africa, where, in 1821, those freed slaves established a government in Liberia. To what extent does Madison's participation in slavery compromise his position in the Bill of Rights?

- **Cause and Effect** Cornel West says, "Democracy is not just a system of governance, as we tend to think of it, but a cultural way of being." As a citizen living in a democracy, describe what you perceive to be the "cultural way of being" that West describes? How does the democratic system produce a culture of behavior and a cultural attitude that is distinct enough to set people apart in their behavior and thinking from those who do not enjoy democracy? What are your general expectations from governance and from society as a member of a democratic nation?

- **Response** Give a careful description of your views on modern democracy based on how you currently see your government at work. Which of the five requirements for a functional democracy do you see at work in your experience? In what ways have you developed a full understanding of the political choices you are offered? How much do people you know understand about their choices? Cite a specific instance in which your choices were either very clear or very unclear to you. What specific examples can you point to that demonstrate how people feel their vote is "counted equally"? Which parts of Robert A. Dahl's argument struck you as most personally relevant to your views on democracy?

- **Example** The oligarchs that Fareed Zakaria refers to in Russia are extremely wealthy businesspeople, almost all men, who wield a considerable amount of power because of the wealth they control. Putin keeps them in control by threatening them with legal action. One oligarch explains that breaking some law or other is impossible to avoid if one is to become wealthy. Extremely wealthy people are the equivalent of Russia's oligarchs in liberal democracies. In our democracy, do you detect the power of oligarchs trying to influence our government's policies? Are those influences for the good or not?

- **Research** One surprising detail in Cornel West's discussion is his suggestion that the work of John Coltrane and Tupac Shakur, both modern musicians with a wide popular audience, supports his position by their criticism of the culture. If you know the work of Tupac Shakur, examine his music and his lyrics and explain to someone who may not know him how he supports West. Why might contemporary politicians feel that it is inappropriate to cite Tupac as a critic of our culture? What other major musical figures are cultural critics? Is their criticism effective? Is it fair?

- **Testimony** In "I Have a Dream," Martin Luther King Jr. alludes to many passages in the Bible, including Psalm 30:5, Isaiah 40:4–5, and Amos 5:24. Take an inventory of the quotations he references and examine them to see how closely they support King's views in his speech.

In the text itself, I also refer to **Development by Rhetorical Question**, but I do not offer writing prompts with that title because any useful rhetorical question must come not from a writing prompt but from the student. You may wish to remind students that they can develop their own rhetorical question as a writing prompt for any of the essays they read.

ESTABLISHING AN ARGUMENT

Most of the selections in *Approaching Great Ideas* are structured as arguments for or against a position or a series of positions. In the process of creating arguments, the writers also make recommendations and draw conclusions concerning their views. In the process, they usually encourage the reader to share their views. In this section of the introduction to rhetoric, students are introduced to three forms of argument, any of which they are encouraged to understand and potentially use.

- **Classical argument** Most of us ordinarily use the classical form of argument, in which we marshal a number of reasons for believing the truth of our thesis. We use facts and point to evidence that is well known or recently proved to support the reasons that we offer to demonstrate our position. Supporting data includes examples from history, from recent events, and from the statements of experts, all of which may constitute evidence in favor of the writer's position. Personal anecdotes can also help convince a reader of the writer's view. The classical argument uses logic where necessary. The purpose of a classical argument is to persuade the reader of the truth of the writer's thesis.

- **Toulmin argument** The Toulmin argument begins with a claim, which is sometimes a version of the thesis statement. The claim is followed by support — the data, facts, observations, and conclusions that bolster the claim. Once the evidence has been examined, the argument continues by examining counterarguments. The analysis of counterarguments reveals why they are insufficient. Underlying the Toulmin argument is an agreed-upon position, something that is taken for granted by the writer and the audience. Such a position might be as simple as assuming that justice is one of the highest values expected of a democracy.

- **Rogerian argument** The Rogerian argument is distinctive because it is not structured only to persuade an audience but often to help inform. It depends on finding a common ground on the subject of the essay. It is a common ground that most people would agree upon as important and relevant to the discussion. James Madison in the Bill of Rights finds common ground with his American audience by assuming that a democracy should guarantee human rights to citizens. Usually the Rogerian argument aims at showing that the author's position is reasonable and desirable as well as preferable to alternative positions on the same subject. The Rogerian argument is less confrontational than other forms of argument.

THINKING CRITICALLY: ASKING QUESTIONS

At one level, education is a matter of learning how to ask the right questions. It is very important to point out that the authors in the text are often answering questions in their essays. The questions posed by students based on Alfred North Whitehead's essay, for example, are only a fraction of those that could be asked.

SUGGESTIONS FOR WRITING

1. Ask your students to come up with as many questions as there are in the book. None of these questions is actually developed into an essay in the introduction, but all are indirectly relevant. Coming up with more questions can be very useful in discussing how to find ideas for writing. You might use some of the questions as vehicles for your students' writing. See if your students can produce good ideas for essays as they discuss the questions.

2. This is a good place to develop thesis statements and to discuss the ways in which a thesis statement merges from questions. If you use this book with a rhetoric text, you can introduce such

material as is relevant. I have provided a good deal of emphasis on thesis statements in the book, but you will want to modify my advice depending on your own views. Thesis statements probably work best for students who are less secure about their writing. More confident students may be able to "spread" their thesis over a few sentences. This is often the way professional writers work, so it's not something you should recommend unless you have a way of making that process work.

3. Go over some sample arguments in class. If you feel it useful, link them with the methods of development and show how each method of development can yield an appropriate thesis statement from the same or similar concerns. Students need drilling in this, and no matter how many times you go over it, you will find students proposing theses that are too broad, too narrow, or too obvious for an essay. Sometimes no thesis statement at all will surface. If you feel this is important, you should allow some time for it in the opening days of the course. Working up questions on the text is a good beginning exercise in class. You can begin by proposing some questions and then showing how they can be answered in an essay. To me, the important issue is to teach students how to raise questions of depth and complexity. Try to steer students away from any questions that require too simple a response. If the question is deep enough, the student will need to think carefully, and that will help produce an essay that might even surprise the student. I asked two basic types of questions. One kind limits itself to how an author works with an idea by articulating a concept and then examining it. Other questions examine life and experience outside the text. You probably will want to stress one kind of question on some occasions and another kind on others.

USING SUGGESTIONS FOR WRITING

In addition to suggestions for writing after each selection, there are a few more suggestions in this manual. One tip for the first papers is to limit their length. I was particularly finicky about the first set of papers. I urged even my best students to write no more than three pages, but I really think two pages for the first paper is acceptable. That way, you can go over the paper in detail and inform your students about what kind of performance you expect. If you review the first papers carefully, you should have a better experience with the second papers.

DEVELOPING IDEAS IN WRITING

METHODS OF DEVELOPMENT

If you were trained in rhetoric, you will recognize my reference to methods of development as allusions to many common topics. The use of definition, comparison and contrast, causal analysis, and discussion of circumstances can be important initial issues for most students. If you are not interested in rhetorical terms or techniques, I doubt that what I have to say in this section will bother you very much. You can use it as you like and tell your students to read it all but take only what they feel is useful.

However, I worked with my students very closely on these matters and found that methods of development help them think more clearly and write more confidently. If you agree with me about the usefulness of studying these methods of development, especially as such methods are evident in the selections, I suggest that you try my approach of having your students develop single-paragraph essays guided by one of the methods of development. I often ask my students, once they have gotten used to thinking in terms of the methods of development, to try writing an essay using each method in turn.

SUGGESTIONS FOR WRITING

1. Assign the class the job of writing a single paragraph using any one of the methods of development. Give your students a choice to ensure some variety in your reading. Be sure to ask them to identify at the beginning of the essay which method they are using. If you would prefer that everyone use the same method of development, try causal analysis or analysis of circumstances. Or, for one that is less difficult, try definition, which is important for first-year students.

2. Assign a one-paragraph essay, but do not allow students to identify the method they used. Read some aloud in class (or photocopy them), and see whether the class can identify them.

3. Request an essay, like the sample essay, that uses a different method of development in each paragraph. This type of assignment may not appeal to you. However, you will see that it serves the important purpose of connecting the act of writing to the act of reading the essays in a way that is helpful for improving your students' writing. I feel that these methods of invention can be learned from watching how good writers work, even when the writers are formidable thinkers. The final result is that your students think much more about how they write something. Not

only should their writing improve, but their thoughts about the subject at hand should deepen. My suggestions have produced some probing essays and have also given some of the most problematic student writers approaches they never knew before. Often, such students show the most rapid progress.

SAMPLE ESSAY

Give your students a chance to go over the sample essay with you. You may find it contains elements that you do not want your students to repeat. If so, give the essay a thorough critique. Your students will want to critique it on their own terms, and they should be given a chance to do so.

SUGGESTIONS FOR ESSAYS

I make an agreement with my students: if they hand in each essay on time, I grade it and give it back in the next meeting. This helps build morale. Students know how well they did almost immediately, and I know what needs to be done to have them writing at the level I think appropriate for them. The reward for turning in the essay on time is that if the student truly underperforms, I permit the student to resubmit the revised essay for a better grade. This works. My most helpful practice is to photocopy some samples from my students' work and offer critiques of them in class. The rule is that no one knows whose work is being discussed, and there is to be no cruel or nasty criticism. Everything is directed toward the goal of writing better. Students are impressively helpful to one another. They become good editors, make good suggestions for revision, and develop a keen eye that extends to the examination of their own work. In one way, this makes their writing part of the subject matter of the entire course. I have not found a faster way to improve student writing than this. Naturally, I make sure every student contributes at least one sample in these "publications," and usually two or three. I choose a wide range, from excellent to good to not-so-good writing samples for them to read.

HOW MANY READINGS TO ASSIGN?

Judging from my mail, this is impossible to answer. Some instructors will use ten to fourteen of the readings. Others will use twice that number. Many look for essays that relate to each other in some way. For those of you who are interested in possible pairings, see "Suggested Pairings of Essays," which follows the syllabus in this manual on page 17.

SAMPLE SYLLABUS

What follows is a sample syllabus of the kind I used when I last taught the first-year composition course. I know it's a workout. I was often exhausted after class, and I know that I could have gotten by without having the students read so many essays. But the truth is that I wished we could read more. The only way to do that is to eliminate assignments in the rhetoric text. You must gauge how hard you want your students to work and how hard they can work. Set your own pace, knowing that whatever you read, you will be working with rewarding ideas.

ENGLISH 105 COMPOSITION
FALL 2016
T-TH: 9:30-11:00
OFFICE HOURS: T-TH 11:00-12:00

The basic purpose of this course is for you to master the fundamentals of rhetoric while also confronting the ideas of some of the most important writers and texts in Western culture. Your responsibilities will include reading the assignments carefully and generating appropriate essays that test your thinking and help craft your writing.

TEXTS: Lee A. Jacobus, *Approaching Great Ideas* (Boston: Bedford/St. Martin's, 2016).

ESSAYS: *Format.* Your essays will be typewritten on standard 8 ½-by-11-inch paper. Leave a margin of 1 ½ inches on the left for my comments. The essays will be given to me on their due date. Their length may vary from assignment to assignment, but one important point is that they should be as short as you can humanly make them. Essay length will be about three pages at first and then will escalate to a maximum of eight pages (but only when I give the word).

ESSAYS: *Style.* We will practice what rhetoricians call the *plain style*, which means that you ought to aim for the simplest, most direct, unadorned, and unaffected style possible. As a guide, you should think in terms of short sentences, averaging twenty words or so. Your paragraphs should have a clear topic, with every subsequent sentence growing naturally from your intentions regarding its development. Your paragraphs ought to be relatively short (five to eight sentences) and structured with a clear plan. Style is to be thought of as an instrument to achieve clarity of expression. Your vocabulary should be jargon-free and designed to inform, not to impress.

ASSIGNMENTS: The pattern throughout the course will be for you to hand in essays on Tuesday or Thursday. We will discuss some of your essays on the second class following the deadline as well as new assigned readings.

> Sept. 3 Tuesday: Introduction to Rhetoric, Reading, and Writing.
> Sept. 5 Thursday: Read: "Examining Ideas," pp. 3-18.
> Sept. 10 Tuesday: Read: Madison, "The Bill of Rights," pp. 65-70.
> Sept. 12 Thursday: Read: "Writing about Ideas," pp. 19-46, and Lafayette, "Declaration of the Rights of Man and Citizen," pp. 71-76.
> **1st essay due.**

ASSIGNMENT: Write a brief essay on a topic chosen from those at the ends of the selections.

> Sept. 17 Tuesday: Read Plato, "Democracy and the Democratic Man," pp. 56-64, and West, "The Deep Democratic Tradition in America," pp. 111-119.
> Sept. 19 Thursday: Read Dahl, "Why Democracy?", pp. 96-110.
> Sept. 24 Tuesday: Read Wollstonecraft, "A Vindication of the Rights of Woman," pp. 77-83.
> **2nd essay due.**

ASSIGNMENT: Write an essay on a topic chosen from those at the ends of the selections.

> Sept. 26 Thursday: Read Rousseau, "Of Slavery and the Social Pact," pp. 136-145.
> Oct. 1 Tuesday: Read Delaney, "Struggles for Freedom," pp. 146-152 and Baldwin, "My Dungeon Shook: Letter to My Nephew on the One Hundredth Anniversary of the Emancipation," pp. 169-175.
> Oct. 3 Thursday: Read Rawls, "A Theory of Justice," pp. 159-168, and Sen, "The Idea of Justice," pp. 183-189.

Oct. 8 Tuesday: Read Roosevelt, "The Four Freedoms," pp. 153–158.
3rd essay due.

ASSIGNMENT: Write an essay on a topic chosen from those at the ends of the selections.

Oct. 10 Thursday: Read Lucretius, "The Nature of Sleep," pp. 206–211, and Sacks, "The Mind's Eye," pp. 236–243.

Oct. 15 Tuesday: Read Darwin, "Of Sexual Selection and Natural Selection," pp. 212–220.

Oct. 17 Thursday: Read Kaku, "Physics of the Impossible," pp. 252–262.

Oct. 22 Tuesday: Read Ackerman, "Molecules and Genes," pp. 263–271.
4th essay due.

ASSIGNMENT: Write an essay on a topic chosen from those at the ends of the selections.

Oct. 24 Thursday: Read Smith, "The Value of Labor," pp. 281–288.

Oct. 29 Tuesday: Read Carnegie, "The Gospel of Wealth," pp. 289–302.

Oct. 31 Thursday: Read Gilman, "Women and Economics: 'Cupid-in-the-Kitchen,'" pp. 303–316.

Nov. 5 Tuesday: Read Galbraith, "Inequality," pp. 317–328.

Nov. 7 Thursday: Read Warren, "The Vanishing Middle Class," pp. 344–356.

Nov. 12 Tuesday: Read Chang, "Factory Girls in Dongguan," pp. 357–366.
5th essay due.

ASSIGNMENT: Write an essay on a topic chosen from those at the ends of the selections.

Nov. 14 Thursday: Read Aristotle, "The Aim of Man," pp. 374–392.

Nov. 19 Tuesday: Read Nietzsche, "Good and Bad," pp. 393–399.

Nov. 21 Thursday: Read Nagel, "The Objective Basis of Morality," pp. 406–413.

Nov. 26 Tuesday: Read Gazzaniga, "Toward a
Universal Ethics," pp. 414–429.
　Nov. 23 Thursday: THANKSGIVING
　Dec. 3 Tuesday: Read Singer and Mason, "Ethics and
Animals," pp. 430–439.
　Dec. 5 Thursday: Read Appiah, "If You're Happy and
You Know It," pp. 447–454.
　Dec. 10 Tuesday: Read Dewey, "Education and
Morality," pp. 400–405.
　6th essay due.

ASSIGNMENT: Write an essay on a topic chosen from those at
the ends of the selections.

　Dec. 12 Thursday: Read and discuss an essay of
　your choice.

NOTE: Prompt completion of essays is crucial in this course.
If you feel you cannot keep the pace we have set, you need
to see me. All late essays, except those made late by *real*
problems, will suffer a grade reduction.

Completed essays are due on the following days:
1. September 12
2. September 24
3. October 8
4. October 22
5. November 12
6. December 10

SUGGESTED PAIRINGS OF ESSAYS

Many instructors look for useful connections between two or more essays;
if you are interested in trying that approach, you might consider the following groupings. The "Comparing Ideas" questions also make concrete suggestions for pairings.

1. Madison and Dahl: The question of how to create and maintain a functional democracy is central to these selections.
2. The Bill of Rights contrasts well with Tocqueville's view of democracy as
he saw it at work.
3. Rawls and Rousseau: Trace the influence of Rousseau in Rawls's view of
utilitarianism.

4. Dahl and West are concerned with the durability of democracy.

5. Wollstonecraft, Gilman, and hooks read together will produce some interesting insights. The questions of the rights of women continue to be important.

6. Carnegie and Galbraith make a great pair. The issue of poverty contrasts with the issue of the freedom of the individual to pursue wealth.

7. Zakaria and Durkheim are of different eras, but their views intersect in interesting ways.

8. Wollstonecraft and Chang might be a good combination, concerning women's opportunities.

9. Smith and Carnegie are a natural combination, both lauding capitalism and both viewing the nature of poverty as normal.

10. Aristotle and Appiah are an obvious combination because they both approach the idea of happiness, and Appiah is essentially analyzing Aristotle's position.

11. Aristotle and Nietzsche are another natural combination because they approach the ideas of good and bad from different directions.

12. Nagel's focus on an objective basis of morality contrasts marvelously with Nietzsche's conviction that morality is socially determined.

13. Singer and Mason are good paired with Madison or Lafayette because the concept of rights for people can be mined for establishing rights for animals.

14. Fukuyama and Singer and Mason are also a good pairing.

15. Aristotle's "The Aim of Man" works with all the essays in "How Ethics and Morality Interact."

16. Darwin works well with Jones and Ackerman because their views tend to overlap in interesting ways.

17. Whitehead appears in several sections of the book, and he naturally connects with Darwin and Jones.

Part Two

⊞ THE
READINGS

CHAPTER THREE

How Democracy Relates to Human Rights

⊞

The nine selections in this chapter treat the issues of democracy as it was developed in the ancient world and as it has been connected to the preservation of human rights in modern times. Because democracy is not a simple idea, nor is there only one form of democracy, we need to examine some of its roots and some of the struggles to reinvent it in modern times. We need to avoid a simplistic approach to democracy and understand its complexities, its significance for developing nations, and its promise for modern industrialized nations. The writers here, both classic and modern, connect our rights with the ideals of democracy.

PLATO

Democracy and the Democratic Man (pp. 56–64)

IT SEEMS logical to me to begin with Plato, since so much of our culture depends on his ideas. Students may be interested in his idealist thought, but here we are dealing with some of the realities of politics as expressed in *The Republic*. You might review the concept of oligarchy, which Plato mentions and which he had described before this passage. This is also an opportunity to talk about the concept of the dialogue, which is a signature of Plato's style. You may also wish to alert your students to the fact that he is not entirely pleased with the idea of a democratic government. What he feared was mob rule and misrule, which also concerned our founding fathers. In *The Republic*, he preceded this chapter with comments on the timocratic man and the oligarchic man.

QUESTIONS FOR COMPREHENSION

1. How does Plato think democracies get established?
2. What does Plato tell us about the weakness of oligarchies?
3. What does Plato tell us about the poor and the rich together in battle?
4. Why is Plato concerned about the way young men are raised in their families?

SUGGESTIONS FOR ESSAYS

1. *Definition* How does Plato define *the democratic man*?
2. *Comparison* Describe the ways in which oligarchies differ from democracies, according to Plato.
3. *Response* Plato talks about "the distinction between necessary and unnecessary appetites" (para. 27). What is your understanding of the idea of "appetites," and how do you respond to Plato's warnings? What appetites are characteristic of your own nature? What has he taught you about yourself?

4. **Research** Consult Plato's *The Republic* for his discussion of oligarchies, which comes just before the discussion of democracy. It is often titled "Oligarchy and the Oligarchic Man." It is usually Chapter 30 (viii. 550 c–555 b), and reference to the Greek text is sometimes used.

5. **Analysis of Circumstances** Near the end of his dialogue, Plato makes reference to an observation that "all must have their equal rights" (para. 35). Under what circumstances does Plato disapprove of this statement? Why does he feel there are situations in which this concept can lead to disorder or bad government? If Plato is right, what does that mean for establishing a democratic government that works?

⊞

JAMES MADISON

The Bill of Rights (pp. 65–70)

MADISON WAS aware that the federal government was going to be a strong government and that it would sometimes conflict with the individual state governments, which, before the Constitution, were extremely powerful. Because he was concerned about the issues that did not seem to be addressed directly by the Constitution, he drafted all but two of the amendments that were designed to protect the rights of individuals in the entire nation. He did not call these a bill of rights, but posterity did that for him. Madison and others feared pure democracy partly because they knew the power of a mass of people roused by demagogues. Yet Madison constantly praised the people as the fountain of power in any government.

QUESTIONS FOR COMPREHENSION

1. What does Madison say about punishment by the law?
2. What legal restrictions are applied to establishing a religion?
3. How soon should a lawbreaker be tried in court?
4. The right of trial by jury is reserved for cases that exceed how many dollars?

SUGGESTIONS FOR ESSAYS

1. *Analysis of Circumstances* Explain when soldiers can be billeted in citizens' houses and why Madison is concerned about this provision.

2. *Research* What are people's concerns regarding a speedy trial today? Check the local and national newspapers and online news sources to see how well Madison's amendment is working.

3. *Response* What is your reaction to the provisions made in the Bill of Rights? Which ones do you most approve of, and which do you most question? Which are clearest, and which are obscure? Do you feel your rights are protected by the Bill of Rights?

4. *Definition* Examine Amendment IX and define its terms. Once you have defined them, explain what the amendment means to American citizens. What rights can be in conflict with other rights and what must be done about those conflicts?

5. *Research* Amendment V refers to a grand jury. Write a brief essay explaining what a grand jury is and how it had been used before Madison wrote this document. How is it being used today?

⊞

MARQUIS DE LAFAYETTE AND THE NATIONAL ASSEMBLY OF FRANCE

Declaration of the Rights of Man and Citizen (pp. 71–76)

MENTION IN the introduction that Lafayette was not the only author of the Declaration, but he was surely one of the most influential of the committee assigned to the task. Like Alexis de Tocqueville, Lafayette was an aristocrat, but he could see the need for changes in France before 1789. His experience in our revolution prepared him for his original return to France. He seems to have been committed as a very young man to the efforts of Jefferson and others to separate from English rule. It's possible that his motives were essentially anti-British. Eventually, he was given command of troops and helped defeat the British general Lord Cornwallis. He returned to

France and helped write the Declaration in 1789 when he was a member of the Estates General. He tried to moderate between the government and the revolutionaries, but when the Bastille, the feared Paris prison, fell, extremists took control and Lafayette was a wanted man. He left France but was caught and imprisoned in Austria for five years. He later returned to France and also to the U.S. when it had grown to twenty-four states. He turned down the offer to be the leader of France after Napoleon was defeated.

QUESTIONS FOR COMPREHENSION

1. What does Lafayette mean when he says, "Social distinctions can be based only upon public utility" (item 1)?
2. What kind of action would normally be "interdicted by the law" (item 5)?
3. To what extent is free speech guaranteed?
4. What right is described as "*sacred* and inviolable" (item 17)?

SUGGESTIONS FOR ESSAYS

1. **Comparison** Which of the rights in the Declaration also appear in Madison's Bill of Rights? How do they compare in apparent importance in each document? Are they exactly the same or are there important differences?
2. **Example** Item 12 in the Declaration says that the guarantee of rights depends on a public force. What is a public force and how does it guarantee rights? Give some examples of the ways in which a public force operates to guarantee our rights today.
3. **Analysis of Circumstances** Item 6 says, "Law is the expression of the general will." Under what circumstances in our own time is this statement true? And in what circumstances is it not the case? When would the "general will" not be law?
4. **Definition** Item 4 says, "Liberty consists in the power to do anything that does not injure others." This is a limited definition of liberty. Write your own comprehensive definition of what *liberty* means in today's society. How would you define it, and how would you support your definition with examples or references to events or to the writings of others?
5. **Research** The Declaration was written by a committee of more than twenty leaders, of which Lafayette was the most important. It was created in the summer of 1789 and became part of the French Constitution in 1793. Write a brief essay that describes the historical situation in which it was written and describe the people who were on the committee and their reception.

MARY WOLLSTONECRAFT

A Vindication of the Rights of Woman
(pp. 77–83)

WOLLSTONECRAFT'S STYLE, typical of late eighteenth-century prose, may seem turgid to twenty-first-century readers. Facing up to that issue at the outset can help smooth the way to a good discussion. In any event, the difficulties are not serious, and a careful examination of the points raised in the essay will generally overcome any difficulties with style.

You might point out right away that this is one of the earliest and most important documents in the movement for women's liberation. You may find it useful to comment on Wollstonecraft's background: she was known as a relatively freethinking person regarding marriage and religion. She and her sisters began a girls' school in England at Newington Green. It ultimately failed for financial reasons, but she did write a book on education, *Thoughts on the Education of Daughters* (1787). She also wrote travel literature and wrote about the French Revolution after observing it firsthand. Her essay reprinted here is the product of a generally inquisitive mind.

Wollstonecraft lived with the American adventurer Gilbert Imlay, had a child by him, and attempted suicide when he left her for an actress. When she met William Godwin, well known as a radical thinker, she fell in love, made an unusual marriage (they kept separate circles of friends), and subsequently died from complications in childbirth. Her daughter, Mary Shelley, wrote *Frankenstein*.

QUESTIONS FOR COMPREHENSION

1. What seems to be the conflict between sense and sensibility in this essay?

2. What is the effect on women of "[n]ovels, music, poetry, and gallantry" (para. 1)?

3. What does Wollstonecraft mean by the "peculiar duties of women" (para. 12)?

4. What is meant by saying women must have "an understanding to improve" (para. 11)?

SUGGESTIONS FOR ESSAYS

1. *Definition* Wollstonecraft asks, "[W]hat is sensibility?" (para. 10). Her definition is brief and references Dr. Johnson. What is your definition? Do you think your definition would satisfy Mary Wollstonecraft?

2. *Cause and Effect* Why is ignorance "a frail base for virtue" (para. 9)? Explain what she means by the statement and then go on to argue the case against ignorance as a means of inculcating virtue in women.

3. *Cause and Effect* Wollstonecraft recommends exercise for women because in her time exercise was for boys and not girls. She argues that exercise will cause women to be less fragile and easily frightened. What are the effects of strenuous exercise on modern women?

4. *Response* Wollstonecraft, at the end of the selection, says that men want to weaken women's bodies and "cramp their minds" (para. 13). In your experience and in your social circle, is what Wollstonecraft says about men true? Do men have a "gross appetite"? Is their intention to limit women both bodily and intellectually?

5. *Comparison* Wollstonecraft says that "love and esteem are very distinct things" (para. 6). Explain what you feel she means by this statement and go on to clarify the way in which love and esteem work differently. If you feel they are comparable instead of distinct, explain how that is so. Why does she make the distinction in the first place?

⊞

ALEXIS DE TOCQUEVILLE

The Idea of Rights in the United States
(pp. 84–89)

THIS IS a brief but significant passage from *Democracy in America*. Reading Tocqueville and responding to his amazement at the success of the experiment in democracy in America are invigorating at a time when the question of spreading democracy is one of the most prominent issues in modern politics. Tocqueville knew that things in France were changing profoundly and that the days of the aristocracy were numbered. His sympathies were with the democratizing wave of the future, and he did what he could to further it. Yet he was, at least in 1835, fearful of the force of the "majority" — the poor people who would enact the laws, as he thought they would. He had more reason to fear that force even than James Madison had, because Tocqueville knew from his parents' firsthand experience how bloodthirsty the poor could be when they got power in the French Revolution. Tocqueville also saw the July Monarchy, the revolution of 1848, and the upheavals in French government and society. Yet he held firmly to his beliefs.

One thing that interests me and may interest you as well is Tocqueville's certainty in 1835 and 1840 that there could be no civil war in the United States. Even during Andrew Jackson's presidency, Tocqueville felt that the real source of governmental power was in the states and not in the federal government. He reports that he saw very little evidence of the presence of government in America, which is one reason why he must have thought that the federal arm was not long enough to reach all quarters of the nation.

He also notes in several places that the power of individualism is great among the low as well as among the high in the society. He says in Volume 1, Part 2, Chapter 10, "I am, therefore, convinced that, at present, Americans experience fewer natural difficulties in remaining united than they encountered in 1789; the Union has fewer enemies than at that time. Nevertheless, a careful study of the United States history over the last forty-five years readily convinces us that federal power is diminishing." It is difficult to read these words and realize that by 1860, fifteen years after the publication of Volume 2, the nation was on the verge of war. Among other things, it makes us understand the significance of Lincoln's influence on American politics and also helps us understand the negative reactions to Lincoln both during and after the war. The issues that concerned Tocqueville from 1831 to 1840 were central to the function of democracy and federalism then, and in a touch of déjà vu, they seem to have come back to the forefront in the twenty-first century. If you have students who are aware of this, it would be very interesting to have them write about their views and discuss them in class.

Finally, I also find it important to consider Tocqueville's general reaction to the industry of the American citizens. His views on their efforts to produce wealth cause him to decide that the people are very materialistic and that they are driven almost entirely by a love of money. With the expansion of the country, the growth of the population, and the new advantages of overseas trade, it is natural that people expected to become rich if they worked hard enough. In contrast, Tocqueville was also struck by the role of religion in aiding industry. As he says about American preachers: "It is often hard to know from listening to them whether the main intention of religion is to obtain everlasting joy in the next world or prosperity in this" (Volume 2, Part 2, Chapter 9). He believes that self-interest guides the religions of America, but he also says, "Religious insanity is very common in the United States" (Volume 2, Part 2, Chapter 12).

What strikes the reader is how perceptive Tocqueville was of the nation's government in his few months in America. Much of what he determined to be true is still true today.

QUESTIONS FOR COMPREHENSION

1. What is the source of the "respect for rights" (para. 2) in the United States?
2. What is the relationship between a child's toys and a man's belongings?
3. What does Tocqueville say about religion in the United States?
4. Tocqueville says Americans have been given rights at a time when it is difficult to abuse them. What does he mean by this?

SUGGESTIONS FOR ESSAYS

1. *Comparison* Throughout this passage, Tocqueville talks about the relationship of boys to men, children to adults. What is the point of this comparison? What does he make of it in relation to human rights? What do you see as the point of making this comparison? Does it work for you?

2. *Analysis of Circumstances* Tocqueville says "beliefs are ceding place to rationality and feelings to calculations" (para. 11). Would this statement still be true of the nation as it is today? Consider his views on religion and answer these questions: Is what Tocqueville said relevant today? Is rationality as dominant today as he thought it was in 1840?

3. *Research* Research Tocqueville's purpose in coming to America. What did he hope to learn and how did he begin to develop his opinions about America? What was his background and how well prepared was he for his mission?

4. *Definition* Tocqueville uses a term that needs definition: "the divine conception of rights" (para. 10). Reread the passage that contains that term and define it for a modern audience. You may begin with what you think Tocqueville means, but be sure to define the term in your own understanding and qualify its meaning for modern Americans.

⊞

EMILE DURKHEIM

The Intellectual Elite and Democracy
(pp. 90–95)

DURKHEIM IS interesting for his having essentially invented what we think of as sociology. When he was a student in France, there was no such curriculum, and he took his degrees in philosophy. Because of his interpretation of philosophy, he did not begin teaching in Paris until late in his career. After his studies in France, he went to Germany, where he could study sociology directly, and began writing articles in German. His book *The Division of Labor in Society* (1893) developed his idea of *anomie*, the breakdown of social bonds between the individual and the community, which he blamed largely on society's inability to provide a satisfactory system of norms. He further developed this idea in his book *Suicide* (1897). It is an idea that was influential on modern novelists, such as Camus and Sartre.

Durkheim's ideas about the elite intellectual derive from his experience in France, whose academic system was designed to produce intellectuals and to identify them as elite. The concept of the elite was accepted in Durkheim's Europe as it never was in the United States. It is interesting to connect what Durkheim says to Tocqueville, whose view of the elite, based on his own aristocratic birth, should have been more like Durkheim's than it is.

QUESTIONS FOR COMPREHENSION

1. Who does Durkheim expect will have a strict duty to participate in public life?
2. What does Durkheim say the role of the intellectual is in society?
3. What does he accuse scholars and intellectuals of doing in the early part of the Third Republic?
4. Durkheim seems to be praising anticlericalism. What is anticlericalism?

SUGGESTIONS FOR ESSAYS

1. **Research** Durkheim makes a reference to France's Third Republic and its attitude toward democracy. Find out what you can about the Third

Republic and explain why Durkheim is concerned about that period in France's history and how it treated the idea of democracy.

2. *Definition* Durkheim uses the term *ancien regime* (para. 5). Define this term and find out enough about it so that you can write an essay that describes it and defines it for those who know nothing about it. What do you think the term means for Durkheim and how does it relate to the idea of democracy and human rights?

3. *Example* Durkheim says that scholars do not make good politicians. Find an example of an important politician who began as a scholar of some sort and who became a politician. Some examples would be William Howard Taft, Woodrow Wilson, William Jefferson Clinton (Rhodes Scholar), and Barack Obama. These presidents taught school: John Adams, Millard Fillmore, James Garfield, Grover Cleveland, and Lyndon Baines Johnson. Verify or contradict Durkheim's views on the suitability of scholars to political life.

4. *Response* What is your view of Durkheim's certainty that there is an intellectual elite that must take a role in public life? What constitutes an elite in our democratic society? Does the concept of the elite ring true to you, or do you think, as Tocqueville did, that equality is the most important characteristic of a democracy? Does the concept of an intellectual elite redefine our sense of what democracy means?

❖

ROBERT A. DAHL

Why Democracy? (pp. 96–110)

THIS IS the first longer selection in the text, and it may make extra demands on your students. However, it is also the first modern piece and the language should be manageable. You may want to review the overall stance of the piece with your students when you begin discussing Dahl. My introduction, while brief, should help you put the major points in perspective. What's good about this piece is that it makes a real effort to clarify the nature of democracy as we understand it today. It was published in 1998 in his book, *On Democracy,* and has four sections: "The Beginning,"; "Ideal Democracy"; "Actual Democracy"; and "Conditions Favorable and Unfavorable." This piece is a complete chapter from Part Two. The first chapter in that section is "What Is Democracy?" and if you can find the book, you may wish to consult that chapter. Dahl was an important figure in American political history for many years, and his views of democracy were examined by political scientists during the 1990s, when there was considerable debate about the idea of "spreading democracy" throughout the world. He is still a major figure, and his work has significance today.

QUESTIONS FOR COMPREHENSION

1. What does Dahl mean by the term "popular government" (paras. 8–9)?
2. If a nondemocratic system allows it citizens broad political rights, would it become a democracy?
3. What did Pericles mean when he said, "The freedom we enjoy in our government extends also to our ordinary life" (qtd. in para. 26)?
4. What is the connection between democracy and moral development?

SUGGESTIONS FOR ESSAYS

1. *Definition* Dahl tells us that only a democratic government can develop a high level of political equality. What is *political equality*? What kinds of political equality can be provided in a democracy? To what extent do you find political equality expressed in your immediate political environment?

2. *Analysis of Circumstances* One of Dahl's beliefs is that "fully developed adult persons should possess the capacity for looking after themselves, for acting to take care of their interests and not simply counting on others to do so" (para. 45). Defend this view, or explain its limitations. Why does Dahl think this is an important point to make for our democracy? Would "counting on others to do so" endanger our democracy?

3. *Cause and Effect* Because all modern democracies have a market economy, Dahl says "a modern democratic country is likely also to be a rich country" (para. 58). What do you think causes a country to be rich: the fact that it is a democracy, or the fact that it has a market economy? Review what Dahl says about a market economy. Find out which countries are the richest and analyze whether it is the form of government or the market economy that produces the most wealth.

4. *Research* Learn what you can about a nondemocratic government, such as China, Cuba, Saudi Arabia, Iran, or another of your choice. Which of Dahl's ten "benefits" of democracy (para. 63) are most at risk in those nations? Do those nations consider their governments to be democratic? Are they democratic according to Dahl's definitions?

CORNEL WEST

The Deep Democratic Tradition in America (pp. 111–119)

LIKE FAREED Zakaria, Cornel West is a popular intellectual, at home on the lecture circuit, in films, and on television. He appears often on the Bill Maher show, taking controversial positions on political and other matters. He has taught at a number of elite universities, beginning with an early tenure at Yale and now with a position at Union Theological Seminary, which he feels is his true home. He is very much the preacher when he holds forth on ideas. There have been a number of unflattering articles written about his personal life, primarily because he has married and divorced several times and maintains a relationship with a daughter in Germany who was the result of a love affair. Tavis Smiley is his PR person, and he handles many of West's financial affairs. Leon Wieseltier, editor of *The New Republic*, finds his work to be specious, and like Larry Summers, former president of Harvard, questions his scholarly seriousness. However, none of these issues gets in the way of his being a most effective writer and champion of positions that are liberal enough to imply a socialist leaning. West has been a champion of African American studies and has supported a range of causes that impact students of color. His studies of political science have consolidated his position on democracy as the most desirable political system for all people, rich and poor. On the other hand, he also understands how the United States is perceived in other cultures, especially Islam, for whom democracy seems to be less interesting. West remains a deeply committed Christian apologist who argues for fairness and inclusion in America.

QUESTIONS FOR COMPREHENSION

1. What does West mean by saying the "political discourse is so formulaic" (para. 2)?

2. What is the role of the "pursuit of pleasure" in harming our political culture (para. 4)?

3. Who are the two paradigmatic figures of "the deep democratic tradition" (para. 12)?

4. How do "artists, activists, and intellectuals in American life" affect our democracy (para. 9)?

SUGGESTIONS FOR ESSAYS

1. *Definition* West uses the term "political culture" to include a great many things. In a brief essay, define the term for an audience that has not read West's essay and does not know a great deal about politics. What is our current political culture like? What does it consist of and how does it affect our attitudes about the value of our democracy?

2. *Research* West lauds the "truth telling" of Ralph Waldo Emerson. Read Emerson's essay "Politics" and explain how Emerson's views support West's. What does Emerson tell us about politics, and what is the significance of his essay for our understanding of American democracy? What is Emerson's position on how much government we should have? What are his views on persons and property?

3. *Analysis of Quotation* Analyze West's statement: "Democracy is not just a system of governance, as we tend to think of it, but a cultural way of being" (para.11). Defend or challenge this statement after analyzing its meaning and significance not only in West's essay but in your own observations of democracy at work in your immediate environment.

4. *Definition* What does West mean by "civically engaged religiosity" (para. 6)? Define the term *religiosity* and then examine what West has to say about it. Define, then, the entire term and explain why he is concerned about its significance. West is himself a religious man teaching at a seminary, and his thoughts on this subject must be clarified if they are to be understood as a commentary on our current democratic culture.

FAREED ZAKARIA

Illiberal Democracy (pp. 120–127)

ZAKARIA IS a media maven. He produces material for many sources and apparently overdoes it enough that he has been chastened for plagiarism more than once. The most important case was lifting a paragraph from a Jill Lepore essay in *The New Yorker* about gun control. He admitted having "made a mistake," which may well be true. Working at his pace could have easily led to his thinking his notes were his own product. But whether it was intentional or not, it is unfortunate that he has been under a cloud, even if only for a short time.

Nonetheless, his most recent book, *In Defense of a Liberal Education* (2015) is a good and important work. Moreover, his work on political systems comes from a point of view that includes an important part of the world and offers us new insights. He is a good communicator, which makes this piece on a difficult subject appropriate for your students. He has often been nominated for the National Magazine Award and has a bevy of honorary degrees from American universities, including Brown and Harvard. In addition, he is a naturalized U.S. citizen and has been widely consulted on political issues.

QUESTIONS FOR COMPREHENSION

1. Who was Boris Yeltsin?
2. What makes a democracy illiberal?
3. Why is Russia a freer country than China?
4. What does Zakaria mean by saying "Putin is a good czar" (para. 11)?

SUGGESTIONS FOR ESSAYS

1. *Research* Zakaria mentions Mikhail Gorbachev and the Russian movement called glasnost. What is glasnost, and what was Gorbachev's role in liberalizing Russia? Would glasnost have produced a liberal democracy in Russia?

2. *Research* Zakaria implies that Vladimir Putin is a good czar. But he worries that if he becomes a bad czar liberalism in Russia will be set back. Examine the recent news reports about Vladimir Putin and decide whether or not he has become a good czar or a bad czar. Look at this question from the West's point of view, and then from Russia's point of view. What do Russian citizens say about Putin?

3. *Definition* What does the term *superpresidency* mean (para. 9)? Zakaria uses the term in reference to Vladimir Putin in Russia. Can it be used to describe any United States president? Could it be used to describe Abraham Lincoln? Can it be used to describe any modern president?

4. *Comparison* Zakaria says that "[t]oday, Russia is a freer country than China" (para. 2). He published his comments in 2003. Now, more than a decade later, do you think that Zakaria's statement is still true? Compare the news about China's liberal or illiberal policies with those about Russia. Which country do you think is freer?

CHAPTER FOUR

How Freedom Depends on Justice

⊞

The eight selections in this chapter continue the discussion of ideas in the general political realm, but we move on to some interesting theoretical areas in the field of justice. Given the events of modern life in America, the question of justice, especially for minorities, seems to be in the news on a regular basis. It has been said many times that one cannot have freedom if one does not have justice. But the ideas and ideals of justice are sometimes vague. Two theoreticians in this group of essays, John Rawls and Amartya Sen, have slightly different ideas. Rawls is the ranking theoretician of justice, and all modern discussions must take his theory of fairness into account.

You may want to prepare some comments on utilitarianism, because many of these modern writers refer back to the idea that the purpose of justice is to provide the greatest good to the greatest number. Rawls is not in that group, so it would help to explain to your students how he differs. Of course, the idea of freedom takes shape in the writings of Lucy A. Delaney, whose post-slave narrative deals extensively with the quest for justice during a period when slavery was the law of the land. Both James Baldwin and Martin Luther King Jr. amplify many of her concerns. The question of freedom and justice for African Americans is still in doubt.

JEAN-JACQUES ROUSSEAU

Of Slavery and the Social Pact
(pp. 136–145)

PERHAPS ROUSSEAU'S most romantic belief is in liberty as a value to be held above all. The question of what freedoms the individual forgoes in committing to a social contract is sometimes complex to consider, since it seems on the surface that the individual "alienates" his freedoms when he joins the civil polity. Maurice Cranston, in his introduction to *The Social Contract*, explains that what "Rousseau is saying is that instead of surrendering their liberty by the social contract, they convert their liberty from independence into political and moral freedom, and this is part of their transformation from creatures living brutishly according to impulse into men living humanly according to reason and conscience."

The abstract concepts of political and moral freedom are important to consider with your students. It is also important to ask what freedoms people give up — and which people give them up — when they accept a social polity such as the one we live in. Likewise, it is important to discuss what freedoms the individual gains in the social contract. Discussing the relationship of equality and democracy might be useful, but before doing so, I usually try to give students some idea of the kind of government under which Rousseau lived. The reigns of Louis XV (1715–1774) and Louis XVI (1774–1792) were shabby imitations of the reign of the "Sun King," Louis XIV (1643–1715).

The worst conservatism took hold, and the government avoided the reforms that might have forestalled the French Revolution, which Rousseau never lived to see. If some students have a background in the Revolution, you might give them a chance to say what they think about Rousseau's contribution. You may wish to talk about Rousseau's idea of the social contract. Ultimately, I think, your energies will probably be devoted to helping your students define for themselves what Rousseau has in mind. You may find yourself examining the concept of liberty and the concept of government as Rousseau seems to be establishing it.

QUESTIONS FOR COMPREHENSION

1. What does Rousseau mean when he says "Imbecility does not produce Right" (para. 4)?
2. What is the "right to enslave" in war (para. 12)?
3. What form of government does Rousseau assume in his writing?
4. When does a commander have the right to kill defenders of a town?

SUGGESTIONS FOR ESSAYS

1. *Research* Rousseau mentions Hugo Grotius, one of the most important legal scholars of the seventeenth century. He promoted the idea of natural law. Find out what you can about Grotius and write a brief essay explaining his main ideas and how they relate to Rousseau.

2. *Comparison* Compare what Rousseau has to say about the rights of war in the seventeenth and eighteenth centuries compared with the rights of war today. What rights do armies have today over the defeated that are different from those Rousseau describes. What rights do you think a victorious army should have over the vanquished?

3. *Analysis of Circumstances* Grotius says a people can give themselves to a king. Under what circumstances can you give yourself to a governor of any sort? Think of a political governor, or think of a governor or president of an organization to which you may belong. In what sense do you give yourself to such leaders?

4. *Example* Rousseau talks extensively about a social pact. He is thinking in terms of the pact one makes with a government to which one belongs. But people make many kinds of social pacts. What examples can you come up with by examining your own situation and your own social commitments? What are some examples of social pacts that most of us make and then keep? How do these examples shed light on what Rousseau is saying about our freedoms?

LUCY A. DELANEY

Struggles for Freedom (pp. 146–152)

THERE HAVE been many American slave narratives written by both men and women. Some were written before emancipation and some after, as in the case of Lucy A. Delaney. The most famous may be Frederick Douglass's *Narrative of the Life of Frederick Douglass, an American Slave* (1845). What makes Lucy Delaney's narrative different is that she does not describe the terrors of slavery, as does Douglass, apart from telling us how a mistress treated her and her mother. What she emphasizes is her struggle to get the protection that the laws of Illinois should have provided for her and her mother. The concept of a "freedom suit" may be totally new to your students, and it might be useful to discuss this with them. Obviously, the laws at the time of the narrative were conflicting, and in addition, the slave catchers ignored the laws even in the northern states. Kidnapped slaves were worth money, so bounty hunters ignored state laws and usually got away with their activities.

QUESTIONS FOR COMPREHENSION

1. What did Mrs. Cox mean by complaining that Lucy's mother put on "white airs" (para. 1)?
2. What did Mrs. Cox do to Lucy's mother?
3. How did the Fugitive Slave Law work in the North?
4. What had Lucy Delaney done before she was taken to live with Mrs. Mitchell?

SUGGESTIONS FOR ESSAYS

1. *Analysis of Circumstances* Lucy Delaney complained about being asked to do work that she had not been taught how to do. Explain why she was disturbed. What were the circumstances of her "employment" when she began to be in service to Mrs. Mitchell? Was Lucy treated fairly? Why did she grow angry? What would it mean for a slave to be treated fairly?

2. **Definition** Lucy Delaney said she always had a feeling of independence when she was young, but Mrs. Mitchell said otherwise. She said Lucy was a slave. Define the condition of a slave in the period that Lucy Delaney writes about. What do we learn about the condition of slavery from reading Lucy Delaney's story? What was a slave in the United States at that time?

3. **Cause and Effect** In what ways did Lucy's mother's faith in her lawyer and the laws that characterized freedom suits affect Lucy's behavior? What is the effect of the law of Illinois on Lucy's fate? How did the law appear to be working? What can you discover about the nature of the freedom suit and its legal standing?

4. **Response** What feelings are aroused by Lucy Delaney's story? What emotions does she describe in herself? What do you think she expected you to feel? To what extent do the emotions aroused by this narrative clarify your understanding of the nature of slavery in the United States at that time? How do emotions inform you and give you knowledge of Lucy's situation before she gained her freedom?

FRANKLIN DELANO ROOSEVELT

The Four Freedoms (pp. 153–158)

IT WILL be interesting to see what your students know about Roosevelt and what they think of his legacy. What surprises me is that contemporary politicians are still arguing over his major accomplishments and either attacking them or trying to modify them. When I was very young, I could not understand why some people wanted to abolish Social Security. I doubt that many people in this country over the age of sixty-two regard Social Security as a form of socialism, but there are active politicians who do. You might want to talk about that with your students and see where they stand on that issue and on the later, non-Rooseveltian innovation of Medicare. Passions run high on these issues. Also, you might want to talk about the fact that he was elected to the presidency four times, and as a result, term limits forbid more than two terms in office. Ronald Reagan's supporters came to regret that decision. Further, you might want to talk about the way in which Roosevelt won the hearts of the public by his radio talks and his programs that began to get people back to work. During and before World War II, he was a source of security in a world of complete instability.

QUESTIONS FOR COMPREHENSION

1. What does Roosevelt say government should provide for workers?
2. What things have "toughened the fiber of our people" (para. 1)?
3. What is "mysterious about the foundations of a healthy and strong democracy" (para. 3)?
4. What does Roosevelt say about taxes?

SUGGESTIONS FOR ESSAYS

1. *Definition* Define the fourth freedom, *freedom from fear*. What does this term mean to you now, and what do you think it meant to people who were alive when Roosevelt gave his speech? How can a government go about providing its citizens the freedom from fear? What do you think most people fear today, as opposed to what they feared in 1941?

2. *Analysis of Circumstances* Roosevelt said that "our strength is our unity of purpose" (para. 17). Do you think this is still true? What constitutes unity of purpose, and what evidence do you see today that indicates a unity of purpose? Does a lack of unity of purpose mean that the nation is weak? How important is unity of purpose in any nation?

3. *Response* Study Roosevelt's budget statements about paying more taxes to build up a more vigorous defense program. What is your response to his suggestions? If our current president were to say no person should be allowed to get rich over the program and that taxes will be levied according to one's ability to pay, how would you or those you know respond? Would you approve or disapprove of his plans?

4. *Definition* Roosevelt says that "[w]e should plan a better system by which persons deserving or needing gainful employment may obtain it" (para. 5). In a brief essay, define the term *deserving* in such a way as to explain what must be meant by singling out people who deserve a job. It is obvious to describe those who need a job, but who are the people who deserve a job? What makes a worker deserving? Who makes the decision about who deserves a job? Is this is a serious issue today?

⊞

JOHN RAWLS

A Theory of Justice (pp. 159–168)

B ECAUSE THIS is a challenging selection, I've tried to prepare your students for the central issues raised in each section of the piece. Nonetheless, it is clear that you will need to focus on the issues that you feel are most important and help clarify them for your class.

One point to remember is that in any section on justice, John Rawls, considered to be today's foremost theorist, must be included. The fact that his book has sold more than 300,000 copies tells us that, while Rawls is not a great writer, his work speaks to a huge audience of diverse people. He is not speaking only to specialists.

And while he is not a great writer, he has one interesting gift: he is able to coin key phrases that other commentators focus on and find useful. The terms that you should probably help your students interpret and understand are key to his thought:

- Justice as fairness
- The original position
- The veil of ignorance
- Primary goods

At the same time, you might want to emphasize more general terms such as "social contract," and "state of nature." The questions for discussion that follow the passage in the text and the questions I've developed here should help you move the class discussion in useful directions.

John Rawls had a reputation for being a political liberal; his book *Political Liberalism* (1996) spells out his views. I suppose it would be reasonable to suggest that his liberalism is what underlies his emphasis on the good of the individual as opposed to the good of the collective. It also underlies his commitment to measuring the success of a social decision on the basis of its effect on the least advantaged citizens. Your students will be able to argue about these issues from any number of points of view. One of my efforts in my introduction and in the suggestions for discussion and for writing is to direct students toward issues they can grasp. Rawls (despite a widespread reputation of pragmatism) is relentlessly theoretical, but your students can move toward more concrete discussions if they understand his key phrases and rely on some of my suggestions.

QUESTIONS FOR COMPREHENSION

1. Is the "veil of ignorance" (para. 3) a good thing or a bad thing?
2. What is the "initial position" (para. 5)?
3. How should the effect of taxes be judged?
4. What do you think Rawls means by saying, "Justice as fairness is an example of what I have called a contract theory" (para. 9)?

SUGGESTIONS FOR ESSAYS

1. *Response* In your opinion, does today's society aim primarily to help the least advantaged members have the same opportunities as the more advantaged members? Do you agree with Rawls's thinking that the least advantaged people should have the same opportunities as the more advantaged members? How could a government achieve such a goal?

2. *Response* When you were a child, how did you and your playmates establish rules of fairness in the games you played? How important was fairness to you when you were young? Did you connect the idea of justice to the idea of fairness? Describe the procedures you used collectively with others in order to help guarantee fairness in games. Did your procedures work well? Is fairness as important to you today as it was when you were younger?

3. *Definition* One of the most important of the "primary goods" Rawls considers is equality. Construct an essay in which you define what you think *social equality* means, taking into consideration such individual differences as genetic makeup, health, intelligence, and physical attributes. How should differences in gender, sexual orientation, or physical prowess be considered in any society that values equality? What is equality and how can it be achieved?

4. *Research* Rawls uses the term *utilitarianism*. Research this term and read some of the important utilitarian literature. Write an essay that explains utilitarianism to an audience that knows nothing about the term. What is it, how does it work, and once you have described it in detail, take a stand on whether or not utilitarianism is a desirable goal for our society. Why should it be carefully considered for our time and our nation?

JAMES BALDWIN

My Dungeon Shook: Letter to My Nephew on the One Hundredth Anniversary of the Emancipation (pp. 169–175)

ONE OF the intriguing qualities of this selection stems from its being a letter. In this age of email, it may come as a surprise for your students to know people actually used letters to work out their ideas. The idea of an open letter may also be important to discuss in class. I suggest later that it would be good to write a letter on the 150th anniversary of the Emancipation.

This is a short but powerful selection. Baldwin wrote at a time in American history when racial tensions were very high, when we were on the verge of riots and social explosions that would rock the nation. All this coincided with the civil rights activism of the 1960s and the changes that were being pressed in the South. In this essay, Baldwin explores how the systematic oppression of African Americans — in the form of the ghetto, for example — has been used to preserve a racist way of life that excludes African Americans from prosperity and opportunity. The American dream was something average African Americans could not enjoy because of American society's structure.

One way of working with this essay is to ask how much has changed since Baldwin wrote it. It is now more than 150 years since Emancipation. What has changed? Your students will probably hedge on this at first, but once you get the discussion going, you may become involved in a very lively debate. No two people are likely to see things the same way, which may give you an inroad to discussing the ways in which individual perceptions of reality affect our sense of progress in racial matters.

You may also want to comment on the way in which Baldwin talks about white people and the advice he gives to his nephew about how he should interact with them.

QUESTIONS FOR COMPREHENSION

1. How many times did Baldwin tear up drafts of his letter?
2. What are the "cities of destruction" (para. 1)?

3. Who are the "innocents" that Baldwin talks about (para. 3)?

4. What does it mean for people to be "still trapped in a history which they do not understand" (para. 5)?

SUGGESTIONS FOR ESSAYS

1. *Research* Look up the Negro spiritual in which the words Baldwin quotes appear: "*The very time I thought I was lost, My dungeon shook and my chains fell off*" (para. 5). Write a brief essay that explains the context of the quotation and why Baldwin uses it. What is the significance of Baldwin's referencing the spiritual in his essay? What do you make of it? What does it tell you about Baldwin and his nephew?

2. *Analysis of Circumstances* Baldwin says "the black man has functioned in the white man's world as a fixed star, as an immovable pillar" (para. 5). How do you interpret this observation in light of the rest of Baldwin's essay and in light of what you perceive about the relationship of the races in your immediate environment?

3. *Research* Baldwin makes a reference to Charles Dickens "in the London of a hundred years ago" (para. 3). Why does he cite Dickens? Look up his biography and his work and decide how pertinent the world Dickens portrayed is to the world that Baldwin's nephew is in.

4. *Response* In this letter, Baldwin makes considerable reference to his family and his nephew's place in it. In a letter on the 150th anniversary of the Emancipation to your "future nephew," write about your own family and encourage your nephew to take pride in what your family has been and done for you and ultimately for him.

⊞

MARTIN LUTHER KING JR.

I Have a Dream (pp. 176–182)

PROBABLY THE most important thing to begin with in discussing this piece is to inform your students that this was an oration and that as an oration it is designed to appeal to the emotions and the understanding of the audience. The language is very different in this piece from almost every other selection in the book. The metaphors are large and affective, and for many students there will be an echo of King's impressive delivery. He was a masterful rhetorician in the old-fashioned sense of the word.

Of all the authors in the book, King may be the most familiar to your students. You might ask what they know of him and what they feel his importance has been to American life. I offer a few observations in the head-note to the text, but you will find that opening a discussion about King will stimulate an interesting classroom experience.

QUESTIONS FOR COMPREHENSION

1. What is the point of King's beginning his speech with "Five score years ago" (para. 1)?

2. What "check" does King and the people he speaks to expect to cash (para. 4)?

3. What is the faith and hope King expects to bring back to the South?

4. Who does King expect to be "free at last" (para. 36)?

SUGGESTIONS FOR ESSAYS

1. *Research* Write a brief essay about what happened in racial and polit-ical affairs in the United States in the year 1963. Why was it a hopeful year? What were the most important events of 1963 that seem to have shaped our history?

2. *Research* Throughout most commentary on Martin Luther King Jr., there are references to Mahatma Gandhi; Gandhi is said to have influ-enced King. Write an essay that explains who Gandhi was and how what he did influenced King's position on civil rights. Do you feel King and Gandhi have established a functional and effective method of achieving real change in society?

3. *Comparison* James Baldwin and King both spoke out during the 1960s. Compare their views on racial matters. Baldwin is said to have been pro-foundly influenced by King. Is it clear from what he wrote that King affected his views? Does King seem to have been influenced by Baldwin?

4. *Testimony* One of Martin Luther King Jr.'s most effective rhetorical devices is the use of metaphor. Write an essay that tries to list all of the metaphors King uses. Which ones are extended metaphors (a single met-aphor used over several sentences) and which ones are the most power-ful? What do you think the effect of metaphor is in a speech? How does it affect you when you either read or hear a speech like King's? How hard do you think it is to use metaphor in the manner in which King does?

AMARTYA SEN

The Idea of Justice (pp. 183–189)

S EN IS a remarkable figure in contemporary economic as well as political theory. He and his family come from Bangladesh, but Sen is the son of a professor, so his childhood reflects his moving in intellectual circles at an early age. You might want to read his personal biography written for the Nobel committee that awarded him his prize for economics. Technically, there is no original Nobel Prize for Economics, but the central bank of Sweden established the prize in memory of Alfred Nobel in 1968. The distinction is of no real importance, but if your students ask, you can explain why there is a slight disparity.

I think one of the nice things about this piece, apart from its being a modern statement in language that your students will appreciate, is Sen's awareness of the work of Mary Wollstonecraft. Wollstonecraft's writing is sometimes daunting, and it is important to note that she represents a number of important positions on gender issues that influence us today. It's good to see someone of Sen's stature hailing her work.

QUESTIONS FOR COMPREHENSION

1. What does Sen mean by "reasoned scrutiny" (para. 1)?
2. When is there a need for public reasoning?
3. Why should a legal judgment be able to "withstand public scrutiny" (para. 9)?
4. What kind of inequities existed in the eighteenth century?

SUGGESTIONS FOR ESSAYS

1. *Research* Sen tells us that Mary Wollstonecraft wrote a letter to M. Talleyrand-Périgord concerning her feelings on the rights of women. Who was Talleyrand? And what was his position? Find the letter (in Mary Wollstonecraft, *A Vindication of the Rights of Woman* [1995, Tomaselli ed., p. 70]). Explain why the letter is important and how it connects with the premises of Sen's argument about "wrath and reasoning" (para. 4).

2. ***Analysis of Circumstances*** Sen makes a great deal about the idea of justice seeming to be done rather than simply being done. Recent acts of violence in minority communities, particularly African American communities, have resulted in circumstances in which a demand for justice has been expressed by rioting and protest. Which current protests have demanded that justice appear to be done? How valid is Sen's view on this issue? Has the appearance of justice being done helped to end violent protests?

3. ***Definition*** Sen uses the term "a reason-based theory of justice" (para. 5). It is not clear precisely what he means by this term, so it will need expansion and definition. How would you define the term? What is a reason-based theory of justice and how does it work? Is this the kind of theory of justice that we operate under in our country? Are there countries that clearly do not rely on a reason-based theory of justice? How does Sen try to explain it?

4. ***Analysis of Circumstances*** If we agree that it is important for justice to appear to have been done, how do we go about making that happen? First, it may be essential that justice was actually achieved, but if that is not enough, what is enough? If possible, argue the case by reference to a recent situation in which justice may not at first have appeared to have been done, but then was finally seen to be done by the population most concerned with justice.

⊞

bell hooks

Feminist Politics: Where We Stand
(pp. 190–197)

OBVIOUSLY, BELL hooks sees racism and sexism as aspects of the same ways of thinking about other people. She is interesting in this piece in that she is free to say that women can be sexist just as well as men.

One thing to observe to your students about this piece is that it is essentially an essay in definition. Just as Amartya Sen attempts a definition of justice through his theory of justice (and John Rawls does much the same), hooks make an effort to define feminism. She feels that people really don't understand what it means. But sexism, like racism, is a form of behavior that denies justice to a group. They are forms of oppression. Once that is understood, it is clear what her position is and where she stands on these issues.

QUESTIONS FOR COMPREHENSION

1. What is hooks's definition of feminism?
2. Why is it necessary to understand sexism in order to understand feminism?
3. When did feminists learn that "females could be sexist as well" (para. 5)?
4. Which black women became "stars" of the feminist movement?

SUGGESTIONS FOR ESSAYS

1. *Definition* bell hooks mentions the term *patriarchy* several times. What is patriarchy and how would you define it to someone who may not know the term? How does patriarchy work and is it a good thing? Hooks protests against it, but does she represent it fairly? What experiences have you had with patriarchy? Are you for it or against it?

2. *Analysis of Circumstances* Gender equality is one ambition of a large number of feminists. Under what circumstances is gender equality desirable? Are there any circumstances in which it is not desirable? Some religions simply do not countenance gender equality. Why? Do you observe gender equality in your own personal environment? Do you support and help forward gender equality? Why is it a good thing? Why is it not a good thing? Should there be laws enacted to secure gender equality? Write an essay that clarifies these issues.

3. *Cause and Effect* If there were gender equality achieved in our society, and if sexism and racism were lessened or eliminated, how would women be affected in our society? What would change in their situation? What changes would you most applaud? How would the nation's politics be different? How would religious institutions be different? How would colleges be different? How would families be different? How would businesses and multinational corporations be different?

4. *Definition* hooks uses the expression "lifestyle feminism." She explains that whether a woman was liberal or conservative she could craft a feminist lifestyle. Write an essay that defines a feminist lifestyle for you or for someone like you who is in a similar relationship with your society. Would this be a desirable lifestyle for someone like you? Would it be a lifestyle that you could achieve? How would such a lifestyle be regarded by your friends and others who know you? How would it be regarded by your family?

CHAPTER FIVE

How Science Reads the Book of Nature

⊞

The seven selections in this chapter cover a wide range of issues in science, from the question of scientific method in the work of Lucretius, one of the world's earliest scientists in the modern sense of the word, all the way to concepts of modern genetics and artificial intelligence. Of course, there are also ethical and political questions that come up in relation to most scientific discoveries and practices. The brief selection from Charles Darwin may or may not cause concern in some of your students. I am not making any political statement in this book about evolution — that's something you can deal with in the way you know best. I thought that the question of sexual selection would be interesting enough in its own right to interest even those students who are skeptical of Darwin's ideas. Alfred North Whitehead takes on the perennial issue of how religious institutions can or should deal with threatening scientific discoveries and theories. In any event, you should have some free-ranging discussions with your students, and I hope some interesting essays to read.

One might think of the Oliver Sacks selection as being in the realm of the psychological, but he has a longstanding interest in the ways in which the physical body affects the mind, and here he is worried about how the senses function when under unusual stress. Steve Jones, a definite Darwinist, focuses on the future of the masculine sex in light of recent developments that have made men virtually unnecessary in the lives of many women. Artificial intelligence has been the stuff of science fiction for many years, but recent developments in robot labs around the world have made so much progress in fashioning robots that do many of the things that once only people could do that we must take serious notice, which is the subject of Michio Kaku's essay. The last selection, by Jennifer Ackerman, describes genetics at the molecular level. Her selection is very informative about genetics and how nature works across both genus and phylum categories. Like Jones, Ackerman seems to be a follower of Darwin, which should make your discussion interesting on a level that few students would have anticipated.

⌗

LUCRETIUS

The Nature of Sleep (pp. 206–211)

THIS SELECTION is from *On the Nature of Things*, which Stephen Greenblatt has recently discussed in detail in his book *The Swerve: How the World Became Modern* (2012). I recommend his book as pleasure reading, but the point really is that people are still interested in Lucretius, and Greenblatt provides a marvelous introduction. This selection is useful because it limits us to our own devices in trying to understand something about the nature of a phenomenon we all know about and experience regularly. Observation and imagination, combined with curiosity and patience, are the central issues here, and every one of your students can possess those qualities and write about their experiences in search of the truth about anything that can be observed. I recommend Lucretius as a fascinating figure in the history of science.

QUESTIONS FOR COMPREHENSION

1. Why does Lucretius describe sleep as a "problem" (para. 1)?
2. What does it mean for an answer to be "persuasive rather than exhaustive" (para. 1)?
3. How effective is Lucretius's metaphor of a "smothered fire" (para. 2)?

4. What does Lucretius say about how one's employment affects one's dreams?

SUGGESTIONS FOR ESSAYS

1. *Research* Learn what you can about Lucretius and his reputation among both ancient and modern thinkers. What makes us value his observations about the psychology of people and animals? Why is he an important authority on scientific inquiry? What is the reputation of his book, *On the Nature of Things*?

2. *Example* Analyze Lucretius's selection for his use of examples. What is the nature of his argument and how is he trying to prove it? Which of his examples are most powerful and convincing? What new examples would you introduce if you were arguing his position? Are there good examples that you can develop to contradict his argument?

3. *Comparison* What is the difference between sleep and a coma? Learn what you can about how scientists describe the nature and function of the coma. Then learn what you can about how scientists describe normal sleep. How are these psychological states different from one another?

4. *Comparison* Using your own experience, along with those whom you know, what is the difference between the dreams you had as a child and the dreams you have now? If you need to, ask some children what they dream about and compare their dreams with those you gather from people your own age and older. Is there a major difference? How might the material you gather in your research have affected what Lucretius says about dreams?

⊞

CHARLES DARWIN

Of Sexual Selection and Natural Selection
(pp. 212–220)

MANY SCIENCE majors and even science graduate students follow their studies without ever reading *Origin of Species* on the theory that Darwin is more of a literary figure than a scientific figure. In addition, almost everyone I have heard question or denounce the theory of evolution has never read a word of Darwin. Despite their absolute ignorance of his work, they reject him. I encouraged my students to read Darwin with as receptive a mind as possible, looking for the details that build his argument and establish his views. This selection is good because it is not especially challenging and it connects with experiences that students can understand. It does not force any particular conclusions but promotes thoughtful consideration. Much of what Darwin says here many students will already know, although they may not know where their knowledge originated. In any event, this should provide a lively discussion and maybe some good essays.

QUESTIONS FOR COMPREHENSION

1. Which is more rigorous, sexual selection or natural selection?
2. How low on the scale of nature does battle descend?
3. Between whom is the struggle for existence in sexual selection?
4. In what animals does the struggle for sexual selection become most fierce?

SUGGESTIONS FOR ESSAYS

1. *Research* Choose an animal in which you are interested and research its patterns of sexual selection. Does your research bear out Darwin's ideas? Which animal have you chosen and why? What are the characteristics of its patterns of sexual selection and how fierce are they? Why do you find them interesting?

2. *Comparison* What are the primary patterns of behavior you notice in sexual selection among human beings? Which gender is most active in doing the selecting? In same-gender relationships, how does sexual selection work? How does human sexual selection work in relation to the way it works in the animal world? What insights has Darwin given you about human sexual selection?

3. *Definition* Darwin was not the first to use the term *survival of the fittest*, but it has come to be thought of as his alone. What does Darwin mean by the term? What do people in general seem to mean by it? Why is it connected with natural selection rather than sexual selection? In what circumstances is this term most useful? How does it help confirm the idea of natural selection?

4. *Research* The idea of evolution has not been limited to the world of nature. It has pervaded general thought in a number of areas. Two such areas are politics and the social sciences. Research the term *social*

Darwinism and write a brief essay that explains how the ideas of Charles Darwin have been applied to thought in the social sciences and politics. How pervasive is the idea of social Darwinism? How close is it to Darwin's thinking?

ALFRED NORTH WHITEHEAD

Religion and Science (pp. 221–235)

WHEN HE was delivering the Lowell Lectures, Whitehead was one of the most respected and well-known intellectuals in England and the United States. His book, *Science in the Modern World,* was a very popular early paperback, appealing to a mass audience as well as to specialists in science and religion. He was one of the only intellectuals who could legitimately bridge the gap between religion and science because he was one of the only well-known and accomplished scientists who was also a ranking theologian. The excitement caused by the Scopes Trial spurred him to write "Religion and Science." The trial was not just a local event in Tennessee but a national event with two of the most impressive lawyers in the country squaring off. Clarence Darrow was the Johnny Cochran of his time, the most feared defense lawyer in the country. William Jennings Bryan was also a legend, a major politician who had run for president three times on a populist Democratic ticket: 1896, 1900, and 1908. He was a staunch Presbyterian and had eventually become secretary of state, but he resigned during World War I because he was a pacifist. The trial was high drama throughout the country and because its outcome was so uncertain, the issues that made it important are still with us. Whitehead's effort to balance each side with the other is still relevant to many people in the United States.

QUESTIONS FOR COMPREHENSION

1. Whitehead says the clash between religion and science "has been unduly emphasized" (para. 13). Is that true today?

2. Why is the example of Galileo important when considering Whitehead's argument?

3. Whitehead says that religion has been on the defensive for how long?

4. What does Whitehead mean when he writes, "Religion has been presented as valuable for the ordering of life" (para. 26)?

SUGGESTIONS FOR ESSAYS

1. *Research* Research the Scopes Trial of 1925. Explain how and against whom the charges were brought. Who were the main people involved in the trial and what was the public response? How did the response differ from one part of the country to another? What was the outcome of the trial and how did it affect education in the United States?

2. *Response* Whitehead several times mentions "the modern fading of interest in religion" (para. 26). Given your own experience and the observations of people in your immediate social environment, can you verify Whitehead's statement? Is what you have learned about interest in religion among your own circle also true of the general public in your state or in the country at large? Would Whitehead be surprised by any current religious controversies?

3. *Analysis of Circumstances* One thing Whitehead says is that "[r]eligion has been presented as valuable for the ordering of life" (para. 26). What does he mean by this? Is it true in today's world that religion helps guide people's behavior and that it helps people order their lives? Does it help you and those you know order your lives? How would religion order anyone's life in this modern world? How does the process of ordering one's life through religion work?

4. *Cause and Effect* Whitehead is presenting an ardent argument in this essay. He uses examples to prove his points. He refers to history and presents an argument based on circumstantial analysis. He brings testimony of important authorities to bear on his position. The questions you should answer in a brief essay are these: What has Whitehead's essay done to clarify the clash between religion and science? How has this essay affected you personally? Is his argument convincing? If it is, what is the most effective thing he does in order to convince his audience?

⊞

OLIVER SACKS

The Mind's Eye (pp. 236–243)

S ACKS IS fascinating for his attention to his own mind and the way it
interacts with his body. He observes himself and then observes others.
He takes great interest in the eccentricities of people, particularly the psychological eccentricities that express themselves in physical behavior. Of
course he also observes very carefully the unusual diseases that affect people around the world, such as encephalitis. His studies of his own neurological disorders are remarkable for their candor and for their Lucretius-like
self-examination. For that reason, you will note that most of the questions I
ask in the text for stimulating student essays are response prompts. They
ask students to study themselves in much the way Sacks studies himself in
his work. One useful thing is that because Sacks is such an engaging writer
it would not be difficult for you to assign any willing student to read more of
his work and make a project of responding to it.

QUESTIONS FOR COMPREHENSION

1. What does Sacks mean when he asks: "To what extent are we the
    authors, the creators, of our own experiences?" (para. 1)?
2. Was John Hull born blind?
3. What did it mean for John Hull to become a "whole-body seer"
    (para. 7)?
4. Is the brain more or less hardwired than was once thought?

SUGGESTIONS FOR ESSAYS

1. **Research** Sacks uses the term *haptic perception*. Find out what you
    can about haptic perception and write a brief essay that explains it to
    an audience who never heard the term. In the process ask yourself to
    what extent you have experienced haptic perception. What is the value
    of such perception?

2. *Comparison* Find John Hull's book, *Touching the Rock: An Experience of Blindness*, and compare what he says about his experience with what Oliver Sacks says. Is Oliver Sacks a reliable source of commentary on Hull's experience, or does he leave out important information that would change your view of what Hull says about his own condition? What important information does Hull provide that Sacks leaves out?

3. *Response* If you were to go blind tomorrow, how would you direct your education and your energies to achieve a life that would permit you to be independent and to earn a living doing something that you would find interesting? Naturally, everything in your life would change, but how would you direct the changes that you think might help you live a full life?

4. *Definition* Sacks mentions the idea of the brain being in some ways *hardwired*. That term is a metaphor from computer language, but it is used frequently in neuroscience. Explain what the term means and find out what you can about how neuroscientists use the term and how valid it is. In what ways is the brain currently thought to be hardwired? And what is it hardwired for?

⊞

STEVE JONES

The Descent of Men (pp. 244–251)

BECAUSE JONES talks about the essential biological inferiority of the male, this piece should stimulate considerable controversy in your class discussion. Males will take umbrage partly because they consider themselves superior and partly because they will feel shocked at the strength of Jones's argument. Females may, on the other hand, gloat a bit, but their reaction may be the more interesting. What is good here is that Jones is easy to read and easy to comprehend, but he is also a devoted Darwinian and you will have plenty of opportunity to discuss what he says in Darwinian terms. Evolution always implies change, and not always for the better, as Darwin himself explains. Jones is absolutely convinced of his position and of the changes in the fate of males that he foresees. Connecting this essay with Darwin's sexual selection is one way of exploring what Jones thinks is true.

QUESTIONS FOR COMPREHENSION

1. What book is the model for Steve Jones's selection?
2. Why was Dolly the sheep a wake-up call for men?
3. How soon might the Y chromosome disappear?
4. What is the importance of the story Jones tells of the Mormons heading to Salt Lake City?

SUGGESTIONS FOR ESSAYS

1. *Research* Consult the government statistics on the life expectancy of men and women in the United States. Compare the figures from fifty years ago, a hundred years ago, and a hundred fifty years ago. Is there a trend apparent in those figures? Find out what you can about life expectancies of men and women in other developed countries and in less developed countries. Does what Jones tells us seem to be borne out in these figures?

2. *Research* Learn what you can about the *SRY* gene. What do modern geneticists tell us about the Y gene that helps us better understand what Jones is saying? Does the research you have uncovered bolster Jones's argument or harm it? Does anything that you have learned about the *SRY* gene surprise you? Does anything you learned worry you?

3. *Response* Jones says, "From middle age onward it is a woman's world" (para. 9). How do you respond to that statement? What are your feelings regarding the prospect that when you become middle aged the population will begin to change to the ratio of two-thirds female to one-third male? How do you think your own experience will change as you grow older?

4. *Response* Jones says "Men, it seems, evolved for matrimony" (para. 13). Explain why he feels he can say this, and comment on your observations about men and matrimony. If what Jones says is generally true about the relation of matrimony to the life span of males, what should you and your friends do to help guarantee a longer life span for males in your community? Given the fact that fewer people in the United States are marrying than did a hundred years ago, what seems to be the future for males? What should our nation do to change the current destructive pattern?

MICHIO KAKU

Physics of the Impossible (pp. 252–262)

THE INTEREST in artificial intelligence has been growing over the years, especially since the introduction of robots that can perform many of the jobs that people used to do. The film *2001: A Space Odyssey,* released in 1968, prompted quite a response from pundits and academicians alike with its portrayal of the computer HAL (the letters just before IBM). In that film, HAL took over the ship and gave rise to the fear that if robots did achieve artificial intelligence they might behave in dangerous ways. It has been a long time since 1968, and robots have done more and more amazing things. Their effect on labor has been remarkable, as anyone who has seen footage of automobile production or product packaging of any kind knows. There is no clear accounting for the number of people who have been replaced by machines, but the modern weakness of labor unions across the country should help us understand how manual laborers have been affected by modernization. The reality is that in the near future it will not just be blue-collar workers who will be replaced; many white-collar workers will find themselves made redundant by robots. Already, there are robots that operate on the nation's borders who hold interviews with people seeking admission to the country. Those robots can interpret facial responses on the part of migrants and actually tell with great accuracy whether or not the answers to their questions are true or false. Many office jobs will be performed by robots, and this is something you need to discuss with your students. Competing for jobs with robots may come as a shock to some of your students, but those who work with computers will likely be very stimulating in your class discussions.

QUESTIONS FOR COMPREHENSION

1. When did people first get interested in the possibility of AI?
2. Why did a backlash set in during the 1970s?
3. What is IBM's Deep Blue?
4. What is a Turing machine?

SUGGESTIONS FOR ESSAYS

1. ***Research*** Alan Turing has been the subject of recent books and a major film, *The Imitation Game* (2014). Write a brief essay that explains who Alan Turing was and what he had hoped to accomplish with the Turing machine. What is a Turing machine? How important would it be to have a fully operational Turing machine?

2. ***Analysis of Circumstances*** How do computer chess programs work? Why are powerful chess programs not considered an example of artificial intelligence? What kind of intelligence do these programs possess? If chess programs are not examples of artificial intelligence, is it then true that good chess players are not examples of human intelligence? What is the difference?

3. ***Example*** One of the problems with robots and advanced computers is that even when they perform amazing feats, their "intelligence" is always attributed to the design of the software in the machine. What examples of behavior or performance by an industrial robot would be necessary before we could claim that it possessed artificial intelligence? What would convince you that the robot was "intelligent" in the sense that we use the term when speaking of our friends, or even our pets? Are you anxious to see the time when such machines can be made?

4. ***Analysis of Circumstances*** Kaku mentions two methods of learning as applied to robots: the top-down method, used by STAIR, and the bottom-up method used by LAGR. Examine your own learning processes. The circumstances of your education throughout your life have been designed to help you learn. Has your process of learning been the top-down method or the bottom-up method? Offer examples of either process as you make up your mind as to which version is the one that works best for you. Which method do you think your school or schools have emphasized?

⊞

JENNIFER ACKERMAN

Molecules and Genes (pp. 263–271)

ONE OF the first things I ask in the book concerns the heredity of genes that all of us have experienced. Even before there was such a thing as the human genome, many of us had been told that we bore traits that resembled those of our ancestors. Those insights were based on observation and have been demonstrated as being reliable and in some cases useful. Usually children are told that they look like one or another parent or even like one or another relative, such as a cousin or an aunt or uncle. They are also told, as they grow older, that their behavior resembles that of relatives, especially if they are very quiet or if they are prone to anger or if they possess any other frame of mind common to the family. Talents are also said to be inherited, especially if they skip a generation. For that reason, in the book I ask a number of questions that require the student to observe his or her own circumstances and make connections with the ideas that Jennifer Ackerman presents. However, in the questions that I provide below, I emphasize research because some of this material is easy to search and important for students to get straight.

I will point out that Jennifer Ackerman is not a scientist or an academic, but a person like Rachel Carson, who writes about science matters and has become well informed about the research in her field. As a result, she is a good stylist and a good writer in that she explains her subject with great clarity.

QUESTIONS FOR COMPREHENSION

1. What is the connection between genes and heredity?
2. Why does Ackerman talk about molecules?
3. What does Ackerman mean by "the gnomic workings of the living order" (para. 4)?
4. Why is Ackerman disturbed to "descend into the darkness of a molecular world" (para. 16)?

SUGGESTIONS FOR ESSAYS

1. ***Research*** What is the human genome? When was it decoded and what have we learned as a result of the research that has gone into its discovery? Scientists have said this discovery has great importance for understanding our past and our future. What is most important to you about the discoveries made relating to the human genome?

2. ***Response*** Ackerman says, "Disparate organisms, it seems, are more radically alike than we ever imagined" (para. 8). Review the examples that she offers us in this selection and write a brief essay that describes your reaction to the most important of the examples. How does it make you feel to learn of the connectedness of the various forms of life that Ackerman tells about? What makes you feel hopeful about what she tells us? What is most disturbing?

3. ***Research*** Ackerman mentions having only recently discovered the "Hox body-shaping genes when I was a few months pregnant with my second child" (para. 19). What are the Hox body-shaping genes and how do they work? Is there a connection between the Hox genes and Ackerman's pregnancy? Once you have learned about the Hox genes, how do you find yourself using that knowledge? What do the discoveries about the Hox genes mean to you and to your friends?

4. ***Research*** Write a brief essay in which you explain to an audience that has not studied much biology what RNA and DNA are. If possible, find a drawing of the macromolecules that are identified as RNA and DNA and explain their importance to all life. Why have scientists felt these two macromolecules are so significant? What importance do they have for you? Have they affected the way you regard human nature and/or the world of nature itself? What is the difference between knowing about RNA and DNA and not knowing about them?

CHAPTER SIX

How Society Regards Wealth and Poverty

The seven selections in this chapter range from the eighteenth century to our own time. Adam Smith is the most basic of the "moderns" on the subject of wealth. I chose his comments on labor because of current issues that affect the nature and value of labor, from the weakening of labor unions to demands for higher wages, and even on to the threat of automation in the future. Smith is a classic capitalist, but he also has an ethical concern for how the practices of business affect the individual. He was witnessing major changes in economics in his own time, a period in which the value of land was changing and the interests of factory owners were growing. While we think of him as a major figure in economics, he was himself quite sure that his legacy was in moral thought and not in his comments on business. Smith's emphasis on self-interest as a stimulus to achieving wealth is important to point to when discussing him with students. Their views will vary widely, but many will surely agree with him.

Andrew Carnegie, another Scotsman, spoke for nineteenth-century industrialists in Europe and the United States. His views on who should possess wealth are still echoing in modern times. He is comfortable with gross inequities between the rich and the poor. In his time, there was relatively little governmental concern about how inequities could be addressed and altered. Today, we talk about how the gap between the top 1 percent and the rest of us may damage the nation. Political parties are waging war over this issue, although little or nothing gets done. This was not quite the case in Carnegie's time, when the Rockefellers, Astors, Vanderbilts, Fricks, and Huntingtons lived lives of unimagined luxury. Carnegie thought they deserved their wealth because they were superior people. The use of the term "gospel" implied that they were chosen people with God-given talents and wealth.

Taking up the cause of feminism after Mary Wollstonecraft, Charlotte Perkins Gilman brought the issues of fairness to women to a modern level. Wollstonecraft wrote for a predominantly male audience in her response to Talleyrand, but Gilman addresses women metaphorically in their own kitchens. She pays attention to the ways in which women are oppressed in modern life and discusses the question of the value of women's labor. In addition, she talks about how women are made to be dependent on the men in their lives. Gilman became a powerful voice for change. Most importantly, she yearned for women to make their lives significant. She makes some radical suggestions designed to change the way women live in their own household.

In the 1840s, Alexis de Tocqueville was impressed by the fact of equality in the United States. As a French aristocrat, he may have been shocked to hear how individual Americans addressed him and each other on an equal footing. By contrast, John Kenneth Galbraith sounds something of an early alarm about the growing inequality of wealth in the nation. His point originally is that the 1940s and 1950s produced a general spread of wealth in the nation that had not been known before. Carnegie's era did not see a significant middle class, but in Galbraith's era, the fact of the enormous middle class was a given. Again, this is a concern of modern society, which sees a regression of sorts in which a very small number of people control a very great percentage of the national wealth. The effect on poverty is yet to be fully understood, but it is clear that people today are not as passive about the problem of inequality as they were in Carnegie's time.

Jane Jacobs became famous for her efforts to stop how politicians were changing New York City. She became an expert on modern cities and complained about many aspects of modern urban life. Her love of neighborhood was central to her crusades, which achieved results. She helped stop a crosstown highway that would have bisected Greenwich Village and destroyed its sense of neighborhood. In the selection that appears here, she gives us a clinic on the major economic theories of modern times and helps us understand what her fears and hopes are for the future. Her view is that stagflation, while a reality in her time, is an anomaly for economists. High inflation and high unemployment are not supposed to happen, but it happened when she came to write her book.

Elizabeth Warren is a polarizing figure. She is remarkable for having been able to redirect her life and take advantage of opportunities that might never have come her way. She understands what poverty is and what it is to be a member of the middle class. Her work here defines the middle class for students who may not have thought much about it. As she says, everyone you talk with assumes he or she is in the middle class. On the other hand, many people we speak with will insist that there is no stratification by class in the United States. Tocqueville thought this was true, but there are those who differ. The value of this piece for your students is in helping them decide just how important it is to have a middle class in our time.

Leslie T. Chang is a Chinese American writer. She learned Chinese at an early age and is a successful journalist in China. This brief selection on the fate of factory girls in Dongguan touches on the question of the value of labor in a modern industrial economy. It also touches on the question of how women are valued in such a remarkably changing society. The mass migration of workers from farm to city in China has virtually no similar event in Western culture. The one event it might be compared with is the much smaller-scale migration of African American workers from farm to factory in the 1930s and 1940s. Chang's piece is remarkable since she was able to communicate with the factory girls directly and to give us a view of them that few other Western journalists could.

These selections give us a valuable introduction to the ways in which societies deal with massive wealth and its effects on the middle class and the poor.

⊞

ADAM SMITH

The Value of Labor (pp. 281–288)

*T*HE WEALTH *of Nations* is a daunting book, best read in parts. However, it is also a fascinating book and worth calling to the attention of your students. Because Smith was writing during a period of change in England and other nations in Europe, your students may need some background. For example, most labor was still on farms, and most laborers in England were tenants on the land of great landowners. In the villages, much labor was done in the household and the products of that labor used and sold. In Smith's time, factory work was transforming much of the ordinary life of the English. Land was slowly becoming less important, and work was being done more and more outside the home. You might read some lines from Oliver Goldsmith's poem "The Deserted Village," which was published in 1770, six years before *The Wealth of Nations*. The nature of labor was changing, and the entire question of working for wages was becoming important. Although Smith takes many forms of labor into account, the importance of wages is central here.

QUESTIONS FOR COMPREHENSION

1. Under what circumstances does labor have an advantage?
2. What kind of laborer is described as an "independent workman" (para. 7)?
3. What effect does the rise of national wealth have on the demand for workmen?
4. Under what conditions would there be a "constant scarcity of employment" (para. 11)?

SUGGESTIONS FOR ESSAYS

1. *Research* Read Oliver Goldsmith's poem about the workers and people in small villages in England at the time Adam Smith's book was written. "The Deserted Village" (1770) is a classic describing the effects of industrialization on the traditional ways of the rural people in England. How does Goldsmith help interpret the basic ideas of labor as expressed in Smith's selection? What are the emotional realities that Goldsmith observed?

2. *Analysis of Circumstances* Adam Smith says that "[t]he most decisive mark of the prosperity of any country is the increase of the number of its inhabitants" (para. 10). First, decide what he means by the statement. Then, decide whether or not you agree with him and whether or not you can see evidence of that statement's truth in the circumstances of population and population growth in your own nation. Why would prosperity and population be linked in Smith's time? Why would it be linked in our time? Would our country be less prosperous if there were fewer people in it?

3. *Definition* Adam Smith speaks very frankly about the relationship between master and laborer. The use of the term *master* may be

equivalent to our term *employer*, but it obviously has a different quality to it. People have described Adam Smith as a capitalist. Examine this selection carefully and write a brief essay that defines his concept of capitalism. Is it the same as our ideas of what capitalism is? What is the position of labor in a capitalist economy? How different is it from Smith's time?

4. ***Response*** What are your personal views on the value of labor in today's economy? Who are the people who today stand in for Smith's "masters"? How does society seem to value labor today? Are there any changes that you perceive in the way society values labor in contrast with the way it values management? What is your perception? Is the current prosperity of the nation more a result of the efforts of management, or the efforts and efficiency of labor? Do you think most of those you know agree with you?

⊞

ANDREW CARNEGIE

The Gospel of Wealth (pp. 289–302)

THERE IS no question that I think this is a marvelous essay for students to read and read carefully. Carnegie not only lived in the age of the robber barons, but he was a prince among them. His absolute confidence in his superiority and of having been blessed with massive wealth because he was deserving is surely replicated among many of the world's current billionaires. I make a great deal out of the word "gospel" because it not only ties into the idea of enjoying a god's blessing, but it connects with Jesus and Christian values. Religion in Carnegie's time was especially helpful in regulating society in such a way as to validate the inequalities of wealth by connecting it to moral values. If one were rich, naturally one was deserving. But there is another issue that I think is worth talking over with students because you are almost surely going to get conflicting views. Carnegie assumes that he knows how to spend money better than the individuals who work for him. His philanthropy is undeniably marvelous to those who admire high art and music. He thought his employees would waste their extra money on less elevating fare. What your students think about his views should be enlightening.

QUESTIONS FOR COMPREHENSION

1. What does Carnegie mean by "the ties of brotherhood" (para. 1)?
2. What bothers Carnegie about the way the Sioux lived?
3. What are advantages of the law of competition?
4. What are Carnegie's views on the disposal of surplus wealth?

SUGGESTIONS FOR ESSAYS

1. *Response* What are your personal views on how well the "ties of brotherhood" have been working to keep the "rich and poor in harmonious relationship" (para. 1)? Do you have personal experiences that help clarify the modern situation in terms of how the rich and poor get along harmoniously or inharmoniously? What seems to be the general perception among your friends and relatives concerning this question?

2. *Definition* Examine Carnegie's essay carefully for his views on what he calls "the law of competition" (paras. 5–7). What does he have to say about it and why does he discuss it in detail? After analyzing his use of the concept, explain how you understand the law of competition. Offer your own definition in a brief essay. At the same time, after having defined it — using examples if possible — take a stand on whether you approve competition in Carnegie's sense of the word, or whether your definition differs enough for you to disapprove his views. How has competition worked for you in economic or other pursuits?

3. *Cause and Effect* Carnegie accepts what he feels is the fact that poverty is inevitable. He also accepts that great wealth for the few is inevitable. Decide whether or not there is a cause and effect relationship between great wealth for the few and great poverty for the many. If there is a cause/effect relationship, what is to be done to alleviate the sufferings of the poor? Can the sufferings of the poor be relieved without reducing the wealth of the super rich? Decide whether there is a general view of the cause/effect relationship among the people you know or among public figures who comment on economics.

4. *Response* Write an essay in which you establish exactly what you approve or disapprove of about what Carnegie has to say. What is most admirable about his ideas? Take a stand by writing an essay that defends or challenges his views. Do you think you would have enjoyed knowing him? What would you have talked about?

CHARLOTTE PERKINS GILMAN

Women and Economics: "Cupid-in-the-Kitchen" (pp. 303–316)

FEW ECONOMISTS before Gilman's time had taken into account the special problems that are raised by what she called sex-linked occupations. Obviously, this is a serious issue today, just as it was in 1898, and for many people, the situation has not changed that radically. Gilman's farsightedness, for example, led her to support a scheme to provide common nurseries for children of working mothers from all classes. After publishing *Women and Economics*, she continued to develop her theories in books such as *Concerning Children* (1900) and *The Home* (1903). Her work contributes to home economics, but it also extends far beyond, into the whole question of gender in the workplace. The book that Gilman thought would become her most important was published in 1904, *Human Work*. In this book, she asserts that work is an end in itself and a source of delight to everyone. Although not well received, it contains much of what she most fervently believed in. In 1909, she became editor and publisher of a monthly magazine called *Forerunner*. From 1909 until 1916 when it ceased publication, she is said to have written the equivalent of twenty-eight books. Your students should find this piece interesting and possibly a bit annoying. I doubt they will find it irrelevant.

QUESTIONS FOR COMPREHENSION

1. Why is human nutrition considered as a "sex function" in terms of economics?

2. How competent were women in Gilman's time in determining the value of nutrition?

3. Why is it important to think of women as amateur cooks?

4. How does "the man" affect the kitchen activities of the women Gilman describes?

SUGGESTIONS FOR ESSAYS

1. ***Comparison*** Compare the way women function in their homes today as opposed to the way Gilman describes them in her essay. What remains the same and what seems to have changed? Have the changes moved in the direction that Gilman would have wanted? Have the changes tended to liberate women or to hamper them in new ways? What do today's women need in order to realize the goals that Gilman envisioned?

2. ***Analysis of Circumstances*** Is there any way that an economy can totally eliminate sex-differentiated labor? What are the problems with trying to abolish such differentiations? In what ways might the economy suffer? In what ways might it be improved? If you feel that such differentiation will be obsolete in the twenty-fifth century, why is it not obsolete today? Is it possible that society enjoys the sex-differentiated economic conditions that exist now? What would your plans for change include?

3. ***Cause and Effect*** Gilman says, "Our general notion is that we have lifted and ennobled our eating and drinking by combining them with love" (para. 18). How does love affect our eating and drinking in today's world? Is it possible that Gilman is being ironic here, or is she being totally serious? In a brief essay, examine her observations that support her statement and decide whether she is correct in her views and whether her views are limited to her time, or whether they extend to our own time.

4. ***Definition*** Gilman relies on the term *Cupid-in-the-kitchen* without fully explaining it. In a brief essay, and with reference to Gilman's examples and the development of the idea, define the term for a reader who has not read Gilman's essay. What makes the term effective? Can it still be used to describe most of the women in the kitchens of today? Is it possible that Gilman has gotten it all wrong, and that this term is not really useful in describing the relationship of women to their husbands in their own homes?

JOHN KENNETH GALBRAITH

Inequality (pp. 317–328)

A S I mention in the introduction to the selection, Galbraith was in his time the best-known economist. Although Canadian, he became an American citizen and taught at Harvard throughout his career. The most important point he makes early in his book *The Affluent Society* is that until the middle of the twentieth century most people in North America were considered poor by modern standards. The affluence that marked the 1940s and 1950s was unusual, but it came to be perceived very quickly as a normal condition. This is not included in the selection, "Inequality," but it is a point that you might want to make. Galbraith talks about poverty in other chapters in his book, but he does not explicitly connect the cause or condition of poverty with inequality or with the fact that some people are rich. He does not discuss the question of the zero-sum game, in which there is only a limited supply of money in the system. Modern economies sometimes limit the supply of money, but the wealth of nations increases with productivity and trade, not to mention increased exploitation of resources. The question of whether increased inequality means that when the rich have much more the poor have much less is not at all clear. Galbraith does not immediately address that point.

When it comes to poverty, the question of cause and effect is important because the effects of poverty are felt by everyone. On the one hand, there is the rising toll in taxes required by poverty programs. On the other hand, there is the rising prison population, making the construction of new prisons a necessity for the first time in generations. Much crime is rooted in poverty, if not caused by it, and thus all members of society are affected by poverty. Inequality is of some concern in our society.

QUESTIONS FOR COMPREHENSION

1. Who in society has generally been in favor of equality?
2. What did Marx say about the redistribution of wealth?
3. How is the formation of capital affected by the redistribution of wealth?
4. What does Galbraith say about the public's interest in inequality?

SUGGESTIONS FOR ESSAYS

1. ***Cause and Effect*** How would the formation of capital in our economy be affected by a significant redistribution of wealth? What are the benefits and what are the problems involved in the distribution of enough wealth so that the poor would no longer be poor? How would our capitalist economy be affected? Would it thrive or would it suffer?

2. ***Response*** Galbraith says that "few things are more evident in modern social history than the decline of interest in inequality as an economic issue" (para. 13). What is your personal view regarding the current inequality in contemporary society? Do you feel it is of more concern today, or of less concern? How does inequality affect you today? How will it affect you in the future? Are you willing to urge Congress to take action against the inequality that exists in our country?

3. ***Analysis of Circumstances*** Galbraith says that "for many years no serious effort has been made to alter the present distribution of income" (para. 14). Do you think this is still true today? What are the chief ways in which a government can make a real effort to alter the distribution of income? Is the government making more of an effort than it did in Galbraith's time? Is it up to the government to try to alter the present distribution of income? If the government does not try to redistribute income, who should take on that role in society? How, legally, could a redistribution of income be accomplished without damaging the economy?

4. ***Research*** During the Great Depression, beginning in 1929 and ending with the Second World War, Franklin Roosevelt's New Deal used taxes to provide programs such as Social Security to help citizens in their old age. Many people, even today, decry these programs as socialism. Critics of his programs felt he was taking from the rich to give to the poor. In a brief essay, explain how the main programs of his celebrated New Deal stimulated redistribution of wealth. What were the programs, how well received were they, how effective were they, and which of them are in place today? Did they damage capitalism? Do people today approve of them?

JANE JACOBS

Stagflation (pp. 329–343)

BECAUSE THIS selection is one of the most difficult in this book, you will probably profit from clarifying several ideas up front. Defining stagflation as high inflation and high unemployment is important. Supply-side economy favors capital and demand-side economy favors the consumer. The seesaw effect Jacobs talks about is a kind of logical proposition. A high demand for labor makes wages rise; then costs rise and therefore all prices rise. The opposite is that low demand for labor makes wages fall; then costs fall and prices drop. Clarifying these points in the early discussion of this piece will make the discussion less problematic.

Jane Jacobs is remarkable for her defense of unpopular ideas and for the fact that in many ways she got things right. To begin with, she is interesting for having been a self-taught expert in her field. According to her obituary in *The New York Times*, "in at least five distinct fields of inquiry, she thought deeply and innovatively: urban design, urban history, regional economics, the morality of the economy, and the nature of economic growth." It is remarkable to have been able to learn enough about these fields to make a valued statement about each. Her essay on stagflation is useful to you because it offers you a chance to talk about a number of important economists. Jacobs argues with each of them in turn and in the process gives us a clinic on the historical development of economics.

She is also remarkable because, like Lucretius, she began from observation to develop her best ideas. In her book, *The Death and Life of Great American Cities*, all her best ideas come almost directly from her observations of life in New York's Greenwich Village. Her contention was that the 1950s practice of tearing down slums and building high-rise projects was all wrong. She argued instead for low-rise buildings with commercial space on the ground floor so that there would be neighborhoods and communities rather than just open space and solitude. Today, many planners agree with her. She is an example of a critical thinker who developed many of her ideas from critical examination of events and critical reading in a number of fields.

QUESTIONS FOR COMPREHENSION

1. What do wages do when there is a high demand for labor?
2. What is the effect of rising costs of production?
3. What is meant by "adulterating coinage" (para. 3)? How does it affect an economy?
4. What kind of income-transfer scheme did John Maynard Keynes approve?

SUGGESTIONS FOR ESSAYS

1. ***Response*** Jacobs says that Marx's theory is that "monopolization of capital permits capitalists to take ever larger shares of income for themselves, leaving ever smaller shares for wage earners" (para. 12). Do you think Marx is correct? Does Jacobs think he is correct? Is this description of how capitalism works accurate as far as your personal experience tells you? What is our modern term for monopolization of capital? Is capital monopolized in our corporate world?

2. ***Research*** Jacobs talks about several historical economists. John Maynard Keynes was very important during and after the Great Depression of the late 1920s and the 1930s. In a brief essay, explain to a potential reader who knows little about economics exactly what made Keynes important. What are your views on his economic policies? Some of them are being recommended today. Would you defend or attack the implementation of his ideas?

3. ***Analysis of Circumstances*** According to some theorists, the unemployment rate ought to be below 5 percent. However, in recent years it has hovered above that number. What is the likelihood that this relatively high unemployment rate is the result of an oversupply of laborers? What has happened in recent years that would create an oversupply of laborers? How can the unemployment rate be lowered? Check news outlets to see how commentators have described the unemployment situation. How can a government — local, state, or federal — act to stimulate higher employment?

4. ***Definition*** In a brief essay, define the terms *supply-side economics* and *demand-side economics* in a manner that would make the ideas clear to someone who knows little or nothing about economics. These terms have a political component because one of them is favored by political conservatives and the other is favored by political liberals. Which is which? Where do you stand on these two theories?

ELIZABETH WARREN

The Vanishing Middle Class (pp. 344–356)

E LIZABETH WARREN is a well-known political figure who has risen from a relatively impoverished background to become an important professor of law at Harvard. In a sense, she is an example of upward mobility and rising to the very top of her profession. In addition, because she was a college dropout, she is a valuable example to put before your students. Clearly, she had plenty of obstacles in her way, but she got past them. Another attractive quality she possesses is her willingness to attack the kind of predatory loan system that may beset some of your students. Her work on bankruptcy law is especially helpful for poor people and those who became unwillingly involved in unnecessary debt. She ran a good campaign in Massachusetts to become one of its senators. It is possible that she may have other political ambitions, so it is valuable to have students read what she says about the middle class.

QUESTIONS FOR COMPREHENSION

1. What is the relationship of the middle class to the poor?
2. How do people define *class status*?
3. How much does Warren say the middle-class, two-income family currently earns?
4. What is the relationship between wages and the cost of being middle class?

SUGGESTIONS FOR ESSAYS

1. *Response* Elizabeth Warren talks about the risks that middle-class families face. In a two-earner family, if one earner is ill, the family will suffer greatly. In a one-earner family, the second person could work to help out. As a young person who expects to become an earner in the near future, how should you plan to achieve stability in the middle class? What are the most important decisions you can make at this point in your life about how you wish to live?

2. ***Analysis of Circumstances*** Warren says that one of the chief complaints made about families today is overconsumption. What do people mean by that term? Is it true that families today buy expensive items they do not need? If you agree that overconsumption is a problem, explain what people are buying that they do not need. Begin with yourself. Then look at your own family and at the families you know. Then go to the advertising pages in the newspapers or fliers that are available to you. What are the most expensive advertised items that you think are unnecessary? How much could a family save by avoiding these items? Do you think Warren's position on overconsumption is right?

3. ***Research*** Elizabeth Warren uses the term *middle class*, expecting that we will understand it without much uncertainty. However, we know that Americans dislike the idea of social class, and yet the term is used frequently. Do some research in sociology on the entire concept of social class. What is the strictest meaning of the term and in what nations has it been most clearly distinct? Are the rich a social class? Are the poor a social class? Why is the middle class singled out in the United States when other classes are not? You might consult Paul Fussell's *Class: A Guide Through the American Status System* (1983), but keep in mind that it is snarky and irreverent, however interesting.

4. ***Research*** One of Elizabeth Warren's most important interests is in the nation's current bankruptcy laws. Learn what you can about the way bankruptcy laws work in your state and in our nation. Who are they designed to benefit? How have they changed recently? How will they impact you if you get into debt and cannot pay back what you have borrowed? Write a brief essay that warns people of your age about the risks of debt and the facts about how bankruptcy works.

⊞

LESLIE T. CHANG

Factory Girls in Dongguan (pp. 357–366)

FRANKLY, I know little about Leslie Chang. The fact that her family in the United States is highly educated and her father was a professor of physics helps explain some of her preparation for the journalism that became her career. She credits her mother with insisting that she take Saturday school classes in Chinese, even though she went under protest. The result is that she had enough language to be able to talk with the factory girls she lived among in Dongguan. She and her husband lived in Cairo when her book was published, but I am not at all sure where they live today.

This selection should help your students gain insight into the ways in which Chinese society has changed as it has become one of the most successful of modern capitalist nations. I say that, despite our understanding that China is communist. The decision to permit private industry and private ownership and small businesses to thrive, while maintaining government ownership of major resources, has made China the only communist society that has achieved prosperity and stability.

Another interesting point is that Dongguan has historically been associated with the West. It was the town that was in the center of the Opium Wars in the mid-1800s. It is currently one of the most active Chinese cities in terms of its business with the West and other nations.

QUESTIONS FOR COMPREHENSION

1. Who taught Leslie T. Chang the details of the city?

2. What do China's migrants no longer fear?

3. How did Leslie Chang become "invisible in Dongguan" (para. 6)?

4. What is a Chinese "special economic zone" (para. 9)?

SUGGESTIONS FOR ESSAYS

1. *Research* The Treaty of Nanking was signed between China and England after the Opium Wars. Research the treaty and in a brief essay explain what led up to it and what it guaranteed. What has been the modern result of the Treaty of Nanking?

2. *Response* How do you respond to the details of Leslie Chang's description of the workers in Dongguan? What does she say that might make you feel that the complaints of American jobs being sent abroad may be true? Does Chang seem resentful about the loss of American jobs? Are you? What is the key factor in the movement of jobs from the United States or the West in general to China: skilled labor or lower labor costs?

3. *Analysis of Circumstances* What do you learn about the nature of the labor force in Dongguan? How skilled is it and how much do laborers earn? Since we are all beneficiaries of cheap Chinese labor, how are we to deal with the ethical issues involved in taking advantage of teenage girls? How do the Chinese authorities seem to treat the ethical issues

that face them? What seem to be Chang's views on the exploitation of cheap labor? Who ultimately benefits from such exploitation?

4. **Research** Scour online resources as well as your library for information on China's economic growth rate. Chang tells us China's economy was growing "by 10 percent a year" (para. 35). What can you learn about the rate of growth since 2001? How does it compare with the growth rate of the U.S. economy? Judging by your research, how soon will China's economy be larger than the U.S. economy? What does your research tell you about economic opportunities in the future for workers such as yourself?

CHAPTER SEVEN

How Ethics and Morality Interact

The eight selections in this chapter begin with Aristotle, whose *Nichomachean Ethics* has long been a touchstone for ethical thought in the West. Aristotle's *eudaimonia* has been ordinarily translated as "happiness." Aristotle's term may mean something close to "wellness of spirit," and that's not a bad way to think about it. He means the highest good that man can aim for, and he does not mean a temporary state of well-being. One of the pleasures you may have in your class discussion is working out the idea of happiness and its connection with ethics and a virtuous life.

Nietzsche is quite different in his perception of moral issues. While Aristotle recommends a moral life for achieving happiness, Nietzsche points to the question of morals: Who decides what is moral? In other essays, he looks to nature and does not see the moral concerns that beset him and his time. Ultimately, he thinks of moral injunctions as having been laid down by the power structure — the church, the government, the power elite. Students may find this interesting. John Dewey leaps ahead to questions of education and morality. There is much to be thought about here. Since your students are engaged in education, they will have a useful perspective to bring to the subject. Is it immoral to be uneducated in a democracy? Since a democracy depends on informed voters, there is something of an argument to be had here. Thomas Nagel brings a powerful philosophical mind to the question, looking closely at the reasons for the survival of the species. If Nietzsche thinks morals are a modern invention, Nagel takes us to the Stone Age and the earliest years of *Homo sapiens*. Without a strong ethical center, the species may have disappeared. Michael Gazzaniga, the famous brain specialist, brings neural research to bear on the question and sees issues that seem rooted in the structure of the brain and therefore universal among us all.

Peter Singer and Jim Mason bring a totally different approach to ethics when they accuse us of speciesism for killing animals and eating them. Many young people today are swayed by their arguments and refuse to eat meat on the grounds that killing animals is immoral. Their argument hinges in part on the question of factory farming, which Singer and Mason have described as horrendous. Their argument raises questions in the best way — that is, they cannot be easily answered except, perhaps, by Nietzsche's reflections on the natural world. Francis Fukuyama continues the discussion of the rights of animals, admitting that animals have few rights in the sense that we use that term in the Bill of Rights. But nonetheless, his views deepen our understanding of what it means to take an ethical position and hold to it.

Finally, Kwame Anthony Appiah gets us back, by a complex route, to some of the questions that Aristotle raised. How is the moral life connected to the possibilities of human happiness? Appiah is interested in that question and more. This section of the book introduces ethical and moral questions in such a way as to sometimes confuse them. Your students will find it a useful challenge to see how they may differ.

⊞

ARISTOTLE

The Aim of Man (pp. 374–392)

YOU WILL notice that I ask mostly response questions for writing in the book because I think that any student has a good deal to think about in reading Aristotle. This selection was written, according to tradition, to his own son as a guide for living a sensible life. If this is true, then it makes sense to ask students to apply some of the advice to their own lives. Their attitude toward happiness is of importance to them, as it is to most of us, and it needs examination. For that reason, I center most of my suggestions for writing on the personal level. Of course, there are many other approaches, and you will undoubtedly come up with some excellent ones. As always, if you wish to share any with me, please feel free to contact me at leejacobus@aol.com.

One thing I think important to talk about is the relationship of the virtuous life with happiness. This is a moral consideration, to be sure. Aristotle is hoping that whoever reads his work will be moved to maintain a moral life. But there is also something of the pragmatist in his advice. It should be interesting to see how much of that your students will see.

QUESTIONS FOR COMPREHENSION

1. Why does Aristotle content himself with a "rough approximation to the truth" (para. 5)?

2. What is the difference between "the good" and "particular good things" (para. 8)?

3. Why does Aristotle say, "the supreme good must of course be something final" (para. 13)?

4. Why should we not "expect the same degree of precision in all fields" (para. 18)?

SUGGESTIONS FOR ESSAYS

1. *Research* Find a copy of *The Nichomachean Ethics* in your school library, read the introduction, and then check the bibliography. Research the reputation of the book and then read some of the criticism and commentary that discusses its content. Write an essay that encapsulates your research to help someone unfamiliar with Aristotle understand why *The Nichomachean Ethics* is as important as philosophers say.

2. *Cause and Effect* Aristotle recommends a virtuous life in order to achieve happiness. In other words, he promotes morality. There is a possible causal relationship in what he recommends. Decide in a brief essay whether living a moral life causes happiness or whether the pursuit of happiness has the effect of producing a moral life. What is the cause/effect relationship of morality and happiness? Do you agree with Aristotle concerning a life of virtue and the quest for the highest good?

3. *Definition* Late in this selection, Aristotle talks about it being important to "ascertain the proper function of man" (para. 15). He says this when considering how different people will regard happiness in different ways. Yet, he seems to feel that we, as individuals, have a proper function that is different from, say, plants. Write a brief essay that attempts to define the proper function of man, remembering that the word *man* means all people.

4. *Analysis of Circumstances* Happiness is a major goal of most people in our own time. Using your observation and reflections, explain what you think people in our immediate environment expect will bring them happiness. What relevance, if any, does Aristotle's advice on how to attain happiness have for modern people? Do modern people seem to have some of the same concerns? Do they share any of the same hopes or worries? If you have a child, would you have them read Aristotle when they are young?

🔠

FRIEDRICH NIETZSCHE

Good and Bad (pp. 393–399)

NIETZSCHE PROPOSED a theory of recurrence in which he suggested that our fate is to relive this life over again. As a result, he felt that if we came to understand this view and accept it we would live our lives much more deliberately and much more carefully. Other philosophers have held this view, but modern existentialists looked to Nietzsche for their ideas concerning how we should live our lives. The question you might ask your students is whether or not they think that Nietzsche has inherited Aristotle's views and is acting on them in this brief selection. Like Aristotle, he does not posit a loving God, and that detail may be of interest to many of your students because they may feel that a moral life depends on the existence of God. Handling these issues in class will prove interesting, and probably challenging.

QUESTIONS FOR COMPREHENSION

1. Why does Nietzsche say the English psychologists may have "[a] secret, malicious desire to belittle humanity" (para. 1)?

2. What is Nietzsche's complaint about the "historians of ethics" (para. 2)?

3. Who decreed the "highly placed, and high-minded" to be good (para. 3)?

4. Who thinks that the concept *good* is equivalent to *useful*?

SUGGESTIONS FOR ESSAYS

1. *Definition* Nietzsche uses the term *idée fixe*. In a brief essay, define the term and explain what the problems are with it that led Nietzsche to use it as he does. Why is *idée fixe* not used in a positive sense? How can an *idée fixe* become a problem? In modern politics there are sometimes numerous *idées fixes*. How many can you identify in our current society?

2. *Response* Review what Nietzsche has to say about the useful in the last paragraph of his selection. How do you respond to him concerning the relationship of the useful to the moral? Does he express your views, or do you find yourself in disagreement with him? What is your position on the question of whether the issues of morality are really just issues of what is or is not useful in a society like ours?

3. *Definition* Nietzsche mentions the *egotism-altruism dichotomy* in the last paragraph in Part II. What does this term mean? How does it relate to the question of morality in society? How does it figure in his argument about what the word *good* means? What is the role of the "herd instinct" in this question?

4. *Research* Find out what you can about Friedrich Nietzsche. He is regarded as one of the most important modern philosophers. After you have read some of his work and read about how other thinkers and philosophers regard him, write an essay introducing him to an audience that does not know him or his work. What is your view of the value of his work to a modern person such as yourself? What insight does he give you into the nature of modern morality and modern thought? Is he an admirable figure in modern thought?

⊞

JOHN DEWEY

Education and Morality (pp. 400–405)

DEWEY IS an American pragmatist. He was interested in results and practicality. Pragmatism developed in the late 1870s with the work of the American philosopher Charles Sanders Peirce (pronounced *Perse*), who was one of Dewey's teachers at Johns Hopkins. William James was also part of the pragmatist group. In essence, they evaluated ideas in terms of their consequences rather than by any abstract values. In this sense, they were empirical, depending on observation and perception of effects. Dewey called his version of pragmatism "instrumentalism" or "experimentalism." He felt he could evaluate an idea in terms of what experience warranted as reasonable. In any event, the emphasis on the empirical works readily in examining the effectiveness of the classroom — a method that begins with providing experience to the student, from which then develop problems to be solved, which then demand information or data to help solve them, leading naturally to a situation in which students will learn.

There is a certain amount of pragmatism in this selection because Dewey saw the connections of education not only to morality but also to politics and the social realities of modern life. It is really interesting to consider the possibility that refusing an education is an immoral act. If one accepts Dewey's ideals and his commitment to both democracy and society, it is difficult to reject the idea. It will be interesting to see how your students react to his ideas, given the fact that they have embraced education.

QUESTIONS FOR COMPREHENSION

1. Why does Dewey say "the educative process is all one with the moral process" (para. 1)?
2. Why is education considered necessary?
3. When do the young arrive at "emancipation from social dependence" (para. 1)?
4. What is Dewey's attitude toward politics?

SUGGESTIONS FOR ESSAYS

1. **Definition** Dewey uses the term *process of education*. What do you think he means by that? What, for him, constitutes the process of education? What "process" are you aware of in your own education? Dewey has a large vision regarding education. Help him define that vision by referencing your own ideas about education. Define his term in a brief essay.

2. **Analysis of Circumstances** Dewey says that some people think of childhood as a preparation for adult life. Analyze the ideas in that concept. How could anyone say that childhood is a preparation for anything? Does Dewey think this is true? If it were true, what is the role of education in childhood? What do you think was the role of your childhood education? Do you have any sense that your teachers were preparing you for something other than childhood?

3. **Example** Using your own education as a source of examples, write a brief essay that explains the moral lessons that were implied in your school experiences. What aspects of education informed your moral nature? Did your teachers intend to shape your views of morality, or did your views of morality result from the interaction of the classroom or the significance of the materials you studied?

4. **Response** In the last paragraph of the selection, Dewey discusses the purpose of education. Explain, in a brief essay, what he thinks the purpose of an education should be. Then, respond to him with your own view of what an education should be. Is your education meeting your needs and satisfying your view of what an education should be? Why are you pursuing an education? Do you feel it a moral obligation to do so? Do you agree with Dewey or not?

⊞

THOMAS NAGEL

The Objective Basis of Morality
(pp. 406–413)

WHILE THOMAS Nagel has a reputation for being difficult, this essay is fairly clear and carefully written. His best known article, "What Is It Like to Be a Bat?" is cited frequently and is a challenging piece of work, although the idea behind it is always intriguing to anyone who has heard of it.

His newest book, *Mind and Cosmos*, may be of interest to some of your students because it takes a totally different view of evolution and evolutionary development. In a sense, he sees the direction of life as a given, a natural and perhaps necessary development. Like Teilhard de Chardin, the priest who wrote *Phenomenon of Man* (1959), which anticipated an "Omega Point" to which the cosmos was evolving, Thomas Nagel sees the pattern of life as having an end goal, the development of higher-level reasoning. The idea that the universe is teleological is very appealing to religious thinkers. However, it is interesting to know that Chardin's original work was banned by the Catholic Church. In recent years, the Church has rescinded its ban and considers his work no longer heterodox. I have no idea what the Catholic Church thinks about Thomas Nagel and his ideas. In fact, I have no idea if the Church has taken any notice of his work. See what your students think of him and his ideas.

QUESTIONS FOR COMPREHENSION

1. What does it mean for consciousness to be metaphysical?
2. What is the relation of wrong and right to the rules?
3. What makes something wrong?
4. If God did not exist, would everything be permitted?

SUGGESTIONS FOR ESSAYS

1. **Response** How do you respond to Thomas Nagel's discussion of "the religious foundation for morality" (para. 13)? Is his analysis as reasonable as he seems to feel? Does it jibe with your own views on the religious foundation of morality? Morality is ordinarily thought to be connected to religious teaching, while ethics has traditionally been related to sociological teaching. In what ways do you find your own moral values shaped by religious teaching?

2. **Analysis of Circumstances** Nagel's opening paragraphs offer many circumstances in which there might be a question about whether a specific behavior should be considered wrong or not. In a sense, he asks the question, "What makes an action wrong?" Review the circumstances he discusses and then offer an answer to that question. In your view, what makes something wrong? Is the question of what makes something wrong a moral question?

3. **Example** Thomas Nagel gives several examples of questionable moments in which morality may or may not be in question. The question of the library's reference book and the possibility of giving it to a friend is one example. However, we all have instances in our lives in which the question of behavior has become a moral issue. What example or examples of behavior have you experienced that are similar in character to those that Nagel describes? How did you behave, and how did you regard it in moral terms? What do you think about it now as you reflect on your behavior?

4. **Definition** After reflecting on all the issues that Thomas Nagel raises about various possibilities of moral behavior, and disregarding the religious basis of morality, define for a reader who does not know Nagel's work the concept of the sociological basis of morality. Nagel is correct in saying that people who have no religious commitment still behave morally. They do not need the Bible or the concept of God. Why do they then behave well? How do you describe and define the moral behavior of those who pay no attention to religion? Do you know people who fit that description? Do you think religious people act more morally than nonreligious people?

⊞

MICHAEL GAZZANIGA

Toward a Universal Ethics (pp. 414–429)

THE BEGINNING of this selection may be controversial for some students. Gazzaniga has been criticized in reviews for giving short shrift to philosophers such as Kant and Hobbes in this particular chapter of his book. It is true that he reduces the work of several millenia's worth of philosophical and religious consideration of human nature to mere "stories." He puts this in such a severe way so as to distinguish supposition and guesses from scientific research, much of which is also guesses (but he doesn't mention that). The basic point is that science is beginning to be ready to take up the issues of ethical behavior and moral reasoning from an evolutionary point of view and perhaps overthrow some of the moral wisdom that is central to established religions. All of this may be upsetting to some of your students, but that should help stimulate class discussion.

I have suggested questions for class discussion that should open up the central issues and give students a chance to work out their thinking on whether a universal ethics could be derived from what is known of how the systems of the brain function and how a social animal such as humans must behave if the species is to survive. Some of this will be a novelty to most of your students, so you may find the interplay of student opinions very stimulating.

One important issue in the passage has to do with the so-called hardwiring of the brain. This computer metaphor may be distracting both to you and to some students, so it would not hurt to mention that it is only a metaphor and that its force may distort the idea. The point is that there seem to be predispositions of certain brains — something we all know about when we look at our talented neighbors or when we are told that we get one trait or another from "Uncle Louie" or some other forebear. If it is true, as language experts now tell us, that the brain is hardwired to develop language, then is it also possible that Gazzaniga's idea that it is hardwired to respond to moral and ethical issues realistic? However, you'll see that the selection mainly aims at pointing to the beneficial effects of good moral judgment. What about bad moral judgment? If Gazzaniga is right about good social behavior, would it not also be reasonable to consider that antisocial behavior can be hardwired, too? And if so, what does that say about the role of evolution and the survival of the species?

QUESTIONS FOR COMPREHENSION

1. Why does Gazzaniga call the wisdom of the ancients "stories"?
2. What is the difference between close-up and long-distance altruism?
3. Are human beings big animals? What is the point of Gazzaniga's suggesting so?
4. Why has Gazzaniga introduced the "trolley problem" (para. 16)?

SUGGESTIONS FOR ESSAYS

1. ***Response*** Review what Gazzaniga has to say about theory of mind, beginning with paragraph 15 ("Research on moral cognition . . ."). Test his ideas by keeping track of your own encounters with people and your sense of whether or not his theory of mind is at work in you. Review his ideas on mirroring, and again explain either how your mind works in parallel with what he points out or how it does not mirror others.

2. ***Research*** Search online and in your library for books and journal articles on brain imaging. The research on the imaging of the brain is developing rapidly, and many discoveries about how the brain functions are being made daily. What is the most important modern research in brain imagery? Does any of it support Gazzaniga? Does any of it tend to contradict him? What are the most startling discoveries? How might they affect you and the way you think?

3. ***Response*** How well developed is your emotional "gut response" in reacting to a moral situation in which you are able to act altruistically? Do you feel your emotional moral response is immediate and instantaneous, or is it simply an aspect of your moral reasoning? Do you think of yourself as an emotional person? Or do you think of yourself as more a logical and reasoned person? How does your view of yourself affect the way you react in situations that demand a moral response? Use your own experiences to examine this question.

4. ***Testimony*** Write an essay that tries to convince an audience that ethics is the key to our survival as a species. Assume a doubting audience, but also an audience that is responsive to careful analysis and evidence. Read some of the authors Gazzaniga cites and include their testimony in your essay. In the process of writing the essay, include some of the brain research that implies a moral center or a moral function in the brain.

PETER SINGER AND JIM MASON

Ethics and Animals (pp. 430–439)

PETER SINGER has become a major figure in the study of modern ethics. In addition to his work on our approach to eating meat and our nation's practices of factory farming, he has become a spokesman for animal liberation. His book *Animal Liberation* (1975) made him famous. His range is considerable: *Democracy and Disobedience* (1973); *Marx* (1980); *Hegel* (1982); *The Most Good You Can Do: How Effective Altruism Is Changing Ideas about Living Ethically* (2015). He is also the editor of the Oxford Reader *Ethics*.

His work on factory farming and what we should eat begins with an analysis of eating the standard American diet, with conclusions that we have come to expect. It's not that good. The recent revelations about chicken in our diet were long anticipated by Singer and his coauthor, Jim Mason. Singer also talks about eating locally, eating seafood, and eating conscientiously whether we eat in or eat out. He also discusses the ethics of raising one's children to be vegan, a very interesting question. Your students will find much to say about the material in this selection because Singer is one of the most powerful voices affecting the current awareness of how we treat animals we intend to eat. Moreover, many young people have become vegetarian as a way of improving their diet and avoiding the pain and guilt of killing animals.

Apart from what I mention in the headnote to the selection in the book, I know virtually nothing about Jim Mason apart from the fact that he is a farmer.

QUESTIONS FOR COMPREHENSION

1. Is the question of animal rights likely to be a politically left or politically right issue?
2. What did Pope Benedict XVI say about factory farming?
3. What are the arguments in favor of factory farming?
4. What is the Benjamin Franklin defense?

SUGGESTIONS FOR ESSAYS

1. *Response* Given the growing awareness of the problems of factory farming and the popularity of becoming vegetarian, explain in a brief essay how your own patterns of eating have changed since you were younger. Keep a journal for a few days that lists everything you eat: breakfast, lunch, dinner, snacks. To what extent do you concern your-self with the question of eating meat? To what extent do you find yourself interested in changing your eating patterns? How have Singer and Mason affected your thinking about food?

2. *Research* The Benjamin Franklin defense based itself on the fact that animals eat other animals. Singer rejects that defense. Some authori-ties recommend that we eat a paleo diet, which is interpreted variously. Find out what the paleo diet is and examine it in relation to the con-cerns that Singer and Mason have raised. Does the paleo diet find fac-tory farming adequate or inadequate for its dietary demands? Would you practice the paleo diet?

3. *Response* If you are an omnivore, defend your dietary choices. What, if any, are your limits when it comes to choosing food? When do you feel it is ethical to eat meat, fish, and game? How do you deal with the ethical issues that Singer and Mason raise? What makes you comfort-able eating beef, chicken, cod, tuna, or any other delicacy? Are there foods you will not eat? Would that be because of an ethical issue or is it a matter of taste or health?

4. *Research* Many foods are prohibited for religious reasons. Until recently, Catholics were expected to avoid meat every Friday. Lent is a period in which certain foods are restricted for Christians. Jews and Arabs are prohibited from eating pork and cats, among other foods. Jews are prohibited from eating frogs and shellfish. Buddhists are gen-erally vegetarian. Find out which foods are taboo for which people and what the apparent reasons are. Are the religious taboos based on eth-ical and moral decisions? Why do religions ban some foods and not others? What foods are taboo for you? Why? Write a brief essay that accounts for the ethical underpinnings of religious food taboos.

FRANCIS FUKUYAMA

Human Specificity and the Rights of Animals (pp. 440–446)

MANY OF your students will feel that animals have rights, just as people do. You might refer students to the first group of selections in this book. "How Democracy Relates to Human Rights" may or may not provide a stimulus for discussion of animal rights. The first suggestion for writing in the book asks students to review the Bill of Rights and the Declaration of Rights as a beginning point from which to start a consideration of what rights animals might have. Interestingly, this particular selection is something of a side issue for Fukuyama, who is much more well known for his work in politics, such as his recent book *Political Order and Political Decay* (2014). One question to ask students is: If we guarantee rights to animals, are we then creating an animal politics? The idea of rights hardly exists outside of a political spectrum.

QUESTIONS FOR COMPREHENSION

1. What does pain and suffering have to do with rights?
2. What is an animal ethologist?
3. What makes macaques different from chimpanzees?
4. Why is it important that an animal can be embarrassed?

SUGGESTIONS FOR ESSAYS

1. *Research* Fukuyama mentions that some chimpanzees have been taught a limited number of words to communicate with humans. Research the field of primate research and language acquisition and write an essay that brings your reader up to date on what has been achieved in primates learning enough language to communicate with people. What kinds of thoughts or ideas have the primates expressed? What are their concerns? What is particularly human about their thought processes?

2. *Response* Fukuyama, commenting on chimpanzee behavior, says, "Some scientists revel in debunking traditional claims about human dignity, particularly if they are based in religion" (para. 6). Why would a scientist have such a reaction? What are the conflicts in religion's views

cf human dignity and the experiments that de Waal describes? Is anything that de Waal reveals contrary to standard religious thinking? Is this another Galileo moment?

3. *Response* Animals are routinely tested in laboratories in which they are injected with various diseases to see which medicines work and which do not. This is a very emotional situation for many people who condemn all such practices. On the other hand, many people, including the scientists who conduct the experiments, insist that the practice saves human lives. What is your position on this matter? What would you say to someone who opposes your views? How would you try to convince that person to accept your thinking and change theirs?

4. *Analysis of Circumstances* Fukuyama writes about many kinds of animals, from viruses to chimpanzees, when considering the question of animal rights. Write an essay that considers a more limited variety of animals: pets. What are the rights that should be accorded to dogs? What are the rights that should be accorded to cats? What rights must be accorded to pet birds, chickens, hamsters, rabbits, goldfish, tropical fish, rats, and mice (add others if necessary)? How does the status of "pet" change the ethical situation for animals? How do your ideas square with Fukuyama's demands for considering animal specificity?

⊞

KWAME ANTHONY APPIAH

If You're Happy and You Know It
(pp. 447–454)

ONE NICE thing about Appiah's essay is that it connects back to Aristotle and the question of happiness as the greatest good. It also connects with Amartya Sen's consideration that justice must be seen to be done, not just done. Then, the word *eudaimonia* is worth spending some time discussing. It is sometimes translated simply as happiness, but you might note that "eu-" is a prefix meaning "good," while the root, "daimon," means spirit. So happiness in this sense implies a goodness of spirit in the individual, and that translates into a happy spirit. However, you will probably have a number of students who will argue that practicing certain vices can make a person happy. Let your students examine that conundrum.

You can also find it valuable to have your students enumerate the virtues that they think are indispensable to a good person, then enumerate the vices that they see in action among their peers. What are the basic virtues? What are the basic vices? You might refer to the seven vices and the seven virtues. Then the question of whether happiness is a feeling or experience may create a bit of discussion in your classroom.

QUESTIONS FOR COMPREHENSION

1. Is happiness a feeling or an experience?
2. How did the Vlach become Romanians?
3. What is the relation of felt desires to happiness?
4. Who sets the standards for happiness?

SUGGESTIONS FOR ESSAYS

1. *Research* Search online, then consult your library, for discussions of the word *eudaimonia*. What philosophers talk about this word? Is their discussion limited to Aristotle or Appiah or another writer? In your essay, explain how the word figures in Western thought.

2. *Response* Now that you have read Aristotle and Kwame Anthony Appiah, what do you think you mean when you tell someone to be happy? What are you wishing for that person? Is it different for each person you tell to be happy? Give specific examples of what you mean to specific people. Is your thinking in line with Aristotle and Appiah, or is it different?

3. *Comparison* Appiah talks about feelings and experiences. Examine what he says about feelings and experiences, and write a brief essay that clarifies the differences between them as well as what they have in common. When you think about happiness — or when you think you are happy — are you responding to feelings or experiences? Do you think Aristotle limits happiness to feelings? Does he limit it to experiences?

4. *Response* Consider what vices you have indulged in and whether they have given you pleasure. If they have given you pleasure, have they made you happy — or contributed to your happiness? Reviewing your own experience, decide just how likely it is that a life that includes vices will make you happy. If you feel it will, how then do you react to the idea expressed from Socrates onward that the secret to happiness is a life of virtue? Is it not true that our current society encourages a number of vices that give pleasure?